Johnson Did It

LBJ's Role in the JFK Assassination

Alex P. Serritella

JOHNSON DID IT

LBJ's ROLE IN THE JFK ASSASSINATION

Alex P. Serritella

www.bookstandpublishing.com

Published by
Bookstand Publishing
Morgan Hill, CA 95037
4585_10

ISBN 978-1-63498-623-6

Printed in the United States of America

Cover photo credits:

John F. Kennedy photo- Wikipedia/Public Domain

Lyndon B. Johnson photo- Wikipedia/Public Domain

Grassy knoll photo by author

For the wrongly accused

Contents

1

INTRODUCTION

I had just turned six when John Kennedy was shot. I have only the vaguest recollections of the event and the aftermath. At the moment when Walter Cronkite announced it to the world, I was in my first grade class at Resurrection Grammar School in Chicago. When we got the news, I'm sure we stopped whatever we were doing and said a prayer for him. I don't actually remember that, but we always said a prayer for any kind of tragedy or suffering.

I naturally asked the same questions as everyone else: "Who?" and "Why?" At the time, no one could really answer either one. I recall my mother telling me that Lee Harvey Oswald killed the president, and naturally I believed it without question. Then she told me that Jack Ruby killed Oswald. When she told me that, I remember that I felt a sense of vindication, as if justice had been served. The good guy killed the bad guy who killed the other good guy, so everything was all right now. If only things were that simple.

I recall seeing John and Jackie Kennedy on TV, and they seemed so happy, bright, and energetic. When Lyndon Johnson took over as president, it just seemed to bring everyone down. It seemed like there was a dark cloud of gloom hanging over everyone's life. I didn't blame Johnson for not having Kennedy's personality. He is who he is, and I understood that. I certainly never thought that he was part of the murder plot. But I missed John Kennedy's enthusiasm. My six-year old assessment was simply, "I liked the other guy better."

It always seemed to me that Lyndon Johnson failed to show proper grief for John Kennedy's death. On the day of the assassination, Johnson made the following short statement to the public:

> This is a sad time for all people. We have suffered a loss that cannot be weighed. For me, it is a deep, personal tragedy. I know that the world shares the sorrow that Mrs. Kennedy

1

and her family bear. I will do my best; that is all I can do. I
ask for your help and God's.[1]

It sounds diplomatic enough on the surface, but there should have been
much more. Johnson made that statement only because he had to. As the
new president, it was the proper thing to do. How would it look if he didn't?
Knowing now how he felt about John Kennedy, I'm surprised he could keep
a straight face when he said it was a "deep, personal tragedy." The
statement was insincere, and was done only for show. Johnson attended
Kennedy's funeral for the same reason- because he had to. Again, how
would it look if he didn't? He declared a day of mourning for John Kennedy,
which was just a token gesture. But at no time did I ever hear Johnson make
a long, impassioned speech about what a great man Kennedy was, and what
he meant to the world and how he will be missed. If you think about it,
Johnson minimized how much he ever spoke about Kennedy at all. Any
mention of him was always brief. It was an affront to Kennedy's memory
that he was virtually ignored post mortem. A true ally of Kennedy would
have spoken at great length about his life, his accomplishments, and his
legacy. All of this was conspicuously missing from Johnson's leadership.

Besides the assassination, all we would hear about on the news after that
was the Vietnam War. I had heard that John Kennedy was going to
withdraw from the war, but now Johnson was escalating it. I just thought
that the escalation of the war was an unfortunate by-product of Kennedy's
death, but I did not see it as a deliberate connection. I still could not fathom
that Johnson played a role in JFK's murder.

As time went by I questioned the war, which was at the heart of the
assassination. I realized I did not understand the political complexities
involved, but the war just did not seem necessary. We were always taught
in school that America was the land of the free, and that people in
communist countries were not as fortunate as us because they did not have
the freedoms that we enjoy. To some extent that is true, but it was greatly
exaggerated for the sake of propaganda. We were told that our military was
protecting us from the evil communists, but I could not understand why we
had to fight a communist country 10,000 miles away, yet we can co-exist
peacefully with communist countries that are only 100 miles away, meaning
Russia and Cuba. I had heard about the domino theory, which was almost

---

[1] http://www.presidency.ucsb.edu/ws/index.php?pid=25976

semi-reasonable to me as a kid, yet we were never harmed by the two dominoes that are closest to us.

In 1975, most of the world saw the assassination for the first time when the Zapruder film was shown on national TV. This was the home movie of JFK getting shot. I was naturally shocked and horrified when I saw it, as were most people. I clearly remember seeing it, and there was not a doubt in my mind that the shot came from the front. I assumed that was unanimously accepted, but it was not. Like most people, I had not studied the case closely, and I didn't know the details of the event. I had always heard that Lee Harvey Oswald killed JFK, and I never questioned it. Even when I saw the film, I just thought that Oswald shot Kennedy from the front. I was still oblivious to the truth, even after I had just seen absolute proof to the contrary.

For about 40 years, I accepted the official version of the JFK assassination. I never really took the time to study it carefully, and I just assumed that the government was right, or at least that they told the truth as best they knew it. Like most people, I just figured our government would never be involved in a crime like that. There was really no basis for that assumption. I just thought that the political overthrow of governments was something that only happened in banana republics in third-world countries. That could never happen in the good ol' USA. I realize now that that was wishful thinking. Most people in the USA probably shared the same wishful thinking, which is exactly why the government gets away with crimes like this.

My interest in the JFK case began in 2003 when I saw a documentary on TV called *The Men Who Killed Kennedy*. This was a nine-part series that was shown repeatedly in November of that year to coincide with the 40th anniversary of JFK's death. It turned out to be a bit of luck that I was able to see the program at all, because that was the last time the series was ever shown on TV. It was broadcast on the History Channel, which ran into legal trouble over the show because one of the segments, called "The Guilty Men," stated in no uncertain terms that Lyndon Johnson was responsible for John Kennedy's murder. Johnson's people threatened to sue. To avoid litigation, the History Channel caved in and ran a lame rebuttal to the segment, and agreed to never air the program again. I was fortunate to be able to see it when I did. Although I don't agree with everything that was said in the nine segments, the series as a whole was very enlightening, and it was then that I realized that our government had lied about the event and that Lee Harvey Oswald was innocent. Suddenly, Johnson's apathy about Kennedy's death made sense. He killed him, so that's why he showed no emotion afterwards.

The official version of the JFK assassination goes like this: As President Kennedy rode through Dallas in an open motorcade, Lee Harvey Oswald killed him by firing three shots from the Texas School Book Depository (TSBD) where he worked. Oswald acted alone, with no accomplices. There was no conspiracy of any kind, foreign or domestic. Oswald was a communist, a loner, and mentally unstable. He killed John Kennedy so he could be famous, then Jack Ruby killed Oswald to avenge Kennedy's death.

As millions of people have already realized, the official story is an obvious lie. A multitude of researchers have proven that Oswald was framed. There were at least four shooters that day, but it was Lyndon Johnson who orchestrated the plot. This was treason at the highest level, and that is difficult for patriotic Americans to accept. Much of the country is still in collective denial about having a murderer in the White House.

People will ask what the proof is that Johnson killed Kennedy. That would depend on how you define "proof." If there was a trial with a judge and jury, there would probably not be enough physical evidence to convict him. Johnson was too smart to leave evidence. Most of the planning was done through subordinates and intermediaries, so we do not see Johnson's fingerprints directly on it. No conversations of the plot were recorded, and there is nothing in writing that would put Johnson away. But if we look at the case closely and objectively, it's plainly obvious that Johnson was the main man behind the assassination plot.

At some point, I think Lyndon Johnson was proud of the fact that he killed John Kennedy. That is not to say that he didn't repent or have regrets, but I think at some point he was proud of what he did. When he became president, he must have felt like king of the world, and maybe he was. This is not a judgment of the man. I don't know if he went to Heaven or not when he died. For his sake, I hope he did. I am only stating the fact that he did play a role in the JFK assassination, in addition to a slew of other crimes.

Many researchers nowadays believe that Johnson was a part of the plot to kill JFK, although they disagree as to the level of his involvement. Some, like myself, believe that he initiated and orchestrated the plot. Others believe he may have known about it and simply chose to do nothing, which is still complicity. Still others believe he had no foreknowledge of it, but when it happened he made no attempt to find the killers because he hated John Kennedy anyway and he was happy to be president now. But to believe that Johnson had nothing to do with either the plot or the cover-up is simply not confronting the obvious truth.

When we see John Kennedy get shot, we naturally feel great sympathy for him. We also feel a lot of other things: shock, horror, fear, anger, confusion, etc. This emotional content gives the JFK assassination a special place in our collective consciousness. You just can't help but feel for the man, even if you didn't like him. The Lincoln assassination was also a tragic event, but it does not grip us emotionally as much because we have not seen a film of Lincoln getting shot. But when we see Kennedy get hit, it brings us all down to Earth. It is an instant reminder of our own frailty and mortality. Kennedy was arguably the most powerful man in the world at the time, yet he was brought down by one finger- the finger of a trained assassin. As Kennedy rode through the streets of Dallas, he had so much on his mind. He was thinking about Castro. He was thinking about the mess in Vietnam. He was wondering if he could achieve détente with Russia. He was wondering how to handle the economy and the civil rights issue. He also thought about his family and his responsibilities to his wife and kids. Then it all ended suddenly in one moment. What about all his big plans and hopes and dreams? All of it was gone instantly. We know all too well that something like that could happen to any one of us at any time, even if not in the same way. Seeing John Kennedy get shot brings us face to face with the ultimate paradox: Life is everything and life is nothing.

Every day in Dallas, in an area known as Dealey Plaza, thousands of people drive past the corner of Elm and Houston, unaware of the historical significance of the location. There is a small plaque near the curb on Elm Street that commemorates John Kennedy, and there is an "X" on the street used by researchers to do various calculations, but otherwise the scene appears innocuous. There is no huge monument or shrine to distinguish the location as historically unique. Even the picket fence from where the fatal shot came is still there, the same as it ever was. It has not been preserved or consecrated; it's just rotting and full of graffiti. If you didn't know better, you'd never guess that the whole world changed right there.

Admittedly, the title of this book is overly simplistic. The JFK case is a tangled web of complexity, and after more than half a century researchers are still trying to sort it all out. The job was far too massive for any one person, even LBJ, to pull off on his own. The list of co-conspirators is long, but ultimately they were all under Johnson's direction. No matter what anyone else did, they could not have gotten away with it without the complicity of Johnson. Even if he took no part in the planning of the crime, he was in control of the investigation afterwards, and it was he who allowed the murderers to get away scot-free.

Some people don't like to hear the word "conspiracy," but in this case it's undeniable. John Kennedy was killed by an assemblage of sinister forces. The "X" on Elm Street marks the spot where these forces converged. They had various reasons why they wanted him dead, but in the end they all colluded to get the job done, and in the end they all needed Lyndon Johnson to cover for them. And he did.

2

ENEMIES

John Kennedy was the youngest president elected to office, and when he was assassinated on November 22, 1963, he was the youngest president to end his tenure. During his short time as head of state, Kennedy was controversial, to say the least. He definitely polarized people. Some loved him and some hated him. There were more of the former than the latter, but those who hated him did so with passion. He seemingly came out of nowhere to win the 1960 election, and the established power structure could not accept the drastic changes he was making. Kennedy was truly a man of the people, and he exuded hope, confidence, and enthusiasm. Together with his photogenic wife Jacqueline, they formed Camelot- a fairy tale without a happy ending.

John Fitzgerald Kennedy was born on May 29, 1917, in Brookline, Massachusetts. His father, Joseph Kennedy, made his fortune in real estate, stocks, banking, and bootlegging. Joseph foresaw a bright political future for his sons, of which John was the second oldest. They all attended the finest schools, and John graduated from Harvard University in 1940.

John Kennedy served in the U.S. Navy from 1941-1945, during which time he suffered a back injury when his boat was hit by a Japanese destroyer. His PT-109 was broken in half by the attack, and Kennedy was credited with saving the life of his fellow crewman. While recovering from his injury, he learned that his older brother, Joe Jr., was killed flying a secret mission over Europe.

As the eldest surviving Kennedy brother, it was up to John to fulfill the political ambitions of his father. As a member of the Democratic Party, Kennedy was elected to the House of Representatives in 1946. He was elected to the Senate in 1952. In 1960, Kennedy ran for president on the Democratic ticket. At the national convention he was nominated on the first ballot and went on to win a close election against Richard Nixon.

In 1952, John Kennedy met Jacqueline Bouvier, who was a photographer for the *Washington Times-Herald*. They married in 1953. The couple had four children, but two died in infancy. Jackie Kennedy was one of the most popular and highly visible First Ladies. She was known for her emphasis on arts and culture, and for her highly publicized restoration of the White House.[2] [3]

John Kennedy liked to associate with Hollywood stars, including Frank Sinatra, Marilyn Monroe, and brother-in-law Peter Lawford. His alleged affair with Monroe was the stuff that tabloids dream of. Whether it was true or not, her sultry rendition of "Happy Birthday, Mr. President" certainly fed the rumor mills.

Jackie Kennedy knew of her husband's numerous infidelities and was easy-going about it, at least on the surface. Once, when Jackie found a pair of pink panties in her pillow case, she turned to John in bed and said, "Would you find out who these belong to, because they are not my size?"[4]

On another occasion, Marilyn Monroe called the White House and spoke directly to Jackie Kennedy, telling her about her affair with her husband. Jackie replied:

> Marilyn, you'll marry Jack, that's great. And you'll move into the White House and you'll assume the responsibilities of first lady, and I'll move out and you'll have all the problems.[5]

But John and Bobby Kennedy considered Monroe to be a loose cannon, due to her emotional frailty and the fact that she knew intimate secrets that could become a problem if exposed. When Monroe died mysteriously on August 5, 1962, rumors began to circulate that her death was somehow related, directly or indirectly, to her associations with the Kennedys. Bobby Kennedy and Peter Lawford were witnessed by neighbors entering Monroe's house earlier in the day. Supposedly, Bobby asked Marilyn for her diary and notes, which she refused to give to him, even after being offered a million dollars. This led to a heated argument. Later, two men were seen entering Monroe's house carrying a big briefcase. They ordered the

---

[2] http://spartacus-educational.com/USAkennedyJ.htm
[3] https://en.wikipedia.org/wiki/Jacqueline_Kennedy_Onassis
[4] http://www.anusha.com/exner.htm
[5] http://www.telegraph.co.uk/news/worldnews/northamerica/usa/10221582/How-Jackie-Kennedy-could-not-ignore-Marilyn-Monroe.html

domestic staff to leave, then emerged a half-hour later. Shortly afterwards, an ambulance arrived to take Marilyn to Santa Monica Hospital. At some point her body was returned to the house and placed face-down on the bed. It was made to look like a suicide, but it could not have been. Marilyn Monroe died from an overdose of barbiturates, yet no traces of barbiturates were found in her stomach or intestines, and there were no needle marks on her. The barbiturates could only have been administered by suppository, which means that she was murdered. The coroner was pressured into signing a death certificate that said she committed suicide.[6][7]

The Marilyn Monroe saga is just one chapter in the short but intriguing life of John F. Kennedy. That life was complicated by his associations with unsavory characters. As popular as John Kennedy was, he had more than his share of enemies. There were a lot of people who would have benefitted greatly from having Kennedy eliminated. Among them were organized crime figures.

The Mafia

John and Robert Kennedy had waged an unprecedented war against organized crime. Robert Kennedy, as Attorney General, headed the Organized Crime and Racketeering Section of the Justice Department. Convictions against organized crime figures rose 800 per cent during this crusade. After John Kennedy's death, the war against the mafia ended. The Organized Crime and Racketeering committee never met again.

It is well-known that Joseph Kennedy, the patriarch of the Kennedy clan, was involved in illegal bootlegging activities in which he amassed a fortune. These activities brought him together with underworld figures, and he used those underworld connections to advance the political career of his son. Through Joseph Kennedy's influence, the mafia helped to get John Kennedy elected by insuring he would carry Illinois in the 1960 election against Richard Nixon.

Here are some of the key figures from the underground who factored into Kennedy's death:

---

[6] Hughes-Wilson, Col. John, *JFK: An American Coup D'etat*, pp. 40-42, John Blake Publishing, 2015
[7] https://22novembernetwork.wordpress.com/tag/james-andrews/

Sam Giancana- Giancana was the mob boss for the Chicago area. His record included charges of theft, burglary, and murder, although the murder charges were dropped after the key witness was murdered. By the 1950s he had emerged as one of the leading crime figures in the Chicago area. He was involved in CIA plots to assassinate Fidel Castro, since the mob had lost a fortune due to Castro's closure of their highly lucrative casinos in Cuba. At the time, Giancana believed that Kennedy would be an ally in the White House, which was not the case. Giancana used his influence to help John Kennedy carry Illinois in the 1960 election. He somehow managed to get 10,000 votes cast for Kennedy by dead people.[8] This swung the election in Kennedy's favor, and he was expected to go easy on organized crime as a result. Instead, Kennedy escalated the aggression against them. Giancana and the mob felt betrayed and wanted Kennedy dead. One or more of the shooters in Dallas may have been Giancana's men.

To complicate matters, Kennedy and Giancana shared the same mistress. In February of 1960, Judith Exner was introduced to John Kennedy by Frank Sinatra, who also introduced her to Sam Giancana. Both Kennedy and Giancana carried on an affair with Exner for about two years. Exner became a conduit between the two men, delivering mysterious envelopes to Giancana from Kennedy. At one point Giancana proposed to Exner, but she declined. By Exner's own account, she became pregnant with Kennedy's child and had an abortion. Exner's association with Kennedy became public knowledge during the Church hearings of 1975, during which she was vilified by the press.[9] [10]

At the time of his death, Giancana had been cooperating with the Senate Intelligence Committee regarding organized crime activities. He was murdered in June of 1975. He was shot six times around his mouth, which is the mob's way of saying, "This guy talks too much."[11]

Carlos Marcello- Marcello was the boss of America's oldest crime family. His rap sheet contained convictions for bank robbery, assault, and narcotics

---

[8] http://www.thirdworldtraveler.com/CIA
[9] http://scandalouswoman.blogspot.com/2009/01/mob-moll-judith-campbell-exner-jfk-and.html
[10] http://channel.nationalgeographic.com/killing-kennedy/articles/the-sex-life-of-jfk/
[11] Benson, Michael, *Who's Who in the JFK Assassination*, Carol Publishing Group, 1993

trafficking. Marcello's territory included Texas and Louisiana. By the 1940s he had taken control of Louisiana's gambling network. Along with Meyer Lanski, he purchased some of New Orleans' most lucrative casinos. In 1959, he appeared before Robert Kennedy's committee on organized crime, but refused to answer any questions, instead taking the Fifth Amendment repeatedly. He had sought revenge on both Kennedys since Robert Kennedy had him deported in April of 1961. Marcello had been dumped in a jungle in Guatamala without being allowed to collect his belongings or make a phone call.[12]Vowing to avenge his deportation, he made the following comment to an associate:

> You know what they say in Sicily: if you want to kill a dog,
> you don't cut off the tail, you cut off the head.[13]

By that he meant that by killing John Kennedy he would render Bobby Kennedy ineffective and neutralize his war on crime. Since Dallas was his turf, Marcello played a major role in arranging the assassination. After John Kennedy's death, Marcello had this to say:

> Yeah, I had the son of a bitch killed. I'm glad I did. I'm
> sorry I couldn't have done it myself![14]

Santos Trafficante- Trafficante was the mob boss for the Tampa area. In the 1940s, he and several other mafia figures set up gambling operations in Cuba, giving Fulgencio Batista a cut of the profits. He was arrested for gambling offenses in the U.S. and did time in a Florida prison. In 1954, Trafficante took control of mob-owned casinos in Cuba after his father died. He controlled the operations until Castro's revolution, and afterwards he worked with the Cuban paramilitary in an attempt to regain control of the Cuban territory. He was held in Castro's prison until he was deported back to the U.S. Like most of the mafioso, Trafficante resented Kennedy for not being more aggressive toward Cuba. Trafficante later became part of a CIA plot to assassinate Castro. He was a key subject in the Justice Department's crackdown on organized crime during the Kennedy administration. He helped to arrange an assassination plot against Kennedy in Miami, which was unsuccessful. Speaking to associate Jose Aleman, Trafficante predicted Kennedy's death in advance:

---

[12] http://spartacus-educational.com/JFKmarcello.htm

[13] http://content.time.com/time/magazine/article/0,9171,956397,00.html

[14] Waldron, Lamar, *Legacy of Secrecy*, p. 754, Counterpoint, 2008

Mark my word, this man Kennedy is in trouble, and he will get what is coming to him. Kennedy's not going to make it to the election. He is going to be hit.[15]

The House Select Committee on Assassinations (HSCA) admitted the role of organized crime in JFK's death. They stated:

Trafficante, like Carlos Marcello, had the motive, means, and opportunity to assassinate President Kennedy…Trafficante's stature in the national syndicate of organized crime, notably the violent narcotics trade, and his role as the mob's chief liaison to criminal figures within the Cuban exile community, provided him with the capability of formulating an assassination conspiracy against President Kennedy.[16]

Meyer Lansky- Early in life, Lansky became involved with Bugsy Siegel and Lucky Luciano. He had his own gang, and was soon involved in bootlegging, drug smuggling, pornography, prostitution and extortion. He was believed to have been involved in the killing of mob bosses Joe Masseria, Salvatore Maranzano, and even his good friend Bugsy Siegel. It was Lansky who obtained incriminating pictures of J. Edgar Hoover, which he used to blackmail the FBI Director into inaction against organized crime. In his entire criminal career, he was never convicted of anything worse than illegal gambling. When he died in 1983, he had an estimated net worth of $400 million.[17]

Jimmy Hoffa- Hoffa became vice president of the Teamsters Union in 1952. David Beck was president of the union at the time, until he was investigated for illegal activities by the Select Committee on Labor, of which Robert Kennedy was the chief counsel. Beck was imprisoned for five years for using union funds for personal reasons, and Hoffa became president of the union. Hoffa was then investigated for corruption by the same committee. He was accused of misappropriating $9.5 million in union funds, but a jury found him not guilty. In spite of that, the Teamsters Union was expelled from the AFL-CIO for their activities. When John Kennedy was elected president, he appointed Robert Kennedy as Attorney General. The Kennedys then

---

[15] http://spartacus-educational.com/JFKtrafficante.htm
[16] https://www.thomhartmann.com/blog/2009/11/legacy-secrecy-introduction
[17] http://spartacus-educational.com/USAClansky.htm

escalated the investigation into Hoffa and the teamster's activities. Hoffa was convicted of jury tampering, attempted bribery, and fraud, and was sentenced to 13 years in prison. After a long appeals process, Hoffa began serving his sentence in 1967. In 1971, Hoffa was pardoned by Richard Nixon. This was in return for Hoffa providing Nixon with suitcases full of cash during his presidential campaign.[18]

Hoffa made no secret of his feelings about the assassination. Author Lamar Waldron describes Hoffa's reaction:

> In Miami, Jimmy Hoffa called Frank Ragano, the attorney he shared with Trafficante, and gloated over the assassination of JFK. However, Hoffa's mood changed after he got a call from a Teamster official in Washington. Hoffa was furious that two Teamster leaders at the union's Washington headquarters had closed the office, lowered its flags to half-mast, and sent condolences to the President's widow. Hoffa yelled at his secretary for crying, hung up on the people in Washington, and left the building.[19]

There was no love lost between Jimmy Hoffa and Robert Kennedy. The two disliked each other intensely. During the hearings, Kennedy questioned Hoffa about a comment, or possible threat, he had made:

> RFK: So whose backs are you going to break, Mr. Hoffa?
>
> JH: Figure of speech - I know you know who I was talking about, and I know what you're talking about.
>
> RFK: Well, Mr. Hoffa, all I'm trying to find out - I'll tell you what I'm talking about. I'm trying to find out whose back you're going to break.
>
> JH: Figure of speech.
>
> RFK: What?
>
> JH: Figure of speech, Bobby.
>
> RFK: Figure of speech about what?

---

[18] http://spartacus-educational.com/USAhoffa.htm

[19] Waldron, Lamar, *The Hidden History of the JFK Assassination*, p. 383, Counterpoint, 2013

JH: I don't know.

RFK: Well, who were you talking about?

JH: I have no knowledge of what you're talking about, and I don't.[20]

Jimmy Hoffa disappeared in 1975. It is believed that he was murdered to keep him from testifying to the House Select Committee on Assassinations. Hoffa's involvement in the assassination has long been suspected by many. Hoffa was closely connected with Carlos Marcello and Santos Trafficante, two of Kennedy's mortal enemies. Hoffa's body was never found, and he was declared legally dead in 1982.[21]

In an interview with *Look* magazine, Robert Kennedy expressed his views on the Teamsters Union:

> At birth, it is a Teamster who drives the ambulance to the hospital. At death, a Teamster who drives the hearse to the grave. Between birth and death, it is the Teamsters who drive the trucks that bring you your meat, milk, clothing and drugs, pick up your garbage and perform many other essential services.
>
> The individual truck driver is honest, and so are the vast majority of local Teamster officials - but they are completely under the control and domination of certain corrupt officials at the top. Picture this power, then, and the chaos that could result in these officials were to gain control over sea and other transportation outlets. Such a force could conceivably cause anyone - management and labor alike - to capitulate to its every whim. With Hoffa at the controls of the union that will dominate the transport alliance, this power would certainly be in the wrong hands.[22]

He was right. The whole country depends on the teamsters to provide the necessities of life. We won't have food if the teamsters don't deliver it

---

[20] http://www.npr.org/2015/07/06/420595057/vendetta-recalls-the-ruthless-rivalry-between-bobby-kennedy-jimmy-hoffa

[21] http://spartacus-educational.com/USAhoffa.htm

[22] Robert Kennedy, *Look* magazine (2nd September, 1958)

to the stores. We won't have medicine if the teamsters don't deliver it to the hospitals. We won't have anything if the teamsters don't deliver raw materials to the factories. They would have the ability to destroy the economy and create absolute chaos if they were not kept in check. The Teamsters Union was all about power, and it was power that killed JFK.

Robert Kennedy wrote *The Enemy Within*, a book which details the results of the McClellan Committee's investigation into Hoffa's illegal and improper activities in labor and management. RFK sent a copy of the book to Hoffa with a note that read: "To Jimmy, I'm sending you this book so you won't have to use union funds to buy one, Bobby."[23]

Some researchers have speculated about the involvement of foreign mafias in the assassination. The French mafia, in particular, has been rumored to have been involved. I see no reason to believe that, because there is simply no need to involve a foreign mafia. Our own mafia is perfectly capable of killing people. They have inside connections that foreign criminals would not have, and they have a proven track record. Why would they need to import killers? That would involve a paper trail. There would be airline tickets, passports and visas, hotel receipts, long-distance phone calls, etc. These could be used as evidence later on. Then they would have to worry about getting them out of the country afterwards, meaning more paper trails. The plotters wanted to keep it as simple as possible, and importing foreign killers just complicates things too much.

The CIA

One month after John Kennedy was assassinated, former President Harry Truman, the founder of the CIA, made the following comment:

> I never had any thought that when I set up the CIA that it would be injected into peacetime cloak and dagger operations.....There is something about the way the CIA has been functioning that is casting a shadow over our historic position, and I feel that we need to correct it.[24]

In 1942, President Franklin Roosevelt established the Office of Strategic Services (OSS). Its purpose was to collect and analyze strategic information.

---

[23] http://spartacus-educational.com/JFKholt.htm
[24] http://www.maebrussell.com/Prouty/Harry%20Truman%27s%20CIA%20article.html

This was done mainly in response to the Japanese attack on Pearl Harbor. The OSS never had complete jurisdiction over foreign intelligence activities, as much of it was left to military intelligence and the FBI. After Japan surrendered in 1945, President Truman dissolved the OSS, whose functions were split between the Department of State and the Department of War. In 1947, Truman signed the National Security Act (NSA). This established the Central Intelligence Agency, which took on OSS functions but with a different organizational structure. The CIA was the nation's first peacetime intelligence service. Its purpose was to coordinate intelligence reports from different agencies.

Under the NSA, the exact authorities and functions of the CIA are left intentionally vague. They are authorized to perform "services of common concern" and "such other functions and duties related to intelligence affecting the national security as the National Security Council may from time to time direct." Since the directive is not clear, it allows the agency to avoid prosecution and to overstep its own authority. The NSA also states that the Director of Central Intelligence is responsible for "protecting intelligence sources and methods from unauthorized disclosure." Who defines what "unauthorized disclosure" means? It just means they don't have to tell what they don't want to tell.[25]

The NSA deliberately structured the CIA so that they would have complete autonomy and everyone else would have plausible deniability. If the CIA commits an illegal act, it would be very hard to prove. They can always invoke the claim of "national security interest" as justification for not revealing their methods. Since the agency is compartmentalized, it is easy to deny any knowledge of the illegal act. Even the head of the CIA does not know all the activities his people are involved in. The president knows even less. They don't have to lie about it. But when someone needs dirty work to be done, they can count on the CIA to pull it off. They are simply told what needs to be accomplished, and no one will question their methods as long as they get the job done. Armed with complete autonomy and no accountability, the CIA became a rogue agency. They set out to change the world by interfering in the internal affairs of foreign countries.[26]

---

[25] https://en.wikipedia.org/wiki/Central_Intelligence_Agency
[26] https://fas.org/irp/offdocs/int022.html

The CIA in Iran

In 1953, the CIA and British intelligence (MI6) orchestrated a coup in Iran. This was known as Operation Ajax to the CIA, and Operation Boot to MI6. Prime Minister Mohammad Mosaddegh was overthrown in favor of dictator Mohammed Reza Pahlavi. Mossadegh sought to limit British influence over Iranian oil reserves. The company in question was Anglo-Iranian Oil Company (AIOC), which is now part of British Petroleum (BP). AIOC refused to allow an audit of the company, leading Mossadegh's government to nationalize Iran's oil industry and expel foreign corporate representatives from the country. This move was widely supported by the Iranian population, and greatly increased the popularity of Mosaddegh. Iran attempted to negotiate with AIOC, offering a 50/50 split of the oil profits, but the company declined. Britain initially responded with an economic boycott against Iran, which was effective at breaking down support for the government and creating factions of dissent. This included an embargo by the British Royal Navy who stopped any ship carrying Iranian oil, claiming that it was "stolen property."

The U.S. and British governments were convinced by their intelligence agencies that Iran's nationalism was a Soviet-backed plot, and that Iran was on the verge of becoming communist. Using this as a pretext, President Eisenhower and Winston Churchill agreed to overthrow the Iranian government. To do this, they provoked a high-profile national incident. Hired infiltrators were brought in, posing as Tudeh (Communist) Party members to fake a communist revolution. Mobsters and mercenaries were used to provoke riots and cause civil unrest, leading to the deaths of up to 300 people. Propaganda and psychological warfare were used to erode support for the government. AIOC contributed funds to bribe Iranian officials, reporters, and businessmen. Mossadegh was arrested, tried, and convicted in a military court. He served three years in jail, then was put under house arrest for life. Many of his supporters were given the death penalty. The new government allowed Pahlavi to rule as a monarch, although he was ultimately controlled by the United States as a puppet ruler.

In 2013, the CIA admitted that it orchestrated the coup. They also admitted to bribing Iranian officials. The CIA called it "an act of U.S. foreign policy, conceived and approved at the highest levels of government."[27] According to former CIA staffer Nick Cullather, the agency burned most of its documents relating to the coup. Cullather claims there was a "culture of destruction" in the agency, which is not hard to believe, considering the sensitive nature of the material. It's surprising that any documents survived at all.[28] [29]

U.S. Secretary of State Madeleine K. Albright was openly critical of the coup:

> The Eisenhower administration believed its actions were justified for strategic reasons. ... But the coup was clearly a setback for Iran's political development. And it is easy to see now why many Iranians continue to resent this intervention by America in their internal affairs.[30]

The CIA in Guatemala

In 1954, the CIA carried out Operation PBSUCCESS in Guatemala. This covert operation was a coup d'etat to depose the democratically elected President Jacobo Arbenz. This ended the Guatemalan Revolution, which had begun in 1944, and installed military dictator Carlos Castillo Armas. The Guatemalan Revolution was opposed by the U.S. government because they saw it as communist, since Arbenz had legalized the Communist Party in Guatemala. The CIA exaggerated the extent of communist influence in the country, and President Eisenhower authorized Operation PBSUCCESS in August of 1953. The CIA armed, funded, and trained a force of 480 men to invade Guatemala, led by Armas. The U.S. formed a naval blockade around the tiny nation to isolate them. The CIA used psychological warfare against Guatemala. This included broadcasting anti-government propaganda over a radio station, and instigating false reports of the invasion's success. The military campaign did not fare well, but the psychological warfare was successful. After being misled about the scope of the invasion, Arbenz and the Guatemalan Army surrendered.

---

[27] http://www.cnn.com/2013/08/19/politics/cia-iran-1953-coup/?hpt=po_c2
[28] https://en.wikipedia.org/wiki/1953_Iranian_coup_d%27état
[29] http://www.nytimes.com/1997/05/29/us/cia-destroyed-files-on-1953-iran-coup.html
[30] Secretary Albright's Speech regarding Iran, MidEast Info, 17 March 2000

Although the U.S. tried to portray it as a fight against communism, they had actually overthrown a democratic government. Considered the deathblow to democracy in Guatemala, the coup was an international disaster for the United States, and created much anti-U.S. sentiment in Latin America. It was widely decried as a needless act of aggression, drawing comparisons with Hitler's invasion of Austria. The U.S. tried to justify the coup by seeking evidence of Soviet influence in the Guatemalan government, but to no avail. Armas became a dictator, reversing social reforms, banning opposition parties, and imprisoning political opponents. Armas was the first in a series of U.S. puppet rulers in Guatemala. Decades of civil war followed, as the Guatemalan people tried to regain their freedom.[31]

Other CIA foreign interventions over the years include: Indonesia, Guyana, Zaire, Brazil, Dominican Republic, Greece, Chile, East Timor, Nicaragua, Grenada, Libya, Panama, Iraq, Afghanistan, Haiti, and Yugoslavia.[32]

James Jesus Angleton was the chief of CIA counterintelligence. His words sum up the CIA's point of view:

> It is inconceivable that a secret intelligence arm of the government has to comply with all the overt orders of the government.[33]

That may sound like a surprising statement, but the only thing surprising about it is that he would admit it openly. Angleton is just stating the obvious. Intelligence agencies were created for the purpose of bypassing official policy, so it would be self-defeating if they were limited by official policy.

JFK's denouncement of the CIA proved to be prophetic:

> If the United States ever experiences an attempt at a coup to overthrow the government, it will come from the CIA. The agency represents a tremendous power and total unaccountability to anyone.[34]

---

[31] https://en.wikipedia.org/wiki/1954_Guatemalan_coup_d%27état
[32] http://www.huppi.com/kangaroo/CIAtimeline.html
[33] Baker, Judyth Vary, *Me and Lee*, p. 225, Trine Day, 2010
[34] http://www.jfktruth.org/LBJ/index3.htm

Kennedy had only been in office a few months when the failed Bay of Pigs invasion took place. He was just beginning to learn how the CIA operates. The agency had no accountability to the president or anyone. He had promised to "splinter the CIA into a thousand pieces and scatter it to the winds." Kennedy wanted to restructure the agency so that it was under presidential control, but the CIA was not about to give up their autonomy.

Anti-Castro Cubans

Cuban rebels were attempting to reclaim their country after Fidel Castro established a communist regime there. Kennedy promised the Cubans a "free Havana," but he refused to invade Cuba and he was considered a traitor by the Cuban refugees.

Fidel Castro rose to power in Cuba in 1959 when he overthrew dictator Fulgencio Batista. At first, the U.S. did not know that Castro would establish a communist rule there. The U.S. had supported Batista, but they soon saw that the Castro administration was tending toward communism. Castro had forged strong political and economic links with the Soviet Union, and the alliance appeared threatening. Being naturally distrustful of a communist force so close to mainland America, the United States government began a program to eliminate the threat. This program included sabotage and subversion against Castro and his communist rule in Cuba. The plan originated as "A Program of Covert Action Against the Castro Regime," under President Eisenhower in March of 1960. The goals of the program included:

1. Provide a powerful propaganda offensive against the regime.

2. Perfect a covert intelligence network within Cuba.

3. Develop paramilitary forces outside of Cuba.

4. Get the necessary logistical support for covert military operations on the island.[35]

This culminated in the failed Bay of Pigs invasion in April of 1961. The plans for the invasion were inherited by Kennedy, after being briefed by Eisenhower and the CIA. The U.S. had funded, armed, and trained the Cuban

---

[35] https://en.wikipedia.org/wiki/Cuban_Project

paramilitary in preparation for the invasion. The paramilitary consisted largely of Cuban refugees who were exiled from their country. The training for the invasion took place in Guatemala. Although it was intended to be a surprise attack, Cubans in the U.S. were aware of the plans, and even Castro himself had learned of the guerilla training camps.

Kennedy had authorized the attack, but he did not want it to appear to be a U.S. invasion. It was intended to be a revolution by the Cuban paramilitary, with limited assistance from the United States. In Kennedy's words:

> I have emphasized before that this was a struggle of Cuban patriots against a Cuban dictator. While we could not be expected to hide our sympathies, we made it repeatedly clear that the armed forces of this country would not intervene in any way.[36]

The goal was to establish a non-communist government that was cooperative with the United States. Jose Miro Cardona, head of the Cuban Revolutionary Council, had already been chosen to be the provincial president if the invasion was successful. The success of the plan depended on the support of the Cuban people. Kennedy had been told by his advisors that the landing of the paramilitary in Cuba would spark an uprising among the Cuban population and elements of their military. That was not the case, as Kennedy had been misled by intelligence reports that showed a greater groundswell of support than really existed.

The original plan called for two air strikes, originating from Nicaragua, against Cuban air bases. The first air strike was launched on April 15, 1961, and it was a failure. The bombers missed many of their targets, doing little damage to Castro's air force. The planes were obsolete WWII B-26 bombers painted to look like Cuban Air Force planes. Photos of the painted planes were published, which revealed involvement of the U.S. military. The second air strike was cancelled by President Kennedy. The plan called for a 1,400-man invasion force, known as Brigade 2506, to land on a remote swampy area on the southern coast of Cuba at night. A smaller force was set to land on the east coast of Cuba to cause confusion. Paratroopers were dropped in advance to disrupt transportation. But as Brigade 2506 landed

---

[36] https://www.jfklibrary.org/Research/Research-Aids/JFK-Speeches/American-Society-of-Newspaper-Editors_19610420.aspx

on the beaches of Cuba, they came under heavy fire from Castro's military. They were attacked by airplanes with machine guns, two ships were sunk, and half of the air support was destroyed. Castro ordered 20,000 troops to fight off the invasion. It became a disaster for the exiles. 114 were killed in action, and 1,183 were captured. After spending 20 months in captivity, the U.S. negotiated a deal with Castro. With Robert Kennedy involved in the negotiations, Castro received $53 million worth of baby food and medicine in exchange for the prisoners. In December of 1962, the freed prisoners returned home. In a ceremony at Miami's Orange Bowl, the flag of Brigade 2506 was handed to Kennedy, who responded, "I can assure you that this flag will be returned to this brigade in a free Havana."[37]

Kennedy's failure to provide adequate air support is often cited for the reason for the failure of the Bay of Pigs operation. Kennedy publicly accepted the blame, but he knew that the CIA had tried to trap him into escalating the invasion. The Bay of Pigs fiasco made Kennedy look weak and indecisive to the public. This was the low point in Kennedy's tenure as president, which was only three months at that point.

In reaction to this failure, Kennedy signed two National Security Action Memoranda to try and bring the CIA under his control. In June of 1961, he signed NSAM 55, stating that the chairman of the Joint Chiefs of Staff would be held responsible for military activity in peacetime as well as wartime. He also signed NSAM 57, which divided paramilitary activity between the military and the CIA. This stated that the CIA would only be allowed to conduct small covert operations, while large operations would be handled by the military. It was a reasonable policy, yet it was an attempt to reign in the power of the CIA, which was met with resistance.[38] [39] [40]

Operation Mongoose

In spite of the Bay of Pigs debacle, Kennedy was more determined than ever to remove the communist threat to the U.S. That led to the development of the next phase of the plan to eliminate Castro. President Kennedy created a committee to construct plans to overthrow Castro's government. The committee was headed by Robert Kennedy, and also

---

[37] https://en.wikipedia.org/wiki/Bay_of_Pigs_Invasion
[38] Marrs, Jim,*Crossfire*, Carroll and Graf, 1989
[39] https://www.jfklibrary.org/JFK/JFK-in-History/The-Bay-of-Pigs.aspx
[40] https://en.wikipedia.org/wiki/Brigade_2506

included Allen Dulles and General Ed Lansdale. The plan was officially named Operation Mongoose in November of 1961. The headquarters for the operation was the CIA's JM/WAVE station in Miami, located in the heart of the Cuban community. Ted Shackley and William Harvey were chosen to implement the program. Harvey recruited David Sanchez Morales from the Mexico City station and moved him to JM/WAVE. The plan called for the training of a paramilitary force for guerrilla action. The paramilitary force was to include exiled Cubans, but not the U.S. military.

In addition to the paramilitary forces, Operation Mongoose also included plans for propaganda, psychological warfare, and creation of internal revolt against Castro's government. The goal was to create a groundswell of support from the population for the overthrow of Castro. Some of the plans bordered on comical. One was a plan to secretly lace Castro's cigars with a hallucinogenic drug to make him act and sound crazy when he gave a speech. Another plan was to contaminate his shoes with thallium to make his beard fall out. When plans like these failed, the next option was assassination.

Operation Mongoose was incorporated into Project ZR/RIFLE, which had originated in May of 1961. ZR/RIFLE was a top secret project to assassinate Fidel Castro. The project recruited criminal assets, both foreign and domestic, to perform various illegal activities such as burglary, wire tapping, intimidation, and murder. When the CIA speaks of executive action programs, that is a covert way of saying "assassination." ZR/RIFLE is an example of an executive action program.[41]

Robert Kennedy and CIA Director Allen Dulles began to involve organized crime in the plan to assassinate Castro. They enlisted the aid of well-known mobsters such as Johnny Roselli, Sam Giancana, Carlos Marcello, Santos Trafficante, and Meyer Lansky. In return for their cooperation, the mafia was assured by the FBI that they would be immune from prosecution. The mafia had their own motives to eliminate Castro. They wanted to regain control of the lucrative casino industry that Castro had taken from them. One plan to kill Castro was to use an exploding cigar. Another was to contaminate his diving suit with toxins. Another was to use a poison pen, which was actually a syringe. Yet another involved the use of poison pills. Supposedly, Roselli was offered $150,000 to use the poison pills on Castro.

---

[41] Stockton, Bayard, *Flawed Patriot*, Chapter 8

Why it didn't work is not known, but according to Castro, there were about 20 CIA-sponsored attempts to kill him.

Robert Kennedy was naturally distraught over his brother's death. But it was more than mere grief; it was guilt. Bobby blamed himself for the assassination, because he believed that the plots to kill Castro, which he had led and orchestrated, had backfired on him. He believed that the same apparatus that was used in the Castro plots was turned against John Kennedy. Killing Castro proved too hard to do, so they turned it around and killed Kennedy instead. The thinking was that Johnson would be more willing to invade Cuba, which turned out to not be the case anyway. On the day of the assassination, Robert Kennedy was on the phone with Cuban exile leader Harry Ruiz-Williams. Robert said bluntly, "One of your guys did it." This shows that Robert Kennedy knew the truth right away. He never bought the Oswald story, in spite of his public comments. Those who knew of the Castro plots had little sympathy for Bobby, since they figured he was no better himself. This would explain why RFK was quiet and cooperative during the investigation, since he had to cover up his own inadvertent role.[42]

Fidel Castro was not the only target of the CIA's assassination squad. Col. Fletcher Prouty, former Chief of Special Operations, has written extensively about the role of the CIA in foreign affairs:

> Assassination is big business. It is the business of the CIA and any other power that can pay for the "hit" and control the assured getaway. The CIA brags that its operations in Iran in 1953 led to the pro-Western attitude of that important country. The CIA also takes credit for what it calls the "perfect job" in Guatemala. Both successes were achieved by assassination...[43]

> It's what we call the use of hired gunmen, and this isn't new. In fact, this little manual here which is called *The Assassination Manual for Latin America*, contains a line which says that, talking about Latin America, "If possible, professional criminals will be hired to carry out specific selected jobs," "jobs" in quotes, which means murders. But, if this manual for Latin America, printed in the last few

---

[42] http://educationforum.ipbhost.com/topic/20026-rfk-one-of-your-guys-did-it/
[43] Prouty, *An Introduction to the Assassination Business* (1975)

years, and a government manual, says that, there's no
question that the application of the same techniques was
dated back in Kennedy's time. In fact, I know that from my
own experience. You know, I was in that business in those
days. So, with that knowledge, you begin to realize that hired
criminals, the way this book says, can be hired by anybody
in power with sufficient money to pay them, but more
importantly, with sufficient power to operate the cover-up
ever after. Because, you see, it's one thing to kill somebody;
it's another thing to cover up the fact that you did it, or that
you hired somebody to do it.[44]

Successful CIA assassinations include Salvador Allende (Chile), Patrice
Lumumba (Belgian Congo), Rafael Trujillo (Dominican Republic), Ngo Dinh
Diem (South Vietnam), and Che Guevara (Bolivia). Unsuccessful attempts
include Fidel Castro (Cuba) and Charles De Gaulle (France).[45]

Lyndon Johnson knew about the "executive actions" of the CIA, but true
to form, he did nothing about it:

We had been operating a damned Murder, Inc. in the
Caribbean.[46]

In 1976, President Gerald Ford signed Executive Order 11905, which was
intended to reform the U.S. intelligence community and improve oversight
on foreign intelligence activities. Among other things, it bans political
assassinations. That was a roundabout way of admitting that the CIA
engaged in political assassinations.[47]

Operation Northwoods

In 1962, Operation Northwoods was developed. This project included the
use of false flag operations to justify military intervention in Cuba. This
could mean real or simulated attacks which would then be blamed on the
Cuban government.

Here is a sample of the proposed strategy:

---

[44] https://www.youtube.com/watch?v=0NdtxGiK3WI
[45] Ventura, Jesse, *They Killed Our President*, p. 246, Skyhorse Publishing, 2013
[46] http://www.prouty.org/johnson.html
[47] https://en.wikipedia.org/wiki/Executive_Order_11905

A "Remember the Maine" incident could be arranged in several forms:

a. We could blow up a US ship in Guantanamo Bay and blame Cuba.

b. We could blow up a drone (unmanned) vessel anywhere in the Cuban waters. We could arrange to cause such incident in the vicinity of Havana or Santiago as a spectacular result of Cuban attack from the air or sea, or both. The presence of Cuban planes or ships merely investigating the intent of the vessel could be fairly compelling evidence that the ship was taken under attack. The nearness to Havana or Santiago would add credibility especially to those people that might have heard the blast or have seen the fire. The US could follow up with an air/sea rescue operation covered by US fighters to "evacuate" remaining members of the non-existent crew. Casualty lists in US newspapers would cause a helpful wave of national indignation.

We could develop a Communist Cuban terror campaign in the Miami area, in other Florida cities and even in Washington. The terror campaign could be pointed at refugees seeking haven in the United States. We could sink a boatload of Cubans en route to Florida (real or simulated). We could foster attempts on lives of Cuban refugees in the United States even to the extent of wounding in instances to be widely publicized. Exploding a few plastic bombs in carefully chosen spots, the arrest of Cuban agents and the release of prepared documents substantiating Cuban involvement, also would be helpful in projecting the idea of an irresponsible government.[48]

This would not only justify military action in the public's mind, but it would also turn the Cuban population against Castro. Operations Northwoods was rejected by President Kennedy, but the mere fact that it was even considered is an embarrassment to his administration. Yet, the strategy was not wasted. Operation Northwoods provided the blueprint for the current War on Terror, which is also based largely on false-flag operations.

---

[48] http://www.net4truthusa.com/operationnorthwoods.htm

Cuban Missile Crisis

Kennedy's defining moment as president came in October of 1962, during the Cuban missile crisis. An American U-2 spy plane had photographed nuclear missile sites in Cuba, which had been established by the Soviet Union. The missile sites had been built in response to the Bay of Pigs invasion, which convinced Nikita Khrushchev that the U.S. was planning military action against Cuba. Whether or not that was true, it gave the Soviet Union justification for establishing missile bases on the island. Castro claimed that the missiles were strictly for self-defense, and he refused to allow any inspections. Since Cuba was too small to fight the United States on its own, they would need help from their larger and stronger communist ally. Khrushchev sent Castro 40,000 troops, 1,300 field artillery pieces, 700 anti-aircraft guns, 350 tanks, and 150 jets, in addition to the nuclear missiles.[49] This was intended to deter a U.S. invasion. But Kennedy was uneasy with the situation of having communist missiles pointed at the U.S. from only 100 miles away. He did not immediately let on that he knew about the missiles. After discussing the problem privately with his advisors, he decided to place a naval blockade around Cuba, which he referred to as a "quarantine." This was a ring of ships around Cuba that would prevent the Soviets from bringing in more missiles or military supplies. Kennedy demanded that the missiles be removed and the sites destroyed. He went public with the crisis in a televised address on October 22, 1962. In it he explained his stance:

> It shall be the policy of this nation to regard any nuclear missile launched from Cuba against any nation in the Western Hemisphere as an attack by the Soviet Union on the United States, requiring a full retaliatory response upon the Soviet Union…To halt this offensive buildup, a strict quarantine on all offensive military equipment under shipment to Cuba is being initiated. All ships of any kind bound for Cuba, from whatever nation or port, will, if found to contain cargoes of offensive weapons, be turned back. This quarantine will be extended, if needed, to other types of cargo and carriers. We are not at this time, however, denying

---

[49] http://spartacus-educational.com/JFKmongoose.htm

the necessities of life as the Soviets attempted to do in their Berlin blockade of 1948.[50]

Both superpowers realized the potential for destruction if the situation escalated into a nuclear war. They agreed to a deal in which the Soviets would remove the weapons and dismantle the sites in exchange for a promise from the United States that they would not invade Cuba. The U.S. also agreed to remove its nuclear missiles from Turkey and Italy, although that was not made public until 25 years later. This appeared to the public as a defeat for Khrushchev, since it seemed that he got nothing from the deal. It's possible that the missile crisis was a ploy by the Soviet Union to get the United States to remove its missiles from Turkey and Italy. If that's the case, then Khrushchev got what he wanted, regardless of the public perception of the events.

During the Cuban missile crisis, Robert Kennedy ordered the CIA to cease all covert operations against Cuba. Considering the delicateness of the situation, it was wise to avoid any needless provocations. William Harvey from JM/WAVE ignored the order and dispatched three commando teams to Cuba to prepare for what he hoped was an imminent invasion. Both Kennedys were outraged. Soon after the missile crisis was over, Operation Mongoose was disbanded as a result of the agreement between Kennedy and Khrushchev. Remnants of Operation Mongoose probably continued as a black ops project.[51]

Vietnam

The CIA and the Pentagon wanted to escalate the war in Vietnam, but Kennedy wanted to withdraw troops. On October 11, 1963, Kennedy had signed NSAM 263, initiating a withdrawal of 1,000 troops from Vietnam, and ordering that all troops be withdrawn by the end of 1965. The memorandum stated that no formal announcement of the withdrawal should be made. The plan was to train the South Vietnamese so that they could carry out essential military functions on their own. This was the first step of a complete withdrawal planned by Kennedy. This was one of many acts that made Kennedy an enemy of the war machine.[52]

---

[50] https://en.wikipedia.org/wiki/Cuban_Missile_Crisis#cite_note-upi-57
[51] http://spartacus-educational.com/JFKzrrifle.htm
[52] https://en.wikipedia.org/wiki/National_Security_Action_Memorandum_263

John Kennedy reflected on his previous learning experience:

> The Bay of Pigs has taught me a number of things. One is not to trust generals or the CIA, and the second is that if the American people do not want to use American troops to remove a communist regime 90 miles away from our coast, how can I ask them to use troops to remove a communist regime 9,000 miles away?[53]

As World War II came to an end, the stage was being set for the next American conflict. At the 1945 summit meeting at Potsdam, Germany, the future of Vietnam was determined by President Roosevelt, Winston Churchill, and Joseph Stalin. They agreed to a temporary plan where Vietnam would be divided in two halves, with the Chinese controlling the north and the British controlling the south. Vietnam had been controlled by the French since the days of Napoleon, and they were aided by the allies in re-establishing control over the area. Britain and China both removed their troops within a year. At this time, Ho Chi Minh had formed the Democratic Republic of Vietnam, which was communist, in spite of its misleading name. France did not recognize this government, and continued their fight to regain control. The Viet Minh, led by Ho Chi Minh, established a firm hold in the north, and the French controlled only the south. In 1954, the French surrendered and pulled their troops out of Vietnam. Ngo Dinh Diem was installed as the new president of South Vietnam.

President Eisenhower was concerned about the spread of communism, but he knew the American public would be reluctant to accept another war at that point. The Korean War was still fresh in their memory. The U.S. had just lost about 35,000 soldiers in that conflict, but they feared the effort would be wasted if they allowed communism to spread to South Vietnam. Lacking public support for another war, Eisenhower instead sent a group of military advisors to Vietnam, led by General Ed Lansdale. Lansdale and his team tried to stir up support for a U.S. invasion. They used propaganda to portray communists as aggressive. They planted stories of communist atrocities, and they hired mercenaries from the Philippines to commit acts of sabotage and subversion to be blamed on communists. Lansdale attempted to make Diem's rule appear more successful than it was, and he distorted economic and unemployment statistics to achieve that end. In reality, Diem was no more of a humanitarian than his communist

---

[53] Marrs, Jim, *Crossfire*, p. 307, Carroll and Graf, 1989

counterpart. Diem imprisoned his political opponents, along with socialists, journalists, labor union leaders and religious leaders. This strategy was so successful that Ho Chi Minh felt he had to create armed resistance in an attempt to unify Vietnam. In 1960 he formed the National Front for the Liberation of South Vietnam (NLF), also known as the Viet Cong. One of the goals of the NLF was to replace the Catholic-dominated administration of Diem with one that represented all social classes and religions.[54]

This was the situation that Kennedy inherited in January of 1961. When Kennedy campaigned for president, he did so on a strong anti-communist platform, promising to use military might to ward off communist aggression. He pledged to continue Eisenhower's policy of supporting the South Vietnamese government of President Ngo Dinh Diem, who was a strong opponent of communism. Kennedy believed in the domino theory, the belief that if a country becomes communist, it will lead to surrounding countries also falling to communism. He felt that the spread of communism must be halted in Vietnam or it would spread to Laos, Cambodia, Burma, and other countries. He warned his fellow Americans that "Our security may be lost piece by piece, country by country." He instilled a strong sense of idealism in the people, and his hard military stance was instrumental in carrying him to victory in the election. But now, he was pressured to escalate a war that made no sense. Both sides were guilty of oppressing their people. Kennedy supported South Vietnam because they were not communist, but he must have questioned if they were really more moral.

When Kennedy became president, he was given questionable advice on Vietnam. He was told that with a small increase in military aid, the U.S. could hold off the Viet Cong and preserve freedom in South Vietnam. Kennedy agreed to give the South Vietnamese financial aid and to send 100 military advisors to help train their army. Some had warned Kennedy that Vietnam was a trap he would not be able to get out of, but Kennedy took the advice of the CIA, not knowing that their goal was to escalate the conflict.

In 1962, the U.S. introduced the Strategic Hamlet program in South Vietnam. This was an attempt to separate the South Vietnamese people from the Viet Cong, fearing that they might become indoctrinated with communist ideology. Peasants were forcibly moved into new villages under

---

[54] http://spartacus-educational.com/VietnamWar.htm

the control of the South Vietnamese Army. A stockade was built around the village, and armed guards kept a close watch on the people. The peasants had to travel long distances to work on their farms, and they resented being removed from the place of their ancestors' birth. This strategy backfired, as it caused much hostility and mistrust against the South Vietnamese government. Many of the South Vietnamese people joined the NLF in protest, and the Viet Cong Army grew by 300% in two years as a result of Strategic Hamlet. This pressured Kennedy to increase the military presence in South Vietnam, and by the end of 1962, there were 12,000 advisors in place. These advisors were there to aid with military training and organization, but were not to engage in combat. Supposedly, the U.S. was just helping the South Vietnamese fight their own battle, but they were becoming increasingly caught up in a war they could not win.

Buddhist Uprising

Another example of CIA manipulation in foreign affairs is the Buddhist uprising in South Vietnam in the early 1960s. At the time, Buddhists made up about 70% of the South Vietnamese population, while Roman Catholics made up only 10%. Yet, the Catholics were favored by the French, who ruled South Vietnam. Catholics held privileged positions in the government and they owned most of the land. The French saw Buddhism as a threat to their authority, and they passed restrictive laws against it.

On the night of May 8, 1963, a crowd gathered outside the government radio station in Hue, South Vietnam. Earlier that morning, Buddhist monk Thich Tri Quang gave an inspired speech in support of religious freedom. The crowd demanded that the radio station play a recording of the speech. The station refused, and the unruly crowd began pushing against the station's doors. Firefighters used water hoses to push back the crowd. The station called for assistance, and President Diem responded. Soon security chief Major Dang Sy arrived with officers in armored cars. Suddenly, two powerful explosions struck people in front of the station. Eight were killed and at least 15 others were injured. Major Dang Sy thought that it was a Viet Cong attack, but Sy and the South Vietnamese government were blamed for the incident by Quang and the Buddhist movement.

Doctors at the hospital said the injuries were very unusual. Some bodies were decapitated. There were holes in the corpses, but no metal was found. There were no wounds below the chest. The officials ruled that the casualties were caused by an explosion in mid-air. Since there was no metal in the bodies, they concluded that the injuries were caused by plastic bombs. The Buddhists disagreed with the findings because they exonerated the government, but Diem's security police were incapable of inflicting such injuries. Dr. Le Khac Quyen, the hospital director in charge of the investigation, was imprisoned by the government for refusing to sign a medical certificate saying that the injuries were caused by a type of bomb made by the Viet Cong, but the Viet Cong did not possess any weapon that could inflict that kind of damage. However, the Central Intelligence Agency did.

The use of plastic bombs was nothing new to the CIA. On January 9, 1952, two bombs exploded in Saigon, killing ten and injuring many more. Those explosions were caused by plastic bombs supplied by the CIA to warlord General The. A photographer from *Life* magazine was present at the Saigon bombing. That was no coincidence. The CIA had set the scene and alerted a *Life* photographer so he could be prepared to capture the evils of communist oppression. Only the bombing was not done by communists; it was done by the CIA. The photographer was prepared for the event and managed to capture graphic images that convinced people of the horrors of communism.

After the Hue incident, the furious Buddhists responded with protests, demonstrations, and public suicides by burning. They called for the Diem government to show compassion to all religions, but Diem instead responded by arresting thousands of Buddhist monks. The U.S. government and media accepted the Buddhist version of the event, and blamed the South Vietnamese government. At about this time, Kennedy probably began to question his support of Diem, although he never said so outwardly. Averell Harriman, diplomat and businessman, encouraged the removal of Diem, and sent a cable to Saigon, discreetly advocating an assassination plot. Kennedy did not authorize the assassination plot, but he also made no attempt to stop it. CIA operative Lucien Conein provided South Vietnamese generals with $40,000 and a promise that the U.S. would make no attempt to protect Diem. Diem was assassinated in a military coup on November 2, 1963.[55]

---

[55] http://spartacus-educational.com/VietnamWar.htm

War Hawks

In a 1961 meeting of the National Security Council, President Kennedy discussed the Soviet situation with the Joint Chiefs of Staff (JCS). Kennedy was hoping to achieve détente with Russia, but the war hawks were furious that he would negotiate with communists. His advisors, led by Allen Dulles and Lyman Lemnitzer, were promoting a pre-emptive nuclear attack on Russia. Kennedy reacted with shock and disgust, knowing that a nuclear war could never be won. He stormed out of the meeting and heatedly commented to Secretary of State Dean Rusk:

And we call ourselves the human race![56]

Rusk described the meeting as an "awesome experience." The JCS emphasized that the missile gap was in America's favor, but Kennedy did not see that as justification for initiating a nuclear conflict:

President Kennedy clearly understood what nuclear war meant and was appalled by it. In our many talks together, he never worried about the threat of assassination, but he occasionally brooded over whether it would be his fate to push the nuclear button... If any of us had doubts, that 1961 briefing convinced us that a nuclear war must never be fought. Consequently, throughout the Kennedy and Johnson years we worked to establish a stable deterrent.[57]

But the JCS and the CIA did not want a deterrent; they wanted war. They attempted to sabotage any negotiations with the Soviets. On May 1, 1960, Francis Gary Powers was flying the CIA's top secret U-2 plane over the Soviet Union. The purpose of his mission was to photograph Soviet nuclear and military installations. Powers' plane flew at 70,000 feet, which was believed to be out of the range of Soviet radar and weaponry. Still, the plane was shot down by a Soviet missile. Powers was captured alive and taken prisoner. U.S. officials believed that the plane had been destroyed, and they claimed that Powers was just conducting a routine weather flight when he drifted over Soviet air space due to a malfunction. They were not aware that the Soviets had recovered the plane intact. This caused an embarrassment for Eisenhower when he lied, saying that it was not a spy

---

[56] http://prospect.org/article/did-us-military-plan-nuclear-first-strike-1963
[57] Rusk, Dean, *As I Saw It*, W.W. Norton & Co., 1990

plane. But the Soviets had the recovered craft, complete with spy cameras and pictures of Soviet military installations.

By no coincidence, the Powers incident happened shortly before the upcoming summit between President Eisenhower and Soviet Premier Khrushchev. It is speculated by many that the event was deliberately staged by military hardliners to sabotage the summit. The incident greatly reduced the chances for progress toward détente. The summit was intended to diminish Cold War tensions, but the controversy created even more tension. Eisenhower refused to apologize, and Khrushchev left the summit early. Khrushchev probably knew that Eisenhower did not order the espionage, but he used the incident for political gain.

House Appropriations Chair Clarence Cannon made a statement on May 10 that placed the blame on Eisenhower. Cannon admitted that the project was "under the direction and control of the U.S. Central Intelligence Agency," yet he also said that the mission was "under the aegis of the Commander in Chief of the Armed Forces of the United States." Eisenhower did not admit to authorizing the mission, but it was clear that he did not have control over the CIA.

Khrushchev himself believed the incident was staged. He told an ambassador that he "could not help but suspect that someone had launched this operation with the deliberate intent of spoiling the summit meeting." Khrushchev did not blame Eisenhower for the spying. Instead, he laid the blame on Allen Dulles of the CIA. Khrushchev had his own issues with the KGB, and he was aware of how intelligence agencies function autonomously, devoid of any oversight. Eisenhower was beginning to recognize this too, as would his successor. Over the next few years, Khrushchev and Kennedy would form a bond based on their mutual disdain of their respective intelligence agencies. This led to the establishment of a backline channel where they could communicate directly.[58] [59]

Ike's Warning

On January 17, 1961, President Dwight Eisenhower gave his farewell address to the American people. In it he warned of the "acquisition of unwarranted influence" by the military-industrial complex. This came as a

---

[58] https://en.wikipedia.org/wiki/Francis_Gary_Powers
[59] https://www.fff.org/2015/11/02/bridge-of-spies-and-lee-harvey-oswald/

surprise to many, since Eisenhower was a military leader and a war hero, and was expected to continue the hard-line stance of the cold warriors. Eisenhower had resisted the pressure to increase defense spending, and was generally leaning toward reducing tensions with the Soviets. But he realized that the powerful arms industry, combined with the clandestine influence of the CIA, represented a threat to democracy. This was the situation that Kennedy would be inheriting.

From Ike's farewell address:

> Our military organization today bears little relation to that known by any of my predecessors in peace time, or indeed by the fighting men of World War II or Korea.

> Until the latest of our world conflicts, the United States had no armaments industry. American makers of plowshares could, with time and as required, make swords as well. But now we can no longer risk emergency improvisation of national defense; we have been compelled to create a permanent armaments industry of vast proportions. Added to this, three and a half million men and women are directly engaged in the defense establishment. We annually spend on military security more than the net income of all United States corporations.

> This conjunction of an immense military establishment and a large arms industry is new in the American experience. The total influence-economic, political, even spiritual- is felt in every city, every state house, every office of the federal government. We recognize the imperative need for this development. Yet we must not fail to comprehend its grave implications. Our toil, resources and livelihood are all involved; so is the very structure of our society.

> In the councils of government, we must guard against the acquisition of unwarranted influence, whether sought or unsought, by the military-industrial complex. The potential for the disastrous rise of misplaced power exists and will persist.

> We must never let the weight of this combination endanger our liberties or democratic processes. We should take nothing for granted only an alert and knowledgeable

citizenry can compel the proper meshing of huge industrial
and military machinery of defense with our peaceful
methods and goals, so that security and liberty may prosper
together.[60]

Prior to Eisenhower's term, military weaponry was only produced on an as-needed basis. With the advent of the Cold War, the U.S. felt compelled to stockpile weapons, including nuclear warheads. At the time, 3.5 million Americans were working in the defense industry in some capacity. That was a huge portion of the American economy. The bloated military budget insured that the factories would continue to crank out missiles and bombs by the thousands. Military action was needed to justify the production. From Pentagon officials to factory workers, there were so many people who benefited from the arms industry, there was little motivation to strive for peace. In 1950 the total military budget was $13 billion. In 1961 it was $47 billion. In 2017, that figure is approaching $700 billion.[61]

In addition to the financial incentives, the military was a source of pride for many. America had won a dramatic victory in World War II, and had heroically rescued suffering prisoners from concentration camps while simultaneously deposing a ruthless dictator. Americans were full of bravado at the time. Add to it the hyped-up belief that communists are evil and that we need to protect ourselves from this ubiquitous threat. We were determined to wipe them out like we wiped out the Nazis. When Kennedy came along and wanted détente, it was a complete change of course for the country. Many people considered it treasonous to negotiate with communists. Although Kennedy was a man of peace, he was considered the enemy to those in true power. This set him up for his inevitable fate.

Oil Tycoons

Kennedy was attempting to eliminate the oil depletion allowance that was granted to oil companies. This allowance gave the oil companies a huge, unfair tax break that was unparalleled in any other industry.

In his book *Cronies*, Robert Bryce explains how the oil depletion allowance works:

---

[60] https://www.ourdocuments.gov/doc.php?flash=true&doc=90&page=transcript
[61] https://www.cato.org/blog/budget-snapshot-average-annual-defense-spending-administration

An oilman drills a well that costs $100,000. He finds a reservoir containing $10,000,000 worth of oil. The well produces $1 million worth of oil per year for ten years. In the very first year, thanks to the depletion allowance, the oilman could deduct 27.5 per cent, or $275,000, of that $1 million in income from his taxable income. Thus, in just one year, he's deducted nearly three times his initial investment. But the depletion allowance continues to pay off. For each of the next nine years, he gets to continue taking the $275,000 depletion deduction. By the end of the tenth year, the oilman has deducted $2.75 million from his taxable income, even though his initial investment was only $100,000.[62]

The depletion allowance was obviously unfair and it allowed the oilmen to avoid paying their fair share of taxes. Kennedy was justified in trying to change this. It was pure greed by the oil barons to oppose it, but oppose it they did. LBJ was their man, and he would do whatever it took to keep them happy.

Author Matthew Smith described the oil depletion allowance as an outdated law that was left on the books after it outgrew its usefulness. In his book, *JFK: The Second Plot*, Smith writes:

The oil industry in Texas had enjoyed huge tax concessions since 1926, when Congress had provided them as an incentive to increase much needed prospecting. The oil depletion benefits were somehow left in place to become a permanent means by which immense fortunes were amassed by those in the industry and, well aware of the anomaly, John Kennedy had declared an intention to review the oil industry revenues. There was nothing in the world which would have inflamed the oil barons more than the President interfering with the oil depletion allowance.[63]

In May of 1958, a federal grand jury indicted 29 oil companies on charges of violating anti-trust laws by charging outrageous prices. The charges were based on price increases made by the oil companies the previous year at a time when there was no oil shortage, and in fact, there was a significant surplus of oil at that point. The price increase was initiated by Humble Oil,

---

[62] Bryce, Robert, *Cronies*, Public Affairs, 2004
[63] Smith, Matthew, *JFK: The Second Plot*, 1992

and the other 28 companies followed suit. It was estimated that the price increase cost U.S. consumers half a billion dollars. Public outrage led to the oil companies being brought to court and charged with conspiracy to violate price-fixing legislation. However, the defendants were all acquitted, with the judge saying only that "the evidence in the case does not rise above the level of suspicion."[64] All of this was before Kennedy took office, but it shows the greedy mentality of the oil tycoons. These are the people he would have to deal with in the coming years.[65]

Clint Murchison was an oil millionaire who owned about 500 companies, and had a strong influence in Washington. He extended his influence through the Del Charro Hotel in La Jolla, California. The Del Charro was a high class, expensive hotel that catered to the power elite. For the special guests who stayed there, food and lodging were free. The guest list included J. Edgar Hoover, mob boss Carlos Marcello, Richard Nixon, D.H. Byrd (owner of the Texas School Book Depository), Lyndon Johnson, and his aide, Bobby Baker. Along with partner Sid Richardson, Murchison owned the Del Mar Race Track. Knowing that Hoover was fond of gambling, Murchison gave him a box seat at the finish line. Murchison was a member of the John Birch Society and funded the McCarthy witch hunt against communists. Murchison also financed Dr. Alton Ochsner in his medical practice, which was used as a front for an anti-Castro project.[66]

H.L. Hunt was one of the richest men in America in 1963, with his estimated worth at about 5 billion dollars. Like most oil men, he wanted to preserve the Oil Depletion Allowance. He disliked the social programs of John Kennedy, and he considered Kennedy a communist. He was quoted as saying there was "no way left to get those traitors out of our government except by shooting them out." Hunt's political views were extremely conservative. He was a member of the John Birch Society, and he formed the International Committee for the Defense of Christian Culture. Hunt was a strong opponent of Fidel Castro and helped fund the Cuban Revolutionary Council. He also had two radio shows that were fiercely anti-communist and supported the tactics of Senator Joseph McCarthy. Hunt helped to finance the political career of Lyndon Johnson.[67]

---

[64] Buchanan, Thomas G., *Who Killed Kennedy?*, G.P. Putnam's Sons, 1964
[65] http://spartacus-educational.com/JFKsinvestOil.htm
[66] http://www.jfktruth.org/LBJ/index3.htm
[67] http://spartacus-educational.com/JFKhuntHL.htm

Author Joachim Joesten writes about the suspicions surrounding H.L. Hunt:

> When District Attorney Garrison, in his statement of September 21, 1967, made the startling disclosure that the assassination of President Kennedy had been ordered and paid for by a handful of oil-rich psychotic millionaires, he didn't name any names. But I'm quite sure that all the good people of Dallas, if any of them were privileged to hear the news, instantly thought of their fellow-resident Haroldson Lafayette Hunt, the boss of the immensely rich Hunt Oil Company of Dallas.
>
> Hunt is not only by far the richest of all the Texas oil millionaires but he is also, and more importantly, the one with the most pronounced and most vicious spleen. And, above all, the one who hated Kennedy most.
>
> It so happens that H. L. Hunt is also a long-time friend, admirer and financial 'angel' of the most prominent Texas politician of our time, Lyndon B. Johnson, the man who was destined to become President of the United States automatically the moment Kennedy died. Perhaps this is the reason why Garrison preferred not to be too specific.[68]

D. Harold Byrd was a right-wing oilman and a hater of John Kennedy. He owned the Three States Oil and Gas Company. He was a close friend and partner of Lyndon Johnson and Clint Murchison. Through Johnson's influence as a senator, Byrd's company, Ling Temco Vought, became one of the government's largest contractors. Byrd hired Johnson's henchman, Mac Wallace, as a purchasing manager for Ling Temco Vought after Wallace had been convicted of first degree murder. Byrd was the owner of the Texas School Book Depository building, which was used in the assassination of JFK.[69]

---

[68] Joesten, Joachim, *How Kennedy Was Killed*, (1968)
[69] Guyenot, Laurent, *JFK-9/11: Fifty Years of Deep State*, p. 59, Progressive Press, 2014

Bankers

John Kennedy was planning to restructure the Federal Reserve System (FRS), and return American currency to the gold standard. On June 4, 1963, he signed Executive Order No. 11,110 which called for $4.3 trillion in currency to be issued through the U.S. Treasury, thus bypassing the Federal Reserve System.[70] This was interest-free money, which did not sit well with the FRS. On the same day, Kennedy signed a bill that changed the backing of currency from silver to gold, which would strengthen the economy. He and his comptroller, James J. Saxon, were in opposition to the Federal Reserve Board. They wanted to eliminate Federal Reserve notes and replace them with genuine U.S. dollars. They also favored broader investment and lending powers for non-Reserve banks, along with the autonomy for those banks to underwrite state and local obligation bonds, which would weaken the Federal Reserve banks.[71] Naturally, the bankers did not want to see their power and wealth reduced. The Executive Order gave the Treasury Department the explicit authority "to issue silver certificates against any silver bullion, silver, or standard silver dollars in the Treasury." That means that the government could issue new money based on the actual silver they physically possessed. The $4.3 trillion was issued in small denominations of $1, $2, and $5. Larger denominations were being printed at the time Kennedy was killed, but they were never circulated.[72] Most of the smaller denominations were taken out of circulation, but a few can still be found today. Although not worth a fortune, these United States notes have become collector's items.[73]

From *Called to Serve* by Col. James Gritz:

> When Kennedy called for a return of America's currency to the gold standard, and the dismantling of the Federal Reserve System -- he actually minted non-debt money that does not bear the mark of the Federal Reserve; when he dared to actually exercise the leadership authority granted to

---

[70] http://foundationfortruthinlaw.org/jfk-vs-fed.html

[71] Marrs, Jim, *Rule by Secrecy*, p. 128, Perennial, 2000

[72] http://www.john-f-kennedy.net/thefederalreserve.htm

[73] https://en.wikipedia.org/wiki/Executive_Order_11110 http://www.john-f-kennedy.net/executiveorder11110.htm

him by the U.S. Constitution . . . Kennedy prepared his own death warrant. It was time for him to go.[74]

Kennedy's stance was backed by the Constitution, which states that only Congress shall regulate money. The Federal Reserve System is unconstitutional in that regard. The FRS prints money and then loans it to the government at interest, which increases the national debt. Kennedy's Executive Order would have put the FRS out of business. Kennedy's economic policies were highly criticized by *Fortune* magazine, the *Wall Street Journal*, and David and Nelson Rockefeller. That is a pretty good indication that Kennedy was on the right track.

The "Federal Reserve System" is a misleading moniker. It is not federal. The Federal Reserve System is privately owned by member banks. The FRS makes its own policies and is not subject to oversight by the U.S. government. By controlling reserves, they give banks access to public funds, increasing their lending capacity and profits. They get rich by inflating the economy.[75]

In March of 1964, the U.S. Treasury halted redemption of silver certificates for silver dollars. Most of the remaining silver in mint vaults were sold to collectors. All redemption of silver ceased on June 24, 1968.[76]

Georgetown professor Dr. Carroll Quigley wrote about the goals of the bankers who control the central bank:

> … nothing less than to create a world system of financial control in private hands able to dominate the political system of each country and the economy of the world as a whole… controlled in a feudalist fashion by the central banks of the world acting in concert, by secret agreements arrived at in frequent private meetings and conferences.

> The Bank of the United States (1816-36), an early attempt at an American central bank, was abolished by President Andrew Jackson, who believed that it threatened the nation. He wrote: "The bold effort the present bank had made to control the government, the distress it had wantonly

---

[74] Gritz, Colonel James, *Called to Serve*, Lazarus Publishing, 1991

[75] http://www.hermes-press.com/frs1.htm

[76] http://www.votefortheconstitution.com/executive-order-11110.html

produced…are but premonitions of the fate that awaits the American people should they be deluded into a perpetuation of this institution or the establishment of another like it."[77]

Thomas Jefferson warned of the dangers of a central bank:

> The Central Bank is an institution of the most deadly hostility existing against the principles and form of our Constitution…if the American people allow private banks to control the issuance of their currency, first by inflation and then by deflation, the banks and corporations that will grow up around them will deprive the people of all their property until their children will wake up homeless on the continent their fathers conquered.[78]

In 1933, Congressman Louis T. McFadden brought formal charges against the Federal Reserve, the Comptroller of Currency, and the Secretary of the U.S. Treasury. The charges included conspiracy, fraud, unlawful conversion, and treason. McFadden spoke to the House of Representatives and warned of the dangers of the FRS:

> Mr. Chairman, we have in this country one of the most corrupt institutions the world has ever known. I refer to the Federal Reserve Board and the Federal Reserve banks. The Federal Reserve Board, a government board, has cheated the government of the United States and the people of the United States out of enough money to pay the national debt. The depredations and the iniquities of the Federal Reserve Board and the Federal Reserve banks acting together have cost this country enough money to pay the national debt several times over. This evil institution has impoverished and ruined the people of these United States, has bankrupted itself, and has practically bankrupted our government. It has done this through the defects of the law under which it operates, through the maladministration of that law by the Fed, and through the corrupt practices of the moneyed vultures who control it.[79]

---

[77] http://www.conspiracyarchive.com/2013/12/21/the-council-on-foreign-relations-cfr-and-the-new-world-order/
[78] https://www.wealthdaily.com/articles/gold-backed-bank/2496
[79] http://libertyforlife.com/banking/us-mcfadden-re-frb.htm

McFadden's petition was referred to the Judiciary Committee and has yet to be acted on.

Three years after signing the Federal Reserve Act into law, President Wilson regretted the decision:

> I am a most unhappy man. I have unwittingly ruined my country. A great industrial nation is controlled by its system of credit. Our system of credit is concentrated. The growth of the nation, therefore, and all our activities are in the hands of a few men. We have come to be one of the worst ruled, one of the most completely controlled and dominated governments in the civilized world. No longer a government by free opinion, no longer a government by conviction and the vote of the majority, but a government by the opinion and duress of a small group of dominant men.[80]

Right-Wing Extremists

In 1963, virtually everyone in America was anti-communist. The government convinced us that communism is evil, and after the McCarthy witch hunts, we were sure there was a commie around every corner. Some were fanatical extremists, such as the Minutemen and the John Birch Society (JBS). They hated Kennedy for his policies with Russia, Cuba, and Vietnam. Even though Kennedy was anti-communist, he was not anti-communist enough for the extremists. They wanted him to invade Cuba, but he would not. They wanted him to escalate the Vietnam conflict, but he refused. Kennedy also negotiated nuclear disarmament with Russia, further alienating him from the extremists. From the far right-wing point of view, Kennedy was a communist and had to be eliminated. These delusional people actually thought they would make a better world by eliminating Kennedy.

At the time Kennedy was elected, the country was still segregated. In some areas, black people still could not eat in the same restaurants or use the same restrooms as white people. In those days, people would routinely use the n- word without thinking twice about it. Promoting civil rights was

---

[80] http://www.themoneymasters.com/the-money-masters/famous-quotations-on-banking/

not as fashionable as it is today. Kennedy pushed hard for the Civil Rights Act, which earned him a lot of enemies among racists.

The John Birch Society was made up of political extremists of the right wing. Commie busters and racists comprised their membership list. Two of these members were H.L. Hunt and Clint Murchison. Both were rich oil tycoons who funded the JBS, and both hated Kennedy with passion. Another JBS member was General Edwin Walker. It was Walker who had 5,000 copies of a handbill marked "Wanted for Treason" printed up, bearing the front and profile images of John Kennedy in a manner resembling the FBI's "Wanted for Murder" posters. These handbills were passed out at JFK's motorcade in Dallas. The bills carried the following list of charges leveled against JFK:

Wanted for Treason

1. Betraying the Constitution (which he swore to uphold). He is turning the sovereignty of the US over to the Communist controlled United Nations. He is betraying our friends (Cuba, Katanga, Portugal) and befriending our enemies (Russia, Yugoslavia, Poland).

2. He has been WRONG on innumerable issues affecting the security of the US (United Nations, Berlin Wall, Missile Removal, Cuba, Wheat deals, Test Ban Treaty, etc.).

3. He has been lax in enforcing the Communist Registration laws.

4. He has given support and encouragement to the Communist-inspired racial riots.

5. He has illegally invaded a sovereign State with federal troops.

6. He has consistently appointed Anti-Christians to Federal office. Upholds the Supreme Court in Anti-Christian rulings. Aliens and known Communists abound in Federal offices.

7. He has been caught in fantastic LIES to the American people (including personal ones like his previous marriage and divorce).[81]

Harry Dean was an FBI informant and CIA operative. He infiltrated the John Birch Society for several months, attending their meetings, gathering firsthand information about the group's activities, and secretly tape recording them. Dean said that during these meetings, former Congressman John Rousselot and General Edwin A. Walker planned the murder of John Kennedy. Rousselot was the western director of the JBS, and Walker was a devoted member. Walker supposedly had a personal grudge to settle with the Kennedys after Robert Kennedy had him imprisoned in a mental institution for his role in causing racial incidents. Rousselot and Walker, along with other JBS members, considered John Kennedy to be a "dirty communist" and believed his murder would save the U.S. from falling into red hands. Dean claims to have several tape recordings of the group members making death threats against President Kennedy, in addition to other unspecified evidence. Dean informed the FBI about the plot, but they ignored him. Dean came forth with his story in 1975, after he and his family had lived in constant fear for 12 years.

Here is some of what Dean said:

> I attended many meetings of the John Birch Society prior to the assassination in 1963 and I heard details of the Kennedy kill plan being discussed each time we met…

> I know that John Rousselot organized the murder plot and with other right-wingers financed it. General Walker ramrodded and trained the hired guns…

> I was with a man in September 1963 when he picked up $10,000 from Rousselot. The money was taken to Mexico City to help finance the murder of Mr. Kennedy. The assassination planning team operated out of Mexico City for several weeks before the president was shot in Dallas.[82][83]

---

[81] http://spartacus-educational.com/JFKSinvestBirch.htm

[82] Morris, W.R., *The Men Behind the Guns*, 1975

So the enemies of John Kennedy were many, but his vice president had to be at the top of that list. Johnson had a personal disdain for Kennedy. He felt that Kennedy had belittled him by giving him trivial tasks to perform as vice president. He was sometimes kept out of meetings. Their political ideologies were diametrically opposed. Kennedy tried to do what he thought was best for the country; Johnson basically catered to whoever could give him more power. That meant the oil barons, the war hawks, the CIA, and the mafia- all of Kennedy's enemies. Kennedy favored disarmament, troop withdrawal, and diplomatic solutions as opposed to war. Johnson was the opposite. He escalated the Vietnam War to appease the CIA. Kennedy wanted to eliminate the oil depletion allowance, whereas Johnson wanted to keep it to satisfy his influential friends. Kennedy favored equal rights for minorities, while Johnson was a closet racist. When it came to dealing with organized crime, the two were at opposite poles. Kennedy was at war with the mob, while Johnson was in bed with them.

All this is not intended to paint John Kennedy as a saint. He had his share of personal flaws. His marital indiscretions have been well-documented, and this made him an easy target for blackmail. Also, he colluded with the mob to get elected, so his war against organized crime is somewhat hypocritical. Still, he basically tried to follow his conscience, but he found out that in politics, that doesn't always work.[84]

The Peace Speech

The Cuban missile crisis had brought the world to the precipice of nuclear war. For the first time, it seemed like a reality. This caused Kennedy to rethink his Cold War strategy, and to re-examine his philosophy on life in general. Throughout his campaign and his presidency, Kennedy had taken a hard-line stance against communism, but now he realized that nuclear war was not an option. The risks to humanity were too great. He knew he had to de-escalate the arms race and cease nuclear testing. He realized that this would not be a popular decision among the military brass, but he felt he had to change course.

On June 10, 1963, John Kennedy gave a commencement address at American University in Washington, D.C. This was considered one of his

---

[83] http://spartacus-educational.com/JFKsinvestBirch.htm
[84] http://viewzone.com/lbj/lbj2.html

most inspired speeches, and it outlined the new direction in which he was leading the country. He spoke of his agreement with Khrushchev to negotiate a test ban treaty, and of his plans to curb nuclear arms. He said that his goal was "complete disarmament" of nuclear weapons. He emphasized that the United States was a peaceful nation that will never initiate a war.

Here are some key excerpts from JFK's historical speech:

> What kind of peace do I mean and what kind of a peace do we seek? Not a Pax Americana enforced on the world by American weapons of war. Not the peace of the grave or the security of the slave. I am talking about genuine peace, the kind of peace that makes life on earth worth living, and the kind that enables men and nations to grow, and to hope, and build a better life for their children—not merely peace for Americans but peace for all men and women, not merely peace in our time but peace in all time....

> Today the expenditure of billions of dollars every year on weapons acquired for the purpose of making sure we never need them is essential to the keeping of peace. But surely the acquisition of such idle stockpiles—which can only destroy and never create—is not the only, much less the most efficient, means of assuring peace. I speak of peace, therefore, as the necessary, rational end of rational men. I realize the pursuit of peace is not as dramatic as the pursuit of war, and frequently the words of the pursuers fall on deaf ears. But we have no more urgent task...

> First examine our attitude towards peace itself. Too many of us think it is impossible. Too many think it is unreal. But that is a dangerous, defeatist belief. It leads to the conclusion that war is inevitable, that mankind is doomed, that we are gripped by forces we cannot control. We need not accept that view. Our problems are manmade; therefore, they can be solved by man. And man can be as big as he wants. No problem of human destiny is beyond human beings...

> For in the final analysis, our most basic common link is that we all inhabit this small planet. We all breathe the same air. We all cherish our children's futures. And we are all mortal...

It is our hope— and the purpose of allied policies—to convince the Soviet Union that she, too, should let each nation choose its own future, so long as that choice does not interfere with the choices of others. The Communist drive to impose their political and economic system on others is the primary cause of world tension today. For there can be no doubt that, if all nations could refrain from interfering in the self-determination of others, the peace would be much more assured...

I'm taking this opportunity, therefore, to announce two important decisions in this regard. First, Chairman Khrushchev, Prime Minister Macmillan, and I have agreed that high-level discussions will shortly begin in Moscow looking towards early agreement on a comprehensive test ban treaty. Our hope must be tempered—Our hopes must be tempered with the caution of history; but with our hopes go the hopes of all mankind. Second, to make clear our good faith and solemn convictions on this matter, I now declare that the United States does not propose to conduct nuclear tests in the atmosphere so long as other states do not do so. We will not—We will not be the first to resume...

The United States, as the world knows, will never start a war. We do not want a war. We do not now expect a war. This generation of Americans has already had enough—more than enough—of war and hate and oppression...

We shall also do our part to build a world of peace where the weak are safe and the strong are just. We are not helpless before that task or hopeless of its success. Confident and unafraid, we must labor on—not towards a strategy of annihilation but towards a strategy of peace...[85]

In spite of its controversial content, Kennedy's speech at AU was widely praised as ground-breaking. In the words of Jeffrey Sachs, American economist and director of the Earth Institute at Columbia University:

---

[85] https://www.jfklibrary.org/Research/Research-Aids/JFK-Speeches/American-University_19630610.aspx

I have come to believe that Kennedy's quest for peace is not only the greatest achievement of his presidency, but also one of the greatest acts of world leadership in the modern era.[86]

In the speech, Kennedy walked a fine line as he tried to embrace peace with communists while simultaneously denouncing their aggressive nature. He was asked by a reporter what he meant by "so long as it does not interfere with the choices of others." Kennedy summed up his philosophy:

Well, what we mean is that we cannot accept with equanimity, nor do we propose to, the communist takeover of countries which are now free. What we have said is that we accept the principle of self-determination. Governments choose a type of government, if the people choose it. If they have the opportunity to choose another kind, if the one they originally chose is unsatisfactory, then we regard that as a free matter and we would accept it, regardless of what their choice might be. But what we will not accept is the subversion or an attack upon a free country which threatens, in my opinion, the security of other free countries. I think that is the distinction we have made for a great many years.[87]

Kennedy and Khrushchev both wanted to turn toward peace. They signed a nuclear test-ban treaty on August 5, 1963. But it was not sufficient that the leaders of the two superpowers were both willing to negotiate for peace. They both had to deal with their intelligence agencies, which they felt were autonomous and out of control. Kennedy had no real authority over the CIA, and Khrushchev had the same problem with the KGB. Both agencies pursued the escalation of conflicts through insurgency. Both resorted to dirty tricks. Both had no accountability. Kennedy and Khrushchev sought to bypass the intelligence agencies in an attempt to establish a working relationship with one another. To that end, they established a back-channel hotline where they could talk to each other directly. Kennedy was the first U.S. president to have a direct phone line to the Kremlin in Moscow.[88]

---

[86] Sachs, Jeffrey D., *To Move the World: JFK's Quest for Peace.* New York: Random House. p. xv., 2013

[87] https://en.wikipedia.org/wiki/American_University_speech#cite_note-11

[88] http://www.history.com/this-day-in-history/hotline-established-between-washington-and-moscow

Recap

As a result of the assassination, most of Kennedy's enemies got what they wanted. The mafia was freed from the war on crime waged by John and Robert Kennedy. There was also a measure of revenge extracted, especially by Marcello. The CIA was allowed to keep their independence and autonomy, and they function virtually unimpeded to this day. The Pentagon and the military-industrial complex got the war in Vietnam that they wanted, and they saw it escalate dramatically in the upcoming years. The oil tycoons got to keep their depletion allowance and avoided paying their fair share of taxes. The Federal Reserve continued to reap enormous profits, in spite of the illegality of their operation. Among the ones who did not get what they wanted were the Cubans. They never did get rid of Castro, and Johnson was no more willing to invade Cuba than Kennedy was. They had to wait 50 years for their dictator to die of old age before they were finally freed from his rule. Redneck racists were disappointed too, since the Civil Rights Act was signed and the inevitable integration of society became a reality. But no individual benefited more from the assassination than Lyndon Johnson. Johnson became president and stayed out of jail, leaving it to researchers and historians to unravel his crimes, rather than the courts.

3

SCANDALS, MURDERS, ETC.

E verything about the JFK assassination points to Lyndon Johnson. He had the most to gain, he had the ways and means to accomplish it, and he was in a position to cover it up afterwards. He also had the psychological make-up to commit such an act. Those who knew Johnson say that he would stop at nothing to achieve his ultimate goal of becoming president of the United States. Johnson has been described as power-hungry, ruthless, and manipulative. Those traits alone don't prove that he killed John Kennedy, but when looked at in the context of Johnson's life and political career, there is no reason to doubt that Johnson was at the center of the plot.

Johnson the Man

Lyndon Baines Johnson was born in Stonewall, Texas, in 1908. After working as a Congressional aide, he was elected to the House of Representatives in 1937. He was elected to the Senate in 1948, became Senate Minority Leader in 1953 and became Senate Majority Leader in 1955. He lost the Democratic nomination for president to John Kennedy in the 1960 election, but accepted the vice presidential spot on the eventual winning ticket. Johnson served as vice president under Kennedy, and became president upon Kennedy's death.

Author J. Evetts Haley was one of the first to point an accusing finger at Johnson. His book *A Texan Looks at Lyndon* said what many others, especially in Texas, were secretly thinking. Written and published in 1964, Haley's book expressed misgivings about the character of the then-new president:

> Federal bureaucratic pressure, state demagogues,
> intellectually elite, labor, money and criminal tactics,
> combined to elevate him to high office in Texas. His special
> talents as a wheeler-dealer and political fixer have kept him

51

there. Herein he has always had the financial support of a segment of main-street socialists, who are perennially paraded, for political purposes, as "Texas conservatives." In truth, they are often aligned with the worst of labor leaders, with essentially the same lack of moral and political principle—the same dedication to special privilege and expediency.

Throughout Texas however, among those who have no political axes of their own to grind, and of every political point of view, there is a deep suspicion and distrust of the man who is now President of the United States. It was generally conceded, prior to the assassination of Kennedy, that, despite Lyndon's alleged political magic, Texas would be swept from the Democratic ticket in 1964 if Goldwater were the nominee. The signs were so conclusive that the Johnson forces themselves were privately admitting it.[89]

Along with his vanity, pride, and acute sensitivity is a high and explosive temper and a notoriously intemperate tongue. These sometimes find vicious outlet upon the subordinates around him—which is the certain hallmark, not of nobility and breeding, but of the plebian nature obsessed with power.[90]

From *The Texas Connection* by Craig I. Zirbel, we get a little bit about Johnson's mindset:

When Kennedy took office he was immediately met with Johnson's first unreasonable request. Vice President Johnson proposed to President Kennedy that he should be allowed to move into the White House and to share the presidential power with President Kennedy under a two person presidential system. At first Kennedy thought Johnson was joking, but when the Vice President persisted, President Kennedy flatly refused to create a new governing duet for America.[91]

---

[89] Haley, J. Evetts, *A Texan Looks at Lyndon*, p.7, Palo Duro Press, 1964
[90] Haley, J. Evetts, *A Texan Looks at Lyndon*, p.232, Palo Duro Press, 1964
[91] Zirbel, Craig I., *The Texas Connection*, pp. 132-3, Wright and Co., 1991

It's hard to believe that Johnson was serious about that. It shows his lust for power. Zirbel wrote at length about the kind of individual Johnson was:

> As an initial overview of Lyndon Johnson's character, it can be said that some people viewed Johnson as "a man who could stoop to commit any type of act and who managed to combine the worst elements of mankind's traits into his personality." Others who reported on his political career considered him to be a "total opportunist, devoted only to profit and personal gain." And still others, including a fellow U.S. Senator, felt that Johnson was the "phoniest individual who ever came around." These opinion statements could be considered as only jealous comments by a few enemies if they had not been regularly repeated by hundreds of different people throughout Johnson's career. In fact, Lyndon Johnson's grandmother pulled no punches about her own negative feelings for him. Repeatedly she declared that LBJ was going to wind up in jail- "just mark my words." Even though Johnson missed the penitentiary for the presidency, his grandmother's prophecy still came very close to the mark. While he was never indicted nor convicted of a crime, Johnson led a political life that was constantly embroiled in scandals and a number of his cohorts, who were less politically connected, ended up being convicted of crimes and jailed.[92]

Johnson was not a religious man, but he was a church-going person. That may sound like a contradiction, but Johnson was an unusual individual. He went were the voters were, and the voters were in church. On any given Sunday, Johnson would go church-hopping. When one service was over, he would be on his way to the next service at some other church, anxious to impress everyone with his piousness. He even gave a generous gift of an automobile to a poor minister. It turned out that the so-called gift was actually government property. No one would blame Johnson for simply not being a religious person or for not going to church, but to pass himself off as something he's not is just another form of lying. This pattern of deceit and manipulation defined Johnson's political career.

> One Washington religious leader publicly proclaimed that LBJ was a man "whose public house was splendid in

---

[92] Zirbel, Craig I., *The Texas Connection*, p. 101, Wright and Co., 1991

appearance…but whose entire foundation was rotted by termites."[93]

Much has also been made of Johnson's drinking, which he apparently could not control:

> Johnson normally drank when he was feeling good, but alcohol did not make him a happy drunk. When drunk, LBJ would swear and belittle friends and constituents in public. While a true friend might tolerate drunken obscenities, ordinarily the American public would not be as tolerant. However, because of Johnson's strong political power, his drunkenness was tolerated by his constituents. In fact, when political dinners conflicted with Johnson's drinking schedule, the drinking would take priority and the paying dinner guests were forced to wait hours for his arrival. And when he would eventually appear (sometimes up to two hours late), Johnson, in a state of inebriation would often step to the speaker's platform and begin his speech with a barrage of obscenities and insults at everyone present.[94]

John Kennedy was all too familiar with Johnson's psychological baggage. He made the following statement to Ken O'Donnell regarding LBJ:

> You are dealing with a very insecure, sensitive man with a huge ego.[95]

Robert Kennedy was among those who questioned Johnson's integrity:

> Johnson lies all the time. I'm just telling you, he just lies continuously, about everything. In every conversation I have with him, he lies. As I've said, he lies even when he doesn't have to.[96]

But the clearest example of Johnson's immaturity is told by Robert Dallek, recalling the words of Arthur Goldberg:

> "Why are we in Vietnam?" Arthur Goldberg recalls that, in response to this recurring question during an informal

---

[93] Zirbel, Craig I., *The Texas Connection*, p 102, Wright and Co., 1991

[94] Zirbel, Craig I., *The Texas Connection*, p. 107, Wright and Co., 1991

[95] Marrs, Jim, *Rule by Secrecy*, p. 25, Perennial, 2000

[96] Shesol, Jeff, *Mutual Contempt*, p. 95, WW Norton and Co., 1997

conversation with journalists, "LBJ unzipped his fly, drew out his substantial organ and declared, 'This is why!'"[97]

All of this is not said just to smear Lyndon Johnson. A lot of people have anger control issues, insecurity, and drinking problems, yet they didn't kill anyone. These traits of Johnson's are pointed out only to show his mind set and his temperament. Those who knew Johnson personally knew that he would stop at nothing to become president. He was obsessed with power. He would lie, steal, and even kill to achieve his lifelong ambition of becoming president of the United States. This was a sentiment that has been repeatedly echoed by many throughout the years.

Disgracing Jackie

One of the lowest things that Johnson ever did involved his treatment of the former First Lady who had just been widowed. Aboard Air Force One, Lyndon Johnson took the oath of office. You would think he'd have his loyal wife by his side at a moment like that, but he didn't. Instead, it's Jacqueline Kennedy by his side. Why? Any politician taking an oath of office would naturally have his or her mate by their side. Why did Johnson have someone else's wife standing by him? It was to taunt and humiliate Jacqueline Kennedy. He has just murdered her husband, and Jackie is obviously in shock and traumatized. But Johnson believed she hadn't suffered enough, so he had to cause her additional torment. Jackie was in her private room on the plane, crying her eyes out as you would expect. Johnson knocked on the door and told her to come out for his swearing-in as the new president. Do you really think she wanted to have her picture taken at that point? At a time like that, Jackie only wanted to be alone, or with family and friends. The last thing she'd want is to have to show phony support for her late husband's enemy. We can see Jackie's torment in a well-known photo of the swearing-in.[98] This is the worst moment of her life. She is in terrible psychological anguish, while Johnson is completely insensitive to her suffering. He takes the oath with a straight face, still trying to feign sadness over JFK's death. Meanwhile, Lady Bird Johnson is looking in, wondering why it's not her standing next to her husband. She is, after all, the First Lady now. She is puzzled why Johnson has someone else's wife standing by him

---

[97] Dallek, Robert, *Flawed Giant*, p. 491, Oxford University Press, 1998
[98] https://en.wikipedia.org/wiki/First_inauguration_of_Lyndon_B._Johnson

while he is sworn in. Johnson wanted so badly to torment Jackie Kennedy, he blew off his own wife to be able to do so.

Jacqueline Kennedy knew that LBJ was an enemy of her husband. She also knew the kind of person he was. One can't help but sympathize with what she went through on that horrible day in Dallas. She probably suspected Johnson from the start, although she never said anything.

From *Irish Central*:

> Jackie Kennedy believed Lyndon B. Johnson was behind the 1963 assassination of her husband President John F. Kennedy. In the sensational tapes recorded by the First Lady months after the President's death, broadcast by ABC, Kennedy revealed her belief that Johnson and a cabal of Texas tycoons orchestrated the murder of her husband by gunman Lee Harvey Oswald. Kennedy, who later became Jackie Onassis, claimed that the Dallas murder was part of a larger conspiracy to allow Johnson to become American President in his own right.[99]

Jackie also revealed that John Kennedy had a complete lack of confidence in Lyndon Johnson's ability to lead the country:

> Bobby told me this later, and I know Jack said it to me sometimes, he said, 'Oh god, can you ever imagine what would happen to the country if Lyndon was president?'... I mean, he didn't like that idea that Lyndon would go on to be president because he was worried for the country.[100]

Vice President by Blackmail

John Kennedy never wanted Lyndon Johnson to be his running mate. His first choice was Senator Stuart Symington of Missouri. Through his advisor, Clark Clifford, Kennedy had already offered the position to Symington, who replied, "You can tell Jack I will accept his offer." So Symington had already been offered, and accepted, a spot on the ticket as JFK's running mate. How then, did LBJ end up as vice president?

---

[99] https://www.irishcentral.com/news/jackie-kennedy-blamed-lyndon-b-johnson-for-jfk-murder-127220093-237788131
[100] http://www.npr.org/2011/09/15/140508717/jackie-o-tapes-offer-window-on-an-era-and-an-icon

Shortly after giving the spot to Symington, Kennedy surprisingly withdrew the offer. As he spoke to his staff, he was visibly upset. His words to Clifford were, "During the night I have been persuaded that I could not win without Lyndon on the ticket. I have offered the vice presidency to him, and he has accepted. Tell Stuart that I am sorry." This came as a shock to Symington, to the public, to analysts, and especially to Kennedy supporters. No one in the Kennedy camp liked Johnson, but now they were stuck with him. What caused Kennedy to change his mind?

Between the time that Symington accepted the offer and the time Kennedy withdrew it, Johnson intervened. Johnson and his aides had a talk with Kennedy. The exact details are not known, but it's a safe bet that Johnson relied on his usual tactic- blackmail. He and his ally, J. Edgar Hoover, had extensive files of compromising information on Kennedy, including his sexual affairs. This information was probably used to blackmail Kennedy into putting Johnson on the ticket with him.[101]

Kennedy was evasive about the reason for choosing Johnson, but he made these statements:

> They threatened me with problems and I don't need more problems. I'm going to have enough problems with Nixon.[102]

> The whole story will never be known. And it's just as well that it won't be.[103]

As quickly as possible, Johnson got himself in front of a TV camera and said, "Jack Kennedy has asked me to serve. I accept." Johnson knew that Kennedy would not want to change his mind once the decision is announced. It is always bad for a politician to look indecisive, or to reverse course on something. By making a public announcement, Johnson made it extremely difficult for Kennedy to change his mind. The truth is that the position had already been given to Symington, who had accepted it. But that had not been publicly announced yet. Kennedy offered Johnson a post as Chairman of the National Committee instead, but Johnson declined.

---

[101] Nelson, Phillip F, *LBJ: Mastermind of JFK's Assassination*, pp. 313-318, Xlibris, 2010

[102] https://nodisinfo.com/lyndon-johnson-jfk-assassination

[103] Guyenot, Laurent, *JFK-9/11: 50 Years of Deep State*, p. 20, Progressive Press, 2014

Kennedy's aide, Kenneth O'Donnell was shocked and irate when he heard that Johnson had been given the vice-presidential nomination. He said to Kennedy:

> This is the worst mistake you ever made. You came here... like a night on a white charger... promising to get rid of the old hack machine politicians. And now, in your first move after you get the nomination, you go against all the people who supported you.

Kennedy was not pleased with how things had worked out, but he was stuck with Johnson. He made the following regrettable statement to O'Donnell:

> I'm forty-three years old, and I'm not going to die in office. So the vice-presidency doesn't mean anything.[104]

As Majority Leader of the Senate, Johnson had far more power than he ever would have as vice president. No politician seeks the vice presidency as an end goal. It is really just a figurehead position, involving a lot of ribbon-cutting and menial tasks. For Johnson, it seemed to be a huge step backwards in his career. Everyone, including Kennedy, was surprised that Johnson would even accept the position. It was thought that Kennedy might make a token gesture of offering the spot to Johnson, but if so, it was assumed that Johnson would refuse. Why would such an ambitious politician volunteer for such a demotion?

Unsure of how the election would turn out, Johnson had a special law passed in Texas just for him. This law allowed him to run on the Texas election ballot as both a U.S. Senate candidate and John Kennedy's vice presidential candidate. If the Kennedy-Johnson ticket lost in the election, Johnson would still be allowed to remain the incumbent U.S. Senator. But if his ticket won the election, he could then resign his position as Senator. This created a win-win situation for Johnson that no one had ever had before.[105]

One example of Johnson's reduced role came when he was traveling in Europe. Johnson was scheduled to meet with diplomats of Scandanavia. The U.S. Embassy sent a telegram saying that anything Johnson said should not be taken as representing the views of the American government. This

---

[104] Harris Wofford, *Of Kennedys and Kings*, 1980
[105] Zirbel, Craig I., *The Texas Connection*, p. 113, Wright and Co., 1991

trivialized Johnson's role. He was the vice president of the U.S., yet he could not represent the American government. His diplomatic presence was purely symbolic. This telegram was sent uncoded, so it was not even secret. Johnson took this as a deliberate attempt to embarrass him. Kennedy may have been worried about Johnson's lack of diplomatic skills, and didn't want him to speak on his behalf.[106]

Lyndon Johnson's brother, Sam Houston Johnson, told about how LBJ was miserable as vice president:

> ...they made his stay in the vice presidency the most miserable three years of his life. He wasn't the number two man in the administration; he was the lowest man on the totem pole...I know him well enough to know he felt humiliated time and time again, that he was openly snubbed by second-echelon White House staffers who snickered at him behind his back and called him "Uncle Cornpone."[107]

Evelyn Lincoln was John Kennedy's personal secretary for 10 years. She knew about the dysfunctional relationship between Kennedy and Johnson. She knew that Kennedy had never wanted Johnson as his running mate. During his presidency, he viewed Johnson as a burden to his administration. It was well-known among insiders that Kennedy was going to drop Johnson from the ticket in the 1964 election. In her book, *Kennedy and Johnson*, Lincoln tells that Kennedy had already made that decision:

> As Mr. Kennedy sat in the rocker in my office, his head resting on its back he placed his left leg across his right knee. He rocked slightly as he talked. In a slow pensive voice he said to me, "You know if I am re-elected in sixty-four, I am going to spend more and more time toward making government service an honorable career. I would like to tailor the executive and legislative branches of government so that they can keep up with the tremendous strides and progress being made in other fields. I am going to advocate changing some of the outmoded rules and regulations in the Congress, such as the seniority rule. To do this I will need as a running mate in sixty-four a man who believes as I do." I

---

[106] http://humansarefree.com/2011/07/john-f-kennedy-assassinated-by-lyndon-b.html
[107] Marrs, Jim, *Crossfire*, p. 295, Carroll and Graf, 1989

was fascinated by this conversation and wrote it down verbatim in my diary. Now I asked, "Who is your choice as a running-mate?" He looked straight ahead, and without hesitating he replied, "At this time I am thinking about Governor Terry Sanford of North Carolina. But it will not be Lyndon."[108]

Kennedy spoke those words on November 19, 1963, just three days before he died.

Lyndon Johnson accepted the vice-presidential nomination for one reason only- to kill John Kennedy. He knew that as VP, he would be able to control things like security arrangements and such. He was only one step away from the presidency this way, and he figured it was his best chance. With an army of henchmen at his disposal, Johnson was confident he could pull off the assassination. If that sounds far-fetched, consider his response to Clare Boothe Luce when asked why he accepted the nomination:

Clare, I looked it up: one out of every four presidents has died in office. I'm a gamblin' man, darlin', and this is the only chance I got.[109]

Some have tried to interpret this as a reference to Kennedy's physical ailments, such as Addison's Disease or his back problems. But Kennedy was basically young and healthy. He was not likely to die in office from natural causes. This was a prophecy- one which Johnson made come true. It is shocking that he actually said that to a reporter. This shows how brazen he was about the whole thing, and how confident he was that he could get away with it.

But the execution of the plan was only one part of it. As vice president, he would then become president, which would give him control over the cover-up. As Majority Leader, he couldn't do that. If Johnson had chosen to remain as Majority Leader, it's possible that he might still have been able to somehow arrange the assassination, but he could not control the aftermath. President Symington would have made that sure a proper investigation was

---

[108] Lincoln, Evelyn, *Kennedy and Johnson*, 1968
[109] http://econlog.econlib.org/archives/2012/05/great_moments_i_4.html

conducted. There would be no Warren Commission and no cover-up. The truth would be exposed, and Johnson could do little about it.[110]

Madeleine

> I'd like the entire world to know how I personally feel is the fact Lyndon Johnson knew about the assassination and was a part of it.-Madeleine Brown[111]

Madeleine Brown was a woman who had a 21-year relationship with Lyndon Johnson. She met him in 1948 at the Adolphus Hotel in Dallas. During that time, she gave birth to his illegitimate son, Steven Mark Brown. At the time, Johnson attorney Jerome T. Ragsdale claimed to be the legal father in order to shield Johnson from negative publicity. In 1987, Steven Mark Brown filed a $10.5 million lawsuit against Lady Bird Johnson and two friends, claiming that they had defrauded him of his share of the Johnson estate. In 1989, the suit was dismissed after he failed to show up in court. Steven Mark Brown died from lymphatic cancer in 1990.[112]

Madeleine Brown has given interviews and written a book called *Texas in the Morning*, detailing her experiences with Johnson and the elite. Brown believes that Johnson was part of the plot to kill Kennedy. She claims that the assassination plot was hatched years earlier, when Johnson accepted the offer to be Kennedy's running mate. Since the vice presidency was a demotion for Johnson, many were surprised that he accepted the offer. Brown told how John Kennedy's father, Joseph Kennedy, had cut a deal with H.L. Hunt. This was an agreement that Johnson would be Kennedy's running mate. One has to wonder how H.L. Hunt could influence a political decision like that, and what the terms of this agreement were.

Brown relates what she was told by H.L. Hunt shortly after Johnson's acceptance. According to her, these were Hunt's exact words:

> We may have lost a battle, but we're going to win a war.

That was a subtle prediction of the assassination. Shortly after Kennedy was killed, Hunt referenced that statement, telling her:

---

[110] http://econlog.econlib.org/archives/2012/05/great_moments_i_4.html
[111] Turner, Nigel, 1988, The Guilty Men, *The Men Who Killed Kennedy*, U.K., Nigel Turner Productions
[112] https://en.wikipedia.org/wiki/Madeleine_Duncan_Brown

We won the war.

Brown said, "It was a total political crime and H.L. Hunt actually controlled what happened to Kennedy, he and Lyndon Johnson." So the acceptance of the vice presidential position was just a ploy to get into position to kill John Kennedy. This has long been suspected by researchers, and Brown's statements corroborate that. Right after the convention, Hunt went to work on the assassination plot.

> H.L. Hunt didn't let it rest. He immediately began mapping out a plot to kill John Kennedy. They were just in total disgust with John Kennedy.[113]

Madeleine told of a meeting at Clint Murchison's house the night before the assassination. This was a meeting of the 8F group, a powerful group of influential politicians and businessmen. The group was named after the room they used at a Houston hotel to discuss their plans. Present at the meeting were such names as J. Edgar Hoover, Clyde Tolson, John McCloy, Richard Nixon, George Brown, R. L. Thornton, H. L. Hunt, and a host of others from the group. It is speculated that Jack Ruby was also included, mainly because of his numerous contacts in the underground. Ostensibly, this was a party to honor Hoover. Lyndon Johnson showed up unexpectedly at about 11:00 p.m. or so. Johnson was in Fort Worth earlier that evening, and it wasn't certain if he would be able to make it to the party. Somehow, he managed to get away. This was the most important meeting of his life, and Johnson was not about to miss it.[114]

Madeleine Brown was not present at the meeting, but she was in the house and she saw the men go into their secret room. She thought they were going in there to gamble, as they often did. Madeleine tells the story:

> Tension filled the room upon his arrival. The group immediately went behind closed doors. A short time later Lyndon, anxious and red-faced, reappeared. I knew how secretly Lyndon operated. Therefore I said nothing... not even that I was happy to see him. Squeezing my hand so hard, it felt crushed from the pressure, he spoke with a

---

[113] https://video.search.yahoo.com/search/video?fr=befhp&p=JFK+meeting+at
+Clint+Murchison%27s+house+night+before+assassination#id=
4&vid=29e1f4437a1e7b515c78100143948374&action=click
[114] https://www.prisonplanet.com/articles/august2006/300806jfk.htm

grating whisper, a quiet growl, into my ear, not a love
message, but one I'll always remember: "After tomorrow
those goddamn Kennedys will never embarrass me again -
that's no threat - that's a promise."[115]

Those who doubt Johnson's involvement should remember those words
of his, spoken on November 21, 1963:

> After tomorrow those goddamn Kennedys will never
> embarrass me again - that's no threat - that's a promise.

This was an overt prediction of the assassination. There is no other way
to interpret it. The next day, Kennedy was killed. Brown was immediately
suspicious of Johnson, but was reluctant to ask him directly. Eventually, she
got around to confronting him about it:

> Just a few weeks later (after the assassination) I mentioned
> to him that people in Dallas were saying he himself had
> something to do with it. He became really violent, really
> ugly, and said it was American Intelligence and oil that were
> behind it. Then he left the room and slammed the door. It
> scared me.[116]

Johnson failed to give a direct answer to Brown's inquiry. If he thought
the oil people and the CIA did it, why didn't he investigate them? By
admitting that it was "American intelligence and oil" behind the
assassination, he was conceding that it was not Lee Harvey Oswald. He did
not admit his own involvement, of course, but he was admitting to a cover-
up. He made no attempt to investigate the real suspects, choosing instead
to put all the blame on the dead patsy. When Brown mentioned this on
Geraldo Rivera's talk show, the host and the crowd gasped at her words.
There was no reason to. Johnson did not name any names or admit to his
own role, so nothing ever became of that statement. No one was
investigated because of it. Most researchers know that Johnson did it, and a
statement like that should come as no surprise.

Madeleine Brown knew of Johnson's hatred for both of the Kennedys.
She also knew how passionately he wanted to become president. Like many

---

[115] Brown, Madeleine, *Texas in the Morning*, Conservatory Press, 1997
[116] Brown, Madeleine, *Texas in the Morning*, Conservatory Press, 1997

others shortly after the assassination, she suspected Johnson had something to do with it:

> He hated them with a passion. They were stumbling blocks to him.
> He had always sought the presidency of the United States and John Kennedy definitely had become a stumbling block to him...[117]

Madeleine Brown shows no hint of resentment or negative feelings toward Johnson. In spite of her accusations, she speaks very fondly of him. There is no reason to think that she is making this up to slander or defame him out of spite. She comes across as sincere and genuine. Naturally, lone-assassin theorists have tried to discredit her, but to no avail.

The Murchison meeting has also been confirmed by Mae Newman, a seamstress and companion who worked for Virginia Murchison. She also states that she saw Nixon, Hunt, Hoover, and Johnson at the meeting that night. She also tells how the Murchison family reacted after Kennedy's death:

> The mood in the Murchison family home was very joyous and happy. For a whole week after, champagne and caviar flowed every day of the week. I was the only one in the household at the time that had any grief for his assassination.[118]

Suspicious Draft

John Kennedy had signed NSAM 263 on October 11, 1963. This was the directive to bring home most military personnel from Vietnam by the end of 1965. On November 26, 1963, just four days after Kennedy's death, Lyndon Johnson signed NSAM 273, which reversed Kennedy's order and escalated the Vietnam conflict instead. Johnson always supported the people who would give him power, and in this case it was the war hawks in the CIA and Pentagon.

---

[117] http://www.jfktruth.org/Johnson/index.htm
[118] Turner, Nigel, 2003, The Guilty Men, *The Men Who Killed Kennedy*, U.K., Nigel Turner Productions

But the strange thing about NSAM 273 is that it was drafted on November 21, 1963, which was the day before Kennedy died. The draft of the memo is identified by code OPLAN-34A, and it states:

> The President has reviewed the discussions of South Vietnam which occurred in Honolulu, and has discussed the matter further with Ambassador Lodge.[119]

Who is meant by "The President"? Both Kennedy and Johnson were in Dallas on the 21st when the Conference of the Joint Chiefs of Staff ended in Honolulu. This draft became NSAM 273, which was Johnson's order, and was in direct opposition to the path that Kennedy had chosen. But there seemed to be a foreknowledge that there would be a change of leadership soon, and that foreknowledge was shared by the Joint Chiefs of Staff.[120]

Why was NSAM 273 drafted while Kennedy was still president? Had Kennedy lived, the draft would have been a worthless piece of paper. But since Johnson was now president, this was the official policy of the United States military. Johnson prepared the order the day before the motorcade in Dallas, knowing that he would be president in less than 24 hours.[121]

Other Suspicions

The KGB suspected Lyndon Johnson of being involved, and had requested all possible information on him. Hoover learned about this and sent Johnson the following memo:

> On September 16, 1965, this same source (an FBI spy in the KGB) reported that the KGB Residency in New York City received instructions approximately September 16, 1965, from KGB headquarters in Moscow to develop all possible information concerning President Lyndon B. Johnson's character, background, personal friends, family, and from which quarters he derives his support in his position as President of the United States. Our source added that in the instructions from Moscow, it was indicated that "now" the KGB was in possession of data purporting to indicate

---

[119] Guyenot, Laurent, *JFK-9/11: 50 Years of Deep State*, p.63, Progressive Press, 2014
[120] https://jfkjmn.com/new-page-77/
[121] http://www.prouty.org/johnson.html

President Johnson was responsible for the assassination of the late President John F. Kennedy. KGB headquarters indicated that in view of this information, it was necessary for the Soviet Government to know the existing personal relationship between President Johnson and the Kennedy family, particularly between President Johnson and Robert and "Ted" Kennedy.[122]

Former CIA operative Robert Morrow has written about the role of Lyndon Johnson in John Kennedy's murder:

Lyndon Johnson made a dirty deal with CIA Republicans to murder John Kennedy in the 1963 Coup d'Etat. (People like Clint Murchison Sr., H.L. Hunt, Nelson Rockefeller, David Rockefeller, top Nelson Rockefeller aide Henry Kissinger, George Herbert Walker Bush and Gen. Edward Lansdale all are excellent candidates for elite sponsorship.)

Lyndon Johnson and Allen Dulles may very well have been co-CEOs of the JFK assassination; with the CIA in charge of the killing of JFK, and Lyndon Johnson and (his close friend and neighbor of 19 years in Washington, DC) FBI director J. Edgar Hoover in charge of the cover up.[123]

In his book *American Spy*, E. Howard Hunt implicated Lyndon Johnson in the JFK assassination:

Having Kennedy liquidated, thus elevating himself to the presidency without having to work for it himself, could have been a very tempting and logical move on Johnson's part. LBJ had the money and the connections to manipulate the scenario in Dallas and is on record as having convinced JFK to make the appearance in the first place. He further tried unsuccessfully to engineer the passengers of each vehicle, trying to get his good buddy, Gov. (John) Connally, to ride with him instead of in JFK's car - where... he would have been out of danger.[124]

---

[122] https://nomoregames.net/2013/06/10/lyndon-johnson-and-the-jfk-assassination/

[123] http://jfktruth.org/Johnson/Morrow/index.htm

[124] Hunt, E. Howard, *American Spy*, Wiley, 2007

Evelyn Lincoln, Kennedy's personal secretary, expressed her beliefs about the assassination:

> As far as the assassination is concerned it is my belief that there was a conspiracy because there were those that disliked him and felt the only way to get rid of him was to assassinate him. These five conspirators, in my opinion, were Lyndon B. Johnson, J. Edgar Hoover, the Mafia, the CIA, and the Cubans in Florida.[125]

Attorney Pat Holloway recalled an incident involving Johnson at Parkland Hospital. This was at about 1:00 p.m., just after John Kennedy had been pronounced dead. As Holloway was leaving, he overheard Johnson on the phone with his tax lawyer:

> I heard him say, "Oh, I gotta get rid of my goddamn Halliburton stock." Lyndon Johnson was talking about the consequences of his political problems with his Halliburton stock at a time when the president had been officially declared dead. And that pissed me off. It really made me furious.[126]

This is one of several examples of Johnson acting callous and indifferent about Kennedy's death. This does not prove that Johnson took part in the assassination, but it does show that he was not too distraught over it.

According to Madeleine Duncan Brown, Robert Kennedy suspected Johnson's involvement from the start. She recalled an incident related to her by a White House reporter. RFK suddenly became irate and lost his composure. He struck a post with his fist and shouted at Johnson, "Why did you have my brother killed?" This shows that Robert Kennedy never did believe the Oswald story.[127]

Author Roger Stone stated that Richard Nixon, Henry Cabot Lodge and Barry Goldwater were absolutely convinced that Lyndon Johnson murdered John Kennedy. According to Stone, Nixon made this assessment of Johnson's political ambitions:

[125] Lincoln, Evelyn, letter to Richard Duncan, a teacher at Northside Middle School in Roanoke (7th October, 1994):
[126] Marrs, Jim, *Rule by Secrecy*, p. 34, Perennial, 2000
[127] https://www.youtube.com/watch?v=zzWNDPx4Pm0

Both Johnson and I wanted to be president, but the only difference was I wouldn't kill for it.[128]

In September of 1969, Walter Cronkite interviewed Lyndon Johnson. Cronkite asked Johnson if he was satisfied that there was no international conspiracy in the assassination of John Kennedy. Johnson stumbled his way through some awkward answers, and seemed unsure of how to handle the question. After the interview, Johnson asked Cronkite and CBS News to delete that portion of the interview for the sake of national security. Cronkite and CBS obliged and deleted the unwanted segment. Years later, the censored portion of the interview was revealed. Here is what LBJ did not want anyone to hear:

> LBJ: I can't honestly say that I've ever been completely relieved of the fact that there might have been international connections.
>
> WC: You mean you still feel that there might have been?
>
> LBJ: Well, I have not completely discounted...
>
> WC: Well, that would seem to indicate that you don't have full confidence in the Warren Commission report.
>
> LBJ: No, I think that the Warren Commission study, first of all, is composed of the ablest, most judicious, bipartisan men in this country. Second, I think they had only one objective, and that was the truth. Third, I think they were competent and did the best they could. But I don't think that they or me or anyone else is always absolutely sure of everything that might have motivated Oswald or others that could have been involved.[129]

The acknowledgement of possible international connections was the part he didn't want the public to hear. It is ironic that Johnson's alleged purpose in forming the Warren Commission was to dispel any rumors of international conspiracy. Then he goes on TV and suggests there might be an international conspiracy. Needless to say, he seemed thoroughly confused. If there was a possible international conspiracy, then why didn't

---

[128] http://dailycaller.com/2013/11/22/roger-stone-nixon-thought-lbj-killed-kennedy/
[129] https://www.youtube.com/watch?v=h5psrZmT0tY

he investigate it? At the end, he fell back on the Oswald story again, as if Oswald may have had some legitimate international connections.

Johnson has suggested the involvement of oil tycoons, the CIA, and foreign governments. Yet he stands by the Warren Report. All he is really doing is deflecting attention away from himself.

Avoidable Plane Crash

LBJ's personal plane was a half-million dollar Convair, which was widely speculated to have been given to him as a kickback for some of the political favors he was known for. While the plane itself may not be significant, Johnson's abuse of his pilots was. Two of Johnson's pilots died in a tragic crash that could easily have been avoided.

The tragedy happened on Friday night, February 17, 1961. The weather in Austin, Texas, was extremely foggy and dangerous for flying. Johnson was at his Pedernales River Ranch, roughly 60 miles west of Austin. His Convair was parked at Austin Airport, with pilot Harold Teague and co-pilot Charles Williams on standby as they usually were. Johnson ordered the plane flown to his ranch, where no ground control instruments had been installed. The weather conditions were extremely hazardous, and the pilots would be flying blindly with only a two-way radio for communications. Teague consulted the tower in Austin, and was advised against flying. He then called Johnson to say they could not make the flight. Johnson exploded with rage and profanity, and ordered Teague to get the plane to the ranch. Reluctantly, Teague and Williams set out on the perilous flight. With no visibility, the plane crashed in a cedar-covered hill, killing both men. It was three days later, on Monday the 20th, when the plane was reported overdue. Why did Johnson wait three days before reporting the flight missing?[130]

This is further evidence of Johnson's indifference to human life. While the deaths of Teague and Williams were not murders, Johnson was still responsible for them. His reckless disregard for safety cost those two men their lives. Johnson's own well-being took priority over that of others. Those two men were allies of Johnson's, yet he showed no concern at all for their safety. Would he be expected to show any more concern for his enemies?

---

[130] Haley, J. Evetts, *A Texan Looks at Lyndon*, pp. 248-251, Palo Duro Press, 1964

Box 13

The story of Box 13 stands as one of the worst scandals in America's political history. It is the story of how Lyndon Johnson stole the 1948 Senatorial election and covered it up through manipulation of the judicial system and the Democratic political organization.

In 1948, Lyndon Johnson ran for the Senate against a popular candidate named Coke Stevenson. Stevenson was expected to win. Throughout campaigning, the polls were very close. During the voting in the state primary, Stevenson led by as many as 70,000 votes, yet Johnson somehow forced a runoff. On the morning after the runoff, the Texas election bureau showed that Stevenson was ahead by just 854 votes. There were several days of recounts, corrections, and suspicious vote-shifting. Still, at noon on the Friday after the election, Stevenson was ahead by 150 votes. Six days after the election, the winner was still not decided. Then, a surprising and suspicious thing happened. In the district of Alice, Texas, 202 additional votes suddenly showed up in the Precinct 13 voting box. 200 of the 202 votes were for Lyndon Johnson. This swung the election, and Johnson won by a total of 87 votes out of nearly 1 million votes cast.

Naturally suspicious, Stevenson began an investigation. It was discovered that the 202 names appeared to be added to the list later. They were all in the same handwriting, written in the same ink, and were all in alphabetical order. But Stevenson and his investigators were only allowed a brief look at the ballots before they were locked away. They only had a chance to memorize a few names off the ballots. When they followed up on those names, it turned out that some of the new voters claimed that they never even voted. Stevenson's team was not allowed further access to the ballots, which were destroyed shortly thereafter. Supposedly, a janitor had accidently thrown them out. Accusations flew, and Stevenson charged that Johnson had stolen the election.

But Johnson was not about to give up his victory, whether tainted or not. He and his lawyers found a cooperative judge in Austin to issue an injunction, preventing the Democratic organization from invalidating those 202 new votes, which would have given Stevenson the election. This was a legal ploy to buy time for Johnson to win certification as the winner by the state Democratic Executive Committee.[131]

Stevenson countered with an injunction of his own, claiming voter fraud by Johnson. He tried to get Johnson's name removed from the ballot for the general election. Johnson's lawyers tried to dissolve the injunction, but a judge denied the request. The hearing had begun, and several witnesses had testified that numbers were changed and ballots were lost. It looked bad for Johnson, until one of his lawyers, Abe Fortas, came up with a legal strategy that saved the day for him.

The plan was to take the case to a single circuit court judge and ask for a stay of the injunction on judicial grounds. It was a weakly presented and unpersuasive case that they would inevitably lose. That was the plan. By receiving an unfavorable ruling, that allowed Johnson's legal team to appeal the case to the Supreme Court. After the appeal was filed, the lawyers were somehow able to arrange for the case to be heard by a single justice. That was Justice Hugo Black, who knew Johnson personally and was an ally of his. Also involved in this was Attorney General Tom Clark, who was also a friend and ally of Johnson's. Clark used his influence to see that the case was handled favorably for Johnson. Justice Black then issued a sweeping order in favor of Johnson, staying the injunction by Stevenson, and ending the hearings into the matter.[132] [133]

The legal reasoning here was convoluted. Fortas' request to the single circuit court judge was based solely on jurisdiction—claiming that the federal government had no authority to interfere in state elections. This is completely ignoring the fact that Johnson was accused of voter fraud, which is a federal offense. Yet, according to Justice Black, it is none of the federal government's business. Black's ruling completely subverted the democratic process, robbed Stevenson of the election, and put a murderer in power.

In 1977, Luis Salas, the local election judge involved in Box 13, gave an interview to the *Dallas Morning News*. Salas admitted that he had certified fictitious ballots for Johnson on orders from George Parr, known as the "Duke of Duval County." Salas stated, "Johnson did not win that election; it was stolen for him." Known as a South Texas political boss with a history of

---

[131] Nelson, Phillip F, *LBJ: Mastermind of JFK's Assassination*, pp. 67-71, Xlibris, 2010
[132] Nelson, Phillip F., *LBJ: Mastermind of JFK's Assassination*, pp. 66-74, Xlibris, 2010
[133] http://viewzone.com/lbj/lbj2.html

corruption, Parr probably felt he owed Johnson a favor since Johnson had arranged a political pardon for Parr in 1946. With Parr's history of crime, he wanted to have a U.S. Senator in his corner.[134]

In 1952, a man named Sam Smithwick wrote to Coke Stevenson with an offer of help. Smithwick was a deputy sheriff who claimed to possess the missing ballot box that had cost Stevenson the election in 1948. This would mean that Lyndon Johnson could be prosecuted for election fraud. The problem, however, was that Smithwick was in state prison for killing a man. The man he killed was Bill Mason, a Texas newsman investigating the Box 13 scandal.

Word of Smithwick's claim reached Johnson and Clark. They knew they had to get rid of him. Ed Clark had a contact in the prison who was a guard, and through this contact they had Smithwick killed. Smithwick was strangled in his cell by one or more guards, then hung from the frame of the top bunk bed. When found, his knees were touching the ground, yet it was still considered a hanging death and ruled a suicide. Those who followed the case suspected foul play, but it could not be proven. There was only a token investigation. Texas Governor Allan Shivers personally confronted Johnson and accused him of arranging the murder. Johnson told a reporter, "Shivers charged me with murder. Shivers said I was a murderer!"[135]

TFX Scandal

The TFX/F-111 was a joint Air Force-Navy undertaking. This was a successor to the Air Force's F-105 tactical fighter. The TFX program involved the building of 1,700 planes for the air force and navy, and was estimated to be worth nearly $7 billion, the nation's largest contract for military planes at the time. In October of 1961, the two services sent the aircraft industry the request for bids on the project. A total of six bids were submitted. The bidders were: Lockheed Aircraft Corporation, North American Aviation Corporation, Boeing Company, Republic Aviation/Chance Vought, General Dynamics Corporation/Grumman Aircraft, and McDonnell Aircraft/Douglas Aircraft.

---

[134] Marrs, Jim, *Crossfire*, p.292, Carroll and Graf, 1989

[135] https://www.washingtonpost.com/archive/entertainment/books/1990/03/04/the-mystery-of-ballot-box-13/70206359-8543-48e3-9ce2-f3c4fdf6da3d/?utm_term=.9fc1965b2f84

Analysts expected Boeing to get the contract. The main competitor was the General Dynamics/Grumman Aircraft bid. During much of the Cold War, General Dynamics had been America's leading military contractor. Government contracts accounted for over 80% of the company's business at that time. But the company had lost $170 million in 1960-61, and was close to bankruptcy. General Dynamics desperately needed the TFX project to stay afloat.

The first three times that bids were submitted for the project, the Pentagon found that Boeing's bid was better and cheaper than the General Dynamics bid. All three times the bids were sent back for resubmission. After the fourth bid, the Pentagon still believed that the Boeing bid was the best, but decided that the General Dynamics bid was acceptable, too. To the surprise of many, the project was awarded to General Dynamics. General Dynamics was located in Texas, and it was suspected that the decision was influenced by Lyndon Johnson, former Secretary of the Navy John Connally, and current Secretary of the Navy Fred Korth, all who were Texas-based politicians.[136]

This suspicious decision was later investigated by the McClellan Committee. The committee found no justification for awarding the contract to General Dynamics. The only document they could find in favor of the decision was a five-page memorandum signed by Secretary of Defense Robert McNamara, along with the secretaries of the Navy and Air Force. The committee found that:

> Boeing's bid was substantially lower than its competitor's. Reports indicated Boeing's bid was $100 million lower on an initial development contract and that the cost difference might run as high as $400 million on the total $6.5 billion procurement.[137]

Yet, General Dynamics was awarded the contract. McNamara offered this justification for the decision:

> Boeing had from the very beginning consistently chosen more technically risky tradeoffs in an effort to achieve

---

[136] Nelson, Phillip F, *LBJ: Mastermind of JFK's Assassination*, pp. 233-236, Xlibris, 2010

[137] http://spartacus-educational.com/JFKkorth.htm

operational features which exceeded the required
performance characteristics.

The committee was apparently not satisfied with that explanation. Under further questioning, McNamara was asked if there was any connection between the Pentagon's decision and the fact that Lyndon Johnson was a resident of Texas, where General Dynamics had its principal office. McNamara denied that Johnson was a factor in the decision, but analysts suspected otherwise. Reporters investigated, and discovered that Continental National Bank of Fort Worth was the principal money lender for General Dynamics. The president of Continental National Bank at the time was Fred Korth, who was Secretary of the Navy when the bid was awarded, and co-signed the memorandum that recommended General Dynamics for the project. This was an obvious conflict of interests, which forced Korth to resign his position. Korth had been appointed to his position by John Kennedy, but only after being pressured to do so by Lyndon Johnson.

Don B. Reynolds was an associate of Johnson. He knew that TFX had paid off Johnson, and was threatening to expose the scandal. Johnson and his team worked behind the scenes to keep the information from going public. Johnson enlisted the help of his friend, J. Edgar Hoover. Hoover sent Johnson the FBI file on Reynolds, which Johnson used to start a smear campaign against him. Nothing in the file was really damaging to Reynolds. Among the information revealed was that Reynolds had lied about his academic success at West Point, he had supported Joseph McCarthy, and had made anti-Semitic remarks. Reynolds testified anyway. Ironically, his testimony took place on the exact day Kennedy died.

In front of the Senate Rules Committee, Reynolds told all he knew about the TFX scandal. He described seeing a suitcase full of money being given to Johnson by his aide, Bobby Baker. According to Reynolds, this was a $100,000 payoff to Johnson for securing the TFX contract for General Dynamics. The kickbacks also included a $585 stereo system and $1200 for advertising on Johnson's television station in Austin. In spite of Reynolds' testimony, Johnson survived unscathed. The ten-member Senate Rules Committee contained seven democrats, and Johnson somehow persuaded those seven democrats to vote against hearing the testimony of key witnesses.[138] [139]

Johnson was intimately connected with a construction and engineering company called Brown & Root. In 1937, Johnson secured federal authorization for the Marshall Ford Dam project in South Texas, which was a prosperous endeavor for Brown & Root. He also obtained a contract for them to build a huge navy base at Corpus Christi. In 1941, Johnson helped the company obtain a lucrative navy contract to build four sub chasers. The navy contract is especially surprising, since prior to obtaining that contract Brown & Root had never built a single ship of any kind.[140]

In the 1940s and 1950s, Lyndon Johnson received illegal campaign contributions from Brown & Root. At the time, the law prohibited political contributions from corporations, and limited individual contributions to $5,000. Brown & Root circumvented the law by paying a $5,000 bonus to their employees and associates, who in turn made a $5,000 donation to Johnson's campaign fund. The IRS became suspicious and investigated. At one point, the investigation was ordered stopped by President Roosevelt. After Roosevelt passed away, the IRS renewed the investigation. The probe ended when it was discovered that the evidence in question had been destroyed in a fire. The evidence had originally been stored in a fireproof warehouse, but it had been inexplicably removed and placed into a shanty which burned to the ground.[141]

In 1961, the National Aeronautics and Space Administration (NASA) decided to build their new manned spacecraft center in the Houston area. It was originally believed that Tampa would be chosen as the new site. But Lyndon Johnson was head of the Space Council at the time, and due to political pressure from him and other influential Texans, Houston was chosen as the new site. The center was built on 1,000 acres of land donated by Humble Oil Company. Humble Oil retained all of the surrounding land and used it to build a large industrial park around the Space Center. This led to a 700% increase in the value of the land for Humble Oil. Brown & Root was the company awarded the $90 million federal contract to build the

---

[138] http://educationforum.ipbhost.com/index.php?/topic/6250-tfx-scandal-and-the-jfk-assassination/
[139] http://spartacus-educational.com/JFKbakerB.htm
[140] Marrs, Jim, *Crossfire*, pp. 290-291, Carroll and Graf, 1989
[141] Zirbel, Craig I., *The Texas Connection*, Wright and Co., 1991

Space Center, apparently as a return favor for their generous campaign donations to Lyndon Johnson. After LBJ passed away in 1973, the center was renamed Johnson Space Center.[142]

Bobby Baker

Bobby Baker was an aide of Lyndon Johnson's. He was befriended by Johnson in the 1940s, when young Baker was a page at the Senate. He got the nickname "Little Lyndon" because of his close personal relationship with LBJ. Throughout the years Baker was a loyal associate of Johnson's, willing to do whatever was necessary to further LBJ's political career. When Johnson became vice president, Baker stayed on as Johnson's secretary and political advisor.

In the early 1950's Baker was involved with a company called Intercontinental Hotels Corporation, helping them to establish casinos in the Dominican Republic. In the process, Baker did business with underworld figures such as Sam Giancana, Meyer Lansky, Ed Levinson, and Jimmy Hoffa. When the first of these casinos was opened, LBJ and Baker were invited as official guests. Baker wanted to turn the Dominican Republic into a haven for the mafia, much as Cuba had been. That plan ended when military dictator Rafael Trujillo was assassinated in May of 1961.

In 1962, Baker started another source of income. He established the Serve-U-Corporation with mob associates Ed Levinson, Benny Sigelbaum, and Fred Black. The company provided vending machines to companies working on federally granted programs. The machines were manufactured by a company secretly owned by mobster Sam Giancana. Baker used illegally-gained influence to promote his business.[143]

Another part of Baker and Johnson's illegal activities involved the Quorum Club. The club was located in the Carroll Arms Hotel, near the Senate office buildings. The Quorum Club catered to politicians and businessmen, and provided them with women. In other words, this was a high-class, and very sophisticated, prostitution/blackmail ring. Baker and his associates would set politicians up with women, then secretly film them, either at the club or at a remote location, wherever the encounter took place. Then, the films would be used later to blackmail those politicians into

---

[142] https://en.wikipedia.org/wiki/Johnson_Space_Center
[143] https://en.wikipedia.org/wiki/Bobby_Baker

submission. Johnson was indirectly involved in this scheme. He didn't do the filming, but he did the blackmailing. This way Johnson, through Baker, would always have something to use against his enemies, something he could control them with. This is one reason why people always seemed to capitulate to Johnson, no matter how much initial resistance they provided.

Baker was clearly a very rich man, although his only official income was that of Secretary to the Majority in the Senate. Attorney General Robert Kennedy became suspicious of Baker, and began an investigation through the Senate Rules Committee. Baker was suspected of bribery using money allocated by Congress and arranging sexual favors in exchange for votes and government contracts. He discovered Baker's corrupt activities, and also found that Baker had ties to oil baron Clint Murchison and several mafia figures. Kennedy also was suspicious that Johnson was involved in the corruption. As the investigation intensified, Baker was forced to resign his post.[144]

The FBI became aware of the activities of the Quorum Club, and started to investigate. Several leading politicians had been found to be involved in relationships with women from the club. The list of politicians involved included John and Robert Kennedy. Baker had arranged a meeting between John Kennedy and a woman named Ellen Rometsch. According to Baker, Kennedy told him "...it was the best time he ever had in his life." They saw each other repeatedly, and the relationship went on for some time.

The FBI kept tabs on this relationship. In July of 1963, they interviewed Rometsch to learn about her past. They concluded that she was probably a Soviet spy. Rometsch, of German descent, had worked for Walter Ulbricht, the Communist leader of East Germany. Hoover, who was no friend of either Kennedy, leaked this information to journalists. When Robert Kennedy found out that Rometsch was a Soviet spy, he ordered her to be deported. Later, he sent committee aide La Verne Duffy to West Germany to talk with Rometsch. She was given an undisclosed sum of money to sign a statement in which she denied having intimate relations with important people.

The Kennedys were anxious to kill the story. Robert Kennedy talked to J. Edgar Hoover and tried to persuade him that the story was contrary to

---

[144] Nelson, Phillip F, *LBJ: Mastermind of JFK's Assassination*, pp. 262-268, Xlibris, 2010

national interests, and to the interests of Congress. He was able to arrange a deal to silence any mention of the Rometsch allegations in the investigation. Hoover then used his influence to convince the Senate Rules Committee to not look into the Rometsch matter. In exchange for this, Robert Kennedy had to give the FBI written approval to use wiretaps. He also had to promise Hoover that his job as FBI director was secure. Hoover would have been forced into mandatory retirement on January 1, 1965, his 70th birthday. This was another example of Hoover and Johnson using blackmail as a weapon. Without the testimony of Rometsch, the Senate investigation of Bobby Baker was impeded.[145]

Still, Bobby Baker was found guilty of seven counts of theft, fraud, and income tax evasion. He was found to have accepted large sums of money, deemed "campaign donations," but kept the money for himself. He was sentenced to three years in federal prison, but served 16 months.[146]

Stories abound of Johnson and Baker raking in truckloads of cash from unscrupulous sources. Author Robert Caro told the *Atlantic Monthly*:

> For years, men came into Lyndon Johnson's office and handed him envelopes stuffed with cash. They didn't stop coming even when the office in which he sat was the office of the vice president of the United States. Fifty thousand dollars in hundred-dollar bills in sealed envelopes was what one lobbyist for one oil company testified he brought to Johnson's office during his term as vice-president.[147]

Jack Halfen was the mob's gambling coordinator in Houston. He told federal officials that Lyndon Johnson had received over $500,000 in contributions from the mob during a ten-year period while Johnson was in the Senate. Halfen said that in return, Johnson stopped anti-racketeering legislation and impeded Congressional probes into the syndicate. Johnson had also written a letter to the Texas Board of Paroles in Halfen's defense.[148]

A former senatorial aide, Jack Sullivan, testified that he witnessed Johnson's aide Cliff Carter receive a suitcase full of money from a teamster

---

[145] https://en.wikipedia.org/wiki/Bobby_Baker
[146] http://spartacus-educational.com/JFKbakerB.htm
[147] Marrs, Jim, *Crossfire*, p. 293, Carroll and Graf, 1989
[148] Nelson, Philip F., *JFK: Mastermind of the JFK Assassination*, p. 77, Xlibris, 2013

lobbyist through a Maryland Senator. The payoff was allegedly approved by Teamster president Jimmy Hoffa.[149]

Life Magazine Probe

Robert Kennedy was determined to get rid of Lyndon Johnson any way he could. He ordered the Senate Rules Committee to investigate Johnson's illegal kickbacks and other corruption. He gave them damaging information about TFX, the Baker scandal, and anything else he could find. He also called several of Washington's top reporters into his office and told them it was open season on Johnson. He informed them that it was acceptable to expose Johnson's scandals, in spite of any backlash to the Kennedy administration. RFK fed information to *Life* magazine, which began a huge expose` on Johnson.

The *Life* probe began with reporter William Lambert. Lambert was a Pulitzer Prize-winning journalist who broke the story about the Teamsters Union and their connection with organized crime. That story led to the formation of the McClellan Committee. Lambert was suspicious of how LBJ had accumulated millions of dollars in net worth while being on the public payroll. Managing editor George P. Hunt authorized Lambert to assemble a task force assigned to investigate both Baker and Johnson.

The Baker story broke wide open with the publication of the November 8, 1963 issue of *Life*. The cover read: "Capital Buzzes Over Stories of Misconduct in High Places: The Bobby Baker Bombshell." The article featured East German call girl Elly Rometsch. Not only was Rometsch a prostitute, but as mentioned earlier, she was also suspected of being a Soviet spy. The article told how a Senate committee was investigating Baker on charges of using illegitimate influence to promote his vending machine business in defense plants. It was questioned how Baker purchased a house in Washington for $124,500 when his annual salary was $19,612. The feature also included pictures of scantily clad waitresses working at the Carousel Hotel, which was half-owned by Baker. The article also included a full-page photograph of Lyndon Johnson smiling with his arm around Bobby Baker. The caption called Baker an "indispensable confidant" of Johnson. Baker was also described as "a messenger, a pleader of causes, a fund-raiser, and a source of intelligence."

---

[149] Marrs, Jim, *Crossfire*, p.293, Carroll and Graf, 1989

The second installment of the *Life* series was published the week of November 15, 1963. It was titled: "The Bobby Baker Scandal: It Grows and Grows as Washington Shudders." This feature, authored by Keith Wheeler, went in-depth in the exposure of Baker's sex-for-power operation out of the Quorum Club. It showed how Baker and Johnson had obtained illegitimate power by blackmailing politicians and businessmen is sex scandals which they themselves initiated by introducing them to prostitutes. The article read:

> "Girls," a former Baker business associate said, "were often around as business adjuncts…even to talk business, they had a bunch of girls who, they say, work in the government and during their lunch hour they make a little extra money."[150]

The article made it clear that everything involving Baker also involved Johnson. It said that Baker was "Johnson's bluntest instrument in running the show." It stated that the U.S. Senate was Baker's base of operations, and that that base of operations was controlled by Lyndon Johnson. As majority leader, Johnson had unequaled power in Congress. Wheeler said that the Senate was controlled by a small group of southern Senators and conservative Republicans who he referred to as "the Establishment," headed by LBJ. Wheeler writes:

> In a very real sense the present Establishment is the personal creation of Lyndon Baines Johnson who, from the day he took over as majority leader until he went to the Vice Presidency, ruled it like an absolute monarch.

So the investigation that started out to be about Bobby Baker had now turned its focus to Lyndon Johnson. The goal was now to expose Johnson's criminal activities. On the morning of November 22, 1963, the members of the investigative team held a meeting to discuss plans for the third installment of the series. It was certain to seal Johnson's fate. Then came word that John Kennedy was assassinated. The third article in the series was never published. Instead, the next issue of *Life* featured the Zapruder film.[151] [152]

---

[150] http://www.wnd.com/2013/11/did-jfk-seal-his-fate-with-plan-to-dump-lbj/
[151] http://www.wnd.com/2013/11/did-jfk-seal-his-fate-with-plan-to-dump-lbj/

James Wagenvoord was the Editorial Business Manager of *Life* magazine at the time. He talks about what happened:

> Beginning in later summer 1963 the magazine, based upon information fed from Bobby Kennedy and the Justice Department, had been developing a major newsbreak piece concerning Johnson and Bobby Baker. On publication Johnson would have been finished and off the 1964 ticket (reason the material was fed to us) and would probably have been facing prison time. At the time *LIFE* magazine was arguably the most important general news source in the US. The top management of Time Inc. was closely allied with the USA's various intelligence agencies and we were used after by the Kennedy Justice Department as a conduit to the public.
>
> The LBJ/Baker piece was in the final editing stages and was scheduled to break in the issue of the magazine due out the week of November 24th (the magazine would have made it to the newsstands on November 26th or 27th). It had been prepared in relative secrecy by a small special editorial team. On Kennedy's death research files and all numbered copies of the nearly print-ready draft were gathered up by my boss (he had been the top editor on the team) and shredded. The issue that was to expose LBJ instead featured the Zapruder film.[153]

The *Life* articles made no mention of the murders that Johnson was a part of, probably because there was not absolute proof. But the financial and political scandals would have been enough to put him away. Confirmation of his complicity in murder would come years later.

---

[152] http://delmardustpan.blogspot.com/2008/07/bobby-baker-and-carousel-hotel.html
[153] http://spartacus-educational.com/USAjohnsonLB.htm

The Hit List

It is a little-known fact that a Texas Grand Jury has officially found Lyndon Johnson guilty as a co-conspirator in nine murders, based on his association with Billie Sol Estes, Cliff Carter, and Malcolm Wallace.[154]

Billie Sol Estes was an associate of Lyndon Johnson's. Together, they were partners in crime during the 1960s. Estes served eight years on fraud charges and was released in 1971. In 1979 he was again convicted of fraud and served four more years. In 1984, Estes was willing to speak out on the crimes that he and Johnson committed together. This included at least nine murders. Estes claims that Cliff Carter and Malcolm Wallace also took part in these crimes. In most cases, it was Wallace who carried out the actual murder. The orders to kill were transmitted to Wallace through Cliff Carter.[155]

Estes agreed to provide information to the Department of Justice in exchange for immunity from prosecution and a pardon. This was after Estes had already served his time for his crimes. Johnson had passed away by this time, and Estes just felt the need to come clean about his past. His attorney, Douglas Caddy, sent the following letter to Assistant Attorney General Stephen Trott of the Justice Department:

> Dear Mr. Trott:
>
> My client, Mr. Estes, has authorized me to make this reply to your letter of May 29, 1984. Mr. Estes was a member of a four-member group, headed by Lyndon Johnson, which committed criminal acts in Texas in the 1960's. The other two, besides Mr. Estes and LBJ, were Cliff Carter and Mac Wallace. Mr. Estes is willing to disclose his knowledge concerning the following criminal offenses:
>
> I. Murders
>
> 1. The killing of Henry Marshall
>
> 2. The killing of George Krutilek

---

[154] http://humansarefree.com/2011/07/john-f-kennedy-assassinated-by-lyndon-b.html

[155] https://en.wikipedia.org/wiki/Billie_Sol_Estes

3. The killing of Ike Rogers and his secretary

4. The killing of Harold Orr

5. The killing of Coleman Wade

6. The killing of Josefa Johnson

7. The killing of John Kinser

8. The killing of President J. F. Kennedy.

Mr. Estes is willing to testify that LBJ ordered these killings, and that he transmitted his orders through Cliff Carter to Mac Wallace, who executed the murders. In the cases of murders nos. 1-7, Mr. Estes' knowledge of the precise details concerning the way the murders were executed stems from conversations he had shortly after each event with Cliff Carter and Mac Wallace.

In addition, a short time after Mr. Estes was released from prison in 1971, he met with Cliff Carter and they reminisced about what had occurred in the past, including the murders. During their conversation, Carter orally compiled a list of 17 murders which had been committed, some of which Mr. Estes was unfamiliar. A living witness was present at that meeting and should be willing to testify about it. He is Kyle Brown, recently of Houston and now living in Brady, Texas.

Mr. Estes, states that Mac Wallace, whom he describes as a "stone killer" with a communist background, recruited Jack Ruby, who in turn recruited Lee Harvey Oswald. Mr. Estes says that Cliff Carter told him that Mac Wallace fired a shot from the grassy knoll in Dallas, which hit JFK from the front during the assassination.

Mr. Estes declares that Cliff Carter told him the day Kennedy was killed, Fidel Castro also was supposed to be assassinated and that Robert Kennedy, awaiting word of Castro's death, instead received news of his brother's killing.

Mr. Estes says that the Mafia did not participate in the Kennedy assassination but that its participation was discussed prior to the event, but rejected by LBJ, who believed if the Mafia were involved, he would never be out from under its blackmail.

Mr. Estes asserts that Mr. Ronnie Clark, of Wichita, Kansas, has attempted on several occasions to engage him in conversation. Mr. Clark, who is a frequent visitor to Las Vegas, has indicated in these conversations a detailed knowledge corresponding to Mr. Estes' knowledge of the JFK assassination. Mr. Clark claims to have met with Mr. Jack Ruby a few days prior to the assassination, at which time Kennedy's planned murder was discussed.

Mr. Estes declares that discussions were had with Jimmy Hoffa concerning having his aide, Larry Cabell, kill Robert Kennedy while the latter drove around in his convertible.

Mr. Estes has records of his phone calls during the relevant years to key persons mentioned in the foregoing account.

II. The Illegal Cotton Allotments

Mr. Estes desires to discuss the infamous illegal cotten allotment schemes in great detail. He has recordings made at the time of LBJ, Cliff Carter and himself discussing the scheme. These recordings were made with Cliff Carter's knowledge as a means of Carter and Estes protecting themselves should LBJ order their deaths.

Mr. Estes believes these tape recordings and the rumors of other recordings allegedly in his possession are the reason he has not been murdered.

III. Illegal Payoffs

Mr. Estes is willing to disclose illegal payoff schemes, in which he collected and passed on to Cliff Carter and LBJ millions of dollars. Mr. Estes collected payoff money on more than one occasion from George and Herman Brown of Brown and Root, which was delivered to LBJ.

In your letter of May 29, 1984, you request "(1) the information, including the extent of corroborative evidence, that Mr. Estes sources of his information, and (3) the extent of his involvement, if any, in each of those events or any subsequent cover-ups."

In connection with Item # 1, I wish to declare, as Mr. Estes' attorney, that Mr. Estes is prepared without reservation to provide all the information he has. Most of the information contained in this letter I obtained from him yesterday for the first time. While Mr. Estes has been pre-occupied by this knowledge almost every day for the last 22 years, it was not until we began talking yesterday that he could face up to disclosing it to another person. My impression from our conversation yesterday is that Mr. Estes, in the proper setting, will be able to recall and orally recount criminal matters. It is also my impression that his interrogation in such a setting will elicit additional corroborative evidence as his memory is stimulated...

In connection with your Item #3, Mr. Estes states that he never participated in any of the murders. It may be alleged that he participated in subsequent cover-ups. His response to this is that had he conducted himself any differently, he, too, would have been a murder victim.

Mr. Estes wishes to confirm that he will abide by the conditions set forth in your letter and that he plans to act with total honesty and candor in any dealings with the Department of Justice or any federal investigative agency.

In return for his cooperation, Mr. Estes wishes in exchange his being given immunity, his parole restrictions being lifted and favorable consideration being given to recommending his long-standing tax leins [sic] being removed and his obtaining a pardon.

Sincerely yours,

Douglas Caddy[156]

The most important statement in the letter is this one:

Mr. Estes is willing to testify that LBJ ordered these killings, and that he transmitted his orders through Cliff Carter to Mac Wallace, who executed the murders.

---

[156] http://home.earthlink.net/~sixthfloor/estes.htm

There is no reason to think that Estes is lying. He had served his time, and had nothing to gain by falsely implicating anyone in a crime. He knew Johnson well, and he saw first-hand the criminal mentality that would eventually inhabit the White House.

For the record, Estes wrongly stated that Mac Wallace was the shooter on the grassy knoll. Most likely, Wallace shot from the TSBD, not the grassy knoll. The shooting sequence will be discussed in detail in Chapter 6.

Henry Marshall was a local agricultural official who was investigating one of Estes' illegal activities. This involved the misappropriation of federal cotton allotment funds. Johnson had attempted to bribe Marshall to stop the investigation, but Marshall refused the bribe. Johnson also tried to get Marshall transferred to another post, but Marshall refused the transfer. Seeing no other choice, Johnson gave the order, "Get rid of him." Johnson's henchman Malcolm Wallace was given the job.

On June 3, 1961, Marshall failed to return home. His family launched a search of his home and property in Franklin, Texas. Henry's brother eventually found him dead next to his truck in a remote place in the woods, about ¾ of a mile from the road. There were obvious signs of a struggle: Marshall had been shot five times, the truck had blood on the sides, there were dents in the vehicle where Marshall's head was apparently slammed into it, he had facial injuries, and a rifle was found next to his body.

The local authorities immediately ruled it a suicide.

No evidence was collected from the scene that would prove homicide. No pictures were taken of the crime scene. No blood samples were taken from the stains on the truck. No check for fingerprints were made on the truck or the rifle. The truck was washed and waxed the next day. With virtually no investigation at all, County Sheriff Howard Steggal officially determined that it was a suicide.

Marshall was shot five times with a bolt-action rifle. Five times with a rifle? How is that a suicide? Steggal was obviously in Johnson's pocket. No legitimate investigation could have ruled it a suicide. But Texas was Johnson's power base, and he had enough connections to get away with just about anything. That same power base would later be used to kill John Kennedy and get away with it. The Henry Marshall murder is about as blatant a crime as you'll ever see. Yet, the local authorities turned a blind eye to it because of Lyndon Johnson's influence.

Even J. Edgar Hoover was puzzled by the ruling, stating, "I just can't understand how one can fire five shots at himself."[157]

The case went before a Grand Jury, most of who believed that Henry Marshall was murdered. Yet, the jury ruled that it was "...inconclusive to substantiate a definite decision at this time, or to overrule any decision heretofore made." The verdict was shocking to those who followed the case, but not shocking to those who knew Johnson. Apparently, there was one juror who held out for the suicide verdict. That was Pryse Metcalfe, who was the son-in-law of Sheriff Howard Stegall. According to juror Ralph McKinney:

> Pryse was as strong in the support of the suicide verdict as anyone I have ever seen in my life, and I think he used every influence he possibly could against the members of the grand jury to be sure it came out with a suicide verdict.[158]

So how did the sheriff's son-in-law wind up on this jury? It's a clear conflict of interest. There was obviously some behind-the-scenes manipulation going on, and Johnson must have had a hand in it. Needless to say, Marshall's family refused to accept the verdict, and continued to fight to get it changed to murder.

On June 1, 1962, the *Dallas Morning News* reported on the case. It stated that President Kennedy had "taken a personal interest in the mysterious death of Henry Marshall." As a result, Robert Kennedy "has ordered the FBI to step up its investigation of the case."[159]The Kennedys must have suspected Johnson's involvement in the murder. Even a cursory look at the case would reveal that much. Yet, there was no mention of the Marshall case in the *Life* series that would run a little over a year later. Maybe the Kennedys were holding off until they had more proof. They may had considered the damage it would do to the administration if the truth was known.

---

[157] http://spartacus-educational.com/JFKmarshallH.htm
[158] http://spartacus-educational.com/JFKwallaceM.htm
[159] http://spartacus-educational.com/JFKmarshallH.htm

In 1984, Billy Sol Estes appeared before a Grand Jury and showed them the hit list of Lyndon Johnson's victims. He confessed that Henry Marshall had been murdered for fear he would expose the cotton allotment scam. Estes claimed that Marshall was murdered on the orders of Lyndon Johnson, who had to hide his own involvement. According to Estes, the assignment to kill Marshall was given to Malcolm Wallace, who Estes described as "Johnson's hit man."

Estes told the Grand Jury how Wallace had described the murder: Wallace had waited for Marshall at his farm. He planned to make it look like Marshall had committed suicide by carbon monoxide poisoning. But Marshall fought back and Wallace was forced to shoot him with his own rifle. Wallace basically botched the assignment and Johnson was forced to use his influence to cover it up.

The Grand Jury changed the verdict on Marshall's death from "suicide" to "death by gunshot." So the Grand Jury believed that Marshall was murdered on orders from Johnson.[160]

George Krutilek was an accountant for Billie Sol Estes and his many scams. This scam involved getting federal agricultural subsidies. Estes made $21 million a year for growing and storing non-existent cotton crops, and Krutilek shared in the wealth. Estes was arrested on April 1, 1962, and charged with 57 counts of fraud. The next day, Krutilek was questioned by the FBI.

Krutilek was found dead on April 4, 1962. The killer had tried to make it look like a suicide by stashing Krutilek's body behind the steering wheel and placing a hose from the exhaust in the window. The El Paso County pathologist, Dr. Frederick Bornstein, was certain he did not die from carbon monoxide poisoning. No trace of carbon monoxide was found in Krutilek's body, indicating he was dead before he was placed in the truck. He had a severe bruise on his head, but the coroner eventually ruled it a suicide. Krutilek must have known too much about Estes' crooked dealings.[161] [162]

Harold Eugene Orr was the president of Superior Manufacturing Company, and a partner in crime with Estes. Orr was arrested along with

---

[160] https://jfkunloaded.wordpress.com/category/suspects/
[161] McClellan, Barr, *Blood, Money, and Power*, Hannover House, 2003
[162] Haley, J. Evetts, *A Texan Looks at Lyndon*, 1964

Estes and given a ten-year federal prison sentence. But before he began serving his term, Orr was found dead in his garage. This was ruled accidental death by carbon monoxide. Was Orr about to talk in exchange for his freedom?

Coleman Wade was a building contractor and a business associate of Billie Sol Estes. He built storage facilities for Billie Sol Estes Enterprises, and became involved in the scandal. Wade died in a suspicious plane crash in Texas in 1963. Estes' pilot said that the crash had "ominous overtones."[163]

Of all of Estes' claims, the most shocking one of all is the claim that Lyndon Johnson killed his own sister, along with her lover. Josefa Johnson had a reputation for wild behavior and promiscuity, and was rumored to have had affairs with Mac Wallace and a man named Doug Kinser. Lyndon Johnson had a puritanical attitude toward Josefa's sexual escapades, which made him a hypocrite. Josefa supposedly took part in sex orgies and had a threesome with Wallace and his wife, Mary. She was also known to have loose lips, and disclosed personal information about Lyndon Johnson, some of it relating to his illegal activities. LBJ feared that Josefa might become involved in a scandal that would be a threat to his political career. If that's the case, then she had to be eliminated.

Doug Kinser had been asking Josefa to get LBJ's help in getting a loan to pay off some business debts. LBJ interpreted this as a blackmail attempt, since Kinser probably knew many of his dirty secrets. This further increased Johnson's resentment toward both Kinser and Josefa.

On October 22, 1951, Mac Wallace drove to the Pitch-and-Putt golf course owned by Kinser. Wallace walked into the clubhouse and shot Kinser point-blank five times, in spite of nearby witnesses. One of the witnesses took note of Wallace's license plate, leading to his arrest.

On February 1, 1952, Wallace resigned from his government job in order to distance himself from Johnson. His trial began seventeen days later. Wallace did not testify. Attorney John Cofer admitted his client's guilt but claimed it was an act of revenge, as Kinser had been sleeping with Wallace's wife. Wallace was eventually found guilty of "murder with malice aforethought." Eleven of the jurors were for the death penalty. The twelfth argued for life imprisonment. Judge Charles O. Betts overruled the jury and

---

[163] http://spartacus-educational.com/JFKwadeC.htm

announced a sentence of five years imprisonment. He suspended the sentence and Wallace was immediately freed.

Years later, one of the jurors on the Wallace trial confirmed to interviewers that all the jurors had been threatened. Phillip F. Nelson writes:

> He had carried with him a burden of guilt because of the outcome of the trial, but explained that the jury members, each one, had been threatened. Describing the period of time during the trial, he said that one evening during dinner, he and his wife were interrupted by two well-dressed men who knocked at his door. As he responded to the callers, he noticed that one of them held a shotgun in his hands. After cocking the gun, the visitor pointed the weapon at the man and pulled the trigger. Click. The weapon was empty. "This gun could just as easily have been loaded," warned the visitor. "Be very careful about your decision." And then the men were gone. These kinds of men were plentiful, and Johnson had the knack of finding them and keeping them loyal.[164]

Several of the jurors phoned Kinser's parents to apologize for the verdict, but told them they had to go along with it because they or their families were threatened.

Josefa Johnson died of a cerebral hemorrhage on December 25th, 1961. She had returned home at 11:45 p.m. from a Christmas party at Lyndon Johnson's ranch. She was found dead at 3:15 a.m. Despite state law, there was no autopsy or inquest. The death certificate was issued by a doctor who was not present to examine her. Josefa was embalmed on Christmas Day and buried on the 26th. According to Estes, she was murdered by Lyndon Johnson, although the method is not clear.[165]

According to Estes' testimony, these murders, including JFK, were arranged and coordinated by a man named Edward Clark. Clark was one of Lyndon Johnson's attorneys. Clark met Johnson in 1935 and the two became close friends. Clark opened a private law practice and became a political

---

[164] Nelson, Phillip F., LBJ- *The Mastermind of JFK's Assassination*, Xlibris, 2010
[165] Brown, Walt, The Sordid Story of Mac Wallace, *JFK/Deep Politics Quarterly*, July, 1998

lobbyist for the oil industry. One of his clients was oil baron Clint Murchison. Clark had contacts with the FBI, the CIA, and the mafia. One of his associates was William K. Harvey. Harvey was part of the CIA's foreign assassination squads and a former FBI agent. Through his numerous contacts, Clark was able to arrange the assassination on Johnson's behalf.

Originally, there were three assassination plots against JFK. One was in Chicago on November 2nd, one in Miami on the 18th, and then Dallas on the 22nd. Chances are that Clark had a hand in all three. These three cities represent the mob bosses who hated Kennedy the most. Chicago was the domain of Sam Giancana, Miami belonged to Santos Trafficante, and Dallas was owned by Carlos Marcello. No doubt Clark and Johnson maintained steady contact with all three, even if only through intermediaries. They could arrange for shooters, parade routes, security changes, etc. Johnson himself probably only knew of the Dallas plot, but Clark could have had some involvement in the other two, which were aborted.[166]

Hit List Expanded—RFK and MLK

There are at least two more individuals who were on Johnson's hit list that Estes did not mention. They are Robert Francis Kennedy and Martin Luther King. Estes was in jail at the time these murders were planned and carried out, so he did not know of Johnson's involvement, although he probably suspected as much. Johnson and Hoover both hated the Kennedys and King. They wanted Bobby Kennedy dead because he was a threat to reopen the investigation into JFK's death if he became president. They wanted Martin Luther King dead because they were racists. RFK and MLK were also targets because of their outspoken opposition to the Vietnam War. Both of these assassinations bear the same trademarks as the JFK murder: missing evidence, intimidated witnesses, conflicting testimonies, etc. When JFK, RFK, and MLK were all murdered within a short span of time, people thought the world was falling apart. Everyone wondered why all these murders were suddenly happening. Lyndon Johnson is the reason. Johnson was the common denominator of all three of those assassinations. He was in the White House for all three, and he had the ways and means to orchestrate the murders, and to cover them up.

---

[166] http://www.viewzone.com/lbj/lbj4.html

Unlike JFK's murder, there is no question who shot RFK. On June 5, 1968, just after midnight, Sirhan Sirhan walked up to Robert Kennedy in the pantry of the Ambassador Hotel in Los Angeles, and shot him several times point blank in front of a room full of witnesses. There is some speculation as to a second shooter, but no one questions the fact that Sirhan shot Kennedy. RFK was mortally wounded, and died about 24 hours later. Sirhan's motives have never been clear. Ostensibly, Sirhan, who was Palestinian, was angry at Kennedy for supporting Israel by sending them 50 bomber planes. Sirhan denied that this was a factor, and said that he was fond of Kennedy. Actually, Sirhan was a Christian, not a Muslim. Strangely, he claims to have no recollection of the shooting. He said he recalls the bodyguards wrestling him to the ground and pulling the gun from his hand, but he does not recall what happened before that. Sirhan claims that there is a gap in his memory that he can't explain. While it sounds hard to believe, there is really no motive for Sirhan to make that up. It's not like he would get off, or get a lighter sentence just because he can't remember the incident. He has stuck to the same story for decades after he was convicted of the murder.

There is legitimate speculation that Sirhan was drugged and/or hypnotized into committing the murder. This is the "manchurian candidate" theory we have heard much about. I used to think it was far-fetched, but after learning about the CIA's involvement in mind-control projects like MK-ULTRA, it's a reasonable possibility. Nothing else explains Sirhan's lack of recall. If it was a case of mind control, then that implicates the CIA. MK-ULTRA was their pet project, and if someone is mind-controlled into committing murder, the CIA is probably behind it. Also indicative of mind control was the notebook that was found among Sirhan's possessions. This notebook contained incoherent ramblings, repeatedly stating "RFK must die," and "RFK must be assassinated." Sirhan also claims that he does not remember writing this, and he has maintained that belief long after his conviction. It is believed that Sirhan was acting out post-hypnotic commands when he did the writing. The notebook would seem to indicate some form of mind control, probably through MK-ULTRA or some offshoot of it. This would implicate the CIA in the assassination.[167]

To investigate the assassination of RFK, the LAPD set up Special Unit Senator (SUS) to control the investigation. The SUS was basically the second

---

[167] https://www.maryferrell.org/pages/Robert_Kennedy_Assassination.html

coming of the Warren Commission. Evidence mysteriously disappeared. Doorframes with bullets were inexplicably destroyed by the LAPD. Photographs taken in the pantry vanished. An officer's notes were suddenly missing. Witnesses were intimidated into changing their testimonies.

Officer Enrique Hernandez persuaded witness Sandy Serrano to say that she did not see two escaping suspects:

> Serrano: I seen those people!
>
> Hernandez: No, no, no, no, Sandy. Remember what I told you about that: you can't say you saw something when you didn't see it...[168]

This is reminiscent of the brow-beating of witnesses by Warren Commission investigators. Many of them were also coerced into changing their testimony, and many others were ignored if their statements were out of line with the official story.

"There is no doubt in our minds that no fewer than 14 shots were fired in the pantry on that evening and that Sirhan did not in fact kill Senator Kennedy," said Robert Joling, a forensic scientist who has been involved with the Kennedy case for nearly 40 years. He and Philip Van Praag have published a book on the killing entitled *An Open and Shut Case*.[169]

Robert Kennedy would have reopened the investigation into his brother's murder if he had been elected. That was the main reason for his assassination. It figures that the same parties would be involved, since they have to cover themselves. It is difficult to pinpoint exactly what role Johnson played in the RFK murder, but even if it was only a passive role, that alone would make him complicit. If he suspected something was in the works, but did nothing about it, then he was part of it.

At about 6:00 p.m. on April 4, 1968, Martin Luther King stood on the balcony of the Lorraine Motel in Memphis, Tennessee. He was killed be a single shot that hit him in the jaw. He was pronounced dead an hour later. After the shooting, a bundle containing a rifle and binoculars was conveniently dropped near the crime scene. Fingerprints on the rifle led authorities to arrest James Earl Ray. Ray was considered yet another "lone

---

[168] https://www.maryferrell.org/pages/Robert_Kennedy_Assassination.html
[169] https://www.theguardian.com/science/2008/feb/22/kennedy.assassination

nut," in the tradition of Lee Harvey Oswald and Sirhan Sirhan. There were no eyewitnesses to the shooting, the slug removed from King's body did not match Ray's rifle, and the angle of the shot seemed to come from a different direction than the rooming house that Ray was in. Ray had confessed to the crime at one point, but then recanted his confession, saying that the FBI had offered him a plea bargain if he admitted guilt.

Dexter King, the second son of Martin Luther King, is among those who believe Lyndon Johnson was involved in the murder of his father. In an interview on ABC's *Turning Point* in 1997, Dexter King stated that Lyndon Johnson was part of a military and governmental conspiracy to kill his father. In the interview King said that the assassination plot was "...Army Intelligence, CIA, and FBI. I think we knew it all along." He also stated that, "Based on the evidence that I've been shown, I think it would be very difficult for something of that magnitude to occur on his watch and he not be privy to it." King said he has always believed that James Earl Ray had nothing to do with the assassination.[170]

True Colors

Concerning accusations of racism, LBJ did little to help his own case. He had been a racist throughout his political career. He supported the poll tax and voted against anti-lynching laws. His usage of the n- word is extensive.

In response to King's opposition to the Vietnam War, Johnson once said privately:

> That goddamn n*gg*r preacher may drive me out of the
> White House.

He referred to the Civil Rights Bill as "the n*gg*r bill."

Referring to the poll tax, Johnson said:

> ...but I've got to prove it discriminates and I can't prove it in
> Texas. There's more n*gg*rs voting there than white people.

Johnson's explanation of why he appointed Thurgood Marshall to the Supreme Court:

---

[170] http://www.nytimes.com/1997/06/20/us/son-of-dr-king-asserts-lbj-role-in-plot.html

When I appoint a n*gg*r to the bench, I want everybody to know he's a n*gg*r.

Johnson's comment to his black chauffer, who wished to be called by his name:

As long as you are black, and you're gonna be black till the day you die, no one's gonna call you by your goddamn name. So no matter what you are called, n*gg*r, you just let it roll off your back like water, and you'll make it. Just pretend you're a goddamn piece of furniture.[171] [172] [173]

From *Wrong on Race* by Bruce Bartlett, we see Johnson's true feelings about African-Americans:

These Negroes, they're getting pretty uppity these days and that's a problem for us since they've got something now they never had before, the political pull to back up their uppityness. Now we've got to do something about this, we've got to give them a little something, just enough to quiet them down, not enough to make a difference. For if we don't move at all, then their allies will line up against us and there'll be no way of stopping them, we'll lose the filibuster and there'll be no way of putting a brake on all sorts of wild legislation. It'll be Reconstruction all over again.[174]

Another famous Johnson quote on race comes from the *American Sentinal*:

I'll have them n*gg*rs voting Democratic for the next two hundred years.[175]

But LBJ was not the only racist in Washington. He had a friend in the FBI who shared his feelings. J. Edgar Hoover was also known to harbor negative feelings about black people. FBI agent Arthur Murtagh took part in Hoover's campaign against the civil rights movement. He describes Hoover's attitude toward African- Americans:

---

[171] http://www.maryferrell.org/pages/Martin_Luther_King_Assassination.html
[172] http://thirdworldtraveler.com/FBI/Who_Killed_MLK.html
[173] http://www.msnbc.com/msnbc/lyndon-johnson-civil-rights-racism
[174] Bartlett, Bruce, *Wrong on Race*, St. Martin's Press, 2008
[175] *The American Sentinel*, p. 9 September 1997,

He was brought up in a culture... in that society there was a real sense of belief, a religious belief, political belief, that there was no such thing as equality between blacks and whites, and that's the way he viewed them... Hoover did so many things to discredit the civil rights movement that I hardly know where to start. In the first place, he put about the same emphasis... much more of the facilities of the Bureau toward keeping the Klan... keeping the blacks in place and let the Klan run wild. He was friendly with people in the South, and ... when a situation came up, he would always make his decisions in favor of the local people.[176]

...In the case of King, Hoover's purpose was to destroy him in any way he could. He would leak the information...any information, some true and some not true, in order to embarrass King. ."[177]

Under Franklin D. Roosevelt, the FBI was given the responsibility of investigating both foreign and domestic espionage in the U.S. This allowed Hoover to collect information on anyone whose political beliefs would be considered radical or subversive. Of course, it was Hoover who decided who fell into that category. Hoover believed there was a communist conspiracy to overthrow the U.S. government. He believed that several high-ranking officials in the government were secretly members of the Communist Party. He began to leak information about those he suspected. Hoover was the main source of information for the House Committee on Un-American Activities, formed in 1938, which attempted to weed out suspected communists. Hoover worked closely with Joseph McCarthy and Richard Nixon in their communist hunt. The committee had the full support of racists everywhere. The KKK themselves sent the following telegram to committee chairman Martin Dies:

Every true American, and that includes every Klansman, is behind you and your committee in its effort to turn the country back to the honest, freedom-loving, God-fearing American to whom it belongs.[178]

---

[176] http://spartacus-educational.com/USAhooverE.htm
[177] http://nsarchive2.gwu.edu//coldwar/interviews/episode-13/murtagh1.html
[178] http://spartacus-educational.com/USAhuac.htm

Some critics were calling for the committee to investigate the KKK. But Dies was a supporter of the Klan and spoke at several of their rallies. Other members of the committee were also Klan sympathizers. The committee declined to investigate the KKK, saying that it "lacks sufficient data on which to base a probe." Committee member John Rankin stated, "After all, the KKK is an old American institution." Another committee member, John S. Wood, also defended the Klan by saying, "The threats and intimidations of the Klan are an old American custom, like illegal whisky-making." So the activities of the KKK were not considered "un-American."

Dies and his committee began attacking other activist groups which they opposed. This included the Hollywood Anti-Nazi League (HANL), which the committee saw as a communist front group. This action was supported by Hoover, and only served to discredit the committee. Actress Luise Rainer defended the HANL:

> I do not believe in the so-called revelations made by the Dies Investigating Committee. I believe their purpose is purely destructive, aimed at discrediting worthwhile peace and anti-fascist organizations, which are so much needed in these worried times.

Director John Ford also offered his defense of the HANL:

> May I express my whole-hearted desire to cooperate to the utmost of my ability with the Hollywood Anti-Nazi League. If this be Communism, count me in.[179]

These statements show that even in 1938, people could see that this was a witch hunt with ulterior motives.

The Hoover Files

Cartha Deloach was the FBI's liaison officer to the CIA under Hoover. He spoke of the working relationship between Hoover and Johnson:

> Mr. Hoover was anxious to retain his job and to stay on as director. He knew that the best way for the F.B.I. to operate

---

[179] http://spartacus-educational.com/USAhuac.htm

fully and to get some cooperation of the White House was
for him to be cooperative with President Johnson... President
Johnson, on the other hand, knew of Mr. Hoover's image in
the United States, particularly among the middle-of-the-road
conservative elements, and knew it was vast. He knew of the
potential strength of the F.B.I. - insofar as being of
assistance to the government and the White House is
concerned. As a result it was a marriage, not altogether of
necessity, but it was a definite friendship caused by
necessity.[180]

In 1975, FBI agent Arthur Murtagh testified to the Senate Intelligence
Committee. Regarding Hoover's use of blackmail, he quoted DeLoach:

The other night, we picked up a situation where this senator
was seen drunk, in a hit-and-run accident, and some good-
looking broad was with him. We got the information,
reported it in a memorandum, and by noon the next day, the
senator was aware that we had the information, and we never
had trouble with him on appropriations since.[181]

Even President Truman complained that Hoover was "dabbling in sex-life
scandals and plain blackmail when they should be catching criminals."[182]

Hoover was known to have extensive files on politicians and prominent
persons with political views that he considered subversive. This would
include anyone with views opposed to Hoover's. Hoover would use wire
taps, and in some cases video surveillance, to monitor his enemies. He
would monitor those who were in a position of power, feeling that he
needed to have some control over them. Anti-war demonstrators and civil
rights leaders were included, too. Hoover would collect as much personal
information as he could on people so he could use it against them later on.
It gave him an edge over others. If someone was not cooperative, they
could be threatened with blackmail. Most people have some skeletons in
their closet, and people in Washington have bigger closets. He could dig up
some kind of dirt on anyone. In some cases, he would uncover crimes that
someone has committed. Then he could threaten to have him arrested if he
was not cooperative.

---

[180] http://spartacus-educational.com/USAhooverE.htm
[181] http://spartacus-educational.com/JFKdeloach.htm
[182] http://spartacus-educational.com/USAhooverE.htm

Often he would use people's sexual follies against them. If a man cheated on his wife or patronized a prostitute, that would be used as leverage to get that person to capitulate. In fact, events at parties and clubs were often staged for this purpose. Unwitting victims would be coaxed or entrapped into performing some form of fornication, with wire taps or hidden cameras ready to capture the misdeeds for future use. Even the best of men could be lured into this. If a man is at a party or a club, and an attractive woman comes by and sits on his lap and starts flirting with him, he may find himself doing something he never dreamed he would do. A few drinks would make it a more likely possibility, and Hoover would gladly provide that. A few drinks would also get people to start opening up about misdeeds they have committed in the past. People have been known to talk too much after they've had a few. Hoover simply exploited that.

Maybe Hoover learned the art of blackmail from the mob. Author Anthony Summers tells of their methods:

> The mob bosses had been well placed to find out about Edgar's compromising secret, and at a significant time and place. It was on New Year's Eve 1936, after dinner at the Stork Club, that Edgar was seen by two of Walter Winchell's guests holding hands with his lover, Clyde (Tolson). At the Stork, where he was a regular, Edgar was immensely vulnerable to observation by mobsters. The heavyweight champion Jim Braddock, who also dined with Edgar and Clyde that evening, was controlled by Costello's associate Owney Madden. Winchell, as compulsive a gossip in private as he was in his column, constantly cultivated Costello. Sherman Billingsley, the former bootlegger who ran the Stork, reportedly installed two-way mirrors in the toilets and hidden microphones at tables used by celebrities. Billingsley was a pawn of Costello's, and Costello was said to be the club's real owner. He would have had no compunction about persecuting Edgar, and he loathed homosexuals.[183]

Meyer Lansky had gotten compromising pictures of Hoover and used them against him for decades. Private investigator Gordon Novel saw the pictures:

---

[183] http://edgar-hoover.tripod.com/

What I saw was a picture of him giving Clyde Tolson a bl*wj*b. There was more than one shot, but the startling one was a close shot of Hoover's head. He was totally recognizable. You could not see the face of the man he was with, but Angleton said it was Tolson. I asked him if they were fakes, but he said they were real, that they'd been taken with a fish-eye lens. They looked authentic to me. [184]

Novel mentioned that it was James Angleton, Counterintelligence Chief for the CIA, who showed the photographs to him. That means that the CIA and the mob both used the photos against Hoover. This was not the only time the two entities colluded on a blackmail project, as Summers writes:

At least once, Lansky worked alongside U.S. intelligence officers on exactly the sort of operation likely to turn up smear material on prominent public men. In 1942, he arranged for the surveillance of a homosexual brothel in Brooklyn suspected of being the target of German agents. "Clients came from all over New York and Washington," Lansky recalled, "and there were some important government people among them. . . . If you got hold of the names of the patrons you could blackmail them to death . . . take some pictures through a hole in the wall or a trick mirror and then squeeze the victim for money or information."[185]

Hoover and Johnson were two of a kind when it came to blackmail. Johnson was also known to use whatever means necessary to achieve his goals, and that often meant digging up dirt on people. Recall his involvement in the Quarum Club operation. Johnson was very close with Hoover, and as head of the FBI, Hoover had the ways and means to monitor anyone who was a concern. Hoover and Johnson shared information on mutual enemies. This was one way Hoover helped Johnson to cover up the JFK assassination, as well as the Bobby Baker scandal and other wrongdoings. The friendship between Hoover and Johnson was one of mutual necessity.

---

[184] Summers, Anthony, *Official and Confidential*, p. 288, Putnam Adult, 1993
[185] http://edgar-hoover.tripod.com/

After Hoover's death, FBI Associate Director and close friend Clyde Tolson arranged to have Hoover's private files destroyed, lest they should fall into the hands of their enemies.

Journalist Ray Tucker wrote an article for *Collier's* magazine, in which he hinted at the fact that Hoover was gay. Hoover had Tucker investigated, and information about his private life was leaked to the media. When this became known, it served as a warning and intimidated other journalists from writing about Hoover's private life.

When it came to fighting organized crime, Hoover was impotent. The blackmail neutralized him, and the mob knew it. Hoover let the mafia run wild. In 1959, there were 489 FBI agents spying on communists and only 4 agents investigating the mafia. Until the early 1960s, the FBI had no formal division devoted to organized crime.[186]

Hypocrisy

In 1965, Lyndon Johnson created the President's Commission on Law Enforcement and the Administration of Justice. On the surface it was a monumental crime-fighting effort, but in reality there was no substance to it. After murdering his way into the White House, Johnson had the audacity to present himself as the protector of justice. This was the ultimate hypocrisy. It's like Hitler promoting a civil rights bill.

The commission originated with this message to Congress (excerpted):

> To the Congress of the United States:
>
> Crime has become a malignant enemy in America's midst.
>
> Since 1940 the crime rate in this country has doubled. It has increased five times as fast as our population since 1958.
>
> In dollars the cost of crime runs to tens of billions annually. The human costs are simply not measurable.
>
> The problems run deep and will not yield to quick and easy answers. We must identify and eliminate the causes of criminal activity whether they lie in the environment around us or deep in the nature of individual men. This is a major

---

[186] http://spartacus-educational.com/USAhooverE.htm

purpose of all we are doing in combatting poverty and improving education, health, welfare, housing, and recreation.

All these are vital, but they are not enough. Crime will not wait while we pull it up by the roots. We must arrest and reverse the trend toward lawlessness.

This active combat against crime calls for a fair and efficient system of law enforcement to deal with those who break our laws. It means giving new priority to the methods and institutions of law enforcement:

--to our police, who are our front line, both offensive and defensive, in the fight against crime. There is a great need not only for improved training of policemen but for all people to learn about, to understand, and to assist the policeman in his work.

--to our courts, traditionally the symbol and guardian of our cherished freedoms. Local criminal courts are so overloaded that their functioning is impeded and their effectiveness weakened. More courts and judges is one answer, but every possibility of improvement must be explored.

--to our correctional agencies. We cannot tolerate an endless, self-defeating cycle of imprisonment, release, and reimprisonment which fails to alter undesirable attitudes and behavior. We must find ways to help the first offender avoid a continuing career of crime.

No right is more elemental to our society than the right to personal security and no right needs more urgent protection.

Our streets must be safe. Our homes and places of business must be secure. Experience and wisdom dictate that one of the most legitimate functions of government is the preservation of law and order.

Our system rejects the concept of a national police force. The protection responsibilities lie primarily with state and local governments.

That is right and proper...

...a comprehensive, penetrating analysis of the origins and nature of crime in modern America.

Johnson went on to specifically target organized crime, drug control, and firearms control as areas of focus. Johnson called organized crime a "cancer" in the city, and wrote of its corrupting effects on public officials:

> ...Perhaps the most alarming aspect of organized crime, however, is that it erodes respect for the law. Corrupting a public official may lend respectability to the racketeer, as it destroys the underpinning of law enforcement in a community.[187]

Johnson does, indeed, know a thing or two about corrupting public officials.

None of this can be taken seriously. Most of this is just political rhetoric designed to boost Johnson's public image. This was about a year and a half after the assassination, and there was talk about his involvement. Maybe this was his way of countering that. For Johnson to portray himself as a crime fighter would be laughable if it wasn't so tragic. The best way for him to fight crime would be to come clean about the Bobby Baker scandal, the Billie Sol Estes scandal, the TFX scandal, the Box 13 scandal, and the multitude of murders he was involved in, including that of his predecessor.

The committee's report was predictable:

> The recommendations call for a cooperative attack on crime by the Federal Government, the States, the counties, the cities, civic organizations, religious institutions, business groups, and individual citizens. They propose basic changes in the operations of police, schools, prosecutors, employment agencies, defenders, social workers, prisons, housing authorities, and probation and parole officers.[188]

Johnson had nothing at all to back up his talk. In the first four years after JFK's death, the Justice Department's Organized Crime section barely

---

[187] http://www.presidency.ucsb.edu/ws/index.php?pid=26800
[188] https://www.ncjrs.gov/App/publications/Abstract.aspx?id=42

functioned. Time spent before grand juries declined 72%, while court briefs filed by that section declined 83%.[189]

Johnson's directive was much too broad. To instruct a committee to try to reduce crime might seem like a noble effort, but it would need to be more specific and focused to be practical. I think the committee was confused as to their purpose. I don't see any major social or legal changes that were implemented because of this commission. There were probably minor adjustments to the system, but overall, it was just for show.

The History Channel Denies History

The History Channel aired a nine-part program called *The Men Who Killed Kennedy*. It was originally a six-part program in 1988, with three episodes added later. It was shown on television in 2003 for the last time. One episode, entitled "The Guilty Men", stated plainly that Lyndon Johnson was the main figure in the JFK assassination. This episode was based largely on the book, *Blood, Money, and Power* by Barr McClellan, who was an attorney for Johnson. The episode caused much controversy at the time. A libel claim was filed by Johnson's surviving associates, including Lady Bird Johnson, Gerald Ford, Jimmy Carter, Jack Valenti, and Bill Moyers. An agreement was reached that the entire nine-part series would never again be shown, including the eight episodes that did not implicate Johnson. This was basically censorship, since the episode gave legitimate testimony from credible witnesses. Even if they were wrong about some things, it is still censorship. Freedom of speech means freedom to be wrong.

The History Channel agreed to air a program that gave critics a chance to voice their disagreement. To appease Johnson's people, an hour-long program was aired called *The Guilty Man- A Historical Review.* This pathetic program was nothing more than disinformation designed to discredit the truth. The guests were Robert Dallek, Stanley Kutler, and Thomas Sugrue. Much of the show consisted of psychoanalyzing the public to find out why they believe in conspiracy theories. Some answers were "People love a good mystery," and "People can't accept that Oswald acted alone." They discussed the "cottage industry" of conspiracy theory, and the loss of faith in the government after Watergate. But no one discussed the Zapruder film, and no one asked why Johnson destroyed evidence. No one questioned the

---

[189] Marrs, Jim, *Crossfire*, p. 294, Carroll and Graf, 1989

dangerous motorcade route. No one asked why Dallas Police were told to step down that day. No one mentioned the Oswald sighting on the second floor. It was a desperate attempt to defend the undefendable.

Dallek was asked why the Warren Commission didn't consider Johnson a suspect. His response:

> They never looked at Lyndon Johnson, because they knew that Johnson had nothing to do with it... Because they had plenty of evidence to demonstrate that Lee Harvey Oswald was the sole killer.

I don't know if Dallek is deliberately lying, or if he has just not done his homework. Consider his statement, "They knew that Johnson had nothing to do with it." How did they know he had nothing to do with it? Dallek assumes that. He is a historian, so it's hard to believe he's serious about this. What is "plenty of evidence"? There was no case against Oswald, but there is a strong case against Johnson.

Dallek responded to the charge that Johnson persuaded Kennedy to go to Dallas:

> John F. Kennedy wanted to go to Texas...He wanted to go there for political reasons. Connally was resistant to it. He wasn't eager for Kennedy to go there, and Johnson wasn't eager, either. It was Kennedy himself who promoted this idea and arranged it.

Dallek does not really know, but Kennedy's people have repeatedly said that he didn't want to make the trip, and there is no reason to doubt them. Naturally, Kennedy said openly that he was looking forward to the trip.

Dallek, who had authored a biography about Johnson, was asked about the possible complicity of Johnson and his attorney, Ed Clark. His response:

> ...the notion that they would kill a sitting president is just simply not credible. I followed the lives and careers of these men, and I simply found not a hint of evidence that anything like this could have been possible.

Found no evidence? Does Dallek think that Johnson would tell him about the murder plots just because he is his biographer?

When asked about Johnson's connections to the Bobby Baker and Billie Sol Estes scandals, Dallek responded with this:

> The FBI came back and told Bobby Kennedy Johnson had no connection with either the Bobby Baker or the Estes cases...

So Hoover said that Johnson was innocent. Dallek is buying that? Johnson was clearly connected with both Baker and Estes. Hoover and Johnson were allies. Was there any realistic chance that Hoover would charge Johnson? The Kennedys were investigating the Johnson-Baker connection, and were in the process of exposing their crimes when John Kennedy was killed. Estes himself has testified to Johnson's crimes. Yet, Dallek still believes Johnson is innocent, just because Hoover said so.

What else convinced Dallek of Johnson's innocence?

> ...Johnson, immediately, within days after Kennedy's killing, he was begging, imploring J. Edgar Hoover to insure the safety of himself and his family, because Johnson did not trust the Secret Service, they had failed to protect Kennedy...Is this a man who was involved in the killing of the president? How could it be?

This was a ploy by Johnson to feign innocence. By acting like he was afraid, it makes him look innocent. Was Johnson seriously fearing for his safety? Who did he fear might kill him? Oswald?

Then they gave us this gem:

> JFK and LBJ got along pretty well. In fact, JFK kind of liked LBJ and LBJ liked JFK.[190]

Johnson hated Kennedy's guts. Kennedy was not wild about Johnson, either. This whole show was just an attempt to pacify the Johnson crowd. If this is the best rebuttal they have, it amounts to a validation of "The Guilty Men" episode.

---

[190] https://www.youtube.com/watch?v=ISY_TUVxtSs

Unthinkable

I'm sure it seems incomprehensible to many people that Lyndon Johnson, or any U.S. politician for that matter, would commit cold-blooded murder. Americans in particular seem to think that our leaders are above that. We tend to think that any wrongdoing by our government people is limited to relatively minor things, like illegal campaign funding or cheating on one's spouse, but never flat-out murder. That only happens in banana republics and third-world countries, but never in America. We are simply too good for that. We have been conditioned to think that way. From the time we are kids, we are taught that the USA is the protector of freedom and democracy. Sometimes that's true, but the change in government in 1963 was not democratic, and there is a mountain of evidence to prove that. Many Americans simply cannot accept this, and we tend to live in a false reality that is more comforting than the awful truth.

The assassination saved Johnson from jail. People cannot fathom that Johnson would stoop to murder, but they fail to realize his desperate predicament, all of his own making. Johnson had everything to gain and nothing to lose by killing Kennedy. It made the difference between the White House or prison.

When the plans for the assassination were discussed, especially by Johnson, they were discussed only in the broadest of terms. Johnson would never say, "Let's kill John Kennedy." I doubt if he or any of his associates ever spoke those words. If anyone did speak those words, it was the shooters and the people at the lower levels. Johnson was very careful about what he said. When he and others discussed the plot, they would probably say things like, "Let's take care of our mutual problem," or "Get the job done," or "Eliminate the obstacle." That way, if anyone overheard the conversation, or secretly recorded it, there would be nothing incriminating that could be used against them in a court of law. Even if they said, "Get rid of Kennedy," they could always say later that they meant get rid of him by voting him out in the next election.

Johnson controlled the plot at the macro level. He did not need to know all the details of it. He probably did not know who all the shooters were, and he probably did not know that Oswald was the designated patsy. Most of those details were arranged by the ones who managed at the lower levels. The shooters were the lowest level of the plot, and Johnson was the highest level. In between were the ones who scouted the area for a location and made the detailed arrangements. Johnson's involvement was kept to a minimum, except where his influence was needed, like to change the motorcade route or reduce security. It wasn't Johnson who chose Dealey Plaza for the assassination, it was the mid-level managers of the plot. Those mid-level managers then told Johnson to secure the Trade Mart for Kennedy's speech, thereby justifying the route through Dealey Plaza. No one ever said the reason. They just told Johnson, "We need the Trade Mart," and he got it for them. They didn't have to say why and he didn't have to ask. They all knew with a wink and a nod.

What if the truth were told about the JFK assassination? What would be the implications? If it was known that a murderer inhabited the White House, it would shake the country to its foundation. No one could ever trust the government again, including other governments. The United States would be damaged in its relations with foreign countries. We would no longer be seen as the protectors of liberty and freedom. The history books would have to be rewritten. Children would grow up learning about the horrible things our government has done. We would no longer be the beacon of hope that we were when we rescued prisoners from concentration camps. Many in power, and in the general public, believe that it is in the best interest of the country that we just bury the truth and move forward. Let Oswald take all the blame so no one else has to. I disagree with that. The truth should be known, even if it may lead to temporary upheaval. It is best in the long run. To do nothing is to condone murder and corruption.

As time goes by, it's easier to distance ourselves from the event. After a while, everyone involved will be dead. The assassination will be so far back in time that we will view it from the outside looking in. Even the government could distance themselves from it after a while, saying it was "them," not "us" who did it. What if new evidence emerged that Abraham Lincoln was killed by a conspiracy? Would anyone care at this point? It would not tarnish the country's image or harm foreign relations because it was so far back in the past. Only historians would care, but the general public would not be fazed. After a while, it will be like that with the JFK assassination. When it is so far back in time that no one cares anymore, maybe then the government will tell the truth.

Shortly before his death, Johnson gave an interview to *Atlantic Monthly*. He was quoted as saying:

> I never believed that Oswald acted alone although I can accept that he pulled the trigger.[191]

This was the closest Johnson ever came to making a public confession. Less than a month before his death, he admitted that there was some degree of conspiracy in JFK's death. He does not admit his own involvement, but he inadvertently admitted to a cover-up.

Of all the conspirators, Lyndon Johnson was the first one to hate John Kennedy. Johnson initiated the plot as far back as 1960, when he accepted the role of John Kennedy's running mate. At that point in time, the mafia did not hate Kennedy yet. They were still expecting him to go easy on them, due to their relationship with Joseph Kennedy and also due to their aid in swinging the election his way. It was only later on when John and Robert Kennedy accelerated their war on crime that the mob turned against them. The same is true for the Cubans. Before the election, they were optimistic that Kennedy would help them get their country back, since Kennedy had campaigned as a hard-liner against communism. It was only after the Bay of Pigs that Kennedy became an enemy of the Cuban rebels. The same is true for the CIA, who expected Kennedy to be more cooperative when he took office. All these groups began to hate John Kennedy after he became president, but Johnson had plans on eliminating him before he was even elected. As time went by, more and more people jumped on his bandwagon, but Johnson was the instigator of the Kennedy assassination plot.

---

[191] Marrs, Jim, *Crossfire*, p. 298, Carroll and Graf, 1989

4

MOTORCADE AND SECURITY

The final piece of the assassination puzzle was the arrangement of the motorcade route. For the shooters to have a clear shot at Kennedy, the limousine had to be slowed down. The easiest way to do that was to put turns in the route, and that's what Johnson did. Through his influence, the motorcade route included two needless turns that could easily have been avoided. The limousine naturally slowed to a crawl as it made the turns. The shooting began during the second turn. That was by design.

Route Selection

There were at least three alternate routes to the Trade Mart that would have been safer than the one chosen. One of the options would have been for the final leg of the route to go down Elm Street. This would have led directly to the Stemmons Freeway on-ramp. There would have been no turns at that point, and the limousine would never have slowed down below 50 mph. Through Johnson's influence, that section of the route was moved over a block, to Main Street. That necessitated the turns that cost John Kennedy his life. Even from Main Street, the destination could have been reached safely, but the needless turns were put into the route solely for the purpose of the assassination.

Dallas Police Chief Jesse Curry revealed in his book that all security arrangements were directed from Washington, D.C.[192] This is indirectly saying that Lyndon Johnson was in control. On matters of security, he probably gave orders to the Secret Service, who carried out his orders in Dallas. The Secret Service violated their own regulations and changed their own procedures in so many ways that it can't be coincidence. There is obvious complicity by the SS, although it was Johnson who was actually calling the shots. The choice of the motorcade route is one example.

---

[192] Curry, Jesse, *JFK Assassination Files*, p. 9, Library of Congress, 1969

There was no legitimate justification for choosing the Main Street route over the Elm Street route, so the Warren Commission came up with this flimsy explanation:

> Elm Street, parallel to Main Street and one block north, was not used for the main portion of the downtown part of the motorcade because Main Street offered better vantage points for spectators.[193]

This was the turning point of the assassination plot. Elm Street is safe, Main Street is a death trap. They chose the death trap. Why? "Better vantage points for spectators"? Is that a justifiable reason for choosing the dangerous route over a safer one? How can they ignore the safety factor and base their decision on "better vantage points"?

I doubt that there were better vantage points, anyway. What does that even mean? Does it mean a wider street? Does it mean more tall buildings for viewers? That would also mean more tall buildings for snipers. If "better vantage points" was really the reason for the route choice, then the Warren Commission should detail what that means. The president died because of that decision. It begs for a better explanation.

This was the reason why the Trade Mart was selected as the site for Kennedy's speech. The plotters had already determined that Dealey Plaza was the ideal site for the assassination. Next, they had to have an excuse for the motorcade to go through it. That's why they chose the Trade Mart- it justified having the route go through Dealey Plaza. In a big city like Dallas, there are any number of places where the president can give a speech, and alternative locations were considered and discussed. But in the end, they purposely chose the Trade Mart because the route there goes through Death Valley.

This is also a blatant violation of Secret Service policy. According to SS policy for protecting the president in a motorcade, the vehicle can never be slowed down below 45 mph. There are certain exceptions, such as if the protective bubble top was on, or if the vehicle was in a wide open space with no place for snipers to hide. But none of the exceptions applied in this case. No other safety precautions were taken that would justify allowing the

---

[193] *The Warren Commission Report*, p. 32, Longmeadow Press, 1964

vehicle to slow down. By authorizing this route, the Secret Service is complicit.

In the documentary *The Men Who Killed Kennedy*, Col. Fletcher Prouty spoke of this obvious violation:

> Instead of going straight down the street and then to the Trade Mart, they made this 90 degree turn, and then another sharp turn right in front of the book depository building. Now, the Secret Service have rules against that. The rule is that if the car is slowed down below 44 miles an hour, you must then protect it fully in other ways, such as not digressing and going around corners and all that, because when you slowed him around that corner, you opened him up to field of fire from three directions: from behind him, from the side, and from in front, and of course, he was killed right in that position that had been set up by the selection of that route.[194]

In a desperate attempt to try to justify the motorcade route, the Warren Commission gave this explanation:

> In order to keep motorists from reaching the freeway from Main Street, a concrete barrier has been erected between Main and Elm Streets extending beyond the freeway entrance. Hence, it would have been necessary for the motorcade either to have driven over this barrier or to have made a sharp S-turn in order to have entered the freeway from Main Street. Selection of the motorcade route was thus entirely appropriate and based on such legitimate considerations as the origin and destination of the motorcade, the desired opportunity for the President to greet large numbers of people, and normal patterns of traffic.[195]

All they are saying here is that the motorcade could not reach the freeway directly from Main Street due to the concrete barrier, therefore they had to turn on Elm Street. They are attempting to justify the turn. But they do not address the fact that the route could have easily gone down Elm Street, the concrete barrier would not have been encountered, and no turn would have been necessary.

---

[194] *The Men Who Killed Kenned*, https://www.youtube.com/watch?v=0NdtxGiK3WI
[195] *The Warren Commission Report*, p. 246, 1964, Longmeadow Press, 1964

Even with the route going straight down Main Street, they could still have accessed the freeway with no problem. The concrete barrier that the commission mentioned was nothing more than a speed bump. The motorcade could easily have gotten over the speed bump as motorists sometimes did, although it was illegal. For the motorcade it would have been no problem, since all roads are blocked off and regular traffic laws are ignored anyway for a special event like this. There were traffic signs posted at the barrier, warning motorists not to make the illegal turn. That shows that the turn is physically possible, and naturally would have been allowed for the president's motorcade. It's true that the limousine would have had to slow down for the speed bump, but at that point they would be in a wide open field with no tall buildings for snipers to shoot from. Only the railroad overpass would have to be secured. So either the Main Street route or the Elm Street route could have led directly to the freeway with no need to make the deadly turn.

A third option would have been for the motorcade to continue west on Main Street past the triple underpass to Industrial Boulevard, which would have taken them to the Trade Mart unimpeded. That route was rejected, supposedly because it would have taken them through a neighborhood that was "filled with winos and broken pavement." Again, the safety factor was ignored in favor of some secondary matter. So the Secret Service rejected three legitimate options for a safer route, without any justification for the decision.[196]

The commission did admit this much:

> Because of the sharp turn at this corner, the motorcade also reduced its speed.[197]

The turn at Houston and Elm was not the usual 90 degree turn. It was a sharp-angle turn of about 60 degrees. This was the second turn, where the shooting started. The sharp-angle turn caused the limousine to slow down even more than it would at a normal intersection. That should have made it even more obvious to the Secret Service that this was dangerous. The commission acknowledged the reduction in speed caused by the sharp angle, yet they made no interrogation of any Secret Service agent about why they allowed it.

---

[196] Benson, Michael, *Who's Who in the JFK Assassination*, p. 261, Citadel Press, 1993
[197] *The Warren Commission Report*, p. 246, Longmeadow Press, 1964

The commission stated that the advance preparations for the motorcade route were primarily the responsibility of Secret Service Agents Winston G. Lawson, a member of the White House detail who acted as the advance agent, and Forrest V. Sorrels, Special Agent in Charge (SAIC) of the Dallas office. The commission questioned Sorrels about the route selection:

> Sorrels...testified that the traditional parade route in Dallas was along Main Street, since the tall buildings along the street gave more people an opportunity to participate.[198]

Sorrels avoided the central issue here. It was not Main Street itself that was the problem; it was the turn *off* of Main Street that mattered, and then another turn after that. That was probably not done for the other parades they alluded to, but even if it was, it would not have presented the kind of danger that was present for Kennedy's motorcade.

All of the commission's statements on this issue seem to imply that this route was unanimously agreed upon by all concerned:

> On November 14, Lawson and Sorrels...drove over the route which Sorrels believed best suited for the proposed motorcade.[199]

> The police officials agreed that the route recommended by Sorrels was the proper one and did not express a belief that any other route might be better.

> The route impressed the agents as the natural and desirable one.

> According to Lawson, the chosen route seemed to be the best.[200]

> No member of the Secret Service, the Dallas Police Department, or the local host committee who was consulted felt that any other route would be preferable.[201]

In other words, not one single person objected to the route. Of all the agents and officers who viewed the route, not a single one pointed out the

---

[198] *The Warren Commission Report*, p. 32, Longmeadow Press, 1964
[199] *The Warren Commission Report*, p. 31, Longmeadow Press, 1964
[200] *The Warren Commission Report*, p. 32, Longmeadow Press, 1964
[201] *The Warren Commission Report*, p. 245, Longmeadow Press, 1964

dangers of slowing the limousine down by making turns. There was no protest from the Secret Service agents who are trained to spot such dangers, and who know that it is a violation of their own policy to slow the limousine down below 45 mph. The commission never challenged them on this point. Why didn't the commission ask Sorrels or Lawson about this policy violation?

This violation was obvious, not only to the handful of cops and agents who physically went to Dealey Plaza to scout the area, but to anyone who simply looked at a map of the route. The turns are right there, plainly visible. The average person would not think "assassination plot," but the Secret Service should. Didn't anyone in the entire agency speak up and point out the obvious violation? I'm sure there were many lunchroom conversations about that at Secret Service headquarters.

According to Jerry Behn, the Special Agent in Charge of the White House detail, the motorcade route was definitely changed from its original form. Behn was the top man in JFK's detail, and he was questioned under oath in an executive session of the HSCA. This differs from staff interviews, which were made public. Behn's testimony was in private and remains unpublished.

In 1992, Behn gave an interview to researcher Vincent M. Palamara, in which he described the nature of the testimony. Behn said he was asked directly by the HSCA, "Why was the route changed for Dallas?" Behn's answer was:

> I know it was changed, but why? I forgot completely. I don't know.[202]

The reason he can't remember is because no legitimate explanation was ever given.

SS agent Winston Lawson, however, claims that the route was never changed. In2003 he gave an interview to the Sixth Floor Museum:

> Well, in a couple of words, that's false (the theory that the motorcade route was changed). That myth is wrong. At first, we didn't know what route it was going to be because we didn't know where the speech/luncheon site was going to be.

---

[202] https://vincepalamara.com/the-secret-service-failed-president-kennedy/

It was either going to be at the Women's Building at the state fairgrounds or it was going to be at the Trade Mart, and early on, in the first couple of days of the advance, I went to both places. And it was later determined that, for one reason or another, it would be better to go to the Trade Mart... That route almost had to be what it was except for a couple of places out near the airport. But eventually, we had to go down Main Street, and of course, it's one-way here now. But then, we had to come over towards the School Book Depository and turn left onto Elm here to be able to go onto the Stemmons Freeway, which we needed to do in the best and most practical way to get to the Trade Mart.[203]

Lawson is clearly trying to cover his own involvement, and that of the Secret Service in general. Notice he says, "for one reason or another" they chose the Trade Mart. But what was that reason? It was to kill the president, of course. There was no other reason, but Lawson glosses over that part. Then he says, "That route almost had to be what it was..." No, it didn't. Lawson is flat-out lying. There were three better options: They could have accessed the freeway from Main Street, they could have taken Main Street to Industrial Boulevard, or they could gone down Elm Street and never slowed down below 50mph. Then he says the route was "the best and most practical way" to get to the Trade Mart, but he does not explain how it was the best and most practical way to get there. It was not. This interview was 40 years after the event, and Lawson is still covering it up.

Bob Ritter was a Special Agent of the White House detail. In his book published many years later, he stated:

The motorcade route chosen by agent Lawson was suggested by SAIC Forrest Sorrels of the Dallas Field Office.[204]

It appears that Sorrels and Lawson are two of the main culprits here. Sorrels suggested the route and Lawson approved it. Sorrels even admitted to the commission that he was the one who chose the dogleg turn onto Elm Street.[205]

---

[203] Lawson, Winston, interview by Sixth Floor Museum, May 9th, 2003
[204] Ritter, Bob and Jan, *Breaking Tecumseh's Curse*, p. 217, Calvert Press, 2013
[205] Palamara, Vincent Michael, *Survivor's Guilt*, p. 102, Trine Day, 2013

Chief Curry has stated that agent Lawson was the "central figure and primary planner of all the security arrangements." In his book, Curry makes the following statement:

> Mr. Lawson suggested that additional manpower be assigned at each point where the motorcade would slow down for a turn.[206]

That sounds like a great idea, but what happened to it? Where was the "additional manpower" at the corner of Houston and Elm? This is exactly the point at which the Dallas Police were told to step down. Lawson did not follow up on his own suggestion; in fact, he contradicted it. Yet he did show an awareness of the danger of making turns. That spells complicity.

Site Fight

John Kennedy never wanted to go to Dallas. He was pressured for over a year by both Johnson and Connally to make the trip. Johnson sold it as a political fence-mending trip to improve relations between rival factions in the Democratic Party. The real reason was for the assassination, of course. But Johnson forced Kennedy's hand. When Johnson suggested the Texas trip, Kennedy only said "maybe" in response. But Johnson announced to the press that he and Kennedy would be coming to Dallas later that year. Kennedy had not yet committed to the trip, but now he was stuck. If he backs out, it makes him and Johnson both look like liars. Openly, Kennedy pretended to be looking forward to the trip, but those close to him knew better. His staff had warned him of potential dangers, but Kennedy was reluctantly coaxed by Johnson and Connally into making his fateful trip to Dallas.

About a week before the assassination, Senator George Smathers recorded the following conversation with John Kennedy:

> JFK: Gee, I really hate to go to Texas; I gotta go to Texas next week and it's just a pain in the rear end and I just don't want to go, I wish I could get out of it.
>
> GS: Well, what's the problem?

---

[206] Curry, Jesse, *JFK Assassination File*, Library of Congress, 1969

JFK: Well, you know how Lyndon is. Johnson wants Jackie to ride with him, and all these fights were going on...I hate to go into all that mess and I hate to go and I wish I could think of a way to get out of it.[207]

Johnson's direct involvement in the assassination plot included the planning of the motorcade and the breakdown of security. It had already been determined by the plotters at the lower levels that Dealey Plaza was the ideal site for the assassination. That's why they needed to select the Trade Mart for Kennedy's speech. This would seemingly justify taking the route through Dealey Plaza. However, all of Kennedy's aides were opposed to the Trade Mart for security reasons. This included Kennedy's advance man Jerry Bruno, whose job it was to scout the area ahead of time to look for security issues. Bruno was completely opposed to the site. Not only was the route dangerous, but the Trade Mart itself was considered a security risk. There were catwalks above the stage that could be used by snipers. So anyone who was serious about legitimate security was opposed to the Trade Mart as the site. All of Kennedy's staff agreed that the Women's Building would be safer and preferable. The people who were advocating the Trade Mart were all Johnson's people: Jack Puterbaugh, Cliff Carter, Bill Moyers, Betty Harris, and Governor Connally. They all argued strongly for the Trade Mart with no justification for it at all. They were simply ordered by Johnson to secure the Trade Mart no matter what. In fact, Connally was adamant about the Trade Mart. In Bruno's journal, he made the following entry:

November 15- The White House announced that the Trade Mart had been approved. I met with O'Donnell and Moyers who said that Connally was unbearable and on the verge of canceling the trip. They decided they had to let the Governor have his way.[208]

In his book, *The Advanceman*, Bruno tells the story differently. He said that Connally played a dirty trick on him to get him to accept the Trade Mart choice. When the argument between the two escalated out of control, Connally got on the phone and called the White House in Bruno's presence, and spoke with Ken O' Donnell. The call was not on speakerphone, so Bruno

---

[207] Nelson, Phillip. F, *LBJ, Mastermind of Kennedy's Assassination*, p. 361, Xlibris, 2010

[208] Bruno, Jerry, *The Advance Man*, pp. 88-89

could only hear one side of the conversation. Connally spoke as if the White House agreed with the choice of the Trade Mart. Bruno relented, only because he thought the White House staff had agreed to it. Bruno found out later that the White House staff did not agree to it, and O'Donnell never said that they did. Connally had deceived Bruno into accepting the choice of the Trade Mart.[209]

That seems suspicious. Why was Connally so insistent on the Trade Mart? Why did it even matter to him? Usually those arrangements are made by committees whose job it is to handle those responsibilities. Politicians don't usually concern themselves with little things like that. Why would Connally oppose the Women's Building? It seems strange that he would even care so much. The only reason I can think of is that he was acting on behalf of Johnson to secure the Trade Mart as the site. Does this mean that Connally was part of the assassination plot? I used to think Connally was blameless, since he was shot himself. But if he was the one who insisted on the Trade Mart, then he is either a willing accomplice or a blind servant of Lyndon Johnson.

Secret Service Chief Rowley lied when he testified to the Warren Commission that Kennedy aide Kenneth O'Donnell was responsible for choosing the Trade Mart. Years later, Jerry Bruno told the HSCA that he, O'Donnell, and Special Agent Gerald Behn all favored the Women's Building. Also in the HSCA hearings, John Connally testified, and told the same lie that Rowley had told to the Warren Commission- that O'Donnell had chosen the Trade Mart. O'Donnell had passed away by that time, so there was no way to verify that. Agent Lawson also lied in those hearings, claiming it was Bruno who wanted the Trade Mart, but Bruno was insistent that he never changed his mind, and always favored the Women's Building for the president's speech. Lawson said it was Jack Puterbaugh who recommended the Trade Mart. As mentioned, Puterbaugh was one of Johnson's men. No one wanted to take the blame for the decision, but it was ultimately Johnson's choice to use the Trade Mart, and he would not take "no" for an answer.[210]

It should be noted that Connally was a long-time associate of Johnson. In 1939 he began his political career as an aide to Johnson. In 1960 he was

---

[209] Bruno, Jerry, *The Advance Man*, pp. 88-89
[210] Nelson, Phillip F., *LBJ, Mastermind of JFK's Assassination*, p. 354, Xlibris, 2010

Johnson's presidential campaign manager, and it was LBJ who appointed Connally as Secretary of the Navy. Later, when Connally was indicted on influence peddling and bribery charges, Johnson appeared as a character witness, helping Connally to be acquitted. Not only were the two good friends, but Connally may have felt that he owed Johnson a favor or two. It was probably Johnson who wanted the Trade Mart, but he had Connally argue for it on his behalf.[211]

On the morning of November 22, Johnson and Kennedy had a heated argument in their Texas hotel suite. The argument concerned the seating arrangements for the motorcade. Johnson wanted Governor Connally to ride with him, and he wanted Senator Yarborough to ride with Kennedy. The ostensible reason was that Johnson and Yarborough did not get along; the real reason was to protect Connally from gunfire. The argument became very loud and boisterous, and was overheard by Jackie Kennedy, as well as many of the hotel staff. According to one witness, Johnson "left that suite like a pistol." When Jackie asked John about the yelling, he answered, "That's just Lyndon. He's having a bad day." As it turned out, Connally was injured in the shooting- the exact thing that Johnson tried to prevent that morning. He would rather have had the bullet go through Yarborough instead.[212]

In retrospect, we can understand the reason for Johnson's surprising decision to accept Kennedy's invitation to be his running mate. As vice president, he had input into things like the site selection, the motorcade route, and the security arrangements. As Senate Majority Leader, he would have had no input. He would not have even been in the motorcade. Johnson had been planning the assassination for years. He spent over a year just persuading Kennedy to come to Texas. He could not have done that as Senate Majority Leader. When he accepted Kennedy's offer, he did not know the details of how the assassination would be carried out, but he knew he had the ways and means to do it. He just had to get Kennedy to come to Texas, which was home-field advantage for Johnson. He had his political power base and his connections there. He could manipulate people and events there. He knew that as vice president he could manipulate Kennedy's movements and his whereabouts, so he could get him to come to Texas. People don't like to believe that the assassination was even

---

[211] Zirbel, Craig I., *The Texas Connection*, p. 232, Wright and Co., 1991
[212] Nelson, Phillip F., *LBJ, Mastermind of JFK's Assassination*, Xlibris, 2010

considered that far in advance, but there is no other explanation for why a power-hungry person like Johnson would willingly take a demotion to vice president.

Route Publication

As for the publication of the route, there is some question as to how that happened. Rowley told the Warren Commission that the Secret Service was not to blame for the publication of the route. The decision was traced to White House aide Bill Moyers, who in turn blamed it on "the agent in charge of the Dallas trip." Some newspapers published the original route, while others published the revised route. This shows that the route was changed at some point, which begs the obvious question, "Why?" Ideally, the plotters would have liked the route to be changed at the last possible second. That would leave no time for anyone to protest the violation. If the change was known far in advance, there would have been too much time for people to analyze and question it, especially honest cops and Secret Service agents. It also would have been better for the plotters if the public did not know the revised route in advance. That would mean that there would be less spectators at the point of the shooting, hence less witnesses and less chance for photographic evidence to emerge.[213]

In a report to the Warren Commission, SS Chief Rowley stated the following:

> The Secret Service does not know who released the route to the press, nor by what authority…the Secret Service does not release selected routes of Presidential motorcades to the press and it did not in Dallas…it is conceivable that someone present at the November 18 meeting may have released the details of the route after they had been furnished with this information…the route of the presidential motorcade…is released either by the White House Press Secretary or by the local committee, usually after they have checked with the White House Press Secretary.[214]

So why was the revised route published in the papers three days earlier? That was probably not supposed to happen. The revised route must have

---

[213] http://www.jfklancer.com/LNE/limo.html
[214] Palamara, Vincent Michael, *Survivor's Guilt*, pp. 106-7, Trine Day, 2013

been "leaked," as sometimes happens with sensitive information. There is always someone who talks too much or gets careless, or maybe secretly wants the truth, or some of it, to be known. Who might have leaked it? Only a handful of people knew about the change. One of them was the ubiquitous Jack Ruby. Ruby delivered a map of the revised route to the hit team through a CIA contact. He was seen in Dealey Plaza during the shooting. He was seen at Parkland Hospital shortly afterwards. He was in the Texas Theater when Oswald was arrested. He was at the Dallas Police station during the press conference featuring Oswald. Ruby was up to his ears in this thing, and he was also known to be a loose talker. He was known to frequent the local newspaper offices, mingling with reporters and editors, and sometimes giving or receiving news stories. When something big was happening, Ruby liked to be in the middle of it. If the altered motorcade route was leaked, Ruby was quite possibly the leaker.

Elm and Houston was the ideal spot for the shooting, in part because the crowd had thinned out at that point. Along Main Street, the crowds lined the sidewalks in masses, but when the limousine turned onto Houston Street, there was a noticeable reduction in crowd density. After the turn onto Elm Street, there were relatively few spectators on either side of the limousine, compared to what it was like on Main Street. This is partly because many people did not know the revised motorcade route. For that reason, the plotters did not want the altered route to be published in advance. Naturally, they wanted as few people as possible at the crime scene.

Stand-Down

Dallas Police officer Roger Craig was interviewed by researcher Mark Lane for a video called *Two Men in Dallas*. Craig explains what he experienced that day:

> RC: I was on duty, but a couple of hours before Kennedy was due to arrive, the sheriff called us in, what I call the street people- the plainclothesmen, the detectives, and he instructed us that we were to stand out in front and in no way take part in the security of the motorcade; that we were merely spectators and nothing more.

> ML: Did that seem unusual to you?

RC: It did at the time, because there were so many people around and so few Dallas Police officers…this was one of the first things I noticed- the lack of Dallas Police officers.[215]

It was Sheriff Decker who gave these instructions. Why would he tell his officers "in no way take part in the security of the motorcade"? Why should they be "merely spectators and nothing more"? There were no Secret Service agents on foot in Dealey Plaza, and there were also no Dallas Police officers there, either. No one was protecting the president at that point. Who gave such a ridiculous order? It had to come from someone who wanted Kennedy dead. This is not standard procedure for such events, so why only in this case?

These instructions came from avid Kennedy-haters. Craig tells of the hostile resentment harbored by Decker and many of his Sheriff's Department cohorts:

> From these elite troops came the most bitter verbal attacks on President Kennedy. They spoke very strongly against his policies concerning the Bay of Pigs incident and the Cuban Missile crisis. They seemed to resent very much the fact that President Kennedy was a Catholic. I do not know why this was such a critical issue with many of the deputies but they did seem to hold this against President Kennedy.[216]

Consider the unique security arrangements that were made that day. The Secret Service and the Dallas Police Department had an agreement that the Dallas Police would only be responsible for providing protection through the downtown area. That area ended at the corner of Main and Houston. But the Secret Service did not replace or expand the protection from that point on. That is where the limousine turns, and it's obviously the most dangerous part of the route. Supposedly, that is where the Secret Service should have augmented the protection, but they didn't. The Dallas Police Department was deliberately told to step down from Dealey Plaza that day to create a void in the security.[217]

---

[215] Video-*Two Men in Dallas*, 1976

[216] https://ratical.org/ratville/JFK/WTKaP.html

[217] Nelson, Phillip F., *LBJ: The Mastermind of JFK's Assassination*, p. 367, Xlibris, 2010

If the Dallas Police had had officers on foot patrol in Dealey Plaza, who knows what might have happened? They might have seen suspicious men on the grassy knoll. They might have checked behind the picket fence, because it seems like an obvious place for a shooter to hide. They might have obstructed the shooter's view. Even if they could not prevent the assassination, they would be likely to apprehend the shooter. If there had been police officers on foot patrol anywhere near the grassy knoll, they would have seen the shooter and gone after him. Johnson and Company had to make sure that didn't happen.

Chief Curry spoke of the curious security arrangements:

> The Dallas Police Department carefully carried out the security plans which were laid out by Mr. Lawson, the Secret Service representative from Washington, D.C. The security at the airport, and along the motorcade route to the downtown area was extremely thorough. The security for the Trade Mart was massive. The preparations for security during the downtown parade route were as complete as possible along Main and the buildings overlooking the parade. Security was comparatively light along the short stretch of Elm Street where the President was shot. In the midst of comprehensive security it seems a freak of history that this short stretch of Elm Street would be the assassination site, and that the Texas Book Depository Building was virtually ignored in the security plans for the motorcade.[218]

Curry calls it a "freak of history" that Elm Street had such limited security. He talks as if it were an inadvertent oversight. He mentions all the heavy security all along the rest of the route, at the airport, and at the Trade Mart. Then security is suddenly reduced when the motorcade reaches its most dangerous point, and that's where Kennedy is shot. Curry still thinks that was bad luck or a coincidence. Or maybe he's just saying what he's supposed to say.

Further evidence of collusion comes from Colonel Fletcher Prouty. Prouty served as Chief of Special Operations for the Joint Chiefs of Staff under JFK. He had coordinated security for President Eisenhower. According to Prouty,

---

[218] Curry, Jesse, *JFK Assassination Files*, Library of Congress, 1969

the local military was ordered to stand down and provide no additional security for the Dallas trip. He writes:

> The commander of an army unit, specially trained in protection . . . had been told he and his men would not be needed in Dallas. "Another Army unit will cover that city," the commander was told. I called a member of that army unit later. I was told that the commander "had offered the services of his unit for protection duties for the entire trip through Texas," that he was "point-blank and categorically refused by the Secret Service," and that "there were hot words between the agencies." This leaves an important question: Why was the assistance of this skilled and experienced unit "point-blank refused"? Who knew ahead of time that it would not be wanted in Dallas?[219]

The unit that Prouty referred to is the 112th Military Intelligence Group at 4th Army Headquarters in Fort Sam Houston. This unit was available to provide as much additional security as necessary. William McKinney, a former member of that unit, has confirmed that his group was told that their assistance would not be needed that day. His commanding officers had strongly protested when they were told to stand down. McKinney explained:

> All the Secret Service had to do was nod and these units which had been trained at the Army's top Intelligence school at Camp Holabird, Maryland would have performed their normal function of Protection for the President in Dallas...
>
> ...Highly specialized classes were given at Camp Holabird on the subject of Protection. This included training designed to prepare this army unit to assist the Secret Service. If our support had not been refused, we would have been in Dallas.[220]

As frustrated and surprised as the unit members where, they just assumed some other unit would get the assignment. They were shocked to see no military presence at all in Kennedy's motorcade. This shows the

---

[219] Prouty, L. Fletcher, *JFK, The CIA, Vietnam, and the Plot to Assassinate John F. Kennedy*, p. 294., Skyhorse Publishing, 2009
[220] http://www.prouty.org/comment9.html

126

invisible hand of Lyndon Johnson. Most likely it was Johnson who told the Dallas Police to step down, and he also told the 112th MI group to step down. In both cases they were simply told that other arrangements had been made. It sounds semi-reasonable, and people weren't likely to question Johnson. He may have done this through intermediaries to hide his own involvement.

So the Dallas Police and the local military were both told not to take part in presidential protection in Dealey Plaza. Clearly, there was a deliberate breakdown of security that day.

In spite of the lack of military presence in the motorcade, a military intelligence officer was in the TSBD within a half hour of the assassination. Army intelligence agent James Powell identified himself to police there. He said he worked with the deputies in the rear of the building for six or eight minutes. It has never been adequately explained why Powell was there. Why was a military intelligence agent present after the shooting, yet military intelligence was told not to take part in protection?

Another strange twist also seemed to indicate the involvement of military intelligence. A list of TSBD employees was given to the Dallas Police. Oswald's name was on the list, along with the address "605 Elsbeth" in Dallas. Oswald never lived at that address, but he did live at 602 Elsbeth. Oswald had long since moved, and the Elsbeth address was never given on his application for work in the TSBD. They only had his current address on Beckley Ave. So who gave the Elsbeth address to the police? It had to be military intelligence. The 112th MI group had a file on "Harvey Lee Oswald." This file had his address as 605 Elsbeth, the exact same mistake that was on the list given to police. The address could only have come from Oswald's MI file. Within minutes of the shooting, military intelligence had provided the Dallas Police with information on the alleged gunman. The information must have been prepared in advance.

Lt. Col. Robert E. Jones was the 112th MI group's operations officer at Fort Sam Houston. Jones testified to the HSCA that on the day of the assassination, he got a call from Dallas saying that a man named A.J. Hidell had been arrested. Jones searched his files and found that A.J. Hidell was cross-referenced with Lee Harvey Oswald. But Oswald had only used the alias A.J. Hidell to open a post office box in that name, and allegedly to purchase the murder weapons. He never used that name any other time.

This means that military intelligence had some prior knowledge of Oswald's activities. Apparently, they had been monitoring him for some time.

The Warren Commission requested military files on Oswald, but they were only shown his regular military file, not his intelligence file. The HSCA learned of these files and requested them, but were told that they were destroyed in 1973. The HSCA stated that this was "extremely troublesome," considering that the same files had been withheld from the Warren Commission. In the committee's words:

> This information suggested the existence of a military intelligence file on Oswald and raised the possibility that he had intelligence associations of some kind.[221]

They also made this admission:

> Access to Oswald's military intelligence file, which the Department of Defense never gave to the Warren Commission, was not possible because the Department of Defense had destroyed the file as part of a general program aimed at eliminating all of its files pertaining to nonmilitary personnel.[222]

The HSCA accepted the DOD's explanation that the destruction of Oswald's military intelligence file was routine procedure.

It should not be hard to believe that the military was involved in the assassination. Kennedy was at odds with the military industrial complex-people who kill for a living. They thought nothing of eliminating Kennedy.

Strange Arrangements

Of further suspicion is the inexplicable reduction in the motorcycle escort. In a picture from earlier in the motorcade, we see a motorcycle policeman to the right of Kennedy.[223]Where was that policeman when the limousine passed the grassy knoll? He would have been an obvious obstruction to the shooter. If that policeman had not changed his position, Kennedy would not have been shot, at least not by the grassy knoll shooter.

---

[221] Marrs, Jim, *Crossfire*, p. 310, Carroll and Graf, 1989

[222] http://www.jfklancer.com/RobertJones.html

[223] https://www.politico.eu/article/7-new-findings-from-the-latest-jfk-files-assassination-lee-harvey-oswald/

It is natural that the relative positions of the limousine and the motorcycles would fluctuate somewhat during the ride, but in this case the officers were deliberately instructed to back off from the limousine.

Members of the Dallas Police Department met on November 19 to discuss security arrangements for the president. They agreed that the motorcycle escort would have two cycles on both sides of the limousine, five motorcycles at the rear, and four immediately ahead. But on November 21, in a joint meeting between the Dallas Police Department and the Secret Service, that protection was reduced. It was decided that there would be no motorcycle patrolmen to the sides of the limousine. This greatly put the president in danger, as patrolmen to the sides of the limousine would obscure the president from ground-level shooters. Had there been a patrolman to the right of Kennedy, he would have been in the way of the grassy knoll gunman. What was the excuse for reducing the motorcycle patrol? Here is Captain Perdue W. Lawrence's account of the meeting:

> I heard one of the Secret Service men say that President Kennedy did not desire any motorcycle officer directly on each side of him, between him and the crowd, but he would want the officers to the rear…when it was mentioned about these motorcycle officers alongside the president's car, he said, "No, these officers should be back, and if any people started a rush toward the car, if there was any movement at all where the president was in danger in any way, these officers would be in a position to gun their motors and get between them and the presidential car."[224]

So it was the Secret Service who reduced the motorcycle escort, further implicating them in the crime. According to Lawrence, it was Special Agent Winston G. Lawson who insisted on the reduced escort. The elimination of the side escorts led directly to Kennedy's death. Lawson then tried to avoid responsibility by claiming that President Kennedy wanted it that way. Films of earlier motorcades, including Fort Worth just a day earlier, show motorcycle escorts alongside the limousine. Blaming it on Kennedy was a foolproof cop-out. Others just assumed that Kennedy wanted the crowd to get a better view of him and his beautiful wife. No one bothered to check with Kennedy before the motorcade, and afterwards of course, they couldn't.

---

[224] Nelson, Phillip F., LBJ, *Mastermind of JFK's Assassination*, Xlibris, 2010

SS agents Samuel A. Kinney and Arthur L. Godfrey have both stated that Kennedy never ordered the motorcycles away from the limo. In fact, other Secret Service agents who were interviewed said that Kennedy never interfered with their performance of their jobs, and basically let them make all the arrangements. According to SS agent Robert Lilley, "He was very cooperative with us once he became president. Basically, (his attitude was) 'whatever you guys want is the way it will be.'"

That means that the Warren Commission had been lied to by the Secret Service about this. The commission reported that:

> On previous occasions, the President had requested that, to the extent possible, these flanking motorcycles keep back from the sides of his car.[225]

Police Chief Curry testified to the Warren Commission about the change of plans for the motorcycle escort. This was an open indictment of the Secret Service:

> Curry: In the planning of this motorcade, we had more motorcycles lined up to be with the president's car, but the Secret Service didn't want that many.
>
> Q: Did they tell you why?
>
> Curry: We actually had two on each side but we wanted four on each side and they asked us to drop out some of them and back down the motorcade, along the motorcade, which we did.[226]

From his book, *JFK Assassination Files*, here is Chief Curry's explanation of the motorcycle escort reduction:

> Captain P.W. Lawrence then was asked to outline the arrangement of the motorcycles for the motorcade. Lawrence stated that there would be a motorcycle sergeant and two motorcycle officers between the motorcade and the pilot car. These three motorcycle officers would alert other officers on the route to the advance of the motorcade and assist in any traffic control or security measures that might be present. A

---

[225] *The Warren Commission Report*, p. 45, Longmeadow Press, 1964
[226] Fetzer, Jim, *Murder in Dealey Plaza*, p. 155, Catfeet Press, 2000

motorcycle sergeant and four motorcycle officers would immediately precede the lead car. In addition to the five motorcycles in the front of the lead car Lawrence then said there would be four motorcycles on either side of the motorcade immediately to the rear of the President's vehicle.

Mr. Lawson felt that eight motorcycles around the President's vehicle were too many. Instead he stated that he thought two motorcycles on either side would be sufficient, and that they should be about even with the rear fender of the President's car. Captain Lawrence was instructed to disperse the other two motorcycles along each side of the motorcade to the rear. Lawrence detailed the procedure for entering and controlling the traffic on Stemmons Expressway while the motorcade proceeded to the Trade Mart.[227]

Billy Joe Martin was a motorcycle officer in the Dallas motorcade. His girlfriend, Jean Hill, was a witness to the shooting. Martin explained the instructions that he and the others were given:

Johnson's Secret Service people came over to the motorcycle cops and gave us a bunch of instructions…They also ordered us into the damndest escort formation I've ever seen. Ordinarily, you bracket the car with four motorcycles, one on each fender. But this time, they told the four of us assigned to the President's car there'd be no forward escorts. We were to stay well in back and not let ourselves get ahead of the car's rear wheels under any circumstances. I'd never heard of a formation like that, much less ridden in one, but they said they wanted the crowds to get an unrestricted view of the President. Well, I guess somebody got an "unrestricted" view of him, all right.[228]

"Under any circumstances" is a very telling phrase. It means that someone really wanted those motorcycles out of the way. Martin referred to "Johnson's Secret Service people," so he knew that Johnson was manipulating all of this. Martin had ridden in motorcades before, so he

---

[227] Curry, Jesse, *JFK Assassination File*, p. 16, Library of Congress, 1969
[228] Fetzer, Jim, *Murder in Dealey Plaza*, p. 155, Catfeet Press, 2000

knew that this configuration was most unusual, but he had no reason to question it until after the assassination.

Officer Marion Baker stated that his instructions were changed at the last minute, just as they were leaving Love Field:

> My partner and I, we received instructions to ride right beside the president's car. When we got to the airport, my sergeant instructed me that there wouldn't be anybody riding beside the president's car.[229]

Arrangements for the motorcade had been discussed for weeks. Why would they be changed at the last moment, just as the motorcade is leaving the airport? There is something very sinister about that. By changing the plans at the last second, there is less time for protest or discussion about it, and there is less time for honest cops to do anything about it.

The HSCA determined that security measures had been compromised in Dallas:

> The Secret Service's alteration of the original Dallas Police Department motorcycle deployment plan prevented the use of maximum possible security precautions…it may well be that by altering Dallas Police Department Captain Lawrence's original motorcycle plan, the Secret Service deprived Kennedy of security in Dallas that it had provided a mere day before in Houston.[230]

In a film of Kennedy's limousine departing from Love Field, we see something very odd happen. Secret Service Agents Donald Lawton and Henry Rybka are riding on the back bumper of the limousine. Then suddenly, SAIC Emory Roberts calls them off the bumpers. The agents respond with puzzled looks, shrugging their shoulders and turning their palms upward as if to say, "What's going on?" According to the Secret Service manual for the protection of a president, it is normal procedure for the SS agents to ride on the back bumper of the limo. There are handles back there for just that purpose. This can be seen in numerous other photos of presidential motorcades. The agents here simply took up their normal positions, and were shocked at the instruction to step down. Had they been

---

[229] Palamara, Vincent, *Survivor's Guilt*, p. 132, Trine Day, 2013
[230] HSCA, Secret Service Final Survey Report, p. 6, Mar. 19, 1978

in their usual positions, they would have provided some measure of protection from snipers in tall buildings. Without the agents there, the shooters in the TSBD and the Dal-Tex building had a clear shot at the president. This was yet another change made at the last second so there was no time for a discussion or an appeal of any kind.[231]

Jerry Behn was the Special Agent in Charge of White House detail (WHD) for JFK. In a report issued during the Warren Commission's investigation, Behn stated that Kennedy:

> ...told me that he did not want agents riding on the back of his car.

But in a 1992 interview, Behn stated:

> I don't remember Kennedy ever saying that he didn't want anybody on the back of his car. [232]

Critics and disinformation agents will be quick to show pictures of previous motorcades where the president does not have SS agents on the bumper or motorcycle cops to the sides of him. That is deceptive, because as the motorcade goes along, the exact nature of the protection may change. It may enter a crowded area where the cops and agents may move a little closer to the president to make sure no bystander could reach him. At other points, the crowd might be more sparse, and the agents and cops might back off a bit. If there are a lot of tall buildings for snipers, there should be agents on the bumper to cut down a shooter's angle. In a more wide open area, they might stay off and focus on street-level risks. If you see a photo that shows that any of this protection is missing, it is probably only for a moment. If you were to watch a film of that entire motorcade, you would see that there is usually reasonable protection on the sides and rear of the president.

Dallas Homicide Captain Will Fritz and his men were originally scheduled to ride in the motorcade. Fritz told the Warren Commission about the late change to the plans:

> Well, we had taken some precautions, but those were changed. We were told in the beginning that we would be in

---

[231] https://www.youtube.com/watch?v=XY02Qkuc_f8
[232] Palamara, Vincent Michael, *Survivor's Guilt*, pp. 3-4, Trine Day, 2013

the parade directly behind (the vice president's car) and we did make preparations for that. But at 10:00 the night before the parade, Chief Stevenson called me at home and told me that had been changed, and I was assigned with two of my officers to the speaker's stand at the Trade Mart.[233]

By taking Fritz and his men out of the motorcade, it reduced the chances that one or more of the shooters would be apprehended.

Another last-minute change to the motorcade plans that has gone largely unnoticed is the repositioning of the press car in the motorcade. The press vehicle was usually a flatbed truck, but in this case it was a convertible. The press car was originally set to be placed directly in front of JFK's limousine, as it usually was. At the last minute, it was repositioned at the end of the motorcade-dead last. The press car was filled with photographers waiting to take pictures. If they had been in their usual location, they would have all gotten footage of the assassination. There is no telling what might have happened then. That problem was conveniently avoided by relocating the press car to the rear. No one has been able to confirm where the order for the last-minute change came from. It had to be a Secret Service agent who ordered the rearrangement, although he could have been acting on orders from Johnson.[234]

Open Windows

In the documentary *The Men Who Killed Kennedy*, Col. Fletcher Prouty mentions other breakdowns in protection, such as the failure to secure the open windows in the TSBD. Prouty tells of how under normal circumstances, Secret Service agents would have gone ahead of the motorcade to check for things like that. This was just one of the many reductions in security on that day:

> You've all seen the picture of the school book building, you know, where Oswald is supposed to have shot the president. Well, you notice in those pictures there are open windows. If the Secret Service had been there, and had done their usual job, none of those windows would have been open. And had anyone opened one of those windows at that time, they

[233] Palamara, Vincent Michael, *Survivor's Guilt*, p. 118, Trine Day, 2013
[234] Marrs, Jim, *Crossfire*, pp. 309-310, Carroll and Graf, 1989

would have been on the radio, they would have had a man in that room immediately, and that window would have been closed. You see, that's protection, and that didn't take place. In fact, there were no Secret Service people on the ground around Dealey Plaza that afternoon. They were told they were not needed.[235]

The Warren Commission tried to justify the inaction of the Secret Service:

With the number of men available to the Secret Service and the time available, surveys of hundreds of buildings and thousands of windows is not practical.[236]

It is true that it's not practical to secure all of the thousands of windows along the route. No one would expect them to. It's always possible that a window could be opened at the last second, just as the motorcade approaches. But it is realistic that the Secret Service could have made a concentrated focus on the windows along Houston Street and Elm Street. That is where the motorcade slowed down, so additional security measures would be justified there. This is only a stretch of one block, and only on one side of the street, since an open field is to the west of Houston and to the south of Elm Street. From the moment the motorcade approached the right turn onto Houston, it should not have been allowed to proceed until all windows along Houston and Elm Streets had been checked and closed. That approach would have been reasonable and realistic. Even the Warren Commission admitted that:

This justification of the Secret Service's standing policy is not persuasive. The danger from a concealed sniper on the Dallas trip was of concern to those who had considered the problem. President Kennedy himself had mentioned it that morning, as had Agent Sorrels when he and Agent Lawson were fixing the motorcade route. Admittedly, protective measures cannot ordinarily be taken with regard to all buildings along a motorcade route. Levels of risk can be determined, however, as has been confirmed by building surveys made since the assassination for the Department of the Treasury. An attempt to cover only the most obvious

---

[235] Turner, Nigel, 1988, *The Men Who Killed Kennedy*, U.K.,https://www.youtube.com/watch?v=0NdtxGiK3WI
[236] *The Warren Commission Report*, p. 447, Longmeadow Press, 1964

points of possible ambush along the route in Dallas might well have included the Texas School Book Depository Building.[237]

They are correct about determining levels of risk, and "the most obvious points of possible ambush" would certainly include the TSBD. Instead, the Secret Service merely scanned the buildings, with no ability to do anything even if they did see a problem. Dallas Police officers were available to aid in the survey of the buildings, but they were not given instructions to do so. Their role was limited to controlling the crowd and traffic, and they stood with their backs to the buildings. Instructions from the Secret Service to the Dallas Police Department were given to Captain Lawrence, who testified to the Warren Commission. The commission summarized the DPD's role:

> Captain Lawrence was not instructed to have his men watch buildings along the motorcade route and did not mention the observation of buildings to them. The three officers confirm that their primary concern was crowd and traffic control, and that they had no opportunity to scan the windows of the Depository or any other building in the vicinity of Elm and Houston when the motorcade was passing.[238]

Unwanted Vacation

Col. Prouty was sent to the South Pole to escort a VIP party from November 10th to the 28th, 1963. That is significant, considering the dates involved. The date range includes the day of John Kennedy's assassination. The trip was nothing urgent; it was simply a diplomatic event. This was really just a ploy to remove Prouty from his post temporarily. Prouty was Chief of Special Operations for the Joint Chiefs of Staff, and he was familiar with presidential security. Prouty had experience in protecting presidents, as he had done for Eisenhower. He knew the rules and regulations, and would likely speak out if he saw how those rules and regulations were flagrantly violated in Dallas. Maybe he would have objected to the dangerous turns in the motorcade route. Maybe he would have complained about the lack of motorcycle protection on the sides of the limousine. Maybe he would have questioned the lack of military presence in Dallas.

---

[237] *The Warren Commission Report*, pp. 168-170, Longmeadow Press, 1964
[238] *The Warren Commission Report*, p. 449, Longmeadow Press, 1964

Prouty could have been a problem for the plotters, so it was easy to get him out of the way by offering him what amounted to a free vacation.

Prouty tells of his talk with General Ed Lansdale:

> ...he came to me one day and he said, "Fletch, you've been working pretty hard and I've got an approval to something that might be a nice paid vacation. How would you like to go to the South Pole?" And I thought, I wouldn't mind a paid vacation. I don't know about the South Pole, but if someone is going to fly me down to the South Pole and all. So OK, I'd be glad to go. Then he said, "Go over to the South Pole Office on Jackson Court near the White House and talk to Mr. So-and-So." I went over there and I found out that they were planning to fly a VIP party to the South Pole and they did need a military escort officer. And I was being nominated for that, and I went to the South Pole.[239]

General Lansdale was in charge of Operation Mongoose, the project to remove Fidel Castro from power. Many in this project viewed Kennedy as an obstacle to be eliminated. Now the leader of that project has weakened Kennedy's security by removing Prouty from his post. Prouty has identified Lansdale from a picture taken in Dealey Plaza shortly after the assassination. "He is so clearly identifiable," said Prouty. "That's him and what's he doing there?" So the man who sent a key security figure on vacation during Kennedy's trip to Dallas is now seen in Dallas when Kennedy gets shot. Prouty naturally wondered if that was a ploy to get him out of the way:[240]

> By the fall of 1963, I knew perhaps as much as anyone about the inner workings of this world of special operations. I had written the formal directives on the subject that were used officially by the U.S. Air Force and by the Joint Chiefs of Staff for all military services.
>
> I have always wondered, deep in my own heart, whether that strange invitation that removed me so far from Washington and from the center of all things clandestine that I knew so well might have been connected to the events that followed. Were there things that I knew, or would have discovered, that made it wise to have me far from Washington, along

---

[239] https://ratical.org/ratville/JFK/USO/chp1_p3.html
[240] Prouty, L. Fletcher, letter to Jim Garrison (6th March, 1990)

with others, such as the Kennedy cabinet, who were in midair over the Pacific Ocean en route to Japan, far from the scene?

I do not know the answer to that question, although many of the things that I have observed and learned from that time have led me to surmise that such a question might be well founded. After all, I knew that type of work very well. I had worked on presidential protection and knew the great extent to which one goes to ensure the safety of the chief executive. Despite all this, established procedures were ignored on the President's trip to Dallas on November 22, 1963.[241]

Since Prouty was at the South Pole during the preparations for Kennedy's Dallas trip, he was helpless to do anything. All of these violations occurred in his absence.

PRS

According to the Warren Commission, the Secret Service had no information about Oswald in their PRS (Protective Research Section) files. The purpose of the PRS is to collect and process information about persons or groups who may be a danger to the president. Most of the information they collect comes from other federal agencies, mainly the FBI. Oswald will be discussed more in Chapter 7, but suffice to say he was known to several federal agencies, including the FBI, CIA, Department of State, and Office of Naval Intelligence. It was standard procedure for these agencies to open a file on communist defectors, which Oswald allegedly was. Whether or not someone is a potential threat is a matter of judgment. That judgment is made by the agencies that report to the PRS. The FBI file was opened because Oswald was considered "a possible security risk in the event he returned to this country." He did return to this country, so why wasn't the PRS notified of this "possible security risk"?[242]

The Warren Commission considered the question of whether or not the FBI should have alerted the Secret Service to Oswald's presence along the motorcade route. There is some question of exactly what constitutes a threat against the president, and it is basically a judgment call. The FBI and

---

[241] http://erenow.com/biographies/jfk-the-cia-vietnam-and-the-plot-to-assassinate-john-kennedy/21.html
[242] *The Warren Commission Report*, pp. 429-430, Longmeadow Press, 1964

the Secret Service saw it differently. Robert I. Bouck was the Special Agent in Charge of the Protective Research Section of the SS. Bouck testified that the cumulative effect of the information in Oswald's file should have triggered an alert to the Secret Service about a potential danger:

> I would think his continued association with the Russian Embassy after his return, his association with the Castro groups would have been of concern to us, a knowledge that he had, I believe, been court martialed for illegal possession of a gun, of a hand gun in the Marines, that he had owned a weapon and did a good deal of hunting or use of it, perhaps in Russia, plus a number of items about his disposition and unreliability of character, I think all of those, if we had them altogether, would have added up to pointing out a pretty bad individual, and I think that, together, had we known that he had a vantage point would have seemed somewhat serious to us, even though I must admit, that none of these in themselves would be--would meet our specific criteria, none of them alone.
> But, it is when you begin adding them up to some degree that you begin to get criteria that, are meaningful.[243]

Bouck also mentioned that no agency knew that Oswald was working in a building directly overlooking the motorcade route. But the FBI had Oswald's work address, so how could they not know?

On August 9, 1963, Oswald was arrested in New Orleans for disturbing the peace. He was on the street, handing out pro-communist literature for the Fair Play for Cuba Committee. This led to a fight with some bystanders, which led to Oswald's arrest. The fight was probably staged by the CIA to make Oswald look like a violent-prone person. Witnesses say that it seemed fake, as if it were staged. However, the FBI would not have known that. As far as they knew, Oswald was a communist, a traitor, a nut, and a volatile person. So why wasn't the PRS notified? What does it take for someone to be labeled a "potential threat"? Do they have to have a conviction for murder? The New Orleans incident was only three months before the presidential motorcade, so the information could not have been considered "stale."

---

[243] *The Warren Commission Report*, p. 440, Longmeadow Press, 1964

The Commission tried to create an alibi for the Secret Service, saying that the PRS division "was a very small group, consisting of 12 specialists and 3 clerks."[244] They go on to say how the PRS receives thousands of cases each year and they are overwhelmed and so forth. In other words, they are saying that the Secret Service was understaffed, and that's why they failed to collect and process information on Oswald. But to be cautious, it would only take one phone call from one FBI agent to one Secret Service agent saying, "Watch out for this guy."

James Hosty was the FBI agent in charge of the Oswald file in Dallas. Hosty testified that even if he had recalled that Oswald's job was along the motorcade route, he would not have alerted the Secret Service that he was a threat to the president. He was only required to do so if there was "some indication that the person planned to take some action against the safety of the President of the United States or the Vice President." Nothing in Oswald's files, or in Hosty's experience with him, indicated that this was the case. When Hosty heard that Oswald was a suspect, he was shocked.[245]

The CIA and the FBI both had files on Oswald, and they were both monitoring him. Yet, when the presidential motorcade passed right by the building where this supposedly dangerous person is known to be working, no one did anything. What was the point of monitoring him if they took no action? You would think that when the president's motorcade passed by the TSBD, the Secret Service would have 10 agents inside the building, watching Oswald's every move. Yet, there were none. Didn't these agencies communicate with each other? Doesn't the Secret Service ask about any potential troublemakers in the area? It's hard to believe it's just an honest oversight. It would take major incompetency by all three of these agencies for that to be true. Someone clearly wanted Oswald unguarded so he could take the blame.

For the Secret Service to take no action on a potential threat would be irresponsible. But not only did the motorcade pass by this potential threat, it slowed down for him! Was that a coincidence? The Secret Service approved the route. They tried to pass it off as incompetency, but it clearly shows willing complicity by them. Even if they knew nothing about Oswald, they do know that a slower-moving target is easier to hit.

---

[244] *The Warren Commission Report*, p. 429, Longmeadow Press, 1964
[245] http://spartacus-educational.com/JFKhosty.htm

Remember also that Oswald did not go to the motorcade; the motorcade came to him. He made no effort to seek out Kennedy. He was in the TSBD anyway because he worked there. He was routinely there for eight hours a day, so there is nothing at all suspicious about his presence in the building. Oswald was hired on October 16, over a month before the motorcade route was published. No one knew that the president would pass by in a month. According to the official story, Oswald was a disgruntled loner who wanted to become someone special by killing a high-ranking public official. Then, lo and behold, the president's motorcade passes right by the window where he works every day, anyway. How convenient! On top of that, the motorcade slows down to a near-stop as it approaches. It's all too perfect. The whole situation was tailor-made for a shooting and a framing.

Ideally, the plotters would have liked to have killed Oswald immediately after Kennedy was shot. The longer he lives, the more likely he is to talk. They had probably planned to shoot him as he left the TSBD, but something went awry.

If the plan had worked to perfection, it would have gone something like this: Kennedy is shot and killed by one of the shooters from behind, preferably the one in the TSBD. Since the grassy knoll shooter was only a back-up, he would never have had to fire. There would be no film showing a shot from the front. Abraham Zapruder's film would have shown Kennedy being hit from behind, which would then seem to confirm the Oswald story and reinforce the lone-assassin theory. Then, as Oswald was leaving the building, he would have been shot by a rogue cop who was in collusion. The cop would then say that Oswald was reaching for his gun, so he had to shoot him in self-defense. They might even plant a gun in Oswald's hand. If there were no witness, they could easily have gotten away with it. Would the Warren Commission have challenged it? Oswald would never be able to speak a word to the public. We would never hear him shout, "I'm just a patsy!" And we would never have gotten to see what a mature and civilized person he was. History would then be even more distorted than it is now.

Body Snatchers

If anyone still has doubts about the involvement of the Secret Service in the assassination, consider their actions at Parkland Hospital, which bordered on criminal. SS agent Roy Kellerman confronted Dr. Earl Rose, the forensic pathologist, as Rose pushed Kennedy's body on a gurney down the corridor of the hospital. Kellerman said that they wanted to take Kennedy's body right away because Jacqueline Kennedy refused to leave without it. Jackie never actually said that, but Kellerman was desperately anxious to get the body out of there, obviously to hide or alter evidence. Dr. Rose refused to release the body, pointing out that under Texas law it was his responsibility to conduct the autopsy, and to keep the chain of custody intact. Kellerman was livid, and a struggle ensued. They had a physical tug-of-war, with Kellerman and Rose literally fighting over the dead president's body. It is said that Kellerman drew a gun and pinned Rose against the wall. Rose relented only after being physically threatened.[246]

Shockingly, Dr. Rose has stated that he agrees with the Warren Commission's conclusions, and he rejects the idea of a conspiracy to kill President Kennedy. This man had a gun pointed at his head, yet he still can't believe there's a conspiracy. Why was Kellerman pointing a gun at Rose's head? Was it because he was so anxious to appease Jackie Kennedy that he would threaten the man for her? Apparently, that's what Rose believes. This is coming from a man who had seen the president's wounds close-up. They used physical intimidation against him at Parkland, so one has to wonder if similar intimidation was used to get him to defend those who threatened him. Like many others, Rose is probably not saying what he really believes.[247]

Phony Agents

Several people, including law enforcement officials, have claimed that they encountered Secret Service agents on the grassy knoll. But the Secret Service has stated that they had no agents stationed anywhere in Dealey Plaza. The only SS agents present were in the motorcade itself. The agents on the grassy knoll were fake. That shows the depth of the conspiracy here. The plotters had phony Secret Service agents stationed at strategic points to allow the shooters to get better shots and to help them escape. The phony agents were convincing enough that they fooled the police.

Deputy Constable Seymour Weitzman testified to the Warren Commission that he encountered "other officers, Secret Service as well" on

---

[246] https://www.fff.org/2013/10/14/the-first-step-in-the-jfk-cover-up/
[247] https://profjoeval.wordpress.com/tag/secret-service-agents-were-ordered-off-the-back-bumper-of-jfks-motorcar-to-strip-away-protection-from-a-gunshot-from-the-rear/

the grassy knoll. Later, in a 1975 interview, Weitzman said that the man he saw produced official-looking credentials and assured him that everything was under control. He gave a description of the man, and when he was shown photos of possible suspects, he immediately identified the man as Bernard Barker. Barker was a CIA asset and future Watergate burglar. The reporter asked him, "Is this the man who produced the Secret Service credentials?" Weitzman responded, "Yes, that's the same man."[248]

Dallas Police officer Joseph M. Smith was nearby Kennedy when the shooting occurred. He believed at least one shot came from behind the picket fence on the knoll. He even smelled gunpowder in that area. As he ran up the hill, he encountered a man who pulled a pistol from his holster. Officer Smith testified to the Warren Commission:

> Just as I did, he showed me he was a Secret Service agent ... he saw me coming with my pistol and right away he showed me who he was.[249]

The commission was not interested in hearing about the fake agents, or anything concerning the grassy knoll. During his testimony, Officer Smith was lead in his questioning by assistant counsel Wesley J. Liebeler. Although Liebeler knew about the fake agent Smith had encountered, he avoided questioning him about it. Smith was asked if he noticed the TSBD, and he answered that he did not because he had his back to the building the whole time. Inexplicably, Liebeler asked Smith if he had noticed if the windows in the TSBD were open. A senseless question, Smith naturally responded in the negative. Then Liebeler asked Smith if he saw Oswald leave the TSBD. Then he asked him when he first heard about Oswald's arrest. All this pointless questioning was simply to redirect attention and avoid confronting the delicate subject of the fake Secret Service agents. Liebeler never asked Smith for a description of the agent- his height, weight, attire, etc. The fake agents are obvious proof of conspiracy, and the commission basically chose to ignore any mention of them. In spite of all the corroboration on the subject, it was much too easy for the commission to just say that all the witnesses were mistaken, even highly credible ones like Officer Smith.[250]

---

[248] Canfield, Michael, and Weberman, Alan J., *Coup d'état In America*, Joseph Okpaku Pub. Co., 1975
[249] *The Warren Commssion Report*, Vol. VII, p. 531, 1964
[250] Lane, Mark, *Last Word*, p. 190, Skyhorse Publishing, 2012

During the HSCA investigation, Dallas Police Sergeant Harkness testified:

> There were some Secret Service agents there – on the grassy
> knoll – but I did not get them identified. They told me they
> were Secret Service.[251]

These fake agents on the knoll have never been identified. If they were really Secret Service agents or undercover cops, they would have identified themselves during the investigation. And if they were really law enforcement officials of some kind, then why weren't they chasing after the escaping assassin who was right behind them? What is the point of just turning people away instead of chasing after the shooter?

Witness Malcolm Summers was on Elm Street when the shooting occurred. Like many others, he ran to the grassy knoll to see what happened. In the 1988 documentary *Who Murdered JFK?* Summers told his story:

> I ran across the--Elm Street to right there toward the knoll. It
> was there (pointing to a spot on the knoll)--and we were
> stopped by a man in a suit and he had an overcoat--over his
> arm and he, he, I saw a gun under that overcoat. And he--his
> comment was, "Don't you all come up here any further, you
> could get shot, or killed," one of those words. A few months
> later, they told me they didn't have an FBI man in that area.
> If they didn't have anybody, it's a good question who it
> was.[252]

During Jim Garrison's investigation (1966-69), Dallas Police officer Roger Craig identified Edgar Eugene Bradley as the man who presented himself as a Secret Service agent in Dealey Plaza. Craig had spoken extensively to Bradley that day. Believing that he was a true SS agent, Craig gave him his account of the events. Bradley was a member of the International Anti-Communist Brigade, knew suspects David Ferrie and Loran Hall, and was suspected of having intelligence connections. Craig signed an affidavit that implicated Bradley, and Garrison had Bradley arrested. However, Bradley

---

[251] Harkness HSCA 180-10082-10443 02/07/78
[252] http://whokilledjfk.net/fake_secret_service_agents.htm

was already imprisoned in California, and Governor Ronald Reagan refused to extradite him, costing Garrison a key witness.[253]

Jean Hill was the closest bystander to the president when he was shot. She saw the shot come from behind the picket fence. She saw movement and a puff of smoke there. She ran up the grassy knoll in an attempt to find the shooter, but she was stopped by two men who identified themselves as Secret Service agents.

> I was looking around but I couldn't see anything, when these two guys came up behind me. One of them said, "You're coming with us," and I replied, "Oh, no I'm not. I don't know you." "I said you're coming with us," one of them said and put this horrible grip on my shoulder. I can still feel the pain when I think about it. I tried to tell them, "I have to go back and find my friend Mary." But then the other guy put a grip on my other shoulder and they began hustling me past the front of the depository. "Keep smiling and keep walking," one of them kept telling me.

> They marched me across the plaza and into a building. We entered from the south side and I think it was the sheriff's office. They took me to a little office upstairs and they wouldn't let me out of this room. It was all such a shock. There was a lot of tension and it seemed like a lot of it was focused on this one area. The two men that grabbed me never showed me any identification but after we got to this little room, some men came in who were Secret Service. They began to ask me a lot of questions. One man told me they had been watching Mary and I out of the window. He asked me, "Did you see a bullet hit at your feet?" I told him I didn't realize that one had struck near my feet. "Then why did you jump back up on the curb?" he asked me and I told him how I had started to run at the president's car but thought better of it. Then I heard some booming sounds and it startled me and I jumped back on the curb by Mary. I guess they were up there the whole time and watched the whole thing. Then they sent those two guys to come and get

---

[253] https://ratical.org/ratville/JFK/WTKaP.html

me. I mean, I wasn't too hard to find that day- wearing that red raincoat.[254]

Dallas Police Chief Jesse Curry commented on the phony agents:

> ...certainly the suspicion would point to the man being involved, some way or other, in the shooting, since he was in the area immediately adjacent to where the shots were, and the fact that he had a badge that purported him to be Secret Service would make it seem all the more suspicious.[255]

The HSCA made the following attempt to explain away the mysterious agents:

> The committee did obtain evidence that military intelligence personnel may have identified themselves as Secret Service agents or that they might have been misidentified as such. Robert E. Jones, a retired Army lieutenant colonel who in 1963 was commanding officer of the military intelligence region that encompassed Texas, told the committee that from 8 to 12 military intelligence personnel in plain-clothes were assigned to Dallas to provide supplemental security for the President's visit. He indicated that these agents had identification credentials and, if questioned, would most likely have stated that they were on detail to the Secret Service.
>
> The committee sought to identify these agents so that they could be questioned. The Department of Defense, however, reported that a search of its files showed "no records indicating any Department of Defense Protective Services in Dallas." The committee was unable to resolve the contradiction.[256]

According to Lt. Jones, 8-12 military intelligence personnel were in Dealey Plaza that day. But not one of the 8-12 members were ever identified. Why didn't they come forth during the original investigation? Many witnesses and police officers claimed to have seen these agents. They could have put an end to all the speculation just by identifying themselves.

---

[254] Marrs, Jim, *Crossfire*, p. 323, Carroll and Graf, 1989
[255] Marrs, Jim, *Crossfire*, p. 324, Carroll and Graf, 1989
[256] HSCA, *Final Report*, p. 184, 1979

Jones said the agents would have stated that they were "on detail to the Secret Service." That just means that they were assigned to assist the Secret Service. It is misleading because it would make people think that they are Secret Service agents, especially since they were plainclothesmen. Why would they do that? They are not Secret Service; they are military personnel. Jones is saying that they would deliberately misidentify themselves. The only reason he would say that would be to explain away the fake SS agents. There can be no other reason for such a strange statement. It should come as no surprise that the Department of Defense could find no records of protective service in Dallas. There were no military intelligence personnel assigned to protect the president that day. The HSCA said that Jones' testimony was credible, even though it made no sense.[257]

In a picture taken moments after the shooting, we can see one of the fake Secret Service agents.[258]The picture can be seen on pages 54-56 of Robert J. Groden's book *The Killing of a President*. There is a tall man walking up the steps of the grassy knoll. He is dressed just like you would expect a Secret Service agent to be dressed, including shades and a fedora. The most conspicuous thing about him is that he is so casual. He is not panicking like the rest of the crowd. Everyone else is running frantically toward the triple underpass. The tall man is the only one walking toward the parking lot, which was his escape. He is likely one of the culprits. It's easy to spot the conspirators here. Just look for the ones who are suspiciously calm.[259]

Other Plots

On October 30, 1963, the Secret Service learned of a possible assassination attempt in Chicago on November 2. A man named Thomas Arthur Vallee was arrested. Vallee was said to be an outspoken critic of John Kennedy. He was a Marine Corps veteran with a history of mental health problems, and a member of the John Birch Society. When Vallee was arrested, he was in possession of an M-1 rifle, a handgun, and 3,000 rounds of ammunition. The president's trip to Chicago was cancelled, but the information about the assassination plot in Chicago was not passed on to the protection team in Dallas.

---

[257] http://www.jfklancer.com/RobertJones.html
[258] http://mcadams.posc.mu.edu/arnold/towner3lg.jpg pl
[259] Groden, Robert J., *The Killing of a President*, pp. 54-56, The Penguin Group, 1993

Vallee was probably the designated patsy for the Chicago plot. His background looks the same as Oswald's- disgruntled Marine, mentally unstable, political extremist, prone to violence, etc. Chances are that Vallee was an intelligence operative just like Oswald was. In the Marines, Vallee was stationed at a U-2 base in Japan, just as Oswald was. The CIA commanded the U-2, so Vallee was clearly one of their men. Vallee also trained Cuban exiles, like Oswald did. If the Chicago plot had succeeded, we never would have heard of Lee Harvey Oswald. Instead, it would have been Thomas Arthur Vallee who would have gone down in history as President Kennedy's assassin. And it would have been Vallee who had to be murdered to be silenced.

Like Oswald, Vallee also gained employment at a site that overlooked the presidential motorcade route. It's almost certain he got the job through the CIA. He worked at IPP-Litho-Plate located at 625 Jackson Boulevard in Chicago. The set-up of this area is very similar to that of Dealey Plaza. If the motorcade had proceeded, it would have made a slow turn from the Northwest Expressway to West Jackson Boulevard. It would have slowed down right in front of IPP-Litho-Plate, just as it slowed down in front of the TSBD in Dallas. From Vallee's work site on the third floor, he would have had an unimpeded view of Kennedy, and presumably, a clear shot at him. This would make him the natural suspect. There were nearby spots where other shooters could hide, too, comparable to the grassy knoll in Dallas.

The timing of Vallee's arrest is interesting. The White House announced the cancellation of the Chicago motorcade at 10:15 a.m. ET, which was 9:15 a.m. Chicago time. Vallee was arrested at 9:10 a.m. Chicago time, just five minutes before the announced cancellation. Of course, the decision must have been made at least several minutes before it was announced, so it appears that Vallee's arrest was purposely delayed until after the motorcade had been cancelled. Why? Wouldn't they want to get this potential killer off the streets as soon as possible? What was the purpose of waiting for the cancellation? It appears that the Secret Service goal was not to restrain Vallee, but to shadow him. Since Vallee was the scapegoat, they had to make sure he was free until the assassination. They could not let him leave town, get injured, or take a day off of work. Least of all, they could not let him get arrested. What if Vallee had been in jail when Kennedy was shot? That's an air-tight alibi if there ever was one. Vallee had to be monitored. Like Oswald, he knew a little too much about the assassination plot. Vallee's arrest and interrogation were probably to ascertain if he was a threat to talk.[260]

Kennedy was aware that there were assassination plots against him. This was confirmed by Marty Underwood, DNC advance man for the Dallas Trip. Underwood warned Kennedy of the plot in Miami, but Kennedy told him not to worry.[261] He may or may not have known about the Chicago threat, but probably would have been equally undeterred by it. In fact, Kennedy was surprisingly undaunted by the threats. He made this comment shortly before his death:

> If somebody wants to shoot me from a window with a rifle, nobody can stop it, so why worry about it?[262]

So what was the reason for the cancellation of the Chicago trip? That very same morning in Vietnam, President Ngo Dinh Diem had been assassinated in a military coup. Kennedy received the news that morning during a meeting with his advisors on Vietnam. This was shortly before he was scheduled to leave for Chicago. This international crisis was supposedly the reason why Kennedy cancelled the trip. The timing of the event was just a coincidence, but it spared Vallee from the fate eventually suffered by Oswald, and it may have extended Kennedy's life by three weeks.

The sad story of Abraham Bolden shows the vindictive nature of the cover-up. Bolden was the first African-American to be appointed to the White House detail of the Secret Service. He was first appointed by President Eisenhower in 1959 and worked out of the Chicago office. In 1961, Bolden was then selected by President Kennedy to serve in the Presidential Protection Division of the White House in an attempt to integrate the all-white staff. Bolden was very fond of John Kennedy, who treated him with respect and dignity that he did not always get from others. Kennedy once referred to Bolden as "the Jackie Robinson of the Secret Service." But Bolden lasted only three months on the White House detail, then was reassigned to Chicago. Bolden had complained about separate housing facilities for blacks, and also about the general laxity and heavy drinking of the agents who were assigned to protect the president. He also complained

---

[260] Douglass, James W., *JFK and the Unspeakable*, p. 202, Touchstone, 2008
[261] http://www.jfklancer.com/LNE/limo.html
[262] Powers, David, and O'Donnell, Kenneth, *Johhny, We Hardly Knew Ye*, Little Brown, 1972

about racial epithets and the use of the n-word by SS agents. These complaints were the cause of his reassignment.

Back at the Chicago branch, the Secret Service was told that an informant had sent a teletype to the FBI, giving details of the plot to assassinate President Kennedy when he came to Chicago on November 2. Bolden and his fellow agents were informed of this by SAIC Maurice Martineau. The teletype warned of "right wing paramilitary fanatics" from a dissident group, and said that the assassination "would probably be attempted at one of the Northwest Expressway overpasses." Vallee was arrested and released after the motorcade was cancelled. Supposedly, the tip came from a man named "Lee." Whether or not this was Lee Harvey Oswald has never been confirmed.[263]

Bolden later found out that this information had been kept from the Warren Commission. He knew about the Chicago plot and was anxious to testify to the commission about it. Bolden's superior officer blocked his request. He was told to "keep his mouth shut." Bolden was persistent, and he was perceived as a threat. He traveled to Washington on his own and spoke with Warren Commission council J. Lee Rankin. Shortly thereafter, Bolden was arrested and charged with soliciting bribes for disclosing Secret Service information. He was sentenced to six years in jail. There was really no case against Bolden, but being black in 1963 did not help. The conviction was mainly based on the testimony of a counterfeiter, Joseph Spagnoli. Later in his own trial, Spagnoli confessed that he lied about Bolden. He said in court that he was told to lie by prosecutor Richard Sikes. Still, Bolden was made to serve his full sentence. Notorious mobster Sam DeStefano was one of the men who accused Bolden of the crime. DeStefano was associated with Sam Giancana, Charles Nicoletti, and Richard Cain, meaning that the mafia helped to frame Bolden in order to preserve their own interests. DeStefano himself was murdered in 1973, allegedly by Cain. Bolden was an innocent man who got caught between the mob, racists, and crooked government officials.[264]

In November of 1975, the *Chicago Independent* reported on the warning:

---

[263] http://thechicagoplot.com/The%20Chicago%20Plot.pdf
[264] Douglass, James W., *JFK and the Unspeakable*, pp. 214-6 Simon and Schuster, 2008

> It wasn't a federal crime to kill a president or even threaten him (at the time). And J. Edgar Hoover had decided since it was the Secret Service's province to protect the president, the FBI would not, could not participate in the investigation.[265]

J. Edgar Hoover had refused to take action on the warning, claiming that it was the jurisdiction of the Secret Service to protect the president. Since murdering the president was not a federal crime at the time, Hoover figured he had no legal responsibility on the matter. He showed equal apathy regarding warnings about the Dallas plot. It is shocking that Hoover knew of the plots, but felt no moral obligation to do anything about it. By doing nothing, Hoover was complicit.

In 1995, the Secret Service deliberately destroyed all its records of the Chicago assassination plot, in violation of the JFK Records Act. They shredded two boxes of documents that were considered incriminating. The protective survey reports that were destroyed covered all of JFK's trips from September 24 to November 8, 1963, including three folders on his cancelled trip to Chicago. The ARRB's Executive Director David G. Marwell stated that the records "were destroyed in violation of the law."[266]

Another assassination plot was discovered in Miami. A Miami police informant secretly recorded a conversation with Joseph Milteer, a racist extremist. On the recording, Milteer describes a plot in the works to kill Kennedy "from an office building with a high-powered rifle." This led to the cancellation of the president's planned motorcade on November 18. Miami police gave copies of the recording to both the Secret Service and the FBI on November 10, 1963. Milteer was interviewed and released, even though the FBI had the incriminating tape. Again, this information was not passed on to Kennedy's protection team in Dallas.

Not much is known about the Miami plot, but it's a safe bet that they had a designated patsy set up there. Most likely, the patsy had a history of political extremism, mental illness, and violent tendencies. Most likely, the patsy got a CIA-arranged job overlooking the motorcade route. Most likely, the motorcade route made a turn just as it passed the patsy's place of employment. But neither the Chicago nor the Miami plots were successful,

---

[265] https://ratical.org/ratville/JFK/TheChicagoPlot-Orig-Nov1975.pdf
[266] Douglass, James W., *JFK and the Unspeakable*, p. 438, Simon and Schuster, 2008

because they lacked what Dallas could offer: home-field advantage for the one most responsible for orchestrating and covering up the crime.[267]

After the assassination, Johnson and Hoover discussed the shooting by phone:

> Johnson: How many shots were fired? Three?
>
> Hoover: Three.
>
> Johnson: Any of them fired at me?
>
> Hoover: No.
>
> Johnson: All three at the President?[268]

Why would Johnson ask, "Any of them fired at me?" Doesn't he know? If someone was shooting at you, you would certainly know it. When bullets start whizzing past your head, that would be the giveaway. No shot came within 50 feet of Johnson. All the shots were aimed at Kennedy. Does Johnson really have to ask if they were shooting at him? And how would Hoover know anyway? For what possible reason would he ask Hoover if they were shooting at him? It's simply to feign innocence.

There is too much here to be coincidence. The choice of the Trade Mart, the inexplicable motorcade route, the stand-down orders, and the motorcycle reduction cannot be explained as simple mistakes or oversights. They were deliberate changes made for the purpose of killing John Kennedy. Most of the changes were initiated at the highest level, meaning Lyndon Baines Johnson.

---

[267] http://spartacus-educational.com/JFKSinvestSS.htm
[268] Telephone conversation between Lyndon B. Johnson and J. Edgar Hoover (1.40 pm, 29th November, 1963)

5

AFTERMATH—TWO MORE MURDERS

n the immediate aftermath of John Kennedy's murder, two other murders occurred which were directly related to it. They were the slayings of Dallas Police officer J.D. Tippit and accused presidential assassin Lee Harvey Oswald. We know Oswald's killer; we do not know Tippit's. But both murders involve a string of unanswered questions that leave the whole assassination puzzle unsolved.

Murder of Officer J.D. Tippit

About 45 minutes after John Kennedy was shot, a Dallas Police officer was shot less than three miles away. The slain officer was J.D. Tippit, and it was thought that his death was related to the Kennedy shooting. It was generally believed that the officer stopped the escaping assassin, who then shot him. The Dallas Police tried to pin the Tippit slaying on Oswald, as did the Warren Commission. But there is no credible evidence that Oswald killed Tippit. Since Oswald did not kill Kennedy, he would have no motive to kill Tippit.

Officer Tippit was one of the few Dallas Police officers who were not called to Dealey Plaza to aid in the assassination investigation that day. At 12:44 p.m., the radio dispatcher ordered all police cars downtown to report to Elm and Houston for a Code 3 emergency. At 12:45 p.m., the dispatcher ordered Officer Tippit to move into the central Oak Cliff area. The reasons for this are not clear. At 1:16 p.m., Officer Tippit approached a man walking along East 10th Street. Reports vary as to exactly what happened, but Tippit was shot dead and the killer, or killers, escaped.[269]

This is the exact description that was sent out to all Dallas Police officers:

> Attention, all squads, the suspect is believed to be a white male, age 30, 5 feet 10 inches, slender build, 165 pounds,

---

[269] *The Warren Commission Report*, p. 165, Longmeadow Press, 1964

armed with what is thought to be a 30-30 rifle. No further description or information at this time.[270]

That description could fit thousands of guys, except for the rifle. Tippit, or any cop at the time, would have been on the lookout for a man with a rifle. The killer in this case did not have any visible weapon on him, so there is no apparent reason for stopping him. It is strange that Tippit did not draw his gun on this alleged assassin, but instead seemed to engage him in light conversation.[271]

Oswald returned to his Beckley Street home right after the assassination. This was in the Oak Cliff section of Dallas. His landlady, Mrs. Roberts, said it was about 1:00 when he came in, and he only stayed briefly. About a minute after 1:00, Mrs. Roberts heard a car horn honk twice from the street in front of the house. She looked out the window and saw a Dallas Police patrol car parked outside. She claimed that two uniformed officers were seated in it. A few minutes later, Oswald came hurrying out of his room, zipping up a light jacket. He left the house, and walked to a nearby bus stop. Mrs. Roberts last saw him standing at the bus stop, waiting for a northbound bus. At this point it was a few minutes past 1:00. Researchers have established that the only patrol car in the area was that of Officer Tippit, who was murdered a few minutes later, about a mile from Oswald's home.

The Warren Commission claimed to have nine witnesses who positively identified Oswald as Tippit's killer. Only two of them were eyewitnesses who saw the shooting, and seven others only witnessed the escaping of the suspect. Some had already seen Oswald's picture in the paper, then they picked him out of a line-up. Those who did witness the shooting expressed uncertainty at first, then picked out Oswald.

Helen Markham was considered the star witness for the Warren Commission. She saw the shooting and identified the killer as "short, a little on the heavy side," and with "somewhat bushy hair." That description does not fit Oswald at all, yet she picked Oswald out of a police line-up and identified him as the culprit. Markham changed her story several times, and seemed to be overdramatizing her descriptions. She is generally considered not credible among researchers.

---

[270] Ventura, Jesse, *They Killed Our President*, p. 130, Skyhorse Publishing, 2013
[271] http://spartacus-educational.com/JFKtippet.htm

Another of the commission's witnesses was Domingo Benavides. Benavides was present when Tippit was shot, and he was the one who used Tippit's car radio to call the police. Benavides told police he did not think he could identify the man. He later saw Oswald on television, and thought he bore a resemblance to the man who shot Tippit. Based on this, he was also one of the commission's top witnesses.[272]

Taxi driver William Scoggins was eating lunch in his cab when he saw a patrol car pull up to a man. He lost sight of them both, as some shrubs obscured his view. Scoggins did not see the shooting, but he heard three or four shots and saw the policeman fall. Then he saw the shooter run across the yard through some bushes. He identified Oswald in a line-up after seeing his picture in the paper.

Warren Reynolds did not see the shooting, but he saw the gunman running from the scene of the crime. In November of 1963, he said that the man was not Lee Harvey Oswald. On January 23, 1964, Reynolds was shot in the head, but he miraculously survived. Later, he changed his testimony and said that Oswald was Tippit's killer.[273]

William Arthur Smith had told the FBI that the escaping gunman had darker hair than Oswald's, yet he still chose Oswald from the line-up. Smith was on probation at the time. He told the Warren Commission that he did not give his name to the police that day for fear that it might hurt his probation record. That sounds suspicious right there. How could it hurt his probation record to help the police catch a cop-killer? Smith mentioned his experience to the son of witness Helen Markham, which is how the FBI found him.[274] They may have used his probationary status as leverage to get him to identify Oswald as the killer.

Contrary to the Warren Report, no witness has made a reliable identification of Oswald as Tippit's killer. The witnesses who did identify him picked him out of a police line-up which was conducted unfairly. Most likely, there was an Oswald look-alike at work here, which would account for the mistaken identifications. Chances are that Oswald was instructed to go home and put on a light-colored jacket after the assassination. This was to match the jacket of Tippit's true killer, thus confusing the identification.

---

[272] Marrs, Jim, *Crossfire*, pp. 341-342, Carroll and Graf, 1989
[273] Groden, Robert J., *The Search for Lee Harvey Oswald*, 1995
[274] https://www.jfk-assassination.com/warren/wch/vol7/page84.php

There were six witnesses who claimed that Oswald was shot by two men. None of these witnesses were called before the Warren Commission. Acquilla Clemons and Frank Wright were among those who claimed that two men shot Tippit. Clemons said that the two men ran in opposite directions.[275]

It appears that Tippit was shot by two men. One of them resembled Oswald and wore a similar jacket. The two men ran opposite ways, with the Oswald look-alike throwing shells in the air so police and witnesses would find them. The four shells matched Oswald's pistol, but none of the bullets recovered from Tippit's body matched.[276]The Oswald look-alike then headed to the Texas Theater to continue the frame-up. It's possible that it was the double who entered the theater without paying.

Officer Tippit was shot with an automatic handgun; Oswald's gun was a revolver. According to the Warren Commission, the cartridge cases found at the scene of Tippit's murder "were fired from the revolver in the possession of Oswald at the time of his arrest, to the exclusion of all other weapons." The commission's statement has no basis in fact. Dallas Police Sergeant Gerald Hill responded to the call about Tippit's slaying. Hill radioed the dispatcher, saying, "The shells at the scene indicate that the suspect is armed with an automatic .38 rather than a pistol." When Oswald was arrested, he was in possession of a revolver. Automatic shells look completely different from revolver shells, and an experienced police officer like Sergeant Hill would certainly know the difference at a glance.

The Warren Commission found that the shell cases allegedly found at the scene of the crime did not match the slugs that were taken from Tippit's body. The four cases included two that were manufactured by Winchester-Western, and two by Remington-Peters. Of the bullets removed from Tippit's body, three were Winchester-Western and one was Remington-Peters. The Warren Commission tried to reconcile this by suggesting that maybe a fifth shot had been fired but not recovered. Yet, no witnesses heard more than four shots. They also speculated that there may have already been an expended Remington-Peters case in the revolver prior to

---

[275] Video- *Two Men in Dallas*, 1976
[276] Sprague, Richard E., *The Taking of America*, 1976

the shooting of Tippit, but this would not explain why only two Winchester-Western cases were found instead of three.[277]

Witness Domingo Benavides picked up two of the cartridge cases from the crime scene and handed them to Officer J.M. Poe. Poe marked the cases with his initials "JMP" before turning them over to the Dallas Crime Lab. In an FBI report, Poe had stated with certainty that he marked the cartridge cases. But six months later, when the FBI showed him the four .38 special cases which were allegedly used in the killing, Poe was unable to find his initials on any of them. The FBI reports state:

> (Poe) recalled marking these cases before giving them to (lab personnel), but he stated after a thorough examination of the four cartridges shown to him...he cannot locate his marks; therefore, he cannot positively identify any of these cartridges as being the same ones he received from Benavides.[278]

When Poe testified before the Warren Commission, he was no longer certain that he had marked the cases. When asked to identify the cartridges, he could only say, "I want to say these two are mine, but I couldn't swear to it." Poe's inability to identify the cases casts doubt on the whole case against Oswald being Tippit's killer. What happened to the cases with Poe's initials? Also, the cartridge cases were not turned over to the FBI until six days after the other evidence, which is further cause for suspicion. It appears that the cases had been substituted at some point. In a fair court of law, the cases would not be allowed as evidence.

The Warren Commission made an issue of Oswald's jacket. Many of the identifications of Oswald were based on his jacket, since not many of them got a good look at the suspect himself.

> When Oswald was arrested, he did not have a jacket. Shortly after Tippit was slain, policemen found a light-colored zipper jacket along the route taken by the killer as he attempted to escape.[279]

---

[277] Marrs, Jim, *Crossfire*, p. 343, Carroll and Graf, 1989

[278] Marrs, Jim, *Crossfire*, p. 343, Carroll and Graf, 1989

[279] *The Warren Commission Report*, p. 175, Longmeadow Press, 1964

Markham described the assailant as wearing a white jacket. Based on that description, the Dallas Police sent out a bulletin about the suspect. Later, a light-colored jacket was found by police under the rear of a car at a nearby service station. It was believed that the escaping gunman ditched the jacket to avoid being identified by it. This jacket was then used to try to incriminate Oswald. Whether or not the jacket found in the service station is the same one as in the Warren Commission exhibits is uncertain. The one found at the service station was white, as described by witnesses. Oswald's jacket was gray. The jacket shown by the Warren Commission as exhibit 162 was gray. According to the Dallas Police radio log, a white jacket was found at the service station. There is no record of who actually found the jacket. It appears to be another instance of evidence being planted or switched.

From the commission:

> There is no doubt, however, that Oswald was seen leaving his rooming house at about 1 pm wearing a zipper jacket, that the man who killed Tippit was wearing a light-colored jacket, that he was seen running along Jefferson Boulevard, that a jacket was found under a car in a lot adjoining Jefferson Boulevard, that the jacket belonged to Lee Harvey Oswald, and that when he was arrested at about 1:50 p.m., he was in shirtsleeves. These facts warrant the finding that Lee Harvey Oswald disposed of his jacket as he fled from the scene of the Tippit killing.[280]

The commission's star witness, Helen Markham, was shown Oswald's gray jacket, and was asked if she had seen it on the suspect. Markham replied, "No, I did not...that jacket is a darker jacket than that, I know it was."

Cab driver William Whaley allegedly drove Oswald home after the assassination. He claims that Oswald wore a gray jacket in the cab. But Oswald did not put on his jacket until he got home, as confirmed by his landlady, Mrs. Roberts. So how could Oswald have had the gray jacket on already in the cab? This seems like part of the set-up. It may have been the Oswald double who was in the cab, since the real Oswald probably took off in a Nash Rambler station wagon, as described by other witnesses.

---

[280] *The Warren Commission Report*, p. 176, Longmeadow Press, 1964

Witness Barbara Davis also failed to identify the gray jacket as the one worn by the killer. She told the commission that the jacket worn by the suspect was more of a "dark coat," with a "wool fabric...more of a sporting jacket."

Ted Callaway did not see the shooting, but he saw the escaping gunman. This was near the crime scene, and Callaway ran over to the fallen officer. Knowing he could do nothing for him, he got into a cab, possibly that of William Whaley, and gave chase to the suspect, but with no success. Callaway was shown the jacket that the Warren Commission claimed was Oswald's. Callaway did not positively identify the jacket, saying, "I thought it had a little more tan to it."[281]

The role of J.D. Tippit in all of this is not clear. Some researchers believe that he was part of the assassination plot, and had to be eliminated for some reason. Maybe he knew too much, or maybe he screwed up somehow. Some believe it was his role to eliminate Oswald, but that went awry. Killing Tippit might have been Plan B. I think that ideally, the plotters wanted to kill Oswald as he left the TSBD. They could easily have shot him, claiming he had pulled a gun on a cop. Maybe Tippit was supposed to be that cop. But since Oswald escaped the TSBD alive, they had to resort to another option. By having Tippit murdered, it cements the notion of Oswald's guilt in the public mind.

At least five witnesses, all of who knew Tippit well, claim to have seen him at the GLOCO gas station at the north end of the Oak Cliff area at 12:45. That is the time when the first reports of the assassination suspect went out over the police radio. Oswald was not mentioned by name. At 12:55 Tippit suddenly took off down Lancaster at high speed. He reported to the dispatcher that he was "in the area of Keist and Bonny View," which was not true. He was next seen at the Top Ten record store, where he asked to use the phone. The store clerk stated that Tippit dialed a number, waited for several rings, then hung up and left. This was at about 1:00, the time when a police car stopped at Oswald's house and honked the horn twice, according to Oswald's landlady. This seems to indicate that it was not Tippit in that squad car.

At about 1:02, Jim Andrews was driving west on West 10th St. when a police car pulled him over to the curb. Andrews noticed the officer's badge,

---

[281] Marrs, Jim, *Crossfire*, pp. 345-346, Carroll and Graf, 1989

which said "Tippit." Tippit scanned the inside of Andrews' car as if he were trying to find someone or something. Without saying a word, Tippit got back into his squad car and took off. Andrews described Tippit as "very upset (and) agitated," and "acting wild."

The actions of J.D. Tippit appear suspicious. He was away from his usual patrol area and he misrepresented his location. He missed at least two radio calls that day, which is a serious offense for a police officer. He seemed anxious and rushed to those who saw him. He gave every indication of a worried person desperately searching for someone.

Also of suspicion are the actions of off-duty police officer Harry Olsen. Olsen was on foot that day, and he was seen in the area of the Tippit slaying. He claimed he was guarding a house for an elderly woman. Yet, he could not remember who owned the house, who referred him for the job, or the address of the property. Olsen testified to the Warren Commission, but requested that much of his testimony be deleted. Some of his testimony is still sealed today, for reasons unknown. Incidentally, Olsen was a good friend of Jack Ruby, and Olsen's girlfriend, Kathy Coleman, was a dancer at Ruby's Carousel Club.[282]

James Files knew Oswald, and he knows that Oswald did not kill Tippit. Files was the alleged grassy knoll shooter, and his interviews will be discussed more in Chapter 6. In his most recent interview in 2003, Files said that he knows who killed Officer Tippit, but he will not reveal his name because he was still alive at that point in time. Files has never given up a living person. He will only talk about another person's crimes after that person is deceased. Here is a portion of Files' first taped interview in 1994:

> JF: The man that killed J.D. Tippit is still alive. He was alive as of three years ago. I haven't talked to him in the past three years. Lee Harvey Oswald did not kill J.D. Tippit, because the man that killed a police officer that afternoon had come by my motel and told me...he said that things got messed up today he said "and I killed a cop"...and my remark to that was "Well, you did what you had to do," and he left shortly thereafter.

---

[282] Hughes-Wilson, Col. John, *JFK: An American Coup Detat*, pp. 213-214, John Blake Publishing, 2015

Q: So then there was one other person that was part of the team other than you, Nicoletti and Roselli?

JF: The person that I am referring to now was not a part of the team to assassinate JFK...as far as I know his job would have been to kill Lee Harvey Oswald from what I understood without asking any direct questions because I did not want to know what anyone else was doing. All I wanted to know was what my assignment was, what I was to do, and the least I know about other people, the better off I am, because I didn't want very many people knowing who I was or what I'm doing .

Q: Would you have known who would have given him orders to kill Officer Tippit?

JF: No, I would not, because that contract would have come from a different source.[283]

In his second recorded interview in 2003, Files talked about the Tippit shooting again:

JF: The Tippit killing is related to Oswald, because Oswald is the one who was supposed to die, not Tippit. Tippit was just one of those people who stopped the wrong person, that got called into the wrong place.

Q: So the party that killed Tippit was actually after...

JF: He was after Lee Harvey Oswald

Q: Okay, make a statement.

JF: Okay. The party that killed J.D. Tippit , he wasn't there to kill J.D. Tippit. He had parked a little ways from Oswald's boarding house. They went down there to kill Oswald. They wanted to kill Oswald. They didn't want to make a big spectacle out of it. They wanted to silence him at that point of the game, before anybody could get to him. But I guess, I don't know if Lee got spooked or whatever it was, but then he went to the theater. And he knew who he was going to when he left there, because he was supposed to meet the controller there, which is David Atlee Phillips. He

---

[283] Video- *Confessions of an Assassin*, 1994

was the one who was supposed to be at the theater as far as I understand…

… My understanding was that Lee, that he was gonna meet his controller, which is David Phillips, who was my controller. He was gonna meet him. I didn't know it was gonna be at the theater. I have no knowledge of that at that point. But if Lee Harvey Oswald ran to a theater, that had to be where the meeting was going to take place. Lee must have left his house earlier or for whatever reason, I don't really know, but the party that went there didn't find Lee there. And when he started to leave, he was stopped by the police. This is when he shot Tippit. What transpired there, I can't tell you, who saw this guy there. I can't tell you whether he ran, I can't tell you whether he walked, I don't know. All I understand is this: A party that I know, that had come to my motel room, told me he had to burn a cop. The cop he burned was J.D. Tippit. That was the only cop burned in Dallas that day. It had to be the one that he burned…

Q: So this party that shot Tippit, he was more connected to the agency than the mob?

JF: To the agency. He wasn't tied to the mob. He might have done some work for them along the way, but he was strictly one of David Phillips' people. Because he did not even know Charles Nicoletti.[284]

Files said that this party was on stand-by and was brought in at the last minute by the agency. That seems to imply that this was not the original plan. They probably wanted to kill Oswald at the TSBD. When that didn't work, they sent an extra man over to his house to find him. Oswald had left his house by that time. The predator then walked the streets aimlessly and must have looked suspicious for some reason. That's when Tippit stopped him. It sounds like the party must have panicked, because by all accounts it started with a casual exchange. None of the witnesses described a heated argument or any kind of shouting. Officer Tippit got out of his car and calmly approached the man. Tippit did not have his gun drawn, so he was not expecting trouble. What happened after that is a mystery.

---

[284] Dankbaar, Wim, *Files on Files*, pp, 206-207, Trafford Publishing, 2005

According to Tippit's wife, Marie, Tippit had been ordered to be on the lookout for Oswald. She was told this by his fellow police officers. Waitress Mary Dowling had seen Oswald and Tippit in a restaurant two days earlier, although they did not sit together. This means that Tippit and Oswald may have had some contact prior to the assassination.[285]

Oswald's Arrest

Supposedly, the identification that led police to the Texas Theater came from Johnny Brewer, the manager of Hardy's Shoestore, located a few doors away from the theater. Brewer saw a man outside, and thought he was acting suspiciously. Brewer watched the man and saw him duck into the theater. He talked to the ticket seller, Julia Postal, who confirmed that the man did not buy a ticket. She then called the police. This was about 1:00, or shortly after.

Once inside, the man began acting strangely. He squeezed into a seat right next to witness Jack Davis. Davis thought this was strange, since the whole theater was almost empty. But the man only stayed seated for a moment. He got up quickly and sat next to someone else in the near-empty theater, and then next to someone else after that. Davis said he thought the man was looking for someone. Apparently he was sitting by each new person just long enough to look for a signal of some kind. If the man was Oswald, he could have been looking for his contact. There might have been a code word or hand signal of some kind that would identify him. If this man was not Oswald, then he is someone trying to set him up by looking like him and acting suspiciously. Whichever was the case, this man went out to the lobby. That is confirmed by the concession stand worker Warren Burroughs, who said he sold the man popcorn at about 1:15. The man then went back into the theater and continued his attempt to find his contact, if in fact that's what he was doing. He sat down next to a pregnant woman, who got up a few minutes later. It was at this point that the police came into the theater. According to Jack Davis, this was about 20 minutes after the man returned from the lobby. That seems about right. The man went to the lobby at 1:15, was back in his seat at 1:20- 1:25, and the arrest of Oswald was at 1:45.

---

[285] http://assassinationofjfk.net/looking-at-the-tippit-case-from-a-different-angle/

Bernard J. Haire was the owner of Bernie's Hobby House, which was just two doors away from the Texas Theater. When Oswald was arrested, Haire saw the police cars and the commotion in front of the theater. At this point, he did not know that President Kennedy had been shot. Haire walked through his store and out to the back alley. According to Haire, the alley was also filled with police cars. He saw the rear door of the theater open, and the police emerged with a struggling suspect who was not Lee Harvey Oswald. The police put the suspect in the squad car and drove off. Haire learned about the assassination and the ensuing arrest later. He assumed it was Lee Harvey Oswald who he saw being arrested in the alley. It was 25 years later when Haire finally learned that Oswald had been taken out the front door, not the rear. The identity of the suspect taken out the back door remains unknown. "I don't know who I saw arrested," said Haire.

Burroughs said that Oswald came into the theater between 1:00-1:07, and that he bought popcorn at 1:15. Burroughs witnessed the arrest of Oswald in front of the theater, but then saw a second arrest just a few minutes later. In an interview with author James Douglas, Burroughs said that the police arrested "an Oswald look-alike." He said that the second man "looked almost like Oswald, like he was his brother or something." Douglas asked Burroughs if he could see the second man as clearly as he saw Oswald, Burroughs answered, "Yes, I could see both of them. They looked alike."[286]

So Haire and Burroughs have corroborated each other's stories. They both saw a man who they thought was Lee Harvey Oswald being arrested behind the Texas Theater. They both got a clear view of the man arrested in the alley, and they both said he looked like Oswald. Their time frames are consistent, too. They both claim that the arrest in the alley came a few minutes after the arrest in the front of the theater. So what became of the man arrested in the alley?

The DPD homicide report on officer Tippit reads:

> Suspect was later arrested in the balcony of the Texas
> Theatre at 231 W. Jefferson.[287]

Also, Dallas Police detective L.D. Stringfellow reported:

---

[286] Marrs, Jim, *Crossfire*, pp. 350-354, Carroll and Graf, 1989
[287] DPD Homicide Report on J.D. Tippit, November 22, 1963

> Lee Harvey Oswald was arrested in the balcony of the Texas
> Theater.

Both reports say that Oswald was arrested in the balcony of the theater. But Oswald was actually arrested on the ground floor. Who are these reports referring to? It's possible that the Oswald double was arrested in the balcony, and it could have been the double who was led out the back door. The real Oswald was probably inside the theater shortly after 1:00, as Burroughs said. The double entered the theater at about 1:30 or shortly after. That fits with the time frame of Tippit's murder at 1:15. The double's job was to lead police to the real Oswald. A deluge of police cars converged on the theater, so there were easily enough cops to make two separate arrests. Some officers were directed upstairs to arrest the double, whether they knew his identity or not. They may have been instructed to take the suspect out the back door. Certainly, the public could not be allowed to see two Oswalds being arrested. The double was probably released shortly after, with two arrest reports being combined into one.

The manner in which the police arrested Oswald was strange. The lights went on in the theater, and Officer M.N. McDonald and three other officers emerged from behind the movie screen. Oswald was sitting in the third seat from the rear on the ground floor. Johnny Brewer identified Oswald as the man he saw enter the theater without paying. Whether or not Oswald was really the man that Brewer originally saw is not clear, but he was the one that Brewer pointed out to the police. That may have been the reason for the jacket switch. In any case, the police did not immediately go toward Oswald. They walked slowly, and began searching other patrons as they walked toward him. It seemed that they were giving Oswald a chance to escape, or to at least try. That would give the police an excuse to shoot him. But Oswald made no attempt to escape. He waited calmly for the approaching officers. When McDonald and the others got near him, Oswald pulled out his pistol. The officers converged on him and wrestled the gun away. They arrested Oswald and led him outside to the squad car in front of the mob that had gathered.[288]

This is how the Warren Commission described the arrest of Oswald:

> Oswald then struck McDonald between the eyes with his left
> fist, with his right hand he drew a gun from his waist.

---

[288] https://ratical.org/ratville/JFK/Unspeakable/TwoLHOs.html#BB

McDonald struck back with his right hand and grabbed the gun with his left hand. They both fell into the seats. Three other officers, moving toward the scuffle, grabbed Oswald from the front, rear and side. As McDonald fell into the seat with his left hand on the gun, he felt something graze across his hand and heard what sounded like the snap of the hammer.[289]

According to the statements of Officer McDonald, Oswald not only resisted arrest, but he assaulted an officer. Worse than that, McDonald is saying that Oswald tried to shoot him. He claims that Oswald "drew a gun from his waist." Then he heard the "snap of the hammer." He said that Oswald was trying to fire the weapon, but it misfired. In a separate interview, McDonald said that his thumb got in between the hammer and the firing pin and prevented it from firing. Either way, it means that Oswald tried to kill a cop in the Texas Theater. If that's true, it was witnessed by not only McDonald, but also by the swarm of cops who were present. So why wasn't Oswald charged with trying to kill Officer McDonald? It would be an open-and-shut case, with half a dozen cops as witnesses. Certainly, at this early stage they could not have known if Oswald would be convicted on charges of killing Kennedy or Tippit. Collection of evidence had only begun. From what they knew at that point, Oswald might be acquitted, or the charges might be dropped. But if they charged him with attempting to kill Officer McDonald, that would be a sure conviction. Maybe the argument could be made that the gun wasn't pointed at a cop, but at the very least, they could have charged Oswald with assaulting an officer. This was witnessed by all the cops, and Oswald himself even admitted to striking an officer. Yet, no assault charges were filed. Why not? It seems that they were totally out to get Oswald, yet they let him off the hook on this.

Two Wallets

A wallet was supposedly found at the scene of J.D. Tippit's murder. This wallet is said to have contained identification for both Lee Harvey Oswald and Alik J. Hidell. A half-hour later, when Oswald was arrested, he allegedly had another wallet on him which contained identification in both names. Why would there be two wallets? The obvious reason for planting a wallet at the scene of Tippit's murder would be to incriminate Oswald. But the

---

[289] *The Warren Commission Report*, p. 178, Longmeadow Press, 1964

plotters must have gotten their signals crossed, because two wallets with the same identification looks extremely suspicious.

The "arrest wallet" was kept in the Dallas Police Department property room until it was turned over to the FBI. The "Tippit scene" wallet was kept in Captain Fritz's desk. On November 25, Oswald's possessions were returned to the Dallas Police from Washington. The FBI inventory listed two wallets, but neither of them was originally from the Dallas Police. Instead, the FBI claimed that the wallets were found at Ruth Paine's house, where Oswald and his wife had stayed. Neither wallet was listed on the original Dallas Police inventory, and neither wallet was initialed by Dallas Police. That makes a ridiculous total of four wallets to account for. On November 27, FBI agent James Hosty picked up the "Tippit scene" wallet from Captain Fritz and sent it to the Washington FBI office, never to be seen again.[290]

Detective Paul Bentley was the one who took the wallet out of Oswald's pocket in the Texas Theater and examined it, yet he never mentioned the Hidell alias in his report or to the press. None of the other officers present ever mentioned the name Alik Hidell in their police reports, either. When the arrest was announced to the public, only the name of Lee Harvey Oswald was given. The name of Alik Hidell was not mentioned to the public until it was discovered that the alleged murder weapon had been purchased under that name.[291]

The first officer to arrive at the Tippit murder scene was Sergeant Kenneth H. Croy. Croy claims that an unknown man handed him the wallet as soon as he arrived, yet no other witnesses at the scene saw a wallet there.[292] It appears that the wallet at the Tippet scene was planted to frame Oswald. It just seems much too convenient that a murderer would drop his identification at the scene of the crime. Where did it come from if no witnesses saw it laying there? Croy attributed the discovery of the wallet to an "unknown man." That is ridiculous, because if someone was at the scene of the crime and found a wallet there, that person would be a significant witness in the case. The police would naturally get his name and contact information. Why would an experienced police officer let such an important

---

[290] https://www.jfkassassinationforum.com/index.php?topic=5103.0

[291] http://readersupportednews.org/opinion2/277-75/33005-the-murder-of-jfk-part-2-counterfeit-id-planted-in-oswalds-wallet

[292] http://jfkfacts.org/oswalds-wallet-planted-at-the-tippit-crime-scene/

witness get away? Either Croy planted the wallet or it was given to him by an accomplice.

Since the Hidell alias was not mentioned by any of the Dallas Police officers on the day of the assassination, it appears that Oswald did not have the Hidell identification on him at the time of his arrest. That makes sense, because Oswald never used the Hidell name in his everyday life, and he did not have the Hidell ID on him when he was arrested in New Orleans three months earlier. The Hidill ID was probably taken out of the "Tippit scene" wallet and placed in Oswald's wallet after his arrest.

Murder of Lee Harvey Oswald

On Sunday morning, November 24, at 11:21 a.m. CST, Lee Harvey Oswald was being transferred from the Dallas Police Headquarters to a nearby County Jail. Strip club owner Jack Ruby stepped out from a crowd of spectators and shot Oswald in the stomach. Oswald died shortly afterwards.

Ruby's motive was said to be revenge for killing Kennedy, but that makes no sense at all. This was less than 48 hours after Kennedy was shot. It was much too soon to know if this was the real killer or not. There was far too much uncertainty at that point. Ruby was not a big fan of Kennedy, anyway, so why would he care to avenge his death? After his arrest, Ruby said he wanted to spare Jackie Kennedy from having to come to Dallas to testify. It is far-fetched to say that he did it for Jackie Kennedy, but he was playing on the public's emotion. Since Jackie was well-liked and people naturally sympathized with her, Ruby looked like a hero for sparing her from suffering, while at the same time slaying her husband's killer. What was his real motive for killing Oswald? He probably owed a debt of some kind to the mafia, and it was agreed that killing Oswald would effectively pay off that debt.

The Warren Commission concluded that Jack Ruby acted on his own. They said this was a spontaneous act. They also concluded that Oswald and Ruby did not know each other. They said they found no connection between Ruby and organized crime. None of that was true.

Ruby had to have help getting into the Dallas Police Station. The entrances to the basement were closed to the public, and only those with press credentials or proper clearance were allowed in. How did Ruby get in? He claims to have entered by the Main Street ramp. But if that were true, he would have had to pass through one of the five doors into the basement. According to police testimony, all of those doors were secured.

The commission believed Ruby, yet they expressed doubt about one of the doors:

> Although the sum of the available evidence tends to support Ruby's claim that he entered the Main Street ramp, there is other evidence not consistent with Ruby's story. If Ruby entered by any other means, he would have had to pass through the Police and Courts Building, and then secondly through one of the five doors into the basement, all of which, according to the testimony of police officers were secured.[293]
>
> Despite the thoroughness with which the search was conducted, there still existed one and perhaps two weak points in controlling access to the garage. Testimony did not resolve positively whether or not the stairway door near the public elevators was locked both from the inside and outside as was necessary to secure it effectively.[294]

So the commission believed it was possible that one of the basement doors may have been unlocked, yet they did not pursue the issue any further. This would have shown deliberate collusion by the Dallas Police, but it was written off as an oversight.

The HSCA found that Ruby could have entered the basement through an alleyway at the side of the building. A door opens from the alley to the ground floor of the building, and Ruby probably entered from that door. However, he would still have to get through one door that leads to the basement, and there is some question about whether or not that door was locked. Sergeant Patrick Dean was questioned about the door. Dean's testimony is not convincing. He keeps saying, "I believe," as if he's not sure. Dean said that he was told by a maintenance man that the door was locked from both sides. Dean was asked if he knew the maintenance man's name, and he answered that he did not. Dean's story cannot be confirmed. However, two other maintenance men and a porter claimed that the door could be opened without a key from Ruby's side.

---

[293] *The Warren Commission Report*, pp. 221-2, Longmeadow Press, 1964
[294] *The Warren Commission Report*, p. 212, Longmeadow Press, 1964

It seems strange that Dean, a police sergeant in charge of protecting a prisoner, would entrust an unknown maintenance man with the responsibility of confirming that the doors are locked.

Here are the HSCA's conclusions on the matter:

> ...Ruby's shooting of Oswald was not a spontaneous act, in that it involved at least some premeditation. Similarly, the committee believed it was less likely that Ruby entered the police basement without assistance, even though the assistance may have been provided with no knowledge of Ruby's intentions... The committee was troubled by the apparently unlocked doors along the stairway route and the removal of security guards from the area of the garage nearest the stairway shortly before the shooting... There is also evidence that the Dallas Police Department withheld relevant information from the Warren Commission concerning Ruby's entry to the scene of the Oswald transfer.[295]

Ruby probably did not enter the police station from the Main Street ramp. He took a less conspicuous route through an alley. He needed police assistance to ensure that the side door was not locked. Also, the HSCA noted the removal of security guards just before the shooting, which is undeniable collusion.

Jack Ruby knew most of the Dallas Police officers personally. He was on a first-name basis with them, and often visited them at the station, bringing them sandwiches and donuts. He welcomed them all into his Carousel Club free of charge, and he treated them like royalty. Police officers were never charged for anything at the Carousel Club- not drinks, food, or women. Ruby did everything he could to endear himself to the police, and to anyone in a position of power, for that matter. Since he crossed paths with gangsters on a daily basis, he knew he might need an inside connection at some point to help him get out of trouble. Ruby was involved in gambling, narcotics, prostitution, pornography, and gun running. Yet, the absence of convictions on his record shows that he had some kind of inside help.

Ruby's relationship to the mob and to the Dallas Police made him the natural candidate to eliminate Oswald. Ruby certainly knew his way around

---

[295] *HSCA Final Assassinations Report*, pp. 157–158, 1978

the police station. Both sides knew and trusted Ruby to get the job done, and since he was not a public official, it could be made to appear that he acted on his own.

The transfer of Oswald had been scheduled for 10 a.m., but Ruby was not ready yet. He had gotten a call from one of his dancers who needed money, so he told her he would go to the Western Union Station, which was only a block from the police station, and wire her the money. To explain the delay to the press, Chief Postal Inspector Harry Holmes arrived and said he needed to interview Oswald about his use of post office boxes. There was really no such need for the interview. It was just a stalling tactic to justify the delay while they waited for Ruby to be ready. There must have been a phone call or some kind of signal to the police that Ruby was ready to go, then the police brought Oswald out to be executed.

Ruby did not want to shoot Oswald. He was coerced or threatened into doing it by the mob. He tried to back out of it by tipping off the police. If Oswald was not transferred at the prearranged time, Ruby would be unable to shoot him and he could not be blamed for it. An unidentified male called the Dallas County Sheriff's office at 2:15 a.m. Sunday, warning that Oswald would be killed if they tried to transfer him. An unidentified male also called the Dallas FBI office at 2:30 a.m. with the same warning. Then at 3:00 a.m., presumably the same caller reached the Dallas Police Department. Dallas Police dispatcher Billy Grammer said that he received a telephone threat against Oswald the night before he was murdered. The caller did not identify himself, but he called the officer by name. This would be typical of Ruby, who knew all the Dallas Police officers personally and called them all by their first name. Ruby recognized Grammer's voice, but Grammer did not recognize Ruby's. The anonymous caller implored the police to change the plans for Oswald's transfer the next morning. The caller was urgent, saying, "We are going to kill him!" After Oswald was killed, Grammer then realized it was Ruby who made the call the previous night. "It had to be Ruby," he said.[296]

Yet, in spite of the three warnings, the police made no changes in their plans for Oswald. They could have transferred him in the middle of the night when there were no reporters or spectators around, but they didn't. They

---

[296] https://deeppoliticsforum.com/forums/showthread.php?16003-Jack-Ruby-Oswald-and-the-Murder-of-JFK#.WgUUYltSzcs

could have arranged for added security measures, but they didn't. In fact, they didn't even adhere to the usual security measures for protecting a prisoner.

The shooting of Oswald by Ruby can be viewed on YouTube.[297]You can see the way the police bring Oswald out into the hall. He is flanked by officers on both sides of him and there are officers behind him, but there are no police officers in front of him. When police are protecting a suspect in custody, especially in a high-profile and volatile case like this one, they surround him on all sides. They form a human shield around him. There is no such protection for Oswald. The large group of cops made it look like they were protecting him, but he was fully exposed from the front. This is practically an invitation to shoot him. The Dallas Police colluded to have Oswald killed. They knew Ruby was waiting. There is no other explanation for such a lack of protection. The police know the protection procedures, and it's not likely they all forgot at once.

But the authorization for the transfer may have come from a higher level. It's possible that the order came from Dallas Mayor Earle Cabell. Cabell's involvement is suspected by many. He was a known Kennedy-hater, and his brother, Charles Cabell, was former Deputy Director of the CIA, and was forced to resign by Kennedy after the Bay of Pigs. Cabell is likely to have pressured Chief Curry into making the transfer against normal procedures, which would have been for the Sheriff's Department to handle it. Several members of the Sheriff's Department thought it was strange that the Dallas Police handled the transfer instead of them.

Deputy Sheriff Bill Courson told a researcher:

> Very seldom did the Dallas Police Department transfer any prisoner to the county jail. I think it's a fact that Jesse Curry yielded to political pressure from Mayor Earle Cabell for the city to transfer Oswald. Normally that was a sheriff's department function.[298]

Deputy Sheriff Jack Faulkner also concurred:

---

[297] https://www.youtube.com/watch?v=r6PcVCqg3tg
[298] Douglass, James W., *JFK and the Unspeakable*, p. 489, Simon and Schuster, 2008

It was our normal procedure that we (the sheriff's department) transferred everyone after they filed on from the city hall.

When Chief Curry testified to the Warren Commission, he lied about the procedure:

I said (to Sheriff Decker), "If you want us to bring him, we will bring him to you." This is not an unusual procedure at all.[299]

Faulkner commented on Curry's testimony:

I understand that the Warren Commission asked Jesse Curry if it was the usual procedure for them to transfer prisoners to the county and he told them, "yes," which was a lie.[300]

Why did Curry lie to the commission about routine procedures? He was probably covering for Cabell. Saying that Cabell ordered the transfer would arouse suspicion, since the mayor is not usually directly involved in such decisions.

Cabell must have believed that the chances of killing Oswald were greater if the police made the transfer. Maybe there were more officers in collusion in the DPD. Maybe it was because Ruby had more contacts in the police department. Whatever the reason, the goal was to eliminate Oswald, and changing the procedure increased the likeliness of success. To further insure that success, Cabell kept Curry out of the transfer protection. Just as Curry was about to leave his office to escort Oswald out to the waiting vehicle, he got a phone call from Mayor Cabell. The call kept Curry in his office while Oswald was shot.[301]

Ruby and the Mob

William Abadie, a small-time bookie who briefly worked for Ruby, gave an interview to the FBI. According to Abadie:

…it was obvious that to operate gambling in the manner that he did, that he must have had racketeering connections with

---

[299] *The Warren Commission Report*, v.15, p.126, 1964
[300] Douglass, James W., *JFK and the Unspeakable*, p. 489, Simon and Schuster, 2008
[301] Groden, Robert J., *The Killing of a President*, p. 107, Penguin Books, 1993

other individuals in the city of Dallas, as well as Fort Worth, Texas…(This) applied also to police connections with the two cities.[302]

Abadie also said that he had observed many policemen coming and going while he served as a bookie for Ruby. This could have been a ploy by Ruby. If police officers have engaged in illegal activities, then Ruby could use that as leverage someday when he is in trouble. He introduced them to prostitutes for the same reason. There were probably many instances when Ruby used blackmail to stay out of prison.

Another big-time gambler, Jack Hardee, was interviewed by the FBI in December of 1963. He told agents that if someone wanted to set up a numbers game in Dallas, it would be necessary to get the approval of Ruby, since any arrangement with the local authorities would have to come through him. This means that the police would take bribes to look the other way, and since Ruby was the middleman, he made sure to get his piece of the action.[303]

In a similar way, Ruby was also involved in narcotics dealing. Ruby was part of a large narcotics ring operating in Mexico, Texas, and the east. He was a contact for James Breen, and has been identified as such by Breen's girlfriend. Breen was probably only one of many dealers who interacted with Ruby. Dallas was Ruby's domain. No drug dealer could operate there without Ruby's approval, and his approval had a price. Suppose there are ten drug dealers operating in the area. Nine of them give Ruby a kickback and one doesn't. Ruby would then call the cops to squeal on the one stingy dealer, who would then get busted. Ruby is a hero for helping to nab a notorious drug dealer. Forget about the nine he helped get away.

J. Edgar Hoover had notified the Warren Commission that Jack Ruby was an informant for the FBI. A three-page letter was found in the National Archives from Hoover to J. Lee Rankin, and was dated June 9, 1964. In 1959, Ruby had met with Special Agent Charles W. Flynn on eight occasions from March 11 through October 2. Agent Flynn had initiated the contact. Ruby

---

[302] https://www.history-matters.com/archive/jfk/wc/wcvols/wh23/pdf/WH23_CE_1750.pdf
[303] Benson, Michael, *Who's Who in the JFK Assassination*, pp. 170-171, Citadel Press, 1993

had expressed a willingness to provide information, but according to Flynn, "no information or other results were obtained."

> Certain information regarding the contact of Special agent [*sic*] Charles W. Flynn with Jack L. Ruby on March 11, 1959, is herewith acknowledged. The purpose of this contact was to determine whether or not Ruby did have such knowledge, and if so, if he would be willing to furnish information to this bureau. A personal description of Ruby was obtained by Special Agent Flynn on the occasion of this contact on March 11, 1959, but no information or other results were obtained.[304]

It's hard to believe that Ruby furnished no information in eight meetings with the FBI. The letter mentions that Ruby was an FBI informant because his position as a nightclub owner brought him in contact with the underground. He probably furnished a wealth of information to the FBI. Like so much else, the commission felt that this letter had to be suppressed, so it was not included in the final report.

It's likely that Ruby was also an informant for the Dallas Police. He was in contact with the criminal element on a daily basis. Ruby was also a police buff, and he knew all the local cops personally. Being around cops and criminals all the time, it would seem natural that Ruby would act as an informant.

Jack Ruby was allowed to speak at a news conference. Here is a sampling of his statements:

> Ruby: Everything pertaining to what's happening has never come to the surface. The world will never know the true facts, of what occurred, my motives. The people that had so much to gain and had such an ulterior motive for putting me in the position I'm in, will never let the true facts come above board to the world.

> Reporter: Are these people in very high positions Jack?

---

[304] http://jfk.hood.edu/Collection/Weisberg%20Subject%20Index%20Files/ T%20Disk/Tattler%20National/Item%2005.pdf

Ruby: Yes.[305]

Those statements are loaded. Remember that the Warren Commission found no conspiracy, and that Oswald and Ruby each acted alone. Then what is meant by "The world will never know the true facts...my motives"? That right there tells us there's a whole lot more to this story than we've been told. Then Ruby mentions "the people." Who are "the people"? The mere fact that that word is plural denotes conspiracy. Ruby is telling the reporters about the biggest conspiracy of all time, yet the truth was still known by relatively few.

Other quotes by Ruby:

> Gentlemen, I want to tell the truth, but I cannot tell it here. If you want a fair shake out of me, you have to take me to Washington.

Ruby feared for his life in Dallas. He knew he would be killed if he spoke out. He said he would be more willing to talk in Washington, but he was never taken there. Warren responded to Ruby's plea by saying, "If you don't think it is wise to talk, that's okay." Why is it okay to not talk? This was supposedly an investigative body.

Also from Ruby:

> When I mentioned about Adlai Stevenson, if he was vice president there would never have been an assassination of our beloved President Kennedy...Well the answer is the man in office now.

Here, Ruby has overtly fingered Lyndon Johnson in the murder of John Kennedy. He said, "The man in office now" is responsible. Who could he mean other than LBJ?

Ruby told the Warren Commission:

> Well, you won't see me again. I tell you that a whole new form of government is going to take over the country, and I know I won't live to see you another time.[306]

---

[305] http://www.jfkmurdersolved.com/ruby.htm
[306] http://www.jfkmurdersolved.com/ruby.htm

"A whole new form of government" does not mean democracy. It means the assassination was a coup d'etat.

While Ruby was in jail, he wrote a letter and discreetly handed it to Dallas Deputy Sheriff Al Maddox as they shook hands. Ruby told Maddox "If you will keep your eyes open and your mouth shut, you're gonna learn a lot."

From the letter:

> ...you must believe me that I know what is taking place, so please with all my heart, you must believe me, because I am counting on you to save this country a lot of blood-shed. As soon as you get out you must read "A Texan Looks at Lyndon," and it may open your eyes to a lot of things. This man is a Nazi in the worst order... isn't it strange that Oswald who hasn't worked a lick most of his life, should be fortunate enough to get a job at the Book Building two weeks before the president himself didn't know as to when he was to visit Dallas, now where would a jerk like Oswald get the information that the president was coming to Dallas? Only one person could have had that information, and that man was Johnson who knew weeks in advance as to what was going to happen, because he is the one who was going to arrange the trip for the president, this had been planned long before the president himself knew about, so you can figure that one out. The only one who gained by the shooting of the president was Johnson, and he was in a car in the rear and safe when the shooting took place. What would the Russians, Castro or anyone else have to gain by eliminating the president? If Johnson was so heartbroken over Kennedy, why didn't he do something for Robert Kennedy? All he did was snub him.[307]

In 1959, Jack Ruby made two trips to Cuba. At the time, the island nation had just been taken over by Fidel Castro. The mob had supplied Castro with arms for his revolution. This was before Castro had established a communist regime and closed down the casinos owned by the mob. Ruby was an instrumental part of the gun-running operation for the mafia. This operation was under the jurisdiction of mob boss Santos Trafficante. Ruby's involvement has been confirmed by several witnesses, including FBI

---

[307] http://jfkmurdersolved.com/ruby.htm

informant Blaney Mack Johnson. Johnson said that Ruby arranged for illegal flights of weapons to Castro. While in jail, Ruby wrote a letter to an unnamed friend. In the letter, he described how he broke down under stress and admitted to a guard that he had sent guns to Cuba. Unbeknownst to Ruby, the guard was wearing a bugging device, further adding to Ruby's paranoia.

The gun-running operation was shaken when its leader was arrested in connection with a Canadian bank robbery. Norman Rothman was an associate of Santos Trafficante and managed his casinos in Cuba. It was Rothman who oversaw the gun-running on behalf of Trafficante. Rothman was connected with a theft of arms from an Ohio National Guard armory, which was linked to the bank robbery by investigators. Authorities believed it was part of a huge gun-running operation.[308]

A significant player in all of this was Lewis J. McWillie. McWillie was involved in gun running, drug smuggling, and contract hits. He was also a big-time gambler and operated top gambling establishments in the U.S. and Cuba. He was also under the rule of Santos Trafficante, and worked with Rothman in the arms smuggling. McWillie was an idol of Jack Ruby. Ruby expressed his sentiments to the Warren Commission:

> I idolized McWillie. He is a pretty nice boy and I happened
> to be idolizing him...I always thought a lot of him...I have a
> great fondness for him.[309]

The Warren Commission never called McWillie to testify. Instead, they simply stated that they found no evidence of anything connecting McWillie to Ruby or Castro. McWillie's mob connections were never mentioned. The commission accepted Ruby's claim that his trips to Cuba were purely social.

The HSCA admitted what the Warren Commission would not. G. Robert Blakey explains:

> ...we established beyond reasonable doubt that Ruby lied
> repeatedly and willfully to the FBI and to the Warren
> Commission about the number of trips he made to Cuba and
> their duration...It was clear, for example, that the trips were
> not social jaunts; their purpose, we were persuaded, was to

---

[308] Marrs, Jim, *Crossfire*, p. 392-3, Carroll and Graf, 1989
[309] Marrs, Jim, *Crossfire*, p. 393, Carroll and Graf, 1989

courier something, probably money, into or out of
Cuba…the evidence indicated strongly that an association
(with Trafficante) existed and that Ruby's trip was related to
Trafficante's detention and release. We came to believe that
Ruby's trips to Cuba were, in fact, organized-crime
activities.[310]

By "detention and release" they are referring to the fact that Trafficante
was imprisoned by Fidel Castro. Castro probably made some kind of
agreement with Trafficante for his freedom, and Ruby was a courier to fulfil
that agreement.

Jack Ruby's phone records have been analyzed by investigators. In the
days and weeks leading up to the assassination, the number of calls made
by Ruby increased dramatically. Many of the calls were made to, or received
from, known organized crime figures. The list included Barney Barker, Dusty
Miller, Lenny Patrick, Dave Yaras, Lewis McWillie, Irwin S. Weiner, and Nofio
Pecora. He was also known to have made contact with Santos Trafficante
and Carlos Marcello.[311]

The Warren Commission collected some of Jack Ruby's phone records,
but failed to carry out a proper analysis of them, supposedly due to limited
time and resources. J. Lee Rankin vetoed a request for the rest of the
records, saying that a full analysis of them would be too burdensome and
far-reaching.[312] They recklessly concluded that Ruby acted alone and that
the mafia played no role. The HSCA did analyze the records and noted the
calls to underworld figures, which should be conclusive proof of Ruby's
connections with organized crime. Ruby explained that the calls were in
relation to labor problems he was having. The committee bought it, and in
their final report, the HSCA concluded that "the national syndicate of
organized crime, as a group, was not involved in the assassination of
Kennedy."[313]

On March 20, 1964, Warren Commission assistant counsels
Leon Hubert and Burt Griffin sent a memo to General
Counsel J. Lee. Rankin, stating, "The most promising links

---

[310] Blakey and Billings, *The Plot to Kill the President*, pp. 293-4, Times Books, 1981
[311] Michael Kurtz, *Crime of the Century*, 1982
[312] https://groups.google.com/forum/#!topic/alt.assassination.jfk/dtsXDIoefYQ
[313] http://jfkcountercoup.blogspot.com/2013/01/oswald-and-ruby-phone-records-rfk-jr.html

between Jack Ruby and the assassination of President Kennedy are established through underworld figures and anti-Castro Cubans, and extreme right-wing Americans."[314]

Ruby, Nixon, and Johnson

A 1947 FBI document has come to light. The document, signed by staffer "L.S.," shows a connection between Jack Ruby and Richard Nixon:

> It is my sworn statement that one Jack Rubenstein of Chicago, noted as a potential witness for hearing of the House Committee on Un-American Activities, is performing information functions for the staff of Congressman Richard Nixon, Republican of California. It is requested that Rubenstein not be called for open testimony in the aforementioned hearings.[315]

This document shows that Jack Ruby worked for Richard Nixon in 1947. Is that proof of conspiracy? No, but it's one of those things that makes you go "Hmmmm."

Roger Stone, author of *The Man Who Killed Kennedy*, spoke with Nixon, who confirmed his affiliation with Ruby. Nixon said he recognized Ruby when he shot Oswald. In Stone's words:

> Nixon stirred. "It's a hell of a thing. I actually knew this Jack Ruby fella. Murray Chotiner brought him back in '47. Went by the name of Rubenstein. An informant. Murray said he was one of Lyndon Johnson's boys ...we put him on the payroll," Nixon's voice trailed off.[316]

So Jack Ruby was one of Johnson's boys, and LBJ encouraged Nixon to hire him. Lyndon Johnson knew Jack Ruby. Johnson's relationship with Ruby is unclear, but he knew him well enough to recommend him. Recall that Billie Sol Estes had stated that Johnson and Mac Wallace recruited Jack Ruby into the JFK plot, and Ruby in turn recruited Oswald. This was mentioned in the letter written by Estes' lawyer to the Justice Department. The world should be very interested to know this, but by now the world doesn't care

---

[314] http://jfkfacts.org/the-man-and-the-mobster-jack-ruby-and-santos-trafficante/
[315] http://www.jfkmurdersolved.com/nixonruby.htm
[316] Stone, Roger, *The Man Who Killed Kennedy*, pg. 18, Skyhorse Publishing, 2013

anymore. Those same revelations would have been earth-shattering years earlier.

Further evidence that Johnson knew Ruby comes from Madeline Duncan Brown, who was a mistress of Lyndon Johnson for 21 years. She claims to have met Jack Ruby through one of Johnson's lawyers, and she also visited his club:

> We were playing poker at the Carousel Club and Jack Ruby came over and he said 'you know what this is?' and I looked up....he had this motorcade route....it stung me that he would be this involved in knowing where the President of the United States was....at that time in my life I thought they were untouchable.[317]

She also claimed that Ruby was at the meeting at Clint Murchison's house the night before the assassination, when that same motorcade route was no doubt discussed in detail.[318]

In spite of overwhelming evidence to the contrary, the Warren Commission concluded that Ruby acted on his own and had no help from anyone. They blamed Oswald's murder on "the pressure of the press...for information," as well as "the acceptance of inadequate press credentials," and "the failure of the police to remove Oswald secretly or control the crowd in the basement." In other words, honest mistakes, but no conspiracy.[319]

Ruby Knew Oswald

Ruby and Oswald knew each other. The exact nature of their relationship is unclear. By all accounts, they were allies and friends, yet Ruby murdered Oswald in cold blood. There are many witnesses who had seen them together.

Beverly Oliver was a dancer at the Colony Club, next door to Jack Ruby's Carousel Club. Oliver frequently visited the Carousel Club on her breaks.

---

[317] https://www.prisonplanet.com/articles/august2006/300806jfk.htm
[318] Benson, Michael, *Who's Who in the JFK Assassination*, p. 61, Carol Publishing Group, 1993
[319] https://en.wikipedia.org/wiki/Warren_Commission

One night when she was there, she saw Jack Ruby sitting at a table with a dancer named Jada and another man.

> I sat down with them to have a drink. As I sat down at the table, Ruby introduced me to the man sitting there at the table with he and Jada, and he said, "Beverly, this is my friend, Lee," and after Jack Ruby went into the police station and killed Lee Harvey Oswald, it was then that I realized this was the man I had met in the club two weeks prior to the assassination of Kennedy. Lee Harvey Oswald and Jack Ruby were linked together, and I don't know how, and probably I never will. But I know in my heart that man, Lee Harvey Oswald, or the man who was shot in the basement of the police station, was the man that was in the club two weeks prior to the assassination. As a matter of fact, the next day, Jada gave an interview to the newspaper, and she said the same thing that I'm saying to you now, that she met Oswald two weeks prior to the assassination of Kennedy. However, unfortunate as it is, Jada is dead, or so they tell me.[320]

On another occasion, Oliver was told by Ruby that this was "Lee Oswald of the CIA." She also said she saw David Ferrie at Ruby's club. She said that Ferrie was there so often she thought he was one of the managers.[321]

Carousel Club emcee Bill Demar identified Oswald as a recent patron, and his story has been verified by patron Harvey Wade. Demar performed a magician-ventriloquist act at the club. He claims that Oswald had taken part in his "memory act":

> I have 20 customers call out various objects in rapid order. Then I tell them at random what they called out. I am positive Oswald was one of the men that called out an object about nine days ago.[322]

---

[320] Turner, Nigel, 1988, The Witnesses, *The Men Who Killed Kennedy*, U.K., Nigel Turner Productions
[321] http://garyrevel.com/jfk/Beverlyoliver.html
[322] *Los Angeles Times*, November 26, 1963.

Comedian Wally Weston also performed and emceed at The Carousel Club. He said that Oswald was in the club at least twice before his arrest.[323]

Karen Carlin, a.k.a. "Little Lynn," spoke to Secret Service Agent Roger Warner two days after the assassination. Warner gave his assessment of her statement:

> She was under the impression that Lee Harvey Oswald, Jack Ruby, and other individuals unknown to her, were involved in a plot to assassinate President Kennedy and that she would be killed if she gave any information to authorities.[324]

Carlin was shot to death in 1964 in Houston.[325]

Carroll Jarnigan, a Dallas attorney, saw Oswald and Ruby together in the Carousel Club on October 4, 1963. He told the FBI that he overheard them discussing plans to shoot Governor Connally.[326]

Madeleine Duncan Brown also confirmed that Ruby and Oswald were acquainted. In a 1988 interview, she said:

> In the fall of 1963 I was in the Carousel Club with other advertising people and Jack Ruby was saying that Lee Harvey Oswald had been in the club and he had been bragging that he had taken a shot at Major General Edwin Walker.[327]

Rose Cheramie was a stripper at Jack Ruby's club. She was found unconscious two days before the assassination and tried to warn officials about it. She claims to have heard the plans being discussed. No one believed her, but after the assassination, they were interested in talking to her. Cheramie said that she had met Oswald at Ruby's club. She said that Ruby and Oswald were good friends. She also claimed that the men who discussed the assassination plot were connected to Ruby.[328]

---

[323] *New York Daily News*, July 19, 1976

[324] Scheim, David E., *Contract on America*, p. 268., Shapolsky Publishers, Inc., 1988

[325] Benson, Michael, *Who's Who in the JFK Assassination*, p. 72, Citadel Press, 1993

[326] http://crimemagazine.com/did-jack-ruby-know-lee-harvey-oswald

[327] Benson, Michael, *Who's Who in the JFK Assassination*, p. 61, Carol Publishing Group, 1993

[328] http://22november1963.org.uk/was-jack-ruby-involved-in-jfk-assassination

Judyth Vary Baker knew both Oswald and Ruby, and she knew that they knew each other. The three of them took part in clandestine research for the CIA. Ruby was first introduced to Baker by the nickname "Sparky." Oswald already knew Ruby at that point and was present when Baker first met him. Judyth recalls asking Lee about Ruby:

> "Is this guy allowed to know about the lab?" I queried.
>
> "He brings money to help finance it," Lee said.

Not only was Ruby involved in the project, but he was an old friend of Oswald's. Referring to a joke Ruby had made earlier, Judyth recalls Ruby's words:

> "I thought you understood my jokes by now, Lee," Sparky mused. "You've known me long enough." Turning to me Sparky said, "I've known Lee ever since he was a little boy."[329]

When Jack Ruby began working for Carlos Marcello in Dallas, he attended parties hosted by Marcello. Oswald's mother, aunt, and uncle attended those parties. Oswald's uncle was Dutz Murret, who was tied to organized crime. Ruby remembers Lee Oswald as a child playing with other children at the parties. When Lee and his mother moved to Fort Worth, Lee's Uncle Dutz asked Ruby to keep an eye on Lee. "Watch over my boy Lee," Dutz told Ruby.[330]

Ruby said that he had tried to interest Oswald in working for Marcello, but Lee had already decided on a military and intelligence career. It was David Ferrie who recommended Oswald for intelligence training. "I did it because he knows how to keep his mouth shut," Ferrie said. Then Ferrie turned to Judyth and said, "It's okay, J., Sparky cares about Lee like a son. And he's a patriot, like Ochsner."

That's why Ruby didn't want to shoot Oswald. He had known him since he was a kid. That's why he called the Dallas Police Station to warn them of the plot to kill Oswald. He wanted them to change the transfer arrangements so he could not kill Oswald and he would not be blamed for it.

---

[329] Baker, Judyth Vary, *Me and Lee*, pp. 235-6, Trine Day LLC, 2010
[330] Baker, Judyth Vary, *Me and Lee*, pp. 235-6, Trine Day LLC, 2010

Stalking

Ruby was stalking Oswald. He was seen running from the TSBD while Oswald was still having his Coke. He was seen at the Texas Theater when Oswald was arrested. He was at the press conference at the police station when Oswald was allowed to talk briefly to reporters. The ideal situation for the plotters would have been to have Oswald killed immediately after Kennedy was shot. For some reason, it didn't work out like that, and so Ruby was given the assignment to eliminate Oswald.

George J. Applin was a patron at the Texas Theater that day. Applin witnessed the arrest of Oswald, and he told the police what he had seen. What he did not know at the time was that he had just spoken to the man who would become Oswald's killer. In Applin's words:

> Ruby was sitting down, just watching them. And when Oswald pulled a gun and snapped it at a policeman's head, and missed, and the darn thing wouldn't fire, that's when I tapped him on the shoulder and told him he had better move because those guns were waving around. He just turned around and looked at me, then he turned around and started watching them.

Applin did not mention Ruby to the police because Ruby was just a random stranger at the time. But after Ruby shot Oswald, Applin recognized him as the man he had spoken to at the Texas Theater. Applin testified to the Warren Commission about Oswald's arrest, but he made no mention of Jack Ruby. He did mention that he spoke with a stranger at the theater, but when asked, he did not identify the man as Jack Ruby. Later, he explained why:

> I'm a pretty nervous guy anyway, because I'll tell you what. After I saw that magazine that said all those people they said were kind of connected with some of this had come up dead, it just kind of made me keep a low profile.[331]

Later that night at the Dallas Police Station, Oswald was brought out in front of a room full of reporters. This was considered a press conference, although questioning was limited, and Oswald was only allowed to make a

---

[331] http://jfk.hood.edu/Collection/Weisberg%20Subject%20Index%20Files/ A%20Disk/Applin%20George%20Jr/Item%2001.pdf

brief statement. D.A. Henry Wade told the reporters that Oswald was a member of the Free Cuba Committee, which was wrong. He was corrected when someone called out, "Fair Play for Cuba Committee." The man who made the correction was Jack Ruby. Since Ruby was not a reporter, how did he even get into the secured room without press credentials? And how did he know the correct name of Oswald's organization?

It's possible that the press conference was held just to give Ruby an opportunity to shoot Oswald. Texas law at the time required that any person charged with a felony crime must be transferred from the city jail to the county jail within 12 hours. Oswald was charged with the murder of Officer Tippit at about 2:00 p.m. Friday, so Curry would have had to transfer him by 2:00 a.m. Saturday morning. It would have been harder to kill Oswald in the county jail, with tighter security and less known connections with Ruby, so Curry probably wanted to avoid the transfer. He put Oswald in front of a room full of reporters, which also included the armed Jack Ruby. Some officers had suggested to Chief Curry that Oswald should be placed behind a protective barrier, but Curry refused. Oswald was a sitting duck. It is not clear why Ruby didn't shoot Oswald during the press conference. Chief Curry broke the law for 36 hours after that by keeping Oswald in the city jail beyond the 12-hour limit.

It was during the press conference that Oswald was first informed that he had been charged with the murder of President Kennedy. At first he stated that he had not been charged, but then a reporter told him that he had been charged. Oswald was noticeably shaken by the news. It's interesting that as soon as Oswald heard this, he was whisked away by police officers so he could not talk anymore. It was probably feared that Oswald might start saying things he would not have otherwise said, now that he was officially the assassination suspect. It's also strange that a reporter informed him of this instead of a cop or a judge. Why hadn't they told Oswald that he was charged with Kennedy's murder? Oswald's sudden departure may have been the reason Ruby why didn't shoot him then.

Jack Ruby seemed to be everywhere that weekend. He was at Parkland Hospital shortly after Kennedy was shot. This was confirmed by reporter Seth Kantor. Kantor knew Ruby well, as Ruby had supplied Kantor with feature stories for his newspaper. They talked briefly at the hospital, each expressing grief for Kennedy's death. Yet, Ruby later denied this encounter to the Warren Commission. Kantor also gave his testimony to the commission, but they chose to believe Ruby instead. Kantor recalls the incident:

> An hour after the shooting of President Kennedy I encountered Jack Ruby at Parkland Hospital. Ruby was someone I had known at the start of the Kennedy administration, when I had been a reporter on a Dallas newspaper. He sought me out at Parkland, called me by name and, later from jail, wrote me a warm, personal note. But he later denied that he had been inside Parkland Hospital at that critical time. As a result, the Warren Commission questioned both Ruby and me in June, 1964, about the Parkland encounter. In the end, page 336 of the Warren Report declared that "Kantor probably did not see Ruby in Parkland Hospital."[332]

Since Ruby was Oswald's killer, they had to minimize any involvement of his. Ruby's presence at Parkland appears suspicious. The commission could not explain it, so they denied it. One possible reason for Ruby being at Parkland was to plant evidence. It's possible that he was the one who planted the magic bullet that mysteriously appeared on Connally's stretcher. Why else would he lie about being at Parkland? If he was there for some innocent reason, he could have just said so. Another possibility is that Ruby had to report to someone that Oswald escaped alive. From there, Ruby might have been given instructions to go to the Texas Theatre, either to kill Oswald or to watch him get arrested.

Ruby was seen in Dealey Plaza at the time of the shooting. This was confirmed by several witnesses, and there are pictures of a man who appears to be Jack Ruby standing in front of the TSBD. Reporter Wes Wise was one of the witnesses. Wise told fellow reporter Malcolm Couch that he saw Ruby walking around the side of the TSBD moments after the shooting. Wise was not called to testify before the Warren Commission.[333]

Jean Hill was another witness who said that she saw a man she thought was Ruby running from the TSBD to the grassy knoll. Recall that Hill had been roughly interrogated by two thugs who pretended to be federal agents. In her words:

---

[332] Kantor, Seth, *Who Was Jack Ruby?*, 1978
[333] Waldron, Lamar, *Legacy of Secrecy*, p. 206, Counterpoint, 2008

> ...Then I saw a man walking briskly in front of the Texas
> School Book Depository. He was the only person moving.
> Everybody else seemed to be frozen with shock. Because of
> my earlier thoughts, I became suspicious of this man and
> thought he might be connected with that truck I saw.[334]

When Hill saw Ruby's picture on TV after he shot Oswald, she immediately recognized him as the man she had seen running in Dealey Plaza. The truck that she referred to was a van that was parked in front of the grassy knoll before the motorcade arrived. She had noticed this van as she was waiting with a friend. The van said "Uncle Joe's Pawn Shop" on the side. Hill thought it was suspicious because this vehicle had been let into the area when no other vehicles were allowed to cross the police lines.

Another Ruby sighting was by Julia Ann Mercer. She also said she saw a vehicle parked near the triple underpass before the motorcade, but it was not the same one that Jean Hill saw. Mercer said that about 11 a.m. that day, she saw a green Ford pickup truck parked at the curb. She saw a man get out of the truck and remove something from the tool compartment on the side. It was a long bag, and Mercer said she could see the outline of a rifle in the bag. She said the man walked up the grassy knoll with the bag. Mercer must have gotten a good look at the man because she described him in detail. She said he was in his late twenties or early thirties, wearing a gray jacket, brown pants, a plaid shirt, and a wool stocking cap with a tassel. She also said that she saw three Dallas Policemen standing nearby. A policeman did confirm that the truck was there, but he thought it had broken down. As Mercer passed the parked vehicle, she got a good look at the driver. The next day, she was brought in to the sheriff's office where she was shown some photos of possible suspects. She picked out two that she recognized as the men in the truck. One of the photos was of Jack Ruby. When she saw the news coverage of the Oswald slaying the next day, she again recognized Ruby as the man she had seen in the truck. She said that the other man resembled Oswald. It's possible that this could have been the Oswald double that was seen repeatedly by witnesses.

Mercer was not called to testify before the Warren Commission. She gave sworn testimony to the FBI, but later said that her testimony was changed before it was given to the commission. According to Mercer, there were

---

[334] http://www.jfk-info.com/whitmey1.htm

three major changes. She had given a positive identification of Jack Ruby, but that was changed to say that she was unable to identify the driver. Second, her description of a plain green truck was altered to say that the vehicle said "Air Conditioning" on the side. Third, the date of the statement was changed from November 23 to November 29. That is significant, because then the commission can say that her identification of Ruby was influenced be her seeing his picture in the news. Worse yet, Mercer claims that a phony affidavit was created to correspond to the FBI's altered report. She said, "I never signed any such document. That affidavit is a crude forgery. That is not my signature."[335]

Victoria Adams saw a man outside the TSBD after the shooting. The man was asking questions of people in such a way that she thought he was an undercover policeman or a reporter. She later said the man was Jack Ruby.[336]

Another clue as to Jack Ruby's involvement comes from off-duty police officer Tom G. Tilson. Tilson and his daughter, Judy, were going downtown to pick up his other daughter who was watching the motorcade. As they approached the area, Tilson heard on his police radio monitor that Kennedy had been shot. He saw a man run down the slope on the north side of Elm Street, throw something into the trunk of a waiting black car, get into the car, and take off. Tilson thought it was very suspicious that everyone was running toward the scene of the shooting while this one man was running away from it. He gave chase and had his daughter write down the license number of the black car. As he caught up to the vehicle, he got a good look at the driver. He identified him as Jack Ruby. "If that wasn't Jack Ruby, it was someone who was his twin brother," said Tilson. He gave the information to the homicide bureau, but nothing ever came of it. Dallas Police radio logs for the day do not show any alert being sent out based on Tilson's descriptions.[337]

---

[335] http://jfk.hood.edu/Collection/Weisberg%20Subject%20Index%20Files/ T%20Disk/Truby%20J%20David/Item%2002.pdf

[336] Marrs, Jim, *Crossfire*, p. 325, Carroll and Graf, 1989

[337] https://groups.google.com/forum/#!topic/alt.conspiracy.jfk/N3vm811F67E

Ironically, Tilson had taken this day off, and his shift was covered by his good friend J.D. Tippit, who would be dead by early afternoon. A few days later, Tilson was a pallbearer at Tippit's funeral.[338]

Jack Ruby was deeply involved in the assassination plot, and so he had to be silenced. But it would look far too suspicious if he was simply shot, so it had to be done discreetly. Jack Ruby was murdered by cancer.

Judyth Vary Baker worked on a cancer research project designed to kill Fidel Castro by injecting him with cancer cells. (This is discussed further in Chapter 7). She worked on the project with Oswald and Ruby. Baker knew that Ruby's cancer was artificially induced. She described the process in a forum:

> The bioweapon is not well-described by my detractors. It must be accompanied by radiation and/or chemotherapy to be useful - and those adjunct forces could be manipulated. For example, I have a newspaper article stating Jack Ruby was placed in front of x-rays for forty-five minutes. Do you know what that kind of potential exposure would do to your immune system? It was destruction of the immune system that would allow strengthened cancer cells to survive and reproduce in the victim's body...[339]

Officially, Jack Ruby died of cancer on January 3, 1967. In reality, he was murdered by the bioweapon described by Baker. Ruby was injected by a prison physician, ostensibly for a cold, but he was certain that he was injected with cancer cells. He was given 45 minutes of radiation to destroy his immune system. Ruby's death is just one of many suspicious cancer deaths involving people related to the JFK assassination.

Dallas Deputy Sheriff Al Maddox recalls this encounter with Ruby:

> Ruby told me, he said, "Well, they injected me for a cold." He said it was cancer cells. That's what he told me, Ruby did. I said, "You don't believe that bull***t." He said, "I damn sure do!"[340]

---

[338] http://flyingtigercomics.blogspot.com/2013/01/julia-ann-mercer-her-real-testimony.html
[339] Baker, Judyth Vary, Assassination of JFK Forum, April 18, 2004
[340] https://en.wikipedia.org/wiki/Jack_Ruby

Ruby, Oswald and Tippit knew too much about the assassination plot, so they all had to be eliminated. The world would love to know what these individuals had to say.

6

EVIDENCE

Contrary to what you might have heard, there is no evidence at all that Lee Harvey Oswald killed John Kennedy. Any so-called evidence is either planted or fabricated. Many witnesses were coerced into changing their testimony. The obvious reason why Oswald was killed was because there was no chance of convicting him in a trial. There was zero evidence against him, and there could not be one honest juror who would have voted "guilty" in a fair trial.

After Oswald was arrested in Dallas, he was interrogated for a total of 12 hours over the next two days. During that time, there were no tape recordings made of the interrogation. No stenographer was present. Most of the notes taken have been destroyed. There is no official written record of what was said during those intense sessions of questioning. It definitely gives the impression that there was something to hide. The public would be interested to know what Oswald had to say. If there had been a trial, how could Oswald's statements be used as evidence? No one seemed to be concerned about that.

The actions of Police Chief Curry after the assassination are puzzling. He was at Parkland Hospital when the president was pronounced dead. But instead of heading back to the police department to help solve the crime of the century, he remained at Parkland with Johnson. It was not to protect him, since Johnson had the Secret Service with him. When Johnson left for the airport, Curry went along with him. The reason is not known. When they arrived at the airport, Johnson invited Curry to come inside, which he did. He spent 90 minutes sitting with Johnson while an assassin was roaming the streets of Dallas. Curry should have been looking for evidence or questioning suspects. What purpose did he serve by remaining with Johnson? It was at this time that his men were collecting evidence in the president's murder, but Curry was not with them. It's a safe bet that this was not his choice. Lyndon Johnson probably asked Curry to stay with him, ostensibly for protection, but in reality to impede the investigation by taking the Chief of Police out of the picture for a few hours.

In the absence of a legitimate investigation, the House Select Committee acknowledged that Oswald's guilt was a foregone conclusion. In a 1976 report, they stated:

> Almost immediately after the assassination, Director Hoover, the Justice Department, and the White House "exerted pressure" on senior Bureau officials to complete their investigation and issue a factual report supporting the conclusion that Oswald was the lone assassin.[341]

The evidence for Oswald's innocence is overwhelming.

The Zapruder Film

The single most convincing piece of evidence of Oswald's innocence is the infamous Zapruder film. You've probably seen it, and have been as horrified by it as anyone else. The film shows Kennedy riding in the open limousine, and being hit in the right temple by a shot from the right front. The shot drives him forcefully back and to the left. It is a known fact that Oswald was in the Texas School Book Depository (TSBD), which was behind Kennedy about 100 feet or so. So if Oswald is behind Kennedy, and the shot comes from the front, it could not have been fired by Oswald. That is absolute proof that the Warren Commission lied, since they concluded that Oswald shot Kennedy. They also claimed that there were no accomplices, so all shots must have come from behind. It is unfathomable how someone could see the Zapruder film and conclude that the shot came from behind.

Yet, the Warren Commission did:

> Based on the evidence analyzed in this chapter, the Commission has concluded that the shots which killed President Kennedy and wounded Governor Connally were fired from the sixth-floor window at the southeast corner of the Texas School Book Depository Building. Two bullets probably caused all the wounds suffered by President Kennedy and Governor Connally. Since the preponderance

---

[341] HSCA, *Final Report of the Select Committee to Study Governmental Operations*, 1976, Book V, p. 32.

of the evidence indicated that three shots were fired, the Commission concluded that one shot probably missed the Presidential limousine and its occupants, and that the three shots were fired in a time period ranging from approximately 4.8 to in excess of 7 seconds.[342]

The commission ignored the most obvious physical evidence. With our own eyes we see the shot hit Kennedy in the right temple. In frame 313 we see blood coming from his temple before any blood comes out the back of his head. That alone is physical proof of a shot from the front. Kennedy's backward movement is also proof. Obviously, if the shot had come from behind, it would have driven him forward.

Also in the film, we see Jackie Kennedy crawl onto the trunk of the limousine. The commission tried to say that she was signaling for agent Clint Hill to come and help, but that is not what we see in the film. The real reason she crawled onto the trunk was to retrieve a piece of her husband's head that had been blown off by the head shot. We can see that she grabs something, then gets back into the seat. As grotesque as it sounds, that is the truth of what happened. Jackie's reaction makes no logical sense, but was simply a reflexive response when she saw the top of her husband's head fly off. While sitting in the back seat on the way to the hospital, she was holding the retrieved piece of scalp onto his head, as if she could somehow fix it. She was heard saying, "I have his brains in my hands." When they arrived at Parkland, she handed the blood-covered scalp portion to a doctor.

Jackie recalls the moment as if she lived it in slow-motion:

> I could see a piece of his skull coming off. It was flesh-colored, not white. I can see this perfectly clean piece detaching itself from his head. Then he slumped in my lap.[343]

Second Floor Sighting

The next most significant proof of Oswald's innocence was his sighting on the second floor of the TSBD about a minute or so after the shooting. The Warren Commission claimed that Oswald shot Kennedy from the sixth floor of the TSBD. That is proven false by the testimony of two credible witnesses.

---

[342] *The Warren Commssion Report*, p. 117, Longmeadow Press, 1964
[343] Andersen, Christopher, *These Precious Few Days*, p. 15, Gallery Books, 2014

Officer Marion Baker was riding on his motorcycle as part of the motorcade security. He saw and heard shots come from the TSBD as he approached the building. He looked up and saw a rifle being drawn back into a window on the sixth floor. He pulled over to the curb and ran into the building. As he entered the building, he encountered Roy Truly, who was the building manager and Oswald's boss. The two started up the stairs to the sixth floor. But when they got to the second floor, they spotted Oswald standing alone in the lunchroom. The officer pulled his gun on Oswald, who must have been puzzled about this. Oswald did not yet know that Kennedy had been shot. Oswald stood there calm and relaxed, something that would have been hard to fake if he had really shot the president, and now a cop was holding a gun on him. Oswald was not nervous, shaking, stammering, or sweating. He also was not out of breath, as he would have been if he had just ran down four flights of stairs at full speed. He had apparently been in the lunch room for some time, and could not have fired the shots from the sixth floor. If Officer Baker had had any suspicion at all about Oswald, he would have arrested him, or at least held him for questioning. Truly told Baker that Oswald was an employee of his, and Baker was satisfied that Oswald was innocent. Baker and Truly are both credible witnesses with no reason to lie. Their testimony confirms Oswald's own story that he was in the lunch room at the time Kennedy was shot.[344]

As if the official story was not ridiculous enough already, the Warren Commission acknowledged that this escaping assassin had time to stop and buy a Coke:

> Within about 1 minute after his encounter with Baker and Truly, Oswald was seen passing through the second-floor offices. In his hand was a full "Coke" bottle which he had purchased from a vending machine in the lunchroom.[345]

The Warren Commission performed a re-enactment of what they claimed were Oswald's movements immediately after the shooting. They determined that it was possible for Oswald to have fired the shots, stashed the rifle behind some boxes, and made it down to the second floor lunchroom within about a minute and a half, which was the time interval between the shots and the Oswald sighting by Baker and Truly.

---

[344] Marrs, Jim, *Crossfire*, pp. 50-51, Carroll and Graf, 1989
[345] *The Warren Commission Report*, p. 6, Longmeadow Press, 1964

A series of time tests made by investigators and by Roy S. Truly and Patrolman M. L. Baker at the request of the Commission, show that it was possible for Oswald to have placed the rifle behind a box and descended to the lunchroom on the second floor before Patrolman Baker and Truly got up there. Oswald did not have a soft drink bottle in his hand at the time he was confronted by Baker and he was not standing by the soft, drink machine. He was just entering the lunchroom; Baker caught a glimpse of him through the glass panel in the door leading to the lunchroom vestibule.[346]

The commission bailed out on this. Their re-enactment was purely physical. They only said that it was physically possible for Oswald to have gotten down to the second floor lunchroom within the allotted time frame. They did not even address the two most important questions:

Why did Oswald stop on the second floor?

If Oswald had fired the shots, he would naturally have wanted to get out of the building as quickly as humanly possible. He would have been flying down the stairs like greased lightning, knowing that the place would be swarming with cops within minutes. For him, it would be a matter of life and death. So why would he stop when he got to the second floor? Was he that thirsty that he just had to stop and get a Coke? With his life hanging in the balance? Seriously? It sounds more like a bad commercial for Coke.

Why was Oswald not out of breath or nervous?

If Oswald had just ran down four flights of stairs at full speed, he would have been huffing and puffing and out of breath. That was not the case. It's true that Oswald was young and healthy, but even an Olympic sprinter would have been at least slightly winded at that point. Oswald was not out of breath, and he was completely unruffled by a cop pulling a gun on him. It is unlikely he could fool a cop by feigning innocence.

The Warren Commission did not even address these two critical questions, which shows that they had no real interest in uncovering the truth.

---

[346] *The Warren Commission Report*, p. 41, Longmeadow Press, 1964

Carolyn Arnold was a secretary in the book depository. She saw Oswald in the second floor lunchroom at about 12:15. She said that Oswald often came into her office to get change for the vending machine, so she recognized him. In Arnold's words:

> About a quarter of an hour before the assassination…about 12:15, it may have been later, I went to the lunchroom on the second floor for a moment…Oswald was sitting in one of the booth seats on the right-hand side of the room as you go in. He was alone as usual and appeared to be having lunch. I did not speak to him but I recognized him clearly.[347]

When she said "alone as usual," that implies that she has seen him many times before, so there is no mistaken identity here. Oswald was definitely in the lunchroom at 12:15, then was seen there again by Officer Baker and Mr. Truly at 12:31. It stretches the imagination to think that Oswald dashed upstairs, shot the president, then dashed back downstairs and was standing there calmly. It is far more likely that he was there all along. Also consider that the motorcade was scheduled to pass the TSBD at 12:25, and Oswald could not have known that it would be five minutes late. In fact, he would have to consider the chance that it might arrive early, and prepare accordingly.

Carolyn Arnold was not called to testify before the Warren Commission. In the FBI report concerning her statement, it reads "…she could not be sure that this was Oswald." Yet, Arnold was absolutely certain that this was Oswald. She knew the man and saw him clearly. She never gave any indication of uncertainty about it. But the Warren Commission ignored her and concluded that Oswald had been on the sixth floor since about 11:55 a.m.[348]

It might seem that the plotters would have wanted Oswald to be on the sixth floor at the time of the shooting, but that may not be true. If he was on the sixth floor, he may have seen the real shooters. They would try to avoid that, since the less Oswald knows, the better for them. He might become suspicious or start talking. All that was needed was for Oswald to be anywhere in the building at the time of the shooting. At some point, Oswald was told to wait for a phone call, which he believed would give him

---

[347] Marrs, Jim, *Crossfire*, p. 49, Carroll and Graf, 1989
[348] http://22november1963.org.uk/carolyn-arnold-witness-oswald

instructions. That kept Oswald in the building. If he had gone outside and been seen there, or worse yet, been photographed there, it would have blown the whole plot. So Oswald stood diligently by the phone, and was still there after Kennedy had been shot. The call, if it ever came, would have been from David Atlee Phillips, or whoever was in charge of manipulating Oswald's movements that day.

Captain Will Fritz recalled Oswald's explanation when he was interrogated:

> I asked him what part of the building he was in at the time the president was shot, and he said that he was having his lunch about that time on the first floor. Mr. Truly had told me that one of the police officers had stopped this man immediately after the shooting somewhere near the back stairway, so I asked Oswald where he was when the police officer stopped him. He said he was on the second floor drinking a coca cola when the officer came in.[349]

There is no reason to doubt Oswald's story. It has been corroborated by Baker, Truly, and Arnold.

The presence of two other depository employees also confirms Oswald's alibi. James Jarman and Harold Norman were outside waiting for the motorcade. As it was coming closer, they decided to go inside to view it from a fifth floor window. They went inside and passed by Oswald having lunch. Oswald later told police that when he was having lunch, he saw Jarman and Norman pass by. Jarman stated that they went back into the building at about 12:20- 12:25, which would place Oswald in the lunchroom just shortly before the assassination.[350]

Officially, there was a role call in the TSBD, and Oswald was the only employee missing. This was given as a reason for the early suspicions of Oswald. According to Kent Biffle of the *Dallas Morning News*, that is not true. Biffle was in the TSBD shortly after the shooting. There had been an earlier roll call which was inconclusive because several employees were missing. By the time they figured out that Oswald was missing, he was already in jail. The first roll call was pointless, because people were obviously outside watching the motorcade. After the shooting, they weren't

---

[349] http://22november1963.org.uk/lee-harvey-oswald-alibi
[350] Marrs, Jim, *Crossfire*, pp. 47-49, Carroll and Graf, 1989

concerned with hurrying back to work. Some were being interviewed by police, others were just talking amongst themselves. There was no reason to suspect an employee just because he wasn't back yet. It shows that the Oswald story was predetermined.[351]

It is standard police procedure to seal off a crime scene, but in the case of Kennedy's murder, that was not done. Captain Will Fritz said that he arrived at the TSBD at exactly 12:58. In his words:

> After I arrived, one of the officers asked me if I would like to have the building sealed and I told him I would.[352]

So at 12:58, the building had not yet been sealed, then Fritz gave the order. That means that it was a half an hour before the crime scene was sealed off. It shows the sloppiness and carelessness of the investigation. They didn't care if the crime scene was tampered with. It also makes the roll call meaningless if people are still coming and going.

Paraffin Test

Oswald was given a paraffin test on his hands and cheeks, and that test proved that Oswald did not fire a rifle. The test was positive on Oswald's hands, but negative on his cheeks. The positive reading on his hands can be attributed to other things besides gun powder. Ink, for example, can leave traces of nitrates on the subject's hands, and since Oswald worked in a book warehouse, it is likely he contacted ink with his hands. Another possible explanation for the positive test is that Oswald was picking up shell casings at a shooting range a day or two earlier. So the hand test is basically irrelevant. But there is no way to say Oswald fired a rifle that day if the paraffin test on his cheek was negative. A right-handed shooter would inevitably have traces of gun powder residue on his right cheek if he had recently fired a rifle. These paraffin tests are admissible in a court of law, something Oswald never lived to experience.[353]

The FBI analyzed the paraffin test results and sent the following conclusion to the Warren Commission:

---

[351] http://the-puzzle-palace.com/files/220120_jfkbiffle.html
[352] Marrs, Jim, *Crossfire*, p. 314, Carroll and Graf, 1989
[353] http://22november1963.org.uk/oswald-rifle-and-paraffin-tests

...as a result of these [neutron activation analysis] examinations, the deposits found on the paraffin casts from the hands and cheek of Oswald could not be specifically associated with the rifle cartridges...At best, the analysis shows that Oswald may have fired a pistol, although this is by no means certain. ... There is no basis for concluding that he also fired a rifle.[354]

The Warren Commission simply responded to that by saying that paraffin tests don't prove anything:

... the test is completely unreliable in determining either whether a person has recently fired a weapon or whether he has not... In a rifle, however, there is no gap between the chamber and the barrel, and one would therefore not expect nitrates to be deposited upon a person's hands or cheeks as a result of his firing a rifle.[355]

There was no explanation given as to why paraffin tests are routinely used in court, and a positive test is considered proof that the suspect has fired a gun, even though the tests are "completely unreliable."

On the day of the assassination, Dallas Police Chief Jesse Curry was interviewed by the press. He was asked about the results of Oswald's paraffin test. He responded with, "I understand the tests are positive." That is misleading. The test on Oswald's cheek was negative, and that's the only one that matters. The positive test result that Curry was referring to was on Oswald's hands. As mentioned, that test is irrelevant in this case. Police Chief Curry deliberately misled the public on this, obviously because he was pressured to promote Oswald as the lone assassin.

No Fingerprints on Rifle

The public is under the misconception that Oswald's rifle was found in the TSBD with his fingerprints on it. That is simply not true. The rifle that was found there could not be connected to Oswald, and it did not have his fingerprints on it. The chain of custody was broken regarding possession of the rifle, so it would have been worthless in a court of law anyway.

---

[354] FBI Report, March 6, 1964

[355] *The Warren Commission Report*, p. 561, Longmeadow Press, 1964

On the morning of November 23, 1963, the rifle was turned over to the FBI in Washington, who examined it for fingerprints. J. Edgar Hoover himself wrote:

> No latent prints of value were developed on Oswald's revolver, the cartridge cases, the unfired cartridge, the clip in the rifle or the inner parts of the rifle.[356]

FBI expert Sebastian Latona told the Warren Commission:

> We had no personal knowledge of any palm print having been developed on the rifle…

After Oswald was killed, the rifle was sent back to Dallas. District Attorney Henry Wade was asked about the strongest evidence of Oswald's guilt. He replied:

> Let's see…his fingerprints were found on the gun. Have I said that? If I had to single out any one thing, it would be the fingerprints found on the rifle and the book cartons which he used to prop the weapon on.[357]

This was on Monday the 25th. It was the first time there was any mention of fingerprints being found. The FBI had already said there were no fingerprints on the rifle. The fact that Oswald's prints were on boxes in the TSBD is irrelevant. He worked in the building, so naturally his prints were all over the place. That evening the *Dallas Times Herald* ran the headline: OSWALD'S PRINTS REVEALED ON RIFLE KILLING KENNEDY.[358]

The day after the assassination, Wade had already told the media he had an open and shut case against Oswald. This was before the prints had been allegedly found. Wade has already declared Oswald guilty. That is highly unusual. Usually, law enforcement officials will say things like, "We will wait until all available evidence has been analyzed," or, "We have faith in the judicial system." It is unheard of to openly proclaim the suspect guilty, especially with virtually no evidence.

---

[356] http://jfk.hood.edu/Collection/Weisberg%20Subject%20Index%20Files/F%20Disk/Frazier%20Robert%20A/Item%2022.pdf
[357] Marrs, Jim, *Crossfire*, p. 443, Carroll and Graf, 1989
[358] Marrs, Jim, *Crossfire*, p. 444, Carroll and Graf, 1989

Wade was heavily pressured by Johnson to present Oswald as the lone killer. In his words:

> Washington's word to me was that it would hurt foreign relations if I alleged conspiracy, whether I could prove it or not. I was just to charge Oswald with plain murder and go for the death penalty. Johnson had Cliff Carter all over me that weekend.[359]

Paul Groody was the director of the Miller Funeral Home, which embalmed Oswald. Groody told interviewers about how two federal agents came to the funeral home and asked to spend time alone with Oswald's body. Groody obliged, and when the agents left, he noticed that there was ink on Oswald's hand. Said Groody, "I had a heck of a time getting the black fingerprint ink off of his hand." Oswald had been fingerprinted in the Dallas Police Department. But that did not include his palm print. The palm print was needed to incriminate Oswald, so the agents took the palm print off Oswald's dead body and placed it on the rifle. So when you hear that Oswald's prints were found on the rifle, this is what they mean.[360]

In 1978, FBI agent Richard Harrison acknowledged in an interview that he had personally driven another agent to the funeral home for the purpose of obtaining Oswald's palm print. He said it was for "comparison purposes." This is an admission of complicity in the cover-up by the FBI.[361]

On November 26, the rifle was sent back to Washington. The incriminating palm print arrived on November 29. The FBI then announced that they had found a palm print on the rifle that matched Oswald's print.

In a 1985 interview, FBI agent Vincent Drain spoke of his doubts about the evidence:

> I just don't believe there ever was a print...All I can figure is that it was some sort of cushion, because they were getting a lot of heat by Sunday night. You could take the prints off

---

[359] Nelson, Phillip F., *LBJ, Mastermind of JFK's Assassination*, p. 420, Xlibris, 2010
[360] Turner, Nigel, 1988, The Patsy,*The Men Who Killed Kennedy*, U.K., Nigel Turner Productions
[361] Marrs, Jim, *Crossfire*, p. 444, Carroll and Graf, 1989

Oswald's (arrest) card and put it on the rifle. Something like that happened.[362]

The Warren Commission did not initially accept the print as legitimate. An internal FBI memorandum shows their skepticism:

> Rankin advised because of the circumstances that now exist there was a serious question in the minds of the Commission as to whether or not the palm impression that has been obtained from the Dallas Police Department is a legitimate latent palm impression removed from the rifle barrel or whether it was obtained from some other source and that for this reason this matter needs to be resolved.[363]

The commission also questioned the suspicious actions of the Dallas Police Department concerning the prints:

> At about 8 p.m. on the day of the assassination, Day had made photographs of the fingerprint traces around the trigger, and had covered this area with cellophane. He claimed that he lifted the palm print using adhesive tape, but did not photograph it.[364]

> It was standard procedure to make a photograph of a fingerprint or palm print before attempting to lift the print. When asked why he had not made a photograph of the palm print, Day claimed that he had been told by Jesse Curry, the chief of police, "to go no further with the processing." In an earlier interview with the FBI, however, Day had claimed that he had not received this instruction from Curry until immediately before the rifle was due to be sent to Washington, more than three hours after he had worked on the prints.[365]

Why did Lt. Day violate standard procedure by not taking a photograph of the palm print? It would have settled the question of whether or not the print was there prior to the trip to the morgue. Day tried to bail out by

---

[362] Marrs, Jim, *Crossfire*, p. 445, Carroll and Graf, 1989
[363] Marrs, Jim, *Crossfire*, p. 445, Carroll and Graf, 1989
[364] *The Warren Commission Report*, p. 261, Longmeadow Press, 1964
[365] *The Warren Commission Report*, Exhibit 3145, p. 7, 1964

saying Curry told him not to process the rifle any further, but as mentioned, that was after Day had worked on it for three hours.

Mauser

The rifle that was found on the sixth floor of the TSBD was a Mauser. At least five Dallas Police officers have confirmed this. They are: Deputy Sheriff Roger Craig, Deputy Constable Seymour Weitzman, Deputy Eugene Boone, Deputy Sheriff Luke Mooney, and Police Captain Will Fritz. Boone was the one who found the rifle, and he and Weitzman both signed sworn affidavits that the weapon they found was a Mauser. They described the weapon in detail, including the color of the sling and the scope. Craig was also present when the weapon was found, and stated that he saw "7.65 Mauser" stamped on the rifle. Fritz was also there, and agreed that the weapon was a 7.65 Mauser. District Attorney Henry Wade stated to the press that the weapon found on the sixth floor was a Mauser, so the early news reports said that a Mauser was the murder weapon.[366]

Boone and Weitzman, the two officers who signed the affidavits, were questioned by the Warren Commission about their identification of the weapon. They were both absolutely certain that the weapon was a Mauser. They both gave detailed descriptions of the rifle. Yet, they were both heavily pressured by the Warren Commission to change their testimony. In the end, they both gave in and said they might have made a mistake. Here is Weitzman's lame capitulation:

> To my sorrow, I looked at it and it looked like a Mauser, which I said it was. But I said the wrong one; because just at a glance, I saw the Mauser action....and, I don't know, it just came out as words it was a German Mauser. Which it wasn't. It's an Italian type gun. But from a glance, it's hard to describe; and that's all I saw, was at a glance. I was mistaken. And it was proven that my statement was a mistake; but it was an honest mistake.[367]

Here Weitzman states that he only got "a glance" at the rifle. Would he really be that irresponsible that he would sign a sworn affidavit after only "a glance" at it? A conscientious officer would not sign a legal statement like that unless he was absolutely certain of the facts.

---

[366] Smith, Matthew, *JFK: The Second Plot*, Mainstream Publishing, 2002
[367] http://www.jfkassassinationforum.com/index.php?topic=6023.60;wap2

But Roger Craig never changed his story. He gave an interview to researcher Mark Lane in which he clung steadfastly to his original story, claiming the weapon found was a Mauser. For this, he was fired from the Dallas Police Department and ostracized by his peers. Worse than that, there were attempts on his life. He was shot at and driven off the side of the road. In one instance, he got in his car and started the engine, and the car exploded. These injuries left him in constant physical pain, and the harassment caused him to have a breakdown. Craig committed suicide in 1975.[368]

Lieutenant J.C. Day is seen on the news the day of the assassination holding a rifle high above his head. The narrator says, "As you see, they are bringing in the weapon that was allegedly used in the assassination of President John F. Kennedy at 12:30 this afternoon, here in Dallas." Asked to identify the rifle, Day looks at it and says, "6.5, apparently made in Italy, 1940." Day logged it in as a 6.5 Mannlicher-Carcano with serial number C2766, which was the make and serial number of Oswald's rifle.[369]

Day's identification of the rifle gives the impression that it was the one found in the book depository. Some think that it disproves the claim that a Mauser was found at the site, but it does not. There could easily have been two rifles found in the book depository. That could mean that two shooters were in the building, or else one rifle was used for the shooting and the other was used for the framing. Another possibility is that only the Mauser was found at first, then it was switched for the Mannlicher-Carcano later. There is no proof that the Mannlicher-Carcano was actually found in the book depository. We only see Lt. Day holding up the rifle, but there is no verification that it was found at the scene of the crime. Films of the TSBD discovery do not clearly identify the rifle. There is no mention of who the officers were who found the second rifle. Instead, the story of the Mauser discovery is transposed to the story of the Mannlicher-Carcano discovery. It is told that the same cops, Boone and Weitzman, found the rifle shortly after the shooting.

According to Weitzman's affidavit, the Mauser was found at 1:22 p.m. When we see Lieutenant Day holding the rifle on the news, it is 6:16 p.m,

---

[368] https://jfk007.com/wowzer-a-mauser/
[369] https://www.youtube.com/watch?v=YY9MrOTbhaY

according to the video on YouTube.[370]I could not verify if that was a live broadcast or a tape. If it was live, it means that almost five hours had elapsed since the Mauser was found, which would have been enough time to switch rifles. Someone may have planted the wrong rifle and it took some time to correct it. On the other hand, if the video was a tape, then it is not known when the Mannlicher-Carcano was found, if it was found in the book depository at all.

To confuse the issue further, the shell casings that were found at the sniper's nest were from a 6.5 Italian rifle, which would seem to indicate that there were two rifles used, or at least two rifles found, on the sixth floor. Another possibility would be that the shooter in the sniper's nest used a Mauser simply because it was his personal preference. He or someone else could have then thrown down the three casings just to frame Oswald. The casings were found in the southeast corner of the TSBD, which was the sniper's nest, and the Mauser was found at the northwest corner of the building, where Oswald allegedly attempted to make his escape. The fact that the rifle and the casings don't match would seem to indicate multiple conspirators in the TSBD.[371]

It appears that there were at least two rifles found in the book depository that day. In early reports, NBC radio identified the alleged murder weapon as a British Enfield .303:

> The weapon which was used to kill the president, and which wounded Governor Connally, has been found in the Texas School Book Depository on the sixth floor- a British .303 rifle with a telescopic sight.[372]

Dallas TV station WBAP reported at 2:14 p.m. CST that the rifle found was a British Enfield .303. At 2:24 they reported that it was a 7.65 Mauser.[373]The Enfield was rarely ever heard about after that, and the Mauser became a Mannlicher-Carcano.

An internal CIA document shows the confusion over the rifle identification. Five days after the assassination, CIA officials noticed that

---

[370] https://www.youtube.com/watch?v=YY9Mr0TbhaY
[371] http://www.jfkmurdersolved.com/warren2.htm
[372] Ventura, Jesse, *They Killed Our President*, p. 65, Skyhorse Publishing, 2013
[373] https://www.assassinationresearch.com/v1n2/gtds.html

two different types of Italian-made carbines were being identified as the murder weapon. The document reads:

> ...The weapon which appears to have been employed in this criminal attack is a Model 91 rifle, 7.35 caliber, 1938 modification...The description of a Mannlicher-Carcano rifle in the Italian and foreign press is in error.[374]

This memo is in error, because the gauge is mentioned as 7.35 instead of 7.65. It must be a mistake, otherwise it would mean yet another rifle was found.

After the ARRB released files relating to the JFK assassination in 1994, an interesting discovery was made. Researcher Michael Griffith discovered an empty FBI evidence envelope with a notation on the front indicating that it contained a 7.65mm rifle shell that had been found in Dealey Plaza after the shooting. The envelope was dated December 2, 1963. Nothing had ever been mentioned about this in the Warren Report or the HSCA report, but it is solid evidence of conspiracy. The 7.65 shell must have come from the Mauser that never officially existed.[375]

Rambler

At about 12:40, Officer Craig witnessed Lee Harvey Oswald running down the slope from in front of the Texas School Book Depository and get into a light-green Rambler station wagon that had pulled over to the curb on Elm Street. Craig gave his description to Mark Lane:

> RC: As I was searching the south curb of Elm Street, I heard a shrill whistle. And I looked up, it just drew my attention. It was coming from across the street, and there was a light-green Rambler station wagon driving real slow west on Elm Street. And the driver was leaning over to his right looking up at a man running down the grass. So I immediately tried to cross the street to take these two people into custody for questioning. Everybody else was coming to the scene; these were the only two people leaving. And this was suspicious in my mind, you know, at the time, so I wanted to talk to them.

---

[374] Marrs, Jim, *Crossfire*, p. 440, Carroll and Graf, 1989
[375] http://michaelgriffith1.tripod.com/extras.htm

Due to the traffic jam, Craig was unable to question the men or follow them. Later, when he called Captain Fritz to give him the description of the man getting into the Rambler, it turned out Oswald was already in custody. "It sounds like the suspect we have in custody," said Fritz. So Craig went to the station to identify the suspect.

> Fritz turned to me and said, "Is this the man that you saw?" And I said, "Yes." And it was, it was. So he turned to the suspect and said, "This man saw you leave," at which time the suspect became a little excited. And he said, "I told you people I did." And Fritz said, "Now take it easy, son," talking to the suspect, "We're just trying to find out what happened." He said, "What about the car?" He didn't say "station wagon," he said "car," at which time the suspect leaned forward and put both hands on the desk, and said, "That station wagon belongs to Mrs. Paine. Don't try to drag her into this." Then he leaned back, and very disgustedly said, "Everybody will know who I am now." Now this was not a brag. I know it's been blown up to be a brag, in the Warren Commission, but this was not a brag. This was a man that was, like, in a building at night after it's locked. This is like, he's trying to steal something and you catch him at it, disgusted that he had blown his cover or been caught or something, it wasn't a brag.[376]

Craig's description of Oswald's departure has been corroborated by witnesses Helen Forrest, Marvin Robinson, Richard Randolph Carr, Carolyn Walther, and James Worrel. The driver of the Rambler has been described as a dark-skinned man. Since Oswald knew that the vehicle was a station wagon before anyone told him, that should be considered conclusive proof that Oswald did get into the vehicle. That is probably how he got to his rooming house. He was driven there in the Rambler by the dark-skinned man, because it makes no sense that they would switch vehicles.

After Craig left Fritz's office, a strange thing happened. Fritz got a call from Sheriff Decker, urging him to come and see him immediately. Decker insisted that Fritz come and talk to him in person rather than by phone. The nature of the call is not known, but it must have been incredibly urgent for Captain Fritz to suspend his interrogation of Oswald and travel almost two

---

[376] Video- *Two Men in Dallas*, 1976

miles to the Sheriff's office. Why the urgency? Why couldn't they have talked by phone? With all that needed to be done that day, it must have been of the utmost importance to require a person-to-person meeting. Decker could not risk having the conversation overheard on the phone. We can only speculate about the purpose of the meeting.[377]

We have heard conflicting testimonies about Oswald's movements after the assassination. Oswald was identified in a Rambler, on a bus, and in a cab, all within minutes of the shooting. Stranger yet, he admitted to Captain Fritz that he was on all three, although the commission would not admit he got in the Rambler.[378] So what really happened?

The official story has Oswald boarding a bus at 12:40, then getting off after the bus was stuck in traffic. To begin with, this is ridiculous because the bus that he was allegedly seen on was going *toward* Dealey Plaza. This sighting was made by passenger Mary Bledsoe, who was also Oswald's former landlady. No other witness confirmed Oswald's presence on the bus, and no one else could confirm Bledsoe's presence either. She said that Oswald had a "maniacal look on his face," which was strange because no one else ever described him that way, and even after his arrest, he seemed remarkably composed in the police station. During her testimony to the commission, Bledsoe read off of notes prepared for her by Secret Service Agent Forrest Sorrels. When she was asked by the commission why she was reading from notes, she answered, "Because, I forgot what I had to say." Bledsoe is not a credible witness, and she was obviously coached by Sorrels, whose involvement is suspected by many. Remember that Sorrels was one of the agents who approved the motorcade route.[379]

Supposedly, confirmation of Oswald's presence on the bus was provided by a bus transfer that was found on him. However, no mention of the transfer was made on the first day, and it would have been very easy to plant one among his belongings. When Chief Curry was asked how Oswald left the area, he responded, "We have heard that he was picked up by a Negro in a car." Of course, that story had to be squelched, because it implies that someone else was in collusion with Oswald. They had to make it look like he "escaped" on his own in order to maintain the lone-assassin line.

---

[377] Nelson, Phillip F., *LBJ, Mastermind of JFK's Assassination*, pp. 276-7, Xlibris, 2010
[378] https://www.maryferrell.org/showDoc.html?docId=29105
[379] http://www.jfk-online.com/bledsoe.html

After getting off the bus, the Warren Commission has Oswald in a cab at 12:48. However, the cab driver, William Whaley, logged the time as 12:30 when he picked up Oswald. That would be impossible, since that was the exact time that Kennedy was shot. The Warren Commission tried to say that Whaley rounded his times in his log to the nearest quarter-hour, but if that was the case, then Whaley would have recorded it as 12:45, not 12:30. Besides, Whaley's other pick-up times were logged as 6:20, 7:50, 8:10, 8:20, 9:40, 10:50, and 3:10.[380]

Whaley's identification of Oswald is highly suspect. He claims that Oswald wore two jackets, when he really had on none at that point. He had taken his jacket off at work, and it was found there the following week. Whaley said that Oswald's shirt had a light-colored stripe on it, but Oswald's shirt had no stripe. But worse than that, Whaley actually told the Warren Commission that he had picked the wrong man out of the line-up. He had originally said he had chosen suspect #3, which was Oswald. During his testimony, he corrected that and said it was actually suspect #2 who he drove in his cab. Whaley explained this by saying that he got confused during the line-up because the suspects kept moving around and changing location while he was trying to identify them. Although Whaley had signed an affidavit confirming his identification of the suspect, he admitted to the Warren Commission that he signed the affidavit *before* he viewed the line-up. At one point, Whaley told the commission that he was very confused.[381]

Oswald was seen by at least five credible witnesses getting into the Rambler, and he knew that it was a station wagon before anyone told him. It appears certain that Oswald did get into the Rambler. If he admitted to being on the bus and cab, he was probably just going along with it. The testimonies of Bledsoe on the bus and Whaley in the cab are just not credible. They seemed to be coerced into making statements they weren't sure of, and both gave questionable identifications of Oswald. It is possible that Bledsoe and/or Whaley saw the imposter that was sent around to implicate Oswald in the crime. It's also possible that one or both are simply honest cases of mistaken identity. Oswald's picture was shown repeatedly on TV, and it may have prompted false sightings of him.[382]

---

[380] https://www.giljesus.com/the-cab-ride.html
[381] http://orwelltoday.com/jfkrogercraig.shtml
[382] http://jfkthelonegunmanmyth.blogspot.com/2012/10/oswalds-escape-from-tsbd.html

The testimony of Richard Randolph Carr adds further intrigue. Carr said that he saw a man near the sniper's nest in the TSBD, but the man was not Oswald. His testimony was corroborated by Carolyn Walther, who also saw the man. After the shooting, Carr saw this man leave the depository and walk briskly south. Carr followed the man for a couple of blocks, then saw him get into the same green Rambler station wagon described by several others. Carr added the additional details of a luggage rack on the roof and Texas license plates. Carr also identified the driver as a dark-skinned man.[383]

In an attempt to refute the Rambler story, the Warren Commission resorted to changing Craig's testimony. Craig had said that the Rambler was light green; the commission changed it to white. Craig said the plates were not Texas plates; the commission said they were Texas plates. Craig said the driver had a tan jacket; the commission made it a white jacket. Craig got a good look at the driver; the commission said he did not get a good look at him. I can only guess that all this was done so that when different witnesses give varying reports of the Rambler incident, it discredits them all.[384]

Researchers suspect that the dark-skinned man driving the Rambler may have been David Sanchez-Morales. Morales was a CIA hit man, and was known to hate both Kennedys. He later made the following bold statement:

> I was in Dallas when we got the son of a bitch and I was in Los Angeles when we got the little bastard.[385]

Curtain Rods

Lee and Marina Oswald were separated by November of 1963. Lee would visit his wife and baby on the weekends at the home of Ruth Paine. The week of the assassination, Lee came to stay with them on Thursday instead of Friday. His arrival was unannounced. Oswald was employed at the Texas School Book Depository, and he rode there daily with his friend and co-worker, Wesley Frazier. Oswald had asked Frazier if he could ride home with him that Thursday afternoon, which was unusual. Frazier asked why, and Oswald responded that he was going to pick up some curtain rods. On the morning of the day that Kennedy was shot, Oswald went to work carrying a long, narrow package. Oswald said that the package contained the curtain

---

[383] Schoener, Gary Richard, *Fair Play Magazine*, A Legacy of Fear (May, 2000)

[384] Craig, Roger D., *When They Kill a President*, 1971

[385] http://forum.jfkmurdersolved.com/viewtopic.php?f=1&t=879

rods. The Warren Commission said that the package contained the rifle used to kill John Kennedy. With the sloppy investigation and the suspicious handling of evidence by the DPD and the FBI, that cannot be accepted at face value.

Two witnesses saw Oswald carrying the package. They were Wesley Frazier and his sister, Linnie Mae Randle. Randle saw Oswald place the package in the back seat of Frazier's car. She described the package as being about two feet long. Frazier saw the package in the back seat of his car, and assumed it was the curtain rods that Oswald had mentioned the previous day. Frazier said it was about 27 or 28 inches. Either way, it was too small to be a Mannlicher-Carcano rifle, which is 40.12 inches when assembled. Frazier testified that when Oswald held one end of the package cupped in his hand, like a soldier would hold a rifle during a military drill, the top end of the package was below Oswald's armpit. Frazier had gotten a good view from behind. Whatever was in the package, it was definitely too small to be the murder weapon.[386]

In spite of the statements by Randle and Frazier, the commission tried to put a sinister spin on Oswald's actions:

> When they reached the Depository parking lot, Oswald walked quickly ahead. Frazier followed and saw Oswald enter the Depository Building carrying the long bulky package with him.[387]

They said that "Oswald walked quickly ahead," implying that Oswald was in a hurry to get inside the building and hide the rifle without Frazier seeing it. According to Frazier, that is not what happened. They parked in the employee lot, which was two blocks north of the TSBD. When Oswald got out of the car, Frazier said he needed to charge up his battery. Oswald offered to wait for him, but Frazier told him to go ahead. Frazier raced the engine for a short time, then turned it off. When he got out of the car, Oswald was far ahead of him.[388] This may seem like a minor point, but it shows the commission's tendency to tweak the truth in their favor.

---

[386] Kurtz, Michael, *Crime of the Century*, University Press of Kansas, 2006
[387] *The Warren Commission Report*, p. 15, Longmeadow Press, 1964
[388] Kurtz, Michael, *Crime of the Century*, University Press of Kansas, 2006

Although the package may have contained curtain rods, it does not explain Oswald's early arrival on Thursday instead of Friday. Even if he did need curtain rods, was it so important that he couldn't wait one more day? Oswald never said anything to Marina or Ruth Paine about curtain rods. According to Oswald's landlady at his boarding house, his room already had curtain rods. If the package did contain curtain rods, it is not known where they came from.

But even if the package did contain a rifle, it does not mean that Oswald shot the president. It simply means that this was another step in the process of setting him up to take the blame. Oswald could have been instructed to bring his rifle to work that day. He would probably not ask why. He would have assumed it would be used only for defensive purposes, like to save the president's life. It's also possible that the package really did contain curtain rods. He could have been instructed to bring in curtain rods to make it appear that he was bringing a rifle to work. Again, he would probably not ask why. Judging from the descriptions of the package, it sounds like it was too small to be a rifle. Most likely, the package contained curtain rods which Oswald was instructed to bring to work to implicate him in JFK's assassination.

No Lawyer for Oswald

The goal of the Warren Commission was to convince the public that Lee Harvey Oswald would have been convicted in a fair trial if he had lived. But Oswald was held in custody for two days and interrogated for a total of 12 hours without being allowed to have a lawyer present. How could there possibly be any trial at all? Before a trial, there is always a preliminary hearing. Any violation of the suspect's rights would be grounds for dismissal of the case. If the judge knows that the suspect was not allowed to have a lawyer, he would throw the case out. There would be no trial.[389]

Here are Oswald's statements to the press and public on the afternoon he was arrested:

> Reporter: Did you shoot the President?

> LHO: I didn't shoot anybody, sir. I haven't been told what I'm here for.

---

[389] *The Warren Commission Report*, p. 199, Longmeadow Press, 1964

Reporter: Do you have a lawyer?

LHO: No, sir, I don't.

Then later:

LHO: I'd like some legal representation. These police officers have not allowed me to have any. I don't know what this is all about.

Reporter: Did you kill the President?

LHO: No sir, I didn't. People keep asking me that.

Reporter: Were you in that building?

LHO: Naturally, if I work in that building, yes, sir.

Reporter: Did you shoot the President.

LHO: No sir. They're taking me in because of the fact that I lived in the Soviet Union. I'm just a patsy!

At the midnight press conference, Oswald still did not have a lawyer:

LHO: I positively know nothing about this situation here. I would like to have legal representation. Well, I was questioned by a judge, however, I protested at that time that I was not allowed legal representation during that very short and sweet hearing. I really don't know what this situation is about. Nobody has told me anything, except that I'm accused of murdering a policeman. I know nothing more than that, and I do request someone to come forward to give me legal assistance.

Reporter: Did you kill the President?

LHO: No, I have not been charged with that. In fact, nobody has said that to me yet. The first thing I heard about it was when a newspaper reporter in the hall asked me that question.

Reporter: You have been charged.

LHO: Sir?

Reporter: You have been charged with killing the
President.[390]

So we have at least three separate occasions where Oswald said that he
did not have a lawyer, but he wanted one. How could this happen? Any
suspect has a constitutional right to a lawyer, but the Dallas Police and the
FBI took the liberty of violating that right. Oswald was interrogated in a
room filled with police officers and FBI agents. No one protected his rights,
even when Oswald was protesting. If someone did speak up, they were
quickly silenced. This was obviously not an oversight or an honest mistake.
Why was no one held accountable? No one was ever charged, fired, sued, or
fined over this blatant violation of a citizen's constitutional rights. At worst,
they were reprimanded. It shows that those in power cared nothing about
this one expendable person. They were mostly covering themselves, or
covering for someone else.

But the American public, and the whole world, for that matter, heard
Oswald's words. His statements were replayed over and over. It's shocking
that everyone knew that Oswald was denied a lawyer, but nothing was done
about it. Where was the outcry? Apparently, the public was so convinced of
Oswald's guilt, and so outraged by it, they were willing to overlook this little
transgression by the police. I'm sure some did protest, but their voices were
drowned out by the hysteria of the day.

The Warren Commission was deliberately vague on this subject. Under
the subheading of "Oswald's Legal Rights" we read:

> Before the first questioning session on Friday afternoon,
> Fritz warned Oswald that he was not compelled to make any
> statement and that statements he did make could be used
> against him.

That is standard procedure, and I don't doubt that Fritz said that. But did
he follow up on it? If Oswald was not compelled to make any statement,
then why was he interrogated for 12 hours? Oswald could not just say, "No
comment" for 12 hours straight. Even if he was not legally obligated to say
anything, he obviously felt pressured and intimidated to make statements,
which he did. What else could he do when he's locked in a room full of cops
for 12 hours? Since he did not have an attorney present, any statements he

---

[390] https://www.youtube.com/watch?v=4FDDuRSgzFk

did make could not be used in a court of law. It seems that no one there was really anticipating a court of law.

From the commission:

> On each occasion the justice of the peace advised Oswald of his right to obtain counsel and the right to remain silent…
>
> …Throughout the period of detention, however, Oswald was not represented by counsel.[391]

So they are saying that Oswald was told he could have a lawyer, yet he did not have one. What does that mean? They make it sound like Oswald himself chose not to have a lawyer. Is that really true? We heard him speak in front of cameras, pleading for a lawyer. The truth is that Oswald clearly wanted a lawyer, but was denied one. But the Warren Commission will not dare say that. They beat around the bush, trying to avoid the obvious truth. They don't actually say that he wanted a lawyer. They don't actually say that he didn't want a lawyer. They don't actually say that he was denied a lawyer. You can tell they really struggled with this. The denial of a lawyer was a key part of the cover-up.

Oswald had said that he would accept a lawyer from the American Civil Liberties Union (ACLU). That Friday night, Gregory Lee Olds, president of the Dallas Civil Liberties Union, had a phone conversation with Captain Will Fritz, who told him that "Oswald had been given the opportunity (of legal counsel) and declined." Olds and three other representatives of the ACLU went to the Dallas Police Station and were told by Captain King that "Oswald had not made any requests for counsel." That is a proven lie, based on the videos we have seen of Oswald calling for legal assistance.[392]

The commission reported on the ACLU's visit:

> They were assured by police officials and Justice of the Peace Johnston that Oswald had been informed of his rights and was being allowed to seek a lawyer.[393]

---

[391] *The Warren Commission Report*, p. 200, Longmeadow Press, 1964
[392] Douglass, James, W., *JFK and the Unspeakable*, pg. 487, Simon and Schuster, 2008
[393] *The Warren Commission Report*, p. 201, Longmeadow Press, 1964

But Oswald still did not have a lawyer. At the time of the ACLU's arrival at the police station, Oswald had already been interrogated for 7 hours without an attorney present. That means that his rights had been violated for 7 hours. If the ACLU offered an attorney, and Oswald said that he would accept an attorney from them, then what was the problem? This sounds suspicious. The interrogation should not have begun until Oswald had an attorney. It is true that he was allowed to make phone calls, but he still did not have legal representation during questioning. He had tried to reach a lawyer by the name of John Abt, but to no avail. Mr. Abt was not someone who Oswald knew personally, but he was known for handling cases involving conspiracy crimes against the government. Abt was Oswald's preference, but an ACLU lawyer would have been his second choice. It's certainly better than no lawyer at all. So supposedly, the ACLU offered a lawyer, and Oswald wanted one, yet he did not get one. That simply cannot be true. Although it was not his first choice, an ACLU attorney could have represented Oswald temporarily until he was able to contact Mr. Abt. The ACLU did make an effort to help Oswald, but it seems that they gave up too easily. After that Friday night, we never heard from them again. Why didn't they file suit against the DPD on Oswald's behalf?

The Dallas Bar Association tried to help, too. The commission reported:

> Later in the afternoon, H. Louis Nichols, president of the Dallas Bar Association, visited Oswald in his cell and asked him if he wanted the association to obtain a lawyer for him. Oswald declined the offer, stating a first preference for Abt and a second preference for a lawyer from the American Civil Liberties Union.[394]

It's hard to believe that Oswald declined the offer. Even if he couldn't get his first or second choice for a lawyer, why would he decline a lawyer from the Dallas Bar Association? Would he prefer to have no lawyer at all? Of course not. This story is not believable. It's possible that they offered him some crooked lawyer who was in collusion, and Oswald was too smart to accept it. But there is no way that Oswald would have refused any legitimate offer of legal assistance. The Commission said that "Oswald preferred to get his own lawyer." They are still trying to make it sound like it was Oswald's fault he did not have an attorney.

---

[394] *The Warren Commission Report*, p. 201, Longmeadow Press, 1964

Did any member of Congress speak out about the blatant violation of a citizen's rights? Did anyone in the media speak out? Was there any individual or agency who cared enough to safeguard the constitution? Oswald was the loneliest man in the world at this time.

Most of all, where was our new leader? Lyndon Johnson must have been following the developments of the case. He was constantly on the phone with the Dallas Police and the FBI at this time. He certainly must have known that Oswald was denied a lawyer. Why didn't he simply order the police to grant the suspect a lawyer like they should have already done anyway? He should have been raising holy heck about this. His inaction speaks volumes. He knew that Oswald would have to be the sacrificial lamb.

Rifle Purchase

The Warren Commission determined that Oswald had purchased the murder weapon in March of 1963 by mail order. The order was from an ad in *American Rifleman* magazine for a 6.5 Italian carbine from Klein's Sporting Goods in Chicago. The overall cost for the rifle was $21.45. The purchase was made under the name A.J. Hidell, and was delivered to P.O. Box 2915 in Dallas. In January of that year, Oswald had purchased a .38 Smith and Wesson revolver, also by mail order, and also under the name A.J. Hidell. That purchase was from Seaport Traders, Inc. for $29.95, plus shipping and handling, and was also shipped to P.O. Box 2915 in Dallas. Both weapons were received in March of that year.[395]

The U.S. postal money order was purchased on March 12, 1963 for $21.45. A bank deposit was made by Klein's on March 13, 1963, which included the item for $21.45.[396] The Warren Commission never questioned how the money order could be purchased on the 12th and deposited on the 13th. This was long before there were computers and online purchases. It would have taken several days to a week for the money order to reach its destination and be processed. This has never been adequately explained.

Also, there is no record of Oswald signing for either weapon. By law, postal form 2162 should have been filled out and signed by the addressee to acknowledge receipt of the rifle. It is required by law that the receipts for

---

[395] *The Warren Commission Report*, p. 174, Longmeadow Press, 1964
[396] *The Warren Commission Report*, p. 119, Longmeadow Press, 1964

firearms purchase through the mail must be kept on file for four years.[397] If Oswald had signed for either weapon, the signed form would certainly have been used by the Warren Commission to strengthen their weak case against him.

The delivery of the revolver did not go to the post office. That delivery was handled by a private mail company called Railway Express Agency (REA). State law required that to ship firearms, form 5024 must be filled out, showing proper identification. The purchaser must also submit a certificate of good character. REA would have sent a postcard to Oswald's P.O. Box, notifying him that he had a package waiting for pick-up. Oswald would then have to go to the REA location and present his identification, along with his certificate of good character. These would have been recorded in the REA logs. But there was no 5024 form. There was no certificate of good character. There was no signed receipt. There was nothing at all to show if the revolver was picked up at all, or by who and when. There is no proof of payment to REA or Seaport Traders. The FBI never even contacted REA in an attempt to confirm the sale.[398]

The Warren Report states:

> Michaelis (office manager for Seaport Traders) furnished the shipping copy of the invoice, and the Railway Express Agency shipping documents, showing that $19.95, plus $1.27 shipping charge, had been collected from the consignee, Hidell. (See Michaelis Exhibits Nos. 2, 4, 5, p. 173.)[399]

I looked at the exhibits and I did not see a signed receipt by A.J. Hidell. The total should have been $21.22. There is nothing to show that Oswald ever picked up this package, and there is nothing to link him with the revolver.

It seems strange that if someone was planning to commit a murder, that they would purchase the murder weapon by mail order. That leaves an obvious paper trail that could be used as evidence later on. The weapon could have easily been purchased at a retail outlet with little or no chance of being traced. In those days it was much easier to buy a gun than it is today.

---

[397] DiEugenio, James, *Reclaiming Parkland*, pg. 60, Skyhorse Publishing, 2013
[398] DiEugenio, James, *Reclaiming Parkland*, pg. 104, Skyhorse Publishing, 2013
[399] *The Warren Commission Report*, p. 174, Longmeadow Press, 1964

No background checks were necessary. It was like buying a pair of shoes. So why would Oswald deliberately leave so much physical evidence? There were the order forms, the cancelled money orders, the P.O. Box rentals, the delivery signatures, and so forth, all of which were evidence, and all of which could have been avoided. It's as if an implicating trail of evidence was deliberately being left. If Oswald made the purchases, it's because he was instructed to, not knowing he was being set up.

Researcher Mae Brussell has reconstructed Oswald's statements from notes and recollections of officers and agents who were present at his interrogation. Here are some of Oswald's words to his captors:

> I have no receipts for purchase of any gun, and I have never ordered any guns. I do not own a rifle, never possessed a rifle...

> I never ordered a rifle under the name of Hidell, Oswald, or any other name. . . . I never permitted anyone else to order a rifle to be received in this box. . . . I never ordered any rifle by mail order or bought any money order for the purpose of paying for such a rifle. . . . I didn't own any rifle. I have not practiced or shot with a rifle...

> I never received a package sent to me through the mailbox in Dallas, Box No. 2915, under the name of Alek Hidell, absolutely not...[400]

> I observed a rifle in the Texas School Book Depository where I work, on Nov. 20, 1963. . . . Mr. Roy Truly, the supervisor, displayed the rifle to individuals in his office on the first floor. . . . I never owned a rifle myself.

> There was another rifle in the building. I have seen it. Warren Caster had two rifles, a 30.06 Mauser and a .22 for his son. . .

> . . I will not say who wrote A. J. Hidell on my Selective Service card. (It was later confirmed that Marina Oswald wrote in the name Hidell.) . . . I will not tell you the purpose of carrying the card or the use I made of it. . .

---

[400] http://whokilledjfk.net/george_and_the_cia.htm

> I don't recall anything about the A. J. Hidell being on the post office card. . .
>
> The name Alek Hidell was picked up while working in New Orleans in the Fair Play for Cuba organization.[401]

Oswald mentioned seeing three other rifles that had been brought to the building, one by his boss, Roy Truly, and two by TSBD worker Warren Caster. These rifles were seen in the building a day or two prior to the assassination. There is no reason to believe that any of these three rifles were used in the assassination. The Warren Commission did question Truly and Caster about the rifles, but found them to be unrelated to the crime. It just shows how easy it would have been to plant a rifle to frame Oswald. People were very casual about guns back then. Someone could bring a rifle to work just to show it to their co-workers. Imagine how we would react today if someone walked into a building carrying a rifle.

It was legal to own a rifle and it was legal to have a P.O. Box, so there was no reason for Oswald to lie about any of this. It appears that someone else ordered the rifle in the name of A.J. Hidell for the sole purpose of incriminating Oswald in Kennedy's murder.

The name A.J. Hidell was the same name Oswald used to start up the Fair Play for Cuba Committee in New Orleans. There, he had also opened a post office box using the Hidell alias. When Oswald was arrested, he had two identifications on him. One said "Lee Harvey Oswald" and the other said "Alek J. Hidell." The Hidell identity was a project name used to access funds. Oswald never used it in his regular day-to-day activities. Even when representing the FPCC in an interview, he used his real name. It is known that Army Intelligence had a file on an A.J. Hidell. However, the contents of the file were destroyed before it could be viewed by investigators.[402]

The Backyard Photos

When Oswald was arrested, police found three photographs of him among his possessions. These have since come to be known as "the backyard photographs." These three pictures show Oswald standing outside, holding a rifle and a newspaper which is apparently a communist

---

[401] https://ratical.org/ratville/JFK/LHO.html
[402] Smith, Matthew, *JFK, The Second Plot*, 1992

publication of some kind. These photographs have been used to convince the public that Oswald was a communist supporter. *Life* magazine played along and used one of the photos on their cover to promote Oswald as the guilty party. There is much debate as to whether or not the photos are fake. Researchers have analyzed them to pieces, doing updated tests over the years as technology has developed. I will not go into analyzing these tests here, because it's not really a crucial issue when you think about it. These photographs were used to frame Oswald, and that is equally true whether they are real or fake. If they are fake, then that is obvious proof of a frame-up. It means somebody created phony pictures of Oswald to make him look guilty. If they are real, it still means he was framed. Someone probably said, "Hey, Lee, let's get some pictures of you with your new rifle. Hold that newspaper, too." Whoever told him that was CIA-connected and was setting him up. It would have been someone he knew and trusted. Naturally, Oswald had no clue that he was being set up. He would not have objected, since his mission at the time was to play the role of a communist sympathizer. Oswald willingly followed orders from the agency, so there is no reason why he would have refused to do this. He went to Russia and openly advocated Marxism. That was to portray himself as pro-communist, so why would he object to holding a communist newspaper for a picture?

Personally, I think the pictures are fake. They just look fake. It looks like Oswald's head is too big in relation to his body, and the pictures seem to have the identical expression. It also seems typical of the kinds of things the agency had been doing to set him up, and this is just one more.

The pictures themselves are not proof of anything. Even the cops know that. Even if Oswald really was a communist supporter and owned a rifle, that still doesn't mean he shot Kennedy. The public will naturally overreact, but law enforcement officials should know better. For what it's worth, Oswald claimed that the photos were fake. He could have just said, "Yeah, that's me. So what." It would not have made things any worse for him. But when these pictures were shown to Oswald, he just casually said, "Oh, that's just someone else's picture with my face on it." Critics might say that he just lied to cover himself, but he really didn't need to.

So if the photos are fake, it means Oswald was framed. If they are real, it still means he was framed. That's why the debate is irrelevant. It is natural for people to wonder about the pictures, and they will continue to do tests on those photographs forever. But Oswald is still an innocent man either way.

The same logic applies to the debate over whether or not Oswald's rifle was found at the scene of the shooting and whether or not his prints were on it. The truth is that it was not his rifle that was found, but consider for a moment that it was. What if they really did find Oswald's rifle there, and it really did have his prints on it? It still means he was framed. It would mean that someone took Oswald's rifle and planted it at the scene of the crime. Saying that his fingerprints were on it is pointless because if he owned the rifle, it's likely that his fingerprints would be on it already. That would be a classic frame-up. If someone wanted to frame you for a murder, that's how they would do it. They would somehow get your gun, which is registered to you and has your fingerprints on it already. Then they would use that gun to commit the murder, wearing gloves, of course, then leave the gun laying there. Police would investigate and find your smoking gun laying at the scene of the crime with your fingerprints on it. Good luck explaining that to the cops. That's what they tried to do to Oswald, except they screwed up. The shooter in the TSBD was supposed to use a Mannlicher-Carcano rifle and leave it there, since that was the type of weapon that Oswald possessed. For some reason, he used a Mauser instead. Maybe he got the instructions wrong, or maybe he just liked the Mauser better. Whatever the reason, the wrong weapon was left in the TSBD, leaving the plotters to have to scramble to switch rifles and explain away the Mauser. In short, if Oswald's rifle was found at the crime scene, it means he was framed. If his rifle was not found at the crime scene, it means he was framed badly.

Studies and reenactments have been done to see if Oswald could have gotten off three shots in the allotted time frame. For the record, that time frame is estimated at 4.8 to 7 seconds, according to the Warren Commission. I find that pointless, since it is known that there were multiple shooters. Why bother doing tests to see if one person could fire all the shots? From all accounts, there were at least four shooters, and Oswald was definitely not one of them. His negative paraffin test and his second floor sighting are conclusive proof of that. The Warren Commission just wanted to waste time with fancy reenactments to make it look like they were conducting a legitimate investigation. It was all for show, and it is a waste of time and space to discuss the reenactment figures.

Of equal non-importance is the question of Oswald's marksmanship skills. The commission went to great lengths to say that Oswald was a top marksmen who had gotten high marks in the Marines for his shooting ability, and was therefore capable of assassinating the president. That, too, is a pointless argument. It is proven that Oswald did not fire a shot that day, so any discussion of his marksmanship skills is moot.

Ballistics

The Warren Commission performed neutron activation analysis on the bullet fragments. As it relates to ballistics, this is the process of determining the concentration of elements in bullet fragments. The commission did extensive questioning of experts in this field, asking about the relative amounts of barium and antimony, and whether or not the fragments could have come from Oswald's rifle, and so on. As expected, the so-called experts verified the magic bullet theory:

> Neutron activation analysis.--In addition to the conclusions reached by the committee's forensic pathology panel, the single bullet theory was substantiated by the findings of a neutron activation analysis performed for the committee. The bullet alleged to have caused the injuries to the Governor and the President was found on a stretcher at Parkland Hospital. Numerous critics have alleged that this bullet, labeled "pristine" because it appeared to have been only slightly damaged, could not have caused the injuries to both the Governor (particularly his shattered wrist) and the President. Some have even suggested the possibility that the bullet wounded neither Connally nor Kennedy, that it was planted on the stretcher. Neutron activation analysis, however, established that it was highly likely that the injuries to the Governor's wrist were caused by the bullet found on the stretcher in Parkland Hospital. Further, the committee's wound ballistics expert concluded that the bullet found on the stretcher--Warren Commission exhibit 399 (CE 399)--is of a type that could have caused the wounds to President Kennedy and Governor Connally without showing any more deformity than it does.
>
> In determining whether the deformity of CE 399 was consistent with its having passed through both the President and Governor, the committee considered the fact that it is a

relatively long, stable, fully jacketed bullet, typical of ammunition often used by the military. Such ammunition tends to pass through body tissue more easily than soft nose hunting bullets. Committee consultants with knowledge in forensic pathology and wound ballistics concluded that it would not have been unusual for such a fully jacketed bullet to have passed through the President and the Governor and to have been only minimally deformed.

The neutron activation analysis further supported the single bullet theory by indicating that there was evidence of only two bullets among the fragments recovered from the limousine and its occupants. The consultant who conducted the analysis concluded that it was "highly likely" that CE 399 and the fragments removed from Governor Connally's wrist were from one bullet; that one of the two fragments recovered from the floor of the limousine and the fragment removed from the President's brain during the autopsy were from a second bullet. Neutron activation analysis showed no evidence of a third bullet among those fragments large enough to be tested.[403]

These tests are needless and the complexities are designed to discourage people from reading further. There is a mountain of evidence to prove multiple shooters, but these complicated tests that no one understands are supposed to prove otherwise. If these tests confirm the magic bullet theory as truth, then the tests were a waste of time.

The commission claimed that the amount of deformity is normal. That is proven false when we look at other pictures of bullets that have been fired. They always show some degree of deformity, even when shot into animal carcasses. The magic bullet appears to have been shot into water or cotton, then retrieved. The claim that a jacketed bullet passes through tissue more easily does not come close to explaining the lack of deformity of CE399- the magic bullet. The commission also did not mention that the total weight of the fragments taken from Connally's wrist weighed more than the missing fragments from the bullet.[404]

---

[403] *The Warren Commission Report*, p. 45, Longmeadow Press, 1964
[404] https://www.maryferrell.org/pages/Single_Bullet_Theory.html

Ballistics analysis showed that 40 to 50 bullet fragments were found in Kennedy's brain and skull. The Warren Report described "numerous small, irregular metallic fragments most of which are less than 1 mm in maximum dimension."[405]That's because the fatal head shot used an exploding bullet, which should be obvious just from a simple viewing of the Zapruder film. The Warren Commission never acknowledged that such a missile was used, because it would raise too many questions. How could they explain why the head shot exploded but the back shot did not, even though they supposedly came from the same weapon with the same ammunition?

Researcher Gary Revel responds to a CNN broadcast implicating Oswald:

> Dr. Hughes testified that 40 to 50 bullet fragments were found in JFK's brain and skull at autopsy. This clearly makes it impossible for the mortal wound to have come from Oswald's rifle. This would be from a fragmentation type round like a hollow point or exploding cartridge. The full metal jacket military rounds used in the Italian Carcano rifle owned by Oswald, if it were used and fired from behind JFK, could not and would not have resulted in the type of head explosion clearly visible in the Zapruder film. Three spent cartridges found on the 6th floor were full metal jacket rounds, none were hollow point fragmenting rounds. It was impossible for the shot that killed JFK to have come from the rifle found on the 6th floor.[406]

Oswald's rifle only fired a fully jacketed bullet. The jacket prevents the dispersion of fragments, so that alone is forensic evidence that the fatal head shot did not come from Oswald's rifle.

Consider also the manner in which the shell casings were found. Deputies Roger Craig and Luke Mooney have both stated that when they found the three shells on the sixth floor of the book depository, they were laying side by side, only inches apart under the window, and all pointing in the same direction. It looked as if someone had placed them there manually, as opposed to being ejected from the rifle, in which case they would have been

---

[405] https://en.wikipedia.org/wiki/John_F._Kennedy_autopsy

[406] http://www.garyrevel.com/News/press_release_11.html

scattered randomly. Right off the bat, that makes the casings very suspicious as evidence.[407]

An interview with news cameraman Tom Alyea casts even more doubt upon the casings as evidence. Alyea entered the TSBD just before it was sealed off by police. He took pictures of the authorities searching for evidence. Alyea noticed the shells laying on the floor, but couldn't photograph them because of a stack of boxes that was in his way. Captain Fritz noticed the problem Alyea was having. Inexplicably, Fritz picked up the shells and held them in his hand for Alyea to photograph, then threw them down on the floor. This occurred before the crime scene search unit had arrived. Alyea said that some film of the depository search was thrown out upon orders from his news director.[408]

Fritz's actions were outrageous. Why would a police captain pick up the shells, throw them down, and then rearrange them? This was before they were photographed by the crime scene search unit, so Fritz was tampering with evidence. There are no known photos of the casings in their original position. There are photos of the scattered shells after Fritz threw them down, which would be inadmissible as evidence in court. After he threw them down, Fritz or someone else must have rearranged them in a neat row, which was how they were when Craig and Mooney found them.

Also of suspicion is a copy of the Dallas Police evidence sheet published by the Warren Commission. The evidence sheet shows that three shell casings were taken from the book depository. But the FBI receipt for assassination evidence from the DPD states that only two shell casings arrived in Washington the night of November 22, 1963. This was confirmed by a copy of the same evidence sheet which was found in the Texas Department of Public Safety files. That evidence sheet also shows that only two casings were found.

That means there were two shell casings for three shots. What happened to the third casing? Dallas Police Detective Will Fritz acknowledged that he held on to one of the casings for several days before forwarding it to the FBI. He said that he held on to it for "comparison purposes." This violated

---

[407] Underwood, H.R., *Rendezvous with Death*, p. 179, Trafford, 2013
[408] Kritzberg, Connie, *Secrets from the Sixth Floor Window*, pp. 39-46, Consolidated Press Int., 1995

the chain of custody, and the third casing could not be considered legitimate evidence.

When the FBI examined the hulls, they found that two of them showed markings that were compatible with being fired from Oswald's weapon, but the third one did not. The third one had a dent on its lip which would have prevented the fitting of a slug. The FBI determined that the casing had been loaded and extracted from a rifle at least three times, but could not confirm that it was in Oswald's rifle.[409]

Medical Evidence

On the day of the assassination, the doctors at Parkland Hospital gave a press conference shortly after Kennedy was pronounced dead. They stated that Kennedy had been shot in the head from the front, and also that the throat wound was an entrance wound. The Secret Service confiscated tapes of the press conference as part of the cover-up, and only a couple of brief segments of the tapes have survived. The official autopsy report from Bethesda would later contradict the Parkland doctors, saying that no shots came from the front.

Dr. Malcolm Perry spoke at the press conference at Parkland. He stated three times that Kennedy's neck wound was an entrance wound.[410] But when questioned later by the Warren Commission, he had suspiciously changed his mind. In front of the commission, he testified that he now believes that:

> ...a full jacketed bullet without deformation passing through the skin would leave a similar wound for an exit and entrance wound and with the facts which you have made available and with these assumptions, I believe that it was an exit wound.[411]

Dr. Perry is just one of many witnesses who suspiciously changed their mind about what they saw. Perry was probably coerced into making the above statement to implicate Oswald. There is no way he could honestly mistake an exit wound for an entrance wound.

---

[409] Marrs, Jim, *Crossfire*, p. 438, Carroll and Graf, 1989

[410] https://en.wikipedia.org/wiki/Malcolm_Perry_(physician)

[411] https://www.jfk-assassination.de/warren/wch/vol3/page373.php

Dr. Charles Crenshaw was one of the Parkland doctors who tried to save Kennedy's life. In his 1992 book *JFK: Conspiracy of Silence*, he states his belief about the fatal head shot that killed John Kennedy:

> From the damage I saw, there was no doubt in my mind that the bullet had entered his head through the front.

Dr. Crenshaw did not testify to the Warren Commission. He describes his feelings at the time:

> I was as afraid of the men in suits as I was of the men who had assassinated the President...I reasoned that anyone who would go so far as to eliminate the President of the United States would surely not hesitate to kill a doctor.[412]

Dr. Robert McClelland's testimony was graphic:

> As I took the position at the head of the table...I was in such a position that I could very closely examine the head wound, and I noted that the right posterior portion of the skull had been extremely blasted. It had been shattered, apparently, by the force of the shot...This sprung open the bones...in such a way that you could actually look down into the skull cavity itself and see that probably a third or so, at least, of the brain tissue, posterior cerebral tissue and some of the cerebellar tissue had been blasted out.[413]

Dr. McClelland's testimony has been confirmed by a multitude of other doctors, nurses, agents, staff, and photographers who claim that they also saw a huge, gaping wound in the back of JFK's head. This was clearly an exit wound, as determined by the medical personnel involved. Yet, when we look at the official autopsy photos that were considered to be evidence, we see nothing like that. Instead, we see a small, round bullet hole, while the rest of his scalp is still perfectly intact. This looks more like an entrance wound. There is no doubt that the autopsy photos do not show the condition of the president's head when he was brought to Parkland Hospital. The obvious reason for the deception is to hide a shot from the front. There was a small wound on Kennedy's right temple, which was an entrance wound from the fatal head shot. An exit wound is always larger

---

[412] Crenshaw, Dr. Charles, *JFK: Conspiracy of Silence*, Signet, 1992
[413] Lifton, David, *Best Evidence*, p. 39, McMillan Publishing Co., 1980

than an entrance wound, and even more so when an exploding bullet is used, as it was here.

From *Best Evidence*, by David Lifton:

> In addition to this large wound of exit, the Bethesda doctors reported that beneath it was a small hole, a bullet entrance wound, approximately a half inch by a quarter inch in size, located "approximately 2.5cm (1 inch) laterally to the right and slightly above the external occipital protruberance."[414]

This is proof that Kennedy was hit in the head with two bullets. There was a small entrance wound below the large exit wound in the back of his head. The shot from the grassy knoll was a fragmenting round; the one from behind was not. The bullet from behind did not exit, but was instead blown apart by the explosion from the frontal shot, which came a split-second later. This can be verified by a slow-motion viewing of the Zapruder film.

In 1968 the Clark Panel, headed by Attorney General Ramsey Clark, studied the X-rays and photographs available to them. They made the following discovery:

> Also, there is, embedded in the outer table of the skull close to the lower edge of the hole, a large metallic fragment which on the anteroposterior film lies 25 mm to the right of the midline. This fragment as seen in the latter film is round and measures 6.5 mm in diameter immediately adjacent to the hole on the internal surface of the skull, there is localized elevation of the soft tissues.[415]

The 6.5 mm fragment they referred to was a result of the rear head shot. The Bethesda doctors had also reported a bullet hole in the same location. The measurement of 6.5 mm is the exact diameter necessary to incriminate Oswald, so the Warren Commission emphasized that while ignoring the 40-50 fragments from the exploding round. So the medical evidence shows both an exit wound and an entrance wound on the back of Kennedy's head, yet it was supposedly done by one shooter.

Researcher and photographic expert Robert Groden made the following analysis:

---

[414] Lifton, David, *Best Evidence*, p. 39, McMillan Publishing Co., 1980
[415] https://en.wikipedia.org/wiki/John_F._Kennedy_autopsy

The vital autopsy photos of the back of the President's head were altered immediately after the autopsy in order to cover up the fact that the President received two bullets in the head, one from the rear and one from the front, and this second shot blew out the back of his head, as Jackie Kennedy testified to the Warren Commission.[416]

An FBI report from the night of the autopsy shows that the doctors were puzzled by what they saw:

Further probing determined that the distance traveled by this missile was a short distance inasmuch as the end of the opening could be felt with the finger. Inasmuch as no complete bullet of any size could be located in the brain area and likewise no bullet could be located in the back or any other area of the body as determined by total body X-rays and inspection revealing there was no point of exit, the individuals performing the autopsy were at a loss to explain why they could find no bullets.

So the report states that there was no bullet found in the back, but also no exit path. So where did the bullet go? The agents who filed the report phoned the FBI laboratory and were informed that the bullet had been found on a stretcher at Parkland. The agents then came up with the following theory:

...since external cardiac massage had been performed at Parkland Hospital, it was entirely possible that through such movement the bullet had worked its way back out of the point of entry and fallen on the stretcher.[417]

But as we know, the Warren Commission arrived at their own conclusion:

A bullet had entered the base of the back of (Kennedy's) neck slightly to the right of the spine. It traveled downward and exited from the front of the neck, crossing a nick in the left lower portion of the knot in the President's tie.[418]

---

[416] Marrs, Jim, *Crossfire*, p. 377, Carroll and Graf, 1989

[417] Marrs, Jim, *Crossfire*, p. 371, Carroll and Graf, 1989

[418] *The Warren Commission Report*, p. 3, Longmeadow Press, 1964

The Zapruder film gives the impression that when John Kennedy was shot, he died instantly. He did not. One of the saddest things about the assassination is that Kennedy survived for about a half an hour in his incapacitated state. When the limousine was on its way to Parkland Hospital, John Kennedy laid with his head on his beloved wife's lap. Kennedy was quivering and shaking, according to witnesses on the railroad overpass who saw him. When they arrived at Parkland, the doctors said that Kennedy was gasping for breath. In desperation, they inserted a tube down his throat to help him breathe. There was a faint pulse, and they attempted heart massage. They knew he had no chance for survival, but as doctors and human beings, they felt obligated to do everything in their power to save him. Kennedy struggled for survival for a half an hour until mercifully, his heart stopped beating. One can only imagine the suffering he endured during the final 30 minutes of his life.

Perfect Patsy

Many of those who believe that Oswald is guilty base their conclusion on the kind of person he was. He was an ex-marine with an undesirable discharge, a high-school dropout, an oddball, and a loner with a reputation for being short-tempered. He even had a misdemeanor charge on his record for a public brawl he was involved in. People who believe in his guilt will say, "He seemed like the kind of person who would do it." Actually, those very same traits are what made him the perfect patsy. Because of his undesirable discharge, his dismal work history, and his criminal record, Oswald makes a very believable assassin. That's why he was chosen to be the patsy. If they chose someone with an immaculate past to be the patsy, no one would believe it because such a person would not shoot the president. Whether or not the aforementioned traits actually portray the real Oswald or not is questionable. All we know of Oswald is his manufactured identity. His undesirable discharge was probably staged by the CIA to give him a background as a disgruntled loser. His public scuffle in New Orleans was probably also staged for the same reason- to cultivate a persona that would be used for a later assignment.

As Oswald is being dragged away by police, we hear him shout, "I'm just a patsy!" By saying that, he is admitting foreknowledge of the assassination. "Patsy" means that he was set-up, that somebody framed him for the crime. It's not a claim that would be made by a person with absolutely no knowledge of the crime. Imagine you were perfectly innocent of any crime, just sitting on a park bench minding your own business, when suddenly squad cars pull up, cops jump out and arrest you. Shocked and confused as you are, you would not shout, "I'm just a patsy!" You would say, "I didn't do it," or "You got the wrong guy," or "I'm innocent." That would be the natural spontaneous reaction. You would assume the police made an honest mistake. But to say, "I'm a patsy" would not make sense unless you knew that someone had set you up to take the blame. You wouldn't figure that out unless you knew, or at least suspected, who it was that set you up.

You can see the moment when Oswald first realized he had been framed. A reporter had asked him if he had shot the president. Oswald replied, "No, I have not been charged with that." The reporter responds, "You have been charged with that." Oswald looks stunned and says, "Sir?" The reporter repeats, "You have been charged with killing the president." Oswald is visibly shaken by the news. Up until that moment, he had not been charged with killing President Kennedy; he had only been charged with the killing of Officer Tippit. When informed of the second charge, Oswald suddenly realized the truth. You can see it in his puzzled expression when he is told about it. Up until then, he was waiting for someone from the CIA to come and identify him to the Dallas Police. Now he realizes that won't happen. He has been hung out to dry. One has to feel for Oswald at a time like this. He kept his mouth shut because he was a patriotic American trying to help his country. But his country betrayed him. No one from the CIA will come to save him at this point.

The Fingerprint

A fingerprint was found in the TSBD which researchers believe connects Lyndon Johnson with the assassination. According to an expert in fingerprint analysis, the print matches that of Malcolm Wallace, a known hitman for Lyndon Johnson. Recall that Wallace was implicated in numerous Johnson-related murders by the sworn statement of Billie Sol Estes, and that Wallace was convicted of the 1951 murder of Doug Kinser.

The print in question was found on a box in the sniper's nest on the sixth floor. The match was made by A. Nathan Darby, a latent print examiner certified by the International Association of Identifiers, and was verified by researcher and former Justice Department member Walt Brown. According to Darby and Brown, the print showed a 34-point match between the retrieved print and the print on Wallace's fingerprint card. Brown called that a "slam dunk" in any murder case. Darby has confirmed the match in a notarized affidavit.[419]

On the day of the assassination, the FBI fingerprinted every TSBD employee and every DPD officer who was in the sniper's nest to eliminate them as possible sources. No match was found anywhere, and the print was stored in the National Archives for 35 years. Brown retrieved the print and showed it to Darby, along with Wallace's fingerprint card from his 1951 arrest for the murder of Doug Kinser. Darby was not told that this was related to the Kennedy assassination. Darby had 35 years of experience analyzing prints for the U.S. military and the Austin Police Department. Darby was absolutely certain of his conclusion:

> There was no question about it. They matched. The inked and the latent print were made by the same finger. The other evidence I was presented with was Malcolm Wallace's left little finger, without a reasonable doubt.

Brown pointed out that fingerprints do not last long on cardboard, meaning that Wallace had been in the sniper's nest recently. The results of the tests were sent to the Dallas Police Department, who forwarded it to the FBI. The FBI took 18 months to respond. Their simple response was "No, it's not a match." There was no explanation and no evidence to the contrary was given.

Darby was flabbergasted by the FBI's statement:

> I don't know why they could say that it didn't match. It did match. There's no question about it. My experience…I've just had too much experience. I know what I'm talking about. I'm positive. No question about it. My dying declaration…If I was to drop dead right now, they match.[420]

Some have speculated that Johnson would not send Wallace to Dealey Plaza to commit the assassination because Wallace was an obvious link back to him. But the shooters had to be someone that could be trusted. Whether they were working for Johnson or some mob boss, it had to be someone they knew they could rely on to do the job and keep quiet about it. They certainly would not get strangers to do the job. Remember that Wallace had

---

[419] http://www.whokilledjfk.net/malcolm_wallace.htm
[420] https://www.youtube.com/watch?v=XdF64wl-3Fg

been convicted of murder in 1951, yet he still committed other murders for Johnson after that, even though he was a known associate. Johnson was not inhibited by the known connection. He got Wallace off with cold-blooded murder in the case of Doug Kinser, and he was only a senator then. He knew that once he became president, he would have control over the investigation, so he was not worried. The only way it would have been a problem was if the assassination attempt failed. If Kennedy had been wounded, but lived, then he would have controlled the investigation into his attempted murder, and then all heck would have broken loose. Johnson would have been nailed, along with many others. Johnson just knew he had to get the job done, and worry about the cover-up later. His best chance for success was to have old reliable Mac Wallace do what he had done many times before.

Destroying Evidence

Less than three days after John Kennedy's death, Lyndon Johnson set about destroying evidence. The presidential limousine that Kennedy died in was shipped to Detroit, where the body was replaced and the interior refurbished. This was a blatant destruction of evidence. The limousine itself is the crime scene, and it should have been untouched after it reached Parkland. Bullet holes, bullet fragments, and blood splatter are all evidence that needs to be analyzed. Some fragments were collected, but the limousine as evidence was rendered useless by Johnson's action. This led to inevitable controversy later on.[421]

Two Dallas motorcycle patrolmen, Stavis Ellis and H.R. Freeman, both observed a bullet hole in the windshield of the limousine at Parkland Hospital. In an interview, Ellis described that hole:

> There was a hole in the left front windshield...You could put a pencil through it...you could take a regular standard writing pencil...and stick (it) through there.[422]

Freeman verified the description:

> (I was) right beside it. I could have touched it...it was a bullet hole. You could tell what it was.

---

[421] Nelson, Phillip F., *LBJ: Mastermind of JFK's Assassination*, p. 538, Xlibris, 2010
[422] Lifton, David S., *Best Evidence*, Signet, 1992

Richard Dudman wrote in *The New Republic*:

> A few of us noted the hole in the windshield when the
> limousine was standing at the emergency entrance after the
> President had been carried inside. I could not approach close
> enough to see which side was the cup-shaped spot which
> indicates a bullet had pierced the glass from the opposite
> side.[423]

Evalea Glanges was a medical student at Southwestern Medical
University, next to Parkland Hospital. She also saw the bullet hole:

> It was a real clean hole....it was very clear, it was a through-
> and-through bullet hole through the windshield of the car,
> from the front to the back...it seemed like a high-velocity
> bullet that had penetrated from front-to-back in that glass
> pane.[424]

George Whitaker was a senior manager at the Ford Motor Company
plant in Detroit, Michigan, at the time of the shooting. In a tape recorded
interview with his attorney, Whitaker told how when he reported to work
on Monday morning, November 25th, he saw the JFK limousine there, with
the interior stripped out and the windshield removed. He was told to report
to the glass lab, where he found the limousine windshield.

> When I arrived at the lab the door was locked. I was let in.
> There were 2 glass engineers there. They had a car
> windshield that had a bullet hole in it. The hole was about 4
> or 6 inches to the right of the rear view mirror, as viewed
> from the front. The impact had come from the front of the
> windshield. If you have spent 40 years in the glass (illegible)
> you know which way the impact was from.
>
> ...the windshield had a bullet hole in it, coming from the
> outside through...it was a good, clean bullet hole, right
> straight through, from the front. And you can tell, when the
> bullet hits the windshield, like when you hit a rock or
> something, what happens? The back chips out and the front

---

[423] Dudman, Richard, *The New Republic*, December 21, 1963
[424] http://www.jfksouthknollgunman.com/index.php/04-2-bullet-hole/

may just have a pinhole in it…this had a clean round hole in the front and fragmentation coming out the back.[425]

They were instructed to make a new windshield for the limousine, which was being rebuilt. The original damaged windshield was ordered to be broken up and scrapped. But who gave that order? If these witnesses are correct, then the windshield would be proof of a shot from the front.

When Whitaker originally gave the interview, he did so on the condition of anonymity. After Whitaker died in 2001, his family released more of his statements, with their permission to reveal his name. His full account was given to film producer Nigel Turner, who used it in his documentary, *The Men Who Killed Kennedy*. Whitaker's story was told in episode 7, "The Smoking Guns."

Secret Service Agent Charles Taylor Jr. wrote a report on November 27, 1963 concerning the whereabouts of the limousine after the assassination. He said the limousine and the follow-up car arrived at Andrews AFB aboard a C-130 cargo plane at about 8:00 p.m. the night of the shooting. Taylor rode in the limousine as it was driven from Andrews AFB to the White House garage. During the vehicle's inspection inside the garage, he noted:

> In addition, of particular note was the small hole just left of center in the windshield from which what appeared to be bullet fragments were removed.[426]

Like so many other witnesses, Taylor changed his mind about what he saw. During the HSCA investigation, he said:

> I never examined this apparent hole on November 22, 1963 to determine if there had been any penetration of the glass, nor did I even get a good look at the windshield in well-lighted surroundings…

Taylor's retraction is not believable. Taylor rode on the passenger side of the limo while SS agent Kinney drove to the White House from Andrews AFB. It is hard to believe he would not notice a hole in the windshield during that ride. In his written statement of November 27, 1963 he had said that he

---

[425] Turner, Nigel, 1988, The Smoking Guns, *The Men Who Killed Kennedy*, U.K., Nigel Turner Productions

[426] http://www.jfksouthknollgunman.com/index.php/04-2-bullet-hole/

noticed it. The agents inspected the limo in the garage that night. Taylor was somehow forced to recant his earlier statements:

> ...it is clear to me that my use of the word 'hole' to describe the flaw in the windshield was incorrect.[427]

Here we have witnesses saying that the impact on the windshield appeared to come from the front, but the Warren Commission concluded:

> The physical characteristics of the windshield after the assassination demonstrate that the windshield was struck on the inside surface.[428]

So was the impact on the inside or the outside? If it's from the outside, then it means another shot from the front. How can the truth be determined without the windshield? Lyndon Johnson destroyed evidence when he had the limousine refurbished. Why was he so anxious to fix it up? Certainly it's within the federal budget to buy another limousine for the president. The FBI and police agencies will often keep evidence stored for years, even decades, depending on the significance of the crime, and no crime has ever been more significant than this one.

It might come as a surprise to learn that JFK's limousine was not retired after his death. It was fully rebuilt, upgraded with bulletproof armor, and continued to be a part of presidential motorcades for another 13 years. Lyndon Johnson himself rode in the rebuilt limousine.[429] Personally, it would give me the creeps. But to Johnson, it was a symbol of his triumph.

Johnson destroyed other evidence, too. He ordered Governor Connally's clothes to be retrieved and laundered, destroying blood stains and gun powder marks that could officially be used as evidence. What was the purpose of washing Connally's clothes? It's not likely that he would wear a shirt and jacket with bullet holes in them, no matter how clean they are. Johnson didn't care how brazen he was. Did anyone ever question him about this?

---

[427] https://www.lewrockwell.com/2012/06/douglas-p-horne/photographic-evidence-of-bullet-hole-in-jfk-limousine-windshield-hiding-in-plain-sight/
[428] *The Warren Commission Report*, p. 77, Longmeadow Press, 1964
[429] https://www.lewrockwell.com/2012/06/douglas-p-horne/photographic-evidence-of-bullet-hole-in-jfk-limousine-windshield-hiding-in-plain-sight/

Besides destroying evidence, Johnson also withheld evidence. He signed Executive Order 11652, which locked up undisclosed files and evidence relating to the assassination until 2039. He claimed it was to protect innocent people who might be harmed by their relationships with those involved. Yet supposedly, no one was involved except Oswald. There is no justification for this act. It is simply a show of power by Johnson. He did it because he could. If the information in those files is relevant, then it is evidence, whether it relates to Oswald or the real killers. What about the Garrison investigation? What about the HSCA investigation? They were limited because they did not have access to those files. It shows a complete disregard for the truth, and a complete disrespect for the public who has a right to know the truth. Due to the JFK Assassination Records Collection Act of 1992, some of these files have since been made public. The act states that all files must be made public within 25 years of the date of their enactment. It's not likely that they will all be made public. Anything that is too sensitive will be redacted or removed.[430]

Grassy Confessions

Most of the world is unaware that the grassy knoll shooter confessed to killing John Kennedy. That confession was made in 1994. You would think that would be really big news. Instead, all the major media outlets chose to ignore it. When people hear about the confession now, they will scoff at it. They will reason that if the true killer really confessed, then they would naturally have heard about it on the news. People who think this way are unaware of the government's control of the media. They naively believe that the media is independent of the government, and will report on the government's wrongdoing. That is only true for relatively minor infractions. When it comes to the biggies, like the JFK assassination and 9/11, you will never hear the truth on TV. The factions that committed these crimes control most of the major media, which is how they are able to get away with it all.

The grassy knoll shooter was James E. Files, born James Sutton. He made his first videotaped confession public in March of 1994. At that time, he gave an interview that was about 75 minutes long. NBC was in the process of making a program for national TV that would allow the public to hear what Files had to say. Edward J. Epstein, a suspected CIA disinformation

---

[430] http://listverse.com/2010/08/07/10-fascinating-sealed-and-secret-documents/

specialist, was hired by NBC as a "consultant." Inexplicably, the program was cancelled. The video of the interview was made available only in a few select retail outlets.

Almost 10 years later, in November of 2003, he gave a second videotaped interview that was about three hours and 20 minutes long. I have seen both interviews, and I believe that Files is telling the truth. In the two interviews 10 years apart, he was consistent and never changed his story on anything. He knew details, like Oswald's CIA handler. He knew about black operations. He knew other CIA operatives. In almost five hours of testimony, he never once flinched or gave any indication that he was hiding something. Files comes across as totally sincere. He is the kind of person who would rather just say, "I don't want to talk about it," rather than lie about something. He has been discredited by critics because he is a convicted felon and a mafia hit-man. How does that discredit him? That is exactly the kind of person who would commit such a crime. Are they saying they would believe a confession from Mr. Nice Guy? But Mr. Nice Guy would not shoot the president. Files' confession is detailed and logical. He was not paid for the interview. In fact, he had to be persuaded to speak about the assassination.

The Files confession came about as a result of the efforts of private investigator Joe West. West was attempting to have John Kennedy's body exhumed to prove multiple shooters. The case was in court at the time that West met Files. West had received a tip from former FBI agent Zack Shelton in 1992. Shelton had suspected the involvement of Files as far back as 1964. Acting on Shelton's tip, West tracked down Files, who was serving time for the attempted murder of an Illinois policeman. West spent months getting to know Files and earning his trust. The two formed a working relationship, and Files agreed to tell West what he knew about the Kennedy assassination.[431]

Then suddenly, West needed heart surgery. He came through the surgery fine and was recovering, when he unexpectedly relapsed and died. Files believes that West was murdered to prevent him from exhuming Kennedy's body. He believes this was done by tampering with his medication. The court case died, but the investigation into James Files' story was resumed by researchers Bob Vernon, Jim Marrs, and Wim Dankbaar. Bob Vernon conducted the first interview, Marrs and Dankbaar conducted the second

---

[431] Video- *Confession of an Assassin*, 1994

one. The powers-that-be went to great lengths to prevent the interviews from airing. Vernon and Files both received death threats, and Vernon was shot at from a car. Files has been verbally attacked and discredited on the internet. Plans for the video's marketing were mysteriously altered after the distributor was invited to the White House by Bill Clinton. Files' daughter has been harassed by mobsters and has had to move twice. Files was told through his attorney that a $50,000 contract had been put out on his head. Through all of this, the two interviews survived. They are available for viewing on *Youtube*, and for sale on Wim Dankbaar's website.

Here is some of what Files had to say:

> Joe West had the case in court, he wanted to exhume John F. Kennedy's body. And that's what he was fighting for. And at this point when I talked to Joe West, I explained to him that John F. Kennedy had been hit in the head with a mercury round, a special load. At this point I explained to him he can use this in the court to have the body exhumed because there would still be traces of mercury because the traces of mercury do not disappear. That will always be there. So this is what Joe West wanted to go back with, more evidence, and use this to get Kennedy's body exhumed, to look for traces of mercury...[432]

Prior to his conversations with Files, West was unaware that Kennedy had been hit with a mercury round. He wanted Kennedy's body exhumed to prove multiple shooters. He knew there would be exit wounds from different directions and bullet fragments from different weapons, but he was unaware of the mercury round, which had been custom-made for Files. From the visible effects of the head shot, West may have believed it was a defragmenting round, since it appeared to explode upon impact. This is one more reason why no legitimate autopsy was performed on Kennedy- it would have revealed traces of mercury. They would then have to explain how Oswald obtained the mercury-laden fragmenting bullets. The Warren Commission made no mention of the obvious exploding round.

Files explained that the mercury round was custom-made for him:

> Well, it was a .22 round and he took the tips off, he drilled them out and he inserted with an eyedrop, he put mercury

---

[432] Dakbaar, Wim, *Files on Files*, p. 167, Trafford, 2005

into the end of the round and he resealed them with wax. This is to make them explode on impact.

Files said that six mercury rounds had been customized for him. He said the rounds were made for him by a party he identified only as "Wolfman." Joe West was interested in talking to Wolfman, and Files made arrangements for the two of them to meet. But before that could happen, Wolfman died suddenly of a heart attack.

Files went on to describe his preparations for the event:

> ...I don't remember the date, but I went down like a week before the assassination. I wanna say I was in the Dallas area five days before the assassination took place.
>
> Q: And what was the purpose of that?
>
> JF: The purpose of that was for me to go to Dallas, look over the area, learn dead-end streets, railroad crossings, time of train crossings. They already knew the regular motorcade route that he would be taking, and they had already looked that over and they wanted to see if there were any better places. A lot of people had already decided on, I'm not the one that chose Dealey Plaza, but I was told to look it over very closely and see if I thought there was any place better. And I did the whole area from the route they had. All the way through I had Lee Harvey Oswald with me.
>
> Q: You say you were shocked to see him, but did you know Lee Harvey Oswald?
>
> JF: I had known Lee Harvey Oswald prior to that, yes.
>
> Q: How did you know him?
>
> JF: I knew him from earlier operations we were on with David Phillips when I was running semi-automatic .45 caliber submachine guns down to Clinton, Louisiana...[433]

It is significant that Files mentions Clinton, Louisiana. This is where Oswald was allegedly seen with Clay Shaw and David Ferrie. During the trial of Shaw, prosecutors were unable to establish a definite connection

---

[433] Dakbaar, Wim, *Files on Files*, p. 173, Trafford, 2005

between Shaw and Oswald. Witnesses had seen them together in Clinton, but they were discredited by the defense. Files' story verifies the Clinton sighting as true. The reason for the weapons was probably for the training of Cuban rebels in their quest to overthrow Castro. Files and Oswald both took part in the training, which took place in the Lake Pontchartrain area in southeastern Louisiana.

Q: And how did you meet Lee Harvey Oswald? Who introduced you?

JF: I met Lee Harvey Oswald through David Atlee Phillips. When I got down there, he introduced me to Lee…And upon doing this, he also explained to me that he was Lee Harvey Oswald's controller, the same as he was mine, that he was always in contact with Lee…

We drove around Dallas, Lee Harvey Oswald and I, we drove around Dallas for five days right up to before the assassination. I did not see Lee Harvey Oswald on the morning of the assassination. But prior to that, Lee Harvey Oswald had been with me every day. We drove around, he showed me different streets, different areas. He was the one that took me out to the place southeast of Mesquite there, next to a big junkyard. We went out in a field, he said, "Nobody is going to bother you out here." Because I wanted to calibrate the scopes, you know, not only for the Fireball, but for the other weapons as well. And while I was out there firing weapons and ejecting shell casings, Lee was picking them up and holding them in his hand. Because I didn't want to leave no casings or nothing behind and I'm busy firing, so I looked at Lee and said, "Lee, grab them casings," and that's what he did. He picked them up and held on to them. I calibrated my scopes, set things up, put the stuff back into the car and we got back in. We were driving around and I wanted to know the railroad crossings, I wanted to wait and see what time trains come through, I wanted to know if they were passenger or freight trains. Whether they stopped, intersection is gonna be blocked. Dead-end streets, construction work, where every intersection was at, where

all the lights were at, how long the lights were staying red. I
wanted to know all these little details.[434]

Here, Files has confirmed that Oswald was a CIA operative, and that his
handler was David Atlee Phillips. Although this information is available from
other sources, Files is not known to be a student of the event, and most
likely speaks from experience. Files acknowledges that he, too, was a CIA
operative and that Phillips was his handler. He repeatedly gives specific
names, dates, and places to indicate he is legitimate. This includes the alias
"Maurice Bishop," used by Phillips.

Files says that Oswald spent five days with him, preparing for the
assassination. This may lead people to believe that Oswald was part of the
plan. He was not. He was duped into this. Oswald thought he was going to
stop the assassination. He had infiltrated the inner circle of the plot. He
acted as though he was part of it, and Files believed that he was. Files was
asked what Oswald's role was:

> I think his part was to plant evidence to mislead everybody. I
> don't believe that Lee Harvey Oswald had any inkling that
> his life was in any danger whatsoever.

Files was unaware that Oswald had been chosen to be the patsy. This is
because of compartmentalization. Each person in the operation only knows
whatever they need to know to accomplish their own role. The less they
know, the better. That way, no one will spill the beans. What if Files knew
that Oswald was being set up? It's possible he might have warned him, or he
might have inadvertently let it slip out, which sometimes happens. That
would have ruined the whole plan. Files in not one to talk loosely anyway,
but some people are. If Oswald found out he was to be the patsy, he would
have bailed out on the mission. He would have known that he cannot trust
the people he is working for. Oswald could have called in sick at work on the
22nd, or he could have watched the motorcade outside with coworkers.
Then he would have had an alibi. Through compartmentalization, that was
prevented.

Q: Why did you go all the way to Fort Worth?

---

[434] Dakbaar, Wim, *Files on Files*, p. 174, Trafford, 2005

JF: That morning when I got there, Johnny Roselli went
there to meet somebody by the name of Jack Ruby. I had
never known Jack Ruby, nothing about him.

So Files has implicated Ruby in the conspiracy, as if it wasn't obvious
already. According to Files, it was Ruby who delivered the altered
motorcade route and the fake Secret Service identification to Roselli.

JF: Johnny opened the envelope, takes the stuff out and is
looking at it. While he is looking at it, he noticed I am
watching over while I am driving, and he's got them little
black wallets, like half-size, like identification wallets. And
he opened them up and there is identification plates in them
and there's badges on them. At that point I didn't know what
the identification on it was. Because he is sitting there and
looking at it, and I'm not going to lean over and I'm not
going to say, "Give me one of those," or anything like that. I
wait. When he wants me to know, he will tell me. And then
he opened up a piece of paper and he unfolded it. And there
has been a lot of discrepancy over this part now. But Johnny
Roselli said, "They only made one change in the route."

Q: That was the motorcade?

JF: It was a map of Dealey Plaza, the motorcade route. When
he looked at it, for Dealey Plaza, he said that they have only
made one alter, one change in it. He said, "That's all." And I
said, "What's that?" And he said, "They are going to go
down Elm Street. They're going to stop and make a detour,
coming around this little street here. And he held it up and I
kinda glanced over but I didn't get a chance to look at it real
good at that point. But I had already reconned the area so I
knew what he was talking about. And I know that everybody
says, "They had the motorcade in the newspaper, weeks and
months ahead of time. Sure they did. But they didn't have
that one change. And if anybody wants to show somebody a
newspaper clip, anybody check real close, because the
original route they were not coming down Elm Street there.
On that little detour, where they had the slowdown.[435]

---

[435] Dakbaar, Wim, *Files on Files*, pp. 177-178, Trafford, 2005

Files' role was to be a back-up shooter. He was to wait for Nicoletti and the others to shoot from behind first. If they got Kennedy, Files would not have to shoot. They did not want a shot coming from the front unless it was absolutely necessary. Files probably did not know the reason for that.

Files told how Johnny Roselli tried to abort the assassination on orders from his faction of the CIA. Nicoletti refused to honor the abort order, saying that only one man could call it off at that point. According to Files, that one man was Sam Giancana.[436]

> Chuck's exact words were, "F**k 'em. It's going anyway."
> And I told him, "What about Johnny?" "Well," he says,
> "Johnny will be with me, but he is not gonna be a shooter.
> He doesn't want to go against the orders. He's been told, he
> flew in here specifically to abort this assassination."

Even though Dallas was the territory of Carlos Marcello, Files and Nicoletti were Sam Giancana's men. Marcello did not want to use his own people for the crime, as explained by the HSCA:

> …Marcello also made some kind of reference to the way in
> which he allegedly wanted to arrange the President's murder.
> Marcello "clearly indicated" that his own lieutenants must
> not be identified as the assassins, and that there would thus
> be a necessity to have them use or manipulate someone else
> to carry out the actual crime.[437]

The weapon that killed John Kennedy was not a Mannlicher-Carcano, as the Warren Commission claimed. The murder weapon was a Remington Fireball. The XP-100 Fireball became commercially available in 1963, but prototypes were available before that, and the CIA naturally had the prototype. This was a .222 caliber single-shot bolt action pistol, described by Files as a "cut-down rifle." The weapon in this case had a scope mounted on it. Files stated that the Remington Fireball was given to him by David Atlee Phillips about 8-12 months prior to the assassination, and that he had used it twice prior to that day in Dallas.[438]

Files recalls the day clearly:

[436] Dankbaar, Wim, *Files on Files*, p. 180, Trafford Publishing, 2005
[437] http://spartacus-educational.com/JFKmarcello.htm
[438] Dankbaar, Wim, *Files on Files*, p. 184, Trafford Publishing, 2005

...I had walked away from the fence and I come back over, secured everything, got it ready, I could hear the rumble, the people murmuring, so you know the motorcade is approaching. So I got ready and opened it up. I'm holding the Remington Fireball down below the fence at this point. The motorcade comes down, I believe that's Main Street, there, come down at Houston, turn back around onto Elm and come down that little side drive there. And when it came down and made its first right, that's when I brought the weapon up.

And then I'm over the fence, and as they come down, made the turn onto Elm Street there, that's when I started focusing through the scope and following the car. As shots started ringing out, I started counting the shots, but I'm not counting like 1, 2, 3, and 4. I'm counting them as miss, miss, miss, because I know we are going for the head shot. So I don't care how many rounds are being fired as long as we get a headshot. So as I hear the shots being fired, I'm counting them as a miss, as a miss, miss. And that's the only thing I'm concerned about. I've got the sign there for the Stemmons Freeway that is fixing to come into my field of fire. As far as I could see at this point, the president has not been hit in the head at this time. I've seen the body lurch, I know he has been hit, how serious I don't know. But my last instructions were: We're going for a head shot. If you have to take a shot, take it, but don't fire unless it's a necessity, unless you really have to. He said, "Jimmy, don't fire unless you have to. We want everything from the backside." I am not asking why. Okay, whatever you say. At this point, as he starts to approach and come from behind that freeway sign...and I've already been instructed not to hit anybody but Kennedy, because they didn't want Jackie to get hurt or anybody else. I'm fixing to lose my field of fire, and at this point, either I shoot or I put it in the suitcase and leave, one or the other. I took the shot. I fired one shot, one shot only.

Q: Where were you aiming?

JF: I was aiming for his right eye which to me is the left side of his head looking head on. But for him it would be his right eye, and when I pulled the trigger, and I'm right in on it, and it's almost like looking six feet away through the

248

scope. As I squeezed, take off my round, his head moved forward, I missed and I come in right along the temple, just right behind the eye.[439]

Files' recollections are graphic and moving. His shot changed the world. I can only imagine what he must have been thinking and feeling at the time.

He mentions that Kennedy's head moved forward. To the observer that does not appear to be the case, but upon closer analysis we see that it's true. When the Zapruder film is slowed down, we see that Kennedy's head moved forward very slightly just before the fatal head shot. That is because he had been hit in the head from behind just a fraction of a second earlier. This was the shot from either the TSBD or the Dal-Tex building. Files must be telling the truth, because the average observer would never notice that. It is not perceivable at normal speed, but Files saw it through the scope. To him, everything was magnified and time was frozen. He was focused on Kennedy, and he was the only one who saw the slight forward movement of the head, causing Files' shot to be very slightly off from where he aimed. We can see this on the film in slow motion. Frame 312 shows Kennedy's head moving slightly forward from frame 311, and then 313 is the fatal head shot. Most people don't realize that Kennedy was hit in the head twice. Recall the medical evidence that showed a small entrance wound in the back of Kennedy's head, and a 6.5 mm fragment found in his brain. That confirms Files' version of the event.

> …the only thing that was said to me was, Mr. Nicoletti asked me, "Jimmy, don't you think you overreacted?" I said, "What do you mean?" He said, "Don't you think you fired too fast?" And I told him I was fixing to lose my field of fire, either I shoot then or I put it in my gun case and leave. I said I had one choice. I said at this point, you told me we were going for a head shot, there had been no head shot. I said I was just following my orders. I didn't want to explain to you why I didn't shoot.[440]

So Nicoletti thought that Files fired too soon. Files was only supposed to fire if necessary. All shots were supposed to come from behind, if possible. Nicoletti knew that Kennedy had been hit in the back of the head. Then

[439] Dakbaar, Wim, *Files on Files*, p. 190-91, Trafford, 2005
[440] Dakbaar, Wim, *Files on Files*, p. 200, Trafford, 2005

Files' shot came a split-second later and was really unnecessary. All it did was ruin the cover story. If Files had not shot, then there would be no bullets coming from the front, which is how they wanted it. They almost achieved that, but Files fired the shot that was caught on film and changed the whole complexion of the case. Without Files' shot, Kennedy would have been driven forward by the shot from behind. Kennedy would still be dead, but with no proof of a shooter from the front, the Oswald story would be more believable. It would naturally be assumed that Oswald's shot drove Kennedy forward.

> ...All the time I was there, I was alone. But in front of the fence the two people that I was mostly concerned about, they were a couple of guys wearing suits, roughly on top of the grassy knoll there, and they were a little away in front of me, 15, maybe 20 feet away, whatever, you know, I did not know who they were...They are between the fence and the sidewalk, between me and the motorcade. They are on top of the knoll, there. They are kinda like, looking over everybody and watching people. And this had me a little bit concerned, because I don't know who they are...I figured maybe they were just a couple of businessmen, people that wanted to see the president go by.
>
> ...But I took the shot, and as I was walking away, and like I say, I had seen Jackie crawl out there, a motorcycle cop, he threw his bike down, he jumped off, and as he came running in a little zigzag, or what you want to call it, like he's really into combat or something, it's still a wide open target, anybody can shoot him, he has got his pistol out, and he's running up the knoll there, the two men at the fence, the guys in the suits, they go over and they open up their identifications, so I have to figure, these were probably my cover that I've never been informed about, but I was told not to worry. They stopped him and he never came no farther. He went back down off the knoll.[441]

Files noticed the fake Secret Service agents on the grassy knoll. He saw them before the shooting and didn't know who they were. After the shooting, he saw them turning a police officer away from the knoll. This was Officer Joseph Smith. Smith testified to the Warren Commission and the

---

[441] Dankbaar, Wim, *Files on Files*, pp. 43-108, 166-235, Trafford Publishing, 2005

HSCA that immediately after the fatal shot was fired, he jumped off his motorcycle and ran up the grassy knoll, where he was turned away by a man who identified himself as a Secret Service agent. Smith said the man showed him Secret Service identification, or so he thought. James Files has confirmed Officer Smith's story as true. Several others have also told of their encounters with these imposters.

Files told of something he did spontaneously following the shot:

> I did something that I shouldn't have done, but I did do it. I took the shell casing and I bit down on it. I took it out and I looked at it and I set it on the stockade fence. And there was an indentation from my teeth on the shell casing…and I left it sitting on the stockade fence there, and I walked away.[442]

That might have been a risky move, but Files said he did it because he felt "cocky" and "indestructible." It was considered a calling card of sorts. It was something that could have come back to haunt him, but it didn't. The shell casing was not found until 1987, when John Rademacher was digging around the area with his stepson. He found it buried five inches deep in the soil, which would be expected after 24 years. The casing had teeth marks on it, which were verified as such by independent dentist Paul G. Stimson. The discovery of the shell casing was not widely reported, and the teeth marks were not mentioned at all. It's not likely that Files had heard about it, and this independent corroboration makes him even more credible.[443]

Files has identified Eugene Brading (Jim Braden), Frank Sturgis, Jack Ruby, Richard Cain, Orlando Bosch, Aldo Vera, Tony Diaz, and Felix Alderisio as being present in Dealey Plaza that day. All are considered possible co-conspirators.[444]

Personally, I believe Files. He comes across as sincere and credible. In spite of his criminal past, he values integrity and made it a point to be as honest as possible about all of this. One example is that he originally stated in his first interview that he had been paid $15,000 for the hit on Kennedy. In his second interview, he said he received $30,000 for the job. Bringing this up on his own, Files clarified the discrepancy. He said that he had been given $30,000, but that was for two jobs, the Kennedy hit and one other. He

---

[442] Dankbaar, Wim, *Files on Files*, p. 201, Trafford Publishing, 2005
[443] http://www.jfkmurdersolved.com/MARKSb.htm
[444] Dankbaar, Wim, *Files on Files*, pp. 187-188, 166-235, Trafford Publishing, 2005

took the $30,000 and figured it was $15,000 for each job, and that's why he initially said he got $15,000 for killing Kennedy. He later clarified that he had received $30,000 in total. Critics tried to use this to discredit Files by saying he changed his story, but it actually gives him more credibility. It shows that he values honesty that much that he wanted to clarify the contradiction so he is not perceived as lying about it.

The testimony of Lee Bowers adds credence to Files' story. Bowers was a railroad towerman situated in the control tower behind the grassy knoll. He claims that he saw two men behind the picket fence. He described one of them as being in his "mid-twenties in either a plaid shirt or plaid coat." Files was 21 at the time, and he said that he turned his jacket inside-out because it was plaid on the inside. He thought that would make him fit in more with the railroad workers. But Bowers knew all the railroad workers who were in the area daily, and he did not recognize Files.[445]

In a photograph taken moments after the assassination, we see a man walking away from the scene of the shooting.[446]He is visible behind the low concrete wall. He has his left arm bent in such a way that he might be clutching a handgun, which is how Files described his departure. This picture was shown to Files, and he stated that he believes it might be him.

Not everyone believes Files. One of the more humorous examples of skepticism involves author Edward J. Epstein. Epstein was the CIA asset planted as a consultant to NBC. In an e-mail to an associate, Epstein described his view on Files:

> In brief, NBC retained me as a consultant for their planned story on Files. I hired the detective firm of Jules Kroll. JK established from telephone records Files was in Chicago, not Dallas, on November 22, 1963. We then placed a call to Files from Dick Clark's office (DC was producer), and I interviewed Files about Kroll findings. He said he had a twin brother, who no one knew about, and whom he met shortly before November 22, and who he murdered after November 22. He said it was his twin brother in hospital with his wife, not him. His wife, however, said there was no twin, and Kroll confirmed there was no twin. My view then and now is

---

[445] http://www.jfkfiles.com/jfk/html/badgeman_4.htm
[446] http://www.jfkmurdersolved.com/figure.htm

that Files invented the story for the money it would earn him.[447]

Epstein just doesn't get it. Files was putting him on. Files believed that Epstein was a fake, so he was toying with him by giving him this bogus story about a twin brother who never existed. Epstein failed to recognize that and thought that Files was just a pathological liar. Epstein doesn't recognize a brush-off when he sees one. As for his claim that telephone records prove Files was in Chicago, that is nonsense. That only means that someone else used his phone in Chicago, but it was not Files.

Umbrella Man Revisited

One of the lesser-known aspects of the assassination involves an individual known as "Umbrella Man." Not much has been written about Umbrella Man, and some researchers write him off as fantasy or fiction. That is unfortunate, because he is a key part of the assassination puzzle. When properly understood, it becomes clear that Umbrella Man was one of the shooters that day. In fact, as we will see here, Umbrella Man shot John Kennedy *twice*.

The Umbrella Man theory explains eight anomalies that cannot be adequately explained any other way. They are:

- No bullet found in front or back
- Throat wound
- Back wound
- JFK's strange reaction
- No forward movement
- No backward movement
- 4 shots heard, 6 shots seen
- Umbrella man and companion

No Bullet Found in Front or Back

No bullet was found in either Kennedy's throat wound or his back wound. Dr. Humes probed both wounds and found that neither one exited. It is extremely unlikely that a bullet would fall out of a wound, but for it to happen twice in the same case defies probability. The bullets did not exit,

---

[447] Epstein, Edward J., e-mail to Barb Junkkarinen, 4-24-01

and they did not remain in the wound. So where are they? There are no bullets in these two wounds. They were both caused by the flechettes from the umbrella gun, which dissolved upon impact. No other theory can explain the absence of these two bullets.

Throat Wound

Kennedy had a small, circular-shaped wound in his throat, just below the Adam's apple. The wound was estimated at 3-5 mm wide. The hole is too small to have been made by either a Mannlicher-Carcano or a Mauser. The throat wound came from a flechette fired by the umbrella gun. Also of note is that the throat wound was described as perfectly round. If it had been an exit wound like the Warren Commission said, it would have been jagged and shredded, and much larger than 3-5mm.

One of the most questionable theories currently in circulation is that the throat wound was caused by an exiting bone fragment or bullet fragment from the fatal head shot. That is clearly wrong for a couple of reasons. As mentioned, an exit wound would not be neat and round as described. The doctors at Parkland Hospital unanimously agreed that the throat wound was one of entrance. Second, the throat wound occurred several seconds before the fatal head shot. We see Kennedy reacting to the throat shot as he emerges from behind the freeway sign. Researchers say that he was hit in the throat at Z-188 (frame 188 of the Zapruder film), and the fatal head shot was at Z-313. With a film speed of about 18 frames per second, that leaves about six or seven seconds between the throat shot and the head shot.

Back Wound

Contrary to popular belief, John Kennedy was NOT shot in the back with a rifle. There was no bullet found in Kennedy's back. Dr. Humes put his finger into the wound and he could feel the end of the pathway. If no bullet was found and the pathway did not exit, then he was not shot with a rifle. It is highly unlikely that the bullet would fall out. Kennedy was shot in the back with another flechette.

The back wound was measured at about 7mm, slightly larger than the throat wound, even though they were caused by the same weapon. The discrepancy can be easily explained by the fact that the back shot had to penetrate Kennedy's clothes, while the throat shot did not. The throat shot hit Kennedy's skin directly without touching any fabric. The flechette dissolves immediately upon impact. Since the shot to the back went through Kennedy's clothes first, it dispersed slightly in the few millimeters of space between his clothes and his skin. That accounts for the slightly larger measurement of the back wound, compared to the throat wound. It also accounts for the unevenness of the back wound compared to the perfect roundness of the throat wound. Yet, they both came from the same weapon. The depth of each wound was only about an inch, because the poison began dissolving upon impact, and was completely dissolved by the time it reached a depth of one inch.

If Kennedy had been shot in the back with a rifle, you would have seen a huge explosion of blood coming out of his back. We see nothing at all like that. Kennedy was not hit in the back with any kind of bullet, so there is no such explosion, just as there was no explosion from his throat. Also, there is no blood on Kennedy's jacket. Exhibit 59 of the Warren Commission's supplemental report shows the hole in the jacket from the projectile, but there is no blood from that point downward.[448] How can a man get shot in the back with a rifle and have no blood on his jacket? If Kennedy had been hit in the back with any kind of bullet, the entire back of his jacket would be covered with blood.

No Forward Movement

We see no sudden, violent movement of the body forward. Kennedy would have been driven into the seat in front of him by the force of a shotgun blast to his back. Critics argue that he wore a back brace that prevented such movement. That is nonsense. Even if his entire body was strapped into the seat, we would still see more of a reaction than we did if he was shot with a rifle. There would have been a violent, jerking movement upon impact. We see nothing close to that. Researchers say Kennedy was hit in the back at Z-228, but we see nothing there to confirm that it was a rifle shot. We only see a slight movement of the shoulders, and nothing more. Kennedy's reaction is more like a hiccup than a gunshot reaction. So what could have caused the back wound without driving him forward? It must have been a flechette from the umbrella gun. It is not a powerful weapon. The only reaction it caused is the slight flinching of the shoulders

---

[448] https://ratical.org/ratville/JFK/HWNAU/EMSapplll.html

that we see at about Z-228, hardly what you would expect from a gunshot.[449]

If we look at Umbrella Man's location in relation to the motorcade, we see that he was in position to hit Kennedy twice. As the motorcade approaches Umbrella Man from his left, he hits Kennedy in the throat. The motorcade continues past Umbrella Man, and now Kennedy is to his right. He then hits him in the back. So Umbrella Man shot Kennedy twice, first in the throat at Z-188, then in the back at Z-228 or later.

No bullet + no thrust + no blood = no gunshot to the back.

No Backward Movement

If Kennedy was hit in the throat with a bullet of any kind, even a low-caliber pistol, he would have been driven forcefully backwards. We see no backwards movement at all that could account for the throat wound. Kennedy is seen reaching for his throat before he disappears behind the freeway sign, so whatever caused the throat wound has already happened by then, and there was no backward movement at all. What could have caused the throat wound without driving him backwards? It could only be the flechette from the umbrella gun. Since it's not an actual bullet, it would not have the power to drive the victim's body forward or backward. It is only a dart. Its power is in the poison, not the impact.

We also do not see an explosion of blood from the throat, which you would expect to see if he had been hit with any kind of bullet, even one from a small handgun.

No bullet + no thrust + no blood = no gunshot to the throat.

4 Shots Heard, 6 Shots Seen

Although there is some dispute as to how many shots were fired that day, most witnesses report hearing either three or four shots. That discrepancy can be easily explained by the fact that two of the shots were nearly simultaneous, and some people perceived one shot as being the echo of the other. Most likely, four gunshots were heard that day. Yet, when we look at the damage, we see at least six shots. That includes Kennedy being hit four times (throat, back, and head twice), Connally being hit once, and

---

[449] http://www.personal.utulsa.edu/~marc-carlson/history/zapruder.html

one shot missing completely. Why do we see six shots, but only hear four? This can easily be explained by the fact that the umbrella gun fired two shots which were not heard. Since it does not fire bullets, there is no loud "Bang!" to be heard. The weapon only fires a dart, which makes more of a "ffffft" sound, which would never be heard in a noisy crowd, and would not be detected on the dictabelt recording.

JFK's Strange Reaction

The first two shots that hit Kennedy were from the umbrella weapon. Kennedy's reaction to these shots is very peculiar, and it is obvious that he has not been hit with any gunshots at this point. On the Zapruder film, Kennedy appears to be hit just before he disappears behind the freeway sign. He has stopped waving at this point, and his hands begin to move toward his throat. As he emerges from behind the freeway sign, we see that his hands are at his throat. It is often said that Kennedy was clutching his throat at this point, but he is not. Look closely at his hands and arms. His fists are clenched and his elbows are up. That is unnatural for someone who has just been hit with a gunshot. He is not clutching his throat, as you would expect if he had just been shot there. "Clutching" would mean that his hands are open, and he is grabbing his injured throat. That is not the case. His fists are clenched instead. Why? It's probably a reaction to the poison in the flechette. The poison affects the central nervous system in such a way that it causes the muscles to contract and stiffen. That's why his fists are clenched. It also explains why Kennedy's elbows are up instead of down. If someone were clutching their throat, their elbows would likely be down. Here we have a man who is teetering on the brink of consciousness, and it seems strange that his elbows are up, defying gravity. It would seem that the elbows would naturally sink down as he is losing consciousness. This shows the stiffness and rigidity caused by the poison from the dart. That is why Jackie Kennedy is looking at him with a puzzled expression. She can tell that something has happened, but she doesn't know what. She did not hear a gunshot, there is no blood, and Kennedy has not been knocked down. There is no reason to think he has been shot at this point, yet, something has definitely happened.

Kennedy's reaction to the second shot is minimal. The second shot was also from the umbrella gun, and it hits Kennedy at Z-228 or later. We see almost no reaction at all here, except for a slight flinching of the shoulders. There is no way that could be a reaction to a gunshot. As mentioned, a rifle shot would have driven him violently forward, with blood spurting out of his back. That is not what we see here. It is ridiculous to try and call the back shot a rifle shot. The second shot was a flechette, but since Kennedy was already paralyzed from the first flechette, the second one caused almost no reaction. We saw the effect of the first flechette. It caused Kennedy to stiffen up, his fists clenched, and his elbows rose. The second one would have done the same thing, but since Kennedy was already paralyzed from the first flechette, the second one had minimal effect.

Umbrella Man and His Companion

The mere presence of Umbrella Man in Dealey Plaza that day is cause for suspicion. Why did he have an open umbrella on a sunny day? It's true that it was raining in Dallas earlier that morning, but it had been clear for hours. In the entire motorcade route, we don't see any open umbrellas. Some people may have had umbrellas due to the earlier rain, but their umbrellas were closed. It is very strange that this one man would have the only open umbrella in Dealey Plaza, and he is standing just a short distance from Kennedy when he is hit. Some critics have tried to say that the man may have had sensitive eyes or a skin condition that requires him to avoid direct sunlight. That is not the case, because in a picture taken just after the shooting, we see the same man sitting at the curb with the umbrella folded up and laying in the street.[450] The umbrella was open as Kennedy passed, then folded up after he was shot. That should make it obvious that the umbrella weapon was a part of the assassination.

Also of interest is the unidentified accomplice. At the moment of the shooting, Umbrella Man is standing next to another man. The second man has a dark complexion, possibly being of Cuban descent. The two appear to be working together on this. As the limousine passes and Kennedy appears to be hit, the second man is seen raising his fist. Some have interpreted this as a signal to other shooters that more shots were needed, or maybe a signal to the limousine driver to slow down. It's not likely that it's a signal to the shooters. The other shooters would have their sights on Kennedy at this point, and would probably not be looking for a signal from anyone. The shooters could see if he was hit, so there is no need for a signal. The raised fist seems to be more of an emotional reaction. He seems to be expressing his joy that Kennedy was hit. He must be part of the plot, because no one

---

[450] https://www.jfk-assassination.eu/articles/umbrella.php

258

else even knows at this point that Kennedy was hit. How could the second man have known that he was hit? Kennedy is still sitting upright and not bleeding. No one in Dealey Plaza knows that Kennedy was hit. Even Jackie Kennedy hasn't figured it out yet. But this second man somehow knows instantly that the President has been hit. How did he know it when no one else knew it yet? It had to be because he was familiar with the umbrella weapon. He has seen it used, at least in demonstrations, so he knows what kind of reaction to look for. The moment Kennedy's fists are clenched and his elbows raised, this second man immediately pumps his fist, either in celebration or to indicate a hit. He was ready for this and he expected it. There is no way he could have otherwise figured it out so fast. Even someone who hated Kennedy would not have reacted so quickly like that. At this point, it is not yet obvious that Kennedy has been hit, and even if it was, the initial reaction would be one of shock and surprise, even to a Kennedy-hater.

As if that wasn't suspicious enough, we then see this second man sitting at the curb along with Umbrella Man after the shooting.[451] Everyone else in Dealey Plaza is running and panicking, while these two calmly sit at the curb and chat. Their indifference shows their involvement.

Who Is Umbrella Man?

Considering the suspicious actions of these two individuals, I would think they would be the subject of investigation. Instead, the Warren Commission, the Dallas Police, and the FBI ignored them. How could these two *not* be considered suspects? In any legitimate investigation, they would have at least been brought in for questioning.

During the HSCA investigation in the 70s, there was renewed talk about the Umbrella Man. By this time, the public had seen the Zapruder film, and a multitude of books had been written on the assassination. The HSCA wanted to know more about Umbrella Man. The public was starting to ask questions, and they had to be silenced. Lo and behold, they claim to have found Umbrella Man, and he was brought up in front of the HSCA to testify. It seems strange that no one could locate this man 15 years earlier, but now they are able to find him. The man who testified identified himself as Louis Steven Witt. He claimed that he didn't know that he was the subject of

---

[451] https://www.jfk-assassination.eu/articles/umbrella.php

controversy, and said that he brought the umbrella with him that day to heckle Kennedy.[452] His explanation is laughable:

> I just knew it was a sore spot with the Kennedys; I just knew the vague generalities of it. It had something to do with something that happened years ago with the senior Joe Kennedy when he was Ambassador to England.[453]

Supposedly, the umbrella symbolizes the policies of British Prime Minister Neville Chamberlain, who often carried an umbrella. So holding an umbrella is supposed to send some kind of political message to Kennedy? I doubt that Kennedy or anyone else would see the political significance in that. But they had to put the Umbrella Man talk to rest, so they needed some kind of explanation, no matter how flimsy. Once again, the public bought it with little or no protest. To further add to this fiasco, Witt brought with him the umbrella he claimed to have had in Dealey Plaza that day. The committee made a spectacle of the whole thing, examining the umbrella in detail, as if they were expecting to find a trigger mechanism or something to indicate that this was a weapon. If it was really a weapon, do you think Witt would bring it with him to show to the HSCA? Obviously, this is neither the right man nor the right umbrella. It was done only to pacify the public. Witt was probably a CIA contact who was chosen for this charade because he vaguely resembled Umbrella Man. As would be expected, Witt denied knowing the dark-skinned man who was obviously an accomplice.

How were they even able to allegedly locate Umbrella Man after 15 years? Supposedly, it was from an anonymous tip to author Penn Jones. This "tip" was actually staged by the CIA. It was their way of getting their man into the HSCA to have the story told their way. When Penn Jones interviewed Witt, he found him unconvincing:

> I felt the man had been coached. He would answer no questions and pointedly invited us to leave. His only positive statement, which seemed to come very quickly, was that he was willing to appear before the House Select Committee on Assassinations in Washington.[454]

---

[452] https://en.wikipedia.org/wiki/Umbrella_man_(JFK_assassination)
[453] http://www.aarclibrary.org/publib/jfk/hsca/reportvols/vol4/pdf/HSCA_Vol4_0925_7_Witt.pdf
[454] Marrs, Jim, *Crossfire*, p. 32, Carroll and Graf, 1989

So who is Umbrella Man? I don't know his name, but he is definitely not Louis Steven Witt. He could be anyone *except* Louis Steven Witt. Along with so much else, the identities of Umbrella Man and his accomplice will remain a mystery.

How the Weapon Works

Critics have dismissed the umbrella gun theory as being far-fetched. Even grassy knoll shooter James Files has stated that he doesn't believe the weapon was used, claiming that it would be too conspicuous to be used in public. This shows a common misconception about how the weapon is used. When properly understood, it's not so far-fetched anymore.

The misconception is that the weapon fires from the tip of the umbrella. Critics, including Files, think that the shooter holds the handle horizontally, while firing from the tip. That would, indeed, look very conspicuous. But that is not how the weapon fires. It fires from within the webbing of the umbrella. The shooter simply holds the umbrella the same way an average person would hold an average umbrella, so it is not conspicuous at all. Then he just squeezes the handle to fire a flechette from the webbing. No one around him knows that he has just shot someone. In the case of the Kennedy shooting, Umbrella Man shot him in the front and back without moving an inch. He only had to turn his wrist slightly to change his shooting angle about 90 degrees.

Robert Cutler and Richard Sprague are two of the leading researchers into photographic evidence regarding the JFK case. Richard Sprague was the original Chief Counsel to the HSCA. Robert Cutler has published five books on the JFK assassination. Cutler and Sprague have written an article on the umbrella weapon, called "The Umbrella System: Prelude to an Assassination." The article addresses the public skepticism of government involvement in the JFK assassination, and does much to dispel that skepticism. The authors recount the revelations of the Church Committee in 1975. During those hearings, the details of the weapon system were made public by the testimonies of CIA Director William Colby, former CIA Director Richard Helms, and CIA contract weapons designer Charles Senseney. They described the variations of the CIA's secret poison and weapons systems, including the umbrella weapon. After reading the testimonies of those involved in the project, there is no reason to doubt that the umbrella weapon was used in the murder of JFK, and probably others.

The article is revealing:

> The system is based on launching devices of various types, used to launch a self-propelled, rocket-like dart, or flechette. The flechette can carry either a paralyzing or fatal poison.

> The flechette itself is very simple. It is about the same size and looks like the tip of a large chicken feather. It is plastic and has tiny tail fins. Many varieties were developed for different uses. The great advantage of this weapon is that it is recoilless, almost silent, and the flechette travels at a high velocity which increases after launch. The flechettes can be fired singly or in high-impact clusters.

> It is propelled to its target by a solid-state fuel, ignited electronically at the launcher. It strikes its target, animal or human, dissolves completely in the body leaving no observable trace, and totally paralyzes its victim within two seconds.

> The launching devices developed by Mr. Charles Senseney at Fort Detrick, Maryland for the CIA included a cane, a fountain pen, soda straws, and an umbrella.

> The umbrella was used to shoot President Kennedy.

> The flechette struck JFK in the throat, causing a small entrance wound, but leaving no other trace. The missile was about 5 millimeters in diameter, and the wound was 4 millimeters. The size of the wound as compared to the size of the flechette is consistent with other findings of this nature. This particular wound, officially called an exit wound by the Warren Commission, puzzled medical examiners and critics of the Warren Commission alike. The critics charged that had the throat wound been an exit wound, it could not have been so small.

> JFK was paralyzed by poison contained in the flechette in less than two seconds--so paralyzed that the first rifle bullet that hit him did not knock him down, but left him in a nearly upright position. A second volley of shots fired at JFK a few seconds later struck a stationary, visible target. The

paralyzing flechette shot was fired by a man holding the umbrella launcher.[455]

There is one point where I disagree with the Cutler/Sprague article. They claim that the first flechette left Kennedy "...so paralyzed that the first rifle bullet that hit him did not knock him down, but left him in a nearly upright position." They are saying that Kennedy was hit in the back with a rifle, but he was so rigid with paralysis from the flechette that his entire body was frozen stiff. That is their explanation for why Kennedy's body did not move when he was hit in the back.

Their claim is wrong for two reasons: One, no bullet was found in Kennedy's back. The wound was only about an inch deep, as confirmed by the autopsy doctors. So the bullet did not exit, and it's extremely unlikely that it fell out. There was no bullet, so there was no rifle shot. Second, the shot from the grassy knoll drove Kennedy's body down. If the paralysis prevented movement from the back shot, why did the same paralysis not prevent movement from the grassy knoll shot? The article did not explain that, and the authors never considered the possibility of a second flechette shot. They assumed the first one created the necessary paralysis, which it did. The second flechette was frivolous. Maybe the shooter just got carried away and fired a needless shot. The Cutler/Sprague article is enlightening, but they underestimated their own theory. Umbrella Man shot Kennedy not just once, but twice.

According to researcher Rich Della Rosa:

> The guy that we call "the Umbrella Man" was seriously pumping the umbrella up and down. He wasn't just holding an open umbrella as we've been said [sic] by a number of other researchers. He was pumping the umbrella up and down. There was a lot of movement.[456]

This could have been done to reload the weapon. After the first flechette was fired into Kennedy's throat, the man pumped the umbrella to reload another flechette into the shaft to prepare it for firing. He then hit Kennedy in the back with a second flechette.

---

[455] Sprague, Richard E., and Cutler, Robert, "The Umbrella System: Prelude to an Assassination," *Gallery* magazine, 1978
[456] https://www.youtube.com/watch?v=UAYynHj9htk

The Church Committee hearings in 1975 gave us some degree of transparency into the workings of the Central Intelligence Agency. Among the many revelations was the use of discreet weapons capable of killing or incapacitating a suspect. The umbrella gun was one such weapon. CIA Director William Colby talked extensively about the workings of what he called "dissemination devices":

> The primary Agency interest was in the development of dissemination devices to be used with standard chemicals off the shelf. Various dissemination devices such as a fountain pen dart launcher appeared to be peculiarly suited for clandestine use.

> A large amount of Agency attention was given to the problem of incapacitating guard dogs. Though most of the dart launchers were developed for the Army, the Agency did request the development of a small, hand-held dart launcher for its peculiar needs for this purpose. Work was also done on temporary human incapacitation techniques. These related to a desire to incapacitate captives before they could render themselves incapable of talking, or terrorists before they could take retaliatory action. (Or to prevent guard dogs from barking.) ....such operation involved the penetration of a facility abroad for intelligence collection. The compound was guarded by watchdogs which made entry difficult even when it was empty. Darts were delivered for the operation, but were not used.

Former CIA Director Richard Helms also testified. He was asked if he would be surprised to learn that the weapon was used on humans:

> I would be surprised if it had been used against human beings, but I'm not surprised it would have been used against watchdogs. I believe there were various experiments conducted in an effort to find out how one could either tranquilize or kill guard dogs in foreign countries. That does not surprise me at all.

Charles A. Senseney was a contract weapons designer for the CIA. Senseney also testified:

Senseney: The fountain pen was a variation of an M-1. An M-1 in itself was a system, and it could be fired from anything. It could be put into....

Q: Could it fire a dart or an aerosol or what?

Senseney: It was a dart.

Q: It fired a dart...a starter, were you talking about a fluorescent light starter?

Senseney: That is correct.

Q: What did it do?

Senseney: It put out an aerosol in the room when you put the switch on.

Q: What about a cane, a walking cane?

Senseney: Yes, and M-1 projectile could be fired from a cane; also an umbrella.

Q: Also an umbrella. What about a straight pin?

Senseney: Straight pin?

Q: Yes, sir.

Senseney: We made a straight pin, out at the branch. I did not make it, but I know it was made, and it was used by one Mr. Powers on his U-2 mission.[457]

So not only could a paralyzing projectile be fired from an umbrella, it could also be fired from a fountain pen, a cane, or a straight pin. Such devices would have myriad uses in the world of espionage. Incapacitating watchdogs would be one of them. Any burglar would love to have such a gadget. The weapon was probably used to incapacitate humans too, even though Helms refused to admit that. But if the agency admits to having such a weapon, and they admit that it can cause paralysis, then it's' not at all far-fetched to believe that it was used in the Kennedy assassination. It does appear that Kennedy was paralyzed, and the paralysis occurred just as he approached the man with the unexplained umbrella. So who was Umbrella

---

[457] Sprague, Richard E., and Cutler, Robert, The Umbrella System: Prelude to an Assassination, *Gallery* magazine, 1978

Man? We may not know his identity, but he has some connection with American intelligence. Umbrella guns were not available at Sears, so if someone possessed this weapon, then they had contact with the Central Intelligence Agency.

The reality of the umbrella weapon was confirmed by none other than Col. Fletcher Prouty himself. Prouty saw the beta version of the weapon in 1960, along with a live demonstration of it in the Pentagon. He described it as "a pistol with a flashlight-size chamber above the grip." This early version fired flechettes in clusters rather than individually. Prouty did not know that the umbrella variation was used until years later when he saw it in a book by Robert Cutler.

Prouty has stated:

> I am able from personal and official experience to support
> the Sprague- Cutler thesis that an umbrella weapon was used
> as part of the JFK murder plot.[458]

The public is reluctant to accept the umbrella gun theory as reality. Even after the CIA's testimony at the Church Committee hearings, which most people did not follow, it is still regarded as fantasy. It is reminiscent of Maxwell Smart chasing after KAOS agents, or James Bond pursuing a cast of notorious characters. We have seen such gadgets in movies and TV shows: a shoe is really a phone, a tie clip is really a camera, and a walking stick is really a gun. So the notion of an umbrella weapon is also considered fictitious, just by association. Actually, such movies and TV shows are based on the true-life activities of the CIA, although they are embellished for the sake of drama or comedy.

Chauncey the Tramp

Chauncey Holt was a CIA covert operations specialist, weapons modification expert, and artist. He parlayed his artistic skills into a career in forgery, creating false documents, identification, police badges, etc. He was part of Operation Mongoose, the top secret plan to overthrow Fidel Castro. Holt worked closely with mobster Meyer Lansky, who owned the Los Angeles Stamp and Stationary Company that provided a cover for the forgery operation. Holt was also associated with CIA covert operations man

---

[458] https://ratical.org/ratville/JFK/TUM.html

Phillip A. Twombly. It was Twombly who instructed Holt to create fake IDs for Lee Harvey Oswald under the name Alek J. Hidell. This was the alias that was used to order the rifle and pistol that were eventually used to frame Oswald. He also used the ID to open a P.O. Box for the Fair Play for Cuba Committee in New Orleans. It was Holt who created 15 sets of fake Secret Service credentials that were used to keep people away from the grassy knoll shooter and other sensitive areas. On November 22, 1963, Holt drove mob hit man Charles Niccolletti to Dallas, unaware that Kennedy would be assassinated that day, and that Nicoletti would be one of the shooters.

Holt was one of the "three tramps" arrested that day, shortly after Kennedy's murder. This has been verified by forensic expert Lois Gibson, considered one of the top experts in her field. She has verified Chauncey Holt as the third man being led away by the police officer in the pictures.[459]

In a 1991 interview, Holt spoke extensively about his unwitting involvement in the assassination:

> … we received orders on November 15th, on the type of pins that were going to be worn in Dallas that day. The pins themselves… it wasn't the background, that never changed. It was the markings on the pins that determined what was going to be used that day. We were under a time constraint for when we received the order November 15th, and were told that we had to be in Dallas on the night of the 21st.

The Secret Service lapel pins are a different color every day to prevent forgery. The assigned color for the day is not known until the start of the day, so Holt could not produce the finished lapel pins until the morning of the assassination.

Holt did not know in advance that an assassination was going to take place. He had been led to believe that an incident of some kind would be staged which would be blamed on the FPCC and other pro-Castro groups. This was believable to Holt because it's typical of intelligence work. Holt's role was to create the fake Secret Service identifications. He had been told that an open box car in the railroad yard would be available to him if he needed refuge. It was in the railroad yard that Holt encountered the other two tramps, who he had worked with before. Dallas Police searched the box

---

[459] http://spartacus-educational.com/JFKholt.htm

cars and discovered the three men hiding. Holt and the other two identified themselves as federal agents. The three men were not handcuffed, but were escorted to the Sheriff's Department in Dealey Plaza. This led to the famous photos of the three tramps that have been a subject of debate for years. Holt talked about the pictures:

> In the photos, the individual in front is the individual I knew as Richard Montoya. The individual behind him I knew as Charles Harrelson. I had reason to believe that's who he actually was, even though I didn't know him that well. I'm confident that's who it was. And I'm the gentleman in the back, carrying the bag with the radio in it...
>
> We were not placed under arrest. We were taken across, and someone interviewed us momentarily, and turned us over to someone else. A person I later learned was Captain Fritz, he said not two or three words to us. He said he was turning us over to the FBI. His name was Gordon Shanklin...
>
> Jim Braden was there. I didn't recognize him at first because he had a hat on with some kind of Texas-style hat band on it, and I didn't know him all that well, if you know what I mean. But I knew that I recognized him like I recognize you...
>
> ...they were very careless. We were strolling around, people were coming around. They didn't treat us like dangerous suspects. They didn't handcuff us. Plus, they didn't search us, and we were heavily armed...
>
> We were taken to the Sheriff's Department, right there on Dealey Plaza. Didn't walk far. We didn't make a statement. Weren't fingerprinted. Weren't taken to the jail, where I assume we would have been taken. Then Gordon Shanklin said, "You're free to go."[460]

Holt mentioned the arrest of Jim Braden. Braden was a known criminal with 35 arrests on his record. He was found in the Dal-Tex building where at least one shot came from, and he did not have authorization to enter the building. In spite of this, he was released after just three hours. Braden had recently had his name legally changed to Eugene Hale Brading, and it's not

---

[460] Dankbaar, Wim, *Files on Files*, pp. 155-163, Trafford Publishing, 2005

clear if the police were aware of this. His criminal past may have escaped them. Braden's record included convictions for burglary, embezzlement, mail fraud, illegal bookmaking, and interstate transportation of stolen property. He also had connections with Carlos Marcello, Santos Trafficante, and David Ferrie. The night of the assassination he stayed at the Cabana Motel, and was visited there by Jack Ruby. Braden, who was on parole, claimed to be in the Dal-Tex building to have a meeting with his parole officer, but the parole officer could not recall such a meeting. But it wouldn't matter, anyway. Once Oswald was in custody, the authorities soon lost interest in all other suspects.[461]According to James Files, Braden was there because he had contacts in the Dal-Tex building. Braden's role was to get Charles Nicoletti into the building and help him gain access to a private office to shoot from.[462]

Holt and Gibson have identified the first tramp as Richard Montoya, whose real name is Carlos Rogers. Rogers was a friend of David Ferrie, who he knew from the Civil Air Patrol. Like Ferrie, Rogers was an associate of mobster Carlos Marcello. Rogers joined the CIA in 1956. Rogers later became known as "The Icebox Killer" because in 1965, his parents' dissected bodies were found in the freezer in his home. Rogers was the prime suspect, but he could not be found and was never seen or heard from again.[463]

The second tramp is Charles Harrelson. He is the father of actor Woody Harrelson, best known for his role on the TV series, "Cheers." Charles Harrelson was a contract killer. He was convicted of the contract killing of a businessman in 1968, and he was convicted of killing federal judge John A. Wood in 1979. When he was arrested for killing Wood, he confessed to being one of the gunmen who killed John Kennedy. He later recanted his confession, which the authorities had ignored anyway.

Harrelson was once interviewed by reporter Chuck Cook, who asked him about his involvement in the Kennedy assassination. According to Cook, Harrelson "got this sly grin on his face." Later, Harrelson told Cook, "Listen. If and when I get out of here and feel free to talk, I will have something that will be the biggest story you ever had." Cook inquired what he meant by that, and Harrelson replied, "November 22, 1963. You remember that."

---

[461] Marrs, Jim, *Crossfire*, p. 338, Carroll and Graf, 1989
[462] Dakbaar, Wim, *Files on Files*, p. 188, Trafford Publishing, 2005
[463] http://spartacus-educational.com/JFKrogersC.htm

After Harrelson's arrest for killing a judge, he admitted to being part of the Kennedy murder plot. He was asked about this in an interview. He responded:

> At the same time I said I killed the judge, I said I had killed Kennedy, which might give you an idea as to the state of my mind at the time. It was an effort to elongate my life. Well, do you believe Lee Harvey Oswald killed President Kennedy alone, without any aid from a rogue agency of the U.S. government, or at least a portion of that agency? I believe you are very naïve if you do.[464]

The testimony of Chauncey Holt seems believable, and if so, it solves the mystery of the three tramps. These men were arrested in a box car behind the picket fence where the fatal head shot came from. They were taken to the sheriff's office and questioned, but there is no record of their interrogation. It was Gordon Shanklin who interviewed them and let them go with no written record. Two days later, the same Gordon Shanklin would order FBI agent James Hosty to destroy a note from Lee Harvey Oswald.

The following excerpt is from the *Wikipedia* entry for The Three Tramps:

> In 1992, journalist Mary La Fontaine discovered the November 22, 1963, arrest records that the Dallas Police Department had released in 1989, which named the three men as Gus W. Abrams, Harold Doyle, and John F. Gedney. According to the arrest reports, the three men were "taken off a boxcar in the railroad yards right after President Kennedy was shot," detained as "investigative prisoners," described as unemployed and passing through Dallas, then released four days later. An immediate search for the three men by the FBI and others was prompted by an article by Ray and Mary La Fontaine on the front page of the February 9, 1992, *Houston Post*. Less than a month later, the FBI reported that Abrams was dead and that interviews with Gedney and Doyle revealed no new information about the assassination. According to Doyle, the three men had spent the night before the assassination in a local homeless shelter

---

[464] Marrs, Jim, *Crossfire*, p. 334, Carroll and Graf, 1989

where they showered and ate before heading back to the railyard.[465]

Supposedly, the DPD released the arrest records of the three tramps in 1989. They identified them as Gus W. Abrams, Harold Doyle, and John F. Gedney. This sounds highly suspicious for several reasons. First, why did it take 26 years for the Dallas Police to identify these men? They were seen the day of the assassination. Reporters were asking, "Who are these men?" Why didn't the DPD identify them immediately? The Warren Commission made no mention of them, and probably did not see the pictures. Jim Garrison had the pictures but didn't know who they were. The HSCA also didn't know who they were. Thousands of researchers have wondered for decades who these men are, but the DPD would not identify them. They claimed to have no record of their arrest or interrogation. Then suddenly, after 26 years, they decide to tell us who they are. Why the delay?

Second, the article mentions arrest reports, but it doesn't seem that the men are being arrested. They are not in handcuffs, and the police do not have their guns drawn on them. They all seem to be very casual. Then, the article says that they were released four days later. That means that they were held for four days, and still no one could identify who they were. When reporters were asking the Dallas Police to identify these men on November 23, the Dallas Police claimed no knowledge of them. But according to this story, the three were still in custody at the time. Why did no one hear about them? No announcement was made of the arrest of Abrams, Doyle, and Gedney. The only announced arrest was that of Oswald. In fact, if these men were held for four days, as the article says, that means that they were still in custody for two days after Oswald was killed. In the interview with Doyle, he claims that they were booked, fingerprinted, and charged with vagrancy. Yet, no one has seen the mug shots.[466]

But the strangest thing about the article is that it says, "An immediate search for the three men by the FBI and others was prompted by an article by Ray and Mary La Fontaine on the front page of the February 9, 1992, *Houston Post*." So Ray and Mary La Fontaine did what the FBI could not do. They are saying that the FBI could not locate these men for 29 years, but these independent researchers did. Then, the FBI finally acts in response to

---

[465] https://en.wikipedia.org/wiki/Three_tramps
[466] http://whokilledjfk.net/tramps.htm

their story. Why is the FBI searching for these men in 1992, when they were totally uninterested in them in 1963? Keep in mind that Chauncey Holt's confession and detailed interview were in 1991, so the FBI may have had an interest in discrediting his story, hence the quick action on the La Fontaine article.

Witnesses

The Warren Commission interviewed 121 witnesses to the assassination. Of the 121, 32 said the shots came from the TSBD, 38 had no clear opinion, and 51 said at least one shot came from the grassy knoll area.[467] Yet, the commission decided that those 51 witnesses must be mistaken:

> No credible evidence suggests that the shots were fired from the railroad bridge over the Triple Underpass, the nearby railroad yards or any place other than the Texas School Book Depository.[468]

How can 51 witnesses all be mistaken? These witnesses either heard, saw, or felt a shot come from the grassy knoll. There is no reason to doubt them, especially when the Zapruder film confirms their testimonies to be true. Yet, the commission never doubted the witnesses who said shots came from the TSBD, because that's what they wanted to hear.

The description of Oswald that was sent out over the police band was said to have come from Howard Brennan, who saw a man in the TSBD window. This description said the man was a white male, in his early thirties, about 5-foot-10, 165 pounds. But Brennan only saw the man from a distance, and could not possibly have known the shooter's height, since he would have been kneeling down at the time. It appears that the description of Oswald was pre-written by the plotters. They just needed someone like Brennan to justify it.[469]

Victoria Adams and Sandra Styles watched the motorcade from the fourth floor of the TSBD. They saw the fatal head shot and ran down the back stairs to see if they could see the escaping shooter. This presented a problem for the Warren Commission, because the stairs that they took were

---

[467] Feldman Harold, *Fifty-one Witnesses: The Grassy Knoll*, 1965
[468] *The Warren Commission Report*, p. 51, Longmeadow Press, 1964
[469] http://jfkassassination.net/russ/testimony/brennan.htm

the same ones allegedly used by Oswald to escape. But neither Adams nor Styles saw Oswald there, nor did they hear anyone coming down. Adams said that it was about 15 or 20 seconds after the shooting before they started heading for the stairs. That would give the shooter two floors above time to get a head start, and they should have been on the stairs at about the same time. Styles was not called to testify. Adams gave a deposition, but claims that it was altered.[470]

Motorcycle patrolman Bobby Hargis was riding to the left of the limousine and slightly to the rear of it. Hargis was splattered with blood from the fatal head shot, which is an indicator that the shot came from the right front, meaning the grassy knoll:

> As...Mrs. Kennedy turned toward (JFK)...he got hit in the side of his head, spinning it around. I was splattered with blood. Then I felt something hit me. It could have been concrete...but I thought at first I might have been hit."[471] [472]

Sandy Speaker was a witness to the shooting:

> I was less than a half a block away and heard the shots. I heard at least five shots and they came from different locations. I was a combat marine with 1st Marine Division in World War II, hand-to-hand combat, and I know what I'm talking about. I've said for years that there were more than three shots fired.[473]

Beverly Oliver was originally known to researchers as "the babushka lady" before anyone knew who she was. She is seen in the Marie Muchmore film taking a film of her own. Her undeveloped film was confiscated by two FBI agents who promised to return it to her within ten days. Oliver never got her film back and it was never seen by the public. From her viewpoint on Elm Street, the film would have shown the activity on the grassy knoll. We might have gotten a glimpse of the shooter's head over the top of the picket fence, and we might have seen a puff of smoke from the muzzle blast. The film must have shown something significant, because if it didn't, it would

---

[470] Marrs, Jim, *Crossfire*, p. 44, Carroll and Graf, 1989

[471] *The Warren Commission Report*, p. 294, Longmeadow Press, 1964

[472] http://jfk50d.blogspot.com/2013/06/bobby-hargis-hit-by-jfks-blood-and.html

[473] Hughes-Wilson, *JFK: An American Coup D'etat*, p. 164, John Blake Publishing, 2015

have been returned to her. Oliver has fought the bureaucracy for years to try and get her film returned, but to no avail. Oliver did not testify to the Warren Commission. She was later interviewed by the HSCA staff, but did not testify at the hearings. She did testify to the ARRB in 1994.[474]

One witness who was especially problematic for the Warren Commission was James Tague. Tague is the reason why the magic bullet theory was developed. Tague was standing on the south side of Elm Street near the railroad overpass as he watched the motorcade approach. During the shooting, Tague was struck on the right cheek by a stray bullet fragment or a piece of concrete. This was proof of too many shots to say that Oswald acted alone. The commission wanted to say that Oswald fired three shots, and no other shots were fired. But if Tague was hit, that leaves only two other shots to account for all the wounds we saw. That lead to the creation of the magic bullet theory. By claiming that Kennedy and Connally were hit by the same bullet, it allowed them to say Oswald was the only shooter.[475]

Even without Tague's injury, the commission would have had a problem with the number of shots. Looking at Kennedy and Connally, we see evidence of at least five shots. Kennedy was hit in the throat and back, and twice in the head, and Connally was hit in the back. That is five wounds, although the commission did not acknowledge the second head shot, so they counted four wounds. Tague's injury would have meant five wounds and five shots. With the magic bullet theory, the commission combined three wounds into one shot. Kennedy's throat and back wounds, along with Connally's wounds, were all caused by the same bullet, according to the commission. This reduced the alleged number of shots from five to three, keeping the lone-assassin scenario intact.

On the day of the assassination, the *Dallas Times Herald* reported that a man was arrested in Dealey Plaza after TSBD employees pointed him out from a third-story window. The man wore horn-rimmed glasses, a plaid coat, and a raincoat. He was taken to the Sheriff's Department under protest while bystanders shouted, "I hope you burn" and "I hope you die." Nothing further was ever said about him. This could have been Larry Florer,

---

[474] http://garyrevel.com/jfk/Beverlyoliver.html
[475] http://michaelgriffith1.tripod.com/tague.htm

who was taken into custody after he had entered the TSBD building to look for a phone. But no arrests other than Oswald's were ever announced.[476]

Officer Roger Craig arrested a woman behind the picket fence as she was attempting to leave a secured parking lot that she was not authorized to be in. In all the confusion, this potential witness/conspirator was somehow lost. Craig wondered:

> How did this woman gain access and, what is more important, who was she and why did she have to leave? I turned her over to deputy sheriff C.L. "Lummie" Lewis and…(he) told me that he would take her to Sheriff Decker and take care of her car…I had no way of knowing that an officer with whom I had worked for four years was capable of losing a thirty-year-old woman and a three-thousand pound automobile. To this day, Officer Lewis does not know who she was, where she came from, or what happened to her. Strange![477]

Witnesses Not Called

Although the Warren Commission claims to have done a thorough investigation, a closer look tells us it was anything but that. There were scores of witnesses who were not called to testify before the commission. These were witnesses who had given verbal or written testimony to the FBI or the Dallas Police, but their testimony conflicted with the lone-assassin theory, so they were ignored by the commission. Here are some of those witnesses:

Carolyn Arnold- saw Oswald in the second floor lunchroom at 12:15.

James Chaney- motorcycle policeman who was closest to Kennedy when he was shot; said he saw Kennedy get hit in the face; said Connally and Kennedy were hit by separate shots.

Bill and Gayle Newman- witnesses north of Kennedy when he was shot; both consistently maintained that the fatal head shot came from behind them and to their right, which would be the grassy knoll.

---

[476] https://groups.google.com/forum/#!topic/alt.assassination.jfk.uncensored/QFsq385n9Ok
[477] Marrs, Jim, *Crossfire*, p. 329, Carroll and Graf, 1989

Charles Brehm- one of the closest witnesses to the shooting.

J.C. Price- witnessed the assassination from atop the Terminal Annex building; said he saw a man with a rifle running behind the picket fence on the grassy knoll.

Ed Hoffman- a deaf mute who saw two men on the grassy knoll; confirmed Price's story; said he saw one man throw a rifle to a second man, who disassembled it, put it in a toolbox and walked away.

Mary Dowling- said that Oswald and Officer Tippit were in a restaurant at the same time two days earlier.

James Simmons- Union Railroad employee who said shots came from behind the picket fence on the grassy knoll.

Richard Dodd- another Union Railroad employee who heard shots and saw smoke coming from behind the picket fence.

Alonzo Hudkins- Houston reporter who said that Dallas officials told him that Oswald was an informant for the FBI.

Ray Rushing- evangelist who saw Jack Ruby at Dallas Police Headquarters about two hours before Ruby killed Oswald; Warren Commission said that Ruby was home at that time.

Lt. George Butler- present when Oswald was shot; gave contradictory information to the FBI about Ruby's criminal past.

Admiral George Burkley- Kennedy's personal physician who was present at the Bethesda autopsy and received all the autopsy information.

John T. Stringer and Lt. William Pitzer- took photographs and x-rays during the autopsy.

James Sibert and Francis O'Neill- FBI agents present at the autopsy; made statement about the location of the back wounds that contradicts official conclusions.

Richard Randolph Carr- witness who saw two men run from behind the TSBD and drive off in a Rambler station wagon.

Marvin Robinson- saw Oswald enter a west-bound Rambler station wagon in front of the TSBD minutes after the assassination.

Julia Ann Mercer- claims to have seen a man walking up the grassy knoll carrying what she thought was a rifle case, about 75 minutes before the shooting; saw Jack Ruby in Dealey Plaza before the shooting.

Frank Wright and his wife- lived on the street where Tippit was shot; heard the shots; saw a man run from Tippit's car and get into a small, old gray car and drive away.

T.F. Bowley- gave time of Tippit's death that was in conflict to official story.

E.E. Taylor- Dallas Police detective who made a list of witnesses to Oswald's arrest in the Texas Theater; list of witnesses has since disappeared.

All of these witnesses had significant information for anyone doing a sincere investigation. They were not called to testify. Yet, other witnesses with trivial information were called. Here are a few:

Mrs. Anne Boudreaux- woman who was Oswald's baby sitter for two weeks when Oswald was less than three years old; never knew Oswald as an adult, yet she gave four pages of testimony.

Mrs. Viola Peterman- neighbor of the Oswalds when Lee was two years old; hadn't seen or heard from any of the Oswalds in 23 years, but gave seven pages of testimony.

Prof. Revilo Pendleton Oliver- discussed his article "Marxmanship in Dallas," suggesting Oswald was part of a Soviet plot; gave 35 pages of pointless testimony.[478]

Witnesses Intimidated

Several other witnesses have claimed that the commission distorted their testimony or changed their words. Butch Burroughs, Jean Hill, Phil Willis, Orville Nix, James Tague, Roland Fischer, and others have all made such charges.

Roland Fischer was a witness who saw a man in the sixth floor window just prior to the assassination. Fischer claims he had a heated argument with Assistant Counsel David Belin, who tried to get him to change his testimony:

---

[478] https://ratical.org/ratville/JFK/NotesForNewInves.html

(Belin) and I had a fight almost in the interview room over the color of the man's hair. He wanted me to tell him that the man was dark-headed and I wouldn't do it. (Oswald's hair) doesn't appear to me in the photographs as light as the man that I saw and that's what Belin was upset about.[479]

Phil Willis was a witness who took photographs of the assassination. He was asked to give a deposition, rather than testify. In two separate interviews, Willis expressed his frustration with the Warren Commission:

This guy came to Dallas and took my deposition. He took down only what he wanted to hear. I tried to tell him about the shots and the echoes, but he wasn't interested. He just seemed to want to get it over with. The Warren Commission never subpoenaed any photographer. They weren't interested in talking to me or Zapruder. It seemed strange to me. It's not much of a way to conduct an investigation.[480] All they wanted to know was that three shots came from the book depository. That's all that got into the Warren Commission report. I'm certain that at least one shot came from the right front. I'll stand by that to my grave.

Willis's daughter, Mrs. Linda Pipes, was also a witness. She echoed the sentiments of her father:

I very much agree that shots came from somewhere else other than the depository. And where we were standing, we had a good view. (The Warren Commission) talked to me later, but they didn't seem to be investigating very thoroughly.[481]

Richard Randolph Carr had seen two men running from the TSBD, which was not what the authorities wanted to hear. Carr described his treatment at the hands of the FBI:

The FBI came to my house--there were two of them--and they said they heard I witnessed the assassination and I said I did. They told me, "If you didn't see Lee Harvey Oswald up

---

[479] Marrs, Jim, *Crossfire*, p. 480, Carroll and Graf, 1989
[480] Marrs, Jim, *Crossfire*, p. 481, Carroll and Graf, 1989
[481] Turner, Nigel, 1988, The Witnesses, *The Men Who Killed Kennedy*, U.K., Nigel Turner Productions

in the School Book Depository with a rifle, you didn't witness it." I said, "Well, the man I saw on television that they tell me is Lee Harvey Oswald was not in the window of the School Book Depository. That's not the man." And [one of the agents] said I better keep my mouth shut. He did not ask me what I saw, he told me what I saw.[482]

Shortly afterwards, Carr's home was raided in the middle of the night by over a dozen Dallas Police officers armed with a search warrant. They claimed they were searching for stolen property. They ransacked the house while holding Carr and his wife at gunpoint. The next day Carr received an anonymous phone call advising him to "get out of Texas." Carr eventually moved to Montana to escape harassment. Yet, one day he found dynamite taped to his car's ignition, and on another occasion he was shot at. Carr testified at the trial of Clay Shaw, during which time he suffered another attack, this one by knife. During the knife attack, he was wounded in the back and arm, but managed to fatally shoot one of his assailants.[483] [484]

Sandy Speaker was the work supervisor of Howard Brennan, who was supposedly the Warren Commission's key witness. Yet, Brennan failed to pick Lee Harvey Oswald out of a police line-up. Brennan, like many others, was intimidated by the authorities. Speaker was interviewed by author Jim Marrs, and he talked about Brennan:

> They took (Brennan) off for about three weeks. I don't know if they were Secret Service or FBI, but they were federal people. He came back a nervous wreck, and within a year his hair had turned snow white. He wouldn't talk about (the assassination) after that. He was scared to death. They made him say what they wanted him to say.[485]

Speaker received a hysterical phone call from friend and co-worker A.J. Millican in early 1964. Millican was a witness who heard way more shots than the Warren Commission cared to deal with, and he also saw the same van that Jean Hill described prior to the shooting. Millican was almost in tears on the phone and told Speaker to never talk about the assassination.

---

[482] http://dealeyintimidation.tripod.com/#

[483] http://spartacus-educational.com/JFKcarrR.htm

[484] http://dealeyintimidation.tripod.com/#

[485] Marrs, Jim, *Crossfire*, p. 25, Carroll and Graf, 1989

He said he had just received an anonymous phone call threatening him and his family, and warning him to keep his mouth shut.

Speaker was interviewed by Jim Marrs:

> That call really shook me up because Millican was a former boxing champ of the Pacific fleet. He was a scrapper, a fighter. But he was obviously scared to death. And I still don't understand how they got my name because I was never interviewed by the FBI, the Secret Service, the police or anyone. They must be pretty powerful to have found out about me.[486]

Suspicious Deaths

For a thirty-year period following the JFK assassination, there were 115 people who died suspicious deaths that were somehow related to it. These were witnesses, participants, law enforcement officials, and researchers. 18 of them died in the first three years, many of them during the Warren Commission's investigation. These suspicious deaths all had one thing in common: they were all advantageous to the conspirators in Kennedy's murder. All of the victims knew too much, and all of them were a threat to expose the truth. Of the 115 deaths, it's likely that a few of them were just coincidence, but it's virtually impossible for all of them to be coincidence. Most of the deaths occurred during one of the three investigations into the crime- the Warren Commission, the Garrison investigation, and the House Select Committee on Assassinations. In many cases, witnesses who were preparing to testify suddenly died. Law enforcement officials also became victims if they were a threat to the guilty parties. Independent researchers sometimes got too close to the truth and paid for it with their lives. Some of the victims were driven to suicide by the fear or stress caused by their knowledge or their involvement.[487]

The government could never admit that these deaths were in any way related to the assassination of John F. Kennedy. According to the official story, Oswald was the only guilty party, and he's dead, so no one alive has any involvement in the crime, and so no one else would have a motive to silence people. If they admit that these deaths are related, they sure can't

---

[486] Marrs, Jim, *Crossfire*, p. 309, Carroll and Graf, 1989

[487] Roberts, Craig, and Armstrong, John, *JFK: The Dead Witnesses*, p. iii, CPI, 1995

blame them on Oswald. There must be somebody else, and as soon as there is somebody else, then by definition that's conspiracy. So the government has turned a blind eye to these deaths, as demonstrated by the ridiculous conclusion of the HSCA on the matter:

> Our final conclusion on the issue is that the available evidence does not establish anything about the nature of these deaths which would indicate that the deaths were in some manner, either direct or peripheral, caused by the assassination of President Kennedy or by any aspect of the subsequent investigation.[488]

Here are some of the more significant deaths related to the case:

Jack Zangretti- Zangretti was a mob figure who owned an expensive resort in Oklahoma. The day after the assassination, he told friends "...a man named Jack Ruby will kill Oswald tomorrow, and in a few days, a member of the Frank Sinatra family will be kidnapped just to take some of the attention away from the assassination." Both predictions came true. Ruby killed Oswald and Frank Sinatra Jr. was kidnapped two weeks later. Shortly after that, Zangretti was found floating dead in a lake with bullet holes in his chest.

Eddy Benavides- Eddy was the brother of Domingo Benavides, who was a witness to the murder of J.D. Tippit. Domingo found two shell casings from the shooting and gave them to a Dallas Police officer, then gave the police a description of the killer. There were two problems caused by Domingo. The casings he gave to the officer were from an automatic weapon, while Oswald only possessed a revolver. Also, the description of the suspect given by Benavides did not match Oswald. He said the killer had dark, curly hair and wore different clothing than Oswald. Domingo Benavides began receiving death threats shortly after it was publicized that his description did not fit Oswald. In February of 1964, Eddy Benavides was shot and killed. Domingo and Eddy bore a great resemblance to each other, and it's likely that Eddy's murder was a case of mistaken identity.

Bill Hunter- Hunter was an award-winning journalist for *The Long Beach Press-Telegram.* Hunter was one of five men who visited Jack Ruby in jail the night he shot Oswald, then convened for a meeting at Ruby's apartment.

---

[488] Marrs, Jim, *Crossfire,* p. 556, Carroll and Graf, 1989

The five men must have learned something earth-shattering, because by March of 1965, four of them were dead and one had disappeared. Hunter was shot in the press room of the Long Beach Police Station by an officer in what was ruled an accident. The officer, Creighton Wiggins, said that he dropped his gun, causing it to discharge. This was proven false, as the trajectory of the shot showed it did not come from the ground up. Another officer present said he had his back turned when the shooting happened. Wiggins later said he was playing a game of "quick draw" when the accidental shooting occurred. Either way, another potential witness was dead.

Tom Howard- Howard was Jack Ruby's attorney, and was conspicuously present in the Dallas Police Department when Ruby shot Oswald. Howard was also at the meeting at Ruby's apartment later that night. It was Howard who suggested to Ruby that he should say he shot Oswald to spare Jackie Kennedy from having to testify at a trial. Howard died of a heart attack while Ruby awaited trial. There was no autopsy.

Maurice Gatlin, Sr.- Gatlin was a bagman for Guy Banister, who employed Oswald at his detective agency in New Orleans. Gatlin was a member of anti-communist extremist groups, and probably a CIA operative. His job was to transport cash payments made by Banister for illegal activities. He knew about Oswald and others connected with Banister. The Warren Commission tried to get his testimony, but before they could, Gatlin was found dead. His throat was cut open and his body was thrown through a store window in Florida. The police first said it was a suicide, but the coroner late said it was a heart attack/accident. They said that Gatlin suffered a heart attack on a sixth floor balcony, causing him to fall over the railing. There was no explanation of how he went through a plate glass window.

Guy Banister- Banister was a former intelligence operative and FBI agent. He ran a private investigation agency in New Orleans, where he employed Lee Harvey Oswald. Banister was connected with Clay Shaw, David Ferrie, and others involved in the assassination. Banister died from a heart attack in June of 1964 before he could testify to the Warren Commission. Witnesses say he had a bullet hole in him.[489]

---

[489] http://www.maebrussell.com/Disappearing%20Witnesses/Disappearing%20Witnesses.html

James F. Koethe- One of the five men who visisted Ruby in jail. He had just stepped out of the shower when someone killed him with a karate chop to the throat. His apartment was ransacked, but the only things determined to be missing were his notes and materials for a book he was working on. The book was about the Kennedy assassination.

Mary Pinchot Meyer- She was the wife of CIA official Cord Meyer, and JFK's mistress in the spring of 1962. She was probably killed because of a diary she kept detailing secrets she learned from associating with high-ranking officials. Meyer was shot to death while jogging, and her diary disappeared immediately. A friend said she wanted the diary burned after her death.

Rose Cheramie (real name Melba Christine Marcades)- She was a stripper in Jack Ruby's club. Three days before the assassination, Cheramie was found lying unconscious by the side of the road just outside of New Orleans. Two of Ruby's associates decided that she knew too much, and decided to kill her by making it look like a hit-and-run accident. They shoved her out of a moving car, but she survived. She told authorities of the plot to kill Kennedy, but they ignored her because she was a drug addict and seemed incoherent. After the assassination, Louisiana State Police relayed the story to the Dallas Police, but they ignored it. Cheramie not only knew of the plot to kill Kennedy, but she also knew that Ruby and Oswald knew each other. She had seen them together on several occasions. About two years later, she was killed by the same method that failed the first time. She was pushed out of a moving car, and an oncoming vehicle could not stop in time. Her death was ruled an accident.

Dorothy Kilgallen- Kilgallen was a syndicated newspaper columnist and radio/television personality. She covered the trial of Jack Ruby, then was granted an exclusive private interview with him in March of 1964. She privately told friends that she had information that would "blow the whole Kennedy case wide open." Kilgallen was found dead in her apartment. The medical examiner said the death was from "acute ethanol and barbiturate intoxication," yet the official cause of death is listed as "natural causes."

Mrs. Earl E.T. Smith- Mrs. Smith was the best friend and confidant of Dorothy Kilgallen. She died three days after Kilgallen's death. It is believed that she had Kilgallen's notes from her research and her interview with Ruby. Officially, she suffered a cerebral hemorrhage at her home. Foul play was suspected, but there was no further investigation.

Captain Frank Martin- Martin was present when Ruby shot Oswald. He was critical of the handling of such an important prisoner. Testifying to the Warren Commission, he stated, "There's a lot to be said but probably be better if I don't say it." Martin officially died from cancer, which developed very suddenly.

Lee Bowers Jr.- Bowers was a railroad towerman for the Union Terminal Company. He was in a 14-foot radio control tower in the parking lot behind the grassy knoll on the day of the assassination. He witnessed vehicles driving around the parking area, which he thought was strange because the area was supposedly secured by police. One of the men Bowers saw appeared to be talking into a radio microphone. Bowers also saw two men behind the picket fence, and he described them in detail. His testimony to the Warren Commission was suddenly cut short before he could finish telling all he knew. He later told author Mark Lane what he witnessed that day: "There was some unusual occurrence- a flash of light or smoke or something which caused me to feel like something out of the ordinary had occurred there." Bowers died in a single-car accident in 1966. The medical examiner said that Bowers appeared to be in some kind of "strange shock." It's possible that he was drugged, but his death was ruled an accident.

Lieutenant Commander William Bruce Pitzer- Pitzer was an X-ray technician who filmed the Kennedy autopsy. He told friends he was "horrified" by what he saw. He was threatened and intimidated by military and intelligence personnel, and was told to never reveal what he saw for reasons of national security. He was shot with a .45 caliber pistol in what was ruled a suicide. But paraffin tests showed no nitrates on his hand, indicating he had not fired the pistol. It was also determined that the shot came from at least three feet away. The autopsy report on Pitzer was never released to his family or the public. All references to Pitzer being present at Kennedy's autopsy have been removed from government records. Pitzer's death is discussed further in Chapter 8.

Jack Ruby- Ruby was heavily involved in the assassination from the start. He had to kill Oswald on behalf of the mob. Ruby could not be allowed to talk. His interview to Dorothy Kilgallen was probably secretly recorded, and Kilgallen was closely monitored until she was killed. Ruby wanted to be taken to Washington, where he felt he could talk more freely, but Earl Warren wouldn't allow it. The few statements he did make to the press were very incriminating of the government, and of Johnson in particular.

Those involved wanted Ruby dead, but it would look too suspicious to just shoot him after he had shot Oswald. They had to make it look like something other than murder. Jack Ruby was injected with cancer cells and given massive amounts of radiation to produce tumors in him. Like many others, Jack Ruby was murdered by cancer.

David Ferrie- Ferrie was being questioned by D.A. Jim Garrison concerning his knowledge of the JFK assassination. Ferrie would have been arrested soon, but he was found dead in his apartment. The circumstances surrounding his death are extremely suspicious. Ferrie left a suicide note and a bequeathment- both typed and unsigned. Yet, the coroner ruled that he had died of a massive brain hemorrhage. They finally settled on the suicide verdict.

Eladio Del Valle- Del Valle was murdered at almost exactly the same time as David Ferrie. His head was damaged by a machete and he was shot through the heart. He was an anti-Castro activist and an associate of Ferrie and Banister. Del Valle was also being sought by the Garrison investigation team.

Dr. Mary Sherman- Dr. Sherman was a cancer researcher, and Oswald and David Ferrie worked with her. Dr. Sherman was murdered two weeks after Ferrie's death. Her arm was virtually disintegrated. She had been stabbed repeatedly, then placed in bed, and the bed was set on fire as the killer attempted to hide what really happened. Dr. Sherman's death is discussed further in Chapter 7.

Dr. Nicholas Chetta- Dr. Chetta was the coroner who performed the questionable autopsies on David Ferrie and Dr. Mary Sherman. Dr. Chetta was a key witness in the investigation of Clay Shaw. He died from a heart attack during the Garrison investigation.

Philip Geraci- Geraci was a friend of David Ferrie and Perry Russo, and he had personal knowledge of the connection between Oswald and Clay Shaw. He also knew of the connection between Oswald and anti-Castro activist Carlos Bringuier, who had a staged altercation to promote Oswald's pro-commi image. Geraci was being sought for questioning by Jim Garrison, but he died from electrocution before he could talk.

Dr. Henry Delaune- Delaune was an assistant and colleague of Drs. Nicholas Chetta and Mary Sherman. He was murdered during the Garrison investigation. Delaune was shot twice in the chest in his apartment.

Rev. Clyde Johnson- Johnson was scheduled to testify in the Jim Garrison investigation. He had information connecting Oswald, Ferrie, and Shaw. He was assaulted and hospitalized before he could testify. Upon his release from the hospital, he was shot to death.

Hale Boggs- Boggs was a dissenting member of the Warren Commission. Although he did sign the final report, he express doubts about its conclusions. He believed that evidence had been withheld by both the CIA and the FBI, and that there was some degree of conspiracy. In 1972, Boggs' twin engine plane disappeared over a remote section of Alaska. The plane was never found and Boggs was presumed dead.

Joseph A. Milteer- Milteer was a racist extremist who was secretly recorded predicting Kennedy's assassination. After being interviewed by the FBI, he was released. He had foreknowledge of the event, which may have cost him his life. He was killed in a freak accident when a heating stove exploded.

Clay Shaw- Shaw was the only person ever charged with taking part in the Kennedy assassination. The trial ended in acquittal, mainly because Garrison's witnesses kept dying. Shaw's death was also very suspicious. He had recently given an interview for the *Washington Post*. A neighbor saw an ambulance pull up in front of Shaw's house. According to the neighbor, two attendants got out and pulled a stretcher out from the rear door. There appeared to be a body under the sheet on the stretcher. The attendants carried the stretcher into the house, and a few minutes later, they emerged with an empty stretcher. A few hours later, Shaw was found dead. The body was quickly rushed to a local mortuary, where it was embalmed and buried before any autopsy could be performed. The local coroner protested and demanded that the body be exhumed and autopsied, but to no avail. The cause of death was ruled lung cancer. I can't help but wonder how they figured that out without an autopsy.

Roger Dean Craig- Craig was a Dallas Police officer on duty in Dealey Plaza when Kennedy was shot. He was one of three officers who found a Mauser in the TSBD. This was inconsistent with the Oswald story, since Oswald did not own a Mauser. The other two officers changed their story, but Craig did not. Craig maintained that the weapon found was a Mauser, and he was eventually fired, harassed, and threatened. After a meeting with Jim Garrison, someone took a shot at Roger's head and narrowly missed. A few years later, Craig had an accident when someone forced him off the road, leaving him with severe back pain. Later, he answered a knock on his door, and he was instantly shot with a rifle, but survived. In 1975, Craig was found dead from a rifle shot. It was ruled a suicide.

Sam Giancana- Giancana was the mafia don that controlled organized crime activities in the Chicago area. In 1975, as the Senate Intelligence Committee was preparing to question him, he was murdered in his home. He was shot multiple times, including several around the mouth, the M.O. for a standard mafia hit on someone who talks too much. Even the dons are not immune from the unwritten mafia code.

Alan Sweatt- Sweatt supposedly told a reporter that Oswald was an FBI informant. He claimed that Oswald was paid $200 a month by the FBI, and that he knew Oswald's informant number. The Warren Commission made no attempt to verify the accuracy of the claim. Sweatt died before he could be questioned by the HSCA. It was ruled death by natural causes.

Ralph Paul- Paul was Jack Ruby's best friend and business partner in the Carousel Club. The night before the assassination, Ruby made four phone calls to Paul. Paul died of a heart attack in 1976.

James Chaney- Chaney was a Dallas Police motorcycle patrolman. He was the nearest person to JFK when he was shot, yet he was not called to testify before the Warren Commission. Chaney had maintained that Kennedy and Connally were hit by separate shots, and that Kennedy was hit in the face. This contradicted the single-bullet theory and therefore, the lone gunman theory. Chaney died of a heart attack in 1976.

Dr. Charles F. Gregory- Dr. Gregory was one of the doctors who treated Governor Connally at Parkland Hospital. Gregory knew that the bullet that was conveniently found on Connally's stretcher could not have gone through him, because it contained less missing grains of lead than what was found inside Connally. His testimony to the Warren Commission was limited due to leading questioning by Arlen Specter. Before he could testify to the HSCA, he died of a heart attack.

Johnny Roselli- Roselli was a mafia figure based in Las Vegas. He was also a CIA asset. In 1975 he gave closed-door testimony to the Senate Intelligence Committee regarding plots against Castro. Roselli was scheduled to testify again in 1976 about the JFK assassination, but before he could, his dismembered body was found in an oil drum dropped off the coast of Florida.

Charles Nicoletti- Nicoletti was one of the shooters in Dealey Plaza. A Chicago-based hit man, NIcoletti had strained relations with the mob, claiming that the CIA was taking over their operations. Nicoletti was being sought for questioning by the HSCA in 1977, when he was executed gangland style. He was shot three times in the head while sitting in his car, then the car was set on fire.

George De Mohrenschildt- De Morenschildt was a CIA-connected geologist. He was asked by the CIA to befriend Oswald. Over a period of a few months, De Mohrenschildt got to know Lee and Marina fairly well. He helped them find work and housing. De Mohrenschildt testified to the Warren Commission, but did not tell them what they wanted to hear. He insisted that Oswald was innocent and by doing so, made a permanent enemy of the CIA. He was hounded and harassed thereafter. He was driven to a near-nervous breakdown, and had to be hospitalized. In 1977, the HSCA attempted to summon him to testify, but before they could reach him, De Mohrenschildt was killed by a shotgun blast. It was ruled a suicide.

Donald Kaylor- Kaylor was the FBI fingerprint expert. The palm print that was found on the rifle was lifted from Oswald's dead body at the funeral home. Kaylor could tell that the print was planted, and he may have been considered a threat to expose it. He died of a heart attack during the HSCA investigation.

J.M. English- English was the head of the FBI Forensic Science Laboratory. He oversaw the testing of the rifle and pistol that supposedly belonged to Oswald. He also knew about the lack of authentic prints on the weapons. English died of a heart attack the same month as Kaylor.

Regis Kennedy- Regis Kennedy was not related to John Kennedy. Regis Kennedy was one of the FBI agents who visited Beverly Oliver a few days after the assassination. Oliver had taken a home movie of the event from the south side of the street facing north- the opposite view of the Zapruder film. Oliver's film would have shown the picket fence on the grassy knoll. She said that she recalled some kind of flash or movement in that area. Oliver gave her undeveloped film to Regis Kennedy. The film was never seen by the public, and its whereabouts are not known. Regis Kennedy died in 1978 of unknown causes shortly after his testimony to the HSCA.

David Sanchez Morales- Morales was a hit man for the CIA. He admitting to killing people in Vietnam, Venezuela, and Uruguay on behalf of the CIA.

These were not military killings in the heat of battle. These were undercover hits orchestrated by U.S. intelligence, just like the JFK assassination. Morales was rumored to be in Dealey Plaza when Kennedy was killed. Morales feared for his life, and installed a high-tech alarm system in his home. Morales said to a friend, "It's my own guys I am worried about. I know too damned much." Morales died of a heart attack at age 52. No autopsy was performed.

William Sullivan – Sullivan was a senior FBI agent in charge of counterespionage and domestic intelligence. Sullivan testified to the Senate Intelligence Committee that Hoover had leaked a memo to the press saying that Oswald was the lone assassin. According to Sullivan, Hoover tried to "blunt the drive for an independent investigation into the assassination." Sullivan was scheduled to testify before the HSCA, but he was killed in a hunting "accident." Supposedly, Sullivan was mistaken for a deer, even though he was wearing bright orange.

Roscoe White- White was a Dallas Police officer and a military operative. As a Marine in 1957, he was stationed at Atsugi, Subic Bay, and Indonesia along with Lee Harvey Oswald. White was identified in Dealey Plaza from photographs. White left a diary detailing his involvement in the assassination. His son, Rickie, went public with the diary in 1990. In 1971, after White had left the police force, he died in an industrial accident.[490] [491]

John Kennedy, Jr.- John Kennedy's son was murdered in 1999 as part of the continuing cover-up of the assassination. His plane crashed 18 miles off the coast of Martha's Vineyard, Massachusetts, but several witnesses say they saw the plane explode. JFK Jr's death is discussed in Chapter 8.

Murder by Natural Causes

Considering the disproportionate number of suspicious deaths attributed to cancer or heart attacks, one has to wonder if all of those deaths were really from natural causes or lifestyle choices. There is justification for such suspicion.

It is well-known that the CIA engaged in cancer-producing research in the 1950s and 60s. The purpose of that research was to create a product that

---

[490] Robert, Craig, and Armstrong, John, *JFK; The Dead Witnesses*, CPI, 1995
[491] La Fontaine, Ray and Mary, *Oswald Talked*, 1996

would cause a person to contract cancer, thus allowing them to kill someone and make it look like it was a death due to natural causes. (This was a project that Lee Harvey Oswald was involved in.) The drug is administered by injection, along with massive doses of radiation. The victim quickly develops cancer. That is one of the tell-tale signs of this drug- the rapidity with which the cancer develops.

A 1952 CIA memo mentions the drug beryllium and its ability to cause cancer:

> This is certainly the most toxic inorganic element and it produces a peculiar fibrotic tumor at the site of the local application. The amount necessary to produce these tumors is a few micrograms.[492]

This drug causes cancer which appears to be from natural causes, or from lifestyle issues, such as smoking. This was useful in the cover up, since it silenced witnesses without causing too much suspicion. Some might suspect foul play, but it could never be proven.

Similarly, the CIA also had the ability to cause a heart attack as a covert way of committing murder. They have long ago developed a poison that induces a heart attack and leaves no trace of residue in the body. This drug is administered by a special gun, which fires a dart made of frozen poison. The dart penetrates clothing, pierces the skin, and leaves only a tiny, red dot. The victim, and maybe even the medical examiner, might think it was a mosquito bite. The poison enters the bloodstream and induces a heart attack. The poison then denatures quickly, making it virtually undetectable. The only way the poison would be detected in an autopsy would be if the examiner deliberately checked for this unique substance. In most of these suspicious deaths, there was either no autopsy or a sloppy one. No one would suspect that the victim was shot with a heart attack gun. This was another useful way of eliminating anyone who was a threat to expose the truth.[493]

---

[492] http://www.assassinationresearch.com/v1n2/deaths.html
[493] https://www.sott.net/article/232912-Assassinations-by-induced-heart-attack-and-cancer

The CIA has had this technology since the 1950s. During the Church Committee hearings in 1975, the CIA admitted to possessing such a weapon. CIA Director William Colby was asked about it:

> Senator Frank Church: Does this pistol fire the dart?
>
> William Colby: Yes, it does, Mr Chairman, and a special one was developed which, potentially would be able to enter the target without perception.
>
> Senator Frank Church: But also the toxin itself would not appear in the autopsy?
>
> William Colby: Yes, so that there was no way of receiving that the target was hit.[494]

This weapon is reminiscent of the umbrella gun described by Cutler and Sprague, and used in the assassination of JFK. The same technology is applied in the umbrella weapon. The dart enters the body without perception, and the toxin does not appear in the autopsy. In the case of John Kennedy it was use to cause paralysis, but a different type of dart can be used to cause a heart attack.

Within months of the JFK assassination, people began talking about suspicious deaths connected with the event. Naturally, they were ignored by our government. Supposedly, no living person had anything to do with the crime at all, so how could there be suspicious deaths? The CIA had to go into disinformation mode to discredit the notion of people dying mysteriously because they knew too much. But anyone who has studied the suspicious deaths knows that they are far beyond anything that could be expected just by random chance. It's not just how many deaths there were, but who they were, and when, how, and why they died that matters. In most cases, it was a witness or associate who knew too much and had to be eliminated. Often, someone would turn up dead shortly before they were scheduled to testify or be interviewed by the authorities.

Yet, the CIA is admittedly involved in the elimination of those it considers hostile or inconvenient. They admitted as much during the Church hearings.

---

[494] http://www.declassifieddocuments.com/2017/02/church-committee-cia-heart-attack-gun.html

The acronym for this practice is TWEP- Terminate With Extreme Prejudice. This is what it means:

> In military and other covert operations, terminate with extreme prejudice is a euphemism for aggressive execution (playing on the expression "termination with prejudice" of an employment contract)...In a military intelligence context, it is generally understood as an order to assassinate.[495]

During the Church Committee hearings the CIA testified on a variety of TWEP techniques, including the aforementioned heart attack gun and toxins of various kinds that cannot be detected in standard autopsies.

A declassified CIA document spells it out plainly:

> You will recall that I mentioned that the local circumstances under which a given means might be used might suggest the technique to be used in that case. I think the gross divisions in presenting this subject might be:
>
> 1. bodies left with no hope of the cause of death being determined by the most complete autopsy and chemical examinations
>
> 2. bodies left in such circumstances as to simulate accidental death
>
> 3. bodies left in such circumstances as to simulate suicidal death
>
> 4. bodies left with residue that simulate those caused by natural diseases.
>
> There are two techniques which I believe should be mentioned since they require no special equipment besides a strong arm and the will to do such a job. These would be either to smother the victim with a pillow or to strangle him with a wide piece of cloth such as a bath towel. In such cases, there is no specific anatomic changes to indicate the cause of death...[496]

---

[495] https://en.wikipedia.org/wiki/Terminate_with_extreme_prejudice
[496] http://www.assassinationresearch.com/v1n2/deaths.html

This states the truth quite graphically: the CIA kills people. They have admitted it. They are instructed to do so and are advised on how to cover it up. This memo says it, the Church Committee testimony says it, and former CIA people have said it. So why can't people believe that they would conspire to kill the president?

Senator Frank Church commented on the potential for abuse inherent in this and other technologies possessed by the CIA:

> I know the capacity that is there to make tyranny total in America. We must see to it that this agency and all agencies that possess this technology operate within the law and under proper supervision, so that we never cross over that abyss. That is the abyss from which there is no return.[497]

Alternate Patsy?

Another man arrested on November 22 was Jack Lawrence. Lawrence was a salesman at the Lincoln-Mercury dealership just two blocks away from Dealey Plaza. On the day of the assassination, Lawrence did not show up for work in the morning. About 30 minutes after the shooting, Lawrence came running into the showroom, sweating and covered with mud, and threw up in the men's room. He told his co-workers that he had been sick that morning. He had borrowed the firm's car the day before, but got stuck in traffic and had to park it. Later, his car was found parked behind the picket fence on the grassy knoll. Lawrence's actions were so suspicious that the others at the showroom called the police. Lawrence was arrested later that evening but released the next day. Ironically, it was Lawrence who then called the FBI.[498]

The involvement of the Lincoln-Mercury dealership must be considered. Allegedly, Lee Harvey Oswald had test driven a car at that location in an incident that was to be used against him later on. Lawrence had worked at the dealership for only a month, and got the job using phony references from New Orleans. He had never sold a car in the time that he worked there. He heard two other salesmen, Albert Bogard and Frank Pizzo, saying that Oswald had been into the dealership to test drive a car. Pizzo told Bogard to get the papers on Oswald, but there were none. No tentative sales report was drawn up on Oswald, which was strange, since any

---

[497] https://www.wanttoknow.info/mk/liftingtheveil#13
[498] Marrs, Jim, *Crossfire*, p. 340, Carroll and Graf, 1989

prospective customer would have paperwork filled out for a follow-up call and a possible sale. When the salesmen heard that Oswald had been arrested, Lawrence insisted on calling the FBI, but Bogard was opposed to the call and appeared nervous about it. Lawrence was told not to make the call, but he did anyway. Lawrence was fired shortly afterwards. Lawrence believed he was terminated in retaliation for notifying the FBI about the Oswald incident.

Of the 16 employees of the dealership on the day of the assassination, only six remained a few months later.[499] That seems like a surprisingly high turnover rate. It's possible that the dealership was used to somehow monitor the assassination plot, considering its close proximity to Dealey Plaza. One has to wonder about Bogard's involvement in the plot. He was the one who said that Oswald had test driven a car, yet there was no paperwork on this potential customer, indicating that Bogard lied about the incident. Bogard also opposed calling the FBI, which gives the impression that he was reluctant to get involved or had something to hide.[500]

What was the role of Lawrence in all of this? A possibility is that he was an alternate patsy. The plotters had to have a back-up plan in case things didn't go right with Oswald. What if Oswald had called in sick that day? What if he had been photographed outside watching the motorcade? What if he had some air-tight alibi? A lot of things could have gone wrong, and they had to have a Plan B. The fact that Lawrence's car was parked behind the picket fence on the grassy knoll is just too obvious. Lawrence said he parked the car there because he was stuck in traffic, but that makes no sense. He hadn't shown up for work, anyway, claiming to be sick. What was his hurry? Supposedly, he was due back at the showroom for reasons not specified. But he had no reason to rush. Certainly, he could not be blamed for being late, considering the circumstances. Was he being set up? Was he deliberately loaned the company car to incriminate him? Lawrence was a sharpshooter in the Air Force, so he would make a believable assassin. His phony job references from New Orleans are further cause for suspicion. There was no explanation for why Lawrence was covered with mud. He blamed his vomiting on the fact that he had been out on the town the night before, combined with the shock of learning about Kennedy's death. Lawrence may have begun to realize he was being set up, and he panicked.

---

[499] http://z313.blogspot.com/2010/05/arrest-of-jack-lawrence.html
[500] http://jfkassassinationfiles.com/hsca_180-10016-10266

Maybe that's why he was so anxious to call the FBI- to put the heat on Oswald and take it off of himself.

Lawrence was, indeed, out on the town the night before. He was at a pre-assassination party at the Cabana Motel, along with Jack Ruby and Jim Braden. He has been identified by Beverly Oliver, who was an acquaintance of Ruby from the neighboring Colony Club. Oliver, who knew Lawrence as Donny Allen Lance, said she danced with him at the Cabana Motel on the 21st. Oliver also said she had seen Lawrence/Lance at Jack Ruby's Carousel Club, as well as David Ferrie and Lee Harvey Oswald. Oliver wrote a letter to the editor of *The Third Decade* in 1993:

> As for Jack Allen Lawrence, I identified a photograph of him that Gary (Shaw) presented to me as someone I knew as Donny Allen Lance, who frequented the club often visiting with George Senator and as someone I had dances with at the Cabana Hotel on November 21, 1963. His not claiming to frequent the Carousel Club is nothing unusual, there were probably ten thousand men in Dallas back then who would say the same. Regardless of the assassination, it was not a place that men publicly stated they frequented. I can't say anything more about Donny Allen Lance. I don't know anything else.[501]

Most Likely Scenario

From the available evidence and testimonies we can construct a most likely scenario of how the assassination happened. It appears that there were a minimum of four shooters. One was on the grassy knoll, one in the TSBD, one in the Dal-Tex building, and the umbrella man was the other.

The testimony of James Files seems credible, so he was probably the grassy knoll shooter. He has identified Charles Nicoletti as the shooter in the Dal-Tex building, which seems reasonable. Malcolm Wallace was probably the shooter in the TSBD. I cannot name the umbrella man, but he was not Louis Steven Witt.

The umbrella man was the first to hit Kennedy. That was the shot to the throat, which paralyzed him and made him an easy target. The umbrella man then fired a needless second dart into Kennedy's back, eliciting minimal

---

[501] http://educationforum.ipbhost.com/topic/4187-jack-lawrence/

reaction but creating a puzzling hole for investigators. The third shot was the shot that hit Connally, and it was on a left-to-right trajectory. It could have been from Nicoletti in the Dal-Tex building, although the angle seems to indicate an origin more to the south, possibly the County Records building. I could not name the shooter, if that was the case. The fourth shot was probably from Mac Wallace in the TSBD. That was the shot that missed everything and injured bystander James Tague with a stray fragment of some kind. Shots five and six were virtually simultaneous. Either Wallace or Nicoletti fired the fifth shot into the back of Kennedy's head just a split-second before Files fired the fatal head shot, which was the sixth and final shot.

It's possible that another shooter may have been stationed by the railroad overpass, but he did not fire a shot. That shooter would have been a back-up to the back-up. Just in case all the others had missed, there would have been one last desperate chance to finish it off. Recall that there was an alleged bullet hole in the windshield that came from the front, so it's possible that the extra back-up shooter got impatient and fired a needless shot.

The Myth of Badgeman

"Badgeman" is the name given to a shadowy image artificially produced by sophisticated photographic techniques. The image comes from the Mary Moorman photograph. Moorman was standing on the south side of Elm Street, taking pictures with her Polaroid camera when the motorcade passed. Moorman snapped a picture of John Kennedy just a split-second before the fatal head shot. He is seen slumping slightly to the left. In the background we see the grassy knoll and the concrete retaining wall. In relation to Kennedy, the grassy knoll is to his right front and the retaining wall is almost directly to his right. The Badgeman image is taken from the retaining wall, which is not where the fatal head shot came from; it came from the grassy knoll. The image seems to show a man firing a rifle, complete with muzzle blast. The man appears to be wearing a uniform with a badge, hence the nickname. It also appears that there are two other figures standing by him, making it even more inconceivable that the images are real.

If one is familiar with the layout of Dealey Plaza, then it is clear that the retaining wall could not be the location of the shooter. It is too exposed. The retaining wall is closer to the street than the picket fence to the west, and it is shorter. Any shooter in that location would be easily seen by spectators, even if he was kneeling. The picket fence, on the other hand, is the ideal spot for an assassin. It is farther back from the street, with a higher fence for cover. Not only that, but there is a large, overhanging tree covering him at that point, whereas the retaining wall is out in the open and not covered. The tree gives the shooter total coverage. No one could see him from a distance. Only the shooter's head was over the picket fence, so even those close by were unaware of him. Even when he is photographed from across the street, it is so dark and shady under the tree that the shooter still can't be seen. From behind the picket fence, the shooter can escape directly into the parking lot unseen. From the retaining wall, he would have to turn right to the steps to reach the parking lot, and he likely would have been seen.[502]

Badgeman is a myth. As much as we would like to believe that it's real, it's not. It is basically the equivalent of an ink blot test. With enough manipulation of the photographic images, we can find things that aren't there. To see another example of this, check out a British documentary called *The Day the Dream Died*. At the 35-minute mark we see another image from the grassy knoll. This one was taken from the Orville Nix film, and was created using optical enhancement. It shows a completely different shooter. It appears to be a man with a rifle, but he is not Badgeman. Do we really have pictures of two different shooters? It's wishful thinking, but they are both illusions.

Z-Film Altered?

The authenticity of the Zapruder film cannot be guaranteed. There is some question as to whether or not it has been altered to some extent. Two CIA employees working at the National Photo Interpretation Center (NPIC) in Washington were interviewed by the Assassination Records Review Board in 1997. Homer McMahon and Bennett Hunter were working at NPIC the weekend of the assassination. They stated that Secret Service Agent Bill Smith couriered the film from Rochester, NY, to the NPIC in Washington for the purpose of analysis and to create a photographic briefing board. Agent Smith had stated that the film was developed in Rochester, but that contradicts what we were told previously about the film. The official story is that Zapruder took the film on that Friday afternoon and supposedly had it

---

[502] https://www.jfk-assassination.eu/articles/umbrella.php

developed in Dallas the same day. He obtained affidavits from Kodak, who developed the film, and Jamieson Company, who made three copies. The affidavits are dated November 22. The Secret Service was given two copies of the film.[503]

But the Secret Service and NPIC tell a different story. From the ARRB Meeting Report of 7/15/97:

> Smith told McMahon that he had personally picked up the film (in an undeveloped condition from the man who exposed it) in Dallas, flown it to Rochester, N.Y. (where it was developed by Kodak), and then flown it down to NPIC in Washington so that enlargements of selected frames could be made on NPIC's state-of-the-art equipment.[504]

So the paper trail says that the film was developed in Dallas, but that seems doubtful now. It is more likely that agent Smith was right, and the Kodak lab in Rochester developed the film. The Rochester lab was run by the CIA, so it makes sense that this crucial evidence would be put in the hands of conspirators.

But besides the developing, what else was done to the film at Rochester? It appears that some alterations may have been made to the film, which would explain its strange odyssey. There are two things that were described by witnesses which we don't see in the film: the stopping of the limousine and the explosion from the back of the president's head.

Several witnesses have stated that the limousine came to a stop, or at least a near-stop. Reporter Bob Clark told an ABC audience that the limousine "came to an immediate stop."[505] The film shows the limousine moving at a steady speed, although very slowly. At no point does it stop or slow down further. If limousine driver William Greer stopped when he heard shooting, then that would seem to indicate he was a part of the plot. Naturally, such obvious collusion would have to be kept from public viewing.

---

[503] https://www.lewrockwell.com/2012/05/douglas-p-horne/the-two-npic-zapruder-film-events-signposts-pointing-to-the-filmsalteration/
[504] Fetzer, Jim, *Murder in Dealey Plaza*, p. 319, Catfeet Press, 2000
[505] https://www.youtube.com/watch?v=7bytUiavrfw

Researcher Rich Della Rosa has seen an earlier version of the Zapruder film that he claims is significantly different from the one that is commonly seen. This version of the film was circulated at various college campuses in the early 1970s, which was when Della Rosa saw the film. This was prior to the first public viewing of the film on *Good Night America* in 1975. It is not known who made the film or who promoted it, but Della Rosa was one of the few who saw it. He claims that the limousine stopped for about 2-3 seconds. He also claimed that the stop was so sudden, the occupants of the limo were thrust forward by it. We do not see that in the extant film.

Witnesses also described an explosion of blood and brain matter coming from the back of JFK's head. Several have described it as a "halo" around his head, as the image was probably frozen in their minds. Zapruder himself said, "I saw his head come off." Hunter viewed the film and recalled seeing a "skull explosion" and "bone fragments" exiting. In the current version of the film, we do not see anything coming from the back of the head, not even blood. Yet, there was a piece of scalp blown off that was so large, Jackie Kennedy felt compelled to retrieve it. It seems that such a thing would be visible in the film.[506]

If the plotters wanted to hide this critical evidence, they would have to modify the film somehow. This could be done at a sophisticated lab like the one in Rochester. What other reason would there be for flying the film to Rochester? It would not be for simple developing.

Contrary to what Abraham Zapruder says, the Secret Service probably took the negatives and the original of the film. It makes no sense that they would let even one copy of the original be possessed by anyone, because that person would naturally make copies of it and it would circulate. That would only make the conspiracy more obvious, because it would show that someone tried to alter evidence. SS agent Smith told McMahon that he picked up the film in its "undeveloped condition," and that it was then developed in Rochester. I see no reason for either Smith or McMahon to lie about this. Zapruder claims to have had the developed film in his possession on the afternoon of the 22nd, but it seems doubtful. It's possible he may have seen the film late in the day, since the film could have been couriered from Dallas to Rochester and back in about 6-8 hours. Zapruder may have been tricked into thinking he had the original. Another possibility is that

---

[506] Fetzer, Jim, *Murder in Dealey Plaza*, p. 315, Catfeet Press, 2000

Smith is simply mistaken. The film may have been developed in Dallas and then altered in Rochester. Zapruder may have seen the original but was not allowed to keep a copy of it before it was altered.

Life has been accused of making the alterations, since the magazine was owned by Henry Luce, an avid opponent of John Kennedy. That is probably not the case. Any changes to the film would logically have been made before the sale. The film was sold to *Life* magazine on Monday the 25th, so if it was altered, it was altered some time over the weekend. *Life* may have thought they had the original, unaltered film, but they did not.

In spite of any possible alterations, the Zapruder film still shows an undeniable shot from the right front. That much can't be hidden. The alterations only hide a couple of details to make the official story seem more plausible, but that doesn't change the main point. The fact that Kennedy was driven backwards is still obvious, which still means a shot from the front.

Weirdness

There are certain anomalies in the JFK case that defy explanation. The strangest of all of these can be seen by comparing the films of the assassination. The Zapruder film is the best-known and clearest of these. It was taken from the north side of the street facing south. The Orville Nix film, which is not as clear, was taken from the south side of the street facing north. When we compare the two films, we see things that don't make sense. Spectators who are visible in one film are not there in the other at the place where they should be. A frame-by-frame breakdown of the Zapruder film can be found at the site referenced here.[507] Both films can be viewed on YouTube. [508] [509]

If we look at frames 362-372 of the Zapruder film, we see a group of four people standing on the south side of Elm Street. We see a small boy with his parents. The man has his right hand on the back of the boy's head. To the left of his wife, and slightly in front of her, is another man, who seems to be on his own. These people are about even with the limousine at this point. If we look at the corresponding moment in the Nix film, we see the man with

---

[507] https://www.assassinationresearch.com/zfilm/
[508] https://www.youtube.com/watch?v=GU4mAVCprAU
[509] https://www.youtube.com/watch?v=kq1PbgeBoQ4

his hand on the boy's head, but his wife seems to have disappeared, as does the man to her left. Now, four new people have come into the picture. We see someone in a white shirt with a foot off the ground who was nowhere in sight in the Zapruder film. We see a man in a light blue shirt who is behind the spot occupied by the woman in the Zapruder film, but she does not appear to be in front of him. We see two new people in the spot where the unidentified man was in the Zapruder film. One has on a long, black coat, and the other has dark pants and a light shirt. So the group of four has become a group of six by subtracting two and adding four.[510]

In frames 373-383 of the Zapruder film, we can see two spectators, a man and a woman, to the viewer's right of the group of four. There is no one behind these people. We see only open field directly behind them. But in the Nix film at that point, we see a woman wearing a black hat and a long, black coat. She has white hair. She is standing about 10 feet behind the man at the curb. This woman is not visible in the Zapruder film. Why is that? For some reason, the two spectators in front seem closer to the curb in the Nix film, and their shirts appear lighter. That might be attributable to the camera angle, but the woman in black is not. She is simply nowhere to be seen in the Zapruder film. How can that be? Was she added to the Nix film or was she removed from the Zapruder film? Who was this mysterious woman, if she even existed at all?

It appears that someone has tampered with the films, but for what reason? We have discussed possible changes to the film which might have been made to hide evidence of conspiracy, such as the head explosion and the slowing of the limousine. There is a logical reason for those changes. But why would someone add and subtract people from the films? None of these anomalies can be explained by an attempt to destroy evidence. The people who have been added or removed from the film cannot be identified. We either see them from the back, or in a blurry image from the front. There was no chance that someone would be identified from the films and then brought in as a witness, so we can eliminate that as a motive. Why would someone go through all the trouble of manipulating the films like that? For a joke? Not likely, since hardly anyone has noticed this. I cannot see a motive here. This does nothing but add further confusion to a case that is already mind-boggling in its complexity. It does not prove conspiracy, and it does not prove non-conspiracy. It only proves weirdness.

---

[510] Fetzer, Jim, *Murder in Dealey Plaza*, p. 16 (picture section), Catfeet Press, 2000

Recap

As we have seen in this chapter, there is zero physical evidence against Lee Harvey Oswald. He would never have been convicted in a fair trial, so he had to be eliminated. The Warren Commission was formed after Oswald was dead, so they did not have to worry about his rights. Oswald did not have the right to remain silent. He did not have a right to a lawyer. He did not have a right to a fair trial by a jury. He was not considered innocent until proven guilty. That's how he was convicted in the public mind. The plotters knew that most of the public would not look at the case closely, and they exploited that.

In the final analysis, there is no case against Oswald except the manufactured one. In his book, Police Chief Jesse Curry claims that Oswald shot Kennedy, but in a later interview, his true feelings came out:

> We don't have any proof that Oswald fired the rifle, and never did.
> Nobody's yet been able to put him in that building with a gun in his hand.[511]

---

[511] *Dallas Morning News*, Nov. 6, 1969

7

OSWALD THE SPY

Lee Harvey Oswald was born in New Orleans, Louisiana, in 1939. His father died of a heart attack two months before he was born. His mother moved him, along with his two older brothers, to Dallas, Texas in 1944. The family briefly lived in New York from 1952-1954, before returning to New Orleans. They moved again to Fort Worth, Texas in 1956.

At an early age, Lee showed an interest in spy work. His favorite radio show as a kid was *I Led Three Lives*, the story of Herbert Philbrick, the FBI informant who posed as a communist. The show must have impacted young Lee somehow, because he spent the rest of his short life mimicking the main character.

In 1955 Lee joined the Civil Air Patrol where he met David Ferrie, who was later to be a part of the plot to kill JFK. It was Ferrie who recruited Oswald for intelligence work. From that point on, most of Oswald's life was shrouded in mystery, since he was an intelligence operative and his life was largely controlled by the Central Intelligence Agency. It's possible that Oswald's records have been altered somehow.[512]

The Marines

Oswald joined the Marines in 1956 at the age of 17. After basic training he was sent to Keesler Air Force Base in Biloxi, Mississippi for instruction in aircraft surveillance and radar operation, which qualified him as an Aviation Electronics Operator. In July of 1957 he was sent to the Marine Corps Air Station in El Toro, California, and from there he was sent to Japan. He was stationed at the Atsugi Air Base in Japan, in the heart of the CIA's main operational base in the Far East. This is where the top secret U-2 spy planes originated from. The U-2 project was run by the CIA. Oswald's job was to monitor the radar screen for signs of Russian or Chinese aircraft. Oswald

---

[512] Marrs, Jim, *Crossfire*, pp. 91-99, Carroll and Graf, 1989

was later accused of attempting to give away sensitive radar secrets to the Russians. The fact that Oswald was given this assignment seems to indicate that he had already begun his intelligence career.[513] In 1977, former CIA finance officer James Wilcott testified to the HSCA that "Oswald was paid by the CIA while stationed at Atsugi."

Trivia question: Who is the only U.S. serviceman known to have contracted gonorrhea in the line of duty? Answer: Lee Harvey Oswald. Oswald's Marine Corp records show that on September 16, 1958, he was treated for "Urethritis, acute, due to gonococcus...Origin: In line of duty, not due to own misconduct." Servicemen who contract gonorrhea are usually subject to disciplinary measures, yet Oswald's promiscuous activities apparently had the full approval of the United States military. How did that happen?

Oswald's story, told through fellow Marine David Bucknell, is that one day, he was sitting alone at a bar when a lady sat down beside him and started talking. She began asking sensitive questions about his work with the U-2 planes. Since the project was top secret, he reported this to his superior officer. It turned out this woman was a known KGB agent. Oswald was encouraged to continue meeting the woman and give her false information. The woman worked at The Queen Bee, an expensive nightclub. Oswald was given money to spend on this project, since a serviceman's pay would not allow him to patronize the club often. He had to get intimate with this woman to succeed in his mission. Oswald, being the true patriot, did what he had to do and thus contracted gonorrhea in the line of duty.[514]

Oswald returned to the United States on November 2, 1958, and was stationed again at El Toro, California. Here he began studying communism and learning Russian. In 1959, he was recruited by the Military Criminal Intelligence Division (CID) for an intelligence operation against communism. He was selected for the assignment that would eventually send him to Russia. It had to be covert, of course, so he was made to look like a defector. He openly endorsed communism, but those who knew Oswald at the base knew he was neither a communist nor a defector. His army buddies called him "Oswaldskovich," because of his obsession with all things Russian. The CIA needed an ex-marine for this assignment, someone who appeared to be

---

[513] Marrs, Jim, *Crossfire*, p. 103, Carroll and Graf, 1989
[514] Marrs, Jim, *Crossfire*, p. 104, Carroll and Graf, 1989

shifting loyalties. So Oswald had to apply for a hardship discharge, supposedly to take care of his injured mother, who was not really injured. He was surprisingly granted the discharge in just a few short weeks. While waiting for the discharge, he applied for a passport, stating openly that he might travel to Russia or Cuba. This contradicted his discharge request, which stated that he needed to care for his injured mother. But under the guidance of U.S. intelligence, the passport was granted quickly and hassle-free. Oswald was off to Russia.

Oswald in Russia

In October of 1959, Oswald traveled to the Soviet Union. He started his journey on September 20, leaving from New Orleans to Le Havre, France. From there he traveled to Southampton, England, where he arrived on October 9. The same day, he flew to Helsinki, Finland, where he was issued a Soviet visa on October 14. He left Helsinki by train the next day, and arrived in Moscow on October 16.

When he arrived in Helsinki on October 11 of that year, he checked into an expensive hotel. Then he went to the Soviet consulate, where he was issued a visa in only two days, compared with the normal waiting period of at least a week. It appears that the U.S. government was helping Oswald with his finances and with his paperwork. It doesn't make sense that a true defector would get such special treatment.

In January of 1960, Oswald was sent to Minsk. In the fall of 1959, Oswald had $200 in his bank account. His trip to Russia would cost him at least $1,500. Where he got the money for the trip is not clear. According to Oswald, he was given five thousand rubles (about $87) by the Soviet secret police, although he said at the time it came from the Red Cross. He was greeted in Minsk by the mayor of the city, who offered him a rent-free apartment. His furnished apartment was spacious and modern, with private balconies offering a scenic view. He wrote in his diary that he was "living big." It is not clear how a high-school dropout was able to live at such a high standard. He must have been receiving assistance from either the American or Russian governments, or both.

In 1959, urged by the State Department, the Department of Health, Education, and Welfare (HEW) had approved financial aid to Oswald. In HEW records, it states that Oswald went to Russia "with State Department approval." Oswald himself verified that fact in his radio interview in New Orleans.[515]

In Minsk he worked as an assembler at an electronics factory. In March of 1961 he met a young Russian girl named Marina Prusakova, who would become his wife in just three short months, and make him a father in less than a year.

For some reason, when Oswald first met Marina, he was introduced as "Alik." That was a reference to the name "Alik J. Hidell" which Oswald used as a code name for certain CIA projects. No one knows who introduced the two, and Marina herself could not remember. Marina's uncle was a high-ranking officer in the MVD (Ministry of Internal Affairs) and a Communist Party member. He would have had access to Oswald's KGB files, since they were monitoring him at that point. Marina was probably affiliated with the KGB, and she knew of Oswald's intelligence connections. It's possible that their meeting was orchestrated to bring Oswald in contact with the KGB for the purpose of counterespionage.[516]

Oswald spoke fluent Russian, although it's not clear where he learned it. He never took Russian in high school, and he was a dropout anyway. Yet, when he first met Marina, his Russian was so good that she though he was a native-born Russian "with a Baltic area accent." It's amazing that his accent could be so perfect that he could pass for a natural-born citizen. There are immigrants in America who have lived here for decades and they still have an accent. How did Oswald master the language so perfectly? He may have gotten some kind of specialized language training as part of his intelligence work while he was in the Marines. It's also possible that Oswald was taught Russian in the Foreign Language Institute located in Minsk. The institute was located adjacent to a known espionage training school. In his manuscript, Oswald had written, "I was in the Foreign Language Institute." He changed it to read, "I was visiting friends at the Foreign Language Institute." Apparently, his affiliation with the institute was supposed to be secret.

Supposedly, Lee became disillusioned with life in the Soviet Union and decided to return home with his new bride and baby. In May of 1962, Marina applied for documents enabling her to immigrate to the U.S. The

---

[515] Marrs, Jim, *Crossfire*, p. 128, Carroll and Graf, 1989
[516] Russo, Gus, *Live by the Sword*, p. 107, Bancroft Press, 1998

following month, Lee, Marina, and their baby girl June moved back to the United States. [517]

The timeline of Oswald's actions has confused a lot of people who don't see the bigger picture here. Oswald began his affiliation with the CIA in 1957, then he went to Russia in October of 1959. He was probably chosen to be the JFK patsy sometime in the early part of 1963, when plans were in the works for Kennedy's trip to Dallas. Lone-assassin theorists reason that Oswald's time in Russia could not be related to the Kennedy killing because it started before Kennedy was even president. They fail to see the manipulation involved. When Oswald first went to Russia, it was not directly related to the JFK plot. He was acting the part of a communist so that he could infiltrate communist organizations- typical spy stuff. The CIA was fighting communism, and Oswald was helping them. It was all legitimate and well-intentioned. But as the assassination plot was taking shape, a fall guy was needed. Oswald was then chosen because of his background. He had an undesirable discharge, which was probably staged by the CIA to make him appear unpatriotic. He had been to Russia and openly endorsed communism. At the time, the word "communist" created a knee-jerk reaction in the American people. Anyone who endorsed it was considered unequivocally evil. This was coming on the heels of McCarthyism, so rational thinking was not the norm. In short, Oswald's trip to Russia was not initially related to the assassination plot, but was only used in retrospect to convict him in the public mind.

Back in Dallas

Lee and his family settled back in the Dallas-Fort Worth area, near his mother and brother. They became acquainted with many Russian immigrants in the area. Lee began working at the Leslie Welding Company in Dallas, but he quit that job after only three months. He then went to work as a photoprint trainee for the graphic-arts firm of Jaggars-Chiles-Stovall (JCS), where he worked from October of 1962 until April of 1963.

His hiring at JCS is suspicious. The company had contracts to do classified work for the U.S. Army Map Service. A special security clearance was needed to work with such sensitive materials. It seems strange that they would hire a Soviet defector who has proclaimed his allegiance to

---

[517] Marrs, Jim, *Crossfire*, p. 128, Carroll and Graf, 1989

communism and attempted to betray his country. This was probably another one of his cover jobs. Oswald's address book, which was confiscated after his arrest, contained the notation "microdots" next to the entry for JCS. Microdots are a data-sending method that photographically reduces documents to a size smaller than a postage stamp.

Around this time, Lee and Marina were introduced to Ruth and Michael Paine by George De Mohrenschildt. Ruth Paine was a student and teacher of the Russian language, and was interested in meeting people who spoke Russian. Lee and Marina lived with the Paines for a while in their suburban home in Irving, Texas. They relocated to New Orleans in May and returned to Dallas in September. At the time of the assassination they were separated, with Lee living in a boarding house in Dallas while Marina was still at the Paine's residence.[518]

Oswald in New Orleans

Judyth Vary Baker knew Oswald when he lived in New Orleans during the summer of 1963. She is well aware of Oswald's intelligence connections, and she knows without doubt that Oswald did not shoot John Kennedy. Her story is intriguing.

Judyth developed an interest in science at a young age. While still in high school, she drew national attention for her work with cancer research. She continued her research at the University of Florida. She was offered a summer internship by Dr. Alton Ochsner, which she accepted. Unbeknownst to her, this was her recruitment into a top-secret CIA project to kill Fidel Castro. She came to New Orleans in April of 1963 and met Lee Harvey Oswald there.

Oswald was already working on the project for the CIA and Ochsner. Judyth described their meeting as a chance interaction. She was standing in line at the post office when she dropped a paper. The man behind her in line picked it up and handed it to her. The man spoke to her in Russian, which Judyth was familiar with. The man was Lee Harvey Oswald. Judyth and Lee were both having marital problems, and they formed a relationship with each other. They had much in common, and Oswald eventually introduced her to others involved in the project. Their chance meeting was probably staged. Baker was targeted for the project because of her

---

[518] https://en.wikipedia.org/wiki/Lee_Harvey_Oswald#cite_note-56

knowledge of science, and of cancer in particular. Oswald was instructed to make contact with her. He probably followed her into the post office that day and looked for an excuse to strike up a conversation with her. Politically, they were of the same mind set, so they got along well and formed a working relationship that gave them both an escape from their troubled marriages.

In May of that year, Lee and Judyth were both hired at Reily's Coffee Company, which provided them with cover jobs. This allowed them to slip away a few afternoons each week to work in their secret laboratory. The company was owned by William B. Reily, one of the most visible members of the anti-communist movement in New Orleans. It is highly unlikely that a true communist defector would have been hired there, but Reily trusted Oswald enough to allow him to work on a sensitive assignment like this one.

The goal of the project was to kill Fidel Castro, but it had to be done in a way that did not look like a murder. It had to look like an accident or natural causes. If it was an overt assassination, it could lead to an international crisis, and possibly a war. The plan here was to create a product which would cause cancer. The product would be administered to Castro by an undercover CIA agent working on his medical staff. This would cause Castro to contract cancer. People would naturally assume it was caused by his habitual cigar smoking.

Also involved in the project was David Ferrie. Ferrie set up a lab in his apartment to assist in the research. Ferrie was not a doctor, so it's not clear what his role was. He was probably given instructions by Baker or someone else. When Garrison visited Ferrie's apartment after his death, he found the apartment filled with cages with white mice in them. Garrison had no clue what they were there for, since Baker's story was not publicly told until more than 30 years later.[519]

Politically, Alton Ochsner was extremely conservative and strongly anti-communist. With financial help from his friend, Clint Murchison, he established the Information Council of the Americas (INCA). The goal of the organization was to prevent the spread of communism to Latin America. A friend of Ochsner's said he was "like a fundamentalist preacher in the sense that the fight against communism was the only subject that he would talk

---

[519] Turner, Nigel, 2003, The Love Affair, *The Men Who Killed Kennedy*, U.K., Nigel Turner Productions

about, or even allow you to talk about, in his presence." Ochsner was close friends with Clay Shaw, and they were allies in their battle against the reds. Ochsner was president of the International House, while Shaw was its director. Ochsner and Shaw were both directors of the Foreign Policy Association of New Orleans. They were both connected with American intelligence, and they were both strongly opposed to the domestic and foreign policies of President Kennedy.

Dr. Ochsner was one of the first to link cigarette smoking with cancer. He exposed the dangers of tobacco and pioneered the war on smoking. He became president of the American Cancer Society. His hospital was one of 159 research centers set up by the CIA for their covert operations.[520]

Monkey Virus

One such project involved cancer that was caused by a polio vaccine tainted with Simian Virus 40 (SV-40), also known as the monkey virus. Multiple studies have confirmed SV-40 to be a cancer-causing agent. The National Institute of Health (NIH) knew about the contaminated vaccines, but continued to inoculate millions of children anyway. Dr. Ochsner was on the Board of Directors of the NIH. In 1953, Dr. Mary Sherman was recruited to head the research project concerning the monkey virus. In her work she used a linear particle accelerator, which may have played a role in her suspicious death.

In 1961, after it was discovered that SV-40 was present in the polio vaccines, a federal law was passed mandating that future vaccines could not contain the virus. However, the law did not require past contaminated vaccines to be destroyed, so distribution of the tainted vaccines continued for an undetermined period of time. The *Boston Globe* estimated that 198 million Americans were inoculated with the deadly vaccine between 1955 and 1963.[521]

Judyth recounts her reaction when she first learned of this:

> My mind raced. It was 1963. They had been distributing contaminated polio vaccines since 1955. For eight years! Over a hundred million doses! Even I had received it! A

---

[520] http://spartacus-educational.com/JFKochsner.htm
[521] Baker, Judyth Vary, *Me and Lee*, p. 281, Trine Day, 2010

blood-curdling chill came over me. Their words seared into my soul. The scale of the accusation confounded me. The thought of a cynical bureaucracy that put its own reputation over the fate of millions of innocent people settled into me like a poison.[522]

Judyth had stumbled onto one of the biggest scandals in history. Imagine the public outrage if they knew about the contaminated vaccinations. Dr. Sherman and others had protested the marketing of the tainted vaccines, but to no avail.

It is also speculated that a mutated strain of this virus was responsible for the AIDS epidemic 20 years later. The virus could have been mutated when it was exposed to radiation, then it somehow escaped into the general population. This could have been an accident, or it could have been done with sinister intent. For more on this, see the reference cited here.[523]

The research intended to find a cure for cancer was also used to cause cancer. Baker and her associates had successfully developed the biological warfare agent. The next step was to test it on human subjects. It had already been tested on rats and monkeys, and was successful in causing "galloping" cancer, which kills its victims within weeks rather than months. Baker was told that the human subjects would be prisoners who were terminally ill and had only a short time to live. The prisoners would be taken from Angola Penitentiary to East Louisiana State Mental Hospital in Jackson, Louisiana, which was about 100 miles northwest of New Orleans. Oswald and Ferrie had both been instructed by Baker on how to administer the agent, and they were given the bioweapon to take to the hospital. The man who drove them to Jackson was Clay Shaw. The vehicle he drove was a black Cadillac registered to the International Trade Mart. The Cadillac was used because it had air-conditioning, and the product had to be stored at cool temperatures to preserve it.[524]

Due to the clandestine nature of the project, it was necessary to use some chicanery to gain access to the patients. An elaborate scheme was concocted to avoid drawing suspicion to the Cadillac. When the vehicles escorting the prisoners left Angola, a cohort would phone Shaw with the

[522] Baker, Judyth Vary, *Me and Lee*, pp. 281-2, Trine Day, 2010
[523] Haslam, Edward T., *Dr. Mary's Monkey*, pp. 273-281, Trine Day, 2007
[524] Baker, Judyth Vary, *Me and Lee*, p. 465, Trine Day, 2010

signal to proceed. The Cadillac would then sneak in behind the state vehicles, making it look like it was part of the official convoy. The arrival of the test team at the hospital would then appear inconspicuous.

Incident in Clinton

This led to a curious incident in Clinton, Louisiana, about 12 miles from Jackson. This is where Shaw and the others were supposed to wait for the phone call that would alert them to the prison vehicle's departure. The call was to come at a pay phone at the Clinton Courthouse, which was chosen because the Cadillac would be less conspicuous at a municipal building.

Clinton was a small town with a population of about 1,500 in 1963. At the time, the civil rights movement was gaining momentum. With a high concentration of black people, Clinton was the target of a black voter registration drive initiated by the Congress of Racial Equality (CORE). Racial tensions were high in Clinton, as they were throughout the country. Black people in Clinton had been arrested just for writing appeals to the mayor and the district attorney. This also happened to be the day after Martin Luther King's famous "I Have a Dream" speech, so racial awareness was even higher than usual.

On this hot summer day, a long line of people, mostly blacks, waited patiently to go through the tedious process of registering to vote. Local police were present, preparing for any kind of incident that may occur. Then, the large black Cadillac drove up, carrying four white men. Along with Oswald, Shaw and Ferrie, the fourth man was an orderly from the Jackson Hospital. Oswald got out of the car and stood in line with the other registrants. This was significant because witnesses would testify to seeing Oswald and Shaw together when Shaw was on trial a few years later. Being one of very few white people in a long line of blacks, it was certain that Oswald would be remembered clearly.

These four men were on their way to the hospital in Jackson. Their only purpose for being in Clinton was to get a phone call. Oswald stood in line only because they had hours to kill before the call finally came. He was curious to see if he would be able to register to vote because he was white, seeing that so many blacks had been denied registration. The main event of the day was the testing of the bioweapon on a human subject. The Clinton incident was a secondary event. No one knew that it would be so significant in court a few years later.[525]

Judyth had been told that the bioweapon would only be tested on patients who were terminally ill and had volunteered to be injected. That was not the case. These subjects were basically healthy, and had been chosen only because they were of similar physical characteristic to Fidel Castro. Judyth had also been told that there would only be one human subject, but there turned out to be many. When Judyth found out, she was irate. She considered it a violation of the Hippocratic Oath to inject healthy people with a cancer-causing virus. She had been lied to by Ochsner, and was tricked into doing something she believed was murder. She left a message for Dr. Ochsner, which read:

> Injecting disease-causing materials into an unwitting subject who does not have a disease is unethical.[526]

When Dr. Ochsner got the message, he was equally irate. He had instructed Judyth and the others never to put anything down in writing that exposed any details of the project. Ochsner fired Baker, and he also withdrew his offer of a scholarship to Tulane Medical School. Ochsner made it clear to Baker that she was "expendable." She knew what that meant.

In spite of the firing, Dr. Ochsner allowed Judyth and Lee to attempt to finish off the project. About a month later, they tried to get the bioweapon into Cuba. Oswald's role in the project was a courier. The product had a short shelf-life, so Oswald had to learn to handle it safely and keep it alive. He was to deliver the materials to a contact in Mexico City, and from there they would be delivered to Cuba. But the contact never showed up due to Hurricane Flora, which had devastated Cuba at the time. Oswald knew the material had a short shelf-life, and he had to get it to Cuba quickly before it expired. He tried to get a transit visa. The visa was approved in mid-October, but by then it was too late. The biological materials were no good anymore. The mission was cancelled and Oswald returned to Dallas.

Baker knew Oswald better than anyone, and she knew that he was a patriotic American. His trip to Mexico City was life-threatening, but he did it for his country. She also knew that Lee was an informant for the FBI. She

---

[525] Baker, Judyth Vary, *Me and Lee*, pp. 466-469, Trine Day, 2010
[526] Baker, Judyth Vary, *Me and Lee*, p. 470, Trine Day, 2010

believes that he was the one who tipped off the Chicago FBI about the assassination plot there on November 2, and that he had also spoken to an FBI agent on November 16 concerning the Dallas plot. Baker has stated that Dr. Mary Sherman helped Oswald by giving him the names of trusted contacts that she knew. This is supposedly how Oswald knew about the Chicago plot.[527]

Death of Dr. Mary Sherman

On July 21, 1964, Dr. Mary Sherman was found dead in her New Orleans apartment. There had been a fire. Her right arm and thorax had been burned completely off, but burned in a manner different from the rest of her body. There were seven stab wounds on the body, one of which pierced the heart. The coroner ruled it homicide, but the circumstances are very suspicious. Why would someone stab her to death, then start a fire? Neighbors did not hear any screaming or anything unusual. There was no forced entry and no sign of robbery. What was the motive?[528]

Dr. Sherman had been working on a cure for the cancer caused by the tainted polio vaccine. Her research involved the use of a machine called a linear particle accelerator. This machine was so huge, it required a three-story building just to house it. It is believed that Dr. Sherman used a particle accelerator located in the Public Health Service Hospital in New Orleans. The machine created high-level radiation and involved a tremendous amount of electricity. It was used to kill or weaken the monkey virus which caused cancer.

The Homicide report stated:

> The right side of the body from the waist to where the right shoulder would be, including the whole right arm, was apparently disintegrated from the fire, yielding the inside organs of the body.

The Precinct report stated:

> From further examination of the body, it was noted by the coroner that the right arm and a portion of the right side of

---

[527] Baker, Judyth Vary, *Me and Lee*, p. 517, Trine Day, 2010
[528] Baker, Judyth Vary, *Me and Lee*, p. 280, Trine Day, 2010

the body extending from the right hip to the right shoulder
was completely burned away exposing various vital organs.

The cause of death was… Extreme burns of right side of
body with complete destruction of right upper extremity and
right side of thorax (chest) and abdomen.[529]

Investigators were puzzled by the case, and in particular by the damage
to Dr. Sherman's arm and side. Her arm was disintegrated, not just burned.
It was clearly not caused by the fire. Her entire right side, from her scalp to
her hip, was damaged so badly that internal organs were exposed. It was
something that investigators had never seen before, and it's not likely that
they would conclude that a particle accelerator was responsible for the
damage to her body.

The autopsy report stated that there was no hemorrhaging around any of
the stab wounds. That means that Dr. Sherman was already dead when she
was stabbed. Why would someone stab a dead body seven times? It had to
be to cover up the true cause of death. The most likely explanation is that
Dr. Sherman had an accident with the particle accelerator. She was
somehow exposed to a tremendous electrical charge and intense heat from
the machine. Either the radiation or a huge flash of electricity caused her
arm to disintegrate. The associates who were working with Dr. Sherman at
the time must have seen what happened. She suffered a terrible accident
that destroyed her arm and damaged much of her body beyond healing.
Since there was damage to internal organs, it's not likely that Dr. Sherman
could have survived even with the best of medical attention.

At the moment of the accident, Dr. Sherman was either dead or close to
it. Even if she had survived, she would have been seriously incapacitated for
the rest of her life. Her associates had a problem. They could not report the
accident because there would be too many questions asked. This project
had to be kept top-secret at all costs, or it would have exposed one of the
biggest scandals of all time. They had only one choice- to make her death
look like murder. They stabbed the dead body seven times to give the
appearance of a psychopathic killer on the loose. One of the stab wounds
was in the genital area, probably so that they could use the explanation of a
sexual assault. The body was taken back to her apartment, which was then
set on fire. The only reason for the fire was to give a superficial explanation

---

[529] Haslam, Edward T., *Dr. Mary's Monkey*, p. 228, Trine Day, 2007

for the damage to her right arm and side. In reality, a fire could not cause the entire arm to disintegrate. Bones do not burn. Even in cremation, with temperatures of about 1,600 degrees, the bones are not completely burned. Yet, the relatively small fire in Dr. Sherman's apartment was said to have disintegrated her entire arm. This was physically impossible, but it was enough of an explanation to satisfy the public.[530]

One has to wonder why Lee Harvey Oswald was involved in this project. He was not a doctor, and he possessed no special skills or knowledge which would have marked him as a candidate for this assignment. Most of his CIA assignments involved high profile left-wing activities, like attempted defection, leaflet distribution and radio interviews. Yet, this cancer project was completely hush-hush. It added nothing to his sheep-dipped persona. So why was Oswald caught up in all this? A possible explanation would be that since this project was so extremely sensitive, the government would go to great lengths to hide every detail about it. By involving Oswald in the project, it ensured the government's cooperation in the cover-up.

According to the Warren Report, Oswald had among his possessions a vaccination card issued to him by the U.S. Public Health Service. The card said that Oswald had been vaccinated for smallpox on June 8, 1963, when he lived in New Orleans. The card was signed "Dr. A.J. Hidell." In the typed section of the card, the last name was spelled "Hideel," due to the sloppy handwriting. The commission determined that the card was a forgery and the signature was in the handwriting of Lee Harvey Oswald.

The proof of vaccination was necessary for Oswald to travel to certain countries. Dr. Ochsner administered the shots, but could not put his name on the vaccination card for security reasons. That is why Oswald signed the card, using the fake name. "A.J. Hidell" was a project name used on fake IDs to access certain funds. Oswald was aware that other agents had used the same name. In a sworn affidavit in 1976, Richard Case Nagell listed all the aliases he had used in connection with his intelligence activities. "Alek Hidell" is among the names listed.[531] [532]

---

[530] Haslam, Edward T., *Dr. Mary's Monkey*, p. 227-241, Trine Day, 2007
[531] Baker, Judyth Vary, *Me and Lee*, p. 338, Trine Day, 2010
[532] http://whokilledjfk.net/george_and_the_cia.htm

FPCC

Lee Harvey Oswald worked for Guy Banister in the summer of 1963. It was Banister who told Oswald to form the Fair Play for Cuba Committee. He did so using the Alik J. Hidell alias to open a P.O. Box in the name of the FPCC. On August 9, Oswald was distributing FPCC leaflets on a street corner in New Orleans. On the leaflets was the address 544 Camp Street, New Orleans, which was a connection back to Banister. This was a mistake on Oswald's part, as Banister did not want it to be known that he was behind the project. 544 Camp St. was the same corner building as 531 Lafayette St., which was Banister's location. The Camp Street address belonged to Carlos Bringuier, an anti-Castro exile. When Bringuier saw Oswald passing out pro-Castro literature, he became irate. He knew Oswald worked for Banister, but he knew him to be anti-Castro. He thought Oswald was a traitor or a fake, and an argument broke out on the street corner. This led to a fight, with the two of them, along with other anti-Castroites, being arrested. Oswald was let off with a $10 fine, and a few days later, he and Bringuier debated Marxism on a local radio show. All this seems to indicate that Oswald was simply putting on a façade of being a communist sympathizer. When Banister was told about Oswald distributing pro-communist literature, he just laughed and said, "Don't worry. He's one of us." It's worth noting that the leafletting and the fight occurred in front of the International Trade Mart, which was owned by Clay Shaw.[533]

One purpose of the leaflet project was to identify communists in the area. Those who responded positively to the flyer would be put on a watch list. The other reason, unbeknownst to Oswald, was to set him up to look like a communist so the public would believe he killed John Kennedy. It's likely that Oswald's employment with Banister was arranged by the CIA. This was part of his "sheep-dipping," meaning he was creating a persona that would be used for other projects later on. At this point, Banister probably did not know that Oswald was the chosen patsy.

A week after the leafletting incident, Oswald was interviewed on a local station in New Orleans by radio commentator William K. Stuckey. Oswald was asked if the FPCC was communist, and if he himself was a communist:

---

[533] http://spartacus-educational.com/JFKoswald.htm

Stuckey: Mr. Oswald, there are many commentators in the
journalistic field in this country that equate the Fair Play for
Cuba Committee with the American Communist Party. What
is your feeling about this and are you a member of the
American Communist Party?

Oswald: Well, the Fair Play for Cuba Committee with its
headquarters at 799 Broadway in New York has been
investigated by the Senate sub-committees who are occupied
with this sort of thing. They have investigated our
organization from the viewpoint of taxes, subversion,
allegiance, and in general, where and how and why we exist.
They have found absolutely nothing to connect us with the
Communist Party of the United States. In regards to your
question about whether I myself am a communist, as I said I
do not belong to any other organization.[534]

A few days later, Oswald had a radio debate with Bringuer and another
anti-communist, Ed Butler. Oswald was asked about the goals of the FPCC:

The principles of thought of the Fair Play for Cuba
Committee consist of restoration of diplomatic trade and
tourist relations with Cuba. That is one of our main points.
We are for that. I disagree that this situation regarding
American-Cuban relations is very unpopular. We are in the
minority surely. We are not particularly interested in what
Cuban exiles or rightists members of rightist organizations
have to say. We are primarily interested in the attitude of the
U.S. government toward Cuba. And in that way we are
striving to get the United States to adopt measures which
would be more friendly toward the Cuban people and the
new Cuban regime in that country. We are not all communist
controlled regardless of the fact that I have the experience of
living in Russia, regardless of the fact that we have been
investigated, regardless of those facts, the Fair Play for Cuba
Committee is an independent organization not affiliated with
any other organization. Our aims and our ideals are very

---

[534] http://mcadams.posc.mu.edu/russ/jfkinfo3/exhibits/stuck2.htm

clear and in the best keeping with American traditions of democracy.[535]

Oswald came across as intelligent and well-prepared in both the interview and the debate. He probably only expressed the viewpoints that he was told to in order to perform his function. But he seemed to know the subject matter intimately, and he does not fit the image of the lone renegade that the Warren Commission made him out to be.

In 1964, with the assassination still fresh in everyone's mind, a recording of this debate was released on a vinyl LP called *Oswald: Self-Portrait in Red*. The LP was produced by the Information Council of the Americas (INCA), which was established by Dr. Ochsner. Ed Butler was the executive director of INCA. On the record, both Ochsner and Butler give their commentaries and are featured on the back cover, along with Hale Boggs, who introduces the debate.

From the back cover of the LP:

> "I AM A MARXIST"
> - Lee Harvey Oswald, August 21, 1963- With these words, a few weeks before President Kennedy's assassination, Lee Harvey Oswald sketched the indelible outline of this Self-Portrait in Red.
>
> HEAR OSWALD'S OWN VOICE AND LEARN:
>
> *What did Oswald really think of President Kennedy?*
>
> Hear the only recorded statement in existence, as Oswald gives his own opinion of President Kennedy.
>
> *Was Oswald alone?*
>
> Listen to this record, as Oswald defends the Fair Play for Cuba committee. Then decide for yourself.
>
> *Was Oswald insane?*
>
> Listen to this record... then judge for yourself.
>
> *What did Oswald call his enemies?*

---

[535] http://mcadams.posc.mu.edu/russ/jfkinfo3/exhibits/stuck2.htm

Hear Oswald pin a label on people he dislikes, and smear the State
Department and the CIA.

Whom did Oswald admire?

Hear Oswald's own suggestion, that the United States should have dropped weapons "into the Sierra Maestra where Fidel Castro could have used them."

How did Oswald explain his three years in Russia?

Listen to this record, and hear his revealing reply.

The album fed off the public hysteria of the day. Oswald actually handled himself well in the debate, but with the FPCC in his background, he still came across as a crazy commie. In the public mind, Oswald is guilty until proven innocent, and this record does nothing to prove him innocent. Naturally, people were curious to hear what Oswald had to say, since they barely had a chance to hear him in the Dallas Police Station that day.

At the end of side one, Dr. Ochsner gave his commentary on the debate:

Because the full facilities of INCA were available, for a change, the propaganda battle was fought evenly. The results speak for themselves. Oswald dropped out of sight immediately after the debate, and left New Orleans shortly thereafter... Many who have heard this record have expressed the belief that if an INCA branch office had existed in Dallas, Oswald would again have been exposed and the president might be alive today.[536]

Ochsner is simply delusional. He believes that his organization could have prevented the assassination if they'd had an office in Dallas. He said that Oswald dropped out of sight and left New Orleans after the debate, which implies that INCA scared him off. Maybe Ochsner should have mentioned that Oswald worked for him. People might want more details about that.

Oswald's intention was to prevent the assassination. He did not realize he was being used. Judyth was one of the few who knew the reality about Oswald. He had penetrated the assassination ring, in spite of the inherent dangers of the assignment. He was aware of those involved: the mafia, oil

---

[536] LP- Oswald: *Self-Portrait in Red*, 1964

tycoons, racists, anti-Castro Cubans, the Secret Service and the CIA. One faction of the CIA wanted to assassinate Kennedy, while another faction was trying to abort the assassination. Oswald was part of the latter group. When talking to Judyth about the mission, he told her to remember two very important names: Bobby Baker and Billie Sol Estes. Any investigation of those two individuals would lead directly to Lyndon Johnson. So Oswald knew about Johnson's involvement.

After the assassination, Judyth received a call from David Ferrie, warning her to keep her mouth shut about her knowledge of the events, or she would be killed.[537]

Oswald and the FBI

During the time Oswald was in Russia, the FBI kept tabs on him. They were aware that he had defected to Russia, attempted to renounce his U.S. citizenship, applied for Soviet citizenship, described himself as a Marxist, and said that he was willing to give the Russian government any useful information he had acquired as a Marine radar technician. That last part is shocking. They are saying that Oswald was willing to betray his country by giving away sensitive military secrets to the Soviet Union. If that were true, then Oswald was a traitor. He could have been court-martialed and put away for life. In fact, he would probably have been arrested as soon as he stepped off the plane. So how could the FBI not consider him a threat? Yet, at the height of the Cold War, this alleged communist defector/traitor was able to get a passport to return to the United States in 24 hours. This shows that he was under the guidance of federal authorities. According to the CIA, Oswald was not debriefed when he returned from Russia.[538] That is strange, since anyone returning from the Soviet Union at that time would normally have been debriefed by the Domestic Contacts Division of the CIA. It was discovered in 1993 that Oswald was debriefed upon his return to America in 1962. The debriefing was done by CIA officer Aldrin Anderson, and the debriefing report was read by CIA officer Donald Deneselya. The CIA was reluctant to admit it because they wanted to wash their hands clean of Oswald.[539] [540]

---

[537] http://spartacus-educational.com/JFKbakerJ.htm

[538] http://jonathandenby.com/blog/2015/11/22/the-oswald-files-what-american-intelligence-knew-about-kennedys-assassin

[539] http://www.jfkbook.org/lee-harvey-oswald-mysterious-man/

When Oswald was briefly incarcerated in New Orleans, he asked the police to arrange for him to be interviewed by the FBI. That seems like a strange request, since this was only a misdemeanor charge. Oswald was let off with a $10 fine. Why would the FBI have any interest in such a minor event? They certainly have bigger fish to fry. Why would Oswald even think the FBI would waste their time on such a petty offense? And why would the New Orleans police even grant him such a request? But surprisingly, they did. And surprisingly, an FBI agent promptly showed up. His name was John L. Quigley, and he had a brief interview with Oswald. According to Quigley, it appeared that Oswald "was making self-serving statements in attempting to explain to me why he was distributing this literature." Oswald had refused to give any details about the Fair Play for Cuba Committee, and Quigley also had the impression that this event was staged. Apparently, Oswald wanted it to be publicly known that he was endorsing Marxism.[541]

FBI agent James Hosty had reopened the file on Oswald on October 3 after it had been transferred from the New Orleans office. From that time until the assassination, Hosty kept tabs on Oswald's whereabouts and his activities. On November 1, and again on November 5, he was at Ruth Paines' house, interviewing Oswald's wife, Marina. Oswald was not living with his wife at the time, but Marina Oswald informed agent Hosty of his place of residence and his place of employment. The interviews were innocent enough, but they led to an incident that caused the FBI some headaches.

Oswald went to the Dallas FBI office to talk with Hosty, who was not there at the time. This was in regard to Hosty's visit with Oswald's wife. Oswald left a note for Hosty. The note said:

> If you have anything you want to learn about me, come talk to me directly. If you don't cease bothering my wife, I will take appropriate action and report this to the proper authorities.[542]

The note would have been evidence in the trial, but after Oswald was shot, there would be no trial. Gordon Shanklin ordered Hosty to destroy the note. Hosty began tearing it up. "No, not like that," said Shanklin. Hosty was ordered to tear up the note and flush it down the toilet, which he did.

---

[540] Janney, Peter, *Mary's Mosaic*, p. 430, Skyhorse Publishing, 2016

[541] http://spartacus-educational.com/JFKoswald.htm

[542] http://spartacus-educational.com/JFKhosty.htm

Shanklin justified his order on the grounds that Oswald was dead, so there would be no trial. But in theory, Oswald could have conspired with someone else. The other party or parties could still be prosecuted, and any evidence that relates to Oswald would also relate to conspiracy charges against the others. That includes the note.[543]

When Hosty saw Oswald in the Dallas Police Department shortly after his arrest, he made the following statement to the police:

> ...we knew he was capable of assassinating the president, but we didn't dream he would do it...

That statement was quoted in newspapers and caused major problems for the FBI. It gave the impression that Oswald was known to be a potential assassin, but the FBI did nothing about it. That is not the case, of course, but at a time of mass hysteria the public will overreact to something like this. They will wonder why no one was keeping an eye on Oswald. But Hosty simply knew that Oswald was not dangerous. In Hosty's defense, the FPCC was not on the FBI's list of subversive organizations, despite the overtly communist nature of the group.

The FBI and the DPD both tried to cover themselves. Dallas Police Chief Jesse Curry made this comment:

> If we had known that a defector or a Communist was anywhere in this town, let alone on the parade route, we would have been sitting on his lap, you can bet on that.

Hosty was made out to be the goat. He had this to say about Curry's comment:

> The police were blatantly trying to wriggle out from under a rock. . . . I wanted to laugh. The police had a long list of well-known Communists in Dallas, and not one had a police officer sitting on his lap on November 22. In fact, Detective H. M. Hart told me that the police neither picked up nor watched anyone the day of November 22. Clearly, someone

---

[543] Turner, Nigel, The Cover-Up, 1988, *The Men Who Killed Kennedy*, U.K., Nigel Turner Productions

from the police department had fed this story to reporter
Hugh Aynesworth...[544]

To make matters worse, Hosty's name and address were found in
Oswald's address book. It was suspected that Oswald was a paid informant
for the FBI. But Hoover wanted no connection with Oswald at all. To cover
up any involvement with him, the FBI did not turn the address book over to
the Warren Commission. Instead, they provided typewritten transcripts of
its contents, but Hosty's name and address were left out. Hoover explained
that the omission was because the report was not originally intended for
the commission. But the address book was deliberately transcribed to be
presented to the commission. If it was for internal use only, why would
Hosty's name and address be left out?

It was Texas Attorney General Waggoner Carr who first informed the
Warren Commission of Oswald's connection with the FBI. On January 22,
1964, he notified the commission that Oswald had been recruited as an FBI
informant in September of 1962. He detailed that Oswald was being paid
$200 a month, and was assigned informant number S-172. (Some sources
reported the number to be S-179.) Carr said he was informed of this by
Dallas D.A. Henry Wade. The same information had been confirmed by the
Secret Service, who named Dallas Deputy Sheriff Allan Sweatt as the source.
The commission speculated that Oswald's number had been "assigned to
him in connection with the CIA."[545]

This explosive information prompted a special executive session of the
Warren Commission. The minutes of the meeting were classified "Top
Secret" and were not published until 1975. The commission discussed how
to handle the delicate information. J. Lee Rankin, Commission General
Counsel, stated:

> When the Chief Justice and I were just briefly reflecting on,
> we said if that was true and it ever came out, could be
> established, then you would have people think that there was
> a conspiracy to accomplish this assassination that nothing
> the commission did or anybody could dissipate.[546]

---

[544] Hosty, James P., *Assignment: Oswald*, (1996):

[545] http://whokilledjfk.net/george_and_the_cia.htm

[546] Marrs, Jim, *Crossfire*, p. 231, Carroll and Graf, 1989

So Rankin and Warren agreed that the consequences would be dire if the public knew about Oswald's FBI informant status. The consensus among the members was that it should be kept from the public. The subject matter was so sensitive, Hale Boggs commented, "I don't even like to see this being taken down." Allen Dulles agreed, saying, "Yes, I think this ought to be destroyed. Do you think we need a record of this?"[547]

According to FBI security clerk William S. Walter, the bureau maintained two files on Oswald- a security file and an informant file. Walter discovered this when he was requested to do a file check on Oswald. The request came from Special Agent John Quigley, who interviewed Oswald when he was arrested in New Orleans. Walter testified to the HSCA and confirmed that there were two files. But when Quigley testified, he only acknowledged the security file, not the informant file.[548]

Confirmation of Oswald's informant status came from the FBI themselves. An internal FBI memo from 1964, written by Cartha DeLoach to Hoover aide Walter Jenkins, states that Oswald was an informant. The memo mentions that agent Will Hayden Griffin identified Oswald as such, based on an unnamed source. According to the memo, Griffin "assisted in the investigation of the Oswald case and that Oswald, prior to his murder, was definitely an FBI informant. The agent said that FBI files in Washington would prove this fact." Griffin later denied that he made that statement.[549]

Hoover told the Warren Commission he had "entire control over whether a man shall be an informant or shall not be an informant of the FBI." Regarding Oswald, he said that he "can most emphatically say that at no time was he an employee of the bureau in any capacity, either as an agent, or an employee, or as an informant."[550]

Dallas Police Chief Jesse Curry did a flip-flop on his statement about Oswald and the FBI. The day after the assassination, he was questioned by the press:

---

[547] Marrs, Jim, *Crossfire*, p. 232, Carroll and Graf, 1989

[548] Marrs, Jim, *Crossfire*, p. 228, Carroll and Graf, 1989

[549] http://jfk.hood.edu/Collection/Weisberg%20Subject%20Index%20Files/ F%20Disk/FBI/FBI%20Records%20Release%2012-7- 77%20News%20Accounts/Item%20096.pdf

[550] http://jfk.hood.edu/Collection/Weisberg%20Subject%20Index%20Files/ F%20Disk/FBI/FBI%20Records%20Release%2012-7- 77%20News%20Accounts/Item%20096.pdf

Reporter: Chief, did the FBI or your department have him under surveillance prior to yesterday?

Curry: No, sir. We didn't have knowledge that he was in the city.

Reporter: Did the FBI?

Curry: I understand that they did know he was here, and had interviewed him, oh, a week or two ago.

After that statement, Curry must have gotten a phone call that burned his ear off, because a short time later he was back in front of the cameras with this to say:

> I want to correct anything that might have been
> misinterpreted or misunderstood, and that is regarding the
> information that the FBI might have had about this man. I do
> not know if and when the FBI has interviewed this man. The
> FBI is under no obligation to come to us with any
> information concerning anyone. They have cooperated with
> us in the past 100%.[551]

The plotters wanted the FBI to have a file on Oswald just for appearance. Oswald's cover is extremely superficial, and becomes obvious upon closer analysis. In New Orleans, the Fair Play for Cuba Committee consisted of a P.O. Box and a guy with a stack of pamphlets. That was not a major concern for the FBI, but it was just superficial enough for them to have a file on him, which makes him appear criminal. Oswald was technically a defector, which required the CIA and the FBI to have files on him. The agencies will go to extreme lengths to deny their involvement with an alleged assassin.

Mexico City

On Friday, September 27, 1963, a man claiming to be Lee Harvey Oswald visited the Cuban consul's office in Mexico City and said he needed a Cuban transit visa. The person he spoke with was Silvia Duran. "Oswald" showed Duran his passport and communist-related documents, such as his membership card for the Fair Play for Cuba Committee. Duran became suspicious of this man, reasoning that he should have applied in advance by contacting the Communist Party in Cuba. She told him he needed a passport

---

[551] Turner, Nigel, 1988, *The Men Who Killed Kennedy*, U.K., Nigel Turner Productions

photograph to apply for the visa. He returned an hour later with the photograph.

Duran told "Oswald" that he would need confirmation that he had clearance for travel to the Soviet Union. She told him it would be at least seven days before the visa could be issued. He complained that he could only stay three days. He was told to visit the Soviet Embassy to get the required paperwork. After doing this, he was informed that the visa application would take about four months to process. The man returned later and told Duran that he had been to the Soviet Embassy again and that they were willing to give him a visa right away. When Duran phoned the Soviet Embassy, she was told that he was lying. The man became very upset. He shouted, made a scene, and called the employees "bureaucrats" as he left the consulate.

When Oswald was arrested in Dallas after the assassination, Duran immediately remembered the name from that day in the consul's office. The real Oswald had Duran's name and phone number in his address book, further confusing the picture. Duran was ordered to be arrested by Winston Scott, the CIA station chief in Mexico City. He also ordered that she be held incommunicado until she gave all details of her contact with Oswald. Duran was interrogated forcefully, and appeared to be physically abused. Yet, it was reported that she had been "completely cooperative."[552]

Soon afterwards, John M. Witten, the CIA head of the Mexican desk called Scott with orders that Duran not be arrested. Scott told him it was too late. She was released, and the Mexican government agreed to keep the whole thing secret. It was feared that Duran's arrest might compromise U.S. relations with Cuba. In a telegraph from Tom Karamessines, Deputy Director for Plans for the CIA, it reads:

> Arrest of Sylvia Duran is extremely serious matter which could prejudice U.S. freedom of action on entire question of Cuban responsibility...With full regard for Mexican interests, request you ensure that her arrest is kept absolutely secret, that no information from her is published or leaked, that all such info is cabled to us, and that fact of her arrest

---

[552] http://mexicounexplained.com/lee-harvey-oswald-mexico-city/

and her statements are not spread to leftist or disloyal circles in the Mexican government.[553]

Duran had initially told authorities that Oswald was not the man who visited the embassy that day. This was not what they wanted to hear. Duran was held for several days. She was released only when she agreed to say that it was Lee Harvey Oswald at the embassy. Duran made a detailed statement that confirmed Oswald as the man in the consul. But after she was freed, she began to talk about her experience. This prompted the CIA to send another cable ordering Duran to be rearrested, but not to make it known that the American government was behind it. The cable read:

> ...to be certain that there is no misunderstanding between us, we want to insure that Silvia Duran gets no impression that Americans are behind her rearrest. In other words we want Mexican authorities to take responsibility for the whole affair.[554]

On November 27, Silvia Duran was arrested again. Ostensibly, it was for trying to leave Mexico for Cuba. Thomas C. Mann, the U.S. Ambassador in Mexico, sent the following message to Winston Scott:

> Duran should be told that as the only living non-Cuban who knew the full story, she was in exactly the same position as Oswald prior to the assassination. Her only chance of survival is to come clean with the whole story and cooperate fully. I think she'll crack when confronted with the details.[555]

The Warren Commission was never told about the Duran incident. The CIA withheld the information, and used the Mexico City story to reinforce the renegade image of Oswald. Duran's testimony not only would have blown the lid off of that fraud, but it also would have proven an Oswald impersonator, which would have been difficult to explain.

Over the years, Duran has publicly maintained that the man at the consul was Oswald. She was probably still intimidated by her experience with the Mexican police and the CIA. But in a 1979 interview with author Anthony Summers, she admitted that she did not think it was Oswald. Duran stated:

---

[553] http://spartacus-educational.com/JFKduranS.htm
[554] Marrs, Jim, *Crossfire*, p. 194, Carroll and Graf, 1989
[555] http://spartacus-educational.com/JFKduranS.htm

> I was not sure if it was Oswald or not. The man on the film
> is not like the man I saw here in Mexico City.[556]

The Cuban and Soviet Embassies were both under photographic
surveillance when Oswald was allegedly there. Everyone entering and
leaving the building was photographed. Yet, the CIA could offer no proof of
Oswald's presence at either embassy. Oswald supposedly made a total of
five trips to the two embassies, giving a total of 10 chances for surveillance
pictures. Also, there was Oswald's visa picture that should have been in his
file at the consul, making a total of 11 possible chances to produce
photographic evidence of Oswald at the embassies. They could not produce
one. The CIA's explanations were pitiful. They claimed that the camera at
the Cuban Embassy just happened to be out of order when Oswald was
there, and the camera at the Soviet Embassy was turned off on Saturdays,
which is when Oswald was supposedly there. They claimed that the visa
photograph was lost. As lame as these excuses were, the Warren
Commission bought them all without a challenge.[557]

The claim that the Soviet Embassy does not take surveillance photos on
Saturday was proven false by the CIA themselves. The day of the
assassination, the CIA sent at least one surveillance photo taken outside the
embassy the day they said Oswald was there, which was a Saturday. They
claimed that the photo was of Oswald, but it is very clearly someone else.[558]
Years later, the CIA admitted that there had been a mix-up with the photos.
The Oswald pictures were either stolen, lost, or destroyed. Still, no
explanation and no Oswald.

The CIA also failed to produce audio recordings of Oswald's visit to the
embassies. In 1976, David Atlee Phillips testified to the HSCA that the CIA
had tape-recorded conversations of Oswald at the Soviet Embassy. The
House Committee asked Phillips why the tapes had not been given to the
Warren Commission. Phillips said the tapes were destroyed about a week
after the visit since Oswald was not considered important prior to the
assassination. This was proven false by a document dated November 23,
1963. According to the document, FBI agents who questioned Oswald in

---

[556] Summers, Anthony, *The Kennedy Conspiracy*, McGraw-Hill, 1980
[557] http://mexicounexplained.com/lee-harvey-oswald-mexico-city/
[558] http://www.irishexaminer.com/viewpoints/analysis/jfk-files-show-soviets-in-a-state-of-red-alert-461918.html

Dallas were informed by the CIA that Oswald had visited the Soviet Embassy in Mexico City. The document stated:

> Special agents of this bureau, who have conversed with Oswald in Dallas, Texas, have observed photographs of the individual referred to above and have listened to a recording of his voice. These special agents are of the opinion that the above-referred-to individual was not Lee Harvey Oswald.[559]

So the FBI did hear the tape recordings that were allegedly of Oswald. Although it was determined that the voice on the tape was not Oswald's, the mere fact that the recording exists proves that Phillips lied when he said the tape was destroyed in early October. The HSCA had learned of the deception in Mexico City, yet withheld that fact in its final report, in order to protect "sensitive sources and methods" of the CIA.

Another suspicious story concerning Oswald comes from a Nicaraguan man named Gilberto Alvarado. Alvarado contacted the U.S. Embassy in Mexico City three days after the assassination, saying that he had important information about Lee Harvey Oswald. Alvarado was interviewed by the FBI. He claimed that while visiting the Cuban Embassy in September, he overheard two men talking. One was a red-haired African man, and the other was a man he now recognized as Lee Harvey Oswald. According to Alvarado, Oswald made a statement about "being man enough to kill someone." Alvarado also claimed he saw money being exchanged. He had reported this to the U.S. Embassy at the time, but they told him to quit wasting their time. Alvarado was then interviewed by David Atlee Phillips of the CIA. Alvarado told Phillips that Oswald had been given $1500 for expenses and $5500 as an advance.

FBI agents who interviewed Alvarado speculated that it might be a set-up by the Nicaraguan government who wanted the United States to invade Cuba. Alvarado tried to convince the agents that Fidel Castro was behind the assassination. But the message from the White House was that speculation about Oswald's motives was to be cut off, not pursued.[560]

Alvarado has changed his story many times. He signed a statement admitting that his story about Oswald was false. He said that he lied

---

[559] Marrs, Jim, *Crossfire*, p. 196, Carroll and Graf, 1989
[560] https://www.maryferrell.org/pages/Gilberto_Alvarado_Allegation.html

because he was trying to get the U.S. to invade Cuba. It is highly suspected that Alvarado was a CIA informant under the guidance of David Atlee Phillips. This was a feeble attempt to mobilize the American public against Cuba. I doubt that anyone in the CIA or the FBI really believed the story. To think that any two people would discuss plans for a paid murder out in the open is absurd. Wouldn't they talk in private somewhere instead of in the lobby of the Cuban Embassy? And to make it even more ridiculous, $7000 cash is exchanged right out in the open, in front of everyone. Alvarado also knows too much detail. He claims that $1500 was for expenses, and $5500 was for an advance. He must have been standing right next to them to hear so much clear detail. This story is obviously phony, but it adds to the overall confusion of the case and obscures the truth even more.

On November 29th, Hoover talked to Johnson on the telephone regarding this story:

> This angle in Mexico is giving us a great deal of trouble because the story there is of this man Oswald getting $6,500 from the Cuban Embassy and then coming back to this country with it. We're not able to prove that fact, but the information was that he was there on the 18th of September in Mexico City and we are able to prove conclusively he was in New Orleans that day. Now then they've changed the dates. The story came in changing the dates to the 28th of September and he was in Mexico City on the 28th. Now the Mexican police have again arrested this woman Duran, who is a member of the Cuban Embassy... and we're going to confront her with the original informant, who saw the money pass, so he says, and we're also going to put the lie detector test on him.[561]

Hoover was just going through the motions of conducting an investigation. He couldn't really believe such a phony story. As for Duran, she had already stated that she did not see Oswald at the embassy.

When Earl Warren commented on the commission's final report, he stated, "Full disclosure was not possible for reasons of national security." But if Oswald was merely a disgruntled loner, then why would any of his activities require such secrecy? What information about him could possibly

---

threaten national security? Supposedly, he was just a stock boy in a warehouse. Yet, if the whole truth was known, national security would be threatened. So Earl Warren has inadvertently admitted that the Warren Report is wrong, and Oswald was more than just a stock boy.

During the HSCA hearings, former CIA accountant James B. Wilcott swore under oath that Lee Harvey Oswald was a regular employee of the Central Intelligence Agency. According to Wilcott, Oswald received "a full-time salary for agent work, for doing CIA operational work." Wilcott also testified that money he had personally disbursed went to an encrypted account for "the Oswald project."[562]

In 1996, Robert Tanenbaum testified at the ARRB hearings in Los Angeles. He claimed that Dallas District Attorney Henry Wade and his counsel, Leon Jaworsky, stated that they had reliable information that Lee Harvey Oswald was a contract employee of the CIA and the FBI.[563]

In a memo dated June 3, 1960, J. Edgar Hoover himself shows awareness of Oswald's affiliation with the FBI:

> Date: June 3, 1960
>
> To: Office of Security
>
> Department of State
>
> From: John Edgar Hoover, Director
>
> Subject: LEE HARVEY OSWALD
>
> INTERNAL SECURITY- R
>
> ...Since there is a possibility that an imposter is using Oswald's birth certificate, any current information the Department of State may have concerning subject will be appreciated.[564]

This was more than three years before the assassination. It was before Kennedy was even elected president, yet Hoover knows who Oswald is. Regardless of the nature of Oswald's relationship with the FBI, it is

---

[562] http://harveyandlee.net/Wilcott/Wilcott.htm

[563] http://www.harveyandlee.net/index.html

[564] http://www.harveyandlee.net/Comrade/Hoover.jpg

significant simply that Hoover would even know his name. What did he know about Oswald? Why does Hoover suspect that someone is using Oswald's birth certificate? And who is the imposter? The FBI claims that they were monitoring Oswald because he was a communist defector. The true nature of the relationship is not known. It's likely that Oswald was an informant, paid or not, for the FBI.

During the Warren Commission investigation, Senator Russell asked Army Intelligence officer Phillip Corso to research the mysterious past of Lee Harvey Oswald. Corso reported back to Russell that two U.S. passports had been issued to Oswald, and that these passports were used by two different men. This information was obtained from the U.S. Passport Office. Corso also reported that two birth certificates had been issued to Lee Harvey Oswald, and that they were also used by two different men. This information was obtained from the FBI. This dovetails with the memo from Hoover, claiming that someone else was using Oswald's birth certificate.[565]

201 File

By now it is well-known that Lee Harvey Oswald was an operative of the Central Intelligence Agency. After the Freedom of Information Act was passed, assassination researchers discovered a 201 file on him. That is proof that Oswald worked for the CIA in some capacity. According to the CIA's Clandestine Services Handbook, a 201 file was opened on "subjects of extensive reporting and CI (counterintelligence) investigation, prospective agents and sources, and members of groups and organizations of continuing interest."[566]That is the official explanation. In reality, a 201 file is basically a personnel file, the mere existence of which indicates that Oswald worked for the CIA. Several former CIA officers have acknowledged as much:

Victor Marchetti, former executive assistant to the CIA's deputy director:

Basically, if Oswald had a 201 file, he was an agent.

Bradley E. Ayers, CIA officer who trained anti-Castro Cubans:

---

[565] Ventura, Jesse, *They Killed Our President*, p. 81, Skyhorse Publishing, 2013
[566] http://educationforum.ipbhost.com/index.php?/topic/8038-oswald%E2%80%99s-201-cia-file/

(A 201 file meant Oswald was)…either a contract agent working for them full-time, or he was on some kind of assignment for the CIA.

Patrick McGarvey, former CIA agent:

If a guy has a 201 file, that means he's a professional staff employee of the organization.[567]

The person who controlled Oswald's 201 file was Ann Egerter. Egerter testified before the HSCA:

Q: When a 201 file is opened, does that mean that whoever opens the file has either an intelligence interest in the individual, or, if not an intelligence interest, he thinks that the individual may present a counterintelligence risk?

Egerter: Well, in general, I would say that would be correct.

Q: Would there be any other reason for opening up a file?

Egerter: No, I can't think of one.[568]

Supposedly, a 201 file is opened on all defectors. The 201 file on Oswald was opened in December of 1960, but Oswald defected to Russia in October of 1959. Why did it take over a year for the 201 file to be opened on Oswald? What makes it even more puzzling is that a cable from Soviet Embassy Consul Richard Snyder, dated October 31, 1959, warns the CIA that Oswald is threatening to reveal radar secrets to the Soviets. In spite of that, no 201 file was opened at the time. When the file was finally opened over a year later, it simply mentioned that Oswald had defected to Russia and was a radar operator, but no mention was made of his alleged betrayal of his country.

Egerter was aware of anything that entered or left his file. She has been unable to explain the delay in opening the file. She claims that she opened the file when she saw Oswald's name on a list of defectors.

Former CIA Director Richard Helms also testified to the HSCA, but couldn't explain it either. He simply said, "I can't imagine why it would have taken an entire year. I am amazed."[569]

---

[567] Marrs, Jim, *Crossfire*, p. 192, Carroll and Graf, 1989
[568] http://whokilledjfk.net/oswald_and_the_cia.htm

Also of suspicion is that some documents are missing from Oswald's file. Helms' explanation was that those documents were not classified higher than confidential. He said that documents of low national security interest are retained for only five years. However, some of these documents have resurfaced due to the JFK Act of 1992. Among them is the cable from Richard Snyder, informing the CIA of Oswald's threat to give military secrets to the Russians. How is that a "low national security interest"?[570]

William Harvey was the commander of ZR/RIFLE, the CIA division devoted to assassinations of foreign leaders. In his notes, he instructed his agents on cover for assassination planning. In referring to the use of operatives, he wrote:

> Should have phony 201 I files to backstop this, documents therein forged and backdated. Should look like a CE (CounterEspionage) file."[571]

So Harvey instructed his people to create phony 201 files. That should come as no surprise. An accurate file would incriminate not only the operative, but his handler and anyone else involved. They must have some kind of cover in the event they are investigated, and files are requested by the governing body. So Oswald did have a 201 file, showing that he was an operative. Any information in the file, however, is suspect, since it used to obfuscate the truth.

Colonel Fletcher Prouty described the multi-layered world of deception employed by the CIA concerning Marines who are recruited into the agency:

> (The CIA) would give the man a Marine file, in other words, his regular file, because he would have told his friends, etc., that he was in the Marine Corps. They would have to keep that file up—it would have to show promotions and duty assignment changes like a regular Marine. However, since he was a member of the CIA he would also get a CIA "201" file. This would be his file of all his work in the Agency, and this would include all of his duty in the station at Atsugi. There he was really a CIA man under the cover of a Marine.

[569] Newman, John, *Oswald and the CIA*, pp. 48-51, Skyhorse Publishing, 2008
[570] http://educationforum.ipbhost.com/index.php?/topic/8038-oswald%E2%80%99s-201-cia-file/
[571] https://www.maryferrell.org/php/cryptdb.php?id=ZRRIFLE

So he has two files. Then on top of that he might need a
civilian file to account for things he did, or may have done,
as a civilian, so that when he went back to civilian life, for
the Agency, he would have a file which he could use to
account for the continuity of his life. In a sense all three files
would require some fabrication.... This triple file system
permits the Agency to use a surprising amount of flexibility
with certain agents. My office kept such files either with the
CIA—agreeing with their entries, etc.—or independently.
For example, when a man came out of the CIA tour of duty,
we had to make his records appear to show that he had a
normal tour of duty without the CIA periods in his records. It
is complicated, but it works..."[572]

This multiple file system shows the futility of trying to find out the truth
about Oswald, or any CIA operative. There will always be a cover file of
some kind, and the information in the cover file will always be innocuous.
This is even more true in a deep covert operation like an assassination.
Obviously, the CIA will not let specific details of the plot be written down
anywhere.

The Warren Commission acknowledged the inherent paradox in probing
an agency whose very existence depends on absolute secrecy:

Agency files would not always indicate whether an
individual was affiliated with the Agency in any
capacity...[573]

Allen Dulles told the commission about the system used to identify an
operative from his file:

The record may not be on paper. But on paper would have
hieroglyphics that only two people know what they meant,
and nobody outside of the agency would know; and you
could say this meant the agent and somebody else could say
it meant another agent.[574]

When Dulles was asked if the CIA Chief would know who hired Oswald,
he responded that "Someone might have done it without authority." Dulles

---

[572] Summer, Anthony, *Conspiracy*, pg. 138, Paragon House, 1980

[573] *The Warren Commission Report*, p. 197, Longmeadow Press, 1964

[574] Summers, Anthony, *Conspiracy*, pg. 139, Paragon House, 1980

was acknowledging that an agent might be hired at a low level by an unauthorized individual, and there would be no way for the head of the CIA to know about it. With his years of service to the CIA, Dulles was well aware of this. Several CIA officials testified to the Warren Commission. Did Dulles ask any of them about the hieroglyphics? If Dulles knew about this system, why was it never mentioned in questioning during the 10 months the commission spent trying to determine Oswald's role in all of this? This was one of the reasons why Dulles was chosen for the commission. He knows the inner workings of the agency, so he knows what to ask and what not to ask.

The HSCA also stated there was a "remote possibility that an individual could have been run by someone as part of a vest pocket operation without other agency officials knowing about it." By "vest pocket operation," they mean that the individual is being used for personal or private reasons not authorized by the CIA.

Antonio Veciana was the founder of Alpha 66, a violent Cuban exile group. Veciana had met repeatedly with his CIA contact, who he knew as Maurice Bishop. Bishop was actually David Atlee Phillips, who was Oswald's CIA handler. Veciana has stated that he saw Bishop in Dallas in the late summer of 1963, and that Bishop was with Lee Harvey Oswald.[575]

Grassy knoll shooter James Files also acknowledged Oswald as a CIA operative:

> Lee Harvey Oswald had the same control agent...the same controller that I had, David Atlee Phillips...because David Atlee Phillips introduced me to him.[576]

Minox

In the FBI report on Oswald's possessions, it said, "Nothing was noted...which would indicate that these specimens would be particularly useful in the field of espionage." But who said anything about the field of espionage? This report is from the day after Oswald's arrest. No one has yet

---

[575] http://whokilledjfk.net/george_and_the_cia.htm
[576] Dankbaar, Wim, *Files on Files*, p. 51, Trafford Publishing, 2005

mentioned a word about Oswald's affiliation with any intelligence agency. It shows the FBI was already thinking that way early on.[577]

But was the FBI's report accurate? When detectives Gus Rose and Richard Stovall were looking through Oswald's possessions, they found a small Minox camera. The camera was loaded with film. Both the camera and the film were recorded in the inventory. When the FBI took over the investigation, the evidence was cataloged and signed for by agent Warren De Brueys. Listed as item 375 was "one Minox camera." The Dallas Police log book shows that they turned over a Minox camera to the FBI. Later, the FBI contacted Rose and Stovall and reported that there was no camera, but there was a Minox light meter. The FBI pressured them to change their inventory, which they refused to do. A few weeks later, the FBI contacted Dallas Police Property Manager H.W. Hill and made the same request. Hill complied with the request and changed the inventory. Item 375 was changed to "Minox light meter." The altered copy of the inventory was given to the Warren Commission.

The existence of the camera is significan because this type of camera was not commercially available. A Minox camera in Oswald's possession is an indication that he was an intelligence agent. This was a small, three-inch camera that was unlike the big, bulky cameras that were common at the time. The *Dallas Morning News* confirmed that the serial number of Oswald's camera did not exist among those distributed for commercial sale in the U.S. Minox cameras that were commercially available in the U.S. began with serial number 135000. Oswald's camera was number 27259. It was also confirmed that Minox did not sell a light meter in the U.S. in 1963.[578]

Rose told his story to the HSCA:

> We found this camera and of course, we brought it and a whole lot of other property in, as possible evidence in the case. And uh, while we were marking the evidence for later identification by us to be used in evidence we did, Stovall and I, did take a close look at this Minox miniature camera and it did have a roll of film in it. As time passed and after the Warren Commission was appointed, uh, a couple of FBI

---

[577] Marrs, Jim, *Crossfire*, p. 193, Carroll and Graf, 1989
[578] Marrs, Jim, *Crossfire*, p. 191, Carroll and Graf, 1989

agents made three different trips to our office to talk to me about this camera. They said that after they had received all the property they found that I had made a mistake, and that that really wasn't a camera, it was a Minox light meter. However, as I told them at the time, I was sure that I had not made a mistake, it definitely was a camera and definitely did have film in it. However, they wanted me to change that in our property invoice to read Minox light meter and not read Minox camera. We never did change it. Uh, Captain Fritz instructed me if I was sure I was right not to make any changes in any reports, to stay with what was right.[579]

The existence of the Minox camera was also confirmed by Dallas Assistant D.A. William Alexander:

The FBI denied the existence of a very small pocket Minox camera found among Oswald's belongings. We picked up a Minox camera which had some film in it and turned it over to the FBI. Despite their denials, claiming it was a light meter, I examined it, and I know a camera when I see one. We had the Minox camera and that was all there was to it! In those days, a Minox camera probably cost around $200. What inference can be drawn from it? Who knows, unless he was an intelligence buff and had bought it through a PX. Obviously, it leads to speculation about his being involved in some kind of intelligence.

But the FBI said there was no Minox camera among Oswald's possessions, in spite of the claims of two Dallas detectives and an assistant D.A. Instead, a Minox light meter has shown up in its place, which was never seen in Dallas. The reason is obvious: The Minox camera is evidence that Oswald was an intelligence agent. This type of camera was only used for spy work and was not available to the public.[580]

In the following memorandum from John McCone, Director of the CIA, Lee Harvey Oswald is clearly identified as a CIA agent:

Oswald subject was trained by this agency, under cover of the Office of Naval Intelligence, for Soviet assignments. During preliminary training, in 1957, subject was active in

---

[579] http://whokilledjfk.net/minox_camera.htm
[580] http://whokilledjfk.net/minox_camera.htm

aerial reconnaissance of mainland China and maintained a security clearance up to the "confidential" level. His military records during this period are open to your agency and I have directed they be forwarded to the Commission.[581]

The U-2 Incident

The U-2 incident involving Gary Powers happened about six months after Lee Harvey Oswald had attempted to renounce his American citizenship at the Russian Embassy in Moscow. Recall that he had offered to give the Russians top secret radar information that he possessed from his time in Atsugi when he was a radar operator for the U-2 flights. When Powers' plane was shot down, there was an investigation, but no mention was made of Lee Harvey Oswald. Oswald was never arrested, interrogated, or charged with anything relating to this event. Yet, the Warren Commission tried to claim that Oswald was a traitor for attempting to give top secret information to the Russians. The implication was that Oswald may have given the Russians radar information about the U-2 flights which the Russians used to shoot down Powers' plane. This was obviously just another attempt to demonize him. In reality, Oswald probably did not have enough knowledge of the U-2 project to effectively betray his country even if he wanted to. Only CIA personnel with the highest security clearance would know specific transponder frequency and tracking information.

If Oswald had really and truly betrayed his country as they claim he did, he would have been arrested and court-martialed for the Powers incident the moment he stepped on American soil. Not only did that not happen, but Oswald was given a repatriation loan of $435.71 by the U.S. Embassy, and was welcomed back into the U.S. with open arms in June of 1962. The CIA even claimed that they didn't bother to debrief him.[582]

From the HSCA Report:

> Did the CIA ever debrief Oswald?--The CIA has denied ever having had any contact with Oswald, and its records are consistent with this position. Because the Agency has a Domestic Contacts Division that routinely attempts to solicit information on a nonclandestine basis from Americans

---

[581] http://www.viewzone.com/lbj/lbj5.html

[582] https://www.fff.org/2015/11/02/bridge-of-spies-and-lee-harvey-oswald/

traveling abroad, the absence of any record indicating that Oswald, a returning defector who had worked in a Minsk radio factory, had been debriefed has been considered by Warren Commission critics to be either inherently unbelievable (that is, the record was destroyed) or indicative that Oswald had been contacted through other than routine Domestic Contact Division channels[583]

As mentioned earlier, the CIA did debrief Oswald in 1962, but they denied it because they tried to disavow any connection with him.

The Baron

George De Mohrenschildt, a.k.a. "the Baron," was a Russian-born immigrant. He was a petroleum geologist by trade and was associated with the CIA, as well as several well-known oil magnates. Among his affiliations was Pantepec Oil, a CIA-connected company. De Mohrenschildt also belonged to two CIA proprietary organizations, the Dallas Council on World Affairs and the Crusade for a Free Europe. It's safe to say that De Mohrenschildt was an intelligence asset of the U.S. government.[584] [585]

De Mohrenschildt was given Oswald's name and address by an associate in 1961. Over the next two years, De Mohrenschildt got to know Oswald and his family. He took Oswald to anti-Castro meetings and learned about his time in Minsk, where De Mohrenschildt had lived as a child. It was De Mohrenschildt who introduced Lee and Marina Oswald to Ruth Paine in April of 1963. The Oswalds became Paine's boarders, although Lee moved out when the two began having marital problems.

De Mohrenschildt was living in Haiti at the time of the assassination. He gave a deposition at the embassy, stating that he did know Oswald, and that he knew Oswald owned a rifle. He stated in the deposition that he thought Oswald was innocent. He did return to America to testify to the Warren Commission.[586]

De Mohrenschildt was an informant for U.S. military intelligence. He befriended Oswald, but he also helped to set him up for his fall. Military

---

[583] *HSCA Final Report*, p. 207-8, 1978
[584] http://spartacus-educational.com/JFKdemohrenschildt.htm
[585] https://en.wikipedia.org/wiki/George_de_Mohrenschildt
[586] http://spartacus-educational.com/JFKdemohrenschildt.htm

intelligence veteran James Southwood stated that all the information he had about Oswald was given to the 112th Military Intelligence Unit in Houston by George De Mohrenschildt.[587] This was the unit that was told to stand down and not provide any protection for the president in his Dallas motorcade. This was also the unit that wrongly provided the TSBD with Oswald's old address, saying that it was 605 Elsbeth when it should have been 602 Elsbeth, which proved MI involvement. That incorrect information was probably provided by De Mohrenschildt. He probably also told them that Oswald used the alias Alik J. Hidell, since they had that information on file, too.

By 1976, George De Mohrenschildt was suffering from severe depression and anxiety. Out of desperation, he sent a letter to his friend, George H.W. Bush, who was director of the CIA at that point. In the letter he said that he was being followed and his phone was bugged. The constant surveillance was stressing him out. Two months after he sent the memo, he was committed to a mental institution. He underwent electroshock therapy- at Parkland Hospital, of all places.

Willem Oltmans was a friend of De Mohrenschildt. He testified to the HSCA about De Mohrenschildt's condition in 1977:

> I couldn't believe my eyes. The man had changed drastically... he was nervous, trembling. It was a scared, a very, very scared person I saw. I was absolutely shocked, because I knew De Mohrenschildt as a man who wins tennis matches, who is always suntanned, who jogs every morning, who is as healthy as a bull.[588]

Oltmans said that De Mohrenschildt begged him to take him out of the country. "They're after me," he said. Oltmans took De Mohrenschildt to Europe to relax and work on a book. When Oltmans tried to arrange a meeting with a Soviet diplomat, De Mohrenschildt became fearful that he was being set up to look like a communist, the way Oswald was. De Mohrenschildt may have been paranoid at this point, but in any case, he returned to the United States.

Back in the states, De Mohrenschildt was contacted by author Edward Jay Epstein, who offered him $4,000 for a four-day interview. De Morenschildt

[587] Ventura, Jesse, *They Killed Our President*, pp. 217-218, Skyhorse Publishing, 2013
[588] http://spartacus-educational.com/JFKdemohrenschildt.htm

agreed, and they met in Palm Beach, Florida and discussed De
Mohrenschildt's life and career. Epstein asked him about Lee Harvey Oswald.
In his diary, Epstein wrote:

> Then, this morning, I asked him about why he, a socialite in
> Dallas, sought out Oswald, a defector. His explanation, if
> believed, put the assassination in a new and unnerving
> context. He said that although he had never been a paid
> employee of the CIA, he had "on occasion done favors" for
> CIA connected officials. In turn, they had helped in his
> business contacts overseas. By way of example, he pointed
> to the contract for a survey of the Yugoslavian coast
> awarded to him in 1957. He assumed his "CIA connections"
> had arranged it for him and he provided them with reports on
> the Yugoslav officials in whom they had expressed
> interest.[589]

After talking all morning, the two broke for lunch and agreed to continue
the interview at 3 p.m. De Mohrenschildt never returned. When he went
home, he found a card from Gaeton Fonzi, meaning that the HSCA wanted
to talk to him. De Mohrenschildt was found dead later that day, allegedly
from a self-inflicted gunshot wound. De Mohrenschildt became a statistic-
another suspicious death related to the JFK assassination.[590]

But De Mohrenschildt did not commit suicide; he was shot. Researcher
Mark Lane discovered the proof for this in a most unusual way. De
Mohrenschildt's daughter was making an audio recording of a soap opera
while she was at work. In the background of the recording we hear a series
of high-pitched beeps, followed by the sound of footsteps, then a gunshot.
The beeps are from the home security system in the house. The system was
on medium mode, which means it beeps when someone opens a door or
window, but no alarm goes off. Knowing the time that the soap opera was
on, along with the point on the tape when we hear the shot, Lane was able
to determine the exact time when the intruder shot De Mohrenschildt,
which was 2:21 p.m. EST.[591]According to the Florida State Attorney's Office,

---

[589] Epstein, Edward Jay, diary entry, March 29, 1977
[590] http://spartacus-educational.com/JFKdemohrenschildt.htm
[591] Ventura, Jesse, *They Killed Our President*, pp. 218-219, Skyhorse Publishing ,
2013

the cassette recording has been destroyed. The Palm Beach County Sheriff's Office said there was no file or record of the case.[592]

General Walker Shooting

General Edwin Walker was a staunch, conservative, right-wing, racist. He was virulently anti-communist. He was a member of the John Birch Society, and he actively opposed segregation. He aggressively promoted his right-wing views among his troops, and was accused of brainwashing them with John Birch Society materials, and of influencing their votes in elections. He strongly disliked John Kennedy because he supported civil rights for blacks and he negotiated with communists. It was Walker who created the anti-JFK handbills that were distributed at the Dallas motorcade.[593]

On April 10, 1963, General Walker was sitting at his desk in his home in Dallas, when a bullet struck the window frame. Walker was slightly injured by fragments that hit his forearm, but otherwise he was all right. At the time, the police had no suspects in the shooting. After Lee Harvey Oswald was arrested for the murder of John F. Kennedy, he became a suspect in the Walker shooting, too.

When police seized Oswald's possessions, they found among them a photograph of General Walker's home. This led police to believe that Oswald had been stalking Walker and planning to kill him. The photograph showed a car parked in the driveway of Walker's home. The car did not belong to Walker. When the photograph was given to the Warren Commission, a hole had been punched through it to obscure the license plate number of the car. When the photograph was in possession of the Dallas Police, it did not have the hole poked through it. This is verified by a photograph of Oswald's possessions taken by the DPD while he was in custody.[594]Apparently, someone's presence at the Walker home had to be hidden.

The widowed Marina was asked about the Walker incident. She said that she asked Lee what happened that night, and he said he just tried to shoot General Walker. Marina was incredulous that he would try to take

---

[592] http://forum.jfkmurdersolved.com/viewtopic.php?f=1&t=3350

[593] Sokolsky, George E., "Taking Close Look At Overseas Weekly," *The Index-Journal*, Greenwood, South Carolina, May 16, 1961

[594] http://jfk.hol.es/opinion/walker.htm

someone's life. Lee allegedly responded, "Well, what would you say if somebody got rid of Hitler at the right time? So if you don't know about General Walker, how can you speak up on his behalf?" Marina claimed that Lee called him a fascist. Supposedly, Lee had left her a note on the night of the shooting, telling her what to do if he did not return. Marina said she kept the note hidden in a cookbook with the intention of showing it to the police if he tried to kill General Walker again. Marina claimed that Lee had a notebook outlining his plans pertaining to the Walker shooting. She said that he burned the notebook in the bathtub, but that was after the shooting. It's hard to believe that if someone was planning to commit a murder, he would leave such incriminating evidence behind. [595]

The authenticity of the note is questionable. The note was undated, and it did not specifically mention General Walker. Ruth Paine's home was thoroughly searched following the assassination, but the police inventory does not mention the note. Two of three handwriting experts consulted by the HSCA determined that the note was not in Oswald's handwriting, although Warren Commission experts said otherwise. The FBI found seven sets of fingerprints on the note, and none of them belonged to Lee or Marina Oswald. It appears that the note was planted and Marina was coaxed into giving a false story. [596]

There was a witness to the Walker shooting. According to the Dallas Police, 14-year old Walter Kirk Coleman, a neighbor of Walker, saw two men at the scene of the shooting. He saw one of them put something into the trunk of a Ford sedan, then the two men sped away in separate cars. When interviewed by the FBI, Coleman said that neither man resembled Lee Harvey Oswald. [597]

The first suggestion that Oswald may have been involved in the Walker shooting came from a German newspaper called *Die Deutsche Soldaten-Zeitung*. One week after the assassination, the paper ran an article that accused Oswald of having shot at General Walker. It is highly suspicious that the original source of the accusation comes from a newspaper that was founded by the CIA as an American propaganda publication. There was nothing at all to connect JFK's death with the Walker shooting. Dallas Police

---

[595] http://spartacus-educational.com/JFKwalker.htm
[596] http://22november1963.org.uk/did-lee-oswald-shoot-general-edwin-walker
[597] http://whokilledjfk.net/Walker.htm

had no suspects after more than seven months. How was a European newspaper able to supposedly solve the mystery about a little-known American crime?[598]

The testimony of Marina Oswald must be considered in the context of her personal situation. At the time, she was not a legal citizen of the United States. She was threatened with deportation by the authorities if she did not cooperate with them. It is likely that she simply told them what they wanted to hear just to protect herself. Early in the investigation, Marina gave multiple statements that incriminated her husband, only to retract those statements later. She said to the Warren Commission:

> Sometimes the FBI agents asked me questions which had no bearing or relationship, and if I didn't want to answer, they told me that if I wanted to live in this country, I would have to help in this matter.[599]

Later in life, Marina was reflective about the past:

> When I was questioned by the Warren Commission, I was a blind kitten. Their questioning left me only one way to go: guilty. I made Lee guilty. He never had a fair chance… But I was only 22 then, and I've matured since; I think differently.[600]

As with so much else about Oswald's activities, the Walker incident must be looked at with skepticism. It seems doubtful that he fired the shot, based on the testimony of Coleman. The punched-out license plate also indicates that someone is hiding their involvement. The notion of leaving an incriminating note belies logic, as does a notebook outlining his plans. Most likely, this was another attempt to portray Oswald as a disenchanted loner trying to become somebody special by killing an important person. The mere accusation of guilt in the Walker shooting would help to sell Oswald as Kennedy's assassin. Oswald was not able to defend himself against either claim, so it's easy to convict him in the public's mind afterwards. If Oswald did fire the shot, it's probably because he was instructed to do so. He may have been just following orders, knowing that events like that are a routine part of life as a spy.

---

[598] https://en.wikipedia.org/wiki/Edwin_Walker
[599] Marrs, Jim, *Crossfire*, p. 234, Carroll and Graf, 1989
[600] Marrs, Jim, *Crossfire*, p. 129, Carroll and Graf, 1989

Fake Defector Program

At the time Oswald was in Russia, the State Department was running a program to study U.S. defectors to Russia. One of the goals of the study was to determine which ones were really defectors and which ones might be intelligence operatives. Otto Otepka was the official in charge of the program, and one of his subjects of study was Lee Harvey Oswald. Five months before the assassination, Otepka was removed from his position and barred from viewing any research materials on the program. In 1971, Otepka was asked if Oswald was a defector. He simply responded that he never had a chance to find out because he was removed prematurely. This would seem to indicate that someone in the State Department had prior knowledge of the assassination.

In all likelihood, Oswald was part of the fake defector program. Another American who was suspected of being in the program was Robert E. Webster. The story of Webster is very similar to that of Oswald. Webster defected two weeks before Oswald and returned home two weeks before him. Webster was a former Navy man who decided to become a Russian citizen after going there on behalf of his company, Rand Development. Oswald and Webster both took Russian wives who were KGB contacts. Like Oswald, Webster spoke to Russian officials about becoming a citizen, and offered to give the Russians technological secrets. This involved Webster's knowledge of plastics and fiberglass which he had learned as a chemist for Rand. Recall that Oswald had allegedly told the Soviets that he would give them top secret radar information which he knew from his time in the U-2 program. In both cases, the U.S. is monitoring the Soviet response to these offers in an attempt to gauge their need for the technology. Like Oswald, Webster claimed to be disenchanted with communism and decided to return to the U.S.[601]

Apparently, Oswald knew Webster, or at least he had heard of him. When Oswald was planning to return to the U.S., he asked U.S. Embassy officials about a man named Webster who had returned just two weeks earlier. It was later found that Marina Oswald had Webster's address in her address book. A slip of the tongue by Marina gave further evidence of their acquaintance with Webster. Marina had told a friend that her husband

---

[601] https://www.maryferrell.org/pages/Essay_-_Otepka_RFK_Sheridan_Oswald.html

worked for Rand Development and that he was sent to Russia to set up a trade exhibition for them. But that is the cover story for Robert Webster, not for Lee Oswald. It looks like Marina got her defectors mixed up.[602]

This also shows the extreme clandestine nature of intelligence operations. If the State Department wanted to know who is an intelligence operative, you would think they could simply ask the CIA. After all, they're on the same side, right? But the activities of the CIA are so top secret that other government agencies are unable to figure out what they're up to. Even the president is unaware of all their operations, and is unable to control or regulate them. This was something that Kennedy tried to change, but never lived to accomplish it.

The Warren Commission reported on Oswald's possible intelligence connections:

> Rumors and speculations that Oswald was in some way associated with or used by agencies of the U.S. Government grew out of his Russian period and his investigation by the FBI after his return to the United States. Insinuations were made that Oswald had been a CIA agent or had some relationship with the CIA and that this explained the supposed ease with which he received passports and visas. Speculation that he had some working relationship with the FBI was based on an entry in Oswald's notebook giving the name and telephone number of an agent from the FBI office in Dallas. The Directors of the CIA and the FBI have testified before the Commission that Oswald was never in the employ of their agencies in any capacity. The Commission has concluded on the basis of its own investigations of the files of Federal agencies that Oswald was not and had never been an agent of any agency of the U.S. Government (aside from his service in the Marines) and was not and had never been used by any U.S. Government agency for any purpose. The FBI was interested in him as a former defector and it maintained a file on him...[603]

Somehow that was predictable. There was no realistic chance that the commission would admit that Oswald was an intelligence asset of the U.S.

---

[602] http://www.jfk-info.com/verb-4.htm
[603] *The Warren Commission Report*, p. 660, Longmeadow Press, 1964

government. They had to address the issue, of course, but it was a foregone conclusion that the CIA and the FBI would not be acknowledged as co-conspirators.

Allen Dulles acknowledged that the CIA might not admit that an agent was in their employment if such secrecy was required. Dulles also defended the non-disclosure as a necessary part of the business:

> Boggs: Let's say (someone)…was recruited by someone in the CIA. The man who recruited him would know, wouldn't he?
>
> Dulles: Yes, but he wouldn't tell.
>
> Boggs: Wouldn't tell it under oath?
>
> Dulles: I wouldn't think he would tell it under oath, no…He ought not tell it under oath. Maybe not tell it to his own government but wouldn't tell it any other way.
>
> McCloy: Wouldn't he tell it to his own chief?
>
> Dulles: He might or might not. If he was a bad one then he wouldn't.

Dulles also pointed out that the same rule of secrecy applies to the FBI, and extends all the way up to J. Edgar Hoover:

> …if (Hoover) says "No, I didn't have anything to do with it," you can't prove what the facts are. There are no external evidences. I would believe Mr. Hoover. Some people might not. I don't think there is any external evidence other than the person's word that he did or did not employ a particular man as a secret agent. No matter what.[604]

Former CIA official Victor Marchetti tells of a top secret program that may have involved Oswald:

> At the time, in 1959, the United States was having real difficulty in acquiring information out of the Soviet Union; the technical systems had, of course, not developed to the point that they are at today, and we were resorting to all sorts of activities. One of these activities was an ONI (Office of

---

[604] Marrs, Jim, *Crossfire*, p. 474, Carroll and Graf, 1989

Naval Intelligence) program which involved three dozen, maybe 40, young men who were made to appear disenchanted, poor American youths who had become turned off and wanted to see what communism was all about. They were sent into the Soviet Union or into eastern Europe [*sic*], with the specific intention the Soviets would pick them up and "double" them if they suspected them of being U.S. agents, or recruit them as KGB agents. They were trained at various naval installations both here and abroad, but the operation was being run out of Nag's Head, North Carolina.[605]

William Robert "Tosh" Plumlee spent over 50 years in covert operations for U.S. intelligence. He was one of the whistle-blowers who alerted Congress to the Iran-Contra scandal, and was commended by Senator Gary Hart for his help in the investigation. Plumlee knew Oswald since their early days of intelligence training, and has signed a sworn affidavit stating that Oswald was an intelligence operative. From the affidavit:

I first met Oswald at Illusionary Warfare training at Nag's Head, North Carolina in 1957. Oswald was taking language courses at the same complex where I was taking Illusionary Warfare training classes. These courses, at the time, were referred to as "Spook School" and were preparatory to "going covert in international operations." Everybody who was there was CIA or Military Intelligence, or at least they were in some form of government training for their particular covert mission.[606]

He also put it bluntly in an interview with Jesse Ventura:

Oswald was military intelligence. He was operational in military ops. I know that from both direct experience and from liaison with my superior intelligence officers. That's not an allegation- that's a fact. Oswald was military intelligence.[607]

---

[605] Marrs, Jim, *Crossfire*, p. 117, Carroll and Graf, 1989

[606] Beltzer and Wayne, Dead Wrong, "Affidavit of William Plumlee," pp. 111-115

[607] Ventura, Jesse, *They Killed Our President*, pp. 69- 70, Skyhorse Publishing, 2013

FLASH

The FBI's FLASH system is designed to alert agents to a possible threat to national security. When an individual has a FLASH alert issued to his file card, that means that a warning is sent throughout the bureau stating that anyone who receives information or an inquiry about that individual should notify the proper authority. Lee Harvey Oswald had a FLASH alert issued on him in 1959 when he defected to the Soviet Union. Agents with any knowledge of Oswald were instructed to notify the Soviet Espionage Section of the FBI, which was headed by Marvin Gheesling. On October 9, 1963, Gheesling removed the FLASH alert on Oswald, disconnecting him from the federal alarm system. The timing of this removal was significant. The next day, October 10, 1963, was the day the CIA sent a message to the FBI about Oswald's contact with the Soviet Embassy in Mexico City. By lifting the FLASH notice the day before, this prevented a security alert on Oswald before the assassination. Such an alert would have focused too much attention on Oswald in advance. Honest agents would have notified the Secret Service, who would then have been aware of Oswald's presence along the motorcade route, and they could not deny knowledge of him afterwards.[608]

Gheesling's motive for cancelling the FLASH are unclear. He could have been in collusion on the plot to frame Oswald, or he may have been misled by the CIA into making the move. Oswald's visits to the Russian and Cuban embassies were on September 27, and the CIA notified the FBI about it on October 10. Why was there a 13-day delay in the notification? Oswald was closely monitored, so they knew his every move. It would seem that the notification should have been instant. That would cover the CIA, since they could say that they took the proper action immediately. A clue about the delay might come from a CIA memorandum to the FBI, dated September 16, 1963:

> Agency is giving some consideration to countering the activities of (the Fair Play for Cuba Committee) in foreign countries...CIA is also giving some thought to planting

---

[608] http://jonathandenby.com/blog/2015/11/22/the-oswald-files-what-american-intelligence-knew-about-kennedys-assassin

deceptive information which might embarrass the
Committee in areas where it does have some support.[609]

Here the CIA is telling the FBI that they are planning to discredit the Fair Play for Cuba Committee by "planting deceptive information" to embarrass them. This could have tipped the FBI off that any action against the FPCC was staged, or that Oswald is an intelligence operative. Did Gheesling purposely lift the FLASH alert, knowing that information about Oswald was forthcoming? That would imply willful collusion on his part. Or did the CIA wait until after the FLASH had been lifted to issue the notification? That would mean that Gheesling was unknowingly duped. Maybe Gheesling did some research after getting the memorandum and found out how superficial the FPCC was, leading him to conclude that there was no threat there. Or maybe he was somehow coaxed into lifting the alert. The CIA issued the memorandum about the FPCC, then waited for the FLASH to be lifted, which took 23 days. The memo about Oswald was then sent the next day.

J. Edgar Hoover did not know Gheesling's motives, either. The order to lift the FLASH did not come from Hoover, at least not overtly. Hoover was irate that the alert had been lifted, and wrote on a memo, "Send this guy to Siberia!" This was Hoover's way of imposing censure on Gheesling, while also deflecting responsibility from himself. "Siberia" turned out to be Detroit.

Hoover was known to be frustrated by the lack of cooperation from the CIA. In a memo concerning their operations, Hoover wrote:

> O.K., but I hope you are not being taken in. I can't forget the CIA withholding the French espionage activities in the USA, nor the false story re Oswald's trip to Mexico, only to mention two instances of their double-dealing.[610]

By "false story re: Oswald's trip to Mexico," Hoover is possibly referring to the memorandum of September 16, 1963, which misled them about the FPCC. He could also be referring to the fact that the CIA did not immediately inform the FBI about Oswald's meeting with Valeriy Kostikov, who was alleged to be the Soviet head of assassinations. Although that event was

---

[609] Douglass, James W., *JFK and the Unspeakable*, pp. 177-9 Simon and Schuster, 2008

[610] Douglass, James W., *JFK and the Unspeakable*, p. 178, Simon and Schuster, 2008

also staged, it shows the exasperation that Hoover experienced in dealing with the CIA. Hoover summed it up to an associate:

> People think I'm so powerful, but when it comes to the CIA, there's nothing I can do.[611]

Those very same words could have been spoken by John F. Kennedy.

Letter to Soviet Embassy

On November 18, 1963, a crudely typed, mistake-filled letter arrived at the Soviet Embassy in Washington. The letter was allegedly written and sent by Lee Harvey Oswald. With the spelling and grammatical mistakes left intact, the letter reads:

> This is to inform you of recent events since by [*sic*] meetings with comrade Kostin [*sic*] in the Embassy Of [*sic*] the Soviet Union, Mexico City, Mexico.
>
> I was unable to remain in Mexico indefinitely because of my Mexican visa restrictions which was for 15 days only. I could not tke [*sic*] a chance on requesting a new visa unless I used my real name, so I returned to the United States.
>
> I had not planned to contact the Soviet embassy [*sic*] in Mexico so they were unprepared, had I been able to reach the Soviet Embassy in Havana as planned, the embassy there would have had time to complete our business.
>
> Of corse [*sic*] the Soviet embassy [*sic*] was not at fault, they were, as I say unprepared, the Cuban consulate was guilty of gross breach of regulations, [*sic*] I am glad he has since been replaced.
>
> The Federal Bureu [*sic*] of Investigation is not now interested in my activities in the progressive organization Fair Play For Cuba Committee, of which I was the secretary in New Orleans (state Louisiana) since I no longer reside in that state. However, the F.B.I. has visited us here in Dallas, Texas, on November 1. Agent James P. Hasty [*sic*] warned

---

[611] http://thirdworldtraveler.com/Assassinations_page/
The_Assassination%20_RFK.html

me that if I engaged in F.P.P.C. [*sic*] activities in Texas the F.B.I. will again take an 'interest' in me.

This agent also 'suggested' to Marina Nichilayova that she could remain in the United States under F.B.I. 'protection.' That is, she could defect from the Soviet Uion [*sic*], of course, [*sic*] I am [*sic*] my wife strongly protested these tactics by the notorious F.B.I.

Please inform us of the arrival of our Soviet entrance visa's [*sic*] as soon as they come.

Also, this is to inform you of the birth, on October 20, 1963, of a DAUGHTER, AUDREY MARINA OSWALD in DALLAS, TEXAS, to my wife.

Respectfully,

Lee H. Oswald[612]

The letter was dated November 9 and postmarked November 12 in Irving, Texas. The Warren Commission determined that the letter had been typed by Oswald, using a typewriter that belonged to Ruth Paine. It appears that the letter was a further attempt to implicate Oswald in the JFK assassination. The letter seems to imply that Oswald and the Soviets had some kind of business together. What does he mean by "...the embassy there would have had time to complete our business"? The writer of the letter wanted it known that he was colluding with the Soviets. What does he mean by, "...unless I use my real name"? He is implying espionage of some kind.[613]

The "comrade Kostin" he refers to is Valeriy Kostikov, a Russian KGB agent and head of executive action (sabotage and assassination). As mentioned earlier, it is ridiculous to think that the average person could simply walk into a foreign embassy and request a meeting with their head of assassinations. It is even more ridiculous to think that such a request would be granted. It stretches the imagination to think that the assassin would then write a letter about it, knowing it would be read by the FBI.

---

[612] http://jfk.hood.edu/Collection/Weisberg%20Subject%20Index%20Files/A%20Disk/Allen-Scott%20Columns/Item%2003.pdf
[613] https://www.maryferrell.org/pages/Valeriy_Kostikov_and_Comrade_Kostin.html

It was a foregone conclusion that this letter would be intercepted by the FBI. That was standard procedure for J. Edgar Hoover. The author of the letter wanted that to happen. It was intended to show Oswald's loyalty to the Soviet Union, Cuba, and the communist agenda. Hoover knew the details of the letter by November 19. The letter does not specifically mention the assassination or any criminal action, yet it was problematic for the FBI. Hoover had publicly denied any knowledge of Oswald, or any contact with him, prior to the assassination. But now we see that he had read Oswald's letter just a few days beforehand. The writer also mentions that FBI agent James Hosty contacted him on November 1 about his FPCC activities, which would leave Hoover and Company with more explaining to do.

The authenticity of the letter has been questioned by researchers. Several things indicate a forgery, including the multitude of mistakes. Marina's maiden name was spelled wrong (Nikolaevna Prusakova), Oswald's daughter's name was wrong (Audrey Marina Rachel Oswald), and agent Hosty's name was spelled wrong (not "Hasty"). Oswald would have known the correct names and spellings of all three.

Supposedly, Ruth Paine found the handwritten rough draft of the letter in her house. The draft was not found by the Dallas Police on the day of the assassination. It was turned over to the FBI on November 23 by Paine. Paine's involvement in the letter-writing scheme is suspected by some, since it was typed on her typewriter and she was the one who "discovered" the rough draft. Also, Paine is one of the few who knew about Hosty's visit to see Oswald on November 1. The FBI did not test the letter for Oswald's fingerprints. It's conceivable that the letter and/or the rough draft were written by someone else. Possible suspects include Ruth Paine and David Atlee Phillips. When Oswald was interrogated after his arrest, Hosty asked him if he had written a letter to the Soviet Embassy regarding his trip to Mexico City, and Oswald answered that he had not. It appears that Oswald did not write this letter.[614]

One of the oddities of the letter is the fact that the typewritten version that was sent to the embassy contains six words that are spelled wrong, while the handwritten rough draft has those same words spelled correctly. Logically, it would seem to be the other way around, since people correct

---

[614] Scott, Peter Dale, *Dallas '63*, Open Road Media, 2015

their mistakes after a rough draft. This would seem to indicate that the handwritten rough was created afterwards.[615]

The Soviets never sent a reply to Oswald. But immediately after the assassination, they knew that the letter had been designed to implicate them. On November 27, the Soviet Embassy in Washington sent a cable to Moscow regarding the letter. They denounced it as a fraud, and said:

> This letter was clearly a provocation. It gives the impression we had close ties with Oswald and were using him for some purposes of our own... One gets the definite impression that the letter was concocted by those who, judging from everything, are involved in the president's assassination. It is possible that Oswald himself wrote the letter as it was dictated to him, in return for some promises, and then, as we know, he was simply bumped off after his usefulness had ended.[616 617]

On November 24, 1963, Hoover sent an internal FBI memo:

> Oswald made a phone call to the Cuban embassy in Mexico City, which we intercepted. It was only about a visa, however. He also wrote a letter to the Soviet Embassy here in Washington, which we intercepted, read and resealed. This letter referred to the fact that the FBI had questioned his activities on the Fair Play to Cuba Committee and also asked about extension of his wife's visa. That letter from Oswald was addressed to the man in the Soviet Embassy who is in charge of assassinations and similar activities on the part of the Soviet government. To have that drawn into a public hearing would muddy the waters internationally.[618]

---

[615] https://groups.google.com/forum/#!msg/alt.conspiracy.jfk/U5D-6-yfB_k/hWd0gc8VIaOJ

[616] Armstrong, John, *Harvey and Lee*, pp. 760-2, Quasar Books, 2003

[617] https://groups.google.com/forum/#!msg/alt.conspiracy.jfk/U5D-6-yfB_k/hWd0gc8VIaOJ

[618] http://www.jfklancer.com/LNE/LHO-Mexi.html

This gave Johnson a superficial excuse to order a cover-up. Washington and Moscow both knew that there was no connection between Oswald and the Soviets, but the public would not see it that way. The mere suggestion of such a connection would cause mass hysteria, and Johnson simply exploited that. He sold Earl Warren with the "40 million Americans dead" threat, as if the Oswald story would spark World War III. But the responsibility to prevent that was on Johnson, not Warren. Johnson's diplomatic skills were needed to prevent a world crisis. It seems that all Johnson would have to do is tell Khrushchev that he does not suspect the Soviets at all. That should have been sufficient to prevent World War III.

The Odio Incident

Yet another instance of setting up Oswald involves a witness named Sylvia Odio. Odio was active in the anti-Castro movement and helped form an organization called Junta Revolucionaria. Her father was a Cuban refugee who was jailed for attempting to assassinate Fidel Castro. In late September, 1963, Odio received a visit at her Dallas apartment from three men who said they were from New Orleans. Two of the men, named Leopoldo and Angelo, claimed to be members of Junta Revolucionaria, and asked her to help them prepare a letter to solicit funds for the group. The third man, named Leon, was introduced to her as an American who was sympathetic to their cause and was willing to take part in the assassination of Fidel Castro. Odio wanted no part of it, and told the men to leave.[619]

The next day, Leopoldo phoned Odio and talked about Leon. He told her that Leon was a former Marine and an expert marksman. He told her that Leon was "loco" and "nuts." According to Leopoldo, Leon had said, "We Cubans don't have any guts...because President Kennedy should have been assassinated after the Bay of Pigs, and some Cubans should have done that, because he was the one that was holding the freedom of Cuba."[620]

After John Kennedy was killed, Odio saw Oswald's picture on the news and recognized him as the man she knew as "Leon." She testified to the Warren Commission about her experience. However, the commission concluded that they were "almost certain" that Oswald could not have been in Dallas at the time. Odio said the incident took place in late September.

---

[619] https://en.wikipedia.org/wiki/Silvia_Odio
[620] *The Warren Commission Report*, Chapter 6, p. 322, Longmeadow Press, 1964,

She estimated it was the 26th or 27th, but she wasn't certain. Oswald's alleged visits to the embassies were on the 27th, and the commission concluded that Oswald had arrived in Mexico City on the 26th. So Oswald is said to have been in two places at once, which created quite a problem for the commission.[621]

In an attempt to explain away the story, the FBI investigated three men who were known to be anti-Castro activists. They were Loran Hall, Lawrence Howard, and William Seymour. These men claimed to remember visiting a woman in that area around that time for the purpose of soliciting funds. According to the FBI, these were the three men who visited Odio in late September. That would explain everything and put the Odio story to rest. But when Odio was shown pictures of the three men, she stated that they were not the men who came to her apartment that day. Her sister Annie, who was present when the visit took place, also said that they were not the same men. When Hall was shown a photograph of Sylvia Odio, he said he had never seen her. This presented a conflict for the Warren Commission, since it was an unexplained connection between Oswald and anti-Castro Cubans. How did the commission deal with it? They dealt with it by quickly publishing their final report before the FBI had concluded that part of the investigation. The commission's report reads:

> While the FBI had not yet completed its investigation into this matter at the time the report went to press, the Commission has concluded that Lee Harvey Oswald was not at Mrs. Odio's apartment in September of 1963.[622]

One can't help but wonder how they figured that out if the FBI had not yet completed its investigation. The HSCA investigated the Odio incident, and was critical of the Warren Commission's handling of it. They acknowledged that the commission did not receive the conclusions of the FBI investigation until after the Warren Report had been published. Therefore, the commission was uninformed of Odio's denial that Hall, Howard, and Seymour had visited her apartment. The HSCA said that they were "inclined to believe Odio," and that the Warren Commission was wrong when they said that Oswald could not have been in Dallas at the time.

---

[621] http://spartacus-educational.com/JFKodioS.htm
[622] *The Warren Commission Report*, Chapter 6, p. 324., Longmeadow Press, 1964

Oswald could have been in Dallas at the time of the incident. If he was at Odio's apartment, it would make some sense, since he would have been in the company of fellow anti-Castroites. Although Oswald would later be presented as a pro-Castro activist, this incident served to portray Oswald as being crazy enough to commit an assassination. The HSCA continued to promote Oswald as pro-Castro, in spite of the Odio story. They commented that Oswald's actions were consistent with someone who was pro-Castro. They speculated that Oswald may have associated with anti-Castro Cubans in an attempt to implicate the anti-Castro movement in the assassination. The HSCA concluded that "it was unable to reach firm conclusions as to the meaning or significance of the Odio incident to the President's assassination."[623] [624]

More Set-Ups

Another instance of Oswald being set up occurred at the Lincoln-Mercury dealership located near Dealey Plaza. Salesman Albert G. Bogard told the Warren Commission that on or about November 9, a man who introduced himself as "Lee Oswald" came into the dealership. Bogard said to the commission:

> I show him a car on the showroom floor, and take him for a ride out Stemmons Freeway and back, and he was driving at 60 or 70 miles an hour and came back to the showroom. And I made some figures and he told me he wasn't ready to buy, that he would be in a couple or three weeks, that he had some money coming in. And when he finally started to leave, I got his name and wrote it on the back of one of my business cards, and never heard from the man anymore.[625]

Apparently, in those days you didn't need to show a driver's license before test-driving a car. With no identification, we don't know if that was the real Oswald who took the test drive. When "Oswald" was told that he could not get credit because he didn't have a credit rating, he became upset and said, "Maybe I'm going to have to go back to Russia to buy a car." Bogard's story was confirmed by three other salesmen present. Oran Brown said he wrote down the name and remembered it. Salesmen Eugene Wilson

---

[623] HSCA, I.C., p. 140, 1979

[624] http://spartacus-educational.com/JFKodioS.htm

[625] http://www.aarclibrary.org/publib/jfk/wc/wcvols/wh10/pdf/WH10_Bogard.pdf

and Frank Pizzo both remember the man who identified himself as Oswald. Pizzo testified to the Warren Commission, but when shown pictures of Oswald, he said this was not the same man who was in the showroom. This is an indication that Oswald was being impersonated. There was enough resemblance between the two men that the story could pass for truth. The purpose of this was to foster Oswald's persona as a communist sympathizer, simply because he mentioned Russia and spoke of it in positive terms. The imposter said that he had some money coming in soon, which implied that he was going to get paid for killing John Kennedy. When Bogard heard that Oswald was arrested, he threw away the card, knowing he wouldn't be making the sale.[626]

Another piece of this huge puzzle concerns a brief note written by Lee Harvey Oswald to "Mr. Hunt," who could be oil magnate H.L. Hunt or CIA agent E. Howard Hunt. It's less likely that it's E. Howard Hunt, since obvious connections to the CIA would have been avoided. The FBI speculated it may have been intended for one of H.L. Hunt's sons. Either way, it connects Oswald to the plotters, even though superficially. It has been confirmed by experts that the handwriting is that of Lee Harvey Oswald.[627] The note reads:

> Dear Mr. Hunt,
>
> I would like information concerning my position.
>
> I am asking only for information.
>
> I am suggesting that we discuss the matter fully before any steps are taken by me or anyone else.
>
> Lee Harvey Oswald [628]

The note is suspiciously vague. What is meant by "my position" and "any steps"? Either the note concerns an issue so sensitive that it cannot be overtly written, or else it is only intended to create a superficial connection, much like other connections that Oswald had. Who the connection is to is not clear.

---

[626] http://www.kenrahn.com/JFK/The_critics/Griffith/Oswald_impersonated.html
[627] http://jfk.hood.edu/Collection/Weisberg%20Subject%20Index%20Files/O%20Disk/Oswald%20Lee%20Harvey%20Mexico/014.pdf
[628] Marrs, Jim, *Crossfire*, p. 197, Carroll and Graf, 1989

When Marina Oswald testified to the Warren Commission, she said that Lee had failed to pay her a visit on the date of the note, which was November 8, 1963. That was a Friday, the day Lee usually visited his wife. She told the commission that he had said, "There was another job open, more interesting work, related to photography." But why would Oswald need to sacrifice an entire weekend with his wife just for a job interview? Was he serious about another job? He was already employed at the TSBD, and he needed to keep that job for his CIA assignment. The fact that the letter was dated two weeks before the assassination raises some questions.

Hunt's chief aide, John Wesley Curington said that on Saturday morning, November 23, Hunt told him to check on the security surrounding Oswald at the police station. Curington went to the jail and reported back to Hunt:

> Mr. Hunt told me, regardless of what time it was, to come by the house and tell him what I witnessed. It was a little bit after midnight when I reported to him that, in my opinion, there was no security whatsoever around the jailhouse. A lot of news people, but nobody too concerned with security. We did not discuss the merits of this, and I left.[629]

According to Curington, Hunt left for Washington after that and stayed for about a week. One day, after Hunt returned to Dallas, Curington was instructed to go to the lobby of the Mercantile Bank Building and not allow anyone to go to the seventh floor, where Hunt's offices were. After about 15 minutes, Curington saw Marina Oswald get off the elevator and get into an unmarked car. He noted the tag number and later found out it was registered to the FBI.[630][631]

There is yet another letter written by Lee Harvey Oswald. This was sent to Governor Connally while Oswald was still in Russia. In January of 1962, Oswald wrote a letter to Connally, asking for his help in changing his discharge from the Marines to an honorable one. (The letter mistakenly says "dishonorable discharge" when it was actually an "undesirable discharge.") Connally once held the post of Secretary of the Navy, but he had since

---

[629] http://educationforum.ipbhost.com/topic/3933-h-l-hunt-and-richard-nixon/
[630] http://educationforum.ipbhost.com/topic/3933-h-l-hunt-and-richard-nixon/
[631] http://jfk.hood.edu/Collection/Weisberg%20Subject%20Index%20Files/C%20Disk/Currington%20John%20W/Item%2001.pdf

resigned the post, and Oswald was probably not aware of that. The letter was forwarded to the new Secretary of the Navy, which was Fred Korth. Korth and Connally were both associates of Lyndon Johnson. Korth was involved in the TFX scandal that forced him to resign, a scandal that also involved Johnson. Also, maybe by coincidence, Korth was a lawyer who had represented Oswald's mother in her divorce case several years earlier.

When Oswald left the Marines, his discharge was honorable. After his attempted defection to Russia received press coverage in the U.S., the Marines held a court-martial in his absence, which was illegal. His discharge was downgraded to undesirable, based on his attempt to defect. Typically, one's discharge is not changed because of events that occurred after their military service has ended. Oswald wrote to Connally in protest of this.[632]

The letter reads:

> I wish to call your attention to a case about which you may have personal knowledge since you are a resident of Ft. Worth as I am. In November of 1959, an event was well puplicated [*sic*] in Ft. Worth newspapers concerning a person who had gone to the Soviet Union to reside for a short time (much in the same way E. Hemingway resided in Paris).
>
> This person, in answers to questions put to him by reporters in Moscow, criticized certain facets of American life. The story was blown up into another "turncoat" sensation, with the result being the Navy department gave this person a belated dishonorable discharge, although he had received an honorable discharge after three years of service on September 11, 1959 at El Toro Marine Corps base in California.
>
> These are the basic facts of my case. I have always had the full sanction of the U.S Embassy, Moscow, USSR, and hence the U.S. Government.[633]

---

[632] http://educationforum.ipbhost.com/topic/19337-bottlefed-by-oswalds-nana/
[633] http://educationforum.ipbhost.com/topic/19337-bottlefed-by-oswalds-nana/

That last paragraph is huge. Oswald admits that he had the full sanction of the U.S. government. How could that be if he was a true defector? He stated the same thing in his recorded interview about Marxism. This was the closest Oswald ever came to openly admitting he was an intelligence operative.

A few months before the assassination, Oswald went to Connally's office and created a disturbance over his discharge issue. But this was a federal military problem, and Governor Connally had no control over it. Oswald should have known that. It's possible someone misled Oswald to create an incident. This incident added to the fabricated story of a young man who is angry with authority.

Oswald was certainly busy writing letters. Notes written in Oswald's name had been sent to H.L. Hunt, Governor Connally, the FBI, and the Russian Embassy. The Connally letter was written about a year and a half before the assassination, and the other three were written in November of 1963. All of them give cause for speculation, and none of them are fully understood.

Those who believe Oswald is guilty should realize that anything he did can be explained by the fact that he was being set up. The deliberate plot to frame him began in the summer of 1963, and from that point on, his actions were guided by the invisible hand of the CIA. Why was Oswald handing out pro-communist literature in New Orleans? Because the CIA told him to, as part of the plot to set him up. Why did Oswald give an interview to a local station in New Orleans? Because the CIA told him to, to set him up. Why did Oswald carry curtain rods into the TSBD the morning of the assassination? Because the CIA told him to, to set him up. Why did Oswald go home and get his handgun after the assassination? Because the CIA told him to, to set him up. Why did Oswald go to the Texas Theater? Because the CIA told him to, to set him up.

Also keep in mind that an Oswald look-alike was used to frame him. Witnesses who claimed that Oswald killed Officer Tippit were fooled by the double. There also may have been an Oswald double in the TSBD during the shooting. For months prior to the assassination, Oswald doubles were seen in Dallas and New Orleans, engaging in acts that would incriminate the real Oswald. The doubles and their actions were guided by the CIA.

In fact, it was the CIA who got Oswald the job at the TSBD. Oswald was informed of the job opening by Ruth Paine, who had a friend working in the unemployment office. Paine herself was a CIA contact. I don't know if her friend was or not, but the CIA somehow manipulated things so that the job would go to Oswald. Warren Commission apologists claim it was a coincidence that Oswald just happened to work at the location where the presidential motorcade would pass by a month later. That was no coincidence. The plotters scouted Dallas for a possible assassination site. They determined that Dealey Plaza was the best site. The tall buildings, the shaded grassy knoll, the picket fence, and the sharp-angle turn made it the ideal location for the crime. Their next step was to get Oswald there anyway they can. That was accomplished by getting him the job at the TSBD.[634]

It is interesting to note that the day before Oswald began working at the TSBD, he was offered a higher-paying job. Oswald started his job as an order filler at the TSBD on October 16, 1963. On October 15, the Texas Employment Commission phoned the Paine residence and asked to speak to Oswald. He was not there, but a message was taken that a job was available for him. The job was as a baggage handler at Trans Texas Airways and it paid about $100 a month more than the job at the TSBD. Also, the baggage handler job was permanent, whereas the TSBD job was only temporary. Yet, Oswald declined the offer of a much better job. The TSBD job was the one arranged for him be the CIA, so that was the job he took. He still believed he was going to save the president's life, and that was worth more to him than $100 a month.[635]

It should also be mentioned here that the building where Oswald was employed was owned by D. Harold Byrd, a wealthy oilman who hated John Kennedy. The Texas School Book Depository is actually the name of a privately owned company whose officers are military hard-liners. The building itself was nearly devoid of tenants until about six months prior to the assassination when the TSBD company moved in. Prior to that, the structure was known as the Sexton Building.[636]

---

[634] Kroth, Jerome A., *Conspiracy in Camelot*, p. 131, Algora Publshing, 2003

[635] Douglass, James W., *JFK and the Unspeakable*, p. 172, Simon and Schuster, 2008

[636] https://whowhatwhy.org/2013/11/13/bush-and-the-jfk-hit-part-9-planning-a-nightmare-on-elm-street/

A Brother's Betrayal

Robert Oswald is the older brother of Lee Harvey Oswald. He has stated repeatedly that Lee was guilty. He has no basis at all for saying that, and one cannot help but question his motive. Here is a sampling from an interview:

> Q: In your mind, are there questions about whether Lee shot President Kennedy?
>
> RO: There is no question in my mind that Lee was responsible for the three shots fired, two of the shots hitting the president and killing him. There is no question in my mind that he also shot Officer Tippit. How can you explain one without the other? I think they're inseparable. I'm talking about the police officer being shot and the president. You look at the factual data, you look at the rifle, you look at the pistol ownership, you look at his note about the Walker shooting. You look at the general opportunity -- he was present. He wasn't present when they took a head count (at the Texas School Book Depository).[637]

Let's analyze Robert's statements line by line:

> How can you explain one without the other? I think they're inseparable. I'm talking about the police officer being shot and the president.

Robert is saying that since Lee shot the cop, he must have shot the president, and since he shot the president, then he must have shot the cop. It's pretzel logic. There is no proof of Lee's guilt in either crime, but somehow they prove each other.

> You look at the factual data, you look at the rifle, you look at the pistol ownership, you look at his note about the Walker shooting...

What does he mean by "factual data"? Neither the rifle nor the pistol belonged to Lee. Neither had his prints on it. Even if they were his weapons, that still only means he was framed. He mentions the note about the Walker shooting, but a note is not proof unless it's a signed confession.

---

[637] http://www.pbs.org/wgbh/pages/frontline/shows/oswald/interviews/oswald.html

You look at the general opportunity -- he was present.

He was present? Robert has decided that the suspect is guilty based simply on the fact that he was present. I just hope there's not a Robert Oswald on my jury someday.

> He wasn't present when they took a head count (at the Texas School Book Depository).

Of course not. He was in jail! The first head count was taken early, when many employees were still outside after the shooting. The second head count was taken at 2:00, but Lee was arrested at 1:45. Robert seems desperate to find something he can pin on Lee.

The interview continues:

> RO: I watched the deterioration of a human being. You look at that last year -- his work, his family, trying to go to Cuba, trying to go back to Russia. His wife is wanting to go back to Russia. Everything is deteriorating.

> You look at all the data there, and it comes up to one conclusion as far as I'm concerned -- the Warren Commission was correct.

What is deteriorating? Robert doesn't explain that, yet he says, "Everything is deteriorating." It's just an attempt to make it look like Lee's life was falling apart, so the shooting could be explained as an act of desperation.

> Q: What do you say to people who are so convinced or are trying to believe in his innocence? I mean, you're his brother; you would want to believe more than anyone.

> RO: I think that's an understatement. I would love to be able to say that Lee was not involved in any way whatsoever, or much less to the extent that I believe that he was. This is a struggle that has gone on with me for almost 30 years now. This is mind over heart. The mind tells me one thing, and the heart tells me something else.

> But the facts are there. ... What do you do with his rifle? What do you do with his pistol? What do you do with his general opportunity? What do you do with his actions? To

me, you can't reach but one conclusion. There's hard physical evidence there. True, no one saw him actually pull the trigger on the president but… his presence in the building was there. What he did after he left the building is known: bus ride, taxi ride, boarding house, pick up the pistol, leave, shoot the police officer. Five or six eyewitnesses there. You can't set that aside just because he is saying, "I'm a patsy." I'd love to do that, but you cannot. …

Robert simply repeated himself here. He again mentions the rifle, the pistol, and the general opportunity. He calls that "hard physical evidence." He mentions the bus ride, the taxi ride, etc. But what does that prove? He then says that five or six witnesses saw him shoot the cop, but that's not true. Only two witnesses actually saw the shooting, and neither positively identified the killer as Lee Oswald.

RO: He did not and would not talk to any of the interrogators about anything of substance. Anytime they brought anything up that pertained to the assassination of the president and the shooting of the police officer, he knew nothing about it. He would talk about anything else. He had the presence of mind then to do that.

That's because he has the right to remain silent. There is something in the Constitution about that. He also had the right to an attorney, but that didn't mean much, either.

RO: (To those who say) "He didn't own a rifle." We know he owned a rifle. You've got all kinds of documented evidence. They've gone to the extreme measures to prove that he owned that rifle. You've got the backyard picture. They've got the original negative. They've got the camera. You've got all the physical evidence that ties together.

Robert stated that they have the original negative of the backyard pictures. I am not aware of the existence of the negatives. Photographic experts have analyzed the pictures to death in an attempt to determine their authenticity. If the negatives were available, that would certainly have settled the issue once and for all. So where are they? Robert also stated, "They've got the camera." How is the camera evidence?

There is no "physical evidence that ties together," and Robert Oswald has to know it. The backyard photographs would prove nothing even if they were real.

> Q: The big question is why. What's the best answer you come to for yourself regarding his motive?

> RO: To try to understand why Lee did what he did on November 22 is a cumulative effect of all his past plans and efforts and failures. Historically in his life, it was always done by himself. He planned by himself, he executed by himself, he failed by himself. This was a part of his character, that inner self, that we used to say, "Me, myself and I will do something."[638]

The interview went on and on and they discussed Lee's childhood, his lack of a father figure, his overbearing mother, his many failures, etc. Needless to say, they never discussed the Zapruder film showing a shot from the front, or the 50-some witnesses who said a shot came from the front, or the testimony of the cop who saw Lee in the lunch room just a minute after the shooting, or the negative paraffin test, or the Mauser, or anything else that could legitimately be considered evidence. It was just pure slander of a dead person.

When Robert Oswald visited his brother in jail, they had this exchange:

> "I don't know what is going on. I just don't know what they are talking about. Don't believe all the so-called evidence."
> When Robert Oswald looked into Lee's eyes for some clue, Lee said to him, "Brother, you won't find anything there."[639]

By "anything" Lee meant "guilt."

Like many others, I am completely baffled as to the motives of Robert Oswald. I can only think of two possible explanations for his lies. One is that the government made some kind of deal with Robert. This could be a cash payment, or some kind of mutual back-scratching. They could somehow make his life easier if he goes along with them. The other possibility is that they sold him on the patriotic angle- the belief that he must crucify his

---

[638] http://www.pbs.org/wgbh/pages/frontline/shows/oswald/interviews/oswald.html
[639] https://ratical.org/ratville/JFK/LHO.html

brother for the good of the country. It sounds ridiculous, but since Robert was a former Marine, he is used to obeying authority without question. Either way, it's hard to believe that a man would sell out his own brother, but that's what Robert Oswald has done.

That whole interview was nothing more than an exercise in disinformation. There was nothing of substance there, as this analysis shows. But most people do not analyze it like that. Many people will just hear that Lee Harvey Oswald's own brother says he's guilty, and they will accept that as conclusive. An interview like this is not designed to be scrutinized closely. It's only meant to sway public sentiment. As long as someone is defending the lone-assassin theory, no matter how poorly, then the issue is considered "controversial" instead of "proven."

Exhumation

On October 4, 1981, the body of Lee Harvey Oswald was exhumed from his grave and studied by a team of pathologists. The purpose was to confirm the identity of the man who was buried in the gravesite. There was a question of whether it was the real Lee Harvey Oswald or an imposter.

The exhumation was set in motion by British writer Michael Eddowes, who theorized that a Soviet spy had assumed Oswald's identity while he was in Russia. In his book, *The Oswald Files*, Eddowes claimed that the Soviet spy returned to America and carried on his life as Lee Harvey Oswald, and then killed President Kennedy. The alleged spy was Alik Hidell, which was the name that was used to link Oswald to the mail-order rifle, and hence the murder of Kennedy. According to Eddowes, Hidell bore such a strong resemblance to Oswald that he was able to fool his mother and brothers.

Dr. Linda Norton was the head of the team of pathologists who examined the remains at Baylor University Medical Center. She stated the team's conclusions:

> We, both individually and as a team, have concluded beyond any doubt, and I mean beyond any doubt, that the individual

buried under the name Lee Harvey Oswald in Rose Hill cemetery is Lee Harvey Oswald.[640]

The body's identity had been determined by 150 X-rays, and by comparing its teeth with Oswald's Marine Corps dental records. It was also confirmed that the body had the scar of a childhood mastoid operation that was mentioned in his military records.

I don't know how Eddowes got the political and legal clout to have the body exhumed. He is merely a British writer with a far-fetched theory. It's surprising that anyone would take this seriously. It's true that doubles were used to frame Oswald, and there may have been several of them. That has been speculated by many researchers. In fact, the name Alik Hidell has been used by other operatives, too. The part I don't believe is that the real Oswald could be replaced by a fake, and be convincing enough to fool his own family. Certainly they would have noticed subtle differences between the two men. It's rare for two people to look exactly the same. Even identical twins have some minor differences in their appearance.

But what's even more ridiculous is the notion that someone could assume Lee Oswald's identity and not be discovered, even by his own family. What happens when the conversation turns to events in the past that only the real Oswald would know about? What happens when a family event from the past is discussed, but the imposter doesn't know the things he's supposed to know, or remember the things he's supposed to remember? There are childhood events and family gatherings that an imposter would never know about in minute detail, even if he had studied Oswald's life. It would be a dead giveaway that he's a fake. He could never fool Oswald's mother and family.

All the media hoopla surrounding the exhumation did nothing to satisfy those who seek the truth about the assassination. The body that was exhumed, whether Oswald's or Hidell's, was not that of Kennedy's assassin. The event was just more publicity for the lone-assassin theory. It only questioned the identity of the assassin, but it still reinforced the notion that Kennedy was killed by one man alone, whoever he was.

---

[640] http://www.nytimes.com/1981/10/05/us/oswald-s-body-is-exhumed-an-autopsy-affirms-identity.html

Robert Oswald fought against the exhumation, but only succeeded in getting a temporary restraining order. Lee's wife, then Marina Oswald-Porter, was in favor of the exhumation, as she felt it would give her closure on her past. She stated:

> Now I have my answers, and from now on I only want to be Mrs. Porter.[641]

But does she really have answers? While I don't believe that Oswald was replaced by a double, I also don't believe that the exhumation proves it conclusively. All they did was compare their results with Oswald's military records. They overlooked the fact that with intelligence operatives, their military records are sometimes altered.

The media and the Warren Commission tried to portray Lee Harvey Oswald as violent, anti-social, mentally unstable, and rebellious. I find it hard to reconcile that with what I see and hear from Oswald himself. During the time that he was held in custody, he seemed remarkably calm and rational, considering what he was going through. Speaking for myself, I would have been sweating bullets at a time like that. But Oswald exudes a calm, relaxed demeanor that belies his psychological profile. That is amazing, considering that the weight of the world is on his shoulders. He is very diplomatic and polite, responding to questions with "Yes, sir" and "No, sir." He shows no anger or resentment toward his captors. Under the circumstances, no one could blame him for being bitter, but he is not. If he's really such a communist radical, why don't we hear him shouting, "Viva Castro!" or "Down with capitalist pigs!"? He shows tremendous maturity, poise, and grace under pressure. That's because he was a seasoned veteran of the intelligence industry.

Nothing in Lee Harvey Oswald's life makes any sense unless it is looked at as a background for intelligence work. His attempted defection, his quick and easy return, his acceptance back in the U.S. after attempting to betray the country, his lavish lifestyle in Russia, and his unexplained trip to Mexico cannot be explained by the "disgruntled loner" theory. But if we view Oswald as an operative who is being manipulated by external forces, then the pieces of this huge puzzle begin to come together.

---

[641] http://www.nytimes.com/1981/10/05/us/oswald-s-body-is-exhumed-an-autopsy-affirms-identity.html

November 22, 2013 marked the 50th anniversary of John Kennedy's death. There was a slew of documentaries on TV, although none of them dared to tell the truth. There was a commemoration ceremony in Dealey Plaza. Politicians gave interviews about JFK's influence on history. Those who were alive at the time gave their recollections. There was heightened awareness of the event at the time. President Obama said a few words, but that wasn't enough. He should have used the occasion to issue a complete exoneration of Lee Harvey Oswald. Everyone in the government, including all of our presidents, knows that Oswald was innocent. Think of what his family and offspring have had to go through all these years. Even if the government won't admit the whole truth, at bare minimum they should exonerate Oswald. But to do that would open a can of worms that they would rather leave closed.

8

COVER-UP

The moment Kennedy was shot, the cover-up went into effect. In spite of overwhelming evidence to the contrary, Johnson and his cohorts were peddling the lone-assassin theory from the start. In addition to silencing the patsy, the evidence had to be corralled and altered. Although that was completely illegal, Johnson had no reason to fear any consequences.

Illegal Seizure

On the night of the assassination, the FBI seized all evidence of the case from the Dallas Police Department. This illegal act was ordered, or at least approved, by Lyndon Johnson. The FBI had no legal jurisdiction over the case. Assassinating the president was not a federal crime at the time, so the case was simply a Dallas homicide and rightfully belonged to the Dallas Police Department. Johnson wanted to control the investigation, so he wanted all the evidence in the hands of his ally, J. Edgar Hoover.

Police Chief Jesse Curry described this to the Warren Commission:

> The FBI actually had no jurisdiction over (the murder of Kennedy), the Secret Service actually had no jurisdiction over it. But, in an effort to cooperate with these agencies we went all out to do whatever they wanted us to do... We kept getting calls from the FBI. They wanted this evidence up in Washington...there was some discussion. Fritz told me, he says, "Well, I need the evidence here, I need to get some people to try to identify the gun, to try to identify this pistol and these things, and if it's in Washington, how can I do it?" But, we finally...about midnight of Friday night, we agreed to let the FBI have all the evidence.
>
> We got several calls insisting we send this (evidence to Washington), and nobody would tell me exactly who it was

that was insisting, "just say I got a call from Washington, and they wanted this evidence up there," insinuating it was somebody in high authority that was requesting this, and we finally agreed...[642]

"Somebody in high authority" has never been identified, but it's not hard to figure out who that is. Lyndon Johnson made it clear from the beginning that he was controlling the investigation.

Chief Curry had given into pressure, but was concerned about the violation of the chain of custody. The FBI in Washington received the evidence without the proper inventory. That means that all of the evidence would have been inadmissible in a trial.

"Chain of custody" refers to the paper trail that shows the custody, control, transfer, analysis, and disposition of physical evidence. When a police officer takes possession of a piece of evidence, he will document it and give it to a clerk for storage. Every subsequent action performed on the evidence must be documented and witnessed. Whoever handled the evidence is accountable for it. Without the chain of custody being preserved, it is too easy for unscrupulous officials to remove or alter evidence. That is what happened in the JFK murder case. Since the chain of custody was broken, all of the evidence is worthless.[643]

FBI evidence technician James Cadigan received the evidence from the Dallas Police, and stated:

I can't find an inventory for the "four or five hundred" other evidence items that the FBI evidence technicians received during the initial twenty-four hours – breaking the legal chain of custody for all these items.[644]

At the time the FBI took control of the evidence, Oswald was still alive. Supposedly, there was going to be a trial. The trial would have been in Dallas, since it was a Texas crime. So why was the evidence being sent to Washington? What if Oswald had lived? How could there be a trial in Dallas when the Dallas Police no longer had the evidence? How could the Dallas authorities prosecute the case? There would be no way a trial could have

---

[642] Marrs, Jim, *Crossfire*, p. 357, Carroll and Graf, 1989

[643] https://en.wikipedia.org/wiki/Chain_of_custody

[644] https://www.maryferrell.org/pages/State_Secret_Chapter6.html#ftn23

proceeded. It seemed to be a foregone conclusion that there would be no trial.

Ironically, the only way the FBI could justify taking control of the case would be if there was a conspiracy. A murder by a lone gunman would be covered by state law, but a conspiracy that crosses state lines would be a federal crime. The FBI was adamant that there was no conspiracy, even though conspiracy charges would be the only legal justification for their actions.[645]

But after the FBI seized the evidence, it started disappearing. First, there was the Mauser. Three Dallas Police officers claimed they found a Mauser on the sixth floor of the TSBD. But after the FBI took over, the Mauser vanished and was replaced by a Mannlicher-Carcano- lo and behold, the same kind of rifle that Oswald owned. The FBI also lost another film of the shooting. This was the film taken by Beverly Oliver, a.k.a. "the Babushka Lady." Oliver had given the undeveloped film to an FBI agent, and it was never seen again. The FBI denies ever having it. Some time later, they also lost Kennedy's brain, which was in a jar of formaldehyde solution. The brain would show shots from different directions, along with bullet fragments from different weapons. This would be clear evidence of conspiracy, but it was conveniently lost.[646]

Marion Johnson, curator of the Warren Commission material at the Archives, simply said, "The brain's not here. We don't know what happened to it."[647]

Stalling

At the airport on the day he took office, Johnson seemed to be stalling. Before he allowed the flight to depart, he insisted that his luggage be taken off of his plane, Air Force Two, and transferred to Kennedy's plane, Air Force One. This was pointless, since both planes had the same equipment and accommodations, and the designation "Air Force One" simply applies to whichever plane is carrying the president. Yet, Johnson insisted on the change, just to show that he's in charge. Then he insisted on taking Kennedy's body back on the plane, which wasted more time. During all this,

---

[645] Zirbel, Craig I., *The Texas Connection*, p. 21, Wright and Co., 1991
[646] https://groups.google.com/forum/#!topic/alt.conspiracy.jfk/Shl-RXTGOp4
[647] *Los Angeles Free Press*, Special Report No. 1, p. 16

Johnson was reported to be relaxing, watching TV, eating soup, and did not seem to be panicking or stressed out in any way.

Then to add further delay, he insisted on taking the oath of office on Texas soil, so they had to locate a federal judge and bring her to the plane. In reality, there was no need for Johnson to take the oath at all. The moment the fatal head shot hit Kennedy, Johnson was president. No oath is legally required. Even if the president is incapacitated but not dead, the vice-president becomes the president instantly. Johnson knew that, but he seemed like he wanted to waste time. It was several hours before the plane took off.

Why was Johnson stalling? One possibility was that it had to do with alterations to Kennedy's body. At some point in all of this, Kennedy's body was hijacked. This was necessary to make sure the autopsy would conform to the lone-assassin theory. Johnson may not have known details about this, but at some point he was told that the body was needed for alterations. He didn't question it, and he delayed as much as he could to give his cohorts time to snatch the body and make the changes.

Johnson told Jackie Kennedy on the plane that it was Robert Kennedy who said he should take the oath of office in Dallas. Afterwards, Robert Kennedy was surprised to hear that from Jackie, and he insisted he had never said that. Robert Kennedy is believable here because he would have no reason to make such a suggestion. It was Johnson who was stalling for time, and he was simply making a cheap excuse. Later, when Johnson gave his deposition to the Warren Commission, he again lied and stated that it was Robert Kennedy who urged him to take the oath in Dallas.[648]

In that same deposition, Johnson said that Ken O'Donnell told him to take Kennedy's plane because it had better communication equipment. O'Donnell denied this, saying:

> The president and I had no conversation regarding Air Force One. If we had known that he was going on Air Force One, we would have taken Air Force Two. One plane was just like the other.[649]

---

[648] Marrs, Jim, *Crossfire*, p. 296, Carroll and Graf, 1989
[649] Marrs, Jim, *Crossfire*, p. 297, Carroll and Graf, 1989

O'Donnell also said that a commission lawyer had asked him to change his testimony so that it would agree with Johnson's. O'Donnell refused to change his story.

Casket Switch

At the start of the day, the plotters did not know how the assassination would turn out. If it had all gone according to plan, all the shots would have come from behind. Then there would only be shots from one direction, so they could say Oswald was the only shooter. If that was the case, there would be no need for any alterations to the body. But it didn't go down that way. Kennedy was hit twice from in front. That includes the throat wound and the fatal head shot. Some doctors in collusion must have been on stand-by in case any alterations were necessary, which they were. After the shooting, someone in charge made a call to these doctors, alerting them that such alterations would be needed. That led to the hijacking of Kennedy's body.

Of great suspicion is the manner in which Kennedy's body arrived at Bethesda. After Kennedy was declared dead at Parkland Hospital, his body was wrapped in sheets and put in an expensive, ornate casket. The casket was then taken to Love Field, where it was loaded into Air Force One, waiting to take off for Washington with Lyndon Johnson and a grieving Jackie Kennedy. At some point, the body was removed from the casket. It seems most likely that this was done before the casket was loaded onto the plane. Jackie Kennedy thought that her husband's body was on board the plane with her. When the plane landed at Andrews Air Force Base near Washington, the empty casket was removed and placed into a hearse which traveled in a motorcade to Bethesda Naval Hospital in Maryland. The casket was carried into the morgue while Mrs. Kennedy was taken to the VIP waiting room. John Kennedy's body had been surreptitiously placed in a body bag and then into a cheap, plain metal shipping casket. This casket was driven by hearse to the back entrance of Bethesda, where the morgue was located. This casket was secretly carried into the morgue at 6:35 p.m. At this time, Jackie Kennedy was still in the car on her way from AAFB to Bethesda, still believing that her husband's body was in the car with her. It is not clear how Kennedy's body got from Dallas to Maryland.[650]

---

[650] https://www.maryferrell.org/pages/Body_Alteration.html

The unloading of the cheap shipping casket from the hearse was supervised by Navy corpsman Dennis David, who was in charge of security for the autopsy. A team of navy personnel carried the casket from the hearse into the morgue. David described the casket as a gray shipping casket like the ones used in the Vietnam War. Twenty minutes later, David saw the motorcade approaching, knowing that it could not contain Kennedy's body because he had just unloaded it. He later saw Jackie Kennedy in the waiting room, knowing that she had been duped. She was still not aware that the ornate casket she had just ridden with was empty, and that her husband's body had been secretly delivered to the rear. Others who confirmed early delivery of Kennedy's body were Navy corpsmen Paul O'Connor, Floyd Riebe, Jerrol Custer, Ed Reed, and James Jenkins.[651]

Two documents prove the stealth arrival of Kennedy's body. The first one was a written report by Joseph Gawler's Sons, Inc., the funeral home that did the embalming. It read:

> Body removed from metal shipping casket at NSNH at Bethesda.

The second document was an official military report filed by Marine Sgt. Roger Boyajian, who was in charge of a 10-man Marine security detail for Kennedy's autopsy. The report read:

> The detail arrived at the hospital at approximately 1800 (6:00 p.m.) and after reporting as ordered several members of the detail were posted at entrances to prevent unauthorized persons from entering the prescribed area.... At approximately 18:35 (6:35 p.m.) the casket was received at the morgue entrance and taken inside.[652]

Kennedy's body was probably removed from the casket before it was loaded onto the plane. That makes sense because it gave the culprits more time to work on the body. If they had waited for the plane to land in Washington to remove the body, they would have lost three or four hours of time that they needed to do the alterations. Even if the casket had been removed from Air Force One before it left Dallas, they still would have lost too much time. That would have been highly conspicuous, considering the

---

[651] https://www.lewrockwell.com/2012/11/jacob-hornberger/the-ongoing-kennedy-casket-mystery/

[652] https://www.fff.org/explore-freedom/article/kennedy-casket-conspiracy/

swarm of reporters at Love Field at that time. The body was probably stolen at Parkland Hospital.

Officially, Kennedy's body was delivered to the Bethesda morgue at 8:00 p.m. in the expensive, ornate casket it had originally been placed in. This was confirmed by Lieutenant Samuel Bird, head of the Joint Casket Bearer Team. After landing at AAFB, the casket was placed in a Navy ambulance along with Jackie Kennedy. From there, they drove in a motorcade procession to Bethesda, where they arrived at 6:55 p.m. At 8:00 p.m., the casket was carried into the Bethesda morgue by the military honor team headed by Lt. Bird.

Paul O'Connor was an autopsy technician for Kennedy's autopsy, who testified to the HSCA. O'Connor stated that Kennedy's body arrived in a "cheap, metal, aluminum" casket in a "rubberized body bag" with a "zipper down the middle." This description has been verified by Reibe, Custer, Reed, and Jenkins.[653] [654]

We can safely say without doubt that Kennedy's body arrived at Bethesda Naval Hospital at 6:35 p.m. in a plain metal shipping casket with the corpse in a body bag.

The documents and testimonies that have proven secret delivery of the metal shipping casket have been uncovered due to the Assassinations Records Review Board, which allowed previously sealed documents to be available to the public. These records and documents would otherwise have been sealed until 2039, based on an order by Lyndon Johnson. The purpose of sealing the records was obviously to prevent the truth from being known. This is an example of that. We have now seen documentation that a metal shipping casket was secretly delivered to Bethesda Naval Hospital, and this has been verified by several credible navy corpsmen. There is no reason for any of them to lie.

Autopsy

John Kennedy's murder was a Dallas homicide. The investigation should have been done by the Dallas Police, and the autopsy should have been done by Dallas doctors. None of that happened, however, as the cover-up

---

[653] https://www.fff.org/explore-freedom/article/kennedy-casket-conspiracy/
[654] https://www.fff.org/2012/11/21/the-ongoing-kennedy-casket-mystery/

took priority over the law. Secret Service agents literally stole Kennedy's body from Parkland Hospital. Doctors there refused to release the body, as it was their legal responsibility to do the autopsy. Secret Service agents forcefully grabbed the gurney that Kennedy's body was on. The SS agents and the doctors had a physical tug-of-war over the body, until the doctors reluctantly let go, figuring they can't fight the feds. The SS agents were in a panic, as if they desperately had something to hide. The superficial reason for taking Kennedy's body was that Jacqueline Kennedy wanted the autopsy done at Bethesda Naval Base. But Jackie Kennedy was in too much of a state of shock at the time. She probably didn't care where the autopsy was performed. It was obvious that the Secret Service had to get the body out of there to save their own hides.

But what happened between Parkland and Bethesda remains a mystery. At some point, Kennedy's body was removed for alterations. The reason for this was to hide the fact that there were multiple shooters. Kennedy was shot with at least three different weapons from four different directions. It would be hard to make that fit with the lone-assassin theory. The evidence of conspiracy would have to be destroyed.

Every doctor from Parkland Hospital who saw the autopsy photos has said that the pictures of the wounds don't match what they saw with their own eyes. The autopsy photos show a small, neat wound at the back of Kennedy's head. The doctors and attendants all said that the back of the head was blown out completely, which is consistent with what witnesses described. Doctors also said that there was an entrance wound on his right temple. This wound was not visible in the autopsy photos. A diagram drawn by the autopsy doctors shows the back wound to be at the base of the neck, but the Parkland doctors said that the back wound was several inches below the shoulders. The real wounds had to be altered to hide the fact that shots came from the front. They had to make it look like all shots came from behind, so they can pin it all on Lee Harvey Oswald.[655] [656]

Supposedly, the body was hijacked to make alterations to hide evidence of a shot from the front. But what alterations were made to the wounds? None. At Bethesda, the head wound looked just as it did at Parkland. Several members of the Bethesda staff have described the head wound the

---

[655] http://www.jfkmurdersolved.com/doctors.htm
[656] http://www.jfkmurdersolved.com/autopsy.htm

same as the Parkland doctors described it- a large, gaping hole in the back of the head. It appears that no alterations were made to the wounds after the body was stolen from Parkland. It may have been taken just for evaluation. At that point in time, the plotters may not have known what, if any, alterations needed to be made. After seeing the extent of the damage to the head, it may have been determined that they would be unable to repair it. They had limited time, since Jackie Kennedy would soon be arriving at Bethesda with an empty casket that supposedly contained her husband's body. There could not be an extended delay in the arrival of the actual body. The plotters may have abandoned the idea of repairing the head wound before the autopsy. They decided they would have to wait until afterwards, and hope that the threat of court martial would keep everyone at Bethesda quiet about what they saw.

That's why it was critical for the plotters that Kennedy's body be taken to Bethesda Naval Hospital. Since Bethesda was a military institution, the doctors there would be forced to obey their commanding officers under threat of court martial. The autopsy could then be tightly controlled, which it was. The doctors were prohibited from performing the functions that they needed to perform. Clearly, someone wanted to obscure the results.

At Bethesda, the autopsy was performed by Commander Joseph Humes, Lieutenant Colonel Pierre Finck, and Commander James Boswell. All three were military men, but none of them were forensic pathologists. None of them were qualified to do an autopsy, let alone the most important autopsy in history. Dr. Humes was the lead doctor, but he had only taken one medical school course in forensic pathology. The attempt to perform a legitimate autopsy was further hindered by the inexplicable orders the doctors received from their superior officers. When the doctors tried to dissect Kennedy's throat wound, they were not allowed to do so. When they tried to track the wounds to determine the pathways of the bullets, they were stopped. When the doctors wanted to study photographs and x-rays, they were seized by the Secret Service. For some reason, the original autopsy report by Dr. Humes was destroyed and rewritten.[657]

To add even more suspicion to this, none of the doctors or attendants were permitted to talk about the autopsy. Paul O'Connor assisted the

---

[657] http://spartacus-educational.com/JFKSautopsy.htm

autopsy at Bethesda. In an interview, he talked about the orders he received from his superiors:

> O'Connor: On Tuesday of that next week we were called into Captain Stover's office - who was one of the commanders of the Naval Medical School - where we were instructed and told that we were going to sign orders of silence under the penalty of general court martial, and other dreadful things like going to prison, if we talked to anybody about anything that happened that night. Period.
>
> Q: So you were threatened basically with being thrown in jail?
>
> O'Connor: In prison.
>
> Q: In prison if you talked about this to anybody?
>
> O'Connor: To anybody. Now that was the worst experience of my life. The Kennedy assassination autopsy was bad. But that scared me to death because I was a good loyal navy hospital corpsman, had done nothing wrong and was thrown into a situation that I couldn't control. And all of a sudden I was told that if I was to say something to anybody, anybody - and they left that wide open anybody-that if found out, we'd go to prison and be dishonorably discharged from the navy.[658]

After the autopsy, two FBI agents prepared a report to summarize the results. The agents were James Sibert and Francis O'Neill. Sibert and O'Neill stated that Dr. Humes attempted to probe the back wound with his finger. The wound did not transit, and Dr. Humes was able to touch the end of the path with his fingertip. Yet, on Sunday morning, November 24, when the Navy submitted its report to the White House, the non-transiting wound had become a transiting wound. On December 9, the FBI submitted its Summary Report to the Warren Commission, and on January 13, 1964, they submitted a Supplemental Report. Both of these were based on the Sibert-O'Neill report. In both FBI reports submitted to the commission, the wound

---

[658] Law, William Matson, *In the Eye of History* (2005)

is non-transiting. But the Navy's report of a transiting wound is the one used by the Warren Commission to support the magic bullet theory and the lone-assassin scenario.[659]

SS agent Kellerman took the autopsy photographs and x-rays to agent Robert Bouck of the PRS section of the Secret Service. From there, it is not known what happened to them, because the Warren Commission never saw them. The commission's response to the missing evidence was to let Dr. Humes and the Navy doctors present drawings and diagrams in place of the photos and x-rays. This was an outrageous maneuver that allowed the doctors to raise the position of the back shot, thus making it appear that the bullet had transited and exited from the throat.[660]

The throat wound was expanded by a tracheotomy performed at Parkland to help Kennedy breathe. There was still a faint pulse at that point and the doctors did what they could to save him, but the throat wound as evidence of conspiracy had been destroyed. Dr. Perry at Parkland Hospital described the wound as being 3-5 millimeters in diameter, and round and neat. He said he made a lateral incision to facilitate the tracheotomy, but he did not obliterate the wound. But in the autopsy photos, the wound has been obliterated. Somehow, the throat wound has been elongated to about two or three inches in the pictures.[661]

It appears that someone tried to hide the fact that the wound in the throat was one of entrance. By elongating and shredding the wound, it gives the impression that it is one of exit. But what is the point of creating an apparent exit wound without a corresponding entrance wound? There was clearly no wound of entry on the rear of the neck. This was just hours after Kennedy was shot, so no one could have possibly known at the time that a few months later, the Warren Commission would come up with the magic bullet theory. It's preposterous even in retrospect, so certainly no one would have anticipated it in advance. Also, no one could have known that the commission would raise the back wound by several inches. So why would they create an exit wound, knowing that the lack of an entrance wound proves it fake?

---

[659] Marrs, Jim, *Crossfire*, pp. 370-372, Carroll and Graf, 1989

[660] Meagher, Sylvia, *Accessories After the Fact*, Skyhorse Publishing, 1967

[661] Marrs, Jim, *Crossfire*, p. 372, Carroll and Graf, 1989

The Sibert-O'Neill report reads:

> …it was also apparent that a tracheotomy had been
> performed as well as surgery to the head area, namely, in the
> top of the skull.[662]

The tracheotomy slit was still visible at the start of the autopsy, so the elongation happened at Bethesda. It should be noted that several Bethesda staff members were told to leave the autopsy room while photographs were taken, then they were allowed to return.[663]

The doctors at Parkland had only operated on the throat, not the head. Yet, the Sibert-O'Neill report states that there was surgery to the top of the skull. The report does not detail the extent of the surgery. It might be referring simply to the reattachment of Kennedy's scalp. Recall that a portion of his scalp came off during the shooting. That was what Jackie Kennedy retrieved from the back of the limo, and she later handed it to a doctor at Parkland. After Kennedy expired, the doctors probably tried to reattach the scalp, just for cosmetic reasons. What else would they do with it? They would not throw it away, and they would not send it on to Bethesda in a separate container. They probably just attached it with some kind of tentative surgery, just to keep it in place during transit. This might be what the Sibert-O'Neill report is referring to as "surgery." Otherwise, it would contradict the statements of the Bethesda personnel.

The original autopsy report, prepared by Finck, states:

> There is a large irregular defect of the scalp and skull on the
> right involving chiefly the parietal bone but extending
> somewhat into the temporal and occipital regions. In this
> region there is an actual absence of scalp and bone
> producing a defect which measures approximately 13 cm. in
> greatest diameter.[664]

Here Finck is describing the condition of the body when he received it. He described the head wound as 13 cm. (5.1 inches) wide, meaning it had not yet been altered at the time it arrived at Bethesda.

---

[662] Lifton, David, *Best Evidence*, p. 172, Carroll and Graf, 1988

[663] http://www.manuscriptservice.com/Throat-Wound/

[664] http://www.aarclibrary.org/publib/jfk/wc/wr/pdf/WR_A9_AutopsyReport.pdf

In an interview, Bethesda autopsy technician Paul O'Connor described the body upon arrival:

> ... the wound was so massive inside of his head there was hardly any brain matter left. There was no brain really. There was no brain really for us, for myself, to take out. There was no need for me to open up the cranium because the cranium was completely shattered. When I say "shattered," not only was the brain blown open, where nothing was left, but the rest of the cranium - the skull cap - was totally fractured.[665]

So apparently no alterations were made to the head wound between Parkland and Bethesda, in spite of the body hijacking and the casket switch. If the plotters were going to alter one wound, it would have been the one in the back of the head, since that was the most incriminating wound of all. Yet, no alterations were made to the head wound. That makes sense, actually, because it's not likely that any alterations would have fooled the autopsy doctors. If the plotters had stitched Kennedy's head together, do you really think the autopsy doctors wouldn't notice?

It may have been determined that altering the photos themselves would be easier than altering the body. Saundra Kay Spencer from the Naval Photographic Center developed the autopsy photos the weekend after the assassination. She testified to the ARRB that the official autopsy photos were not the ones she developed. When agent O'Neill testified to the ARRB about the photos, he said "This looks like it's been doctored in some way."[666] [667]

It's also possible that some pictures were taken of the body after it had been embalmed. Thomas E. Robinson was the mortician at Gawler's Funeral Home where John Kennedy was embalmed. Robinson testified to the HSCA:

> Q: Were you the one that was responsible for closing these wounds in the head?
>
> Robinson: Well, we all worked on it. Once the body was embalmed arterially and they brought a piece of heavy-duty

---

[665] William Matson Law, *In the Eye of History*, (2005)
[666] https://www.maryferrell.org/pages/ARRB_Medical_Testimony.html
[667] https://www.history-matters.com/essays/jfkmed/How5Investigations/
How5InvestigationsGotItWrong_5.htm

rubber, again to fill this area (area in back of the head). I remember treating the...organs. Like I said, we all tried to help one another.

Q: OK, you had to close the wound in the back of the head using the rubber. What other work had to be done on the head?

Robinson: It had to be all dried out, packed, and the rubber placed into the hair and the skin pulled back over it as much as possible and stitched into that piece of rubber. They were afraid again of leaks, once the body is moved and shaken in the casket and carried up the Capitol steps and opened again, we had to be very careful, there would have been blood on the pillow.[668]

If the embalmer saw the head wound, then certainly the autopsy doctors saw it, too. Robinson also described a wound "at the temple in the hairline." This was the entrance wound from the fatal head shot. Robinson said it was small enough that it could be hidden by the hairline and didn't need to be covered with make-up.

It's possible that at some point, the plotters abandoned the idea of patching up the wounds and decided to either let the embalmer do it, or else just fake the pictures instead. They could have gotten pictures after the embalming, but it's more likely that they altered the photos. So either the body or the photos were altered, or it may have been some of both. But either way, the autopsy photos do not accurately represent Kennedy's wounds.

Thomas Robinson was never asked to alter evidence. Robinson was told that John Kennedy would have an open casket funeral. That was the ostensible reason for the alterations to the head wound. Robinson believed it was for cosmetic purposes only, since he thought that thousands of people would be viewing the late president's body. As we know, there was never a public viewing of John Kennedy's body, neither at the funeral nor elsewhere. We have seen pictures of his flag-draped casket in the Capitol Rotunda. But Robinson meticulously worked on Kennedy's head to make it look presentable to the mourners. The pictures we see as evidence are

---

[668] https://www.history-matters.com/archive/jfk/arrb/master_med_set/md63/html/Image02.htm

either forgeries, or they are pictures taken after Robinson and his associates made the cosmetic alterations to Kennedy's head wound. If the latter is the case, Robinson did not know that his work would be used to dupe the public.

Robinson had seen evidence of a fragmenting round, but he didn't know it:

> Well, it exited in many pieces. They were literally picked out, little pieces of this bullet from all over his head...I watched them pick the little pieces out.

Robinson asked an FBI agent why the bullet was in little pieces, but he did not get a straight answer:

> He just explained to me that on occasion that happens. The bullet will smash into a great many pieces.[669]

The agent's answer was evasive. Kennedy was hit with an exploding round which caused the wide dispersion of fragments that Robinson saw. But the agent could not say that because Oswald's rifle could not fire an exploding round. The agent bailed out by saying it just "happens."

Dr. Humes lied to the Warren Commission when he made this statement:

> ...the bullet penetrated the rear of the President's head and exited through a large wound on the right side of his head.[670]

This was the opposite of what we see in the Zapruder film. Casting further suspicion on Dr. Humes, he made this admission:

> In privacy of my own home, early in the morning of Sunday, November 24th, I made a draft of this report which I later revised, and of which this represents the revision. That draft I personally burned in the fireplace of my recreation room.[671]

The drawings of Kennedy's wounds are clearly not accurate, and were designed to promote the lone-gunman theory. Several months after the

[669] https://www.history-matters.com/archive/jfk/arrb/master_med_set/md63/html/Image04.htm
[670] http://spartacus-educational.com/JFKSautopsy.htm
[671] *The Warren Commission Report*, Vol. II, p. 348, 1964

assassination, the commission still hadn't seen the autopsy photos. In a memo from Arlen Specter to J. Lee Rankin, we read:

> In my opinion it is indispensable that we obtain the photographs and x-rays of President Kennedy's autopsy.[672]

This is a token attempt to create the appearance of a legitimate investigation. Specter was the creator of the magic bullet theory, so he is clearly not serious about finding the truth. But the commission had to go through the motions of conducting a real investigation, and that is why the memo was sent. The commission never did see the autopsy photos.

Dr. Cyril Wecht is the former president of the American Academy of Forensic Medicine. He has been a very vocal critic of the autopsy performed on President Kennedy. Dr. Wecht testified before the Warren Commission:

> ...it is not my responsibility to retroactively justify and defend the investigation that was done, which I think was extremely superficial and sloppy, inept, incomplete, incompetent in many respects, not only on the part of the pathologists who did this horribly inadequate medical-legal autopsy but on the part of many other people. This is the kind of examination that would not be tolerated in a routine murder case by a good crew of homicide detectives in most major cities of America on anybody just a plain ordinary citizen, let alone a President.[673]

Johnson Controls the Cover-Up

The day after the assassination, The *Dallas Morning News* stated the following:

> (DA Henry) Wade said preliminary reports indicated more than one person was involved in the shooting which brought death to the president and left Gov. John Connally wounded.[674]

---

[672] http://mcadams.posc.mu.edu/shootft.htm
[673] Turner, Nigel, 1988, The Cover-Up, *The Men Who Killed Kennedy*, U.K., Nigel Turner Productions
[674] *Dallas Morning News*, November 23, 1963

So Wade believed early on that there was a conspiracy. He was quoted as saying, *"They should all go to the electric chair."* Yet, Wade eventually capitulated and went with the lone assassin story. In an interview years later, Wade explains why:

> Cliff Carter, President Johnson's aide, called me three times from the White House that Friday night. He said that President Johnson felt that any word of a conspiracy- some plot by foreign nations- to kill President Kennedy would shake our nation to its foundation. President Johnson was worried about some conspiracy on the part of the Russians. Oswald had all sorts of connections and affections toward Castro's Cuba. It might be possible to prove a conspiracy with Cuba. But it would be very hard to prove a conspiracy with Russia. Washington's word to me was that it would hurt foreign relations if I alleged a conspiracy- whether I could prove it or not. I would just charge Oswald with plain murder and go for the death penalty. So I went down to the police department at City Hall to see Captain Fritz- to make sure the Dallas Police didn't involve any foreign country in the assassination.[675]

As soon as Johnson made it back to Washington, he was busy orchestrating the cover-up. The call to Wade was just the first step. Johnson did not want a congressional investigation into the assassination for the simple reason that he would not be able to control it. A recorded phone conversation from 11-29-63 between Johnson and John McCormack, Speaker of the House of Representatives, is revealing:

> Johnson: We don't want to be testifying, and some fellow comes up from Dallas and says, "I think Khrushchev planned this whole thing and he got our President assassinated." You can see what that'll lead us to, right quick... You take care of the House of Representatives for me.
>
> McCormack: How am I going to take care of them?
>
> Johnson: Just keep them from investigating!

---

[675] https://www.jfkassassinationforum.com/index.php?topic=7761.0;wap2

McCormack: Oh that. I've been doing it now.[676]

After Oswald was shot, Hoover talked with Johnson aide Walter Jenkins, saying:

> The thing I am concerned about, and so is Katzenbach, is having something issued so we can convince the public that Oswald is the real assassin. Mr. Katzenbach thinks that the President might appoint a Presidential Commission of three outstanding citizens to make a determination.

Since Oswald was dead now, there would be no trial. Hoover did not have to worry about things like "innocent until proven guilty." It has been determined that Oswald was the one and only gunman, and now it's just a matter of convincing the public. There would be no real investigation.

The Katzenbach Memo

On November 25, 1963, Assistant Attorney General Nicholas Katzenbach sent a memo to White House Press Secretary Bill Moyers. This memo provides proof of a cover-up at the highest level. Let's take a look at what the memo says:

> The public must be satisfied that Oswald was the assassin; that he did not have confederates who are still at large; and that the evidence was such that he would have been convicted at trial.

The memo shows that the White House had already decided that Oswald was the lone assassin. In less than 72 hours, they have concluded without a doubt that Oswald, and Oswald alone, shot John Kennedy. How? Katzenbach himself admitted that very little was known at this point. There is a film showing conclusively that a shot came from the front. There were witnesses who said that shots came from the front. There were conflicting identifications of the shooter in the TSBD. At least one rifle found in the TSBD was not Oswald's. Credible witnesses placed Oswald elsewhere at the time of the shooting. Oswald's paraffin test was negative on his cheek. Yet, the White House is absolutely certain that Oswald is their man. This clearly shows that they have made that decision independent of the evidence.

---

[676] http://spartacus-educational.com/USAjohnsonLB.htm

Speculation about Oswald's motivation ought to be cut off,
and we should have some basis for rebutting thought that
this was a Communist conspiracy or (as the Iron Curtain
press is saying) a right-wing conspiracy to blame it on the
Communists. Unfortunately the facts on Oswald seem about
too pat-- too obvious (Marxist, Cuba, Russian wife, etc.).
The Dallas Police have put out statements on the Communist
conspiracy theory, and it was they who were in charge when
he was shot and thus silenced.

The memo says to rebuke any notion that this was a communist
conspiracy. Even if they really believed Oswald was the shooter, how could
they know so soon that he acted alone? How could they know that no one
else assisted in any way? Why do they say, "Speculation about Oswald's
motivation ought to be cut off"? It seems natural to speculate about motive.

I think this objective may be satisfied by making public as
soon as possible a complete and thorough FBI report on
Oswald and the assassination.

But a complete and thorough report would prove Oswald innocent.
Notice the memo doesn't say "accurate."

This may run into the difficulty of pointing to inconsistencies between this report and statements by Dallas
Police officials. But the reputation of the Bureau is such that
it may do the whole job.

The memo admits there are inconsistencies between the FBI report and
the Dallas Police report. But the memo does not say, "Investigate the crime
and find out who did it." It just says that people will believe the FBI over the
Dallas Police. Then it recommends a presidential commission to reinforce
that belief.

We need something to head off public speculation or
Congressional hearings of the wrong sort.[677]

Congressional hearings had to be avoided because they would be more
likely to expose the truth. It's easier to corrupt seven people than to corrupt
535 people.

---

[677] https://www.maryferrell.org/showDoc.html?docId=62268#relPageId=29

The Warren Commission

Lyndon Johnson officially formed the Warren Commission on November 29, 1963. Of the seven members chosen, not a single one volunteered for the assignment. All of them were coerced into accepting the job by Johnson. Reluctant or not, the Warren Commission included: Chief Justice Earl Warren, Senator John Cooper, former CIA Director Allen Dulles, Representative Gerald Ford, advisor John McCloy, Senator Richard Russell, and Representative Hale Boggs. These were all busy men who had a full schedule of responsibilities to attend to. They all agreed to be on the commission only after heavy persuasion from LBJ. But the most reluctant participant of all was the head of the commission.[678]

Johnson had already asked Earl Warren to head the commission, and Warren had turned him down flat. During a second meeting, Warren changed his mind. What was said that caused him to change his mind? Johnson told Warren that he was concerned about relations with Russia and Cuba. Ostensibly, he feared that rumors of Russian or Cuban involvement would damage relations with those countries to the point where it could lead to nuclear war. Johnson persuaded Warren that 40 million American lives could be lost in a nuclear war, and Warren's job was to prevent that. Here is Warren's explanation of why he agreed to the assignment:

> I then told the President my reasons for not being available for the chairmanship. He replied, "You were a soldier in World War I, but there was nothing you could do in that uniform comparable to what you do for your country in this hour of trouble." He then told me how serious were the rumors floating around the world. The gravity of the situation was such that it might lead us into war, he said, and, if so, it might be a nuclear war. He went on to tell me that he had just talked to Defense Secretary Robert McNamara, who had advised him that the first nuclear strike against us might cause the loss of 40 million people.
>
> I then said, "Mr. President, if the situation is that serious, my personal views do not count. I will do it." He thanked me, and I left the White House.[679]

---

[678] https://en.wikipedia.org/wiki/Warren_Commission
[679] http://grandsubversion.com/jfkAssassination/lbjdoubt.htm

This reasoning is preposterous, and it is shocking that an intelligent person like Earl Warren would fall for it. Does Warren really believe that he must slander and defame an innocent person to preserve world peace? Something is very wrong if that's the case. It is Johnson who is responsible for foreign relations, and it is Congress who is responsible for declaring war. War will not happen unless Congress decides so. Congress would be extremely reluctant to declare war on a country with nuclear capabilities. That could only happen under the most extreme of circumstances. If foreign relations deteriorate that badly, it's Johnson's fault, not Warren's.

Theoretically, what if Russia or Cuba really were involved? Is Johnson asking Warren to cover it up? Why would he want a foreign government to get away with killing our president? Why would Johnson want to cover for them? Why would he ask Warren to prove Russia or Cuba innocent if he thought they were guilty? If that were the case, then Johnson is siding with America's enemy. What if the commission investigated, and found that a Russian conspiracy killed Kennedy? Should they say so? Or should they bury it? Johnson seems to imply that they should bury it.

If Johnson was really concerned that charges of foreign conspiracy could lead to a nuclear war, he could have easily remedied that situation himself. Johnson could have simply made a public statement, saying that there is no reason to believe that any foreign government was involved in the assassination. No foreign government had a motive to kill Kennedy, and none of them had anything to gain by it. How would Russia or Cuba benefit from Kennedy's death? Kennedy had good relations with both Khrushchev and Castro. Why would they want to kill him? Johnson could have simply reminded the American public of these obvious facts. Stating this publicly would suffice to maintain good relations with Russia and Cuba.

The thought of a communist conspiracy is simply a knee-jerk reflex by the American people. They have been conditioned to believe that communists are evil, so naturally they will be the first ones suspected. There is no rational basis for this; it is simply conditioning. Johnson was feeding off the hysteria and using it to his advantage.

When the word "conspiracy" is used by Johnson and others in the cover-up, it is always referring to a foreign conspiracy. There is rarely a mention of domestic conspiracy. A domestic conspiracy would not threaten to start a war with any other country. If the Warren Commission concluded that Kennedy was killed by a domestic conspiracy, there is no chance that it will kill 40 million Americans. So why couldn't the Warren Commission pursue a domestic conspiracy? The real reason is because it would land the president in jail. The commission officially stated that they found no evidence of conspiracy, "foreign or domestic." But the thought of a domestic conspiracy was never even considered.

In a recorded phone conversation with Senator Richard Russell, Johnson described his talk with Warren:

> Bobby and them went up to see him today and he turned them down cold and said NO. Two hours later I called him and ordered him down here and he didn't want to come. I insisted he come – came down here and told me no twice, and I just pulled out what Hoover told me about a little incident in Mexico City, and I said now, I don't want Mr. Khrushchev to be told tomorrow and be testifying before a camera that he killed this fellow, and that Castro killed him, and all I want you to do is look at the facts and bring in any other facts you want in here and determine who killed the President. And I think you can put on your uniform of World War I – fat as you are – and do anything you could to save one American life. And I'm surprised that you, the Chief Justice of the United States, would turn me down. And he started crying, and said, "Well I won't turn you down. I'll just do whatever you say."[680]

In the talk, Johnson mentioned "...Hoover told me about a little incident in Mexico City." There are a couple of different interpretations of that statement. Johnson might have been referring to Oswald's trip to Mexico City. Allegedly, Oswald had visited the Russian embassy there and had a meeting with a man named Valeriy Kostikov, who is unofficially the head of the assassinations department for the Soviets. Johnson could have been alluding to the sensitivity of that information. If the public thought that Oswald had a meeting with the Russian head of assassinations, what would they think? It would create mass hysteria, and Warren was supposed to prevent that. This version of the story is absurd for a number of reasons.

First, Oswald was never at the Russian Embassy. Everyone entering or leaving the embassy is photographed, and there is no photograph of Oswald

---

[680] http://spartacus-educational.com/JFKrussell.htm

entering or leaving the embassy. There was allegedly such a photograph, but the man in the picture looks nothing at all like Oswald.

Second, it is ridiculous to think that any country would overtly have an assassinations department. Covertly, every country probably has one, but it is never overt. One cannot just walk into an embassy and say, "I'd like to talk to your head of assassinations, please." Will they even acknowledge that such a person exists? Will they admit that such a department exists? Of course not, and the people who work at the embassies honestly know nothing about it, so they don't have to lie. Such things are controlled by the intelligence agencies of most countries. It's rare that they would get a request like this one; I doubt if they ever have. But the thought that such a thing would be discussed openly is just ridiculous. But the public mind is not rational, and they would react to a story like this with emotion, not reason.

Third, if the Russians did want to kill Kennedy, why would they pick Oswald to do the job? They didn't even know him. A sensitive assignment like an assassination would only be given to someone who could be trusted, not only to succeed at the assignment, but to keep quiet afterwards. The assignment would be given to someone in the intelligence agencies or to one of their assets (i.e., hitmen). The job would only be given to someone who has shown their loyalty through years of service and success on other assignments. They have never met Oswald before in their lives, so why would they entrust him with such a sensitive assignment?

Fourth, why would the Russians believe that Oswald has the capability to assassinate the president? Does he have some special access to the president? Will he be able to penetrate the security? Does he have the ways and means to outwit the Secret Service? Does he have a proven track record of successful assassinations? Does he have inside information that might give him a chance to get close to the president? Does he have superior marksmanship skills? The answer is "no" to all of these questions. The Russians would have no reason to believe that Oswald could successfully kill the president, even if he wanted to. At this point in time, Oswald had not yet gotten the job at the TSBD, and the motorcade route had not been determined yet. So how could the Russians have known that the motorcade route would pass right by Oswald's window and slow down for him?

So what was Johnson referring to when he mentioned "little incident in Mexico City?" Was he alluding to this story? Was he saying that this story is so explosive, it could lead to nuclear war that would kill 40 million

Americans? Is that how he coaxed Warren into accepting the assignment? That makes no sense. Johnson is saying that Oswald had a meeting with the Russian head of assassinations, then he killed the president. If that were really true, I would think that Johnson would want to have a word with the Russian head of assassinations. Covering that up would help the guilty Russians. In fact, covering it up would be treason. Why would Warren go along with that?

If a foreign government had really murdered our president, then from a military standpoint, a retaliatory strike would be justified. Most Americans would have supported military action if that were really true. World War I was started by an assassination. The public will support a war if they feel the cause is justified, like freeing slaves or rescuing prisoners from concentration camps. The killing of President Kennedy by a foreign government could be interpreted as an act of war. If a foreign government did kill our president, then America would have to take some action, or be perceived as cowards to the whole world. In the bravado world of the military this would be unacceptable, and it would practically be an invitation to war. Johnson is a war hawk anyway, so why would he back down from this? It's because he knew darn well that no foreign government had anything at all to do with John Kennedy's death.

There is another possible explanation for the "little incident in Mexico." It is speculated by some that years earlier, Warren had committed some kind of ethical or legal violation in Mexico City. Maybe he cheated on his wife or patronized a prostitute. Hoover was known to monitor people. It was also known that he was not fond of Warren. It is quite possible that Hoover had dirt on Warren, and he shared the dirt with LBJ. Johnson then used the dirt to blackmail Warren into serving on the commission. For Johnson and Hoover, this was their modus operandi. This version of the story is much more believable. Naturally, Warren could not reveal the real reason he agreed to head the commission, so he had to fall back on the "40 million dead Americans" excuse.

In retrospect, it's hard to believe that anyone would fall for that. But this was a time of panic and shock, and everyone looked up to Johnson for leadership. No one wanted to rock the boat. No one wanted to disobey the president, especially when he had such an unexpected tragedy to deal with. Truth be told, it was not so unexpected to Lyndon Johnson.

Johnson had already talked with Russell, and Russell made it clear he would not serve. He told Johnson, "Get somebody else...I haven't got time..." Russell also had difficulty in getting along with Warren, and didn't think he could have a working relationship with him. But later that evening, Johnson informed Russell that he was a member. He had already announced the commission to the public and named its members, including Russell. Once it was announced, it was difficult for Russell to back down. Russell complained, but Johnson said, "Dick, it has already been announced, and you can serve with anybody for the good of America."[681]

Magic Bullet Theory

By now, everyone has heard of the infamous magic bullet theory. The people who still believe it are the people who have just not looked at it closely. This theory was created by Warren Commission staffer Arlen Specter, as a desperate attempt to maintain that Oswald was the lone assassin. I am certain that no one on the Warren Commission believed the magic bullet theory. I doubt that Arlen Specter himself believed it. I am shocked that anyone would accept it. It was created for the two-fold purpose of covering up the crime of the century, while simultaneously insulting the public's intelligence.

The magic bullet theory claims that one shot fired by Lee Harvey Oswald went through the back of Kennedy's neck, came out his throat, continued on and hit Governor Connally in the back, went through his upper torso, came out of his body and hit his wrist and the limo door, ricocheted off the door and went into Connally's leg. As if it's not baffling enough that one bullet could do so much, it's even more baffling that the bullet emerged in virtually perfect condition. It is undamaged, and there is not even blood or tissue on the bullet. This theory shows complete desperation by the Warren Commission. The wounds to Kennedy and Connally were too numerous to have been done by one shooter. The truth is that Kennedy was hit four times, Connally was hit once, and one shot missed. How could that much damage have been done by one shooter who allegedly only fired three shots? To reconcile this, Specter came up with the magic bullet theory. By saying that one bullet hit both men, they can say that there was only one shooter. It's a desperate attempt to explain all of the wounds with three

---

[681] http://jfkfacts.org/nov-29-1963-warren-commission-announced/

shots. Shockingly, the public bought it, which shows the unjustified faith they have in the government.[682]

The theory is also ridiculous because the alleged path of this bullet is not even a straight line. If you look at the way Kennedy and Connally are seated, the alignment is not right for this to happen. If the shot hit Kennedy in the back from a sixth floor window, that means it was on a downward trajectory. If the bullet did exit Kennedy, it would have continued downward and hit the back of the seat in front of him. It would not have hit Connally. Also, if the bullet was on a downward trajectory, then the wound in the back of the neck would be higher than the wound in the throat. That is not the case; it's the opposite. The back wound was lower than the throat wound, or at best, level with it. The Warren Commission tried to maneuver around this by changing the location of the back wound.

The bullet that hit Connally was on a left-to-right path. It penetrated his body and came out on his right side, hitting his right wrist. That means the shot came from behind and to the left, which is southeast of Connally. That shot must have come from a source other than the book depository. It may have come from the County Records building. The shot that came from the TSBD would have been on a right-to-left path, so that shot could not have been the one that hit Connally. Both the vertical and horizontal trajectories are wrong here. This bullet would have had to zig-zag through the air in order to do what the Warren Commission said it did.

But with all the geometry aside, the most obvious proof that one bullet did not hit these two men is simply the time sequence. Kennedy was hit at about Z-188, while Connally estimated he was hit at about Z-231 to 234. If we figure about 18 frames per second, that's a difference of about 2.5 seconds between Kennedy's reaction and Connally's reaction. We see Kennedy react before the limousine goes behind the freeway sign. His hands move toward his throat, so he has already been hit. Connally has not yet been hit at that point. Connally does not react until 2.5 seconds later. We see him grimace in pain when he is hit. How can anyone explain this delayed reaction? If they were both hit by the same bullet, they would react almost simultaneously.[683]

Governor Connally admitted as much in his testimony to the commission:

[682] https://en.wikipedia.org/wiki/Single-bullet_theory
[683] *The Warren Commission Report*, p. 106, Longmeadow Press, 1964

Specter: In your view, which bullet caused the injury to your chest, Governor Connally?

Connally: The second one.

Specter: And what is your reason for that conclusion, sir?

Connally: Well, in my judgment, it just couldn't conceivably have been the first one because I heard the sound of the shot … and after I heard that shot, I had the time to turn to my right, and start to turn to my left before I felt anything. It is not conceivable to me that I could have been hit by the first bullet.[684]

The conclusions of the Warren Commission are offensive to seekers of truth:

There is no medical evidence that the President was struck by a bullet entering the front of the head,) and the possibility that a bullet could have struck the President and yet left no evidence is extremely remote. Because this conclusion appears to be inconsistent with the backward motion of the President's head in the Zapruder film, the committee consulted a wound ballistics expert to determine what relationship, if any, exists between the direction from which a bullet strikes the head and subsequent head movement. The expert concluded that nerve damage from a bullet entering the President's head could have caused his back muscles to tighten which, in turn, could have caused his head to move toward the rear. He demonstrated the phenomenon in a filmed experiment which involved the shooting of goats. Thus, the committee determined that the rearward movement of the President's head would not be fundamentally inconsistent with a bullet striking from the rear.[685] [686]

No medical evidence of a shot from the front? According to the experts, nerve damage caused his back muscles to tighten which caused his head to move toward the rear. Are we to believe that? The commission knows that

[684] http://crimemagazine.com/gerald-fords-role-jfk-assassination-cover
[685] *The Warren Commission Report*, pp. 44-5, Longmeadow Press, 1964
[686] https://www.archives.gov/research/jfk/select-committee-report/part-1a.html

most people won't actually read the report, so they could get away with this. As Allen Dulles said:

> But nobody reads. Don't believe people read in this country. There will be a few professors that will read the record...The public will read very little.[687]

The final insult came when we were shown a picture of this magic bullet. It looks practically new. A small bit of metal was scraped from the bullet for a spectrograph analysis, but otherwise it looks like a brand new bullet. Any bullet that is fired from a gun will be deformed to some extent. As soon as it hits anything, even a relatively soft substance, it deforms at least slightly. So how can a bullet go through two men, hitting hard bones and the interior of the car door, and still be in perfect condition? This was a brazen lie. The plotters could have simply shot a bullet into a tree, dug it out and then planted the smashed-up bullet as evidence. It would at least be slightly more convincing. But they didn't even do that. The bullet found on the stretcher at Parkland may have been shot into water or cotton, but it was not shot into a human being.

Ford's Move

In a memorandum to J. Lee Rankin, Arlen Specter expressed concern over a possible conflict about the location of the back wound:

> Commission Exhibits Nos. 385, 386, and 388 were made from the recollections of the autopsy surgeons as told to the artist. Someday someone may compare the films with the artist's drawings and find a significant error which might substantially affect the essential testimony and the Commission's conclusions.[688]

Specter is referring to the drawings made by the autopsy doctors in lieu of photographs. The "significant error" he mentioned is the discrepancy in the placement of the back wound. It was Gerald Ford who solved that problem for the commission.

---

[687] (September 6, 1964, Warren Commission internal memo)
http://www.jfklancer.com/LNE/report35.html
[688] http://mcadams.posc.mu.edu/shootft.htm

The pictures of Kennedy's back wound, along with the autopsy description sheet, show that the wound was several inches below the shoulder. In other words, it was lower than the throat wound, which would mean an upward trajectory. Ford deliberately altered the location of the wound in the final report, placing it at the base of the neck- a flagrant distortion of the truth. Even in the new location, the alignment is still not right. It is only a slight downward trajectory, and it still could not have hit Connally.

The ARRB released 40,000 pages of Warren Commission records in 1997. Among them were Gerald Ford's handwritten notes. From the notes it was discovered that Ford had urged the commission to change the wording of Kennedy's wounds to make it fit the magic bullet theory.[689]

The commission staff had written:

> A bullet had entered his back at a point slightly above the shoulder and to the right of the spine.

Ford suggested that it be changed to read:

> A bullet had entered the back of his neck at a point slightly to the right of the spine.

The final report read:

> A bullet had entered the base of the back of his neck slightly to the right of the spine.[690]

The wording here is significant. If the shot came from the TSBD, it would be on a downward trajectory. The entrance wound in the back would have to be higher than the exit wound in front. In reality, it was not. The back wound was lower than the throat wound, meaning it would be on an upward trajectory from behind, which makes no sense. The commission moved the back wound up several inches in a desperate attempt to make it fit the magic bullet theory. But even then, it still doesn't work. The point at where the commission placed the wound is only slightly higher than the throat wound. It is still not enough of a downward trajectory to have come

---

[689] http://spartacus-educational.com/USAfordG.htm

[690] http://www.jfklancer.com/Ford-Rankin.html

from a sixth floor window. Drawing CE 385 shows only a slight downward angle of the bullet's path, as if he were shot from a second story window.[691]

Actually, the original wording of the commission's staff was questionable. It said the bullet entered his back "slightly above the shoulder." That must mean the neck, even though it doesn't say so. What else could be above the shoulders? But of the three revisions of the draft, none of them are accurate. The truth is that the wound in his back was several inches below the shoulder, but nowhere in the report does it say that. Maybe the original was intended to say "shoulder blade" instead of just "shoulder," which would have made sense. The exact location of the wound could not be confirmed because the commission did not have the autopsy photos to work with. They only had a hand-made sketch drawn by the autopsy doctors. It was easy for the commission to say that the sketch was drawn in haste and is therefore not accurate.

Regardless of the vertical placement of the back wound, it is unanimously agreed that it was to the right of the spine. If a bullet had hit Kennedy in the middle of the neck, it would have struck a vertebra and he would have had a broken neck, which was not the case. The commission could not say the bullet exited if it hit bone, since anything solid would have stopped its transit. The entrance wound was to the right of the spine, but the alleged exit wound was in the middle of his throat. That means the bullet was on a right-to-left trajectory, making it even more implausible that it would hit Governor Connally. An exiting bullet on a right-to-left trajectory would have been more likely to hit Mrs. Connally, who was seated to her husband's left.

The autopsy sheet was signed by Admiral George Burkley, who directed Kennedy's autopsy at Bethesda. He also signed Kennedy's official death certificate. On the death certificate, Burkley confirmed that the back wound was at Kennedy's "third thoracic vertebra." He was saying that the wound was in the back, not the neck. The vertebrae in the neck are referred to as "cervical vertebrae." So the wound was three vertebrae lower than the base of the neck.

In an interview, Ford gave a dubious explanation for the change:

---

[691] https://www.history-matters.com/archive/jfk/wc/wcvols/wh16/pdf/ WH16_CE_385.pdf

My changes had nothing to do with a conspiracy theory. My changes were only an attempt to be more precise.[692]

After so many years, Ford still lied about it. His changes were not more precise; they only distorted the truth further. Gerald Ford went to his grave promoting the magic bullet theory in vain.

Misgivings

In the final analysis, the Warren Commission could not establish any motive for Lee Harvey Oswald to have killed John Kennedy. Here is their conclusion:

> Many factors were undoubtedly involved in Oswald's motivation for the assassination, and the Commission does not believe that it can ascribe to him any one motive or group of motives. It is apparent, however, that Oswald was moved by an overriding hostility to his environment. He does not appear to have been able to establish meaningful relationships with other people. He was perpetually discontented with the world around him. Long before the assassination he expressed his hatred for American society and acted in protest against it. Oswald's search for what he conceived to be the perfect society was doomed from the start. He sought for himself a place in history--a role as the "great man" who would be recognized as having been in advance of his times. His commitment to Marxism and communism appears to have been another important factor in his motivation. He also had demonstrated a capacity to act decisively and without regard to the consequences when such action would further his aims of the moment. Out of these and the many other factors which may have molded the character of Lee Harvey Oswald there emerged a man capable of assassinating President Kennedy.[693]

Since the commission could not find a motive for Oswald, they had to resort to psychoanalyzing him. Phrases like "perpetually discontented" and "hatred for American society" are simply wrong. Oswald loved his country and tried his best to serve it. In the few short film clips that we have of

---

[692] http://www.whatreallyhappened.com/RANCHO/POLITICS/JFK/ford.html
[693] *The Warren Commission Report*, pp. 423-4, Longmeadow Press, 1964

Oswald talking, he seems civilized and mature, and does not display any aggression or hatred in any way. The commission was simply desperate for an explanation. They figured that if someone is labeled as crazy, then people won't try to figure him out. No motive is needed, because crazy people don't act rationally.

Senator Russell had strong doubts about the conclusions of the commission. He correctly reasoned that Kennedy and Connally could not have been hit by the same bullet. Initially, he refused to sign his name to the final report. After a talk with Warren, Russell agreed to sign the report as long as he could make a written statement of dissent, which would be included in the report. Russell then made his statement in the presence of a stenographer. However, when the final report was published, Russell's statement was not in it. Warren had lied to Russell and withheld his statement from the record. Russell was irate, as you can imagine. Warren had tricked him into signing his name to a conclusion he did not agree with.[694]

Throughout the hearings, the CIA continually withheld information from the commission. This included files relating to their previous contact with Oswald. It also included files that would have revealed plots to assassinate Fidel Castro with the use of Mafia hit men. This would have been doubly damaging to the CIA and the government in general. Not only were they planning to assassinate a foreign leader, but they were colluding with organized crime to do it. If the commission had had this information, it would have been difficult to deal with.[695]

The FBI was no more cooperative than the CIA. Hale Boggs made that clear:

> Hoover lied his eyes out to the Commission - on Oswald, on Ruby, on their friends, the bullets, the gun, you name it.[696]

Others involved have let their true feelings show:

Earl Warren:

---

[694] http://22november1963.org.uk/warren-commission-jfk-assassination

[695] https://en.wikipedia.org/wiki/Warren_Commission

[696] http://spartacus-educational.com/JFKboggs.htm

Full disclosure was not possible for reasons of national security.[697]

Senator Richard Russell:

We have not been told the truth about Oswald.[698]

Senator John Sherman Cooper:

On what basis is it claimed that two shots caused all the wounds? It seemed to me that Governor Connally's statement negates such a conclusion. I could not agree with this statement.[699]

Ken O'Donnell admitted that he capitulated to the Warren Commission:

I told the FBI what I had heard (two shots from behind the grassy knoll fence), but they said it couldn't have happened that way and that I must have been imagining things. So I testified the way they wanted me to. I just didn't want to stir up any more pain and trouble for the family.[700]

Lyndon Johnson:

I'll tell you something about Kennedy's murder that will rock you.....Kennedy was trying to get Castro, but Castro got to him first.[701]

Johnson did not explain how Castro changed the motorcade route. Johnson has openly accused Castro, the CIA, and Big Oil of killing John Kennedy. His finger points at everyone but himself.

No one on the Warren Commission was truly an ally of John Kennedy. None of his staff or aides were chosen. Why wasn't Robert Kennedy chosen to be on the commission? One might answer that he lacks objectivity since he is John Kenney's brother. Yet Allen Dulles, a man who was fired by Kennedy and openly called him a traitor, was chosen to investigate his

---

[697] http://harveyandlee.net/

[698] Weisberg, Harold, *Whitewash IV*, p. 21, Skyhorse Publishing, 2013

[699] Wrone, David, *The Zapruder Film*, p. 247, University Press of Kansas, 2003

[700] O'Neill, Tip Jr., *Man of the House*, p. 178, St. Martin's Mass Market Paperback, 1988

[701] Altshuler, Harry, *How the CIA Plot to Kill Castro Backfired*, 1976

death. Was Dulles objective? Robert Kennedy could have been trusted to pursue a truthful conclusion, not only because he was the president's brother, but because he was the Attorney General. He was J. Edgar Hoover's boss. If the commission's purpose was to evaluate the FBI's findings, shouldn't the Attorney General be a part of it?

After JFK's death, Robert Kennedy's effectiveness as Attorney General basically ended. As Jimmy Hoffa said, "He's just another attorney now." Without the support of his brother and president, he was a distraught individual, and could not function effectively. Racketeering indictments came to a halt after November of 1963. Johnson did not share his predecessor's enthusiasm for the war on crime. The mob had just gotten Johnson into office and kept him out of jail. He was not about to pursue any investigation into their activities, especially when such an investigation was bound to lead back to him. He disliked Robert Kennedy, and not naming him to the Warren Commission was his way of saying that RFK was persona non grata. There was no working relationship between Robert Kennedy and Lyndon Johnson, and within a matter of months, Robert Kennedy had submitted his resignation as Attorney General.

I have often wondered why Robert Kennedy was not more outspoken about his brother's death. Publicly, he endorsed the Warren Commission, and said that he believed Oswald had killed his brother. I cannot believe those were his true feelings on the matter. He said what he had to say to protect his career, his family, and his life. He had privately said to friends that he doubted the Warren Commission, and that he would reopen the investigation if he ever became president. He successfully ran for Senator of New York in 1964, and he was on the campaign trail for the presidency when he was assassinated in 1968.

Another possible reason for Robert Kennedy's silence was the multitude of skeletons both he and his brother had in their respective closets. This included a long list of mistresses, concubines, and courtesans. Both of the Kennedys were known to be promiscuous, and in the end it came back to haunt them. They were repeatedly controlled through blackmail at the hands of Hoover and Johnson. It was through this kind of blackmail that Johnson had been chosen as John Kennedy's running mate. Robert Kennedy may have been blackmailed into silence regarding his brother's murder, since Hoover was known to do extensive wiretapping on the Kennedys, among others. He probably had the goods on them both. Bobby had to consider his brother's legacy. If he had spoken out, Hoover and Johnson could have retaliated against him by releasing proof of the Kennedy's many transgressions. It would be secretly leaked to the press, of course, so that no one would know that Hoover and Johnson were behind it. But if the truth about JFK's many wanton escapades had been made public, it would have permanently tarnished his image. John Kennedy died a martyr, and maybe his brother just decided he would rather have the public remember him that way.

But it was not only the sexual adventures of the Kennedy brothers that was used against them. They had both been less than saintly in their political dealings, too. John Kennedy had colluded with the mafia to get elected. They helped him to carry Illinois in the 1960 election. Robert, on the other hand, was involved in plots to assassinate Fidel Castro. If either of these facts had become known, the Kennedy image would have been stained. Over the years, these facts have become known to researchers, but not to the general public. This effectively silenced Robert Kennedy, who was forced to bite his tongue while the Warren Commission went through the motions of performing an investigation.

Jim Garrison recalled a phone conversation he had with Robert Kennedy in 1964:

> I told him some of my theories. He listened carefully, then said, "Maybe so, maybe you're right. But what good will it do to know the truth? Will it bring back my brother?" I said, "I find it hard to believe that as the top law man in the country you don't want to pursue the truth more ardently." With this he hung up on me.[702]

Pitzer

Lieutenant Commander William B. Pitzer was present at JFK's autopsy. Pitzer was the Assistant Head of the Graphic Arts department at National Naval Medical School. He specialized in closed-circuit TV, which he used to make instructional films. He had taken film and photographs of the JFK autopsy, which may have cost him his life. Pitzer died from a gunshot wound. He was found dead in his studio-office at 7:50 p.m. on October 29, 1966. A revolver was found close by, and like many JFK-related deaths,

---

[702] http://spartacus-educational.com/USAkennedyR.htm

many suspect that Pitzer was murdered for knowing too much. A joint investigation by the Naval Investigative Service (NIS) and the FBI concluded that Bill Pitzer had committed suicide.

Pitzer's name does not appear on any list of personnel who were in the autopsy room at the time. However, since he specialized in closed-circuit TV, it's possible that he took film and photographs of the autopsy without being present in the room. Jerrol Custer was one witness who claims Pitzer was in the autopsy room, and that he was actively taking film and photographs. Whether physically present or not, Pitzer somehow recorded the autopsy and was in possession of extremely sensitive materials which the government desperately wanted.

It seems that if Pitzer was physically in the autopsy room taking pictures, he surely would have been noticed by all the federal agents who were there. If they knew that Pitzer had pictures and film of the autopsy, they would have confiscated them before he was allowed to leave. If Pitzer was actually there, then they probably did take his film, but they did not know about the closed-circuit filming. The cameras may not have been prominent, or the agents just didn't think to look for them, since closed-circuit cameras were new at the time. Pitzer probably went back to his office afterwards and looked at the films he had surreptitiously taken.

A few days later, Pitzer was editing the film when Dennis David came by. Pitzer was a mentor and close friend of David, who had been in charge of security at the autopsy. David found Pitzer working on the 16-mm film, making slides and photographs of Kennedy's autopsy from different angles. Pitzer invited David to look at what he had. Hand-cranking the film through a machine, Pitzer showed him the explosive materials he possessed. What the two of them saw was shocking. They could see Kennedy's body being touched by the hands of unseen people. They saw the body being rolled over on its side and back. The film clearly showed an entry wound in the right temple and a corresponding exit wound on the back of the skull.[703] [704]

In an interview, David described what he and Pitzer saw:

> ...the shot that killed the President had to have come from the front...I had seen gunshot wounds before, and so had

---

[703] http://spartacus-educational.com/JFKpitzerW.htm
[704] http://www.manuscriptservice.com/Pitzer/Article-1.html

Bill. I've seen a lot of them since, and I can assure you that it definitely was an entry wound in the forehead...

...It is inconceivable that anyone even vaguely acquainted with gunshot wounds would conclude that the massive wound in the rear of JFK's skull could have occurred from a rear-entry projectile, unless it was from grenade or mortar shrapnel, which tears and rends flesh and bone rather than pierces it.[705]

FBI files released in 1997 under the FOIA suggest that Pitzer was murdered. The paraffin tests of Pitzer's hand were negative, with no trace of nitrates. That means that Pitzer did not fire the weapon. According to the report, analysis of the gunshot wounds indicate that "the revolver must have been held at a distance of more than three feet when discharged." This was determined by the fact that there were no powder burns around the gunshot wound in his right temple. The FBI could find no record of Pitzer ever acquiring live ammunition. They did, however, find out that in the Firearms Logbook in the Security Office at Bethesda, a .38 caliber revolver had been checked out in Pitzer's name. The signature in the logbook was illegible. This suggests that someone tried to make it look like Pitzer obtained the weapon for the purpose of committing suicide.[706]

Daniel Marvin knows for a fact that Pitzer was murdered. He knows because he was offered the assignment to murder him, but he turned it down. A Second Lieutenant in the army, Marvin led Special Operations Forces in Vietnam and Cambodia. The day after Kennedy was killed, he volunteered for counterinsurgency and guerilla warfare training, and became a Green Beret. He was involved in the assassination of enemies of the United States. Marvin was approached by a member of the CIA and asked to terminate William Pitzer. This request was made in August of 1965. Marvin was told that the target possessed sensitive materials, and that he was a traitor who was selling state secrets to the enemy. Marvin turned down the assignment, only because the execution was to be carried out on American soil. Marvin said he had no hesitation about committing murder on foreign soil, but drew the line when it came to killing Americans in the U.S. A little over a year later, Marvin heard about the death of Pitzer, the man he was asked to kill. He knew that someone else had taken the

---

[705] Douglass, James W., *JFK and the Unspeakable*, p. 423, Touchstone, 2008
[706] Eaglesham, Allan, *Pitzer: An Update*, 1999

assignment that he rejected. He had not known that the request to kill Pitzer was connected with the Kennedy assassination.[707]

Marvin is highly suspicious of the FBI's report on Pitzer's death. In particular, he questioned the odyssey of the revolver that killed him. But he became even more suspicious after he began his Green Beret training. He started to wonder if the CIA was involved in Kennedy's murder. But even then, he rationalized it by believing it was for some morally justifiable reason:

> The training was accomplished by highly motivated instructors, all of whom, with exception of the few CIA "advisors," had seen at least one year of combat as a Green Beret. CIA personnel were involved in instruction related to terrorism and assassination techniques, to the extent of going into detail on how the JFK "hit" was perpetrated, including film footage and photographs taken in Dealey Plaza that fateful day.
>
> I shared a "gut feeling" with a few others in my class that our CIA instructors had first-hand knowledge of what happened in Dallas. A sobering thought, particularly so in view of my motives for joining Special Forces. During a coffee break one day, an instructor casually remarked on the "success of the conspiracy in Dallas," tending to confirm my suspicions that the President's murder was conceived, executed and covered up by high-level echelons within our government. I attempted to rationalize this by believing there had to have been compelling reasons, with no malicious intent as such on the part of loyal Americans who deemed it necessary, at significant risk to themselves, to wrest the White House from one considered ill-equipped to lead our nation in those troubled times.
>
> What I subsequently gleaned led me to believe that evil factions in certain agencies within our government had engineered and executed the conspiracy that left President Kennedy dead.[708]

---

[707] http://spartacus-educational.com/JFKmartinD.htm
[708] Marvin, Daniel, *The Unconventional Warrior*, 2002

After talking with Pitzer's widow and family, Marvin had a change of heart about the Green Berets, the military, and the U.S. government in general. He realized that Pitzer was an innocent man and a loyal American. Pitzer had been presented to Marvin as "a traitor who was selling state secrets to the enemy." That is a gross distortion of the truth. Pitzer was not a traitor, the "state secrets" were the autopsy photos, and the "enemy" was the American public. Marvin is relieved that he turned down the assignment, but regrets that he accepted so many others. After becoming a born-again Christian in 1984, Marvin has crusaded to have the truth about our government exposed. He has written two books, *Expendable Elite* and *Without Smoking Gun*, which detail some of the deplorable acts which Marvin committed, but now regrets.[709]

On his website, Marvin writes about "The Psyche of a Trained Military Assassin." His tone is one of contrition:

> Documented and corroborated testimony of what I had done during 21 years of military service that was of an evil or illegal nature now serve as the foundation of my crusades against evil in our government. I care because the truth matters. Those of us who have the will to must act courageously and with integrity to communicate what we have experienced. We must include direct first-hand knowledge of what happened in Dallas on 22 November, 1963 and in succeeding days, months and years, as those same forces within our government who conspired to kill our president continue to do what is "necessary" to silence those who would bring forth evidence to prove the who, what, when and where of the conspiracy and to judiciously disrupt actions taken to cover them up...

Marvin speaks of the Green Berets who he was once so loyal to. As his loyalty is now to a higher power, Marvin no longer sees the government or the military as authoritative institutions. In fact, he compares them to organized crime:

> ...These men would be the assassins, the persuaders, the terrorists for the intelligence "community." A Green Beret, trained to function in these roles, may be philosophically more akin to a Mafia enforcer or a brother clandestine

---

[709] Marvin, Daniel, *The Fourth Decade*, 1999

operative than would be the educated CIA "handlers," conventional military personnel, or civilians.

Each of the former is in a sense a cold-blooded killer. Does it matter who gives the order or whether the "hit" is for territorial control by the Mob or a call to duty to preserve "national security," if that killing is indeed illegal? Assassinations and other deadly clandestine activities are not legal. They should never be used to "defend the national interests" or for any other so-called "political necessity."[710]

Marvin is not alone in his regret. There are thousands of others who have gone through the same indoctrination, believing it was for the good of our country and the human race in general. It is only much later that they realize they have been duped. After they have committed murder, they have no recourse except to search their souls for redemption of some kind. Telling the truth as Marvin did may help to exorcise some demons, but nothing can bring the dead back to life or console their families. The brainwashing that is done to these well-intentioned men and women is comparable to a cult. Those who are in the cult are held in check by the support of others, support that they don't want to lose. Those who leave a cult and speak out against it are considered traitors. But truth and conscience always win out. It's just a matter of when.

Garrison

Jim Garrison was the District Attorney in Orleans Parish, Louisiana. Garrison began investigating the Kennedy assassination in late 1966, after discussions with Senator Russell Long and former Warren Commission member Hale Boggs. Garrison was interested in the New Orleans-based aspects of the crime, since he believed that the planning had occurred there.

He had come to believe that David Ferrie was the key to understanding the crime. Garrison had originally arrested Ferrie shortly after the assassination, based on a tip from private detective Jack Martin. Ferrie admitted he drove to Texas on the Friday that Kennedy was shot, but he had a weak excuse for it. He claimed he was going to go ice skating at a rink in Houston. He drove through a major thunderstorm to get there, then he

---

[710] http://www.libertytothecaptives.net/reflect_green_beret.html

didn't go ice skating anyway. He spent most of his time waiting at a pay phone. Garrison turned Ferrie over to the FBI, who interviewed him and then let him go. The FBI report on Ferrie's arrest was classified top secret, and has since been reported missing from the National Archives.[711]

When Garrison began his investigation, he talked to Ferrie again. Garrison questioned Ferrie and several others who might have knowledge of the plot. He tried to keep the investigation secret as long as he could until he had collected enough evidence. But word leaked out, and the news of Garrison's investigation was reported in the *New Orleans States-Item* on February 17, 1967, causing a national frenzy. Garrison eventually arrested Clay Shaw on charges of conspiring to murder President Kennedy. Garrison was verbally attacked and slandered for daring to oppose the Warren Commission's conclusions. They tried to make him look crazy or unethical. But Garrison had a solid case, and by all rights, he should have won it. Washington must have known that, because they went to great lengths to destroy Garrison's case. They refused to let out-of-state witnesses be extradited. This greatly hampered Garrison's ability to prosecute Shaw. Still, it was a winnable case, but Shaw was eventually acquitted.[712]

David Ferrie was a key figure in the Kennedy assassination. He was fanatically anti-communist and had a reputation for being a little crazy. Ferrie suffered from alopecia praecox, which caused all of his body hair to fall out. Because of this, he grease-painted on his eyebrows, which gave him an odd appearance. Early in life, Ferrie had studied for the priesthood. He left that calling in 1944 at the age of 26, at which time he obtained a pilot's license. This eventually led him to the Civil Air Patrol in Louisiana, where he met Lee Harvey Oswald. It was Ferrie who referred Oswald for intelligence work. Later, Ferrie worked for Guy Banister in New Orleans, and was also a CIA asset working on a plot to kill Fidel Castro.

David Ferrie was also involved in the top secret project to assassinate Castro by giving him cancer. This was the project that Lee Harvey Oswald and Judyth Vary Baker were working on. Ferrie worked with Dr. Alton Ochsner and Dr. Mary Sherman, two of the most highly respected cancer researcher in the world at the time. Ferrie was not a doctor, but he ran a

[711] http://spartacus-educational.com/JFKgarrison.htm
[712] https://www.maryferrell.org/pages/Garrison_Investigation.html

laboratory in his apartment, conducting various experiments on white mice in cages.

Ferrie and Banister worked for lawyer G. Wray Gill. One of Gill's clients was mob boss Carlos Marcello. Marcello was attempting to fight deportation at the hands of Attorney General Robert Kennedy. Marcello was eventually deported and dropped off in a jungle in Guatemala without so much as a change of clothes. It was Ferrie who flew Marcello back into the United States. The mere fact that Ferrie and Banister would be so concerned about the welfare of a mob boss is interesting. Why would they care? Why would they want to bring a hardened criminal back into the country? It's because they needed Marcello to accomplish their goals. That shows that the anti-Castro extremists were aligned with organized crime.[713]

Guy Banister was a member of the FBI from 1934-54. He worked to fight communism, and took part in the investigation of the American Communist Party. In 1955, Banister became Assistant Superintendent of the New Orleans Police Department. His function was investigating organized crime and internal affairs. His strong opposition to communism earned him a position with the Louisiana Un-American Activities Committee. Banister was dismissed from the NOPD in 1957 after an incident with a gun in a bar. After that he started his own private detective agency, Guy Banister Associates.

Banister was known to be a racist. He published a racist periodical called *The Louisiana Intelligence Digest*. Banister detested the civil rights movement. He believed it was part of a communist plot to create instability in America. He monitored left-wing political activists, and he blamed them for inciting racial riots.[714]

Guy Banister died during the Warren Commission hearings. His death was ruled a heart attack, but witnesses say he had a bullet hole in him.[715]

The arrest of Clay Shaw was announced on March 2, 1967. Naturally, this was met with some resistance from Washington. Attorney General Ramsey Clark said that the FBI had already investigated Shaw in 1963, and cleared

---

[713] http://spartacus-educational.com/JFKferrie.htm
[714] http://spartacus-educational.com/JFKbanister.htm
[715] http://www.maebrussell.com/Disappearing%20Witnesses/
Disappearing%20Witnesses.html

him of any part of the assassination. Garrison quickly pointed out the contradiction inherent in that statement:

> The statement that Shaw, whose name appears nowhere in the 26 volumes of the Warren Commission, had been investigated by the federal government was intriguing. If Shaw had no connection to the assassination, I wondered, why had he been investigated?[716]

Excellent point by Garrison. If Shaw was investigated in late 1963, shortly after the assassination, then the FBI had some reason to suspect him, so Garrison's charges are reasonable. What was their basis for suspecting his involvement? If the FBI investigated Shaw, then why isn't he mentioned in the Warren Report? Clark had no choice but to change his story and say that Shaw had never been investigated. Clark said that somehow erroneous information had been published.

Clay Shaw was considered a prominent and upstanding citizen of New Orleans. He helped restore historic sites, and established the city's International Trade Mart. He was a member of the Centro Mondiale Commerciale (CMC), based in Italy, and was on the board of directors of Permindex, a trade organization in Switzerland. Shaw was known to have intelligence connections, and was also passionately anti-communist. CMC and Permindex were actually CIA fronts, and conduits for subsidies to extreme right-wing groups. Shaw was associated with Dr. Alton Ochsner, who was working on a bioweapon to eliminate Fidel Castro. In 1979, former CIA Director Richard Helms testified under oath that Shaw was a CIA contact who provided information from foreign travels, mostly to Latin America.[717]

On the day of the assassination, Banister and a friend, Jack Martin, went drinking together. They got into an argument about a missing file. Banister became angry and struck Martin over the head several times with the grip of his gun. Martin was badly injured and was hospitalized. Afterwards, Martin began telling people that Banister and Ferrie had been involved in the plot to kill Kennedy. He talked about Oswald working for Banister. He talked about the anti-Castro Cubans who were in and out of Banister's office all summer.[718]

---

[716] http://spartacus-educational.com/JFKshaw.htm
[717] https://en.wikipedia.org/wiki/Clay_Shaw#cite_note-Holland-20
[718] http://spartacus-educational.com/JFKmartinJ.htm

On November 25, 1963, the FBI interviewed Martin. Martin told them what he had seen, but the FBI did not take him seriously, and decided not to investigate Banister or Ferrie. When Jim Garrison began his investigation in 1967, he learned about Martin's claims and interviewed him. Garrison believed Martin and began investigating both Ferrie and Shaw.[719]

A possible connection between Shaw and Oswald might be proven by the incident in Clinton, Louisiana. Recall that Shaw and Oswald were seen together at the voter registration drive there. The registrar at the drive was Henry Palmer. Palmer verified the presence of Lee Harvey Oswald. He remembers not only the face, but the identification:

> I asked him for his identification and he pulled out a U.S. Navy I.D. card…I looked at the name on it and it was Lee H. Oswald with a New Orleans address.[720]

Palmer said that Oswald wanted to be a registered voter so that he would have a better chance of getting a job. Oswald told him he wanted to work at nearby East Louisiana State Hospital. Palmer told Oswald that he had not lived in the area long enough to qualify as a voter. Oswald thanked Palmer and returned to the Cadillac.

During the trial, Palmer identified Shaw as the driver of the car, and said that he believed David Ferrie was the other passenger. Corrie Collins, the chairman of the local CORE chapter, positively identified Oswald as the man standing in line, and said that Shaw and Ferrie were in the car. William E. Dunn, Sr., a CORE volunteer, also remembered the incident, and positively identified the driver as Clay Shaw. Town Marshal John Manchester also identified the driver as Clay Shaw. During the trial of Shaw, the defense tried to discredit these witnesses. The jury must have fallen for it, since Shaw was acquitted. But if these testimonies are accurate, it provides clear proof that Shaw and Ferrie were somehow connected with Oswald.[721] [722]

Ferrie had denied any involvement in the assassination, and he said he never knew Oswald. Yet, Martin insisted that Ferrie knew Oswald, and that they were both seen in Banister's office. It was discovered later that Oswald had been in Ferrie's Civil Air Patrol Unit in the 1950s.

---

[719] http://spartacus-educational.com/JFKferrie.htm

[720] http://jfk-online.com/palmer2.html

[721] http://www.jfk-online.com/impeach.html

[722] http://www.jfk-online.com/palmer.html

Garrison had the impression that Ferrie was willing to talk now. But before he could be arrested, he was found dead in his apartment. His death is puzzling. He left a suicide note and a bequeathment, yet the New Orleans coroner ruled it a death due to natural causes. Officially, he died from a massive brain hemorrhage from artery failure.[723] In reality, he was murdered to keep him from talking. Ferrie joined a long list of witnesses who met with a suspicious death. Garrison made the following statement following Ferrie's death:

> The apparent suicide of David Ferrie ends the life of a man who in my judgment was one of history's most important individuals. Evidence developed by our office had long since confirmed that he was involved in events culminating in the assassination of President Kennedy... We have not mentioned his name publicly up to this point. The unique nature of this case now leaves me no other course of action.[724]

Garrison was preparing to arrest Ferrie when his death occurred. "Apparently, we waited too long," he said. When Garrison said, "leaves me no other course of action," he meant that he had to arrest Shaw immediately before he, too, became a statistic.

Ferrie's death made a prophet out of him. After the news broke about Garrison's investigation, Ferrie had phoned Garrison's aide, Lou Ivon, and said:

> You know what this news story does to me, don't you? I'm a dead man. From here on, believe me, I'm a dead man....

Ferrie was clearly part of the assassination plot and he knew his life was in danger. The suicide notes look suspicious. One was a note to a friend, bequeathing his possessions, and the other was a comment on the intolerable state of his life. Yet, the coroner ruled it a death by natural causes. A puzzled Garrison offered this comment:

> I suppose it could just be a weird coincidence that the night Ferrie penned two suicide notes, he died of natural causes.[725]

---

[723] Phelan, James, *Saturday Evening Post*, May 6, 1967
[724] http://spartacus-educational.com/JFKferrie.htm
[725] https://en.wikipedia.org/wiki/David_Ferrie

It seems that the plotters couldn't make up their minds on this. Were they going to make the murder look like a suicide, or a death by natural causes? Maybe they got their signals crossed somehow. Maybe they started to go with the suicide story, then changed their minds and forgot to destroy the notes. To make it even more dubious, the suicide notes were typed and unsigned. Supposedly, these were Ferrie's final words:

> To leave this life for me is a sweet prospect. I find nothing in it that is desirable, and on the other hand everything that is loathsome.

Grassy knoll shooter James Files knows that David Ferrie was murdered. He knows who did it and he knows how. From his interview with Marrs and Dankbaar:

> Q: Do you know anything about David Ferrie's death?
>
> JF: Yes I do. He had a cerebral brain hemorrhage. But the cerebral brain hemorrhage that David Ferrie had, that was brought on...the tissue tear and the brain itself is just above the palate of the mouth. The hemorrhage was inflicted.
>
> Q: Ice pick?
>
> JF: No sir. Nail file. A nail file gives you the simulation of tear. You could use a stiletto, thin blade knife, icepick, but then you would see what it is. You get a clean cut. With a fingernail file, you got a smooth edge, you've got a preparated [sic] edge. And when it goes through the tissue, it's like a tear. It's like something ripping apart...Who killed David Ferrie, I'm not saying.
>
> Q: But you know?
>
> JF: I know who it was, yeah.[726]

Whoever the culprit was, he tried to make it look like the death was from natural causes. As Files explained, the nail file caused the appearance of a natural tear in the tissue as opposed to a knife cut. This was supposed to make it look natural, and the coroner did, in fact, rule that the death was by natural causes. So what about the suicide notes?

---

[726] Dankbaar, Wim, *Files on Files*, pp. 209-210 Trafford Publishing, 2005

A key witness for Garrison was Perry Russo. Russo was at a party at David Ferrie's home in New Orleans one night. According to Russo, Clay Shaw was there and so was Lee Harvey Oswald, along with some anti-Castro Cubans. At that point, Russo knew Shaw as "Clay Bertrand." Ferrie and Shaw were discussing plans to assassinate John Kennedy. Ferrie promoted the idea of triangulation- ambushing Kennedy from multiple directions. The plan was to blame it on Castro, and hopefully use it as a pretext to invade Cuba. Russo described all this in clear detail. Since the Warren Commission had already determined that Oswald killed Kennedy, and the government stood firmly behind that conclusion, then connecting Shaw with Oswald would prove conspiracy. Here we have eyewitness testimony that the assassination plans were discussed by Shaw and Ferrie in the presence of Oswald.[727]

More than likely, Ferrie was one of the ones who drove around Dallas during the early stages of the planning, looking for a good location for the assassination. He was the one who proposed the concept of triangulation. To make sure they got Kennedy, they would have shooters hit him from three directions. Ferrie discovered that Dealey Plaza provided the perfect set-up for such triangulation. The three spots for shooters were the TSBD, the Dal-Tex building, and the grassy knoll. One or more shooters were added later, which Ferrie was probably not aware of.

To help his case, Garrison subpoenaed the Zapruder film from Time-Life Corp. Time-Life fought the subpoena all the way to the Supreme Court, but was eventually forced to surrender the film to Garrison. Until then, the film had only been seen by a very select few in high places. When Garrison showed the film to the jury, it was the first time that members of the American public were allowed to see it. Since the film proved multiple shooters, it was therefore evidence of conspiracy. Garrison's job was to prove that Clay Shaw was part of that conspiracy. During the trial, bootleg copies of the film were made by investigators, giving it somewhat more exposure.[728]

Garrison subpoenaed Kerry Thornley to appear before a grand jury to question him about his relationship with Lee Harvey Oswald and others. Thornley had known Oswald in the Marines. Thornley testified, but denied that he had any contact with Oswald since their Marine days. Garrison

---

[727] http://garyrevel.com/jfk/russo.html
[728] https://en.wikipedia.org/wiki/Jim_Garrison

charged Thornley with perjury, believing he had associated with Oswald, Shaw, Banister, and Ferrie in covert CIA plots in New Orleans in 1963. He also claimed that Thornley had impersonated Oswald in 1961. Garrison's charges seem legitimate, especially considering that Thornley and Oswald had similar backgrounds. They were both stationed at Atsugi, and both were intelligence operatives. However, the perjury charges were eventually dropped.[729]

When Clay Shaw was arrested, he was asked the standard booking questions. One of those questions was, "Have you ever used an alias?" Shaw responded that he had used the alias "Clay Bertrand." It seemed innocuous at the time, but proved to be a vital key to Garrison's case against Shaw. The day after the assassination, New Orleans attorney Dean Andrews received a call from a man who identified himself as "Clay Bertrand." Bertrand asked Andrews if he would represent Lee Harvey Oswald. Andrews had spoken with Oswald on three occasions during the summer of 1963 concerning his citizenship status, his wife's status, and his undesirable discharge from the Marines. He testified to the Warren Commission about his encounters with Oswald, and also about the phone call from Bertrand. There was no mention that Bertand was Clay Shaw. Garrison later discovered that Shaw and Bertrand were one in the same. This was a breakthrough in the case, since it was a clear connection between Shaw and Oswald. That should have been the decisive factor in the trial, but the judge had other ideas.[730]

In Garrison's possession was a fingerprint card from Shaw's arrest. The card contained Shaw's signature, along with the admission that he had used the alias "Clay Bertand." But Judge Edward Haggerty ruled that the fingerprint card was inadmissible as evidence because Shaw did not have his lawyer present during the fingerprinting. Haggerty claimed that the booking officer violated Shaw's Miranda rights by asking him about his alias, even though it was standard questioning. Garrison claimed that Haggerty's ruling was unprecedented and probably illegal. This cost the prosecution a key piece of evidence, and was a turning point in the trial.

In his book, *On the Trail of the Assassins*, Garrison expressed his exasperation over Haggerty's ruling:

---

[729] https://en.wikipedia.org/wiki/Kerry_Wendell_Thornley
[730] https://en.wikipedia.org/wiki/Dean_Andrews_Jr.

From time immemorial, this had been standard booking procedure at the central lockup. We knew that there was no constitutional requirement that an attorney be present for routine questions at booking. That was not the law then, and it is not the law even today. But Judge Haggerty was changing the law before our eyes.[731]

Garrison's handling of the Shaw case has been criticized by many. One of the main criticisms was his use of truth serum and hypnosis when he interviewed his prospective witnesses. Garrison defended his use of the process:

Before we introduced the testimony of our witnesses, we made them undergo independent verifying tests, including polygraph examination, truth serum and hypnosis. We thought this would be hailed as an unprecedented step in jurisprudence; instead, the press turned around and hinted that we had drugged our witnesses or given them posthypnotic suggestions to testify falsely.[732]

Garrison underestimated the deviousness of his enemy. During the trial, the CIA pulled something new out of their bag of tricks. They planted a phony witness on Garrison's team to discredit him. Charles Spiesel was the bogus witness, and he was questioned by Shaw's chief counsel, Irvin Dymond. Garrison describes the courtroom fiasco:

Then Dymond zeroed in for the kill. Was it not a fact, he asked, that when Spiesel's daughter left New York to go to school at Louisiana State University he customarily fingerprinted her? Spiesel replied in the affirmative.

Dymond then asked if it were not also a fact that he customarily fingerprinted his daughter again when she returned at the end of the semester. Again, the witness acknowledged that this was true.

Dymond then asked him why he fingerprinted her. Spiesel explained that he did this, in effect, to make sure that the

---

[731] Garrison, Jim, *On the Trail of the Assassins*, p. 283, Warner Books, 1988
[732] https://en.wikiquote.org/wiki/Jim_Garrison

daughter who was returning from L.S.U. was the same one
he had sent there.[733]

Garrison knew instantly what had happened. Spiesel was planted by the
CIA to make the prosecution's case look ridiculous. It made Garrison look
incompetent, and it altered the whole perception of the case. Most
importantly, it changed the jurors' votes, or at least some of them. Dymond
was in collusion with Spiesel because he seemed to know exactly what
questions to ask. How could he have known to ask Spiesel if he fingerprinted
his daughter? Garrison blamed himself for not checking Spiesel's
background more thoroughly. Spiesel was a late addition to the witness list,
which should have drawn suspicion to him.

Jim Garrison lamented the lack of cooperation that cost him the case:

> The reason we are unable to extradite *anyone* connected with
> the case is that there are powerful forces in Washington who
> find it imperative to conceal from the American public the
> truth about the assassination. And as a result, terrific
> pressure has been brought to bear on the governors of states
> involved to prevent them from signing the extradition papers
> and returning the defendants to stand trial. I'm sorry to say
> that in every case, these Jell-O spined governors have caved
> in and "played the game" Washington's way.[734]

In retrospect, Garrison's mistake in dealing with the press and the public
was that he emphasized the role of the CIA, while downplaying the role of
the mafia. This made the conspiracy angle difficult for the public to accept.
Americans at that time were still very trusting of their government. They
simply could not believe that any element of the government would kill the
president. But they could accept that the mafia killed him. The public knows
that the mafia kills people, and they knew that Kennedy was at war with
them, so it is reasonable to believe that the mob killed Kennedy. Garrison
should have emphasized the mafia angle to the public. His case would have
been more acceptable and easily believable. Then, any further investigation
into the mafia's role would inevitably lead to the CIA without Garrison
having to promote that angle. The jury would have been more likely to
accept the notion of conspiracy. Garrison had been known for being soft on

---

[733] Garrison, Jim, *On the Trail of the Assassins*, p. 277, Warner Books, 1988
[734] Benson, Michael, *Who's Who in the JFK Assassination*, p. 147, Citadel Press, 1993

organized crime, especially where Carlos Marcello was concerned. Because of that, he steered the investigation in the wrong direction.

A sitting president cannot be prosecuted, so Lyndon Johnson was safe during the trial. But Garrison did make this not-so-subtle reference to LBJ when asking rhetorically who has taken action to cover up the truth:

> The one man who has profited most from the assassination - your friendly President! Lyndon Johnson.[735]

HSCA

The Zapruder film was first shown to the public on March 6, 1975, on ABC's *Good Night America*, hosted by Geraldo Rivera. Researchers Robert Groden and Dick Gregory presented the film to an anxious audience. The gasps in the crowd were audible when they saw the fatal head shot drive John Kennedy down. Putting the shock and horror aside, this was proof that the government had lied about the assassination. Sympathy quickly turned into anger, and the public responded with outrage. There had already been much suspicion about the Warren Commission's conclusions, with most people believing that the truth had not been told. The Zapruder film confirmed those suspicions. This came on the heels of the Watergate scandal, which had caused many Americans to lose faith in their government. Also in recent memory was the hopelessly futile Vietnam War, which most people felt was unjustified. Around the same time the Zapruder film was shown, the Church Committee was conducting its investigation into abusive practices by the CIA, which further eroded the public's confidence in their leaders.[736]

The House Select Committee on Assassinations (HSCA) was formed in 1976, due largely to the outrage sparked by the viewing of the Zapruder film. There had been calls for another investigation, and the American people were hopeful that now they could finally find out what happened to their beloved president. The committee was also assigned to investigate the assassination of Martin Luther King, although that received much less fanfare.

---

[735] Brener, Milton, *The Garrison Case*, pp. 220-221, C.N. Potter, 1969
[736] https://www.youtube.com/watch?v=4DwKK4rkeEM

From the start, the committee was divided among itself, with individual members fighting for the various factions they represent. The original Chief Counsel was Richard A. Sprague. The first chairman was Thomas N. Downing. Downing retired in January of 1977 and was replaced by Henry B. Gonzalez. Gonzalez and Sprague had multiple disagreements which could not be reconciled, leading to the resignation of Gonzalez. Sprague and Deputy Counsel Robert K. Tanenbaum also resigned, citing the restrictions put on the investigation. Louis Stokes replaced Gonzalez as chairman, while G. Robert Blakey replaced Sprague as Chief Counsel and Staff Director.[737]

When Blakey took over, things changed. Blakey was much more secretive that his predecessor Sprague. In Blakey's first statement to the media, he told them, "The purpose of this news conference is to announce there will be no more news conferences." Investigations were conducted in private, supposedly to protect "innocent associates." Blakey required all staff members to sign a nondisclosure agreement. The agreement was mandatory in order to remain on the committee. The agreement stated that the signer could not reveal that they worked for the committee, nor could they reveal anything they learned while working for the committee. This remained in effect indefinitely after the committee disbanded. If there was any legal action resulting from the nondisclosure agreement, the legal fees would be paid by the signer, should they lose the case. At one point, Blakey invited ten critics of the Warren Commission to Washington to exchange information. The critics were required to sign the same nondisclosure agreement. Afterwards, Blakey instructed his staff to have no further contact with those critics.

The legality of the nondisclosure agreement is in question. Some experts claim that it is in violation of the U.S. Constitution, and is therefore not legally binding. Gaeton Fonzi, for one, has written extensively and critically about the inner workings of the committee, and there has been no legal action taken against him. Still, the agreement intimidated most staff members from talking, since they would rather avoid any legal action.

To further inhibit the investigation, Blakey gave the CIA and the FBI full control over who could examine any classified files. A committee report states:

---

[737] https://en.wikipedia.org/wiki/United_States_House_Select_Committee_on_Assassinations

> All staff members on the Committee have received or are in the process of receiving "Top Secret" security clearances. The FBI, as an accommodation to the Committee, conducts the background investigations for these security clearances. The CIA then reviews these background investigations done by the FBI. After consultation with the FBI and the CIA, the full committee makes the determination regarding an individual's security clearance.[738]

In other words, the FBI and the CIA can censor the investigation by not granting a security clearance to anyone deemed unworthy. This gives them control over the investigation. This was a sell-out by Blakey. The intelligence agencies were suspected of being involved in the assassination, and now those same intelligence agencies have control over the investigation. Blakey calls this an "accommodation" to the committee. Several staff members were fired for failing to receive the security clearances.

Richard Sprague, the committee's original counsel, had refused to yield to the demands of the intelligence agencies for security clearances. He naturally saw that as self-defeating. Sprague said in a TV interview, "What's the point of getting material in the first place if they are going to control who sees it and what we can do with it?" Blakey, on the other hand, defended his actions by saying, "I've worked with the CIA for twenty years. Would they lie to me?" If Blakey worked with the CIA for twenty years, then he knows they will lie to him.[739]

Blakey found out that the CIA had a 201 file on Oswald, meaning that he worked for the agency. When Blakey obtained the file from the CIA, it was a nearly empty folder with nothing but a few newspaper clippings about Oswald. But a CIA memorandum from 1979 states:

> ...The files include the Lee Harvey Oswald 201, which fills two four-drawer safes. Oswald's 201 file was not completely reviewed by HSCA staff members.[740]

Oswald's 201 file filled "two four-drawer safes." That means that eight drawers full of files were withheld from the committee by the CIA, who Blakey thought would never lie to him.

---

[738] Marrs, Jim, *Crossfire*, p. 526, Carroll and Graf, 1989
[739] Marrs, Jim, *Crossfire*, p. 527, Carroll and Graf, 1989
[740] http://whokilledjfk.net/george_and_the_cia.htm

Under Blakey's rule, the investigation was severely restricted. The focus moved away from intelligence agencies and anti-Castro Cubans, and began to center more on organized crime. Promising leads in Dallas, New Orleans, and Miami were abandoned. Blakey had said from the start that the committee would not be looking at any new evidence, but instead would concentrate on re-examining old evidence. There was little interest in pursuing new leads. From the start, it seemed that Blakey was serving some other agenda.[741]

Bill O'Reilly was a reporter for a local station in Dallas at the time of the assassination. He related an interesting story:

> ...a guy who was (in Dealey Plaza) at the time watching the motorcade. His son found (a bullet). I can't remember his name...But he wanted to remain anonymous...He gave me this little cylinder. He said that his son had found it on the ground that day...It was definitely a slug. And the guy said he definitely dug it out of there...It was something I came across and held. And then when the committee started, I handed it over to Gaeton...and I don't think anything ever came of it. It was a pistol slug, I'm pretty sure. But again, I'm not positive...But again, I am no ballistics expert so it could have been a rifle slug.

Gaeton Fonzi said he remembers getting the slug from O'Reilly:

> I wound up with the slug just prior to going with the committee. I gave the slug to the chief investigator, Cliff Fenton, with the committee and never heard any more of it. I kept asking Cliff whether he turned it over for analysis or what he did with it. I kept getting noncommittal answers.

Cliff Fenton was asked about the slug, but didn't care to talk about it:

> I don't know nothing about that. The best thing I can tell you is to talk to Rep. Stokes. I don't make any comment on the

---

assassinations committee...You got to forgive me for that
but that's the way I am.[742]

This mysterious story shows that the HSCA was not interested in pursuing
new leads. A slug found at the scene of the crime has got to be considered
serious evidence, or else they're just not trying.

I am puzzled by two things about this story. The first is that a bystander
found a bullet and gave it to a reporter instead of giving it to a cop. The
second is that O'Reilly held on to the bullet for 15 years before turning it
over to the HSCA. Why didn't he give it to a cop right away or to the Warren
Commission? O'Reilly's credibility has been questioned on other occasions,
but in this case Gaeton Fonzi confirmed that he did receive the slug. He said
he gave it to Cliff Fenton, who was very evasive about what happened to it.
It's just one more example of missing or altered evidence, which seemed to
be the norm in both investigations.

In its conclusion, the HSCA turned out to be only slightly less corrupt than
the Warren Commission. In its final report issued in 1979, the HSCA
concluded that:

> A. Lee Harvey Oswald fired three shots at President John F.
> Kennedy. The second and third shots fired struck the
> President. The third shot he fired killed the President.
>
> 1. President Kennedy was struck by two rifle shots fired
> from behind him.
>
> 2. The shots that struck President Kennedy from behind
> him were fired from the sixth floor window of the southeast
> corner of the Texas School Book Depository building.
>
> 3. Lee Harvey Oswald owned the rifle that was used to
> fire the shots from the sixth floor window of the southeast
> corner of the Texas School Book Depository building.
>
> 4. Lee Harvey Oswald, shortly before the assassination,
> had (access) to and was present on the sixth floor of the
> Texas School Book Depository building.

---

[742] Marrs, Jim, *Crossfire*, pp. 524-530, Carroll and Graf, 1989

5. Lee Harvey Oswald's other actions tend to support the conclusion that he assassinated President Kennedy.

B. Scientific acoustical evidence establishes a high probability that two gunmen fired at President John F. Kennedy. Other scientific evidence does not preclude the possibility of two gunmen firing at the President. Scientific evidence negates some specific conspiracy allegations.

C. The committee believes, on the basis of the evidence available to it, that President John F. Kennedy was probably assassinated as a result of a conspiracy. The committee is unable to identify the other gunman or the extent of the conspiracy.

The committee believes, on the basis of the evidence available to it, that the Soviet Government was not involved in the assassination of Kennedy.

The committee believes, on the basis of the evidence available to it, that the Cuban Government was not involved in the assassination of Kennedy.

The committee believes, on the basis of the evidence available to it, that anti-Castro Cuban groups, as groups, were not involved in the assassination of Kennedy, but that the available evidence does not preclude the possiblility that individual members may have been involved.

The committee believes, on the basis of the evidence available to it, that the national syndicate of organized crime, as a group, was not involved in the assassination of Kennedy, but that the available evidence does not preclude the possibility that individual members may have been involved.

The Secret Service, Federal Bureau of Investigation, and Central Intelligence Agency were not involved in the assassination of Kennedy.[743]

---

[743] http://history-matters.com/archive/jfk/hsca/report/html/ HSCA_Report_0005a.htm

The HSCA was very reluctant to commit to the c-word. They said that Kennedy was "probably assassinated as a result of a conspiracy." They had to insert the word "probably," so they could back out of it later. Was there a conspiracy or not? How can they just say that there's a conspiracy, but not tell us who it was? It was up to the Justice Department to pursue the investigation, but no further action was taken. They made no attempt to bust the conspiracy. The committee spoke of the probability of a second gunman on the grassy knoll, but they went no further with it. They just left it hanging. But they went to great lengths to tell us who was *not* part of the conspiracy. The Secret Service was not involved. The FBI was not involved. The CIA was not involved. The Soviet government was not involved. The Cuban government was not involved. The anti-Castro Cubans were not involved. Organized crime was not involved. Yet, there was probably a conspiracy. They did not even venture to guess at the identity of a second gunman. If they had, it would seem to necessitate further investigation.

Ultimately, the HSCA blamed everything on Oswald, the same as the Warren Commission did. They could not refute the lunchroom sighting of Oswald, or the negative paraffin test on his cheek, both of which prove his innocence. They could not explain how Kennedy was driven backwards by a shot from behind. They also could not refute the discovery of the Mauser by three cops. The only mention of the Mauser is that it "was subsequently determined to be a 6.5 millimeter Mannlicher-Carcano Italian military rifle." Like the Warren Commission, the HSCA failed to attribute any reasonable motive to Oswald's alleged actions.

One of the most puzzling conclusions of the HSCA was that a shot was fired from the grassy knoll, but it missed. It missed? Did the HSCA even look at the Zapruder film? That's what motivated the new investigation in the first place. How can they say it missed? If you have seen the Zapruder film, you know that the shot from the grassy knoll definitely did not miss. That is an absurd conclusion. Where did it go? If the shot had missed, it likely would have hit a bystander on the south side of Elm Street, which it did not. No spectator there reported a bullet flying past them. No bullet was found in the grass on the south side of the street, which is where it would have landed. No divot of grass was seen flying up in the air. The committee speculated that the shot might have hit the limousine, but we do not see that in the film. There is no bullet hole in the limousine. We would have seen the bullet hit the limousine, and we would have seen smoke and paint chips flying off. No such thing happened. Their conclusion is utter nonsense, and if someone believes it, they are not paying attention.

One reason for the bogus claim of a missed shot from the grassy knoll is that the HSCA wanted to preserve the magic bullet theory. By acknowledging a shot from the grassy knoll, they were able to explain everything else the same, meaning that three other shots were fired, all by Oswald, etc. The HSCA agreed with the Warren Commission about the magic bullet theory. They agreed that Kennedy and Connally were both hit by the same bullet. They agreed that the bullet emerged in nearly perfect condition. All of that is ridiculous, of course, but we now have two government investigations that have both confirmed this fairy tale as truth. Apparently, accepting the magic bullet theory has become a symbolic way of expressing faith in the U.S. government, and the committee wanted to preserve that.

Strangely, the determining factor in the committee's decision to acknowledge a shot from the front was not the Zapruder film. It was the dictabelt recording, which was somewhat of an 11th hour discovery. The committee was preparing the final draft of their report, with their affirmation of the Warren Commission's conclusion that Lee Harvey Oswald acted alone. When they became aware of the dictabelt recording, they rewrote their findings. This recording occurred because a DPD motorcycle officer accidently left his microphone in the open position, inadvertently creating a vague recording of the assassination. The audio analysis of the gunshots and their echoes led the committee to conclude that one shot was fired from the grassy knoll area.[744]

I find it puzzling that the Zapruder film did not convince the committee that a shot came from the front, but the dictabelt recording did. To me, and many others, the Zapruder film is absolute, unquestionable proof of a shot from the right front. But the committee was unmoved by it. The dictabelt recording, on the other hand, sounds to me like a bunch of static with some vague popping sounds in the background. Yet, this convinced the committee of a shot from the grassy knoll. It is strange that both the Warren Commission and the HSCA considered the Zapruder film to be inconclusive. The Warren Commission did not have access to the dictabelt recording, but

---

[744] https://en.wikipedia.org/wiki/John_F._Kennedy_assassination_Dictabelt_recording

it's not likely that it would have changed their minds. They were determined to hang Oswald, no matter what. The HSCA was slightly more open to a conspiracy claim, mainly because it was 15 years later. Still, the scratchy sounds on the recording are nowhere near the powerful proof that the Zapruder film is, yet that is what changed the committee's conclusion.

But the HSCA's conclusion was soon negated anyway. Shortly after the committee disbanded, the FBI stated that the acoustical evidence was "invalid." The Justice Department authorized the National Academy of Sciences to undertake a study of the acoustical evidence. Known as the Ramsey panel, they concluded that:

> The acoustic analyses do not demonstrate that there was a grassy knoll shot, and in particular there is no acoustic basis for the claim of 95% probability of such a shot. The acoustic impulses attributed to gunshots were recorded about one minute after the President had been shot and the motorcade had been instructed to go to the hospital.
> Therefore, reliable acoustic data do not support a conclusion that there was a second gunman.[745]

The findings of the panel are perplexing, especially the second point. They are saying that the recording they analyzed was actually from about a minute after the president had been shot. It's strange that the HSCA didn't know that. How can they analyze the recording without even knowing the time frame? It would seem obvious, since there would be sirens, screaming, etc. And what were the four sounds that were mistaken for gunshots?

So after all is said and done, we're right back where we started. The HSCA briefly said there was probably a conspiracy, but the results were quickly overturned by the Ramsey panel. So we are back to having Lee Harvey Oswald as the lone assassin.

In an interview in 2003, Blakey blamed the CIA for the obstruction of the investigation:

> ...I no longer believe that we were able to conduct an appropriate investigation of the Agency and its relationship to Oswald.... We now know that the Agency withheld from

---

[745] https://en.wikipedia.org/wiki/John_F._Kennedy_assassination_Dictabelt_recording#cite_note-Report_of_the_Committee_on_Ballistic_Acoustics-27

the Warren Commission the CIA–Mafia plots to kill Castro. Had the commission known of the plots, it would have followed a different path in its investigation. The Agency unilaterally deprived the commission of a chance to obtain the full truth, which will now never be known. Significantly, the Warren Commission's conclusion that the agencies of the government cooperated with it is, in retrospect, not the truth. We also now know that the Agency set up a process that could only have been designed to frustrate the ability of the committee in 1976–79 to obtain any information that might adversely affect the Agency. Many have told me that the culture of the Agency is one of prevarication and dissimulation and that you cannot trust it or its people. Period. End of story. I am now in that camp.[746]

Did Blakey have a change of heart? He and the committee had absolved the CIA, among others. Now here he is, saying that the CIA withheld evidence. He acts like he found out afterwards, when actually it was known to objective investigators all along. Remember that the HSCA investigation came shortly after the Church Committee hearings, so the CIA's dirty tricks were well-known. Blakey and his committee had no excuse for absolving the CIA.

But they also absolved the mafia, too, saying that they were not part of the assassination. Yet in 1981, Blakey co-authored a book with Richard N. Billings called *The Plot to Kill the President*. It's strange to hear the word "plot" from someone who is basically a Warren Commission apologist. Did Blakey also have a change of heart regarding the mafia? In 2003, Blakey was interviewed by ABC News:

> Q: Since you believe that Lee Oswald shot the president, and you also believe that Carlos Marcello was behind the assassination, what connections do you point to between Oswald and Marcello?
>
> Blakey: I can show you that Lee Harvey Oswald knew, from his boyhood forward, David Ferrie, and David Ferrie was an investigator for Carlos Marcello on the day of the assassination, with him in a court room in New Orleans. I

---

[746] *PBS Frontline*, "Who Was Lee Harvey Oswald?" -- Interview: G. Robert Blakey -- 2003 Addendum

can show you that Lee Harvey Oswald, when he grew up in New Orleans, lived with the Dutz Murret family (one of Oswald's uncles). Dutz Murret is a bookmaker for Carlos Marcello.

I can show you that there's a bar in New Orleans, and back in the '60s, bars used to have strippers and the strippers circuit is from Jack Ruby's strip joint in Dallas to Marcello-connected strip joints in the New Orleans area. So I can bring this connection.

Did Lee Harvey Oswald grow up in a criminal neighborhood? Yes. Did he have a mob-connected family? Did he have mob-connected friends? Was he known to them to be a crazy guy? He's out publicly distributing Fair Play for Cuba leaflets. If you wanted to enlist him in a conspiracy that would initially appear to be communist and not appear to be organized crime, he's the perfect candidate. Ex-Marine, marksman, probably prepared to kill the president for political reasons.

Could he be induced to kill the president for organized crime reasons unbeknownst to him? I think the answer is yes and compelling.[747]

Blakey's statements are pointless. There is no case against Oswald, and even less when you try to connect him to organized crime. Blakey points out that Oswald's uncle was a bookmaker, which is true, but that hardly implicates Oswald. Oswald had no connection with organized crime, except for that which he encountered through his CIA activities. Then Blakey mentions strip joints in New Orleans, and their connections with Ruby and Marcello. Is that proof that Oswald killed Kennedy? He mentions that Oswald grew up in a criminal neighborhood. So did millions of other people who did not commit murder. He mentions that Oswald was a crazy guy. That's an opinion, which I don't agree with, but it's irrelevant. Millions of people are considered crazy, but they still did not commit murder. Then he mentions Oswald distributing Fair Play for Cuba literature. Is that anywhere close to proof? All of this is nothing more than wild speculation.

---

[747] http://spartacus-educational.com/JFKblakey.htm

Blakey is a walking contradiction. Whether with the HSCA or on his own, he seems unsure of what he is saying. He acknowledges probable conspiracy, but yet he absolves every possible suspect of involvement. He says that the CIA was not involved, then he rails against them for obstructing the investigation. He says that the mafia was not involved, but then he writes a book saying the mafia was involved. He was unconvinced by the Zapruder film, yet the scratchy dictabelt recording convinced him of a second shooter. He acknowledges a shot from the grassy knoll, but yet he says that it missed. After saying the shot missed, he makes no attempt to tell us where the stray bullet went. He criticizes the Warren Commission for an inept investigation, yet he supports their most absurd conclusion- the magic bullet theory. It appears that Blakey's motive is simply to confuse the heck out of everyone.

Warning?

William S. Walter was a security clerk for the New Orleans FBI office. In the early morning hours of November 17, 1963, Walter received a teletype alert from the FBI office in Washington. The teletype was headed "Urgent" and signed "Director." The message was a warning of a possible assassination attempt on Kennedy in Dallas by a militant revolutionary group. Walter phoned his special-agent-in-charge, Harry Maynard, who instructed him to phone all the relevant agents in charge of criminal informants or potential criminal informants. Walter did as instructed, and wrote down the names of the five agents he contacted. Walter was shocked five days later when he heard that Kennedy had been shot. He wondered how it could have happened with five days notice. J. Edgar Hoover then destroyed original reports on Oswald from New Orleans FBI agents. When Walter checked the relevant file, he found that the teletype was missing. No other agents could confirm his story, and even the HSCA concluded that his testimony was "unfounded."[748]

Under oath, Walter testified:

> I immediately contacted the special agent-in-charge [*sic*] who had the category of threats against the president and read him the teletype. He instructed me to call the agents that had responsibility and informants, and as I called them, I

---

[748] http://jfk.hood.edu/Collection/Civil%20Actions/
JFK%20Appeals%20FOIA%20Chrono/Folder%2038%2004-16-79/38-060.pdf

noted the time and the names of the agents that I called. That all took place in the early morning hours of the 17th of November.[749]

But Judyth Vary Baker, who knew Oswald intimately at the time, stated that Oswald had met with an FBI contact at an unknown location on the 16th of November, and that he was the source of the information. Marina Oswald confirmed the story when she wrote to the JFK ARRB. She stated, "I now believe that my former husband met with the Dallas FBI on November 16, 1963, and provided informant information on which this teletype was based."[750]

The teletype read:

> Bureau has determined that a militant revolutionary group may attempt to assassinate President Kennedy on his proposed trip to Dallas, Texas, November 22-23, 1963.[751]

The teletype states "From: Director." That would seem to indicate that it's from J. Edgar Hoover himself. That makes no sense when you consider that Hoover hated Kennedy and played a key role in the cover-up of the crime. Why would he be sending a warning memo? If Hoover was really sincere about preventing the assassination, I have to believe he would have contacted the Dallas FBI personally instead of just sending a teletype. If this warning is real, it was probably sent by someone else, and was made to look like it came from Hoover. That can't be proven, but it's a reasonable explanation.

Z-Film Sale

TV newsman Dan Rather was the first to report on the Zapruder film- the home movie of John Kennedy being shot. Zapruder had made three copies of the film. He gave two copies to the Secret Service, and kept the original and one copy. Then he arranged for two showings of the film on Monday- one at 8:00 a.m. for the authorities and one at 9:00 a.m. for the media. Richard B. Stolley, a journalist for *Life* magazine, got there at 8:00 a.m.,

[749] https://archive.politicalassassinations.net/2012/03/foreknowledge-and-forewarnings-of-the-jfk-assassination/
[750] Baker, Judyth Vary, *Me and Lee*, p. 516, Trine Day, 2010
[751] https://archive.politicalassassinations.net/2012/03/foreknowledge-and-forewarnings-of-the-jfk-assassination/

before any other journalists. Secret Service agents were present, and Stolley watched the film with them. The other members of the media showed up at 9:00 a.m. to see the film. Zapruder showed it to them, but agreed to talk to Stolley first. Stolley negotiated with Zapruder and bought the film, for $50,000.[752] In Stolley's words:

> In less than half an hour, we had agreed on a price —
> $50,000 for all print rights — and I snuck out the back door
> of the factory with the original film and one copy, leaving
> poor Zapruder to face the angry journalists in the hall.[753]

After the initial sale of the original film for $50,000, Stolley then negotiated a deal to purchase all subsequent rights to the film for $150,000. This included all print and motion picture rights.

Rather knew Stolley and described him as "a tough reporter working for an outfit with deep pockets." Rather had been authorized to bid up to $50,000 for the film, but when he talked to Zapruder, it had already been sold to Stolley.[754]

Another version of the story says that H.L. Hunt was the one who bought the original. It is widely believed that Hunt was one of the plotters of the assassination. In his book *Killing Kennedy*, Harrison Edward Livingstone writes:

> I had high-level information in Dallas that the original
> Zapruder film (from Zapruder's camera) was first obtained
> by H.L. Hunt before *Life* bought what they thought was the
> original...The indication is that Hunt's people obtained it and
> passed it on to the FBI who sent it to headquarters in
> Washington shortly after it was developed...What happened
> to H.L. Hunt's copy? Why won't the Hunt family discuss
> this?[755]

[752] http://www.whokilledjfk.net/zapruder%20film.htm
[753] http://ew.com/article/1992/01/17/richard-b-stolley-remembers-zapruder-film/
[754] http://www.dailymail.co.uk/news/article-2511587/Dan-Rather-recounts-tracking-Zapruder-JFK-assassination-film-50-years-ago--outbid-iconic-footage-Time-magazine.html
[755] http://wherechangeobama.blogspot.com/2013/06/50-years-since-jfk-assassination.html

It is not known who has the original. *Life* thought they had it, but Hunt may have had the inside track somehow. There are currently several different versions of the Zapruder film available, each with different levels of editing.

Before Rather left Zapruder that day, he was allowed to see the film once. He described his horror at seeing the film. "My head was back, my eyes were wide, my mouth was agape," he said. When he reported on it that day on the news, he told the viewing public:

> ...his head could be seen to move violently forward.[756]

Yet, the film clearly shows Kennedy's head going violently backward, not forward. Why did Rather say he went forward, instead? Although it could be a mistake in recollection, it is more likely that he lied that day, trying to make the lone assassin theory more plausible. Since it is alleged that Oswald was shooting from behind, Rather seemed to be conforming to the official line.

In his autobiography, *The Camera Never Blinks*, Rather gave this explanation of his dubious description:

> At the risk of sounding too defensive, I challenge anyone to watch for the first time a twenty-two second film of devastating impact ... then describe what they had seen in its entirety, without notes.[757]

Rather's excuse is lame. In spite of anything he said, Kennedy's head clearly went backward, not forward. Rather either lied about the film or he lied about seeing the film.

Richard B. Stolley has proven to be no more forthright than Rather. Here is Stolley's description of the fatal head shot:

> Brain matter and blood spray up and forward, a trajectory that would have been impossible if the shot had come from

---

[756] https://www.bing.com/videos/
search?q=JFK+Dan+Rather+his+head+could+be+seen+to+move+violently+forward.
&view=detail&mid=03510E4246EB58AC88C703510E4246EB58AC88C7&FORM=VIRE
[757] https://www.reddit.com/r/AskHistorians/comments/3b0iv3/
why_did_dan_rather_say_jfks_head_was_thrown/

anywhere but behind JFK and many conspiracy theorists argue that it came from the grassy knoll in the front.[758]

When we see the word "forward" there, we know it's just not true. Anyone can see it with the naked eye: Kennedy's head clearly went back and to the left, indicating a shot from the grassy knoll. Stolley had been persuaded by someone to deceive the public.

In the Warren Commission's final report, 158 frames of the Zapruder film were reproduced in black and white. However, frames 208-211 were missing, there was a visible splice in frames 207 and 212, frames 314 and 315 were switched, and frame 284 was the same as 283. J. Edgar Hoover tried to say that the switching of frames 314 and 315 was a "printing error." But such an "error" gives the impression of Kennedy's head going forward, which reinforces the Warren Commission's conclusions. It is much too convenient to be a mistake. *Life* tried to explain that frames 208-211 were accidentally destroyed, and frames 207 and 212 were damaged by a photo lab technician. The missing or damaged frames from 207-212 would show the interval between Kennedy's throat shot and the shot that hit Connally. This would prove that they were not hit by the same bullet. That proof might not be as obvious in printed stills, but it would be a reason for the alteration. If there was nothing to hide, there would be no need to alter the film.[759]

Disinformation

Disinformation is the deliberate distortion of the truth for the purpose of swaying public opinion. Sometimes it involves flat-out lies, other times it is a subtle tweaking of the truth. Sometimes it is more a matter of what is *not* said. Sometimes it means changing the subject or the focal point. It takes many different forms, but disinformation was necessary to keep the public from knowing the truth about the JFK assassination. Without such disinformation, certain people would be in jail.

Disinformation works, partly because most people do not really look closely at controversial issues like the JFK assassination. They see a few minutes of a news segment, or they see a headline in the paper, and they base their conclusions on that without looking any farther. Most people will

---

[758] http://ew.com/article/1992/01/17/richard-b-stolley-remembers-zapruder-film/
[759] https://en.wikipedia.org/wiki/Zapruder_film

not take the time to read books or watch documentaries that are not seen on TV, so they never hear alternate viewpoints. It's not really their fault, because the issues are complex, and people have other things in their lives to worry about. They trust the media to tell them what's important. That is naïve, but well-intentioned. We would like to think we can trust the media. Unfortunately, that is only wishful thinking. The government knows that the public's understanding of the issues is superficial, and they exploit that.

If someone believes that Oswald killed Kennedy, they fall into one of two groups: Either they have not looked at the event closely, or they have some motive to obscure the truth. Without exception, all lone-assassin apologists are in one or both of these groups. The average person would fall into the first group- the uninformed. They have only taken a cursory look at the evidence, and their knowledge of the event is limited. But if someone in the government or the media defends the lone-assassin theory, then there is a deliberate deception. Anyone in those fields must at least know the basic facts of the case. It's their job to know. And if they have studied the case like they should, they cannot possible believe that Oswald is guilty.

But most people in the government or media know that their careers depend on supporting the official line on the JFK assassination. Those who speak the truth will have to look for a new line of work. Even today, so many years later, the truth is still a threat to many in power. It's a threat because if people wake up to the truth about the JFK assassination, then they will also wake up to other truths, too. When they realize the government lied, they will naturally wonder what else they lied about. They will look at other events more closely. They will begin to scrutinize events more closely instead of blindly accepting the government's version of things. That would naturally lead to more dissent.

With very few exceptions, any book that says Oswald killed Kennedy is written by the CIA, or some arm of the government. Any documentary that says Oswald killed Kennedy is also put out by the CIA, or some arm of the government. That does not mean that the author or producer is a CIA agent, but it does mean that the government was somehow involved in the creation or publication of the work. The government's influence is subtle or invisible. The author may have been persuaded to write the book by someone connected with the government. He may have been guided along by someone from the CIA. There may have been parts edited out because of pressure from some element of the government. People hear of these books and documentaries, and they think that they are made by independent researchers. That is a gross misconception. I doubt that there is one independent researcher in the world who believes that Oswald was the culprit. But by making it appear non-unanimous, disinformation gives the impression that conspiracy has not been proven.

In many cases, people haven't even read these books or watched these documentaries, yet they are still influenced by them. As strange as that sounds, that is why they're effective. If people really looked at them closely, they would see what frauds they are. These books and documentaries are disinformation tools because they are not meant to be scrutinized by the public. People will hear of a book that says Oswald was the lone assassin, and it will convince them that that is reality. They will be even more likely to believe it when the book gets rave reviews, but those rave reviews only come from other CIA assets working in the media. Most people won't read the book, but they will be influenced by the reviews. They will logically figure that no one could write a nonsense book and get positive reviews. But they don't know the CIA. These are just sock puppet reviews. A CIA asset writes the book, then another CIA asset reviews the book and lavishes it with praise, which was predetermined. The reviewer probably did not even read the book, but the public will not know that. They will naturally believe that the book was a well-intentioned effort to find the truth. Sure, there are other books that say the opposite, but if someone is inclined to believe the government anyway, then it doesn't take a whole lot to convince them. It's saying what they want to hear, so they won't challenge it. They will hear talk of conspiracy later, but they will not believe it because they also heard of this other book that says there was no conspiracy. It puts just enough doubt in people's minds that they can say that it's not unanimous, and therefore conspiracy is not proven. When someone says that conspiracy is proven, skeptics will be quick to point to that book they never read as proof to the contrary.

People don't realize how much the government controls the media in the U.S. A naïve public still believes we have freedom of the press, but there is no freedom of the press when the government controls it. There are a handful of conglomerates that control most of the major media outlets in the country. They are connected with the government so that what the public sees and hears is tightly monitored. Some dissent is allowed, but truly dissenting views on major issues like JFK is not permitted. All the major media outlets eventually conform to the government's line. People watch

JFK documentaries on TV and they think they are getting a wide diversity of viewpoints, but they are not. Seeing a hundred documentaries on TV is like seeing one documentary, because ultimately they all come from the same source.

Not all individuals involved in this deception have malicious intent. To many people, it's important that the public maintains faith in the government, even at the expense of truth. This was especially true in the early days after the assassination, when the country was in turmoil and we looked to LBJ for leadership. Many felt that it was important that the country be unified, not divided, in a time of crisis. We needed our government for support, so we could not allow ourselves to believe that they were involved. We also needed to be respected on the world stage and to maintain good relations with other countries. No one wanted to be a boat-rocker at that time. Besides, in the early days the public had not seen the Zapruder film, so conspiracy was not yet that obvious. Many people in the media may have suspected collusion of some kind, but without absolute proof, they were inclined to give their government the benefit of the doubt. They cannot be faulted for that, but the same is not true for today's media.

Members of the media are never overtly instructed to lie about the JFK assassination. The manipulation is more subtle than that. Anyone who is too outspoken about it will simply not be hired. When someone applies for a position with a media outlet, they are questioned about their viewpoints in their job interview. The company would naturally like to know their opinions on the issues they will be reporting on. If they are vigilantly against the lone-assassin theory, then they will probably not get the job. If a journalist is outspoken about the assassination, they will be less likely to get the upcoming promotion. That is not said outwardly, but they all know it. If someone does rock the boat too much, there won't be a big incident where the journalist is fired for it. That would cause too much controversy. Instead, they will just wait for his contract to expire and quietly not renew it. Then they will hire someone more cooperative. In ways like these, they are able to hide the truth about the JFK assassination without overtly lying.

It is natural to wonder how so many people could go along with an obvious lie. That is why many people can't accept the reality of the conspiracy. They naturally figure that if so many respected people in the government and media go along with the main line, then it must be true. But what they don't see is the thousands of people who *didn't* go along with it. There are many people who once sought a career in politics or journalism, only to realize that they were too idealistic. Many would not go along with the lie, but we just never hear about them. They are working 9 to 5 jobs now. They are unsung heroes because they did not sell out. Maybe only a small percentage of people would knowingly support such a lie, but those are the ones who make it in politics and journalism, and the rest just disappear.

The media shapes our thinking on this by selecting which elements to focus on. When a JFK segment or documentary is shown on TV, they will avoid dealing with proof such as the Zapruder film. They may give mention of it, or gloss over it, but they will not go into a truthful and careful analysis of it. Instead, they will talk about Oswald's childhood and what a bad boy he was. They will talk about his undesirable discharge from the Marines and his treasonous journey to Russia. They will talk about his time in New Orleans and his Castro obsession. The mere fact that they are talking about Oswald at all gives the impression that he must be somehow involved. Yet, they avoid mentioning that the film shows a shot from the front, which could not have been Oswald. That is conclusive proof of conspiracy, but they ignore it or downplay it. The same show will also neglect to mention that Oswald was seen in the second-floor lunchroom by a cop just moments after the shooting. They will not mention that Oswald was denied a lawyer. But they will waste time speculating about whether or not the KGB was involved, or if Castro had anything to do with it. Anything that makes it more complicated works to their advantage. They can fill the whole show with trivial matters, further confusing the viewer who gets bogged down with needless details.

Specialists

A few of the most active disinformation specialists are John McAdams, Gerald Posner, and Vincent Bugliosi. They are all CIA assets. I cannot prove that, but it is basically just obvious. No one else would be motivated to obscure the truth like they do. They all claim that Oswald killed Kennedy, and that he acted alone. I doubt if any of them really believes that in their heart of hearts. Their arguments are so flimsy and weak, they cannot be taken seriously by legitimate researchers. They exist only to confuse the public into thinking that consensus on conspiracy is not unanimous.

John McAdams has written a book called *JFK Assassination Logic- How to Think about Claims of Conspiracy*. The title says it all. This book will tell you

442

how to think, so you won't have to think for yourself. McAdams also spouts his ridiculous theories on his website, simply called *The Kennedy Assassination*. The title of the website gives no indication that this is disinformation, which is the whole point. People who are new to the study of the assassination will go to McAdams' site, thinking they will get an objective viewpoint there. This will shape their thinking early on, and possibly discourage them from forming conspiratorial beliefs.

One of the most ridiculous examples of disinformation involves something called "the jet effect." This is a desperate attempt to un-prove what has already been proven. The Zapruder film clearly shows a shot from the right front, which is proof of a second shooter, hence conspiracy. There is no legitimate argument against that, so they have to resort to disinformation. The jet effect concept was originally developed by Dr. Luis Alvarez, a Nobel Prize winner whose motives are unclear. Using Alvarez's theory, researcher Richard Trott conducted an experiment. In response to the proof of a shot from the front, Trott tried to disprove that using melons. Yes, melons. He did an experiment where he shot at melons and noticed where the melon matter went. Some of it splashed backward toward Trott. Supposedly, this proves the jet effect theory. This theory states that when an object is shot with a rifle, that object may sometimes move back toward the shooter. Is that really true? Of course not. When something is shot, whether it is a person or a melon, the object is pushed in the direction of the shot. This is very basic and simple, and I think we all know it. If you put a tin can on a fence and shoot it, which way will it fall? Will it come back toward you? No, it will be driven forward by the momentum of the bullet. How can anyone challenge that? But disinformation specialists do. Based on the jet effect, Trott concluded that Kennedy was driven backwards by a shot from behind. Since the melon matter rebounded back toward the shooter, Trott reasoned that Kennedy is also rebounding back toward the shooter, who is behind him. That is the twisted logic of Alvarez and Trott. Naturally, some of Kennedy's blood did rebound back toward the shooter. We see it in frame 313 of the Zapruder film. But his body as a whole went back and to the left because the bullet pushed him that way, just like the melon as a whole was pushed by the bullet. The reasoning here is an insult to the public's intelligence, but the public is not paying attention enough to know that they've been insulted.

And look who speaks out in full support of Alvarez. It's John McAdams. On his website, McAdams praises Alvarez as some kind of genius for figuring this out. He is responding to the claim of a shooter on the grassy knoll when he says:

> It's supposed to prove that Kennedy was hit in the head by a shot from the Grassy Knoll. You know, the movement of his head back and to the left in the Zapruder film. But in fact, it's perfectly possible for an object hit by a bullet to move in the direction from which the bullet came. Richard Trott demonstrates this by shooting melons. Here is his first melon (link), and here is his second (link). This "jet effect" phenomenon was first suggested, and experimentally demonstrated by physicist Luis Alvarez. Trott shows that the average citizen with a rifle can recreate the effect.[760]

The second link was broken, but the first link led to a very grainy video of a man shooting a melon. He apparently does not shoot the melon straight-on. He shoots it in such a way that is spins and falls off the stand, still completely whole. If it had been shot straight-on, it would have been obliterated to pieces by the bullet. This is supposed to convince us that the fatal head shot came from behind. Watch the Zapruder film and see if you can possibly imagine that the shot came from behind.

Naturally, McAdams supports the magic bullet theory. On his website he goes into an analysis of the relative positions of Kennedy and Connally, pointing out that Kennedy was seated slightly higher than Connally, and that Connally was seated slightly inward of Kennedy. The adjustment still does not make the alignment right. It just brings it a little closer, but the theory is still implausible. McAdams then tries to explain away the two-second delayed reaction between the two men. He tries to say that they were both hit at Z-224. That is nonsense, because we see Kennedy reacting to the throat wound at Z-188. Then McAdams tries to validate the pristine bullet by showing a view of it from the tip, showing that it is slightly more damaged than we realized. That is trivial. It still does not explain how the bullet could go through two men and ricochet off the car door, and still emerge almost completely intact. Then he goes into a British science journal study about auditory stimulus response times in the human brain. This shows the common disinformation technique of inundating the reader with so much muddled complexity that they get discouraged and give up.

---

[760] http://mcadams.posc.mu.edu/dealey.htm

McAdams tried to discredit the discovery of the Mauser in the TSBD:

> Seymour Weitzman, the officer who first saw Oswald's rifle behind some boxes on the 6th floor of the Texas School Book Depository, said it was a Mauser, and several other officers repeated this statement. Before the Warren Commission, Weitzman said that "in a glance" the gun looked like a Mauser. This photo, taken from *Six Seconds in Dallas*, shows Oswald's Mannlicher-Carcano beside a Mauser. So you be the judge: could someone "in a glance" mistake one rifle for the other?[761]

The website shows photos of the two rifles so we can see how similar they look. But McAdams does not mention that Weitzman signed a sworn affidavit saying that the rifle was a 7.65 Mauser. If Weitzman was not 100% certain of it, he would not have signed a legal document to that effect. Weitzman did not just see the gun "at a glance," like McAdams claims. Weitzman held the weapon by the strap and read "7.65 Mauser" on the barrel. This was confirmed by two other officers, Craig and Boone. Weitzman was pressured into changing his testimony as a concession to the Warren Commission, so that's why he later said he saw the rifle "at a glance."

Keep in mind that many witnesses changed their testimony one way or another due to pressure. Some initially gave true statements that indicated conspiracy, then they were coerced into changing their stories to conform to the official line. In other cases it was the reverse. They were initially pressured into giving false testimony, then their conscience got the better of them and they later told the truth at some point. This gives someone like McAdams two chances to discredit them. They either lied first or they lied later, but either way, that can be used against them. But McAdams never gives the reason why they changed their stories. They were pressured by government officials to do so.

McAdams attacks the single most important element of the plot: the motorcade route. He goes to great lengths to show that the route was never changed, and that it was always intended to make the sharp turn. He thinks this will debunk the conspiracy theorists, but he completely missed the main point. The motorcade route was made the way it was only for the purpose

---

[761] http://mcadams.posc.mu.edu/dealey.htm

of the assassination. It is irrelevant if it was changed or not. It does not matter if that route was the first choice of the planners, or if another route had been chosen first and then changed. What would it matter? Even if the Main Street route really was the original route, and it had never been changed, it still means that it was made like that only to kill the president. There is no other reason or excuse for the sharp-angle turn that cost Kennedy his life. McAdams shows a newspaper from November 19 of that year, which shows the route with the sharp-angle turn. He takes that to mean that the original route was that way all along and not changed. How does he know that it was not changed earlier? Maybe it was changed on the 18th and reported in the paper on the 19th. At some point in the early discussions of the arrangements, the Elm Street route was probably suggested. They may have initially agreed to that, then changed it. The original route was never published in the paper because it had not been confirmed, but it is very possible it was at least discussed, since it seemed to be the most logical route. There must have been some confusion over this, because some newspapers showed the altered route and some did not.[762]

McAdams' analysis of Kennedy's throat wound is pointless:

> ...conspiracy books describe the Dallas doctors as being absolutely sure that the wound in Kennedy's throat was an entrance wound. What they usually omit is the fact that the doctors who actually saw the wound speculated that it was an exit wound from a fragment from the head shot.[763]

To say that the throat wound was an exit wound is ridiculous enough, but to say that it came from a fragment from the head shot is even more far-fetched. On top of that, McAdams just says that the doctors "speculated" such a theory. I don't know where McAdams got that statement. There is no citation for it on his website. But every Parkland doctor's analysis that I have heard concerning the throat wound has said without doubt that it was an entrance wound. It was described as a small, neat, round hole, which would indicate an entrance wound, as opposed to a large, shredded, jagged hole which would be more typical of an exit wound. Also, Kennedy can be seen responding to the throat wound several seconds before the fatal head shot, which proves that a separate shot caused the throat wound.

---

[762] http://mcadams.posc.mu.edu/route.htm
[763] http://mcadams.posc.mu.edu/sbt.htm

Then McAdams wastes time and space by discussing the absurd theory that a Secret Service agent shot Kennedy from within the motorcade. There are variations of this theory, but most of them come from the lone-assassin side for the purpose of disinformation. Such a claim cannot be taken seriously, but McAdams is more than happy to lead truth seekers down another blind alley. It's safe to say that the most preposterous theories come from disinformation agents. When you hear that John Kennedy was shot by aliens with space guns, that's an example of disinformation. It's an attempt to make all conspiracy theories sound ridiculous, even the legitimate ones. It works because people are not aware of the process.

Basically, McAdams just discredits everybody. He discredits Roger Craig, Jim Garrison, Judyth Vary Baker, Oliver Stone, and any witness who contradicts the lone-assassin scenario. That's cheap and dirty, since almost everyone can be found to have some imperfection in their being which would make them unworthy of being taken seriously. Yes, credibility is a factor, but McAdams overdoes it. If he can't prove someone wrong, he just discredits them.

Another disinformation agent of the CIA is Gerald Posner. His book *Case Closed* is a typical disinformation book, hailed by Warren Commission apologists as a brilliant work. But those who praise the book have probably never read it. An example of the inane arguments put forth by Posner concerns the magic bullet theory, which of course, Posner endorses wholeheartedly. Although the Zapruder film clearly shows that the fatal shot came from the right front, Posner claims that it is an optical illusion, and that the fatal shot actually came from behind. His reasoning:

> The backward movement is the result of two factors. First, when the bullet destroyed the President's cortex, it caused a neuromuscular spasm, which sent a massive discharge of neurological impulses from the injured brain shooting down the spine to every muscle in the body. "The body stiffens," said Dr. John Lattimer, "with the strongest muscles predominating. These are the muscles of the back and neck...They contract, lurching the body upward and to the rear. The President's back brace likely accentuated the movement, preventing him from falling forward.[764]

---

[764] Posner, Gerald, *Case Closed*, p. 315, Random House, 1993

All of that is complete nonsense, of course, but Posner uses a lot of big words and quotes a doctor, so it gives it the appearance of legitimacy. If people read Posner's theory and believe it, they would probably have a hard time explaining it in their own words, which would show they don't really understand it. Posner is just putting ink on paper to create the appearance of a real book, but there is nothing of substance here.

Posner took aim at the paraffin tests that concluded Oswald did not fire a rifle that day:

> Law enforcement seldom used paraffin tests in 1963, and the FBI considered them "practically worthless." As for the negative result on Oswald's cheek, the FBI did reconstruction tests where a shooter fired Oswald's Carcano rifle and there was never a positive result from any paraffin cast taken of the right cheek. The Dallas police [*sic*] had never before even conducted a paraffin test on a shooter's cheek. "I was ordered to take it. . . by Captain Fritz," remembered policeman W.E. Barnes. "I didn't ask the questions why he wanted it. . . Common sense will tell you that a man firing a rifle has got very little chance of getting powder residue on his cheek."[765]

None of the above is true. Law enforcement routinely used paraffin tests in 1963. It's hard to believe that the Dallas Police had never before conducted a paraffin test on a shooter's cheek, since it was standard practice in gunshot cases. As for W.E. Barnes, I cannot tell you what his motive is, but he is obviously in collusion here. His statement about "common sense" contains no common sense at all. A person firing a rifle will very likely get gunpowder residue on his cheek. Needless to say, if the paraffin test on Oswald's cheek had been positive, Posner would be raving about the wonderful reliability of paraffin tests.

Posner does not distinguish between spectrograph paraffin tests and neutron activation analysis, the latter being the more reliable. Oswald submitted to both tests, but the Warren Commission claimed that the results of the neutron activation test were considered invalid because the casts were washed with chemicals in the spectrograph test, which contaminated the casts for the second test. They also claimed that the casts

---

[765] Posner, Gerald, *Case Closed*, p. 349, Random House, 1993

contained traces of gun powder residue from the cartridge casings, which further contaminated the results.[766] [767]

Posner tried to distort the testimony of Officer Marion Baker, who saw Oswald just moments after the shooting:

> Baker recalled that Oswald was moving as fast as he was and was "hurrying" through a second door, which would have let him enter the office and conference area where Baker could not have seen him.[768]

Posner tries to give the impression that Oswald was running away from Baker, which would imply his guilt. This contradicts Baker's testimony to the Warren Commission:

> Boggs: When you saw him, was he out of breath, did he appear to have been running or what?
>
> Baker: It didn't appear that to me. He appeared normal you know.
>
> Boggs: Was he calm and collected?
>
> Baker: Yes, sir. He never did say a word or nothing. In fact, he didn't change his expression one bit.
>
> Belin: Did he flinch in anyway when you put the gun up in his face?
>
> Baker: No, sir.[769]

Officer Baker's testimony is among the strongest validations of Oswald's innocence, but Posner refuses to see that.

In 2007, Vincent Bugliosi published *Reclaiming History*, a dizzying dissemination of disinformation. Weighing in at about 2,000 pages, the book obscures the truth with its sheer volume. Very few people will read a book of this size, and I'm sure Bugliosi knows that. The book was given glowing reviews by people who probably never even opened it. These are sock puppet reviews, as described earlier. The assignment to review the book is

[766] *The Warren Commission Report*, p. 562, Longmeadow Press, 1964
[767] http://22november1963.org.uk/oswald-rifle-and-paraffin-tests
[768] Posner, Gerald, *Case Closed*, p. 265, Random House, 1993
[769] *The Warren Commission Report*, p. 252, Longmeadow Press, 1964

given to someone who is known to be a Warren Commission apologist, and so a positive review is a foregone conclusion. Bugliosi simply parrots the usual disinformation phrases like "mountain of uncontroverted evidence against Oswald," but then he produces none.

In 1986, Bugliosi took part in a mock trial of Lee Harvey Oswald. A program of the mock trial, called *The United States vs. Oswald*, was made for London Weekend Television. Bugliosi was the prosecutor and Gerry Spence was the defense lawyer for Oswald. It was a foregone conclusion that Oswald would be found guilty, which he was. Bugliosi would obviously not take part in a program that would prove him wrong.[770]

Without even seeing the program, it can safely be said that the mock trial was a sham. Supposedly, before any trial there is a preliminary hearing. If the suspect's Miranda rights have been violated, the case would be thrown out. That is clearly the case with Oswald. He was interrogated for hours on end and was not allowed to have an attorney. He repeatedly requested one, but was denied. Any fair judge would immediately dismiss the case based on that alone. I did not hear of any preliminary hearing that preceded Bugliosi's mock trial. He conveniently skipped that step because he could never get past it. And what about Gerry Spence? He was obviously a fake, and was not really dedicated to proving Oswald innocent. Why didn't Spence protest Oswald's lack of legal representation?

Bugliosi also ignored the fact that most of the evidence would be considered invalid because the chain of custody had been broken. Because of that violation, evidence could easily be planted or switched. The Mauser disappeared and became a Mannlicher-Carcano. Ballistics evidence was handled improperly. If Spence was sincerely defending Oswald, he would have screamed about the chain of custody breach.

One of the most ridiculous examples of disinformation is the preposterous theory that Kennedy was shot by the limousine driver. This theory does not deserve serious consideration. This will pop up in books and documentaries that appear on the surface to be legitimate attempts to find the truth. One example that I came across inadvertently is a book called *Murder from Within*, by Newcomb and Adams. After browsing the book on Amazon, it looked like a legitimate book. It discussed the motorcade route, Oswald's employment, the autopsy fraud, etc. Since it did not overtly

---

[770] DiEugenio, James, *Reclaiming Parkland*, pp. 26-27, Skyhorse Publishing, 2013

support the lone-assassin theory, it did not seem to be disinformation. I bought the book, but didn't get very far before I realized it was a fake. In Chapter Three, they describe the shooting. They claim that a Secret Service agent in the fourth car opened his door and fired a decoy shot to distract people. Then the limousine driver shot Kennedy in the throat, then he shot Connally, then Kennedy again. That is wrong in so many ways, I won't even bother to list them. A book like this gives ammunition to the Warren Commission apologists, because it makes their critics look ridiculous. The book is 90% truth and 10% garbage, which leaves the reader confused and frustrated. Beware of books and documentaries that appear to denounce the Warren Report, but actually endorse it in a roundabout way.[771]

CIA Instructions on Disinformation

Attorney Mark Lane, author of *Rush to Judgment,* filed a Freedom of Information suit to obtain records that the CIA had refused to release. The CIA had tried to discredit and neutralize Lane after his book questioned the official conclusions of the Warren Report. It was found that the CIA had issued a dispatch called "Concerning Criticism of the Warren Report." This 1967 document was basically a guide on how to disseminate disinformation, although the word "disinformation" is not actually used, since it would imply deceit. The guide assumes that the Warren Commission was right, or at least that they did the best job they could. The dispatch discourages any kind of meaningful dialogue on the subject.[772]

CIA Document #1035-960

RE: Concerning Criticism of the Warren Report

1. Our Concern. From the day of President Kennedy's assassination on, there has been speculation about the responsibility for his murder. Although this was stemmed for a time by the Warren Commission report, (which appeared at the end of September 1964), various writers have now had time to scan the Commission's published report and documents for new pretexts for questioning, and there has been a new wave of books and articles criticizing the Commission's findings. In most cases the critics have

[771] Newcomb, Fred T., and Adams, Perry, *Murder from Within,* pp. 42-55, Author House, 2011
[772] Lane, Mark, *Last Word,* p. 98, Skyhorse Publishing, 2012

speculated as to the existence of some kind of conspiracy, and often they have implied that the Commission itself was involved. Presumably as a result of the increasing challenge to the Warren Commission's report, a public opinion poll recently indicated that 46% of the American public did not think that Oswald acted alone, while more than half of those polled thought that the Commission had left some questions unresolved. Doubtless polls abroad would show similar, or possibly more adverse results.

The document mentions that 46% of Americans did not believe that Oswald acted alone. That is a subtle way of influencing people's thinking, including the agency's own members. The statement implies that it is unanimously agreed upon that Oswald shot the president, and the only question is if he acted alone or if he had help. There is no mention of the possibility that Oswald was completely innocent.

2. This trend of opinion is a matter of concern to the U.S. government, including our organization. The members of the Warren Commission were naturally chosen for their integrity, experience and prominence. They represented both major parties, and they and their staff were deliberately drawn from all sections of the country. Just because of the standing of the Commissioners, efforts to impugn their rectitude and wisdom tend to cast doubt on the whole leadership of American society. Moreover, there seems to be an increasing tendency to hint that President Johnson himself, as the one person who might be said to have benefited, was in some way responsible for the assassination.

Innuendo of such seriousness affects not only the individual concerned, but also the whole reputation of the American government. Our organization itself is directly involved: among other facts, we contributed information to the investigation. Conspiracy theories have frequently thrown suspicion on our organization, for example by falsely alleging that Lee Harvey Oswald worked for us. The aim of this dispatch is to provide material countering and discrediting the claims of the conspiracy theorists, so as to inhibit the circulation of such claims in other countries. Background information is supplied in a classified section and in a number of unclassified attachments.

They are appealing to people's sense of patriotism, claiming that the whole reputation of the American government is at stake if conspiracy theories persist. The implication is that it is un-American to dispute the Warren Report. To even suggest that Oswald may have worked for the CIA is discouraged. Notice also that they emphasize discrediting conspiracy claims, as opposed to proving them wrong.

> 3. Action. We do not recommend that discussion of the assassination question be initiated where it is not already taking place. Where discussion is active [business] addresses are requested:

> a. To discuss the publicity problem with [?] and friendly elite contacts (especially politicians and editors), pointing out that the Warren Commission made as thorough an investigation as humanly possible, that the charges of the critics are without serious foundation, and that further speculative discussion only plays into the hands of the opposition. Point out also that parts of the conspiracy talk appear to be deliberately generated by Communist propagandists. Urge them to use their influence to discourage unfounded and irresponsible speculation.

The authors of this document are assuming that their own people have never looked closely at the Warren Report. If they did, they would know that it was not the thorough job they claim it to be. To blame conspiracy theories on Communist propaganda is a dirty trick, as they are just exploiting the Red Scare hysteria of the day.

> b. To employ propaganda assets to [negate] and refute the attacks of the critics. Book reviews and feature articles are particularly appropriate for this purpose. The unclassified attachments to this guidance should provide useful background material for passing to assets. Our ploy should point out, as applicable, that the critics are (I) wedded to theories adopted before the evidence was in, (I) politically interested, (III) financially interested, (IV) hasty and inaccurate in their research, or (V) infatuated with their own theories. In the course of discussions of the whole phenomenon of criticism, a useful strategy may be to single out Epstein's theory for attack, using the attached Fletcher article and Spectator piece for background. (Although Mark

Lane's book is much less convincing that Epstein's and
comes off badly where confronted by knowledgeable critics,
it is also much more difficult to answer as a whole, as one
becomes lost in a morass of unrelated details.)

This section of the document exposes the CIA presence in the media. This
was before the Church Committee hearings of 1975, so the extent of CIA
influence in the media was not known. But as of this document, they knew
they had enough people in the media to sway public opinion. They
mentioned book reviews and feature articles. The only way they could
influence that is by having their assets in television stations and news
publications. They have their own people who write such reviews and
feature articles, only the public doesn't know that, so they think the reviews
and articles are coming from objective sources. This document encourages
the hidden CIA assets in the media to write reviews that are critical of any
book claiming conspiracy to kill JFK, and to write positive reviews about
books that praise the Warren Report. CIA assets in television stations often
hold an editorial position, which allows them to decide which stories and
features will air, and which ones won't. That is huge, as it allows them to
shape the public's thinking.

4. In private to media discussions not directed at any
particular writer, or in attacking publications which may be
yet forthcoming, the following arguments should be useful:

a. No significant new evidence has emerged which the
Commission did not consider. The assassination is
sometimes compared (e.g., by Joachim Joesten and Bertrand
Russell) with the Dreyfus case; however, unlike that case,
the attacks on the Warren Commission have produced no
new evidence, no new culprits have been convincingly
identified, and there is no agreement among the critics. (A
better parallel, though an imperfect one, might be with the
Reichstag fire of 1933, which some competent historians
(Fritz Tobias, AJ.P. Taylor, D.C. Watt) now believe was set
by Vander Lubbe on his own initiative, without acting for
either Nazis or Communists; the Nazis tried to pin the blame
on the Communists, but the latter have been more successful
in convincing the world that the Nazis were to blame.)

b. Critics usually overvalue particular items and ignore
others. They tend to place more emphasis on the

recollections of individual witnesses (which are less reliable and more divergent--and hence offer more hand-holds for criticism) and less on ballistics, autopsy, and photographic evidence. A close examination of the Commission's records will usually show that the conflicting eyewitness accounts are quoted out of context, or were discarded by the Commission for good and sufficient reason.

To claim that the critics ignore evidence is hypocritical. The commission basically ignored the Zapruder film, which is the single most significant piece of evidence in the whole case. Although the public had not seen the film at this point, I have to believe that CIA officials did.

c. Conspiracy on the large scale often suggested would be impossible to conceal in the United States, esp. since informants could expect to receive large royalties, etc. Note that Robert Kennedy, Attorney General at the time and John F. Kennedy's brother, would be the last man to overlook or conceal any conspiracy. And as one reviewer pointed out, Congressman Gerald R. Ford would hardly have held his tongue for the sake of the Democratic administration, and Senator Russell would have had every political interest in exposing any misdeeds on the part of Chief Justice Warren. A conspirator moreover would hardly choose a location for a shooting where so much depended on conditions beyond his control: the route, the speed of the cars, the moving target, the risk that the assassin would be discovered. A group of wealthy conspirators could have arranged much more secure conditions.

That paragraph is simply loaded with misstatements. Informants receive large royalties? More likely, informants end up dead. Robert Kennedy did go along with the cover-up because he had his own misdeeds to hide. To think that Ford and Russell would be motivated to expose the cover-up is ridiculous. Ford in particular was loyal to Hoover and the FBI, not the American public. And why are they questioning the assassination plot? It worked, and the culprits got away cleanly.

d. Critics have often been enticed by a form of intellectual pride: they light on some theory and fall in love with it; they also scoff at the Commission because it did not always answer every question with a flat decision one way or the

other. Actually, the make-up of the Commission and its staff
was an excellent safeguard against over-commitment to any
one theory, or against the illicit transformation of
probabilities into certainties.

e. Oswald would not have been any sensible person's choice
for a co-conspirator. He was a "loner," mixed up, of
questionable reliability and an unknown quantity to any
professional intelligence service.

Once again, Oswald was not a co-conspirator. This document does not
even remotely consider the possibility that Oswald had no part in the
assassination. Besides, what does anyone really know about Oswald's
personality make-up? He was dead before he barely had a chance to talk.

f. As to charges that the Commission's report was a rush job,
it emerged three months after the deadline originally set. But
to the degree that the Commission tried to speed up its
reporting, this was largely due to the pressure of
irresponsible speculation already appearing, in some cases
coming from the same critics who, refusing to admit their
errors, are now putting out new criticisms.

g. Such vague accusations as that "more than ten people have
died mysteriously" can always be explained in some natural
way e.g.: the individuals concerned have for the most part
died of natural causes; the Commission staff questioned 418
witnesses (the FBI interviewed far more people, conduction
[*sic*] 25,000 interviews and re interviews), and in such a
large group, a certain number of deaths are to be expected.
(When Penn Jones, one of the originators of the "ten
mysterious deaths" line, appeared on television, it emerged
that two of the deaths on his list were from heart attacks, one
from cancer, one was from a head-on collision on a bridge,
and one occurred when a driver drifted into a bridge
abutment.)

Any of the deaths mentioned by Penn Jones could have been murder.
Heart attacks, cancer, and car accidents can all be induced somehow. And
do we know that the cause of death is listed accurately and honestly? Many
of the suspicious deaths lacked a proper autopsy.

Here the CIA is advocating discrediting the notion of mysterious deaths. They exploit the fact that most of the deaths can't be proven to be foul play. The 25,000 interviews is a gross exaggeration. It probably includes Oswald's grade school teacher and Jack Ruby's barber. But it makes the suspicious deaths look less suspicious if there are a great many people interviewed, because the likelihood of someone dying is greater.

> 5. Where possible, counter speculation by encouraging reference to the Commission's Report itself. Open-minded foreign readers should still be impressed by the care, thoroughness, objectivity and speed with which the Commission worked. Reviewers of other books might be encouraged to add to their account the idea that, checking back with the report itself, they found it far superior to the work of its critics.[773]

All in all, the document is a feeble attempt to defend the undefendable. To researchers, it simply proves the infestation of the media with CIA assets, because that's who the document was intended for.

CIA Indicted

On February 6, 1985, a Miami jury officially concluded that the CIA was involved in the assassination of President Kennedy. This will probably come as a surprise to most people, since there was not a single major newspaper or national news broadcast that reported on it. This was a big story to those still interested in the case, but the CIA-controlled media buried it.

The case in question involved E. Howard Hunt, the famous Watergate burglar. Hunt sued the *Spotlight* for a story they ran claiming that Hunt took part in the JFK assassination. The jury decided in favor of the *Spotlight*, and in doing so, they admitted the CIA's involvement in the crime.

On August 14, 1978, the *Spotlight* ran an article by former CIA official Victor Marchetti. In the article, Marchetti stated that the CIA was planning to admit that Hunt took part in the JFK assassination. Their claim was that Hunt acted on his own as a rogue agent, without official sanction from the CIA. This was based on an internal CIA memo from 1966, which apparently was deliberately leaked to congressional investigators at the height of the HSCA hearings. The memo stated that Hunt had been in Dallas on the day

---

[773] http://www.jfklancer.com/CIA.html

that JFK was murdered, and the CIA was concerned about possibly having to explain his presence there. The memo was signed by CIA Director Richard Helms and Chief of Counterintelligence James Angleton. It was Angleton who had leaked the memo.[774]

Hunt had been with the agency since 1949, and was a CIA liaison to anti-Castro Cubans in the early '60s.He was involved in the Bay of Pigs operation, and in multiple CIA interventions in foreign affairs. His involvement in the Watergate scandal in 1972 made him a household name.[775]

Marchetti also stated that since Hunt was considered a villain in the public eye due to Watergate, he was now considered expendable, and the CIA had decided to sacrifice him by acknowledging his involvement in the assassination. This would absolve the CIA, since they did not officially sanction the assassination. It would also assuage the public anger somewhat, since it would finally be an admission that some element of the government was involved, albeit without authorization. Hunt would have to defend himself on his own.[776]

In 1992, Lane recounted the trial in his book, *Plausible Denial*. Until then, the only significant reporting of the trial appeared in the *Spotlight*. There had been scattered reports that Hunt lost a libel case to the *Spotlight*, but its connection to the JFK case was downplayed.

It appeared that Hunt had originally won the case. The jury decided in Hunt's favor and ordered the *Spotlight* to pay him $650,000 in damages. However, the verdict was overturned due to an error in jury instructions. The judge ordered a retrial, which is when Mark Lane took over as the attorney for the *Spotlight*.

The key witness for Lane and the defense was Marita Lorenz, an ex-CIA operative who had worked with Hunt in plots to eliminate Fidel Castro. Lorenz testified that on the day before Kennedy was shot, she arrived in Dallas with several members of the assassination team, most of who were CIA operatives. One member of that team was Frank Sturgis, who later conspired with Hunt to commit the Watergate burglary. The team drove from Miami to Dallas, transporting telescopic rifles along the way. Lorenz

---

[774] Lane, Mark, *Plausible Denial*, pp. 129-132, Thunder's Mouth Press, 1991
[775] http://spartacus-educational.com/JFKhuntH.htm
[776] Lane, Mark, *Plausible Denial*, pp. 129-132, Thunder's Mouth Press, 1991

said she was unaware of the purpose of the mission. She said that they checked into a Dallas motel, and that Hunt showed up later with a bag full of cash. Later, Jack Ruby also showed up with an envelope full of money. Lorenz said she felt uncomfortable about the whole thing. She sensed that something big was about to happen, and she wanted no part of it. She left Dallas the same day she arrived, and was told about the assassination later by Sturgis.

Hunt hurt his own case by providing conflicting stories over the years about where he was the day Kennedy was shot. Lane was quick to point out the inconsistencies. To the jury, Hunt insisted that he had been at home in Washington, D.C. with his wife and kids that day. However, his kids had asked him if he had been in Dallas that day. Reporter Joe Trento also testified that Hunt was in Dallas when Kennedy was shot and that Angleton had sent him there. Trento said that he was told this by Angleton himself.[777]

In the end, Hunt lost the case and the *Spotlight* was absolved. The conclusions of the jury in this case are historically significant. The jury forewoman told the press:

> Mr. Lane was asking us to do something very difficult. He was asking us to believe John Kennedy had been killed by our own government. Yet when we examined the evidence closely, we were compelled to conclude that the CIA had indeed killed President Kennedy.[778]

Hunt's involvement in Watergate can be traced back to Dallas. The Watergate tapes contain discussions in which Richard Nixon mentions the connections between the Bay of Pigs, JFK, and Watergate. The three events are intricately related, and involve many of the same participants, including Hunt and Frank Sturgis. Supposedly, the Democrats had photos of Hunt and Sturgis being arrested for the murder of JFK. The CIA was trying to prevent the photos from being leaked to the press, which led to the break-in.[779]

On the tape of June 23, 1972, Nixon and his Chief of Staff, H.R. Haldeman are discussing how to stop the FBI investigation into the Watergate burglary. Nixon mentioned that he was worried that the investigation might expose "the Bay of Pigs thing." Haldeman stated in his book *The Ends of*

---

[777] Lane, Mark, *Plausible Denial*, pp. 129-132, Thunder's Mouth Press, 1991
[778] http://www.libertylobby.org/articles/2000/20000207cia.html
[779] *San Francisco Chronicle*, May 7, 1977

Power that "Bay of Pigs" was Nixon's code name for referencing the JFK assassination. Nixon mentions the names of E. Howard Hunt, Bernard Barker, Richard Helms, and Bush associate Robert Mosbacher, thereby connecting them to the "Bay of Pigs thing." (Recall that Barker was identified as one of the fake SS agents on the grassy knoll.) After hearing these tapes, the Watergate investigation went into secret session and thereafter released only 12 hours of the 4,000 hours of tapes, while locking up the rest in the National Archives.[780]

In a May 7, 1977 interview with the *San Francisco Chronicle*, Frank Sturgis stated the fact about as bluntly as possible:

> The reason we burglarized the Watergate was because Nixon was interested in stopping news leaking related to the photos of our role in the assassination of President John Kennedy.[781]
> [782]

E. Howard Hunt died in January of 2007. Later that year, *Rolling Stone* magazine reported on his deathbed confession that was recorded by his son, St. John. Hunt named about a half-dozen CIA operatives who were involved in the JFK assassination. He described his own involvement as being limited to a meeting in a Miami hotel room with Frank Sturgis and David Morales. Sturgis mentioned the "big event" and asked Hunt, "Are you with us?" Hunt asked what he was talking about. Sturgis replied, "Killing JFK." Hunt replied, "You seem to have everything you need. Why do you need me?" Hunt said he would not get involved in anything with William Harvey, who he called "an alcoholic psycho."[783]

Hunt acknowledged Lyndon Johnson's role in Kennedy's murder. He gave his son a sheet of paper that diagrammed the assassination plot. It started with LBJ at the top and showed that he was connected to Cord Meyer of the CIA. St. John Hunt told of the plot:

---

[780] http://www.johnfitzgeraldkennedy.net/
thenixonbushconnectiontothekennedyassassination.htm
[781] http://jfk.hood.edu/Collection/Weisberg%20Subject%20Index%20Files/
K%20Disk/Krassner%20Paul/Item%2002.pdf
[782] http://www.johnfitzgeraldkennedy.net/
thenixonbushconnectiontothekennedyassassination.htm
[783] http://www.federaljack.com/nixon-watergate-and-the-jfk-assassination/

Cord Meyer discusses a plot with (David Atlee) Phillips who brings in Wm. Harvey and Antonio Veciana. He meets with Oswald in Mexico City…. Then Veciana meets w/ Frank Sturgis in Miami and enlists David Morales in anticipation of killing JFK there. But LBJ changes itinerary to Dallas, citing personal reasons.[784]

From the statements of St. John Hunt, we see his father's feelings about John Kennedy:

Actually, there were probably dozens of plots to kill Kennedy, because everybody hated Kennedy but the public. The question is, which one of them worked? My dad has always said, "Thank God one of them worked."[785]

Bush

On November 22, 1963, George H.W. Bush was giving a speech at a local Kiwanis Club luncheon in Tyler, Texas. He had just begun his speech when he was informed that President Kennedy was dead. He discontinued his speech at that point, due to the circumstances. He immediately got on the phone and made a call to the Houston FBI office. Bush reported that a man named James Parrott might have been involved in Kennedy's murder. The memo reads:

Bush stated that he wanted to be kept confidential but wanted to furnish hearsay that he recalled hearing in recent weeks, the day and source unknown. He stated that one James Parrott has been talking of killing the President when he comes to Houston.[786]

The reason for the memo is not clear. If Bush had heard Parrott mention that he was going to kill Kennedy, why didn't he report it beforehand? Did he have foreknowledge of the plot but did nothing? Was he trying to implicate Parrott? Did he not know that Oswald had already been chosen to be the patsy? No investigator has ever connected Parrott with the crime,

---

[784] http://www.rollingstone.com/culture/features/the-last-confession-of-e-howard-hunt-20070405

[785] http://www.rollingstone.com/culture/features/the-last-confession-of-e-howard-hunt-20070405

[786] Stone, Roger, *The Man Who Killed Kennedy*, p. 302, Skyhorse Publishing, 2013

and his name is rarely mentioned in assassination research. Parrott was simply a 24 year-old Air Force veteran who was honorably discharged. He had campaigned against Bush when he ran for GOP Chairman of Harris County in 1964. Parrott does not appear to be a major player in the assassination, yet Bush is fingering him just minutes after Kennedy has been pronounced dead.

A memo from J. Edgar Hoover dated 11-29-63 concerns a threat that a "misguided anti-Castro group might capitalize on the present situation and undertake an unauthorized raid against Cuba." The final paragraph of the memo begins:

> The substance of the foregoing information was orally furnished to us and George Bush of the Central Intelligence agency...[787]

This is proof that George Bush worked for the CIA in 1963. Yet, Bush has publicly stated that his first job with the CIA was as its Director in 1976. For some reason, he wants to hide his earlier affiliation with the agency. The memo came to light while Bush was in the White House in the 1980s. When asked about it, Bush remarked that he didn't know anything about it and that it "must be another George Bush." The CIA initially said that there was no other George Bush who was with them in 1963. Then they changed their story and said there was a George William Bush who was affiliated with them in 1963. But George William Bush was merely a clerk and was with the agency only briefly. He was not someone in a high position who would receive personal briefings from Hoover himself on matters of national security. The George Bush mentioned in the memo must have been the future president.[788]

Bush was with the agency as a recruiting officer as far back as the 1950s. The memo from Hoover was in regards to anti-Castro Cubans, and this was of concern to Bush at the time. Bush was involved in Operation 40, which was the Cuban Task Force. His function was recruiting Cuban exiles for the Bay of Pigs invasion. One of his colleagues from Operation 40 was Felix Rodriguez, who was later connected to Bush in the Iran-Contra scandal. So Bush's connection with the CIA goes back to the Bay of Pigs planning.

---

[787] Stone, Roger, *The Man Who Killed Kennedy*, p. 301, Skyhorse Publishing, 2013
[788] Stone, Roger, *The Man Who Killed Kennedy*, p. 300, Skyhorse Publishing, 2013

Col. Fletcher Prouty confirmed Bush's involvement in the Bay of Pigs. He said that in 1961, he helped to deliver three ships to Guatemala to a CIA agent named George Bush in preparation for the invasion of Cuba. He said that Bush had the ships painted to look like civilian ships, then he named them after his wife, his home town, and his oil company: Barbara, Houston, and Zapata. Bush still denies playing any part in the Bay of Pigs invasion or the Cuban exile movement.[789]

Another witness to Bush's involvement in the Bay of Pigs was grassy knoll shooter James Files:

> Q: During that time, during the time of the Bay of Pigs, while you were training and moving around in the Carribean, No Name Key and all that, did you ever hear the name George Herbert Walker Bush?
>
> JF: Oh, yeah.
>
> Q: What was his role?
>
> JF: George Herbert Walker Bush. I don't know if, I think a lot of people are not going to believe this, but he worked for the CIA back as early as 1961, that I know of.
>
> Q: How did he work? What did he do?
>
> JF: I don't know all he did, but he did a lot of recruiting work. I know he was there at the beginning for what we called Group 40, a special operations group, Group 40. If you wonder what Group 40 was, an assassination group.[790]

The appointment of George H.W. Bush as CIA Director in 1976 was part of the continuing cover-up of the truth about the Kennedy assassination. The appointment was made by President Gerald Ford, who had been supervising the cover-up for 13 years at that point, going back to his days on the Warren Commission. It is no coincidence that the appointment was made at the time the HSCA was being formed and preparing to begin their investigation into Kennedy's murder. This was done deliberately so Bush could stonewall the investigation by withholding documents, information,

---

[789] http://www.johnfitzgeraldkennedy.net/
thenixonbushconnectiontothekennedyassassination.htm
[790] Dankbaar, Wim, Files on Files, p. 225, Trafford Publishing, 2005

and witnesses. Bush appointed Ted Shackley, his former associate from JM/WAVE and the Bay of Pigs, to be his Deputy Director for Special Operations.[791]

Another connection between Bush and the JFK assassination involves George De Mohrenschildt, the Russian geologist who befriended Oswald in Dallas. Bush and De Mohrenschildt were close friends and had known each other since at least 1939, when De Mohrenschildt went to work for Humble Oil, which was founded by Prescott Bush, the father of George H.W. Bush. In 1976, De Mohrenschildt wrote the following letter to Bush, then director of the CIA:

> Maybe you will be able to bring a solution into the hopeless situation I find myself in. My wife and I find ourselves surrounded by some vigilantes; our phone bugged; and we are being followed everywhere. Either FBI is involved in this or they do not want to accept my complaints. We are driven to insanity by this situation . . . tried to write, stupidly and unsuccessfully, about Lee H. Oswald and must have angered a lot of people . . . Could you do something to remove this net around us? This will be my last request for help and I will not annoy you anymore.

The CIA staff questioned Bush about the letter. He responded with an internal memo that read:

> I do know this man De Mohrenschildt. I first met him in the early 40's. He was an uncle to my Andover roommate. Later he surfaced in Dallas (50's maybe) . . . Then he surfaced when Oswald shot to prominence. He knew Oswald before the assassination of Pres. Kennedy. I don't recall his role in all this.[792]

By all accounts, Bush was a longtime personal associate of De Mohrenschildt's. At this point in time, the HSCA was just beginning its investigation into Kennedy's murder, and Bush wanted to distance himself from De Mohrenschildt by saying he only had a passing acquaintance with him.

---

[791] http://jfkmurdersolved.com/bush3.htm
[792] https://whowhatwhy.org/2013/10/14/bush-and-the-jfk-hit-part-5-the-mysterious-mr-de-mohrenschildt/

George Bush responded to De Mohrenschildt's letter:

> ... my staff has been unable to find any indication of interest in your activities on the part of Federal authorities in recent years. The flurry of interest that attended your testimony before the Warren Commission has long subsided. I can only speculate that you may have become "newsworthy" again in view of the renewed interest in the Kennedy assassination, and thus may be attracting the attention of people in the media. I hope this letter had been of some comfort to you, George, although I realize I am unable to answer your question completely.[793]

Bush was lying when he said he was unable to find any interest from federal authorities. De Mohrenschildt's letter came the same month that the HSCA was established. The revelations of the Church Committee were still fresh in people's minds, and the government was in damage control mode. De Mohrenschildt was intricately tied to Oswald and to the CIA. Naturally, the federal authorities would be keeping an eye on him. But Bush blamed the harassment of De Mohrenschildt on the media, not the federal government.

The Third Kennedy Assassination

It is common knowledge that John and Robert Kennedy were both assassinated, but it is not widely known that there was a third Kennedy assassination. In 1999, John Kennedy Jr. was murdered when the private airplane he was flying was sabotaged. This was part of the ongoing cover-up of his father's murder. There is surprisingly little that has been written about this, compared to the thousands of books that have been written about the JFK assassination. There are only a few books about JFK Jr., and most of them are biographies that don't really focus on his death. Considering the scarcity of reporting on this subject, it will be dealt with in some detail here.

John Jr. turned three years old on the day of his father's funeral. He is seen in an iconic picture, saluting the flag-draped casket of his father. 36 years later, John Jr. himself was murdered. At the time, he was seriously considering running for the U.S. Senate seat in New York, and he may have

---

[793] https://en.wikipedia.org/wiki/George_de_Mohrenschildt

even considered running for president.[794]Being intelligent, popular, and charismatic like his father, John Jr. had a good chance of winning the election. This was a threat to those in power who were still covering up the truth about the JFK assassination. JFK Jr. would have reopened the investigation, so he had to be eliminated.

On July 16, 1999, John F. Kennedy Jr. was flying his Piper Saratoga from Fairfield, New Jersey to Martha's Vineyard, Massachusetts. On board were his wife, Carolyn Bessette and her sister, Lauren. Visibility was eight miles, contrary to reports that said conditions were foggy and hazy. The flight was going well, and at 9:39 p.m. John checked in with the FAA tower at Martha's Vineyard. At this point he was about 18 miles from the local airport. A minute later, his plane took a steep, vertical dive into the Atlantic Ocean, killing all three aboard. According to the official investigation by the National Transportation Safety Board (NTSB), Kennedy fell victim to "spatial disorientation" and lost control of the plane. However, Kennedy's plane had autopilot, which was capable of flying the plane within 100 feet of the airport. All he had to do was let the plane fly itself.[795]

Inexplicably, it took 15 hours to find the crash site. The media was not permitted to get near the scene of the wreckage recovery, and no photographs of the recovered bodies were allowed. Evidence from the plane was destroyed, a rush autopsy was done in less than four hours, and the bodies were cremated and buried at sea. All of that points to another cover-up.[796]

At about 12:30 p.m. on the day after the crash, the Public Information Office of the Coast Guard made a press announcement, stating that the FAA confirmed that Kennedy had contacted the control tower at 9:39 the previous night, and that his plane was holding steady and was prepared for its final descent. This announcement was shown on TV. Then, the announcement was retracted and the FAA and Coast Guard were silenced. Although this was a civilian crash, the Pentagon took control of the investigation, which suggests their complicity right off the bat. Then they proceeded to lie about it. They said that Kennedy had not contacted the control tower, which was not true. They said that the radar analysis showed

[794] http://nstarzone.com/JFKJR.html
[795] http://themillenniumreport.com/2016/04/who-killed-john-f-kennedy-jr-and-why/
[796] Hankey, John, (Video)- *Assassination of JFK Jr.*, 2006

a normal descent, which was not true. They said they did not know where the plane went down, which was also not true. By controlling all press communication, the Pentagon covered up the crime.

There were two alarm systems that should have been activated the night of the crash. When a plane contacts the control tower, its radar blip is recorded in the FAA system by its aircraft registration number. If the plane then descends below 100 feet outside its normal landing area, an alert is sounded automatically, which initiates a search at the point where the plane descended. At 9:38 p.m. Kennedy was adjusting his altitude to be above the level required to contact the tower for landing, so it makes sense that he made the contact at 9:39. Yet, at 9:40 his plane plunged into the ocean.

Once a plane has contacted the tower and has been cleared for landing, but does not land within five minutes, an alert is sounded that launches a search. Since Kennedy made contact with the tower, both of these alarm systems should have gone into effect. There is no legitimate explanation for the 15 hour delay. Therefore, the fact of the contact with the tower had to be buried. After the Coast Guard's initial announcement, there was no further mention of contact with the tower.[797]

After the Pentagon assumed control of the case, Lt. Colonel Steve Roark told the press:

> I only know for sure that they did not talk to the tower at Martha's Vineyard.[798]

The U.S. Coast Guard stated that at 2:15 a.m., a family friend, Carol Radziwill, called to report the plane missing and asked that a search be launched. This is strange. Why did a family friend call the Coast Guard instead of the FAA? It must be because the FAA was deliberately stalling the investigation. When the plane failed to land, family members probably tried to inquire about its whereabouts, but got nowhere. As a last resort, they had to call the Coast Guard themselves. But it was the Pentagon that now controlled the investigation. They ignored the precise radar data available from the FAA, and instead dispatched the Coast Guard to search an area

---

[797] http://911research.wtc7.net/essays/green/TheAssassinationOfJFKJr.html
[798] https://www.youtube.com/watch?v=Vehk03v23y4

100 miles away from the location of the crash. The Air Force took no other action at that time.

At 6:30 a.m. Ted Kennedy called Chief of Staff Norman Podesta, who called President Clinton at 7:00. Clinton ordered the Air Force to begin a search, which led to the aimless combing of 20,000 square miles of ocean with two planes and two helicopters. This was only a semblance of a search, done to pacify the Kennedy family and the public.

At 5:00 a.m. the FAA had constructed an N-Tap Radar Analysis of the flight path. This analysis provided a three-dimensional graph of the path of Kennedy's plane, as well as the latitude and longitude where the plane went down.[799] This is the most compelling evidence for murder. We can see how the flight path turns sharply downward at the end. This is a near-vertical descent, which could not happen by accident. Even if he was unconscious or disoriented, the plane would not make a straight vertical plunge like we see in the graph. What we would expect to see is a more gradual descent, not a straight vertical descent. Instead, the plane took a nose dive, reaching a speed of 4,700 feet per second when it hit the water.[800]

The graph showed the exact latitude and longitude of where the plane went down, but the Air Force ignored it and continued their pointless scanning of the Atlantic Ocean. Eight hours after they had the N-Tap analysis, Lt. Colonel Roark was asked by the press if he will now change his course of action. He answered:

> We'll continue on the same track that we're on, which is to search the entire area. We have nothing that absolutely pinpoints one area as opposed to another...

Reporter Martha Raditch of ABC asked Roark about the N-Tap Radar Analysis which showed that the plane went into a nose dive 19 miles west of Martha's Vineyard. Roark's lame response was:

> The radar position is just a last possible position, and it can't be confirmed that it's the aircraft we're looking for.[801]

---

[799] http://canucwhatic.blogspot.com/2014/04/who-murdered-jfk-jr.html
[800] http://articles.latimes.com/1999/jul/20/news/mn-57750
[801] https://www.youtube.com/watch?v=Vehk03v23y4

Does that mean that there was another plane crash in that area the night before? What other plane could it be? Roark's lie is totally absurd. The N-Tap graph was specifically generated for Kennedy's plane. It was based on the transponder code the FAA had given Kennedy when he checked in with the tower. Roark was lying and everyone knew it. This was a lie comparable to any that was told in the cover-up of the assassination of John Kennedy, Sr.

Kennedy's plane was equipped with an emergency locator transmitter (ELT). The ELT is a beacon that goes off when the plane crashes and signals the location of the crash via satellite. The ABC news coverage had visuals of the precise location of the crash as determined by the ELT. The Air Force ignored the ELT data and continued to search blindly over the ocean. They also claimed that Kennedy did not file a flight plan outlining his planned course of travel. That is probably also not true, since records of Kennedy's previous flights show that he always filed a flight plan before flying.

Kennedy's plane was also equipped with a flight voice recorder to capture the final moments of communication from the cockpit. When the voice recorder was recovered from the craft, the battery was missing, which caused all the data to be lost. This was another obvious sign of a cover-up.

At 7:30 a.m. the Civil Air Patrol initiated a search for the missing plane. Lt. Colonel Richard Stanley told the press that he had seen Coast Guard helicopters in the area, but the Coast Guard later said that the helicopters were not theirs. Logically then, the unidentified helicopters must have belonged to the murdering faction.[802]

After the FAA tower was contacted at 9:39, the two aforementioned alarm systems should have been triggered shortly thereafter. One alarm system should be activated if the plane descends below 100 feet outside the landing area. The other alarm system should be activated if the plane fails to land within five minutes. Either of these systems should have triggered an alarm and an immediate search, yet the crash site was not found for over 15 hours. The Coast Guard found the site at about 1:00 p.m. the following day, when they saw luggage washed up on the shore. The FAA and the Air Force had to know about the missing plane. Why did it take 15 hours?

---

[802] Hankey, John, (Video) *Assassination of JFK Jr.*, 2006

The most likely explanation is that the delay was caused by the guilty parties having to retrieve evidence that the crash was really murder. A reporter for the *Vineyard Gazette* told WCVB-TV in Boston that he saw a "big white flash in the sky" on Friday night at about the time of the crash.

Another witness, Victor Pribanic, heard the explosion while he was fishing, but he did not see it. "I heard an explosion over my right shoulder," said Pribanic. "There was no shock wave, but it was a loud bang." At the time, he didn't know what it was. The next morning, when Pribanic heard the news about JFK Jr.'s plane crash, he said he felt a sinking feeling in the pit of his stomach.[803]

It appears that Kennedy's plane was blown up in the air. Researcher Tom Flocco interviewed a former Interpol operative and CIA Division 4 team member known only as "Delbert." Delbert talked about the final classified report on JFK Jr.'s death, which he had seen:

> JFK Jr.'s plane broke in half just aft of the cabin. The damage was caused by a plastique (C-4) shape charge which was formed along the bottom of the fuselage and up along both sides of the walls. The charge was caused to be set off or exploded with a large spark generated by a barometric switch device triggered by the altitude of the plane. In other words, the assassins chose the altitude for the explosion of the plane—a standard procedure to make the target's murder look like an accident.[804]

According to Delbert, 30-40 witnesses were interviewed, and 10 of them said they actually saw JFK Jr.'s plane explode in mid-air. What is even more suspicious is that two witnesses, an aircraft mechanic and a maintenance worker, said they saw George H.W. Bush and George W. Bush at the Essex County Airport in New Jersey two days before the crash. This was confirmed by U.S. intelligence sources, who stated that the Bushes were there with two known Mossad agents, and the four of them were standing right next to JFK Jr.'s Cessna. Delbert stated that these sources are willing to testify before a grand jury.

---

[803] Dawson, Dr. Paul, *JFK Jr. Murdered*, pp. 34-35, Vistar Pictures LTD, 2017

[804] http://galacticconnection.com/jfk-jr-s-assassins-identified-in-official-report-sealed-until-2025/

From the report:

> All indication from Forensics and Physical evidence investigations lend themselves to a violent explosion, either from an altitude or barometric pressure device... Aircraft 'broke up' in mid-air, as evidenced by wide spread debris gathered from the ocean and several different beaches. This can only be caused by an onboard explosion...Considering the nature of current political leanings of subject and today's political atmosphere in America, and the before-mentioned facts, there is little doubt that subject was assassinated. In fact, team [Interpol Serial Killer Alpha Team] considers this a Political Assassination of the highest order. It was meant to alleviate a potential threat to the ruling elite. And it succeeded.
>
> At 9:39 P.M. JFK radioed the Martha's Vineyard Airport giving his location. Subject was completely calm, giving no indication of any difficulties, stating that he was making his final approach, no more than 10 miles from shore and 13 miles from the airport...When he radioed at 9:39 P.M., 17-18 miles West of Martha's Vineyard, he was at 2,500 feet. When detected on radar 29 seconds later he was at 1,800 feet, 16 miles West of Martha's Vineyard. He was then lost off radar. No MAYDAY was ever heard. Tower personnel at Martha's Vineyard Airport verified previous data, indicating an immediate catastrophic problem.
>
> All evidence at this time indicates that aircraft was in a fiery, head-long crash dive within seconds after the 9:39 radio transmission. Aircraft was equipped with a radar transponder that transmits a 4-digit ID code and the altitude. Aircraft contained a 406 MHz satellite Distress beacon which would have notified the FAA of exact lat. & long. Device was NOT Activated. Believe reason as aircraft disintegrated instantly.
>
> When SK Alpha team began investigating weather anomalies and any possible phenomenon, (weather), Radar images/data that have proven useful in such investigations, to include the observations of Electromagnetic/radio frequency phenomena, were discovered to be missing from the archives for the Eastern Long Island/Martha's Vineyard area during the two (2) critical hours in which JFK Jr's plane

apparently crashed/disappeared. This is/was more than suspect. After demanding said data from air control personnel, and receiving stammering red-faced explanations as to its whereabouts, team notes data has been intentionally 'misplaced,' or in fact lost.

The head-rest, steering yoke, pieces of the cowling, plexiglass and carpeting were literally torn apart from/off the plane, floating up on Gay Head Beach. This indicates a mid-air explosion, not a stall and crash. Debris from the crash has also been washing up on the West end of Martha's Vineyard, creating a very wide-spread area of destruction (in other words, the remains of the aircraft are spread out over a very large area of space on the Ocean, indicating a mid-air explosion, not a stall and crash).

Recorded conversation with air traffic control all indicate a calm, relaxed pilot in full command of the flight, with no difficulties in the final approach. Seconds after the last transmission, the explosion was observed and contact was lost with subject's plane.

Previously mentioned weather and electro-magnetic/radio frequency data has been lost or misplaced. Since this typically NEVER happens, a cover-up of some sort is strongly indicated....The wings of the aircraft were NOT torn off, which they would have been had subject's plane gone into uncontrollable dive, as being reported by the American press....If aircraft had had engine trouble, as reported, it should /could have simply gone into a slow glide and made a soft-water landing.[805]

Based on the eyewitness accounts of a mid-air explosion, along with the widespread debris, it seems that the most likely explanation for the crash is that the plane was destroyed by plastic explosives. The explosives could have been set off by a sudden drop in altitude. Other possibilities include the use of drone conversion or directed energy weapons (DEW), both of which are within the capabilities of the Pentagon. Of further suspicion is the missing electromagnetic/radio frequency data mentioned in the report.

[805] http://galacticconnection.com/jfk-jr-s-assassins-identified-in-official-report-sealed-until-2025/

Since that never happens otherwise, and no explanation was given, it seems to indicate deliberate sabotage that needed to be covered up.

Kennedy's plane was flying at 2,500 feet when he contacted the tower. It must have blown up just seconds after that. The report states that the explosion was caused by a barometric switch device triggered by the altitude of the plane. But from the plotters' point of view, it would have made more sense to blow up the plane *before* Kennedy contacted the tower. That way, they wouldn't have to cover up the lie that he never contacted the tower at all. Why did they detonate the explosion *after* he contacted the tower? Was this a miscalculation on their part? They knew the approximate altitude that Kennedy would be flying at. Logically, they should have rigged the device to detonate sooner, while he was still at a higher altitude.

When Navy frogmen found the wreckage underwater, they took eight hours of footage documenting the recovery effort. That footage has since been destroyed by U.S. Navy officials. The Navy said they burned the tapes "out of respect for the family." Also, a large quantity of photographs has been lost by both the Navy and the NTSB. One can't help but be suspicious of this. What would we have seen in the footage? Would we see evidence of an explosion? Would we see bodies badly burned? Would we see evidence being removed from the plane, such as the cockpit recorder or the flight log? The Navy said they did not need the footage because they had been able to recover almost all of the wreckage and determine the cause of the accident from that. But if the cause of the accident was spatial disorientation of the pilot, how can that be determined from the wreckage? There must be something to hide.[806]

There is some question as to whether there was a Certified Flight Instructor (CFI) on board the plane. John was an experienced pilot, but he needed to log a required number of hours with a CFI to earn an instrument rating, which would qualify him to fly under Instrument Flight Rules (IFR) when visibility is limited. Early reports said there was a CFI aboard, but he quickly disappeared from all subsequent reports. John Jr.'s flight log would have revealed that information, but it was suspiciously taken from the crash site and disappeared. John had only flown a total of 45 minutes at night without a flight instructor, so he likely would have requested one, and one

---

[806] http://www.federaljack.com/jfk-crash-site-footage-vanishes/

would have been available on short notice at the airport. John was recovering from a broken foot at the time and may have been limited in his ability to fly the plane, so it would figure that he would want a flight instructor aboard. He had, in fact, said to a concerned friend earlier in the day that he would have a flight instructor along with him that night. It is known that John and the others waited at the airport for 45 minutes until they departed. A likely explanation is that they were waiting for the CFI to show up. Members of the Coast Guard rescue team stated that when they arrived at the crash site, one of the seats on the plane was missing. It's possible that the plotters, who were at the crash site first, had to remove the entire seat to get the flight instructor's body out. The presence of a flight instructor on the plane would have blown the cover story. Supposedly, the plane crashed because John Jr. became disoriented, but that story would make no sense if there had been a flight instructor on board to take over.[807]

Robert Merena, a certified flight instructor who knew Kennedy and had flown with him several times before, said that he spoke with him on the day he died. He offered to fly with him, but Kennedy said that he wanted to do it alone. That led to John being quoted in headlines as saying, "I want to do it alone." There is some question as to whether or not he made that statement. Merena was interviewed by the NTSB five days after the crash, and did not mention that statement. If the statement was made at all, it was taken out of context by the press in an attempt to make John seem like a reckless and irresponsible individual who disregarded the safety of his passengers. The many people who knew him and flew with him all said that John was a careful, conscientious, responsible pilot who always followed the regulations. Kennedy was not a novice pilot, having logged 310 hours of flight experience according to the NTSB.[808]

Of further suspicion is the whereabouts of George W. Bush when JFK Jr. was killed. On Friday morning, July 16, 1999, he was campaigning in Iowa. He departed by bus at 10:00 a.m. and was not heard from for three days. His opponent, Al Gore, cancelled all his campaign rallies for the weekend out of respect for the family's loss. The press naturally wanted to hear what Bush had to say. After all, he was a former president's son, so it would be proper for him to make a statement concerning the death of another

[807] Hankey, John, (Video)- *Assassination of JFK Jr*, 2006
[808] http://911research.wtc7.net/essays/green/TheAssassinationOfJFKJr.html

former president's son. But Bush was nowhere to be found. His staff could not say where he was, what he was doing, or when he would be back. On Monday the 19th, Bush finally called a press conference to offer condolences.[809] [810]

To add to the suspicion, President Clinton ordered the bodies cremated and the ashes scattered at sea in a hastily prepared Navy funeral. That is strange, considering that JFK Jr. was never in the Navy, and the family did not consent to a Navy funeral. No pictures of the bodies were allowed, probably because they would show evidence of an explosion that could not be explained.

It may be of interest to know that JFK Jr. was the target of at least three kidnapping plots in his life, the most recent being about four years before his death. The first threat was in 1972, when John Jr. was still in elementary school. The FBI arrested eight Greeks who were planning to abduct young John when he visited the Greek island of Skorpios, which was owned by his stepfather, Aristotle Onassis. The second kidnapping plot was in 1985, two years after John graduated from Brown University. The Herndon, Virginia, Police Department received a call from an intoxicated white male who said that he and seven others would kidnap JFK Jr. that night. Then in 1995, someone called the FBI in New York with information that alleged kidnappers "had determined that Kennedy rode a bicycle in Manhattan and did not have any bodyguards." For some reason, most of the FBI files of the cases have been redacted. We see the words "armed and dangerous" on the FBI report, and some mention that Kennedy's security firm would be notified, but we cannot read much else of significance. These files were obtained by the Associated Press through the Freedom of Information Act.[811]The FBI felt they had to delete anything that was too sensitive, which was a lot.

One interesting tidbit came from an FBI inventory of materials received. It reads:

---

[809] https://www.youtube.com/watch?v=Vehk03v23y4

[810] Dawson, Dr. Paul, *JFK Jr Murdered*, p. 82, Vistar Pictures LTD, 2017

[811] http://articles.latimes.com/2000/jun/20/news/mn-42953

Accompanying handwritten/hand printed letter dated
8/26/94, beginning "Dear Sen. Biden: You are a traitor...,"
and bearing the signature "John F. Kennedy Jr."[812]

Nothing else about the letter is legible, so we are left to ponder the mystery of what John Kennedy Jr. had to say to Senator Joseph Biden.

JFK Jr. opposed the power elite, the war machine, and the crooked bankers, just like his father did. He had dreams of continuing his father's unfinished work. He had started a magazine called *George*, named for George Washington. It was a left-leaning publication, intended to expose the corruption of those in power. John Jr. was the only member of the Kennedy clan to openly denounce the Warren Commission's conclusions.

John Kennedy Jr. was planning to run for either the State Senate of New York or the presidency of the United States. He had a realistic chance of winning either election. Friends and associates say he was leaning toward the presidency. If he had become president, it would have changed history. 9/11 as we know it would not have happened. Bush was complicit, but JFK Jr. would not have gone along with it. This was a huge threat to the power elite and the war machine. They felt they had to eliminate JFK Jr., and the sooner the better. If they had waited until after he had announced his candidacy, it would be obvious to the public that it was a political assassination. That was the key- JFK Jr. had not yet announced his candidacy for president. When he died, it was seen as just an unfortunate accident, but not politically motivated. Imagine how different the public perception would have been if the crash had occurred in the midst of a presidential campaign.

So the government is covering up a political assassination. The media cooperates. Witnesses are silenced. The final FBI report has been classified and sealed away for decades. For JFK researchers, it's déjà vu all over again.

Cover-Up 2017

As this is being written in 2017, the cover-up continues. President Donald Trump has blocked the release of JFK assassination-related files. Trump had earlier said that he would release all of the files "subject to the receipt of

---

[812] https://vault.fbi.gov/John%20F.%20Kennedy%20Jr./John%20F.%20Kennedy
%20Jr.%20Part%201%20of%201/view

further information."[813] That means he expected some resistance, and sure enough, Trump caved in to last-minute requests from national security agencies that some of the files remain secret. According to the JFK Records Act, all records must be released by October 26, 2017. In a memorandum issued on that exact date, Trump stated, "I am ordering today that the veil finally be lifted." That sounds encouraging, but then he added:

> At the same time, executive departments and agencies have proposed to me that certain information should continue to be redacted because of national security, law enforcement, and foreign affairs concerns. I have no choice --today -- but to accept those redactions rather than allow potentially irreversible harm to our Nation's security...
>
> This temporary withholding from full public disclosure is necessary to protect against harm to the military defense, intelligence operations, law enforcement, or the conduct of foreign relations that is of such gravity that it outweighs the public interest in immediate disclosure...
>
> Any agency that seeks further postponement shall, no later than March 12, 2018, report to the Archivist of the United States (Archivist) on the specific information within particular records that meets the standard for continued postponement under section 5(g)(2)(D) of the Act.[814]

In other words, Trump is releasing all the records, except for the ones that the CIA and other agencies don't want us to see. So what is the point? The agencies involved were allowed to redact certain files and withhold others. They were given five months to build a case for "continued postponement." Supposedly, these records would put our military defense at risk. How can that be? If Lee Harvey Oswald was the only guilty party, then there should be nothing to hide. No legitimate explanation is given for the suppression. Once again, they simply fall back on the old reliable cop-out of "national security." After 54 years, it's hard to imagine that any information in the files would be a threat to the nation.

---

[813] http://www.cnn.com/2017/10/21/politics/trump-jfk-documents/index.html
[814] http://www.cnn.com/2017/10/26/politics/trump-memo-jfk-documents/index.html

9

SPECULATIONS

The many enemies of John Kennedy were discussed back in Chapter 2. This included a long list of groups who had a motive to eliminate him. One group not mentioned was secret societies. It is more appropriate to discuss them separately, since their effect on the assassination is more diffuse, as is their effect on society in general. It is very difficult to pinpoint the exact role that secret societies played in the assassination. In subtle ways, they affect policy, appointments, and elections, and in the long run, that affected the assassination.

Freemasonry

The granddaddy of all secret societies is Freemasonry. They have been around for centuries, but the public knows very little about them. They have a significant influence on world events, but that influence is always behind the scenes and covert. It is virtually impossible to prove their role in the JFK assassination. Unless there was a Freemason on the grassy knoll, they can never be directly connected to the crime.

The modern period of Freemasonry dates back to 1717, when the first Grand Lodge was founded in London. The practice was brought to the colonies, and has played a part in American government since the nation was born. Nine of the 56 signers of the Declaration of Independence were Freemasons. 13 of the 39 signers of the U.S. Constitution were Freemasons. 33 of the 74 generals in the Continental Army were Freemasons.[815]Among the more notable Masons in American history are Benjamin Franklin, John Hancock, Sam Houston, Davy Crockett, Paul Revere, and Douglas MacArthur. At least 15 U.S. Presidents have been Freemasons. They are: George Washington, James Monroe, Andrew Jackson, James Polk, James Buchanan, Andrew Johnson, James Garfield, William McKinley, Theodore

---

[815] http://bessel.org/foundmas.htm

Roosevelt, William Howard Taft, Warren G. Harding, Franklin D. Roosevelt, Harry S. Truman, Lyndon B. Johnson, and Gerald Ford.[816]

Lyndon Johnson is included in the list even though he only completed the first two degrees of Freemasonry. There are 33 ascending degrees of Freemasonry in all, achieved through study of the group's symbols and rituals. The Grand Lodge does not consider a man a Mason until he completes the third degree, making him a Master Mason. Johnson was initiated on October 30, 1937, in Johnson City Lodge No. 561, in Johnson City, Texas (named after his cousin). Johnson attained the second level of Freemasonry, called Fellowcraft. Like many people, Johnson dabbled in the practice, but soon lost interest or didn't have time for it. During Johnson's tenure as president, his vice-president, Hubert H. Humphrey, was a confirmed Freemason.[817]

The 33rd degree of Freemasonry can be earned or it can be honorary. Some Presidents and other influential people have been given honorary 33rd degrees for public relations reasons.[818]

Masonic Style Cover-Up

When we look at the people who covered up the truth about the Kennedy assassination, we see Freemasons all over the place. Let's take a look at some of them.

The most significant Freemason involved in the assassination cover-up is J. Edgar Hoover. Hoover was a 33rd Degree Scottish Rite Mason. He was a member of Federal Lodge No. 1 in Washington, D.C. He was a charter member of Justice Lodge No. 46 in Washington, as well as a York Rite Mason and a Shriner. Suffice to say that Hoover was deeply involved in Freemasonry. Even if he was a low-level Mason, that would be cause for suspicion. But Hoover ascended all the way up the ladder to the top. He obviously took it very seriously. How this affected his actions and policies in running the FBI is unclear, but it would be naïve to think it had no affect at all.

---

[816] http://www.cuttingedge.org/news/n1081.cfm
[817] http://freemasoninformation.com/masonic-education/famous/united-states-masonic-presidents/
[818] http://www.ramministry.org/freemasonry.htm

Another Freemason of interest is Earl Warren. He was initiated as an Entered Apprentice in 1934. He became Most Worshipful Grand Master of Masons in California in 1935. He was coroneted a 33rd degree Mason in the Scottish Rite. Warren was one of seven Chief Justices who were Freemasons. The others are: John Jay, John Rutledge, Oliver Ellsworth, John Marshall, William Howard Taft, and Fred M. Vinson.[819]

Yet another Freemason of note is Gerald Ford. Ford was initiated into Freemasonry in 1949, and he was made a 33rd degree Scottish Rite Mason in 1962. His manipulations of the Warren Commission are suspicious, and even more so when one considers his Masonic affiliation.[820]

There are still other Freemasons involved in the cover-up. Senator Richard B. Russell was a member of Winder Lodge No. 33 in Georgia.[821] Arlen Specter was a member of E. Coppe Mitchell Lodge No. 605 in Pennsylvania.[822] Allen Dulles was a 33rd degree Freemason, as was his brother, former Secretary of State John Foster Dulles.[823]

J. Edgar Hoover, as a high-ranking Mason, had been taught that loyalty to the Grand Lodge takes priority over the law. Should this man have been running the Federal Bureau of Investigation? Could he be trusted to fight crime, or even to look at it objectively? As head of the FBI, Hoover must have taken an oath of loyalty to the Constitution, but does that really mean anything? What if there was a conflict between the Constitution and the Masonic agenda? His oath to Freemasonry takes priority. He was in a position to subvert justice, and he exploited that. The Kennedy assassination was only one example of it. He looked the other way on organized crime, and basically denied that it was a serious problem. Was that his choice or was he guided in that thinking by his Masonic superiors? The Grand Lodge was happy to have someone of Hoover's stature in their fold, knowing that he had the power and influence to get things done on their behalf. I'm sure he consulted them on critical matters, and they probably influenced his actions or inactions. At Hoover's level of commitment, he had already accepted the fact that murder was permissible if it satisfied the Masonic

---

[819] http://chicagolodge.org/masonic_articles/marshall_warren.htm
[820] https://en.wikipedia.org/wiki/Gerald_Ford#Freemasonry
[821] http://www.hiddenmysteries.org/themagazine/vol14/articles/masonic-33rd.shtml
[822] http://www.freemasonrywatch.org/freemasonry.and.the.media.html
[823] http://thewebmatrix.net/disclosure/secretsocieties.html

agenda. So it's not hard to believe that he would take part in the Kennedy assassination and the cover-up.

Biographer Jim Newton described Earl Warren's view on Freemasonry:

> Warren thrived in the Masons because he shared their ideals, but the ideals also shaped him, nurturing his commitment to service, deepening his conviction that society's problems were best addressed by small groups of enlightened, well-meaning citizens. Those ideals knitted together Warren's Progressivism, his Republicanism, and his Masonry.[824]

Warren believed that the problems of society should be solved by a "small group of enlightened, well-meaning citizens." This is a twisted point of view that is nurtured by Masonic philosophy. First of all, who is "enlightened" and "well-meaning"? Naturally, Warren considers himself to possess those characteristics, and also his fellow high-ranking Masons. Is Warren really objective about that, or any Mason, for that matter? Masons believe themselves to be on a path to enlightenment, and that every degree they advance brings them closer to that goal. The 33rd degree is the highest degree of Freemasonry, so they are considered the most enlightened of all. But are they truly enlightened, or are they just deluded into thinking that they are? It is self-serving for them to believe that they are more enlightened than others. Based on Freemason's sordid history, it's hard to believe that they are really spiritually advanced. And what about "well-meaning"? Are they objective about that? Do they really have the best of intentions, while others are just selfish? That is what we would all like to believe about ourselves, but people cannot be objective about themselves. Masonic philosophy has polluted the thinking of people like Earl Warren, who believe their superior wisdom gives them the right to dictate the fate of mankind.

Warren's beliefs are antithetical to democracy. Democracy means government by the people. The majority rules. But Warren's beliefs are the opposite. Warren believes that a small group of people should determine the direction society takes. He asserted that belief when he oversaw the Warren Commission. Seven people determined the fate of the nation. Millions of people wanted the truth, but seven people decided it must be withheld. Millions of people knew Oswald was innocent, but seven people

---

[824] https://en.wikipedia.org/wiki/Earl_Warren

said otherwise. Millions of people believed the government should be held responsible for Kennedy's death, but seven people said no. Apparently, they are the enlightened ones. That is not democracy in action.

So why was Earl Warren a Chief Justice? He was sworn to uphold the Constitution, but he did not do so. Like all Freemasons, their Masonic oath takes priority over any other oath. Warren was not serving the public, neither as Chief Justice nor as head of the Warren Commission. His first loyalty has always been to the Grand Lodge. We have seen how that loyalty has subverted justice. It is likely that he consulted with his Masonic superiors on serious matters, both on the bench and on the commission.

Gerald Ford was the FBI's liaison to the Warren Commission. Ford reported back to Hoover about the daily developments in the investigation. If we have one Freemason reporting to another Freemason about an investigation headed by another Freemason, how can anyone think that Freemasonry had nothing to do with the cover-up?

So at least six of the main figures in the Kennedy cover-up were Freemasons, several of them high-ranking. Hoover, Warren, Dulles, Russell, Specter and Ford did all they could to obscure the truth and keep the public from finding out what really happened. How much they were influenced by their Masonic commitment is unclear, but most likely it was a factor.

Other Masonic connections of note:

Dan Rather was a member of the Order of DeMolay, which is basically Freemasonry for young people. After viewing the Zapruder film, Rather lied to the public, saying that Kennedy's head went violently forward.

Guy Banister was a Freemason. Banister employed Oswald at his detective agency in the summer of 1963. He helped to set up Oswald to be the patsy, although it's not known if it was deliberate on his part. Banister's gravestone has a Masonic square and compass on it.

DPD officer Paul Bentley was a 32nd degree Freemason. Bentley was one of the officers who arrested Oswald at the Texas Theater. Freemasons are known for infiltrating police departments, so Bentley was probably not the only Mason in the DPD. As a matter of morbid trivia, the cut on Oswald's forehead was caused by Bentley's Masonic ring during the scuffle.

George Dealey, who Dealey Plaza is named for, was a 33rd degree Freemason and a Knights Templar. He was the publisher of the *Dallas Morning News*.

Abraham Zapruder was a 33rd degree Freemason. There is no reason to suspect Zapruder in either the plot or the cover-up. He did, however, take the historic film that recorded the event. It's possible that the altering of the film could have had Masonic connections.

There is a Masonic obelisk in Dealey Plaza. The plaque at the base of the obelisk states that Dealey Plaza housed the first Masonic lodge in Dallas.[825]

Corruption

Freemasonry exists to corrupt. They corrupt governments, courts, police departments, schools, churches, institutions, and activist groups. Since the founding of modern Freemasonry in 1717, more than a dozen countries have banned Freemasonry from existing within their borders.[826]The Catholic Church has denounced Freemasonry, as have about 20 Protestant denominations. Freemasonry corrupts by means of infiltration. They infiltrate police departments, where they are in a position to destroy evidence or intimidate witnesses to get a fellow Mason acquitted. They can also plant evidence to frame the enemies of Freemasonry. Police who are Freemasons will refuse to testify against a brother Mason. Masons who are judges will give favorable decisions to fellow Masons, in spite of their obligation to remain impartial. Although it is not widely known, Masonic infiltration in the Vatican led to the pedophilia scandal that shook the Catholic Church in the latter half of the 20th century. These are just a few examples of how Freemasons subvert justice and contaminate society.[827]

The evils of Freemasonry became apparent in the early days of the USA. A strong movement against Freemasonry gained momentum in 1826 with the disappearance of Captain William Morgan. Morgan, a disgruntled Mason, was planning to publish an expose` on Freemasonry entitled *Illustrations of Masonry*, which would reveal the inner workings and secrets of the organization. As a Mason, Morgan had taken an oath never to reveal the passwords, grips, and secrets of the fraternity. Masons denounced

---

[825] https://www.youtube.com/watch?v=n3QvQKZFKJs
[826] https://en.wikipedia.org/wiki/Suppression_of_Freemasonry
[827] https://en.wikipedia.org/wiki/Opposition_to_Freemasonry_within_Christianity

Morgan for breaking his word. Morgan was arrested on trumped-up charges, which included non-payment of a loan and allegedly stealing a shirt and tie. His debt was paid by his publisher, who secured his release. After that, Morgan disappeared. It was generally assumed that he was kidnapped and murdered by Freemasons to prevent publication of his book. The book was published after his presumed death and became a best-seller, due to the publicity caused by the events surrounding his disappearance. Public awareness of the evils of Freemasonry grew, and culminated in the formation of the Anti-Masonic Party, which ran William Wirt as a presidential candidate in 1832. It speaks volumes that an entire political party was formed solely for the purpose of eradicating Freemasonry.[828]

President John Quincy Adams stated his feelings about the organization without ambiguity:

> I do conscientiously and sincerely believe that the Order of Freemasonry, if not the greatest, is one of the greatest moral and political evils under which the Union is now laboring...a conspiracy of the few against the equal rights of the many...Masonry ought forever to be abolished. It is wrong-essentially wrong- a seed of evil which, can never produce any good.[829]

Someone may have gotten their position with the help of Freemasons, and they will then feel obligated to repay them. If it involves a politician, the repayment could take the form of supporting legislation favored by Masons. If it involves a judge, his verdict in a case might be influenced by his Masonic affiliations. They are corrupted because they are beholden to Freemasonry, hence their loyalties are misplaced.

Masons do all this because their loyalty to the Grand Lodge takes priority over their loyalty to the law:

> As Masons climb the Masonic ladder, their oaths contain instructions not to testify against a Brother Mason, even though he has committed a crime. The Mason, taken the oath of the Third Degree, promises to conceal all crimes committed by a Fellow Mason, except those of Treason and

---

[828] https://en.wikipedia.org/wiki/William_Morgan_(anti-Mason)

[829] http://www.atlanteanconspiracy.com/2008/06/quotes-from-historical-anti-masons.html

Murder. However, by the Thirteenth Degree, the oath is taken to the effect that all crimes are to be covered and concealed, even murder and treason. This means that, if a Mason has committed murder and the judge is also a Mason, the judge is obligated by his Masonic oath to set the murderer free. This may even mean placing the blame on an innocent person! In fact, this command is given in one handbook: 'You must conceal all the crimes of your brother Masons ... and should you be summoned as a witness against a brother, be always sure to shield him ... It may be perjury to do this, it is true, but you are keeping your obligations."[830]
[831]

So Masons are instructed to cover for fellow Masons who have committed treason and murder. This is at only the 13th degree. That means that by the 13th degree, they are already so indoctrinated with Masonic philosophy that they will defend murderers. So what is their mind-set by the time they reach the 33rd degree? At that point, the Grand Lodge has replaced their conscience as their moral guide.

Freemasonry draws good people into a bad situation, and it does so by deception. Freemasonry is compartmentalized, much like intelligence agencies and organized crime. There are 33 levels, or degrees, of Freemasonry. The introductory levels are very simple and innocent, and not likely to arouse suspicion. But as one ascends up the ladder to the higher levels, the doctrine becomes more sinister. It moves away from what is best for mankind, and instead moves toward what serves the Masonic agenda. That agenda becomes more and more twisted, until at the 33rd level, the individual can no longer distinguish right from wrong. At that point they are fully indoctrinated with Masonic ideology and they cannot see the evil in it.

Researcher Jeff Rense comments on Freemasonry:

> Freemasons portray themselves as a good charitable fraternity of men. They own the media so they get to say what they want. They have infiltrated all of society...

---

[830] Burns, Cathy, *Hidden Secrets of the Eastern Star*, Chapter 4, Sharing Publishing, 1994
[831] http://www.cuttingedge.org/news/n1656.cfm

In defense of most Masons, they were conned in the first place. They were led to believe it was a good fraternity of men, then they were hoodwinked and threatened with violence. If they had known this before they joined, nobody would have anywhere near them. Masons are trapped into this extreme evil, they are too scared to talk freely. They have become FM slaves and most have become crooked benefactors.[832]

Author Stephen Knight interviewed a former Mason named "Christopher," who describes the inner workings of the organization:

… Private information on anybody in the country could normally be accessed very rapidly through endless permutations of masonic contacts – police, magistrates, solicitors, bank managers, Post Office staff ('very useful in supplying copies of a man's mail'), doctors, government employee bosses of firms and nationalized industries etc., etc. dossier of personal data could be built up on anybody very quickly. When the major facts of an individual's life were known, areas of vulnerability would become apparent. Perhaps he is in financial difficulties; perhaps he has some social vice – if married he might 'retain a mistress' or have proclivity for visiting prostitutes; perhaps there is something in his past he wishes to keep buried, some guilty secret, a criminal offence (easily obtainable through Freemason police of doubtful virtue), or other blemish on his character: all these and more could be discovered via the wide-ranging masons network of 600,000 contacts, a great many of whom were disposed to do favours for one another because that had been their prime motive for joining. Even decent Masons could often be 'conned' into providing information on the basis that 'Brother Smith needs this to help the person involved'.[833]

The Masonic system operates very much like an intelligence agency, with various contacts in all walks of life to prepare them for any occasion. Christopher mentioned how areas of vulnerability are exploited. Social vices, like prostitutes and mistresses, can be used against a person. We are

---

[832] http://www.rense.com/general77/freem.htm
[833] Knight, Stephen, *The Brotherhood*, Acacia Press, 1984

talking about blackmail, here, which is something J. Edgar Hoover was intimately familiar with. Hoover blackmailed his enemies into silence, while at the same time being blackmailed by the mob. He was deeply involved with an organization that specializes in exploiting people's weaknesses. The Grand Lodge might have taught Hoover a thing or two about the practice of blackmail.

There are many similarities between Freemasonry and the CIA. They are both highly compartmentalized. They both have an extensive network of contacts available to them. They both insist on absolute secrecy concerning their activities. They both preach a code of ethics that is above the law. There is bound to be some overlap between the two entities. Since they both have a similar mind-set, there are bound to be individuals who are connected with both groups, either as a member or as a contact. The CIA is no doubt aware of the sinister actions of Freemasonry, but would they expose them? Probably not, because Freemasonry can be seen as an asset to the CIA. By working with Freemasonry instead of against them, the CIA can make use of the contacts and resources they possess. Most likely, the CIA has annexed Freemasonry to some extent, thus expanding their sphere of influence.

More from Christopher:

> Masonic police can harass, arrest on false charges, and plant evidence. 'A businessman in a small community or person in public office arrested for dealing in child pornography, for indecent exposure, or for trafficking in drugs is at the end of the line,' said Christopher. 'He will never work again. Some people have committed suicide after experiences of that kind.'

> Masons can bring about the situation where credit companies and banks withdraw credit facilities from individual clients and tradesmen, said my informant. Bank can foreclose. People who rely on the telephone for their work can be cut off for long periods. Masonic employees of local authorities can arrange for a person's drains to be inspected and extensive damage to be reported, thus burdening the person with huge repair bills; workmen carrying out the job can 'find' – In reality cause – further damage. Again with regard to legal matters, a fair hearing is hard to get when a man in ordinary circumstances is in financial difficulties. If he is

488

trying to fight a group of unprincipled Freemasons skilled in using the 'network' it will be impossible because masonic Department of Health and Social Security and Law Society officials can delay applications for Legal Aid endlessly.

Employers, if they are Freemasons or not, can be given private information about a man who has made himself an enemy of Masonry. At worst he will be dismissed (if the information is true) or consistently passed over for promotion.[834]

Thanks to Christopher, we get an idea of the inner workings of Freemasonry. No doubt, he put himself in danger by saying all this, because it's obviously not meant for public consumption. But it shows that Freemasonry will stop at nothing to promote their twisted agenda. It may seem shocking that anyone could accept such a blatantly amoral code, but remember that they are indoctrinated with this a little at a time. It starts off innocently enough, and the new Mason has no idea what he is getting into. At some point, they see things that may seem improper, but they go along with it because their brother Masons do. It is a natural human tendency to do as others do, especially when those others are people you are close to and care about. Freemasonry exploits that natural human tendency.

Masonic lodges are governed at the regional level by a Grand Lodge, and each Grand Lodge is independent. There is no worldwide Grand Lodge that supervises all of Freemasonry. That protects them legally, because if one Grand Lodge is found guilty of illegal activity, all the other lodges are protected because they can claim no legal affiliation with the guilty lodge. This prevents the entire body of Freemasonry from collapsing due to a scandal, of which there have been many.[835]

Former KGB First Chief Directorate Col. Stanislav Lekarev wrote about the connections between Freemasonry and intelligence agencies:

In the "Masonic-intelligence" complex, it's difficult to say who's more central – who's the real "leader," and who's being "led." This has taken shape in various ways. It's well-known that through its men in the Masonic lodges, the CIA

---

[834] Knight, Stephen, *The Brotherhood*, Acacia Press, 1984
[835] https://en.wikipedia.org/wiki/Freemasonry

is able to channel the work of the international business community into directions needed by the United States. But Masons who work in the CIA are also capable of setting the tone they require.

In any case, Masonic techniques have been adopted in the CIA, MI6, the BND, and Mossad. With all conditions equal, during officer selection preference is given to Freemasons. Masonic lodges serve not only as a personnel reservoir, but as their own type of guarantor of a given officer's reliability. In contemporary conditions, the setting out of agents of influence and the use of blackmail; bribery; intimidation; and defamation of one's enemies have entered soundly into the arsenal of these kindred organizations. Consequently, the leaderships of the Masonic lodges and NATO intelligence services were spliced together.

A classic example of this is the founder of the CIA, Allen Dulles. Having become the director of the CIA, he would remain a Mason until the end of his life.[836]

President Harry Truman was given the 33rd degree of the Supreme Council of the Scottish Rite. When Truman was asked exactly what Freemasonry is, he responded:

Freemasonry is a system of morals which makes it easier to live with your fellow man whether he understands it or not.[837]

The last part of his statement is dubious. "Whether he understands it or not" seems to imply that non-Masons are just too stupid to know what's best for them. That is disrespecting the public. We see this same arrogant attitude later on in the Warren Commission investigation. They figured that the public, which is mostly non-Masons, simply does not know what is best for them, so they cannot be told the truth.

President Truman was asked what honor he holds most dear in his life. His answer was not what you would expect:

---

[836] https://espionagehistoryarchive.com/2015/11/21/malta-masonry-the-cia
[837] Roberts, Allen E., *Brother Truman*, p. 62, Anchor Communications, 1985

> Although I hold the highest civil honor in the world, I have always regarded my rank and title as a Past Grand Master of Masons as the greatest honor that has ever come to me. [838]

So Truman stated bluntly that being a Grand Master Mason is a greater honor than being President of the United States. That would come as a surprise to the public, but not to other Masons.

Franklin D. Roosevelt was a 32nd degree Freemason, in addition to holding a number of honorary memberships in various lodges. He was initiated into Freemasonry in 1911 in New York. It was FDR who suggested that the Great Seal be put on the dollar bill. This included the "Eye of Providence," which is the Masonic symbol of the Great Architect of the Universe. Other Masonic symbols on the Great Seal include the pyramid, the eagle, and the notation "Novus Ordo Seclorum" (A New Order of the Ages).[839]

Presidents Franklin D. Roosevelt and Harry S. Truman were both high-ranking Freemasons. These two presidents created the U.S. intelligence apparatus as we know it today. Roosevelt originally created the Office of Strategic Services in 1942, which was replaced by the Central Intelligence Agency in 1947 by Truman. The CIA, and all subsequent branches of it, operate by compartmentalization, the same as Freemasonry does. These two presidents were well-acquainted with this concept, and they applied it to the development of American intelligence. That means that Masonic thinking made its way into presidential policy-making. Two decades later, the CIA was involved in overthrowing the American government. As mentioned, the connection is vague and indirect. Truman could never have foreseen what the CIA would become. After JFK's death, Truman regretted the monster he had created. The significance of it is open to debate, but it is a historical fact that the CIA was created by a Freemason.[840]

Through their subtle influence, Freemasonry is able to get people in place who will be assets later on. That includes politicians, judges, policemen, district attorneys, editors, and reporters. Then when they need them later on, those assets are available to help them get away with crimes, like a presidential assassination. In many cases the assets involved are not

---

[838] Roberts, Allen E. *Brother Truman*, pp. 143-5, Anchor Communications, 1985
[839] http://www.greatseal.com/dollar/hawfdr.html
[840] https://en.wikipedia.org/wiki/Central_Intelligence_Agency

Freemasons themselves, but they are somehow affiliated with others who are, which makes it harder for investigators to trace the connections.

With this in mind, we can see that the magic bullet theory has Masonic origins. It makes no sense any other way. We know that the theory is so preposterous that no one could possibly take it seriously. I doubt that Arlen Specter believes it himself. Yet, he developed the theory, promoted it, and went to his grave proclaiming it to be the truth. Why? Most likely, there was some influence from his Masonic superiors. Either they invented the theory or they encouraged Specter to. It may seem far-fetched, but it is more far-fetched to think that his Masonic affiliation had no influence at all on his actions.

Freemasonry and Racism

Among other things, Freemasonry is a racist organization. The roots of the Ku Klux Klan can be traced to Freemasonry. At least one of the founders of the KKK, General Bedford Forrest, was a Freemason, and well-known Freemason author Albert Pike was Chief Justice of the KKK. If there is any question of Pike's attitude toward blacks, the following quote should settle it:

> I took my obligation to White men, not to Negroes. When I have to accept Negroes as brothers or leave Masonry, I shall leave it.[841]

After the KKK briefly disbanded in the late 1800s, it was re-established by another Freemason, W.J. Simmons in 1915. This was due in part to the silent movie *Birth of a Nation*, which portrayed the KKK as heroic guardians of American morality. The film was directed and co-produced by Freemason D.W. Griffith.[842]

Talk of racism in this context brings us right back to J. Edgar Hoover. Anyone who knew Hoover knew of his racist leanings. His hatred of Martin Luther King was no secret. Hoover created COINTELPRO (Counterintelligence Program) to monitor and control the civil rights movement. Through this program, FBI agents infiltrated and spied on the

---

[841] Darrah, Delmar D., *History and Evolution of Freemasonry*, p. 329, Charles T. Powner Co., 1954

[842] http://www.jesus-is-savior.com/False%20Religions/Freemasonry/ku_klux_klan.htm

meetings of civil rights groups. Hoover wiretapped King in an attempt to find dirt he could use against him. COINTELPRO funded and controlled the KKK, as was determined by the Senate Select Committee to Study Governmental Operations (Church Committee). They described the FBI's use of fictitious organizations:

> For example, Bureau informants set up a Klan organization intended to attract membership away from the United Klans of America. The Bureau paid the informant's personal expenses in setting up the new organization, which had, at its height, 250 members.[843]

The FBI had a disproportionate number of Freemasons, probably due to Hoover's influence. Through Freemason agents and informants, the FBI actually created their own cell of the KKK.[844] If Hoover had been questioned about this, he could have easily said that he was monitoring the Klan for the purpose of controlling them or breaking them up. But the FBI did not break up the Klan and they never had any intention to. Over time, the Klan just withered away in response to social outrage.

Other groups also espouse the same principles as Freemasonry. The John Birch Society and the Minutemen are examples of this. They both promote racism and right-wing extremism. There is no formal connection between these groups and Freemasonry, but there is undoubtedly a large overlap in their memberships. Although the JBS and the Minutemen have faded away due to national acceptance of integration, they were political forces in Kennedy's day.

P2

A connection between Freemasonry and the CIA can be found in the P2 scandal. P2 is the commonly used name for the Italian lodge called Propaganda Due. The lodge was founded in 1945 as a place for visiting Masons who were unable to attend their own lodge. This was in violation of the Italian Constitution, which had banned secret societies since 1925. Licio Gelli took control of the lodge in 1966, and increased membership from 14

---

[843] https://www.intelligence.senate.gov/sites/default/files/94755_III.pdf
[844] https://www.larouchepub.com/eiw/public/1993/eirv20n12-19930319/eirv20n12-19930319_043-hoover_satanism_and_the_scottish.pdf

to one thousand. At that time, P2 had transformed into an ultra right-wing organization that tried to affect the Italian political process.

Gelli was a paid CIA contact, and it was the CIA who funded P2. An Italian court indictment called P2 a "secret structure that had the incredible capacity to control a state's institutions to the point of virtually becoming a state-within-a-state." Italian authorities discovered the P2 plot in 1981. They searched Gelli's home and found a list of Masonic conspirators. The list included 40 members of Parliament, 43 military generals, eight admirals, three cabinet members, 24 journalists, and several police chiefs, security chiefs, industrialists, financiers, diplomats, civil servants, and celebrities.

Also found in Gelli's home was a document entitled "The Strategy of Tension." This was a plan to create artificial terrorism in order to install an authoritarian government. This plan grew out of Operation Gladio, which was a joint program set up by the CIA and NATO after World War II. Ostensibly, it was to thwart a communist takeover in Italy and Western Europe. In reality, it became a state-sponsored terrorist network. They engaged in false-flag operations to subvert democracy and frighten the public into surrendering their freedom. The terrorist acts would be blamed on the communists, giving the government a license to take away civil liberties in the name of national security.[845]

A Parliamentary Commission of Inquiry concluded that the P2 lodge was a secret criminal organization. The commission charged the Central Intelligence Agency with supporting P2.The majority report said that P2 action resulted in:

> ...the pollution of the public life of a nation. It aimed to alter, often in decisive fashion, the correct functioning of the institutions of the country, according to a project which ... intended to undermine our democracy.[846]

In 1976, the Masonic charter of P2 was withdrawn and the Grand Orient of Italy officially expelled the lodge. That legally absolved the Masonic body of the crimes committed by P2. In January 1982 the P2 lodge was abolished by law. However, they continued to function underground. P2 has been implicated in several criminal acts, including the 1980 bombing of a Bologna

---

[845] Marrs, Jim, *Rule by Secrecy*, pp. 256-258, Perennial, 2000
[846] https://en.wikipedia.org/wiki/Propaganda_Due

train station that killed 85 people, the murders of journalist Mino Pecorelli and banker Roberto Calvi, and the collapse of the Banco Ambrosiano. Remnants of the group are suspected in the 1988 bombing of Pan Am flight 103 over Lockerbie, Scotland. According to a report by Pan Am's insurance company, the flight victims included a CIA team investigating drug smuggling and gun running activities which were financed by P2 members. Other CIA agents arrived at the crash scene and are suspected of seizing critical evidence.[847] [848]

From CIA officer Ibrahim Razin:

> P2 was at the center, one of the main participants in the illegal arms traffic, which was connected to the drug traffic from the outset. P2 also made a substantial contribution to the recycling of large amounts of money used for this arms and drugs traffic from one country to another...Suffice it to see how the P2 was involved with Banco Ambrosiano and with Michele Sindona and how the CIA was involved with them in several financial manipulations. For example, in the United States the big scandal involving the S&L banks is big news. The Texas state prosecutor has found evidence of CIA involvement in the bankruptcy of many of these banks which used illegal funds for their operations. The man who knows a lot about this is Richard Brenneke, a former CIA agent from Oregon.

Brenneke stated to an interviewer that P2 was the financial and organizational arm of the CIA to destabilize and run covert operations in Europe. Brenneke elaborated:

> There is no doubt. The P2 since the beginning of the 1970s was used for the dope traffic, for destabilization in a covert way. It was done secretly to keep people from knowing about the involvement of the U.S. government. In many cases it was done directly through the offices of the CIA in Rome and in some other cases through CIA centers in other countries...[849]

---

[847] http://www.truthmove.org/content/operation-gladio/

[848] https://en.wikipedia.org/wiki/Propaganda_Due

[849] http://www.freemasonrywatch.org/propaganda.due.p2.membership.list.html

The P2 scandal occurred after Kennedy's death, so it is not directly related to the assassination, but it shows that there is collusion between the CIA and secret societies. It figures that there would be, since they both exist to deceive and subvert. This collusion was in its infancy when Kennedy died. At the time, the CIA had only existed for 16 years, whereas Freemasonry had been around for centuries. Freemasonry has branched out into other secret societies, keeping some of the same ideology, but changing to attract a different membership and serve different purposes.

Illuminati

No one really knows who the Illuminati are, and unlike other secret societies, I could not name one single individual who is a member of this group. They seem to exist in the abstract. There is not a physical location of Illuminati headquarters. If you think you know of one, it is only a cover or a decoy. If you find a book by someone calling themselves Illuminati, that is also a cover or a decoy. And don't be fooled by the "Official Illuminati Website." They will not tell you 1% of the truth about this group. If someone tells you that they are with the Illuminati, they are probably with one of the many splinter groups that they have dispersed into. That is not to say that the Illuminati does not exist. They do, but it seems to be in some other realm that is intangible to us.

The Bavarian Illuminati was officially formed on May 1, 1776, just two months before the birth of the United States. It was founded by Adam Weishaupt, a Freemason.[850]Groups calling themselves Illuminati claim to have some connection with the original Bavarian Illuminati, although that is not always true. Some groups like to use the name "Illuminati" because it sounds mystical and mysterious, so the term gets tossed around a lot. Also, the word is sometimes used in a more mundane sense to describe the forces of the deep state, so we will occasionally hear terms like "Illuminati bankers" or "Illuminati global elitists."

The Bavarian Illuminati was more or less absorbed into Freemasonry. Freemasonry is much more visible and accessible to the public. You can go to a Masonic lodge, read books about Freemasonry, and talk to a representative of Freemasonry. That is not the case with the Illuminati. It's true that you won't get the whole truth about Freemasonry either, but they

---

[850] https://en.wikipedia.org/wiki/Illuminati

are much more tangible than the Illuminati, whose nebulous existence makes them seem other-worldly. The Illuminati works through other secret societies, but mainly Freemasonry. We can think of Freemasonry as the arm, while the Illuminati is the brain.

Authors Michael A. Hoffman II and James Shelby Downard have written about the JFK assassination in terms of mass psychology and symbolism. Their view is very dark, yet enlightening:

> ...the ultimate purpose of that assassination was not political or economic but sorcerous: for the control of the dreaming mind and the marshalling of its forces is the omnipotent force in this entire scenario of lies, cruelty and degradation. Something died in the American people on Nov. 22, 1963 -- call it idealism, innocence or the quest for moral excellence. It is the transformation of human beings which is the authentic reason and motive for the Kennedy murder...[851]

Hoffman examines the effects of the assassination on the collective human spirit. His view is that the assassination was a symbolic statement of power by the invisible ruling elite:

> The perpetrators deliberately murdered JFK in such a way as to affect our national identity and cohesiveness -- to fracture America's soul. Even the blatancy of their conspiracy was designed to show their "superiority" and our "futility." "They" were doing to the nation what they had been doing to individuals for years.[852]

"Blatancy" is the key word in the above quote. Think of the absurdity of the magic bullet theory. Think of how they could show us a pristine bullet and tell us that it went through two men. Think of how insulting it is to our intelligence when they say that the fatal shot came from behind, in spite of what we've seen in the Zapruder film. Think of how the Warren Commission could just flagrantly ignore key witnesses and distort the testimony of others. It's as if they purposely wanted to thumb their noses at us and laugh at how much they could get away with.

Hoffman continues to lament the effect on society:

---

[851] http://www.whale.to/b/kingkill_33.html
[852] http://www.ctrl.org/essay2/MCIJFKA3.html

The killers were not caught, the Warren Commission was a whitewash. There was a sense that the men who ordered the assassination were grinning somewhere over cocktails and out of this, a nearly-psychedelic wonder seized the American population, an awesome shiver before the realization that whoever could kill a president of the United States in broad daylight and get away with it, could get away with anything.

A hidden government behind the visible government of these United States became painfully obvious in a kind of subliminal way and lent an undercurrent of the hallucinogenic to our reality. Welcome to Oz thanks to the men behind Os-wald and Ruby.

There was a transfer of power in the collective group mind of the American masses: from the public power of the elected front-man Chief Executive, to an unelected invisible college capable of terminating him with impunity...

The role assigned to us is that of zombies called upon by our shadow masters to perform bit parts and act as stock characters in their spectacular show. This mesmerizing process produces a demoralized, cynical, double-mind.[853]

Hoffman views the Warren Commission as a technique of psychological warfare designed to reinforce the power of the hidden elite. He describes the one-two punch conveyed in symbolic murders:

One: the ritual murders are successfully accomplished. The principals get away, the scapegoat conveniently takes the blame. Two: later we learn the truth but no one is prosecuted. We are mocked, disoriented, and demoralized. Occult prestige and potency is heightened.

This is what simplistic researchers miss: the function of macabre arrogance thumbing its nose at us while we do nothing except spread the tale of their immunity and invincibility further. That is the game plan operant here.[854]

---

[853] Hoffman, Michael, *Secret Societies and Psychological Warfare*, pp. 91-95, Independent H & S, 2001

[854] Hoffman, Michael, *Secret Societies and Psychological Warfare*, p. 78, Independent H & S, 2001

It's easy to see what he means by "macabre arrogance." It's not enough that they lie to us; they have to insult us, too. The magic bullet theory is the clearest example of that. I sensed that same macabre arrogance laughing at us again decades later as the Twin Towers lay smoldering for reasons that have still not been adequately explained.

The Core

Manly P. Hall, a 33rd degree Freemason, writes about the secrecy of the organization:

> Freemasonry is a fraternity within a fraternity -- an outer organization concealing an inner brotherhood of the elect ... it is necessary to establish the existence of these two separate and yet interdependent orders, the one visible and the other invisible. The visible society is a splendid camaraderie of 'free and accepted' men enjoined to devote themselves to ethical, educational, fraternal, patriotic, and humanitarian concerns. The invisible society is a secret and most August (defined as 'of majestic dignity, grandeur') fraternity whose members are dedicated to the service of a mysterious *arcannum arcandrum* (defined as 'a secret, a mystery')."[855]

Freemason Albert Pike wrote *Morals and Dogma*, which is considered the Masonic bible. He has this to say about Freemasonry:

> Masonry, like all the Religions, all the Mysteries, Hermeticism, and Alchemy, conceals its secrets from all except the Adepts and Sages, or the Elect, and uses false explanations and misinterpretations of its symbols to mislead those who deserve only to be misled; to conceal the Truth, which it calls light, and draw them away from it...Fictions are necessary to the people, and the Truth becomes deadly to those who are not strong enough to contemplate it in all its brilliance."[856] [857]

---

[855] Hall, Manly P., *Lectures on Ancient Philosophy*, p. 433, TarcherPerigee, 2005
[856] Pike, Albert, *Morals and Dogma*, pp. 104-5, Martino Fine Books, original 1906
[857] http://www.cuttingedge.org/free001a.htm

But what exactly do these authors mean by "secrets," "truth," and "invisible"? Keeping in mind that Lucifer is essentially Satan, here are some revealing quotes from Masons:

> The seething energies of Lucifer are in his hands and before he may step onward and upward, he must prove his ability to properly apply this energy.[858]

> Lucifer is the Logos the Serpent, the Savior...It is Satan who is the God of our planet and the only God.[859]

> Lucifer, the Light-bearer Strange and mysterious name to give to the Spirit of Darkness! Lucifer, the son of the morning! Is it he who bears the Light, and with its splendors intolerable blinds feeble, sensual or selfish Souls? Doubt it not![860]

> The Masonic Religion should be, by all of us initiates of the high degrees, maintained in the purity of the Luciferian Doctrine. ...the true and pure philosophical religion is the belief in Lucifer.[861]

> When a Mason learns that the key to the Warrior on the Block is the proper application of the dynamo of living power, the seething energies of Lucifer are in his hands.[862]

Anton LaVey wrote *The Satanic Rituals*, in which he acknowledged that Satanic rituals are taken from Masonic elements, and that almost all occult orders have Masonic roots. In his book he explains that there are 12 Enochian keys (an occult language) which are the Satanic paeans, or expressions of faith. His source for this was the Order of the Golden Dawn, which was an occult order founded by Freemasons.[863]

So from Freemasons themselves, we learn the truth about this organization: Freemasonry is a huge, international Satanic cult. That

---

[858] Hall, Manly P., *The Lost Keys of Freemasonry*, p. 48, Tarcher Perigee, 2006

[859] Blavatsky, Helena Petrovna, *The Secret Doctrine*, pp. 215-6, 220, 225, 245, 255, 533, TarcherPerigee, 2009

[860] Pike, Albert, *Morals and Dogma*, p. 321, Martino Fine Books, 1906

[861] Pike, Albert, Instructions to the 23 Supreme Councils of the World, July 14, 1889

[862] Hall, Manly P., *Lost Keys of Freemasonry*, p. 50, Tarcher-Perigree, 2006

[863] http://www.ritualabusefree.org/Freemasonry

explains the secrecy, the compartmentalization, the corruption, the infiltration, the ban by the Catholic Church, and the fact that Freemasonry has been expelled from a dozen countries. Masons won't like hearing this, and of course they will deny it. And they are not lying, because most of them honestly don't know. Only a tiny fraction of a percent of Freemasons practice serious hardcore Satanism, meaning the rituals, the human sacrifices, etc. The rest are just cover. It is tragic that thousands and thousands of well-meaning people in Freemasonry are being unwittingly used as a buffer to insulate the inner circle of Satan worshippers. That's why Freemasonry engages in so much public service- it makes the perfect cover. When Freemasons raise money to build hospitals for crippled children, who would ever suspect that Satanism is at the core of it? It goes without saying that if Freemasons knew the truth about their organization, almost every one of them would quit the group instantly and renounce any affiliation with them.

It should be emphasized here that this is coming from a purely secular point of view. Although I come from a Catholic background, I am neither a church-going person nor a Bible scholar. I am not preaching any religion or judging anyone. I do not know who will go to Heaven and who won't. The purpose of this section is to point out the truth about this deceptive organization: its essence is Satanic. Satanism engages in rituals that involve human sacrifices and sexual abuse of children. Opposition to that is not a religious thing; it's a human thing. All people on Earth should be opposed to this. An atheist should be opposed to Satanism on moral grounds.

While I'm not an authority on the subject, I have to believe that Satanic cults are a form of mind control. I cannot see how a free-thinking individual could be involved with something like that. People in these cults do not think for themselves; someone else does their thinking for them. They have surrendered their own critical thinking, and that includes their conscience. The cult has become their conscience instead, and when the cult says it's permissible to kill, then they will kill without remorse. It's not hard to believe that an organization like this could play a role in a multitude of crimes, not the least of which is a presidential assassination. This does not prove that Freemasons played a role in the murder of JFK, but it does show that they had the mind set to do so.

So does that mean that Hoover, Warren, and Ford were all Satan worshippers? I assume that they were not. I would say that about any

Freemason until I find out otherwise. Considering the high-profile positions of these three, it's possible that the truth about the Satanic element may have been kept from them. Like many Masons, they probably heard rumors about it but did not take them seriously. But these and others were still used to do the bidding of the inner core, even without knowing the full truth about it.

JFK and Lucifer

John F. Kennedy was the nation's first Roman Catholic president. That is significant here because the Roman Catholic Church has been feuding with Freemasonry for centuries. According to the Masonic document *Alta Vendita*, the goal of Freemasonry is "the total annihilation of Catholicism." The Catholic Church has prohibited its members from being Freemasons since 1738. Since then, 11 popes have made pronouncements, called Papal Bulls, which state the incompatibility of Freemasonry with Catholic doctrine. Members are threatened with excommunication for joining Freemasonry or other secret societies. In 1963, Pope Paul VI relaxed the restrictions somewhat, although it is suspected that he had been corrupted by Freemasons who infiltrated the Church. The Church still considers members who affiliate with Freemasonry to be in a state of grave sin and may not receive Holy Communion.[864] [865]

When John Kennedy took office, he may not have been aware of the corrupt nature of Freemasonry. It is generally not known, and the organization naturally promotes an image of wholesomeness. On April 10, 1961, a group of Freemasons toured the White House. The group represented the Eighth International Conference of the Supreme Council of Freemasonry. Kennedy can be seen in a picture shaking hands with Masons in the Rose Garden.[866] Just 17 days later, Kennedy made a speech in which he addressed secret societies. Although the speech was mainly about responsibility of the press and transparency in government, it was the only time a president ever mentioned secret societies. From that speech:

> The very word "secrecy" is repugnant in a free and open
> society; and we are as a people inherently and historically
> opposed to secret societies, to secret oaths and secret

---

[864] http://www.cuttingedge.org/news/n1656.cfm

[865] http://www.cfnews.org/page10/page83/paul_vi_beatified.html

[866] https://www.jfklibrary.org/Asset-Viewer/Archives/JFKWHP-KN-C17478.aspx

proceedings. We decided long ago that the dangers of excessive and unwarranted concealment of pertinent facts far outweighed the dangers which are cited to justify it...[867]

This speech was given just a week after the Bay of Pigs debacle. Kennedy was a baby president at the time, having served in office only three months. In that short time, his eyes had been opened as to how the government functions. He lamented the unwanted influence of those who operate in secrecy, and he alluded to this in the speech. Although he did mention secret societies, he did not specifically mention any of them by name. That way, he didn't ruffle any feathers.

Pope Paul VI began his reign of the Catholic Church on June 21, 1963. It is highly suspected that Pope Paul VI was in collusion with Freemasonry, as he later relaxed restrictions against Catholics joining secret societies. It is alleged that on June 29, 1963, there was a ritual held within the Church called the Enthronement of Lucifer. This was a Masonic celebration of their successful infiltration of the Catholic Church. Shortly afterward, President Kennedy paid a visit to the pontiff. This was described by Denise Brondson in *Swiftly Comes the Battle*:

> President John Kennedy made a trip to see Pope Paul VI, on July 2, 1963, just three days after the enthronement of Lucifer. Kennedy met with Pope Paul personally, to give him the message that the FBI had reported to Kennedy about the enthronement, and to ask the Pope to reverse the enthronement. The Pope refused, saying he could not. At the time of the meeting, Paul had no other response; he was taken aback by the FBI's knowledge of the events of June 29, 1963. Obviously, there was a U.S. spy in the Vatican. The Jesuits are not the only ones who know how to infiltrate.[868] [869]

So the FBI was spying on the Vatican. Someone in Washington knew what was happening in Rome, and John Kennedy was sent as an ambassador. His relationship with the Vatican was a unique one. Being both president and

---

[867] https://www.jfklibrary.org/Research/Research-Aids/JFK-Speeches/American-Newspaper-Publishers-Association_19610427.aspx

[868] Brondson, Denise, *Swiftly Comes the Battle*, p. 70, Bronsdon Publishing, LLC, 2014

[869] http://www.denisebronsdon.com/408488055/2312331/posting/

Catholic, the enthronement was naturally an event of great concern for Kennedy. But it's surprising that he would even know about this event. Naturally, it was done with the utmost secrecy, and even the Pope was surprised that Kennedy knew about it. Did Kennedy order the FBI to spy on the Vatican? At some point, he must have become aware of the Satanic element in Freemasonry, otherwise the enthronement of Lucifer would make no sense to him. Two years earlier, Kennedy had given Freemasons a tour of the White House, but now he was aware of their Vatican infiltration and their potential to bring the Church down. To Kennedy's credit, he tried to reverse this abomination of the Church, but the pope himself was powerless to do anything about it.

The pope responded to Kennedy with a diplomatic letter that is vague and gives no actual reason for the refusal to reverse the enthronement:

> With candor your words recall the higher moral principles of truth, of justice and of liberty. We find a spontaneous harmony with that which Our Venerable Predecessor, Pope John XXIII, said in his last Encyclical Letter, '*Pacem in Terris*,' when he presented anew to the world the Church's constant teaching on the dignity of the individual human person, a dignity which the Almighty Creator bestowed in creating man to His own image and likeness....[870][871]

It is a documented fact that Kennedy did meet with Pope Paul VI on July 2, 1963. Upon their initial meeting, Kennedy chose to simply shake hands instead of observing the traditional etiquette of genuflecting and kissing the papal ring. He probably chose this as a conservative act, knowing that the public was still leery of a Catholic president. Naturally, there is no written or oral record of the two leaders discussing the enthronement of Lucifer, but the best source of this information comes from a Vatican insider.

Father Malachi Martin was a Jesuit priest who served in Rome as a close associate of Cardinal Augustin Bea, Pope St. John XXIII, and Pope Paul VI. Martin has written a book called *Keys of This Blood* in which he details the enthronement ritual. This involved concurrent ceremonies in Rome and South Carolina on June 29, 1963. A telephone hookup was established between the two locations. The exact phrases were spoken and the same

---

[870] https://www.jfklibrary.org/Asset-Viewer/Archives/JFKPOF-032-001.aspx
[871] http://www.denisebronsdon.com/408488055/2312331/posting/

gestures performed at both rituals simultaneously. Father Martin's source for this story is a young girl who was forced to take part in one of the ceremonies. She was sexually abused in the ritual, and her puppy was tortured and murdered. This was the Freemason ritual called the Enthronement of Lucifer, and it symbolically represented their conquest of the Catholic Church.[872][873]

According to Father Martin, a human sacrifice was made in the South Carolina ceremony, but not in Rome. I can only assume that's to avoid the bad PR of a dead body at the Vatican. Otherwise, the ceremonies were identical. As shocking as that sounds, it appears to be true. Father Martin is a Vatican insider and seems credible. His claims are believable because they are consistent with centuries of infiltration and subversion by Freemasonry. This could only happen because Pope Paul VI was in collusion with Freemasons.

From *The Cutting Edge*:

> Through this Black Magick ceremony, the first truly Black Magick Pope in history -- Pope Paul VI -- was officially and powerfully enthroned. The Parallel Ceremony was absolutely essential, for the true merger of Satanic forces worldwide could not have otherwise occurred.[874]

Symbolism plays a huge role in Masonic rituals. The Enthronement of Lucifer was a ritualistic expression of their successful infiltration of the Catholic Church. Later, President Kennedy was assassinated in a manner that strangely parallels their Killing of the King ritual. To further symbolize the Masonic victory, Pope Paul VI publicly displayed a bent crucifix with a distorted image of Jesus. He called it a pastoral staff, but it was actually a Satanic symbol used to mock and demean Christ. The next two Pope John Pauls also displayed the distorted crucifix.[875]

Freemason Adam Weishaupt, the founder of the Bavarian Illuminati, predicted that the Catholic Church would be infiltrated and brought down:

---

[872] https://www.newswithviews.com/Horn/thomas130.htm
[873] http://www.tldm.org/news/martin.htm
[874] http://www.cuttingedge.org/news/n1623.cfm
[875] http://www.cuttingedge.org/news/n1623.cfm

We will infiltrate that place [the Vatican], and once inside, we will never come out. We will bore from within until nothing remains but an empty shell.[876]

Weishaupt's prophecy was fulfilled in 1963. Masonic infiltration of the Catholic Church was responsible for the child molestation scandal that shocked everyone. The public started hearing about the molestation charges in the 1980s, but the seeds were planted in 1963. In many cases, Freemasons either committed the molestations, or they were somehow in a position of power where they could stifle any investigation into the charges. This occurred because Pope Paul VI opened the Church to Freemasonry. Not only did Masons infiltrate the priesthood, but they also influenced the seminaries who trained future priests, indoctrinating them with a philosophy that is tolerant of pedophilia.[877] [878]

In 1978, Pope Paul VI wrote a letter to his successor, Pope John Paul I. The letter informed the new pope about the enthronement of Lucifer. John Paul I was considered unsuitable for the plans of the Vatican, and it is suspected that he was murdered for that reason. Pope John Paul I died suddenly on September 28, 1978, after reigning over the Catholic Church for a mere 33 days. It was reported that he had died of a heart attack. The Pope's body was quickly embalmed before any autopsy could be performed, which aroused great suspicion in the Italian press. To add further suspicion, no blood samples were taken, which might have indicated poisoning. The Vatican cleaned up the scene before police could investigate. His blood pressure pills and his will were confiscated and were never to be seen again. The Pope's niece told the press, "In my family almost no one believes it was a heart attack that killed my uncle. He never had heart trouble or any illness of that kind."[879]

The ostensible conspiracy theory is that Pope John Paul I was murdered to prevent him from investigating Vatican bank malfeasance. As much of a scandal as that would have been, it is still minor compared to the true scandal that was covered up- the enthronement of Lucifer.

---

[876] http://michaeljournal.org/corruptionfashions.asp\.

[877] http://www.cfnews.org/page10/page83/paul_vi_beatified.html

[878] http://www.cuttingedge.org/news/n1656.cfm

[879] https://theunredacted.com/pope-john-paul-1-murder-at-the-vatica/

So Freemasonry scored a double victory over the Catholic Church in 1963. In June, they successfully infiltrated the Church by getting their own man into the papacy. Five months later, the nation's only Catholic president was assassinated and the crime covered up by Masonic forces.

John Kennedy never lived to see the pedophilia scandal that tarnished the image of his beloved Church. By asking the pope to reverse the enthronement, he did what little he could to prevent it. He may not have known that the infiltration would lead to child molesting, but he knew in a general way that it was bad for the Church. He is probably the only public official to have taken any pre-emptive action to stave off the scandal. It was a noble gesture, but in reality, he had no better chance of reforming the Vatican than he did of reforming the CIA.

Other Groups

Over the centuries, Freemasonry has branched out into other groups. This is not official, and the Grand Lodge would deny any formal affiliation with other secret societies. But a slew of secret groups have popped up over the years, many with the same goals of subverting society and supplanting the government. When Freemasons interact with other members of society in their everyday lives, they spread the Masonic ideology in subtle ways. They may not be proselytizing on purpose, but it's only natural that when Masons interact with others, their ideology will be spread simply by social osmosis. Others will start groups and societies that have no legal or formal connection to Freemasonry, but they promote the same ideology.

Part of that ideology is the belief that the ends justify the means. This is how good people are coaxed into doing bad things. This belief has been used to justify the Holocaust, slavery, and the atomic bombing of Japan. It is the excuse for every war ever fought. Sometimes it really is true that the ends justify the means, but far too often it is used as a cheap excuse for senseless violence and atrocities. Once people are convinced of their own righteousness, it goes to their heads, and there is no reasoning with them after that. Cults like Freemasonry exploit that tendency in humans. Members are taught that their group has purely altruistic motives. Once they are convinced of that, they are taught that anyone who opposes them must be evil. Then it is easy to convince people to commit unethical acts that they otherwise never would, because they have to eliminate that evil force. Hence, the ends justify the means.

Aside from Freemasonry, there are several other secret societies that have formed over the years that have become social and political forces. A few of the main ones are: Skull and Bones, Bohemian Grove, the Bildeberg Group, Trilateralists, and Council on Foreign Relations (CFR). Although none of these groups are officially related to Freemasonry, there is still an indirect connection. The Masonic influence is present, but not visible.

Skull and Bones is a Yale fraternity founded in 1832. It is similar to Freemasonry in that they follow some Masonic rites. Their meetings and rites take place in a windowless building known as "The Tomb." The group selects 15 new members a year from among Yale seniors. Some famous Bonesmen include William Howard Taft, George H.W. Bush, George W. Bush, Averell Harriman, John Sherman Cooper, Henry Luce, William Buckley, McGeorge Bundy, and John Kerry.[880]

The Bohemian Club was formed in 1872 in San Francisco, and was originally composed of artistic types such as writers and musicians. Over the years, it became more geared toward businessmen and world leaders. Members meet annually for a 17-day retreat at Bohemian Grove in northern California. The membership is estimated at 1,500, although some attendees are not considered members. Some Bohemian Club members/attendees are former presidents William Taft, Calvin Coolidge, Dwight Eisenhower, Gerald Ford, Ronald Reagan, Richard Nixon, and George H.W. Bush. Others are Newt Gingrich, William Randolph Hearst, Herbert Hoover, Colin Powell, George Schultz, Pete Wilson, and Henry Kissinger.[881]

The Bildeberg Group was formed in 1954. They have no official membership list. This group of 120-140 highly influential non-members meets in secret every year, always with extremely tight security. The press is not allowed to attend meetings. Contents of the meeting are kept secret and attendees are sworn not to discuss the proceedings with anyone. Attendance is by invitation only. Bildeberg people include Henry Kissinger, Bill Clinton, Hillary Clinton, Gordon Brown, Bill Gates, Colin Powell, and Condoleezza Rice.[882]

---

[880] http://conspiracyarchive.com/NWO/Skull_Bones.htm
[881] http://bohemiangroveexposed.com/
[882] http://www.therichest.com/rich-list/the-biggest/new-world-order-the-5-oldest-secret-societies/

The Trilateral Commission is also a significant force today. However, they were formed in 1973, so they do not directly relate to anything involving John Kennedy. Other secret societies of note are the Rosicrucians, Ordo Templi Orientis, Knights Templar, and Knights of Malta.[883]Concerning the JFK cover-up, Richard Helms, James Angleton, and John McCone were all members of the Knights of Malta, which is indirectly related to Freemasonry.[884]

The Council on Foreign Relations has developed into the most influential secret society today. Founded in 1921, the CFR is a non-profit organization headquartered in New York City, with a membership of about 5,000. The CFR meetings convene government officials, global business leaders and prominent members of the intelligence and foreign-policy community to discuss international issues. CFR publishes the bi-monthly journal *Foreign Affairs*, and runs the David Rockefeller Studies Program, which influences foreign policy by making recommendations to the presidential administration and publishing on foreign policy issues.[885]

For the past 60 years, 80% of the top positions in every administration have been CFR members. That is true for both Democratic and Republican administrations, proving that there is very little difference between the two parties. Some well-known CFR members are George McGovern, Walter Mondale, Jimmy Carter, Edmund Muskie, John Anderson, Lloyd Benson, Madeleine Albright, Bill Clinton, George H.W. Bush, Nelson and David Rockefeller, Zbigniew Brzezinski, John Foster Dulles, and Richard Nixon.[886][887]

Admiral Chester Ward, a longtime CFR member, explains the objective of the group:

> ...to bring about the surrender of the sovereignty and the national independence of the United States...Primarily, they

[883] http://listverse.com/2007/08/27/top-10-secret-societies/
http://www.businessinsider.com/this-chart-shows-the-bilderberg-groups-connection-to-everything-in-the-world-2012-6
[884] http://www.cuttingedge.org/news/n1623.cfm
[885] https://en.wikipedia.org/wiki/Council_on_Foreign_Relations
[886] http://humansarefree.com/2013/10/the-complete-history-of-freemasonry-and.html
[887] http://humansarefree.com/2016/01/CFR-Mainstream-Media-NWO.html

want the world banking monopoly from whatever power ends up in the control of global government.

Once the ruling members of the CFR have decided that the U.S. Government should adopt a particular policy, the very substantial research facilities of CFR are put to work to develop arguments, intellectual and emotional, to support the new policy, and to confound and discredit, intellectually and politically, any opposition.[888]

The Rockefeller Foundation, formed in 1913, was created with the goal of "promoting the well-being of humanity throughout the world." The foundation has become the "think tank" for the CFR, and a steady source of its funding. The Rockefeller Foundation originally focused on creating and funding medical institutions, like the Johns Hopkins School of Public Health and Harvard School of Public Health. During World War II the Rockefeller Foundation funded Nazi racial studies at the Kaiser Wilhelm Institute of Anthropology, Human Heredity, and Eugenics. It was known to the foundation that these studies were being used to demonize Jews and to justify their oppression, but the funding of the institute continued. The Rockefeller Foundation funded the CFR's War and Peace study from 1939-1945, which advised the U.S. government on wartime activities. The Security and Armaments division of the study was headed by Allen Dulles, future Director of the CIA. The foundation was used to promote the goals of the CFR, and David Rockefeller himself became director of the CFR in 1949. Officially, the Rockefeller Foundation does not make policy; they only make recommendations. However, their recommendations have been consistently implemented by the Joint Chiefs of Staff and the Department of Defense. One must wonder why the U.S. government would even consider the recommendations of Nazi sympathizers.[889]

Prescott Bush was the father of President George H.W. Bush and grandfather of President George W. Bush. All three Bushes were members of the Skull and Bones society at Yale, and all three have CFR connections, although George W. Bush is not officially listed as a member. The financial assets of Prescott Bush were seized by the U.S. government during World War II under the Trading with the Enemy Act. Prescott Bush managed five U.S. enterprises on behalf of Nazi industrialist Fritz Thyssen. Among Bush's

---

[888] Marrs, Jim, *Rule By Secrecy*, p. 35, Perennial, 2000

[889] https://en.wikipedia.org/wiki/Rockefeller_Foundation

business partners were Allen and John Dulles and former New York Governor Averell Harriman.

The Nazi connections of this group were numerous. Harriman's company, Brown Brothers Harriman and Co., was a front for a Nazi espionage ring. Allen Dulles was a director and lawyer for I.G. Farben, a powerful German chemical cartel that financed experiments at the Auschwitz concentration camp. John Foster Dulles was the head of Sullivan and Cromwell, a legal firm representing German cartels. His letters to German clients bore the salutation "Heil Hitler!"[890]

From *The Nazi Hydra in America*, by Glen Yeadon and John Hawkins:

> The two Wall street firms that aided the Nazis the most were Sullivan and Cromwell and Brown Brothers Harriman. Sullivan and Cromwell was the Wall Street firm that employed Allen and John Foster Dulles. Brown Brothers & Harriman was the Wall Street investment firm that employed George Walker and his son-in-law, Prescott Bush....
>
> Direct actions taken by the Harriman-Bush shipping line in 1932 and by the Dulles brothers in January, 1933, are the two gravest (and most treasonous) actions ever taken against the United States and humanity in the 20th century. Those actions led directly to the seizure of power by the Nazis, placing the burden for (World War II) squarely on the shoulders of Harriman, Bush and the Dulles brothers.
>
> .... Unequivocally, John Foster Dulles, Allen Dulles, Prescott Bush and Averill Harriman were the most flagrant in providing aid for the Nazis. Not only did they help Hitler seize power, their actions also facilitated other American aid to the Nazis. Bush and Harriman acted as Hitler's American banker, operating a company (Brown, Brothers, Harriman and Union Banking Co.) that was at the center of the Nazi's espionage ring in the United States. Once it was clear that

---

[890]https://www.globalresearch.ca/bush-nazi-dealings-continued-until-1951-federal-documents/1176

war was immanent, the Dulles brothers attempted to cloak the Nazi investments of their clients.[891]

After the war, the Dulles brothers took part in Operation Paperclip, a project that recruited German scientists to America. These were mostly scientists who specialized in aerodynamics and chemical weapons. The use of Nazis was controversial, but was considered necessary to keep up with the Soviets in the space race. Yet, there may have been a more sinister aspect to Operation Paperclip. This involved mind control experiments. The Nazis had successfully brainwashed the masses, and our government wanted to know how they did it. Some of the recruited Nazis were specialists in propaganda and psychological warfare. Some of them had performed mind control experiments on prisoners at Auschwitz. In a joint effort involving Freemasonry and intelligence agencies, they created the Tavistock Institute. Founded in London in 1947, the institute became notorious for their use of LSD and other mind-altering drugs under the project MK-ULTRA.[892] [893]

All this is mentioned here to show the collusion between secret societies and intelligence agencies, and to show that their motives are not always benevolent. This collusion has existed at least since the end of World War II, and it involves well-known names like Bush, Dulles, Harriman, and Rockefeller. These are influential people who inject a Nazi mentality into the U.S. government. Consider the remorseful words of President Harry S. Truman:

> I never would have agreed to the formulation of the Central Intelligence Agency back in '47, if I had known it would become the American Gestapo.[894]

If Nazi sympathizers are given unchecked power with no accountability, then the "American Gestapo" is the inevitable result. Truman made that statement in 1961, so he hadn't even seen the worst of it yet. Two years later, his American Gestapo would assassinate President Kennedy.

It's interesting that Truman mentioned he "agreed" to form the CIA. That implies that it was not his idea. It was his military advisors and/or Masonic

---

[891] Yeadon, Glen, and Hawkins, John, *The Nazi Hydra in America*, 2007

[892] http://911nwo.com/?p=4335

[893] http://educate-yourself.org/mc/

[894] http://www.takeoverworld.info/bushnazi.html

superiors who persuaded him to do so. Truman realized the need for an agency to coordinate intelligence, but he disagreed with the proposed power structure of the agency. He relented to the pressure put on him by forces whose motives were not in the best interest of the country.

Butler

Smedley Butler was a U.S. Marine Major General. At the time of his death in 1940, he was the most decorated Marine in U.S. history. In November of 1934, Butler alleged a conspiracy among business and military leaders to overthrow President Roosevelt and create a fascist government in the United States. Butler claimed that he was asked to lead the coup by bond salesman Gerald P. MacGuire in what came to be known as "The Business Plot." Butler refused to take part in it. Supposedly, the plot was backed by the J.P. Morgan banking firm, along with a private army of 500,000 ex-soldiers. A special committee of the House of Representatives, known as the McCormack-Dickstein Committee, listened to Butler's claims. The committee stated that it was unable to confirm Butler's allegations, although it did acknowledge that the plot had been discussed and prepared. It seems that that alone would be cause for prosecution on conspiracy charges. However, no prosecutions or further investigations followed.

The committee stated:

> In the last few weeks of the committee's official life it received evidence showing that certain persons had made an attempt to establish a fascist organization in this country...There is no question that these attempts were discussed, were planned, and might have been placed in execution when and if the financial backers deemed it expedient.[895]

The plot that Butler was asked to be a part of was the early structure of what we now know as the New World Order. It was less developed in Butler's day, but it was still a force. Butler is a hero for trying to stop it before it grew out of control. The committee did find evidence of a plot, but chose to look the other way on it, showing that even back then the military/banking complex had control of most politicians in government. This complex grew in strength as it went unchecked for decades.

---

[895] https://en.wikipedia.org/wiki/Smedley_Butler

After 34 years in the Marines, Butler realized the truth about the military:

> War is a racket. It always has been. It is possibly the oldest,
> easily the most profitable, surely the most vicious. It is the
> only one international in scope. It is the only one in which
> the profits are reckoned in dollars and the losses in lives.[896]

In the end, Smedley gave a good effort, but the NWO was not to be denied.

Media and NWO

The forces that orchestrate world events from behind the scenes are part of the New World Order. Collectively, these groups seek to establish a one-world government with a one-unit monetary system and no national boundaries. They have been gradually working toward this for centuries. Most of the wars fought by the U.S. have been orchestrated to achieve this goal.

A century ago, no one saw this coming. In March of 1915, J.P. Morgan and his associates got together 12 men from the newspaper world and employed them to control the policy of the influential print media. This was a huge step forward for the NWO, as it allowed them to control the flow of information and shape public perception. Congressman Oscar Callaway exposed this collusion as early as 1917:

> An agreement was reached; the policy of the papers was
> bought, to be paid for by the month; an editor was furnished
> for each paper to properly supervise and edit information
> regarding the questions of preparedness, militarism, financial
> policies, and other things of national and international nature
> considered vital to the interests of the purchasers.[897]

Today, 90% of the media is owned by a mere six companies, compared with 50 companies who controlled that same percentage 30 years ago. This is due to mergers and buyouts, and it has consolidated control over the media into the hands of these few conglomerations. The six conglomerates are Comcast, News-Corp., Disney, Viacom, Time Warner, and CBS. These conglomerates own almost all of the TV and radio stations, newspapers,

---

[896] https://en.wikiquote.org/wiki/Smedley_Butler
[897] http://humansarefree.com/2016/01/CFR-Mainstream-Media-NWO.html

publishing companies, textbook providers, internet service providers, recording companies, and the Hollywood film industry.[898]The six media conglomerates are all owned by CFR members, which explains why you never hear the CFR mentioned in the news.

This is a movement toward a police state and away from freedom of speech. With control of the media in the hands of a few, it is easier to control the flow of information. There is less chance for dissenters with six companies instead of 50. The ownership groups are loyal to the government, which is obvious because none of them stray too far from the government's version of events. The six owners will hire like-minded subordinates, who will in turn hire like-minded subordinates. This enables the government to censor the media, as dissenters are gradually eliminated. The media has become an arm of the government instead of an independent agency that monitors it.

This plan has been in effect for over 100 years now. The global elitists have gradually gotten their people in place in the media, which gives them more and more control over what people see and hear, and more importantly, what they don't see and hear. Some prominent CFR members in the media are Dan Rather, Tom Brokaw, David Brinkley, John Chancellor, Barbara Walters, Diane Sawyer, George Stephanopuolos, Robert McNeil, Jim Lehrer, Rupert Murdoch, William F. Buckley, Marvin Kalb, Irving R. Levine, Peter G. Peterson, Hodding Carter III, Daniel Schorr, and Michael Posner. At least three CEOs in the media are CFR members. They are Laurence A. Tisch (CBS), Thomas S. Murphy (ABC) John F. Welch (NBC/MSNBC).[899]

This is why people can't comprehend that the media could be so biased. It doesn't seem realistic that so many people would willingly lie to cover up a crime. But what they don't realize is that these groups have been setting this up for a long time. Little by little they have worked their members and associates into positions of influence. CFR people obtain positions in the media where they can make personnel decisions. This helps them to disseminate information as they desire. We have seen how the CIA has infiltrated the media for the same purpose. There is a huge overlap between the CIA and the CFR. Almost every CIA director since 1966 has been a CFR

---

[898] http://www.businessinsider.com/these-6-corporations-control-90-of-the-media-in-america-2012-6

[899] http://humansarefree.com/2016/01/CFR-Mainstream-Media-NWO.html

member. The list includes Allen Dulles, Richard Helms, James R. Schlesinger, William E. Colby, George H.W. Bush, Adam Stansfield Turner, William J. Casey, William H. Webster, Robert M. Gates, R. James Wollsey, and John Deutch.[900]

In a meeting of the Trilateral Commission in 1991, David Rockefeller gave a speech in which he thanked the mass media, without actually mentioning the CFR, for maintaining their secrecy regarding this collusion:

> We are grateful to the *Washington Post*, the *New York Times*, *Time* Magazine and other great publications whose directors have attended our meetings and respected their promises of discretion for almost forty years. It would have been impossible for us to develop our plan for the world if we had been subject to the bright lights of publicity during those years.

> But, the work is now much more sophisticated and prepared to march towards a world government. The supranational sovereignty of an intellectual elite and world bankers is surely preferable to the national auto determination practiced in past centuries.[901]

The last statement there confirms that the goal of the NWO is a one-world government run by the "intellectual elite and world bankers." Is that in the best interests of the common man and the world as a whole?

Even the Associated Press (AP) has been infiltrated by the CFR. Stanley Swinton, Harold Anderson, and Katharine Graham of the AP are CFR members. The AP is useful in promoting media control because their articles appear in thousands of publications, including websites. The contributing journalists who report for the AP are ultimately under the control of the CFR.

AP reports on news stories are brief, concise summaries of the events. They are often the first source of information on breaking news stories. Only the most basic information is given, without a detailed analysis. That helps to promote the CFR agenda because they can give out limited information. To serve the CFR's agenda, the AP doesn't have to lie; they just report

---

[900] http://www.bilderberg.org/roundtable/CIA-LtdHng1.html
[901] http://rense.com/general17/quote.htm

certain facts and omit certain other facts. By doing so, they can shape people's perception of events, especially in the early hours of a breaking story.[902]

The least-censored form of media is simply books. With all the heavy censorship of TV and newspapers, there is relatively little censorship of books for the simple reason that not nearly as many people read books. When a news item is on TV or in the papers, millions and millions of people hear about it all at once. It has a dramatic impact on society, and if the news story involves anything that would be damaging to those in power, there will be a concerted effort to hide it. They have their people in place to be able to do that. But not nearly as many people read books. If a book is written that exposes government wrongdoings, it will only be read by a relatively small portion of society. A few scattered individuals will read the book, compared with 100 million people who would see a news story. The small number of people who read books are not a threat to the NWO, so they don't censor books as much. They attempt to censor the internet, although that is much harder to do, since anyone can post something on the web.

Naturally, researchers will seek to find an explanation for the unexplained, but the plotters are always one step ahead of us. We are but puppy dogs begging for scraps of truth. Now and then they throw us a bone and laugh while we scramble after it. This is psychological warfare, and those who control the media will usually win at that.

Kennedy and NWO

In his famous speech about the press, Kennedy may have discreetly addressed the New World Order:

> For we are opposed around the world by a monolithic and ruthless conspiracy that relies primarily on covert means for expanding its sphere of influence--on infiltration instead of invasion, on subversion instead of elections, on intimidation instead of free choice, on guerrillas by night instead of armies by day. It is a system which has conscripted vast human and material resources into the building of a tightly

---

[902] http://www.morriscreative.com/6-corporations-control-90-of-the-media-in-america/

knit, highly efficient machine that combines military, diplomatic, intelligence, economic, scientific and political operations.

Its preparations are concealed, not published. Its mistakes are buried, not headlined. Its dissenters are silenced, not praised. No expenditure is questioned, no rumor is printed, no secret is revealed. It conducts the Cold War, in short, with a war-time discipline no democracy would ever hope or wish to match.[903]

Analysts have questioned just what Kennedy meant by "monolithic and ruthless conspiracy." Many think that he was referring to a communist conspiracy, and maybe he was. But his words could also have double meaning. He may have been referring to the "shadow government" that he was just beginning to learn about.

John Kennedy opposed the New World Order, although he never knew it by that name. Many of his enemies- such as the CIA, bankers, and military officials- are disproportionately represented in secret societies. Kennedy did not realize the machine he was up against. His enemies gained strength from unity and from secrecy. He learned the hard way that the official government does not control the country. Between the intelligence agencies and secret societies, they have formed a shadow government that runs things behind the scenes. A full discussion of this in not the scope of this book. Suffice to say that Kennedy was the last American president to oppose the New World Order. All subsequent presidents have not only supported it, but owe their careers to it.

Throughout his short tenure as president, Kennedy was consistently pressured by the Joint Chiefs of Staff and others to escalate the U.S. involvement in Vietnam, and he consistently resisted that pressure. In doing so, he stood against a multitude of CFR members, which included Dean Rusk, Robert McNamara, William and McGeorge Bundy, General Maxwell Taylor, Henry Cabot Lodge, and Averell Harriman. Remember that it was Harriman who sent the "green light" cable to Saigon which led to the assassination of President Ngo Dinh Diem.

---

[903] https://www.jfklibrary.org/Research/Research-Aids/JFK-Speeches/American-Newspaper-Publishers-Association_19610427.aspx

So not only did John Kennedy defy the CIA, he also defied the CFR. Both are powerful organizations with the ways and means to eliminate any obstacle that stands in their way. John Kennedy was one of those obstacles.

Lyndon Johnson, on the other hand, was much more cooperative with the CIA, the CFR, and the military machine in general. On December 2, 1963, just 10 days into his illegitimate presidency, Johnson sent a memo to General Maxwell Taylor that read:

> The more I look at it, the more it is clear to me that South Vietnam is our most critical military area right now. I hope that you and your colleagues in the Joint Chiefs of Staff will see to it that the very best available officers are assigned to General Harkins' command in all areas and for all purposes. We should put our blue ribbon men on this job at every level.[904]

Taylor and his CFR associates must have been thrilled to know that they now had the chief executive on board with them. It can't be proven that the CFR helped to orchestrate the JFK assassination, but there is no doubt that they benefited greatly from it.

Kennedy failed to stop the runaway train that is the New World Order. And where has it led? It has led to 9/11, among other things. 9/11 was orchestrated and carried out by the very forces that Kennedy attempted to rein in decades earlier. 9/11 was a pretext to initiate the War on Terror, and to invade Iraq and Afghanistan, which serves the agenda of the New World Order. We can only imagine how different things might have been if John Kennedy had lived and achieved the things he wanted to achieve. The JFK assassination was truly a turning point in world history.

Recap

In summary, let's take a look at the list of people who were involved in the investigation of John Kennedy's murder, and the secret society affiliations they have:

- J. Edgar Hoover- Freemason
- Earl Warren- Freemason
- Allen Dulles- Freemason, Bildeberg, and CFR

---

[904] Marrs, Jim, *Rule by Secrecy*, p. 131, Perennial, 2000

- Gerald Ford- Freemason, Bildeberg, and CFR
- Arlen Specter- Freemason
- Richard B. Russell- Freemason
- John Sherman Cooper- CFR, Skull and Bones
- John McCloy- CFR, Bildeberg
- Richard Helms- Knights of Malta
- James Jesus Angleton- Knights of Malta
- John McCone- Knights of Malta

I'm sure the list is incomplete, but these U.S. officials are the top players in the cover-up, and they all were loyal to secret societies. That loyalty took priority over their oath to defend the constitution. These officials were not serving the public; they were serving an alternate agenda.

Those who have attained positions of power in Washington have become privy to certain secrets that the general public is not aware of. They learn things that the average person will probably never know in their lifetime. It's true that some things must be kept secret for legitimate concerns of national security. Most people can accept that. But does knowledge of these secrets give them a license to kill? Can they exalt themselves as keepers of the truth and look down upon the dumb, deluded masses? Can they lead the nation into endless, pointless wars that kill thousands of civilians, and justify it on the grounds that they know what's best for us? Along with knowledge of these secrets comes responsibility of dealing with it. There is sometimes an air of superiority among political leaders in the sense that they look down on the common people and view them as unenlightened. The prevailing belief seems to be "They don't know what we know, so why should we listen to them?" There's an old saying that a little knowledge can be a dangerous thing. That is true if one lets it go to their head and they lose perspective because of it. Because of their political position, along with their affiliation with secret societies, our leaders are aware of certain truths that are kept from the public on a daily basis. But no matter how huge those secrets are, I do not believe they override one's conscience.

10

SUMMARY

In the JFK assassination, the list of possible suspects is long: the CIA, the FBI, the Secret Service, the mafia, the Cuban rebels, oil tycoons, bankers, racists, right-wing extremists, and more. In the end, it all comes back to Lyndon Johnson. No matter what the CIA did, or the mafia did, or the Cuban rebels did, or the oil tycoons did, it was still up to Johnson to give the green light. He could have nixed it all if he chose not to go along with it. The final piece of the puzzle was the change in the motorcade route. Could the mafia have changed the route without inside help? Could the Cubans have changed the route? It had to be someone with connections in the Dallas Mayor's office to do that. Who could have ordered the Dallas Police and the local military to step down, contrary to normal procedures? Could Castro do that? Could the Russians do that?

Even if Johnson had nothing at all to do with the planning, he is completely responsible for the cover-up. Who else could have ordered all evidence to be seized from the Dallas Police? Who else could have persuaded seven decent people to lie to the world, crucify an innocent man, and defend murderers? In spite of the actions of all the other parties involved, those parties had to have known that Johnson would cover for them, or all their efforts would be for naught. Even if they could somehow pull off the assassination, they would have all been dead meat if Johnson didn't cover for them. If the vice president had been a true ally of John Kennedy, there would have been a legitimate investigation. There would have been no Warren Commission. The Dallas Police would have handled the investigation like they should have. Things would have turned out differently, but that was not the case. During both the planning and cover-up stages of the crime, it was Johnson's eye at the top of the pyramid.

To summarize the lack of a case against Oswald:

- The Zapruder film shows the shot came from the front. Oswald was behind Kennedy.

- Oswald was seen in the second floor lunch room by a cop and Oswald's boss about a minute or so after the shooting. He was standing there calmly.
- The paraffin test on Oswald's cheek was negative.
- Oswald's rifle was not found in the TSBD. A Mauser was found, and later switched for a rifle matching Oswald's.
- The alleged murder weapon did not contain Oswald's fingerprints.
- Oswald was killed so there could not be a trial, because there was no case against him.
- The CIA has a 201 file on Oswald, meaning he was an agent or operative.
- All of Oswald's actions can be explained by the fact that he was following orders from his CIA handler.
- Oswald had no motive to kill John Kennedy.
- The case against Johnson is infinitely stronger than the case against Oswald.

Two subsequent murders were by-products of the assassination. They were the shooting deaths of officer J.D. Tippit and accused assassin Lee Harvey Oswald. Tippit's assailant is not known, but no witness has positively identified Oswald as the killer. Tippit was shot with an automatic, while Oswald owned only a revolver. An imposter might have been used to implicate Oswald in the shootings of both Kennedy and Tippit. Oswald's own murder was coordinated by the Dallas Police, who deliberately led Oswald out unprotected, knowing that Jack Ruby was waiting to silence him. Ruby was deeply connected with organized crime, and probably killed Oswald on their behalf.

Officially, there were two government investigation into Kennedy's murder, the Warren Commission and the House Select Committee on Assassinations. Both were complete whitewashes. Evidence was destroyed, witnesses were intimidated, testimonies were distorted, and key people wound up suspiciously dead. Lyndon Johnson purposely selected seven people who he knew would lie for him to form the Warren Commission and get the predetermined result. The CIA and the FBI both withheld evidence from the commission. Oswald's connections with intelligence were denied, as were Ruby's connections with organized crime. Even most commission members themselves doubted the final conclusion. The HSCA did admit to a probable conspiracy, but left that hanging with no further investigation. Some members of the government did attempt to find the truth, but they were overwhelmed by the opposition's desire to smother the truth. Since the plotters ultimately controlled the media, they were able to deceive the public and get away with their crime. The Jim Garrison prosecution of Clay Shaw also ran into the same problems, and as a result, Shaw was acquitted when he was probably guilty.

The mere fact that the Warren Commission even existed shows Johnson's complicity. Kennedy's murder was legally a Dallas homicide, and it should have been investigated by the Dallas Police. Johnson overstepped his legal authority when he ordered the evidence to be seized by the FBI, and then overstepped it again in forming the Warren Commission. He also destroyed evidence by having the limousine refurbished. He ordered files and evidence relating to the case to be locked up for 75 years to further frustrate investigators. Johnson did not testify to the Warren Commission, providing instead only a written statement.

The Warren Commission will be forever remembered for their absurd magic bullet theory. This was the claim that one bullet went through Kennedy, then went through Governor Connally, ricocheted off the interior car door, and went back into Connally. The alleged magic bullet emerged in virtually pristine condition. As ludicrous as it sounds, they got away with it. Authentic autopsy photos were withheld from the commission and replaced with drawings. The locations of the wounds were altered in the drawings to make the magic bullet theory seem more plausible. The public bought it only because of the credibility of the commission and of the FBI.

The key to the assassination was the motorcade route. By changing the route so that it made turns instead of going in a straight line, it caused the limousine to slow down so the shooters could get a better shot. That could only be done by someone in power, like Lyndon Johnson and Earl Cabell, the mayor of Dallas. Also of significance was the reduction in security—the stand-down orders to the Dallas Police and the local military unit, and the re-arrangement of the motorcycle escort. These changes could only have been made by the Secret Service, who were in collusion with Johnson.

Johnson was highly visible in his position, but most of the plot was carried out by unseen forces that manipulate events surreptitiously. The actual shooters were mafia hit men, but it was the CIA who worked out the specific details of the plot. The CIA also did an extensive frame-up of Oswald by manipulating his actions to create an image of him as a communist sympathizer, and by using doubles to further implicate him.

Much of the cover-up was aided by various secret societies. Most members of Congress owe their careers to secret societies of some kind, and they are obligated to do the group's bidding, hence they are compromised leaders whose loyalty is not to the public. This leads to honest people reluctantly going along with the cover-up. Many of our politicians are not aware that the societies they serve have sinister motives. That's how good people get corrupted and find themselves caught up in something they wanted no part of.

The same is true for the media. Most influential members of the media are connected with intelligence agencies or secret societies, so they take part in the cover-up. The public believes that the media is objective and acts as a watchdog agency to monitor government wrongdoings. They don't realize that those in power have manipulated their own people into strategic positions in the media, giving them the ability to control the flow of information and thereby shape public perception of events.

All of this is part of a larger picture. The forces that orchestrated the JFK assassination are focused on world domination. Eliminating John Kennedy was just one step in that direction. Those same forces are responsible for virtually every war this country has been through. They are also the same forces that planned and executed 9/11 and got away with it using the same kind of propaganda and media manipulation.

In reality, it is much too simplistic to say that the JFK assassination was Lyndon Johnson's fault. Johnson pulled the strings, but he did not pull the trigger. The gunmen who shot John Kennedy must ultimately take responsibility. No one forced them to commit the crime. In spite of any personal or social conditions that may have lead them down the path they were on, the decision to pull the trigger was a free will choice. They cannot blame that on Lyndon Johnson. They each have to deal with their conscience, and like all of us, they will eventually have to face their judgment in the highest of courts.

John Kennedy was a man of very high intelligence, yet at the same time he appeared surprisingly naïve. He knew that the mafia hated him and wanted him dead, yet he rode in an open limousine in what was known to be hostile territory. On top of that, he let his arch enemy handle the motorcade and security arrangements, even while knowing of his criminal past. He knew of the assassination plot in Miami, but he went on to Dallas anyway. If there was ever such a thing as an unconscious death wish, this may have been it.

Kennedy was the only president who ever seriously fought the mafia. They killed him for it, and every president since then has looked the other way on organized crime. Kennedy was the only president to challenge the autonomy of the CIA. He was the only president in modern times to seriously challenge the war machine. He is the only one who tried to bypass the Federal Reserve. Kennedy was one of few presidents who were not beholden to secret societies.

In conclusion, it is much too simplistic to say that John Kennedy was the good guy and Lyndon Johnson was the bad guy. Like all of us, they both had good and bad in them. Kennedy was not a saint, but he died a martyr. All of his personal flaws and weaknesses will be viewed in the context of martyrdom. Anyone who we look up to as a leader is guaranteed to be a fallible human being with inevitable human frailties. That much is a given. In spite of his flaws, Kennedy embodied a certain spirit of freedom, and he basically stood against those who oppressed that freedom. No other president stood up to the forces that he stood up to. He genuinely cared about peace and he genuinely cared about people. Kennedy was far from perfect, but if we're looking for a hero and a martyr, he's about the best we've got.

Rest in peace, John.

A.P.S.

INDEX

128, 130, 133-143, 150, on
Tippit slaying- 153-160, 165,
166, 168, on Oswald slaying-
169, 170, 173-181, 185, 187,
189, on JFK assassination
evidence- 194-242, 247, 250,
254, 259, 271-288, 302, on
Oswald's intelligence
connections- 316, 319, 325-
371, various- 373-438, 445-454,
463, 465, 476, secret society
influence- 481, 482, 483, 490,
497, 498, various- 521, 522,
523
Warren, Earl, 357, 392, 393, 404,
455, 481, 483
Washington Post, 286, 516
Washington Times-Herald, 8
Washington, President George,
479
Webster, Robert E., 347, 348
Webster, William H., 516
Wecht, Dr. Cyril, 388
Weishaupt, Adam, 496, 505, 506
Weitzman, Seymour, 142, 143,
205, 206, 445
West, Joe, 241, 242, 243
Weston, Wally, 183
Whaley, William, 158, 159, 211
Whitaker, George, 237, 238
White, Roscoe, 289
Who Murdered JFK?, 144
Wiggins, Creighton, 282

Wilcott, James B., 304, 332
Williams, Charles, 69
Willis, Phil, 277, 278
Wilson, Eugene, 359
Wilson, President Woodrow, 9,
43, 508
Wise, Wes, 187
Witt, Louis Steven, 259, 260, 261,
295
Witten, John M., 327
Wolfman, 243
Wollsey, James, 516
Women's Building, 117, 119, 120
Wood, John S., 97, 269
World War II, 21, 29, 35, 36, 494,
510, 511, 512
Worrel, James, 209
Wright, Frank, 52, 53, 54, 58, 75,
121, 156, 277, 375
Yeadon, Glen, 511, 512
Zangretti, Jack, 281
Zapruder film, 3, 80, 104, 194,
227, 231, 233, 249, 257, 259,
272, 288, 297, 300, 301, 368,
380, 387, 399, 419, 423, 429,
430, 434-438, 441-447, 455,
497, 521
Zapruder, Abraham, 141, 194,
278, 297, 299, 300, 405, 423,
429, 430, 431, 436, 438, 443
Zirbel, Craig I., 52, 53, 54, 58, 75,
121, 375
ZR/RIFLE, 23, 335

CPSIA information can be obtained
at www.ICGtesting.com
Printed in the USA
LVHW03s2202130818
586837LV00033B/1390/P